Liability Claim Practices

Liability Claim Practices

James R. Jones, CPCU, AIC, AIS
Director of Claims Education

First Edition

American Institute for Chartered Property Casualty Underwriters/
Insurance Institute of America
720 Providence Road, PO Box 3016, Malvern, Pennsylvania 19355-0716

First Edition • Sixth Printing • July 2006

Library of Congress Catalog Number: 2001090694

ISBN 978-0-89462-150-5

Foreword

The American Institute for Chartered Property Casualty Underwriters and the Insurance Institute of America (the Institutes) are independent, not-for-profit organizations committed to expanding the knowledge of professionals in risk management, insurance, financial services, and related fields through education and research.

In accordance with our belief that professionalism is grounded in education, experience, and ethical behavior, the Institutes provide a wide range of educational programs designed to meet the needs of individuals working in property-casualty insurance and risk management. The American Institute offers the Chartered Property Casualty Underwriter (CPCU®) professional designation. You select a specialization in the CPCU program with either a commercial or a personal risk management and insurance focus, depending on your professional needs. In addition to this specialization, the CPCU program gives you a broad understanding of the property-casualty insurance industry.

The Insurance Institute of America (IIA) offers designations and certificate programs in a wide range of disciplines, including the following:

- Claims
- Commercial underwriting
- Fidelity and surety bonding
- General insurance
- Insurance accounting and finance
- Insurance information technology
- Insurance production and agency management
- Insurance regulation and compliance

- Management
- Marine insurance
- Personal insurance
- Premium auditing
- Quality insurance services
- Reinsurance
- Risk management
- Surplus lines

No matter which Institute program you choose, you will gain practical knowledge and skills that will help you to grow personally and professionally.

The American Institute for CPCU was founded in 1942 through a collaborative effort between industry professionals and academics, led by the faculty members at The Wharton School of the University of Pennsylvania. In 1953, the American Institute for CPCU merged with the IIA, which was founded in 1909 and which remains the oldest continuously functioning national organization offering educational programs for the property-casualty insurance business. The Institutes continuously strive to maximize the value of your education and qualifications in the expanding insurance market. In 2005, the Institutes extended their global reach by forming the CPCU Institute of Greater China (CPCUIGC). In addition, many CPCU and IIA courses now qualify for credits towards certain associate's, bachelor's, and master's degrees at several prestigious colleges and universities, and all CPCU and IIA courses carry college credit recommendations from the American Council on Education (ACE).

The Insurance Research Council (IRC), founded in 1977, helps the Institutes fulfill the research aspect of their mission. The IRC is a division of the Institutes and is supported by industry members. The IRC is a not-for-profit research organization that examines public policy issues of interest to property-casualty insurers, insurance customers, and the general public. IRC research reports are distributed widely to insurance-related organizations, public policy authorities, and the media.

Our textbooks are an essential component of the education we provide. Each book is specifically designed both to provide you with the practical knowledge and skills you need to enhance your job performance and career and also to deliver that knowledge in a clear manner. The content is developed by the Institutes in collaboration with insurance and risk management professionals and members of the academic community. We welcome comments from our students and course leaders because your feedback helps us to continuously improve the quality of our study materials. Through our combined efforts, we will truly be *succeeding together*.

Peter L. Miller
President and CEO
American Institute for CPCU
Insurance Institute of America

Preface

This text is used in conjunction with the AIC 36 course, Liability Claim Practices. Our goal in creating this text was to make it relevant, readable, and accessible to AIC 36 students. We took several approaches to help make this text relevant to the work lives of claim representatives.

First, in the chapters dealing with insurance coverages, we went beyond the usual treatment of those coverages and described many of the gritty challenges that claim representatives encounter when trying to apply policy wording to a given claim.

Second, we included, throughout all chapters, sample reports and letters, suggested statement guidelines, investigating checklists, and other aids that liability claim representatives can use in their jobs. In the chapters involving legal concepts, we included claims-related examples and brief descriptions of actual cases to help explain the concepts.

Finally, in the last three chapters, we applied many of the key coverage and liability concepts to real-world case scenarios. The three extensive cases—an auto liability claim, a premises liability claim, and a product liability claim—acquaint students with a cast of characters who must resolve some challenging claim issues.

We sought to improve readability by organizing the material in the sequence in which claim representatives would encounter it when handling liability claims. We included tables, charts, callout boxes, a legal glossary, and exhibits that summarize and clarify key points. We also introduced special sections, such as "Claim Representative Solutions," that recap important legal and investigative issues.

To enhance accessibility, we did our best to present concepts in the most direct manner possible, avoiding legalese and unnecessary qualifiers. By presenting complicated legal issues in such a direct fashion, we run the risk of oversimplifying some concepts. Entire books and periodicals are devoted to topics such as insurance coverage issues, tort law, contract law, litigation management, product liability, and automobile liability, subjects we cover in one chapter or less. We believe these abridgements will enhance students' learning of the material while still providing students with the information they need to handle most liability claims. Students are encouraged to use more detailed reference sources, as needed, on claims involving more complex legal or coverage issues.

I wish to thank West Group Publishing and Ken Brownlee for allowing me to adapt part of their wonderful reference work, *Casualty Insurance Claims*. Some of the section on legal concepts found in this text relied on that reference source.

Creating this text was truly a team effort. Several professionals were involved in writing and reviewing the manuscripts for it. The following people wrote a section of a chapter for this text:

William Stewart, CPCU, AIC

Patricia Doyle, JD

Michael LaPlaca, Esq

Jill Murphy, CPCU

Bradford Purcell, JD

Donald Hirsch, JD

Robert K. Gonter, JD

Eric A. Fitzgerald, Esq, CPCU, ARe

Richard A. Cass, CPCU, RPLU

The following professionals reviewed chapters and made important content suggestions:

Daniel Eidsmoe, JD, CPCU

Scott Brown, CPCU, AIC, ARe

John D. Kearney, JD, AIC

Darnell Pettengill, JD, CPCU

Tom Crumpler, CPCU, AIC

John O'Hara, CPCU, AIC, AIS

J. Michael Bondura, CPCU, SCLA

Clarence Johnson, CPCU, AIC

Mark Hofer, CPCU, AIC

Dwight Snodgrass

Bruce Stauf, AIC

Austin Bowles, CPCU

Jeff Avery, CPCU

Thomas Stout, AIC, AIM

Doris Hoopes, CPCU, AIC, AIS

We would like to thank members of the CPCU Society's Claims Interest Section who helped marshal resources for this project. Finally, we would like to thank all of the busy students and course leaders who took the time to make suggestions about how to improve this course. We encourage feedback and invite students and course leaders to comment on this text so that we can improve the material.

For more information about the Institutes' programs, please call our Customer Service Department at (800) 644-2101, e-mail us at cserv@cpcuiia.org, or visit our Web site at www.aicpcu.org.

James R. Jones

Contents

Overview of Liability Claims

Introduction to Liability Claims

Types of Liability Claims

The Liability Claim Process

Competencies and Characteristics of Effective Liability Claim Professionals

Issues in Liability Claims

Liability Insurance Policy Basics

Conclusion

Overview of Liability Claims

"A desk job. Is that all you see in it? Just a hard chair to park your pants on from nine to five? Just a pile of papers to shuffle around and a sharp pencil and a scratch pad to make figures on, with maybe a little doodling on the side? That's not the way I see it, Walter. To me a claims man is a surgeon, and that desk is an operating table, and those pencils are scalpels and bone chisels. And those papers are not forms and statistics and claims for compensation. They're alive! They're packed with drama, with twisted hopes and crooked dreams. A claims man, Walter, is a doctor and a bloodhound and a cop and a judge and a jury and a father confessor all in one."

- Edward G. Robinson, talking to Fred McMurray, in *Double Indemnity*, MGM, 1941

INTRODUCTION TO LIABILITY CLAIMS

Since Edward G. Robinson's quote in the 1941 MGM film *Double Indemnity*, the world of the claim representative has changed in some ways, but not in others. Today, the term "claims man" is obsolete. Even the term "adjuster" has increasingly been replaced by "claim representative," especially when referring to people handling liability claims. The intrigue of the job, however, remains the same. Being a liability claim representative still requires a broad range of skills, knowledge, and talent.

Liability Claims Basics

The first insurance coverages protected insureds from their own losses, usually those caused by some force of nature. These insurance coverages involved only two parties, the insured (the first party) and the insurer (the second party). Liability insurance is somewhat unique in that it provides coverage for losses experienced by a third party.

Liability insurance coverages were created to help protect insureds from the financial consequences of an insured's legal obligation to a third party. In theory, insurance coverage either exists for a claim or it does not. There is no in-between status. Liability, on the other hand, comes in various shades of gray. Liability cases can range from clear liability without question to no liability at all. Because liability coverages are based on losses caused by legal obligations, historically, liability claim representatives were required to be lawyers. This changed in the 1950s. Today, liability claim representatives need not be lawyers, but they must have a firm understanding of legal principles.

Parties Involved in Liability Claims

Liability insurance claims involve three parties: the insured, the insurance company, and someone who allegedly suffers an injury or damages that the insured is responsible for. First, a contractual relationship exists between the insured and insurer that is based on the policy wording and that determines whether coverage is provided for a loss.

Second, a relationship exists between the insured and the party who is making a claim against the insured, usually known as the claimant or plaintiff. The relationship between the insured and the claimant is one that is based on legal duties under tort law.

A claimant who has filed a lawsuit is known as a plaintiff.

Legal liability coverage is sometimes referred to as third-party coverage. This is because the third party or **claimant** is the liability insurance policy's beneficiary (the one who gets paid). In liability claims, the claimant makes a claim against the insured, and the insurer, based on the insurance policy, generally agrees to perform two things:

1. Provide the insured with a legal defense and
2. Settle the claim by the third party on the insured's behalf.

Exhibit 1-1 describes the relationship of the parties involved in a liability claim.

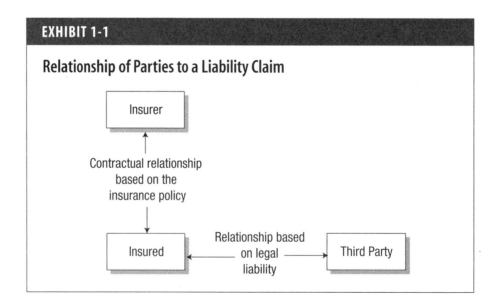

EXHIBIT 1-1

Relationship of Parties to a Liability Claim

Liability and Related Coverage

Some first-party coverages are related to, and sold with, liability coverages. The beneficiaries of these first-party coverages might not be named insureds (parties listed on the insurance policy and who typically pay the insurance premium) but are nonetheless "insureds" because they are entitled to direct compensation from the insurer based on the insurance contract, rather than on liability under the tort law.

These related coverages include medical payments coverage under auto, homeowners, and general liability policies. Complicating liability claim practice is the fact that occupants might potentially have **third-party claims** against the insured as passengers.

Third-party claims arise out of the insured's legal liability to another party. These claims arise with or without insurance.

The term "casualty insurance" is sometimes used to refer to liability and other related insurance claims that result from "casualties." It is an old term that has its roots in historical insurance regulation and includes liability insurance and related coverages such as medical payments. It also includes coverage for workers compensation and theft. Because of the broad and sometimes conflicting meanings of the term "casualty," the term is not used in this text.

TYPES OF LIABILITY CLAIMS

The world of liability claims can be broken down into several categories. Some of these categories have specific liability coverages, while others are covered under broad, comprehensive liability insurance policies.

The following sections give brief descriptions and examples of various liability claims.

Auto Liability Claims

Operators of motor vehicles are required to exercise reasonable care for the safety of others. When they fail to exercise a reasonable degree of care and other people are harmed, the operators are legally liable for that harm. In the United States, this is the most common type of liability claim. More than six million auto accidents occur each year, resulting in more than two million injuries. In 1998, the average auto claim paid was $10,128 in injuries and $2,220 in property damage.[1]

Premises Liability Claims

People and businesses who own and/or control land must exercise reasonable care in using and maintaining their premises. Slip-and-fall claims are the most common premises liability claims. Legal liability for persons injured inside a home or building or on the driveways and parking lots of landowners varies according to the situation.

Product Liability Claims

Product liability refers to the responsibility arising out of the manufacture, distribution, or sale of allegedly defective or dangerous products. Advances in technology have placed an ever-increasing number and variety of products on the market. Free trade has opened markets for products from all over the world. When consumers are injured by these products, retailers, distributors, and manufacturers can become liable. Social philosophy favors consumers, and laws holding businesses liable for products have expanded over the past four decades.

Professional Liability Claims

The first occupations in history to be regarded as professions were those of physician, lawyer, and clergy. Today, this list has expanded to include many other occupations such as registered or licensed practical nurse, dentist, certified public accountant, registered architect, professional engineer, and pharmacist. Other occupations sometimes covered under professional liability insurance policies are registered physical therapist, hairdresser, insurance agent, and, in many states, claim representative.

Being engaged in a professional occupation brings with it the potential for **professional liability** arising from the failure to properly practice the profession, which is called malpractice. Following are some examples of obvious malpractice committed by various professionals.

- A surgeon leaves a sponge inside a patient during surgery. An infection develops, and a second surgery is required.
- An attorney fails to file a summons and complaint within the required time limit, and his client's claim is barred.
- An insurance agent fails to properly advise a wealthy client to carry high policy limits. The client has low limits, an accident happens, and, as a result of the low limits, he is bankrupted.
- An accountant fails to properly audit a business and overstates its financial condition. The business receives loans and investments that it cannot repay. Creditors and investors suffer as a result of the audit.
- A pharmacist fills a prescription incorrectly, and the patient is hospitalized as a result.
- An architect fails to properly design a roof to carry snow loads customary for the northern climate of the region where the building is located. The roof collapses under the weight of normal snow and ice. Occupants of the building are injured, and the building is severely damaged.
- A dentist extracts the incorrect tooth.

Liability in most malpractice claims is not as clear-cut as in the preceding examples. Many medical practice liability claims are highly questionable. Overall, professional liability claims tend to have higher-than-average defendant verdicts (favoring the professional).

An important dynamic exists in malpractice claims that does not exist in typical liability claims. In malpractice claims, the insured's professional reputation may be at stake. This reputation can be adversely affected when claims are paid. Therefore, many professional liability policies include a

consent to settle clause. This clause requires the insurer to obtain consent from the professional to settle the claim. This differs from other types of liability policies, which permit the insurer to settle as it sees fit. The consent to settle clause requires claim representatives to communicate and sometimes negotiate with the professional in order to obtain consent. Sometimes insureds refuse to give their consent. Consequently, a much higher percentage of malpractice claims reaches the trial stage and has verdicts rendered, as compared to automobile and general liability claims, which generally do not have coverages with consent to settle clauses. Most insurance companies try fewer than 2 percent of all reported automobile and general liability claims.[2]

Employer Liability Claims

Employers are liable to injured workers based on workers compensation statutes. However, employers can become liable to workers for workers' injuries that fall outside the workers compensation statutes because of either the type of injury or the circumstances of the injury. In addition, employers can be liable for poor employment practices that violate workers' rights.

Injury Claims Outside of Workers Compensation

Employers have liability exposures for injuries to employees. Employers' liability is normally established according to workers compensation laws. In some unusual circumstances, claims by employees fall outside these laws and subject the employer to greater loss potential than exists under workers compensation laws. If, for example, an employee is injured as a "user" of the employer's product, the employer may face a product liability claim that falls outside what workers compensation covers.

When the negligence of third parties combines with the negligence of the employer, the employer may end up owing more than would be owed under an injury claim directly against the employer. Flagrant violations of safety standards can also create employer liability for damages in excess of limits under workers compensation laws.

Employment Practices Liability

Employers can also become liable for violating workers' rights under various federal and state laws. **Employment practices liability (EPL)** claims are made by employees or job applicants based on harassment, discrimination, wrongful failure to promote, wrongful termination, violation of civil rights, and failure to provide or enforce adequate and consistent company policies.

Numerous state and federal statutes have been enacted within the past forty years that prohibit certain workplace behavior. These laws have created various duties for employers that, if breached, can result in liability. Federal statutes include:

- Title VII of the Civil Rights Act of 1964—This law prohibits discrimination in employment because of race, color, religion, sex, or national origin or on the basis of pregnancy, childbirth, or related medical conditions.

- Equal Pay Act of 1963—This law prohibits differences in pay between women and men for substantially the same work.
- Age Discrimination in Employment Act of 1967 (ADEA)—This law prohibits discrimination by employers against any individual with respect to hiring, terminations, promotions and demotions, compensation, and the terms and conditions of employment on the basis of age when a worker is forty years old or older.
- Americans With Disabilities Act of 1990—This law prohibits workplace discrimination against workers with disabilities and requires employers to make reasonable accommodations in the workplace for workers with disabilities.
- Civil Rights Act of 1991—This law amends and strengthens the Civil Rights Act of 1964 and the Age Discrimination in Employment Act of 1967 while also imposing caps on compensatory and punitive damages.
- Family and Medical Leave Act of 1993—This law permits employees to take an expanded period of leave without losing their jobs. It provides up to twelve weeks without pay for purposes of handling family and medical issues, including pregnancy, childbirth, and adoption.

A number of states have laws that mirror and in many cases exceed the requirements set forth in these federal statutes.

With the exception of the Family and Medical Leave Act of 1993, all of these laws are enforced by the Equal Employment Opportunity Commission (EEOC). The EEOC receives between 75,000 and 80,000 complaints each year. More than one-third of the complaints are for racial discrimination, about 30 percent are gender-based complaints, and the remainder of the complaints received result from other violations such as those related to age or disability.[3]

Sexual harassment is one type of gender-based complaint. Awareness of sexual harassment issues increased significantly in the 1990s following the allegations of Anita Hill during the Clarence Thomas Supreme Court nomination hearings.

Sexual harassment can be broken down into two categories; **quid pro quo** claims and hostile environment claims. *Quid pro quo* in Latin means "something for something." With gender-based claims, it refers to workplace advancement or other job-related favors in return for sexual favors.

Hostile work environment claims are more common than *quid pro quo* claims. In a hostile environment claim, the claimant faces adversity in the job environment because of his or her gender. Some examples of activities causing a hostile environment include displaying sexually explicit photos, using inappropriate language, graphically discussing the physical characteristics of the claimant or other workers, and making unwelcome physical contact. Such activities can make the job environment so hostile that workers must quit or take actions that keep them from properly performing their jobs. Hostile work environment claims may also arise out of racial discrimination.

Today, most companies have adopted corporate policies on sexual harassment and discrimination. In fact, most insurers who write employment practices liability coverage require insureds to have formal corporate policies and training on how to prevent, report, and handle harassment and discrimination claims. Currently employment practices claims are handled mainly by lawyers, but as employment practices liability coverage becomes more commonplace, insurers are likely to have more non-lawyers handle these claims.

Directors and Officers Liability Claims

Liability exposures exist for people who are responsible for the well-being of various businesses or other organizations, including those who serve on the board of directors or are trustees of the organization. Claims made against directors and officers usually address situations that have resulted in loss of value to the organization because of the actions of the directors and officers. The claimant(s) must prove that the directors and officers performed their duties improperly, with resulting damages to the organization or to an entity separate from the corporation.

Personal and Advertising Injury Claims

The commercial general liability (CGL) policy combines coverage of personal injuries and advertising injury. Umbrella policies still separate these two types of claims.

Personal injury claims range from reputation defamation to invasion of privacy. A personal injury may result from advertising, but personal injuries can result from other activities as well. Although these injuries may seem intentional, they may not always be so. For example, a company publishes a newsletter that makes false statements about a competitor. Although the company publishing the newsletter believes them to be true, in reality they are false, and the false information damages the competitor's reputation. This type of defamation could be an advertising injury.

Revealing private information about a person to the public would be an invasion of privacy and grounds for a personal injury claim.

> In the insurance industry, the term "personal injury" is distinguished from "bodily injury." However, outside the insurance community, the term "personal injury" can include bodily injury. "Personal injury lawyers" handle property damage and bodily injury claims.

Intellectual Property Rights Claims

The rise of computers, the Internet, and digital technology has provided the ability for digitized information to be reproduced with little loss of quality. A CD burner can reproduce exact copies of music or software CDs, and documents can be redistributed as e-mail attachments almost instantaneously over the Internet throughout the world. These capabilities have caused a proliferation of copyright infringements. When information can be published throughout the world over the Internet, it becomes more difficult to protect the rights of the creator from people who use the work without permission (copyright infringement). Copyrights, trademarks, and patents protect intellectual property. One value of intellectual property lies in its ability to be used by or sold to others. Intellectual property rights claims are a fast-growing and complex part of the liability claim environment. Coverage for these claims may sometimes be provided under Personal and Advertising Injury coverages found in CGL policies.

Environmental Liability Claims

In general, as a society's level of economic prosperity grows, members of that society become more environmentally conscious. This consciousness is reflected in laws regulating liability for pollution. Rachel Carson's book *Silent Spring* brought environmental awareness to the American public in the early 1970s. Since that time, numerous federal and state laws have been enacted to help curb pollution.

Often pollution discovered today is the result of activities that occurred years ago. Some laws still hold current landowners responsible for activities that occurred years ago. For example, a person who has owned a home for thirty years decides to convert from an oil-fired furnace to gas heat. Upon removing the underground oil tank, it is discovered that the tank has holes in it and has been leaking oil into the ground for numerous years. Laws today would require the homeowner to pay for cleanup costs.

Before 1986, the majority of commercial liability insurance policies provided coverage for pollution on an occurrence basis, without aggregate limits, when the polluting event was "sudden and accidental." Personal lines insurance—in particular, homeowners policies—had no pollution exclusion. Therefore, if a claim occurred during the policy period of any of these previous policies, even if the claim were discovered today, coverage would generally apply under the old policy. Contemporary commercial general liability policies specifically exclude pollution. A small number of companies write environmental liability coverages. These are expensive policies and are underwritten with tight guidelines. Claim representatives handling serious commercial liability claims are likely to encounter claims for environmental liability, even if they are not covered.

THE LIABILITY CLAIM PROCESS

Responsibilities of the liability claim representative can be divided into four critical processes that constitute the entire claim process. Claim representatives must determine coverage; determine and investigate liability; evaluate damages; and then conclude the claim, usually by settlement but sometimes by litigation.

This text is designed to track with these critical processes and follow claims from beginning to end. The liability claim process presented in Exhibit 1-2 may occasionally vary depending on the circumstances of the claim. For

EXHIBIT 1-2

Claim Process With Corresponding Chapters in Text

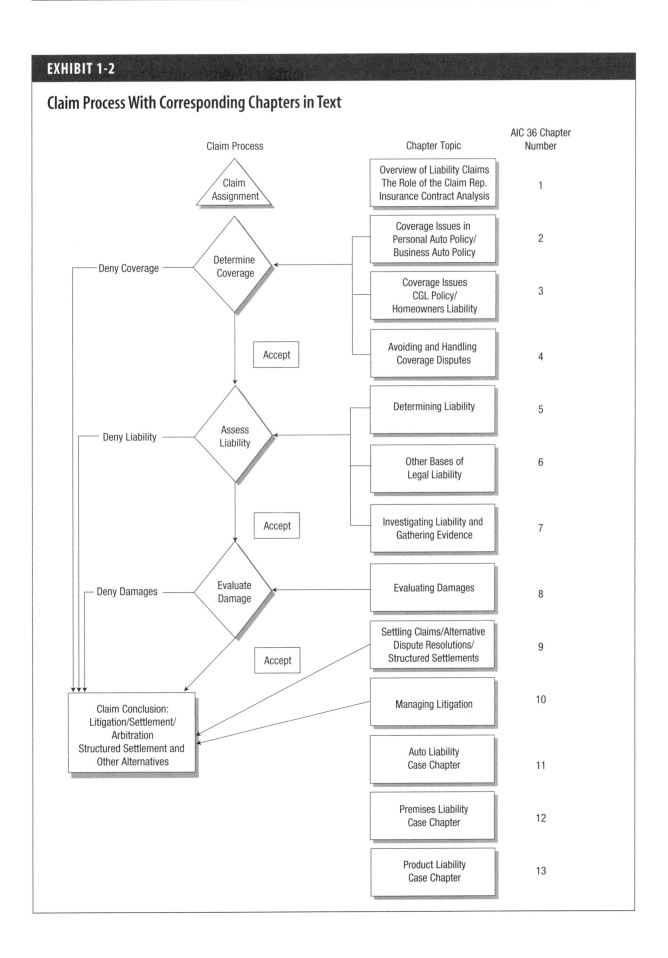

Claim Process	Chapter Topic	AIC 36 Chapter Number
Claim Assignment	Overview of Liability Claims The Role of the Claim Rep. Insurance Contract Analysis	1
Determine Coverage	Coverage Issues in Personal Auto Policy/ Business Auto Policy	2
	Coverage Issues CGL Policy/ Homeowners Liability	3
	Avoiding and Handling Coverage Disputes	4
Assess Liability	Determining Liability	5
	Other Bases of Legal Liability	6
	Investigating Liability and Gathering Evidence	7
Evaluate Damage	Evaluating Damages	8
	Settling Claims/Alternative Dispute Resolutions/ Structured Settlements	9
	Managing Litigation	10
	Auto Liability Case Chapter	11
	Premises Liability Case Chapter	12
	Product Liability Case Chapter	13

Deny Coverage

Deny Liability

Deny Damages

Accept

Claim Conclusion: Litigation/Settlement/ Arbitration Structured Settlement and Other Alternatives example, sometimes coverage issues are discovered while investigating liability. *If the resulting delay in fully identifying coverage issues has not caused the insurer to lose its rights to deny coverage*, then the claim representative can reconsider coverage and investigate coverage issues. Sometimes during settlement, liability or damages issues that the claim representative did not initially assess are asserted by the claimant. Exhibit 1-2 shows the typical liability claim process and the order of chapters for this book.

Determining Coverage

Determining coverage is an important but sometimes overlooked role of liability claim representatives.

First, after receiving a claim notice, coverage must be determined. This includes *routine* coverage activities such as confirming the insured's information, making sure that a policy premium was paid and the policy was in force at the time of the claim, and verifying that the vehicles or building locations involved were listed on the policy. In addition, more potentially complex coverage questions must be answered to ensure that the policy applies to the claim alleged. The following are questions that claim representatives must answer in determining whether coverage applies:

- Who is covered?
- Are the activities causing the injury or damages covered?
- Are the damages (loss consequences) covered?
- Do any policy exclusions apply to the claim?
- Did covered damages occur during the policy period?
- Is the location of the loss covered?
- Did insured and insurer meet their obligations before and after the loss?
- What limitations exist on liability?
- Do any laws or regulations affect coverage?

Who Is Covered?

The named insured is the party listed on the policy. In addition to the named insured, other parties such as spouses, business partners, and employees often meet the definition of an "insured." People who occupy or drive an insured vehicle may also be considered insureds. Liability claim policies provide coverage for many parties other than those who are listed as named insureds in the declarations page of the policy. For instance, the personal auto policy provides coverage for organizations in which the insured is acting as an agent. The auto policy would cover claims against the Boy Scouts if an accident occurred while the insured was acting as a Boy Scout leader and using his car to transport Scouts on an outing.

The personal auto policy is not the only policy that provides coverage for other entities that are not named in the policy declarations. The commercial general liability policy (CGL) provides coverage for real estate managers and parties having certain types of contracts with the insured. Claim representatives must first ascertain whether the person seeking protection under a liability policy qualifies as an insured under the policy.

Are the Activities Causing the Injury or Damages Covered?

The activity that gives rise to the claim must also be covered by the policy. Claim representatives may encounter particular liability coverages that apply to specified activities, such as using a motor vehicle, as well as comprehensive liability coverages such as those offered under the CGL policy.

The personal auto policy is an example of a specific liability policy because it provides coverage for one specific type of liability, "legal responsibility because of an auto accident." Conversely, a general liability policy provides coverage for all activities unless they are excluded. The CGL insurance policy states that it "will pay those sums that the insured becomes legally obligated to pay." A general liability policy usually has more exclusions than a specific liability policy because its scope of coverage is greater. Before considering whether exclusions might apply, claim representatives should always review the policy to see whether the activities of the insured are covered.

For liability policies that cover "accidents," the loss must be definite in time and place and not intended by the insured. Losses occurring because of wear and tear or obsolescence would not be considered definite in time. Deliberate acts may not be "accidents" if the insured intended the harm that was caused. The loss must occur by chance to be considered accidental.

Are the Damages Covered?

Damages occur as a result of loss. In essence, "damages" means money owed to a claimant because of the insured's legal liability. All types of damages are not necessarily covered, and most liability insurance policies specify the damages they will pay for. Homeowners and personal auto policies provide coverage for damages resulting from "bodily injury" and "property damage." Under such policies, "damages" would include not only medical expenses for injuries and the cost to repair or replace damaged property, but damages would also include loss of income, loss of enjoyment because of disabilities resulting from an injury, disfigurement, pain and suffering from an injury, and the loss of use of property damaged. However, such policies might not cover punitive damages awarded against an insured to punish the insured. Also loss of reputation, loss of privacy, or other losses not resulting from a bodily injury or property damage would not be covered under these policies. In insurance terms, these other losses are known as "personal injuries" rather than bodily injuries. An insured who defames a neighbor by wrongly identifying him as a sex offender can become liable and owe the neighbor damages for loss of reputation in the community, but the homeowners policy would not cover these resulting damages.

Do Any Policy Exclusions Apply to the Claim?

Liability policies usually contain exclusions that preclude coverage resulting from certain activities. Homeowners and commercial general liability policies exclude auto liability losses because they are better insured separately. If these policies covered auto liability, then the premiums would have to reflect that loss exposure, which would be unfair to those insureds who do not have auto liability exposures. Personal lines coverages have exclusions for business liability losses for the same reason. Exclusions for intentional injury and damages are specified in liability policies to ensure that only incidents occurring by chance are covered.

Did the Covered Damages Occur Within the Policy's Time Period?

Normally, automobile, homeowners, and general liability policies are written on an occurrence basis. Under an **occurrence-based policy**, the loss must occur during the policy period to be covered. Although this sounds relatively simple, it becomes more complicated when dealing with claims that occur over a long period of time or claims that result from something that happened in one period but whose manifestations were not discovered until much later.

For example, in the 1950s a drug was manufactured called DES that was prescribed to prevent miscarriages by pregnant women with certain health issues. The drug was effective at preventing miscarriages but was found to cause, or contribute to, cervical and uterine cancer. The cancer connection was discovered more than three decades after women began using the drug. The drug was immediately taken off the market, but claims were reported for years. In this example, which policy(ies) would cover the claims and based on what dates? When the drug was taken? When the cancer connection was discovered? When the woman was diagnosed with cancer? Courts have a variety of interpretations on this issue.

Liability claims that arise many months or years after an initial exposure are known as "long-tail" liability claims. This means that the loss event may begin at one point in time and not manifest itself for many years. Medical malpractice and product liability are two types of long-tail claims. As a result of problems determining when an "occurrence" took place, many insurers began to write what are known as **claims-made policies**. For coverage to apply in a claims-made policy, the loss must occur and be reported within a specified time period (with a few exceptions). These policies reduce the possibility of long-tail claims.

Although they are available, claims-made policies are now rarely used with general liability exposures, but most professional liability coverages such as medical malpractice, architects' coverages, or employment practices liability are written on a claims-made basis.

Is the Location of the Loss Covered?

The coverage territory of liability policies varies depending on the type of policy. The personal auto policy provides coverage for losses occurring within the United States, its territories and possessions, Puerto Rico, and Canada. The commercial general liability policy provides limited worldwide coverage. This means that if an insured manufactures a product within the U.S., coverage is provided for loss caused by the product anywhere in the world, provided that any lawsuit arising from the claim is brought in a court within the covered territory. Homeowners policies may limit medical payments to people injured at described locations. Determining where a loss occurred is necessary because the loss location can sometimes affect coverage.

Did Insured and Insurer Meet Their Obligations Before and After the Loss?

Insureds and insurers have certain obligations (policy conditions) that they must meet. Conditions that must be met before a loss are called **conditions precedent**, and those that must be met after a loss are called **conditions subsequent**.

An example of a condition precedent that applies to the insurer is that the insurer properly cancel the policy if coverage is no longer in effect. If the insurer does not cancel the policy properly and a loss occurs, the insurer may still have to provide coverage although the intent was to cancel the policy. Examples of conditions precedent that apply to the insured include honestly completing the application and paying the policy premium on time.

Conditions subsequent to a loss can also affect coverage. An insured must promptly report losses, forward legal papers to the insurer, and cooperate with the insurer during the investigation. Failing to meet these obligations can lead to coverage denials.

What Limitations Exist on Liability?

Liability policies have maximum limits of liability. However, some policy limits are "refreshed" after each claim is paid; that is to say, the amount paid on a given claim may be limited, but the total amount paid during a policy period is unlimited. Other policies set limits by claim and have aggregate limits for all claims made within a policy period.

Policies differ as to whether the payment of legal fees to defend insureds reduces the policy limits or is made in addition to policy limits. In general, defense costs and other associated expenses do not affect the policy limits. Sublimits of liability may also apply. For example, some auto policies establish limits for bodily injury and other smaller limits for property damage.

Do Any Laws or Regulations Affect Coverage?

Although the policy may include provisions whose intent seems clear, courts may make decisions or insurance departments may make regulations that affect how the policy is interpreted. When a court makes a decision that affects a coverage interpretation, it will usually be applied to all other similar claims within the court's jurisdiction. The interpretation that the court makes may differ greatly from what was intended by the insurer's underwriters.

Insurance department regulations can affect coverage, too. For instance, while a policy may merely specify a certain time period that the insurer has to give notice to the insured of cancellation, an insurance department regulation may specify the size of type that must be used in the notice. Failure to comply with the insurance department regulation can not only lead to fines, but also make insurers responsible for claims that would otherwise not be covered.

Much of the discussion in the following chapters on coverage relates to how various laws and regulations affect insurance liability coverage.

Investigating Liability

Investigation is time-sensitive; the "investigative trail" goes cold quickly. Claim representatives do not see losses occur; therefore, they must rely on others in obtaining the facts of what occurred so that a liability determination can be made, damages assessed, and the claim resolved. To a great extent, the amount of information that can be obtained in an investigation depends on what those involved in the claim—including insureds, claimants, and other witnesses—remember about it. Memories quickly fade. The Dietz and Jones Memory Curve illustrated in Exhibit 1-3 shows the effect of time on a person's ability to recall facts.

EXHIBIT 1-3

Dietz and Jones Memory Curve

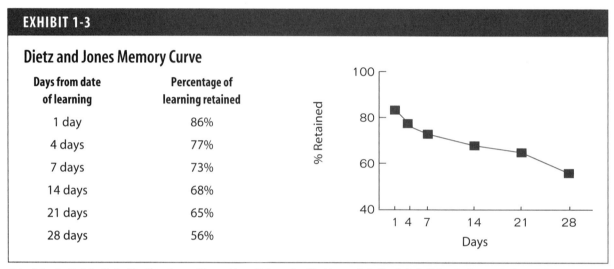

Days from date of learning	Percentage of learning retained
1 day	86%
4 days	77%
7 days	73%
14 days	68%
21 days	65%
28 days	56%

Sister Columba Mullaly, Ph.D., *The Retention and Recognition of Information* (Washington D.C.: The Catholic University Press, 1952), pp. 7-8.

To get the maximum, most accurate facts about an occurrence, claim representatives must promptly conduct investigations. Physical evidence such as skid marks on a road or oil on a parking lot may disappear, and if these physical facts are not documented, the claim investigation will be lacking. Investigation is critical in the liability claims process for two important reasons:

* Insurers have a good faith duty to investigate.
* Investigation provides information needed to evaluate liability and damages and to settle the claim properly.

Good Faith Duty To Investigate

Liability insurance policies require insurers to accept the financial consequences of their insureds' liability to others. Liability insurance policies protect the insured from personal financial loss. But if a claim against an insured exceeds the insured's policy limits, then the insured is responsible for the amount of the claim exceeding the policy limit. Because of this exposure to personal loss, insurance companies have a good faith duty to recognize claims with this potential and perform investigations promptly and thoroughly so as not to jeopardize the insured. Delays in investigations can harm the insured's liability position. Witnesses become difficult to locate, physical evidence is lost, memories fade, and adverse parties begin to "recall" facts in ways that might be less favorable to insureds. A poor investigation adversely affects insureds as well as insurers.

In some circumstances, insurers have been required to pay for damages in excess of the policy limit for not properly conducting an investigation. At the least, insurers are expected to advise an insured when investigations reveal claims that could possibly exceed an insured's policy limit.

Information Needed for Proper Evaluation

Claim representatives need to know about the characteristics of the claim for a number of reasons. First, accurate claim reserves must be established by the insurer. The reserve is an estimate of the insurer's expected loss payment. Overall, reserves help describe whether an insurance company is in good financial condition.

The goal of any claim investigation is the resolution of a claim. Generally speaking, the longer a claim stays open, the more it ultimately costs. Expenses mount, especially if the claim becomes litigated, and settlement values increase.

Investigations may either reveal that an insured is liable and the claim should be settled or that the insured is not liable and that it should be defended. Sometimes investigations reveal that insureds are liable but not for all of the damages claimed. For example, some injuries claimed by the claimant might not be causally related to an insured's accident. A compromise may settle these kinds of claims, but sometimes they must be defended if a compromise cannot be reached. Claim representatives can come to an appropriate decision to settle or defend only through a proper investigation.

Evaluating Damages

The evaluation phase comes after the investigative phase in the claim process because the *final* evaluation of the amount to offer to settle a claim occurs only after liability and coverage have been determined. However, claim representatives evaluate damages as they are conducting their liability investigations. While claim representatives are gathering facts, they are often assessing the value of the damages. These initial evaluations can help set the scope of the investigation. Claims with minor damages usually require less investigation than claims with larger damage potential. In general, damages in liability insurance claims are to compensate a party for a loss and make the injured party "whole" by returning that party to a pre-loss position. Damages that serve this purpose are called compensatory damages, and they include special damages and general damages.

Special damages or "specials" are out-of-pocket expenses that claimants incur as a result of a loss. With respect to specials, claim representatives must:

1. Verify the amount of the damages claimed, and
2. Verify that the specials are related to the insured's accident.

General damages are more difficult to measure than special damages because of the subjective nature of general damages. General damages include items such as the value of the claimant's pain and suffering, inconvenience, disfigurement, and other intangible factors. Because these valuation factors are subjective, liability claim representatives must be comfortable evaluating general damages with some degree of ambiguity.

Settling Liability Claims

The claim settlement is perhaps the most visible phase of the claim process. Many of the claim performance measures are based on settlement criteria—the length of time to settle, the average settlement, the number of settlements per month. This emphasis is somewhat justified because the purpose of the claim department is to pay claims. Claims that are not paid are the exception rather than the rule. Only a small minority of claims are denied, and fewer than 2 percent of all claims end up going to trial.

Claim representatives should be familiar with different methods for settlement so that the highest percentage of claims that are owed can be paid without litigation. Once a decision has been made to pay a claim or deny it, then the claim must be properly concluded through one or more various "release of liability" documents.

Methods

After coverage for a claim has been determined, liability investigated, and damages evaluated, claim representatives must decide either to settle the claim or defend the claim.

The preferred method of claim settlement is through a negotiated, mutually acceptable agreement. Some negotiations are brief; an agreement is reached after one or two phone calls. Other negotiations are protracted, going on for months and involving lengthy negotiations with numerous parties.

A simple negotiated agreement is not always possible without assistance; therefore, claim representatives need to be able to employ other methods as well. Within the past couple of decades, a number of alternative dispute resolution (ADR) processes have been used to help bring claims to a conclusion. Mediation is a settlement conference wherein an intermediary (known as a mediator) acts as a referee between two parties. In claims, this usually involves a claim representative or legal counsel mediating with the claimant and the claimant's attorney. Arbitration is another form of ADR in which an arbitrator makes a decision regarding the outcome of the claim that may be either binding or nonbinding, depending on the agreement between the parties.

Most state courts have adopted procedures for resolving smaller claims. Some courts have mandatory settlement conferences, and others use arbitration or mediation.

Concluding a Claim

Claims are concluded with some type of compromised settlement agreement or with a denial letter. Most liability claims result in some payment to conclude the claim. Once all parties have agreed to a settlement figure, they must conclude the settlement with a settlement agreement. In general, settlement agreements are in writing and involve some type of document releasing the insured of liability in exchange for a specified amount of money.

Claim representatives must occasionally issue claim denials if the insured is not liable or if the claimant's damages are not owed. Denials should be made promptly after concluding a liability investigation. Denials sometimes result in litigation. When this occurs, the insurer hires legal counsel to defend and represent the insured.

COMPETENCIES AND CHARACTERISTICS OF EFFECTIVE LIABILITY CLAIM PROFESSIONALS

No uniform definition exists for the term "competency," but for purposes of this section, a competency is defined as the skills and knowledge required for effective performance. Effective liability claim representatives possess certain personal characteristics as well as competencies. The following section is divided into two areas: skills and knowledge, and personal characteristics.

Skills and Knowledge of Effective Claim Representatives

Liability claim representatives must have a fairly good understanding of the law, especially tort law, because most liability claims are based on torts. They must understand how insureds can become liable and understand what legal defenses might be available to insureds for claims made against them. Knowledge of contract law is useful in understanding the elements of an insurance policy, which is a contract. Liability claim representatives must not only be able to read and understand the wording of an insurance policy to determine whether coverage for a claim exists, but they also must be able to interpret the policy on more controversial types of claims. This means being able to interpret ambiguities and anticipate how courts would apply coverage for a given set of facts.

Experienced claim representatives can become experts in certain aspects of the law related to claims that they handle, but claim representatives should never believe or represent that this narrow expertise gives them the same qualifications as an attorney (unless they are licensed to practice law).

All liability claim representatives must be good students of human behavior. They must be able to assess the credibility of insureds, claimants, and other witnesses. They must understand the motivations of claimants and their attorneys during negotiations. Many insurers have their claim representatives attend trials or hearings to observe the proceedings and the negotiations. This helps them to see and understand the implications and subtleties of how witnesses present themselves. It also helps them to see how well attorneys do in convincing the judge or jury of the insured's version of the facts.

Inextricably tied to the human relations aspect of liability claim practices is the ability to communicate. Claim representatives must be able to establish rapport and explain complex legal and medical issues in simple terms. The wrong tone in a letter or a phone conversation can virtually destroy hopes for a successfully negotiated agreement. But the right words and tone can result in a quick, amicable resolution. Good communication involves characteristics like the ability to establish trust by demonstrating confidence and competence.

Liability claim representatives must have excellent interpersonal skills. They constantly work and interact with co-workers, claimants, attorneys, medical providers, auto body repair shops, mediators, arbitrators, judges, and others. Some of these interactions involve conflict and require good conflict management skills. It is not easy to tell a friendly, cooperative claimant that the investigation revealed the insured to be free of liability. It is even more difficult to explain to a good insured that the liability investigation revealed that the claim was owed. It is sometimes uncomfortable to tell a judge at a settlement conference that the company has reached its highest offer and despite the judge's desire to settle the claim, the insurer can offer nothing further to settle.

Most liability claim representatives must handle bodily injury claims. This requires a fundamental knowledge of anatomy, medical terminology, injury causation, and medical tests and procedures. At the least, liability claim representatives must be able to read and understand medical resources in order to competently review and evaluate medical records. Liability claim representatives should be able to converse intelligently with doctors, nurses, and other medical professionals regarding a claimant's injuries.

Liability claim representatives must be able to conduct liability investigations. They must be able to interview and take statements from insureds, claimants, and other witnesses. They must be able to accurately draw diagrams of accident scenes and take photographs of accident locations and physical evidence such as skid marks, damaged property, or defective equipment.

Most liability claim representatives need to have a basic understanding of property damage estimating. Property damage ranges from the cost to repair or replace automobiles to the cost of reconstructing a building or repairing machinery or equipment. Claim representatives need to at least be able to read and understand property damage reference sources in order to check repair estimates others have written.

Because they often operate with little direct supervision, liability claim representatives must be self-starters who possess good time management and organizational skills. Liability claim representatives must be able to handle heavy workloads and take the initiative to settle claims as soon as is practical.

Characteristics of Effective Claim Representatives

Personal characteristics include qualities such as integrity, intelligence, empathy, a positive attitude, and inquisitiveness. Helpful characteristics for liability claim representatives are practically innumerable, but certain characteristics are critical for them to be effective.

Effective liability claim representatives must be willing and able to embrace frequent changes. The law changes, technology changes, and organizations change. All of these changes affect the claim department. People looking for routine or predictable work will not enjoy or be effective at handling liability claims.

Liability claim representatives must enjoy learning. The knowledge required to be effective is constantly changing; for example, the laws affecting liability are dynamic. New court decisions and new statutes affect liability. Liability claim representatives must also keep up with medical and technological changes that affect injury claims. This environment of change requires liability claim representatives to have a commitment to continual professional development. Professional development can include attending seminars, reading books and trade publications, and taking courses. People who prefer to learn something once and be done with it are not likely to be effective in liability claims.

The job of liability claim representative requires people with inquisitive minds. Liability investigations do not come with a clear road map. The direction and ultimate outcome of each liability claim are based on facts revealed over the course of the investigation. When information is obtained, claim representatives must be able to think of other questions or investigative issues that might be related. People who lack intellectual curiosity and who want to do liability investigations based strictly on a standard, prescribed set of questions or investigative activities will not be as effective.

Effective liability claim representatives are analytical. They sift through tremendous amounts of information obtained from their investigations. This includes statements, police reports, medical reports, and other documentation needed to assess liability and damages. They then have to put all of this information into a logical framework that leads to a well-reasoned assessment. Coverage determination also requires analyzing the policy contract, based on the facts of the loss, and then applying these facts and various laws to a given claim situation to determine coverage.

Strong self-esteem is another useful characteristic. Good conflict resolution skills often come from a strong sense of self-esteem; it can help to prevent claim representatives from taking adversity personally. If claim representatives take their differences with claimants, attorneys, and insureds personally, the conflict escalates and can become impossible to resolve.

Self-esteem also helps claim representatives make, and stand by, decisions knowing others may disagree with them. Effective liability claim representatives are decisive, ethical, and able to make fair decisions based on the information available. Deciding whether a claim should be denied, settled, or sent to trial requires decisiveness, good judgment, and courage of convictions. Because of the subjective nature of liability and damages, liability claim settlements are easy to second-guess. It is not unusual for several liability claim representatives to conclude similar claims for different amounts of money. Ineffective liability claim representatives are paralyzed by the fear that someone will disagree with their liability assessment, which leads to indecision and causes claims to linger without closure.

Handling liability claims involves stress because of the workload, the uniqueness of every claim, and the emotionally charged atmosphere associated with liability claims. People who have suffered traumatic injuries and substantial financial losses are often not completely rational and may react with more emotion than they normally would. Claim representatives must be able to (1) handle these sources of stress and balance the competing pressures of closing claims in a timely fashion with the need to do a thorough, high-quality investigation and (2) balance the interests of the insurance company and its customers (insureds) while at the same time being fair to claimants injured by insureds.

Having a positive attitude can help claim representatives deal with these pressures and improve customer service. Claim representatives have little control over which insureds and claimants they must deal with, and many of these people can be difficult. Liability claim representatives will, without exception, encounter situations that drain their energy, challenge their sense of justice, and make them question the goodwill of others. Effective claim representatives understand that they can choose their attitude and the way they respond to others no matter what the situation. A healthy skepticism paired with a positive attitude is valuable in liability claims, while a defensive, cynical attitude can lead to poor claim service and job dissatisfaction. Claim representatives with poor attitudes usually make themselves as miserable as they make those around them. Consequently, they are not effective. A good sense of humor and camaraderie are potent antidotes to the stresses and conflicts encountered in claims.

Because of the nature of insurance, which involves fulfilling an intangible promise, claim representatives (like insurers) must be trustworthy. This trustworthiness can be established through honesty and integrity. Keeping appointments, using credible information that is accurate and free of exaggeration, listening to all parties before forming a judgment, and making decisions based on facts rather than prejudice are examples of ways to establish trustworthiness.

It is unlikely that any one liability claim representative would always be strong in all of the competencies and personal traits described here. But effective liability claim representatives can identify their areas of weakness and look for opportunities to improve them.

ISSUES IN LIABILITY CLAIMS

The environment of liability claims is constantly changing, and a number of issues affecting the job of the liability claim representative continue to surface. Technology in claims, the changing legal environment, managed care, and claims ethics are perennial issues affecting claims.

Technology in Claims

Evolving technology is enabling liability claim representatives to make better, faster decisions; provide better customer care; and reduce the time from claim notice to claim settlement.

Advances in communication technology allow claim representatives to be in touch with their home office, insureds, body shops, and rental-car companies anywhere in the country. These communication advances can eliminate some of the time lost in returning phone calls. Voice recognition software helps claim representatives dictate and type reports at the same time.

Changes in data-storage capabilities are leading toward the elusive and sought-after "paperless" claims office. Digital cameras can store digital images, and some cameras can even measure distances. Digital technology can now store photos, medical reports, estimates, and even digitized audio statements. In many offices, an entire claim file may exist in an electronic form, and it can be accessed almost anywhere in the world at any time of day. Medical and legal reference resources can be stored and accessed on computers to assist claim representatives with some of the more technical aspects of claims. Interactive databases help liability claim representatives make decisions on liability, coverage, and damages and even to assess the likelihood of fraud.

All of these changes influence customer expectations and the effectiveness of liability claim representatives. Consider the following claim scenario and how it might affect the role of a liability claim representative. The technology for this scenario exists but has not yet become as pervasive or as integrated as described.

Conglomerate Financial Services (CFS) is a full financial services company. An insured with CFS has a car that is equipped to notify the insurer when and where an accident occurs. Upon receiving electronic notification that an insured's vehicle has been in an accident, the claim department contacts the driver via wireless phone or dispatches someone to the scene using global positioning systems (GPS). A digital image is taken of the damaged vehicle and transmitted to a home-office computer. The computer quickly develops a damage assessment profile of the vehicle. Digital imaging permits the claim representative to do "triage" and suggest the most appropriate auto body shops based on the damage assessment profile. Depending on the extent of the damage, towing and rental-car services could also be arranged. After the accident, the vehicle's "black box" is analyzed to supplement the statements of the insured driver, the claimant, and witnesses. Their statements are taken, and the transcription of their statements is reviewed along with the data from the black box indicating the speed at and direction of impact. An electronic signature of the claimant is obtained and transmitted to the hospital and doctor by whom the claimant is being treated. The hospital and doctor's office transmit the medical files electronically to the claim representative. The liability claim representative runs the claim through a computerized bodily injury claim evaluation program. This helps to estimate likely medical expenses and the potential for disability and suggests a settlement range. Within a short time, the cause of the accident is determined and liability assessment is made. An agreement is reached with the claimant via an Internet Web site that permits claimants to settle online with insurers. The claimant is sent a debit card from Conglomerate Financial Services for the agreed-upon amount of the claim.

If such a scenario were common, what skills would liability claim representatives still require to be effective? Would claim operations be organized differently? As technology changes, claim representatives need to consider how their jobs will change and what skills will be valuable.

Because of the changes in technology, insurers should be able to give better service in the future, but the heart of this service is still going to be based on the skills and knowledge of claim representatives. The need for "high touch" service based on soft skills will likely become more important to complement the high-tech ways in which claims are processed. Insurers that offer good customer service will still be able to distinguish themselves from their competition. Without people who understand the customer service role of claim representatives, companies can end up inappropriately using technology. An example of this was common in the 1990s with the use of phone answering machines in claim departments that required insureds to navigate through a series of options before reaching a person. Companies quickly discovered that insureds who had been involved in serious accidents had little tolerance for such systems, and they were dropped in favor of people.

Computerized Evaluation and Negotiation

In the preceding hypothetical claim scenario, the injury claim was evaluated through a computerized evaluation program, and the claimant and insurer settled the claim via the Internet. Computerized evaluation of claims is a relatively new tool that a number of insurers now use routinely as part of their claims processes. Generally, these programs work by requiring a claim representative to enter an extensive amount of data about the claim into a computer program, including medical information and accident facts. These evaluation programs search their database of claims and provide information back to the claim representative about the settlement range of the claim based on the injury type, accident facts, and past claims settlement data.

There are both pros and cons to using such a computerized evaluation program. The programs are good in that they provide claim representatives with knowledge of similar claims and, therefore, tend to prevent the claim representative from dramatically undervaluing or overvaluing the claim. However, over-reliance on these programs can lead to formulaic decision making that does not consider all of the circumstances of a claim. No two claims are ever alike, and values of liability claims with similar facts and damages can vary widely. The vendors of these computer programs suggest they be used as a tool to assist claim representatives in establishing settlement ranges. They caution against using these programs without considering all of the circumstances of a claim.

The Internet has begun to be used as a tool in the negotiation of claims. Allowing the parties to a negotiation to make demands and offers through the Internet or e-mail can help some claims to be settled more quickly. Often, parties cannot reach each other by phone or do not have time to meet in person. Internet negotiations can be more efficient by reducing exchanges of voice-mail messages and canceled appointments. Online settlement negotiations are likely to increase as people become more comfortable with using the Internet for other business transactions.

Dynamic Legal Environment

The legal environment of liability claims is dynamic and requires liability claim representatives to keep up with numerous significant changes that affect their jobs. Liability claim practices are affected most by the following three challenging areas of legal change.

- Changes in laws affecting the application and interpretation of insurance coverages
- Creation and expansion of new areas of liability
- Changes in the types of damages allowable and awarded by courts

Newly trained claim representatives are often distressed when they learn that the insurance coverages do not always apply in the same, straightforward way they learned in basic training classes. This is because insurance coverages are affected by court decisions, statutes, and insurance regulation—all of which can change from one year to the next and vary from one state to another.

Courts have expanded acceptable causes of action (reasons for allowing a lawsuit). New theories of liability are still being invented. Liability claims that were not compensable in the past might now be owed under current laws. Security liability is one example of how changing laws affect liability claims. Security liability arises from crimes involving rape, other forms of sexual assault, assault and battery, and wrongful death committed on the premises of insureds. In the past, liability claim representatives would have denied liability under several defenses, such as the incidents' being unforeseeable by property owners or their being caused by criminals rather than the property owners. Today, courts accept allegations of negligence for failure to provide proper lighting or security guards. Security liability is just one example of how changes in society (increased crime and increased willingness to hold property owners responsible for crime) can expand the circumstances under which insureds can be found liable. Claim representatives can stay informed of some of these changes by subscribing (usually for free) to newsletters written by defense attorneys who have staff paid to keep up with legal changes.

Allowable damages also change. Courts are accepting an increasing number of claims for medical conditions such as sick building syndrome, multiple chemical sensitivity, latex allergies, fibromyalgia, and chronic fatigue syndrome. These new types of injury claims complicate the legal environment for claim representatives trying to assess compensable damages. Mental injury claims such as those involving post-traumatic stress disorder (PTSD) have risen dramatically and are encountered occasionally by almost every claim professional. As mentioned earlier, employment practices liability has spawned new insurance coverages that could become as common as workers compensation insurance. As these and other liability exposures grow in significance to society, they are encountered more frequently in liability claims practice. Liability claim representatives must keep up with legal changes because they affect liability claim reserves, negotiations, settlements, and jury awards. These changes require claim representatives to keep an open mind about how courts might assess compensability in new ways. Going to trial to have a court decide these issues is costly and can set unfavorable precedents for future claims. It is sometimes advisable to settle one claim with unusual coverage, liability, or damage issues in order to prevent having a court decide the issues and then having the decision applied to a host of other claims with less merit.

Managed Care

The term "managed care" refers to a variety of techniques that are used to contain medical costs while providing people with appropriate care for injuries sustained. Managed care has been used in the health insurance industry for a number of years. Its use has spread to the casualty insurance industry, especially for workers compensation and no-fault insurance.

Managed care techniques may include establishing defined networks of medical providers, auditing medical fees, using nurse case managers to define the best care paths based on the injury sustained, and reviewing medical treatment utilization.

In automobile no-fault, several different approaches are used with respect to determining the fee that a medical service provider can charge. For instance, the New York No-Fault Law has adopted the New York Workers Compensation Fee Schedule. In this type of fee schedule, medical service providers are assigned a rating code based on their medical specialty. This specialty rating indicates the amount that the medical service provider is allowed to charge for a given treatment. Various defined medical procedures are scheduled at fixed fees. Other states, like New Jersey, have a different type of fee for medical service providers based on the area within the state where they practice. Many states have no set fee schedule but require medical service charges to be "reasonable and customary."

In an effort to contain medical costs, some states have adopted specific medical protocols, or care paths, for particular injuries. For example, if someone sustains a cervical sprain, the protocol may require that certain types of expensive diagnostic tests be delayed until conservative treatment has been provided. In the small percentage of cases in which the injury does not resolve on its own, more diagnostic tests are permitted to be performed. In New Jersey, for example, insurers have the choice of following state-mandated care paths or, alternatively, filing their own managed care plan that the state must approve before its use.

Utilization review organizations (UROs) have been used extensively in health insurance, and they are now being used in certain states in the areas of no-fault claims and liability claims. Their purpose is to provide a retrospective review, after the fact, on the extent to which treatment rendered for an injury was appropriate.

Case management firms are used in cases involving severe injuries. A case manager acts as the coordinator of the claimant's medical care to ensure that treatment and therapies being provided are appropriate for the injuries sustained and do not conflict with one another.

The way in which liability and automobile no-fault claims are handled is following the trends of the health insurance industry. Given that the United States has an aging population with increasing healthcare needs (and costs), managed care is likely to continue to be an ongoing and ever-increasing component of health insurance. However, laws and regulations reflect public opinion, and to the extent that the public rebels against managed healthcare and seeks greater choice and more privacy, liability and no-fault insurance will be affected likewise.

Liability claim representatives should know what managed care techniques are available in their states. The AIC 34 text, *Managing Bodily Injury Claims,*[4] describes various applications of managed care techniques in detail.

Ethical Issues

The English word "ethics" comes from the Latin word *ethos*, meaning principles of right conduct. Ethical conduct extends beyond the letter of the law. Certain types of conduct may be legal but at the same time may be considered unethical. As insurance becomes more competitive, the need for ethical conduct becomes even greater. As this need grows, claim representatives and insurers must place a greater emphasis on ethical conduct.

In 1986, a widely reported study showed that, on average, one dissatisfied customer told eleven others about the service problems encountered.[5] Today, with the presence of e-mail and the Internet, this number is likely to be much higher. Some people have set up Web sites for logging complaints against various insurers. Online newsletters quickly disseminate information about company misdeeds. These misdeeds have never been more transparent than they are today. Most state insurance departments now have Web sites that enable consumers to find out how many complaints have been made against a given company (adjusted for the size of the company).

Insurance regulation is often based on these complaints; consequently, insurers are sometimes the "authors" of their own regulation. Insurance regulation has been and is likely to continue to remain in a state of flux. Bills regulating information privacy and the use of managed care are likely to remain numerous and high-profile, and the way insurers deal with information and use managed care can influence bills that are proposed and enacted. Unethical conduct, or even the appearance of unethical conduct, can be costly for the insurance industry.

Identifying Ethical Issues in Claims

Ethical dilemmas arise because of the nature of liability insurance. As mentioned earlier, liability insurance involves three interrelated parties who often have diverse interests. This three-party dynamic of liability claims is called a *tripartite relationship*. The tripartite relationship is sometimes the source of conflict that creates ethical dilemmas. Consider a defense attorney who has been hired by an insurer to defend an insured. While the defense attorney is being paid by the insurer, he or she is also representing the insured. What if the defense attorney, during a privileged conversation with his client, the insured, discovers that there is no coverage for the particular claim and that a defense should not be provided? In such a situation, it would be unethical for the lawyer to tell the insurer of the coverage issue even though the insurer is paying the legal fees for the insured. It would also be unethical for claim representatives to ask the lawyer to find out and report to them about coverage information. Instead, claim representatives would have to hire another lawyer to examine any coverage issue.

"Unfairness" is a common complaint insureds and claimants make with insurance claims. Complaints of "unfairness" sometimes arise from the heavy-handed manner in which claimants and insureds are treated when claim representatives fail to negotiate in good faith or fail to adequately explain settlement offers. More troubling complaints arise from the unethical conduct of improper handling of confidential information, making offers to settle below a reasonable settlement range, using "experts" who always favor insurers, and failing to disclose the use of aftermarket or used auto parts.

A claim representative investigating a no-fault law claim for lost income might accidentally discover that the insured has been cheating the government on income taxes. Would it be proper to report the insured's tax evasion to the Internal Revenue Service if the insured does not drop the claim? In the absence of a statute requiring the claim representative to report the evasion, this would be inappropriate. The reason is because the claim representative obtained knowledge of the tax evasion through a privileged relationship to the insured.

Sometimes, payment to third parties will increase the insured's premium. Some insureds may attempt to influence the claim representative's decision and pressure claim representatives to deny claims even when the evidence indicates that the insured is responsible. The ethical way to handle such situations is (1) to pay third-party claims promptly and fairly and (2) to explain to insureds the legal basis for the payment and why it is in the insured's long-run best interest to pay claims that are owed. This is not always easy to do, and ethical challenges are presented with insureds who are persuasive or influential.

Resolving Ethical Dilemmas

Three methods for resolving ethical conflicts are (1) asking stock questions that give guidance, (2) establishing rules or guidelines to resolve dilemmas that occur frequently, or (3) eliminating the conflict causing the ethical dilemma. Consider the following claim situation.

A claim representative has evaluated the bodily injury claim of an unrepresented claimant at $5,000, and when entering into negotiations, the claim representative asks the claimant what the claimant thinks would be a fair settlement. The claimant responds by telling the adjuster that $1,000 would be acceptable. Is it wrong for the adjuster to settle the claim for this amount? Most people would argue that the claim representative is underpaying the claim and taking advantage of the unrepresented claimant's ignorance. However, others would say that $1,000 is all the claimant asked for and paying $5,000 on a claim that can be settled for $1,000 is a disservice to the insured who has paid a premium for liability insurance coverage.

How can a claim representative resolve such a dilemma? One common way is by asking some stock questions such as the following:

- Do any laws exist to give me guidance? (Even if the exact wording of the law does not cover the action, the intent of the law might give some guidance.)
- How would I feel if my actions were publicly reported? (This is an increasingly likely occurrence in claims.)
- How would I want a family member to be treated in a similar situation?
- Would society be better or worse off if every claim representative acted in a similar fashion?
- Would this action lead to unfavorable laws or increased insurance regulation if my actions became a widespread claim practice?
- How would my actions appear to friends and family members whose opinion I respect?

Claim representatives are often required to select or rate the performance of service providers, including lawyers, auto body shops, medical reviewers, and various contractors. However, a conflict of interest arises when these service providers give gifts to claim representatives, such as tickets to ballgames, dinners at nice restaurants, or liquor. It creates the appearance that selection and rating is based on some form of payola. Conflicts of interest can sometimes be resolved by setting company rules and guidelines or by eliminating the potential for conflict. For example, some insurers strictly prohibit their claims staff from accepting any form of gift or gratuity. They set restrictive rules that have no room for ambiguity. A problem arises when the rules appear so restrictive that claim representatives, and even management, ignore the rules.

Some insurers prefer not to set steadfast rules. They either allow each claim representative to decide these issues, which places the claim representative in an ambiguous ethical predicament, or they eliminate the conflict by not allowing claim representatives to select or rate the service providers they work with. The conflict is eliminated when the service providers are reviewed objectively by others who look at the service provider's results.

Many insurers find that claim representatives benefit from having a good rapport with these service suppliers, especially lawyers they work with in litigated claims, and permit business relationships outside the office. These companies would view going to a ballgame or a restaurant (especially for lunch at a reasonably priced restaurant) as acceptable. However, gifts of ballgame or concert tickets if the lawyers do not plan to attend would be unacceptable.

LIABILITY INSURANCE POLICY BASICS

Understanding insurance policies is essential to good liability claim practices. To understand these issues, claim representatives must first understand insurance policy basics. The remainder of this chapter discusses the basics of insurance policies that are needed to analyze more complicated coverage issues. Because auto policies are the most commonly used liability policy, the auto-policy format will be used to present insurance policy basics. Most of these basics apply to other liability policies.

Auto Insurance Policy Basics*

An insurance policy, like any written document, is a combination of headings, words, phrases, sentences, and paragraphs. The components of an insurance policy are called policy provisions and constitute the distinctive agreements that collectively make up an insurance contract. Depending on the purpose it serves, every property-liability insurance policy provision can be placed in one or more of the following categories or parts:

- Declarations
- Definitions
- Insuring agreements
- Exclusions
- Conditions
- Miscellaneous provisions and endorsements

Some provisions can have more than one function; for example, a definition can act to exclude coverage, and exclusions sometimes contain definitional terms. Examples from the Personal Auto Policy (PAP) and the Business Auto Coverage Form are used to illustrate the wording found in these different policy parts.[6] Some of the examples are specific to auto policies, but most of the provisions have counterparts in other types of liability policies.

Declarations

The **declarations** section of a policy contains information that is "declared" by both the insured and the insurer. The insured declares information when completing the application for insurance, and the insurance company declares details on the coverage it provides. This information is shown on the declarations page (usually the first page) of the insurance policy.

Exhibit 1-4 shows a sample declarations page for a Personal Auto Policy.

Coverage issues sometimes involve information in the declarations. For example, the declarations page might indicate that an insured has paid a premium for Medical Payments and Uninsured Motorists Coverages. If the insured was injured in an accident that exhausted the limits of both coverages, some courts have required the insurance company to pay the limits of both coverages even if a policy provision indicates that payment for the Uninsured Motorists Coverage should be reduced by the amount paid under the Medical Payments Coverage. The court may reason that the declarations state that the insured paid a premium for each type of coverage and was therefore entitled to coverage from both.[7] Similarly, declarations on business auto policies can cause misunderstandings over how vehicles are classified or how they are used.

---

*This section is adapted from the essay written by Eric A. Wiening entitled "Reading an Insurance Policy," *CPCU Handbook of Insurance Policies*, 3d ed. (Malvern, Pa.: American Institute for CPCU, 1998), p. 68.

Exhibit 1-4

Declarations Page—Personal Auto Policy

Personal Auto Policy Declarations

POLICYHOLDER: **(Named Insured)**	David M. and Joan G. Smith 216 Brookside Drive Anytown, USA 40000
POLICY NUMBER:	296 S 468211
POLICY PERIOD:	**FROM:** December 25, 2000
	TO: June 25, 2001

But only if the required premium for this period has been paid, and for six-month renewal periods if renewal premiums are paid as required. Each period begins and ends at 12:01 A.M. standard time at the address of the policyholder.

INSURED VEHICLES AND SCHEDULE OF COVERAGES

VEHICLE	COVERAGES	LIMITS OF INSURANCE		PREMIUM
1	2000 Toyota Sienna	ID#JT2AL21E8B3306553		
	Coverage A—Liability	$300,000	**Each Occurrence**	$301
	Coverage B—Medical Payments	$ 5,000	**Each Person**	$ 40
	Coverage C—Uninsured Motorists/ Underinsured Motorists	$300,000	**Each Occurrence**	$190
			TOTAL	$531
2	1997 Ford Taurus	ID#1FABP30U7GG212619		
	Coverage A —Liability	$300,000	**Each Occurrence**	$280
	Coverage B—Medical Payments	$ 5,000	**Each Person**	$ 40
	Coverage C—Uninsured Motorists/ Underinsured Motorists	$300,000	**Each Occurrence**	$168
	Coverage D—Other Than Collision	**Actual Cash Value Less** $100		$ 39
	—Collision	**Actual Cash Value Less** $250		$215
			TOTAL	$742

POLICY FORM AND ENDORSEMENTS:	PP0001, PP 03 06
COUNTERSIGNATURE DATE:	December 1, 2000
AGENT: A.M. Abel	

Coverage issues sometimes involve the application of policy endorsements. A common endorsement to auto policies is Personal Injury Protection (no-fault insurance).

Definitions

Both the PAP and the Business Auto Coverage Form contain a section titled **"Definitions,"** which defines the terms used in each policy. The PAP defines terms such as "family member" and clarifies what it means to "occupy" an automobile. These seemingly self-explanatory terms are the subject of a great deal of litigation, even when they are specifically defined.

Words defined in the policy are set in quotation marks, boldface, or italics each time they are used. For example, "accident" is defined in the Business Auto Coverage Form as follows:

> "Accident" includes continuous or repeated exposure to the same conditions resulting in "bodily injury" or "property damage".

The terms "bodily injury" and "property damage" are defined in the policy and therefore are set in quotation marks in the definition of "accident" as well as when used elsewhere in the policy.

Insuring Agreements

An **insuring agreement** is any policy statement in which the insurer agrees to make a payment or provide a service under certain circumstances. The body of most insurance policies begins with the insuring agreement.

Some policies provide more than one coverage, each based on a separate insuring agreement. For example, auto policies typically provide liability coverage and physical damage coverage, each with its own insuring agreement. The insuring agreement for the liability coverage provided by the Business Auto Coverage Form reads (in part) as follows:

> We will pay all sums an "insured" legally must pay as damages because of "bodily injury" or "property damage" to which this insurance applies, caused by an "accident" and resulting from the ownership, maintenance or use of a covered "auto".

Common insuring agreements found in a typical auto policy are:

- Liability
- Medical Payments
- Uninsured Motorists
- Underinsured Motorists
- Damage to Insured Autos

Some insurers combine Uninsured and Underinsured Motorists Coverages into one insuring agreement.

Liability Coverage

In terms of the protection it provides for the insured, **Liability Coverage** is the most important coverage provided under an auto policy. It provides protection against legal liability arising out of the ownership or operation of an automobile. In the insuring agreement, the company agrees to pay damages for bodily injury and property damage for which the insured is legally responsible because of an automobile accident. In addition to the payment of damages, the insuring agreement provides coverage for all legal defense costs. Courts frequently consider the insurer's obligation to defend insureds and pay their legal costs (often referred to as the "duty to defend") to be a broader duty than the duty to pay damages.

Medical Payments

Medical Payments Coverage is an optional accident benefit that pays reasonable and necessary medical expenses and funeral expenses up to a certain specified limit. This coverage applies, without regard to fault, to named insureds as well as any occupants of the insured car if they are injured in an automobile accident.

Uninsured/Underinsured Motorists Coverage

Uninsured Motorists (UM) Coverage is designed to address the problem of bodily injury caused by a motorist who does not carry liability insurance, by a hit-and-run driver, or by a driver whose insurer is insolvent. The insurer agrees to pay damages that the insured person is legally entitled to recover from the owner or operator of the uninsured/hit-and-run motor vehicle. This includes medical expenses, wage loss, and general damages such as pain and suffering. Several states include property damage as well as bodily injury as part of the Uninsured Motorists Coverage. The insurer is responsible for paying only damages for which the uninsured motorist is legally liable. For example, if an insured rear-ended an uninsured motor vehicle at a stop light and the insured was 100 percent liable for the accident, then the insurer would have no responsibility to pay for the insured's bodily injury claim under Uninsured Motorists Coverage. However, Medical Payments Coverage (if included in the insured's policy) would provide limited coverage. If the situation were reversed, however, and the uninsured motorist rear-ended the insured at a stop light, the insured's UM Coverage would pay for the insured's bodily injury claim.

Underinsured Motorists (UIM) Coverage is designed to meet the need of insureds who are injured by drivers who are inadequately insured. Most states require insureds to carry only $25,000 or less in liability insurance coverage. One week in a hospital can now exceed that amount. Wage loss is another factor making limits inadequate. The $25,000 sum is less than the average American's annual income. Anyone who suffered a permanent injury would probably not have adequate compensation even if he or she had a separate health insurance policy to pay the medical bills.

Damage to the Insured Auto

An auto policy can also include auto physical damage coverage on autos owned, leased, hired, or borrowed by the insured. Most commonly, auto policies provide Collision Coverage and Comprehensive Coverage.

Collision Coverage insures against loss to an insured auto resulting from its collision with another object or its overturn. **Other Than Collision Coverage** (also known as **Comprehensive Coverage**) covers loss to an insured auto resulting from any accidental loss other than collision and from a few specified causes, including collision with an animal, vandalism, theft, fire, hail, flooding, and windstorm.

A less expensive alternative to Comprehensive Coverage in the Business Auto Coverage Form is specified causes of loss coverage, which covers *only* those causes of loss specifically stated (such as fire, windstorm, theft, and so forth). Auto policies may also include Transportation Expense Reimbursement Coverage (also known as Rental Reimbursement Coverage) for the cost of renting a substitute auto/vehicle while the insured auto is unusable because of a covered loss.

Exclusions

Exclusions eliminate coverage for certain situations. The first exclusion in the PAP reads as follows:

> A. We do not provide Liability Coverage for any "insured":
>
> > 1. Who intentionally causes "bodily injury" or "property damage."

This is an example of a provision that seems to be clearly worded but is difficult to apply. Applying this exclusion is difficult because it requires the claim representative to analyze the intentions (the mindset) of the person at the time of the accident. If, for example, an insured is overcome with "road rage" and deliberately sideswipes another vehicle, it is unlikely that the insured would, after time for reflection, admit that the accident was intentional. The claim representative would have to make a coverage decision based on the observable actions of the driver, which indicated that the incident was "intended or expected." Applying this contentious and imprecise terminology to specific facts requires a thorough investigation and careful analysis of the circumstances before making a decision.

Reasons for Exclusions

The following are purposes for policy exclusions:

1. Eliminate coverage for uninsurable loss exposures
2. Assist in managing moral hazards
3. Reduce the likelihood of coverage duplications
4. Eliminate coverages that the typical purchaser does not need
5. Eliminate coverages requiring special treatment
6. Assist in keeping premiums at a reasonable level (which applies to virtually all exclusions)

Uninsurable Loss Exposures   One purpose of exclusions is to eliminate coverage for exposures that are considered uninsurable by private insurers. Private insurers consider exposures to be uninsurable for several reasons. For example, most property and liability insurance policies exclude losses arising out of war because war can affect many insureds simultaneously. Covering such losses would disrupt the insurance mechanism because insurance premiums are pooled collectively from all insureds, but compensation is paid to a much smaller number of insureds who suffer losses with damages that are often many times greater than the premiums they have paid.

Nuclear radiation is another example of a risk that is considered uninsurable because the potential for it to affect many insureds at the same time is so great that it becomes impossible for insurers to spread the risk of loss.

Moral Hazards   A second purpose of exclusions is to reduce moral hazards (also known as attitudinal hazards). A hazard is a condition, risk, or danger that increases the probability that the event insured against will happen. With a moral hazard, the increase in probability is because of the character or habits of the insured.[9] Without exclusions, a condition would exist that causes insureds to be less careful than they would be otherwise.

Although there is no legal distinction, some insurance authors refer to indifference to loss as a "morale hazard" and reserve the term "moral hazard" to describe the possibility that a covered loss will be deliberately caused by an insured. Either hazard is a legitimate reason for an exclusion.

Coverage Duplications   A third purpose of exclusions is to reduce the likelihood of coverage duplications. Coverage is usually eliminated from one type of policy because it is probably provided by another type of policy that is better suited to the task. For example, the Building and Personal Property Coverage Form eliminates autos from the description of covered property because auto physical damage insurance is readily available and better suited for covering auto physical damage exposures. The Business Auto Coverage Form does not cover liability arising out of the operation of "mobile equipment" such as bulldozers because the Commercial General Liability Coverage Form covers that loss exposure.

In general, different types of standard insurance policies are designed to dovetail with each other. This is particularly true when the policies are written by the same insurance company or service organization. For example, the exclusion for "loading and unloading" items that is found in the Business Auto Coverage Form dovetails with the exclusion for "handling" items found in the Commercial General Liability Coverage Form. This helps to define which policy applies when someone is injured by an item that is being loaded into or unloaded from an auto.

Unnecessary Coverages   A fourth purpose of exclusions is to eliminate coverages that are not needed by the typical purchaser of a particular type of insurance. For example, most people who purchase automobiles for their personal use do not face the same frequency or severity of exposures as do taxi drivers and truck drivers. It would be inequitable to require all insureds to share the cost to cover the business exposures faced by only some insureds. For that reason, the PAP excludes these automobile exposures.

Another purpose of excluding the business use of commercial vehicles is to eliminate coverages requiring special treatment. As used here, the term "special treatment" means rating, underwriting, or loss control that is substantially different from what is normally applied to the policy containing the exclusion. Certain policies require different underwriting, rating, and loss control methods.

Reasonable Premiums   Finally, exclusions assist in keeping premiums at a level that most insurance buyers would consider reasonable. Insurers and rate regulators both share this goal. To some extent, all exclusions serve to keep premiums reasonable; however, it is the sole purpose of some exclusions. Consider the following exclusions from the physical damage section of a Business Auto Coverage Form:[10]

> We will not pay for "loss" caused by or resulting from any of the following unless caused by other "loss" that is covered by this insurance:
>
> a. Wear and tear, freezing, mechanical or electrical breakdown.
> b. Blowouts, punctures or other road damage to tires.

The excluded losses are insurable. Auto dealers, tire shops, and various other organizations offer insurance-like service warranties covering just such losses. However, many individuals and organizations would prefer to pay for such predictable losses out-of-pocket as the need arises rather than to pay insurance premiums to cover them.

Some exclusions are added as endorsements. The ISO Liability Coverage Exclusion Endorsement is an endorsement available with the PAP in several states. It excludes Liability Coverage for bodily injury to "you" or any "family member" and prevents insurance payments in states that otherwise permit one insured family member to collect bodily injury damages from another insured family member. For example, a husband injured as a passenger while his wife was driving would not be able to collect under the Liability Coverage if this endorsement were attached. By limiting coverage, the premium is kept at a reasonable level.

Although the Liability Coverage Exclusion was once a common endorsement or policy provision, it is now prohibited or significantly restricted by several courts ruling that it was against public policy, especially in states that mandate Liability and/or Uninsured Motorists Coverage. Currently, this endorsement is not approved in thirty-six states.

The **Named Driver Exclusion** is another common example of an exclusionary endorsement. Where permitted by law, some companies may specifically exclude coverage for a specifically named driver who has access to the car but, because of a history of accidents or dangerous driving habits, is considered to be an unacceptable risk. Instead of eliminating coverage for the entire family, the company specifically identifies this driver and excludes him or her, typically with a signed endorsement. Eliminating the one driver permits other family members to continue having coverage (at an affordable rate) rather than losing coverage altogether or being placed in a high-risk plan. Many courts and state legislatures do not support these exclusions because they do not protect innocent victims and view forcing the entire family into a high-risk plan (at higher rates) that covers the risky driver as a better alternative.

Exceptions to Exclusions

Exceptions to exclusions should not be overlooked because they give coverage back to the insured. For example, the PAP has the following business exclusion with an exception:

EXCLUSIONS

A. We do not provide Liability Coverage for any "insured":

    7. Maintaining or using any vehicle while that "insured" is employed or otherwise engaged in any "business" (other than farming or ranching) not described in Exclusion **A.6.**

    This Exclusion **(A.7.)** does not apply to the maintenance or use of a:

    a. Private passenger auto;

    b. Pickup or van; or

    c. "Trailer" used with a vehicle described in **a.** or **b.** above.

Because of exception (a), coverage applies to parties who are using their own car for business purposes.

Exclusion A.6. applies to nonowned autos used in the business of selling, repairing, parking, servicing, or storing vehicles.

Conditions

As previously mentioned, an insuring agreement obligates an insurer to make a payment or provide a service under certain circumstances. The insurer's promises are invariably subject to several conditions. **Conditions** can be thought of as qualifications an insurer attaches to its promises.

Common policy conditions obligate the insured to do the following:

- Pay premiums
- Report losses promptly
- Provide appropriate documentation for losses
- Cooperate with the insurer in legal proceedings
- Refrain from jeopardizing an insurer's rights to recover from responsible third parties (subrogation actions)

Miscellaneous Provisions and Endorsements

Insurance policies often contain various provisions that do not strictly qualify as declarations, definitions, insuring agreements, exclusions, or conditions. They may deal with the relationship between the insured and the insurer, or they may help to establish working procedures for carrying out the terms of the contract, but they do not have the force of conditions. Endorsements are attached to a policy to add coverages, name additional insureds, add exclusions, or otherwise clarify or amend policy provisions.

CONCLUSION

In addition to computerized evaluation and negotiation that will continue to evolve, no doubt other technological tools will be produced to help claim representatives perform their jobs more efficiently and better. However, there will never be a substitute for claims people having the ability to comprehend the issues presented by each individual claim. All claims are unique. Each requires individual understanding from the claim representative.

Liability claim representatives never know it all. Their job requires a broad range of knowledge and skill. The law constantly changes. Injuries vary greatly. New insurance coverages are introduced. No two claimants have the same personality, nor do any two trials have the same jury. By no means is this a boring, mundane occupation. The profession of liability claim representative is one that is interesting and both personally and professionally rewarding.

Welcome to the world of liability claims.

CHAPTER NOTES

1. Insurance Information Institute, *III Fact Book 2000* (New York: Insurance Information Institute, 2000), p. 31.
2. *III Fact Book 2000*, p. 36.
3. EEOC, World Wide Web: www.eeoc.gov/stats/index.html.
4. James R. Jones, *Managing Bodily Injury Claims* (Malvern, Pa.: Insurance Institute of America, 2000).
5. Technical Assistance Research Programs Institute, *Consumer Complaint Handling in America: An Update Study, Part III* (Washington, D.C.: United States Office of Consumer Affairs Council, 1986).
6. The Insurance Services Office, Inc. (ISO) policies used are the PAP (PP 00 01 06 98) and the Business Auto Coverage Form (CA 00 01 07 97).
7. Webb v. State Farm, 479 SW 2d 148.
8. Standard Venetian Blind Co. and Sheldon Morris v. American Empire Insurance Co., Supreme 503 Pa. 300,469 A.2d, 563.
9. Henry Cambell Black, Joseph Nolan, Jacqueline M. Nolan-Haley, *Black's Law Dictionary* (St. Paul: West Publishing, 1990).
10. This is an ISO policy.

Coverage Issues for Automobile Insurance

How Court Decisions Affect Coverage

Definitions in Auto Policies

Liability Coverage Insuring Agreement

Exclusions in the Liability Coverage

Limit of Liability for the Liability Coverage

Other Insurance

Medical Payments Coverage Insuring Agreement

Uninsured Motorists Coverage Insuring Agreement

Limit of Liability—Uninsured Motorists Coverage

Underinsured Motorists Coverage

Duties of the Insured After an Accident or a Loss

General Provisions

Conclusion

Coverage Issues for Automobile Insurance

This chapter is devoted to specific coverage issues and practical concerns related to the more controversial or complicated provisions in personal and commercial auto policies. Although actual cases in numerous jurisdictions were reviewed in developing this chapter, a deliberate attempt has been made to avoid exhibiting a summary of how each **jurisdiction** views a given coverage issue (although actual cases are cited as endnotes). In addition to being an onerous task, compiling a summary list would be potentially misleading because the dynamic nature of case law that affects coverage could make any such list obsolete in a short period of time.

The purpose of this chapter is to identify and describe important policy definitions, exclusions, limits, and other policy provisions that have coverage interpretations varying by jurisdiction. The chapter describes these various interpretations and suggests ways to investigate coverage issues.

Claim representatives might find many of these coverage issues disconcerting because they could contradict their own comprehension of the policy. After reading this chapter, some claim representatives might feel discouraged and believe learning the policy is not worth their time because laws invalidate the wording. This assessment is not accurate. Most policy provisions apply as stated, and those that do not usually have some consistent interpretation (at least within a given jurisdiction). Furthermore, a familiarity with policy coverages provides the basis for understanding the significance of how the law affects coverage.

> Companies may be reluctant to put case summaries, or state-specific laws, on a company intranet because of the potential for case summaries to be misleading or for state laws to change. Claim representatives should be cautious about making decisions based on any case summary because many of the unique facts of the case are not presented in the case summary.

A claim representative should identify local, reliable resources that state how a given coverage issue has been decided in the jurisdictions where he or she works. This is an implicit educational objective of this chapter. Larger companies sometimes list this information on a company intranet. Most large

The term **jurisdiction** as used in this text means the geographic area in which a court has power to hear a case. Because most of the law affecting coverage comes from state courts, the text often uses the term "states" interchangeably with "jurisdictions." Although there is a technical distinction, the term "states" is used because it is less cumbersome.

law firms publish newsletters and report on changes in the law that affect coverage in the jurisdiction where they practice. Every company should have a claim manager, a litigation manager, or legal counsel who can assist claim representatives with specific coverage questions. Claim representatives should consult with these resources when they are assigned claims in unfamiliar jurisdictions. The policies quoted in the chapter come from the 1998 edition of the Personal Auto Policy (PAP) (PP 00 01 06 98) and the 1997 Business Auto Coverage Form (CA 00 01 07 97). The issues and concerns follow the order of the PAP.

Many of the topics presented in this chapter are further highlighted in a section entitled "Claim Representative Solutions." The purpose of these sections is to give guidance and a suggested investigative approach for handling claims involving the respective topic. These solutions are not necessarily comprehensive but are intended to provide a framework for determining coverage. Individual insurers may have their own approach for resolving a given coverage issue.

Examples of the type of coverage issues described in this chapter include:

- If a person borrows a friend's car and is involved in an accident, whose insurance coverage is primary if both people have personal auto policies?
- If a teenager moves away from home, is the teenager still covered under the parents' personal auto policy?
- If a delivery truck driver claims he was forced off the road, but not struck, by an unidentified motorist, would the uninsured motorists coverage apply?

These coverage questions have one definitive answer: "It depends." Coverage interpretation in claims is not simply a matter of reading the policy. Courts must deal with situations not addressed by policy language and have complicated the legal landscape by interpreting policies in ways unexpected by insurance companies. Legislatures also play a role in coverage interpretation by writing statutes that mandate or define specific insurance coverages. Consequently, claim representatives must interpret coverage with the policy in one hand and case or statutory law in the other. This is true because, among other reasons,

- Claim representatives are more likely to handle claims in multiple states.
- Courts are willing to depart from decades of tradition and interpret policies in new ways.

The increase in the cost to the company for claim representatives' misinterpreting the policy is due to the increased exposure to bad faith claims and the increased cost of litigation. Courts have been lowering the threshold required to make a bad faith claim, while bad faith jury awards have escalated.

Many insurance companies have reorganized and consolidated their claim offices across the United States. As a result, remaining claim offices, and the claim representatives who staff these offices, now have responsibilities for claims in several states. Different states often have different court interpretations or statutory wording that affects insurance coverage.

Although numerous automobile coverage issues are related to physical damage to an insured vehicle, most of them involve relatively nominal sums compared to the disputed amounts in other coverages. Insurance company guidelines are the most common method of resolving these issues, because the amounts do not justify litigation unless the company has a pattern of handling these claims that consumers may see as inconsistent or unfair. While some of the largest awards given in recent litigation are based on class-action suits for physical damage claims, these kinds of first-party coverage disputes are outside the scope of this chapter.

HOW COURT DECISIONS AFFECT COVERAGE

Because the insurance company, in most cases, offers the insurance policy to policyholders on a take-it-or-leave-it basis and does not permit individual policyholders the right to alter a policy's wording, courts will find in favor of policyholders whenever policy wording is found to be ambiguous. For this reason, lawyers for policyholders only need to prove that the meaning is not clear in order to prevail in court. However, courts will not normally rule against insurers if the policy language is clearly written and comprehensible to a layperson. An insured who fails to read or understand clearly worded policy language is not likely to obtain a favorable coverage decision from the court.

For terms not specifically defined, courts apply a "plain talk" standard. A description of this standard as declared by one court is as follows:

> Generally, the terms of an insurance policy must be considered not in a technical but in a popular sense, and they should be construed according to their plain, ordinary and accepted use in common speech, unless it affirmatively appears that a different meaning was intended.[1]

Using this standard, claim professionals cannot rely on industry usage of a term to be applied by the courts. If the term is specifically (affirmatively) defined in the policy, then the courts will use the term as defined, but otherwise they will consider the common meaning of the term. This chapter will elaborate on some of the terms that are subject to controversy.

For example, the insuring agreement for the liability coverage provided by the business auto coverage form reads (in part) as follows:

> We will pay all sums an "insured" legally must pay as damages because of "bodily injury" or "property damage" to which this insurance applies, caused by an "accident" and resulting from the ownership, maintenance or use of a covered "auto."

To the casual reader, this may seem like a simple provision that has little chance for differing interpretations. In reality, this one provision is fraught with several potential coverage issues. For example, the term "use" is not defined and is not always equated with the actual operation of a vehicle. "Using" the auto may mean loading or unloading tools or supplies from the auto.

Knowing the purpose of an exclusion is useful, because courts will often contemplate the reasons for it when assessing the intent of the wording. Consider the following commentary of two Pennsylvania Supreme Court Justices on the reason for the "care, custody or control" exclusion:

> There are several different reasons for such an exclusion in the policy. Fundamentally, were it not for the exclusion there would be a greater moral hazard.
>
> There is usually some form of insurance available to cover the excluded property. This exclusion is to eliminate the ability to secure coverage under a liability policy at a cheaper rate.[2]

Some jurisdictions apply the **doctrine of reasonable expectations** to policy wording interpretation. The application of this doctrine is rare and varies by state. The most liberal application provides coverage for insureds—even if the policy wording unambiguously denies coverage—if the outcome is contrary to the objective, reasonable expectations of the insured. Although advocates for policyholders often cite this doctrine as a reason to provide coverage, this doctrine is applied only in very unusual circumstances, usually when information such as an agent's statement or an advertising brochure contradicts policy wording. The doctrine is sometimes applied if an insurance company changes its policy wording by adding an exclusion but fails to notify the insured of the changes when the policy renews. In this case, the insured's reasonable expectation would be that the policy renews with the same coverage unless the insured is informed otherwise.[3]

Finally, one of the most common reasons for courts to find coverage is because a policy provision is against the interests of the general public. This is referred to as being "contrary to public policy." **Public policy** refers to principles and standards that are a fundamental concern to society as a whole. The most common example occurs when an insurance company tries to enforce a policy provision that excludes coverage, but the state mandates automobile insurance coverage for the protection of third parties. States permit many policy exclusions, but some are considered to be against public policy because the insurance policy fails to provide the coverage specifically mandated by legislatures. Numerous examples of contravening policy interpretation are described later in this chapter. Many states place an affirmative duty on claim representatives to act in good faith in properly interpreting insurance coverages. A statement by the New Jersey Supreme Court summarized this duty:

> Insurance policies are contracts of utmost good faith and must be administered and performed as such by the insurer. Good faith demands that the insurer deal with laymen as laymen and not as experts in the subtleties of law. . . . In all insurance contracts, particularly where the language expressing the coverage is deceptive to the ordinary layman, there is an implied covenant of good faith and fair dealing that the insurer will not do anything to injure the right of its policyholder to receive the benefits of his contract.[4]

This good faith effort requires claim representatives to understand the policy and then apply any jurisdictional interpretations to the policy wording. The purpose of this chapter is not to provide a complete state-by-state analysis of coverage provisions, but instead to give guidance on some commonly disputed provisions in the personal and commercial automobile policies, such as the Insurance Services Office (ISO) Personal Auto Policy (PAP) and the ISO Business Auto Coverage Form. As claim representatives encounter claims involving these coverage provisions, they should check with claim managers or legal counsel to ensure that they understand how their jurisdiction handles the coverage issue. Many of the challenging coverage issues related to these automobile policies are found in other types of insurance.

DEFINITIONS IN AUTO POLICIES

Policy definitions are a common source of coverage litigation. Certain definitions are more often litigated than others. The purpose of this section is to identify those definitions and to describe the tests that courts may apply in interpreting them. Four such definitions examined here are "family member," "occupying" (a motor vehicle), "bodily injury," and "employee." These terms are often interpreted differently by courts in different states.

Who Is a "Family Member"?

All of the insuring agreements for the liability, medical payments, uninsured motorists, and underinsured motorists coverages in the PAP include "family members" as insureds. The PAP defines **family member** as follows:

> "Family member" means a person related to you by blood, marriage or adoption who is a resident of your household. This includes a ward or foster child.

Some questions that arise from this definition are:

- Who is a resident of your household?
- Does the definition include children away at college or in military service who no longer live in their parents' home?
- And what about children of divorced parents who spend alternate weekends with their father but live with their mother the rest of the time?

Because the policy does not define the term **"resident,"** courts may look to dictionary definitions to help resolve these questions. Courts view dictionary definitions as the "plain, ordinary, reasonable meanings."[5] Webster's *New International Dictionary* contains the following definition of "resident:"

> One who resides in a place; one who dwells in a place for a period of more or less duration. Resident usually implies more or less permanent abode, but it is often distinguished from inhabitant as not implying as great fixity or permanency of abode.[6]

Against this background, courts have declined to equate a resident with a permanent domicile. Although a truly short-term visitor who expects to stay for a definite period of time is probably not a resident, it is not necessary that a resident have a permanent or even long-term living arrangement.[7] The term "resident" will therefore have different shades of meaning depending on the context.

Factors To Consider in Determining Whether a Person Is a Resident of a Household

What objective actions and behaviors should claim professionals look for in determining residency? Usually, no individual factor will decide the issue, but instead the court looks at all relevant factors. This requires claim professionals to conduct a thorough investigation.

To determine whether a person is a resident, courts will consider a person's actions and intentions.[8] If the person intends to remain for an indefinite period of time, the person is more likely to be considered a resident than someone whose intention is to stay for a fixed, limited time. A person need not remain physically within the household to be considered a resident. As long as the person maintains some regular, permanent attachment to the family household, most courts will find the person to be a resident. Courts seem to view residence as a matter of intention and choice rather than one of geography. Furthermore, some courts find that a person can be a resident of more than one household.[9]

Temporary Residents

Persons who temporarily or occasionally stay in a home present particularly troublesome residency issues. The following cases illustrate how courts look at the overall circumstances in determining residency in these situations:

> A husband separated from his wife, leaving the house and taking almost all of his belongings. Four months later the man was in an accident and sought coverage under an auto policy issued to his wife. The court concluded that the man was not a resident of the woman's household because nothing the man did indicated that he intended to reconcile with his wife or return home.[10]

> A niece lived at her aunt and uncle's house. She maintained her own room there with personal belongings, ate meals with her aunt and uncle, and received correspondence there. She had frequent contact with her aunt and uncle. The court noted the close relationship the woman had with her aunt and uncle and determined that she was a resident of their household.[11]

> A twenty-five-year-old man stayed with his uncle after being released from jail. He intended to stay with his uncle until he could find employment. He did his own laundry and slept in the den of the uncle's house. The court concluded that the nephew was not a resident and reasoned that the nephew's intent was to leave the house.[12]

> A nephew who was raised by his aunt left her house after high school. He lived with several different friends but returned to his aunt's house to mow her yard, use her swimming pool, pick up mail, and occasionally spend the night. The court held that although the nephew enjoyed substantial privileges at his aunt's home, his visits were insufficiently permanent for him to be considered a member of her household.[13]

These cases illustrate the importance of a person's intentions, the duration and nature of time spent in the household, and the closeness in the relationship of the person to the named insured.

When the claim issue involves the insured's children, several additional issues must be considered in determining residency. The following topics examine the residency issue as it arises in situations involving children away at school or in the military, emancipated children, and children of divorced parents.

> ### CLAIM REPRESENTATIVE SOLUTIONS
>
> ## Determining Residency
>
> The following questions can serve as guidelines to assist claim representatives in investigating the residency issue.
>
> - How frequently and for how long does the person stay at the residence?
> - Does the person eat meals at the residence?
> - Does the person keep clothes or other personal belongings in the residence?
> - Does the person maintain a room in the residence?
> - Does the person receive mail at the residence?
> - Does the person pay rent, utilities, telephone bills, or maintenance expenses for the residence?
> - Do the person's living and working circumstances indicate that the person is likely to return to the residence?
> - Where does the person keep his or her vehicles?
> - What address does the person list on his or her tax return?
> - What is the address on the person's driver's license?
> - Where is the person registered to vote?

Children Away at School

As mentioned earlier, children away at school in temporary residences generally may remain residents of the parental household.[14] Courts may allow a transitional period after graduation even if the intent appears to be not to return to the parents' home.[15] Exceptions to this rule sometimes exist when the children demonstrate that they have no intention of returning home. The following case illustrates this point.

> Two sisters attended college. Their mother claimed them as dependents on her tax returns. The sisters listed their mother's address as their home address on their own tax returns. Despite the mother's claim of dependency for tax purposes, the facts indicated that the sisters were financially independent from their mother, including paying for their own automobile insurance. Their mother told them that they were on their own after they had turned eighteen. The sisters had moved their personal belongings out of their mother's house. The court ruled that they were not residents of the mother's household.[16]

Children in the Military

Adult children in military service who have not acquired a separate domicile may also remain residents of the parental household. Courts have recognized that the nature of military service requires children to leave home but often with the intent of returning to the parents' home. The following case illustrates this point:

> Before entering the Navy, Davy resided continuously with his parents. After entering the service, he continued to keep his personal belongings at his parents' home. He also continued to use his parents' home as his permanent mailing address. Even though he had lived at several Navy bases, he was still considered a resident of his parents' household.[17]

Emancipated Children

Children who live on their own, free of parental control and support, are not normally considered residents of the parental household; however, numerous circumstances occur when children have not completely separated from their parents. These circumstances create difficult coverage decisions. As a general rule, courts consider teenage children to be residents. The following cases illustrate the facts that courts weigh in determining residency.

> A sixteen-year-old was, at the time of an automobile accident, staying at his grandmother's house. Based on disciplinary problems at his parents' home, the juvenile had moved into his grandmother's guest room, bringing with him a partial wardrobe and other belongings. Eventually, the juvenile moved from his grandmother's home to live with various friends. The court weighed his testimony against his young age and strained family relationships and concluded that emancipation is governed by the parents' intent, not simply determined by the acts of the child. Characterizing his move from his grandmother's home to his friends' as an "experiment with independence," the court was unable to conclude that the youth was freely able to terminate his residency in his grandmother's household.[18]

> A daughter lived alone at her mother's house in Spokane, Washington. Her mother, who owned the house, lived with her new husband in another city. The girl did not pay rent or utilities. The mother and her second husband returned to the house in Spokane once each month. The court concluded that the mother did not maintain a residence in Spokane with her daughter because she showed no intent to move back to Spokane. The courts did not accept that the mother had dual residency because the time divided between the two households was not close to being equal. Therefore, the daughter was not covered under her mother's policy.[19]

> Paul, a thirty-five-year-old man, moved from his parents' New Jersey home to Greenwich Village, New York. Paul kept his clothes, some other personal belongings, and three cars at the parents' home in New Jersey. He spent two nights each week at the New Jersey home. This arrangement continued for five years. When an underinsured motorist struck Paul's father, the father sought coverage under Paul's policy as a "family member" of Paul. The court ruled that Paul was a resident of the New Jersey household and therefore his father was a "family member" under Paul's auto policy.[20]

> An adult son lived in an upper unit of a house owned by his mother. The unit had its own living area, sleeping quarters, bathroom, entrance, mailing address, telephone line, and electricity. The son paid his mother

monthly rent for the unit. Even though the son spent time downstairs with his mother, the court considered the son to have a separate residence and not to be a resident of the mother's household; thus he was not covered by his mother's policy.[21]

Children of Divorced Parents

The increased existence of nontraditional family situations has caused many courts to liberally construe the issue of residency for minor children of divorced or estranged parents. In some states that acknowledge the concept of dual residency, one parent's having legal custody of the minor child will not always preclude the child from being considered a resident of the other parent's household.

The following cases illustrate what factors courts apply:

> A nine-year-old child of divorced parents lived with her mother, who had custody of the child. The child visited her father's house every weekend. The court ruled that the minor child was a resident of both households. The court stated that it was sufficient that the child spent regular time at her father's residence even if her principal residence was with her mother.[22]

> A teenage daughter resided with her father and visited her mother once each week. When visiting her mother, she brought a suitcase and slept on the mother's pullout couch. The court ruled that the circumstances (such as a pullout sofa instead of her own room and no clothes kept at her mother's house) indicated a transitory visit rather than a residency.[23]

> A seventeen-year-old son of divorced parents lived with his mother for several years. He visited his father infrequently and irregularly. The court concluded that the father was no longer integrated into the routine of the son's household and would therefore not permit the son to collect as a "family member" under the father's policy.[24]

In summary, coverage as a "family member" under the PAP depends on the context of the person's residency. As illustrated by the cases presented, the term "relative" is in the words of one court "flexible, elastic, slippery and somewhat ambiguous."[25] The elastic nature of the term requires claim professionals to be open-minded and diligent in investigating the circumstances that might affect the determination of coverage.

CLAIM REPRESENTATIVE SOLUTIONS

The Residency of Children

Courts look at several factors in determining the residency of children. Claim representatives should investigate these factors, which include the following:

- Is the child in college or in the military and planning to return home?

- Is the child self-supporting or still substantially dependent on his or her parents?

- What are the child's and parents' intent?

Continued on next page.

- How often is the child present in the home?

- What is the nature and permanency of the child's place of lodging?

- What is the child's relationship with the parents?

- Does the child have a key to the home, have his or her own room, or keep personal belongings in the parents' house?

- What is the age of the child?

- Does the noncustodial parent have regular visitation rights?

- Is the parent current in child support (this might make a difference in a few states)?

"Occupying" a Vehicle

The term "occupying" appears in the medical payments, uninsured motorists, and underinsured motorists coverage sections of the PAP and in the business auto endorsements for those coverages. For this reason, it is important for claim representatives to understand what circumstances constitute **occupying a vehicle**. The following excerpt from the medical payments section of the PAP illustrates the usage of the term "occupying" in the insuring agreement and the exclusion:

B.   "Insured" as used in this Part means:

1. You or any "family member":
   a. While "occupying"; or
   b. As a pedestrian when struck by a motor vehicle designed for use mainly on public roads or a trailer of any type.
2. Any other person while "occupying" "your covered auto".

EXCLUSIONS

We do not provide Medical Payments Coverage for any "insured" for "bodily injury":

1. Sustained while "occupying" any motorized vehicle having fewer than four wheels.

The term "occupying" is defined in the definitions section of the PAP. The definition reads as follows:

Occupying means in, upon, getting in, on, out or off.

Although the term "occupying," as defined by the policy, may seem clear to a casual observer, it becomes cloudy when applied to certain factual circum-stances[26] such as the following:

- When a person slips on ice and falls onto the insured vehicle.

- When a person is struck by another vehicle while standing two feet away from the insured car after exiting the car door.

Courts would probably find in favor of a person who slips on ice and falls into the car. The person in that instance has made physical contact with the car.[27] However, the second situation is more controversial. Courts have two ways of looking at this. One view is to require physical contact with the vehicle, while the other is to provide coverage if the person is in "sufficient proximity" to the vehicle.

The Physical Contact Test

An ordinary reading of the definition of "occupying" would suggest that the person would need to be in physical contact with the car and, in fact, some courts require that a person be in physical contact with the vehicle in order to meet the definition of "occupying." However, physical contact might include circumstances not envisioned in the everyday usage of the "in, upon, getting in, on, out or off" definition. For example, physical contact could include a person who is leaning against the vehicle or a person who is pushing the vehicle.[28] The investigation of coverage in such jurisdictions can be challenging because it requires claim representatives to determine whether the person was touching the vehicle at the time of the accident. Such a determination can be difficult to make after the accident, especially if there were no independent witnesses, such as in a hit-and-run accident or when the victim was rendered unconscious and does not recall the specific details of the event.

Even when physical contact with the auto exists, courts are reluctant to give coverage for circumstances unrelated to the normally intended use of the vehicle. For example, physical altercations involving drivers or passengers of vehicles often occur around vehicles. Using a car door as a weapon by intentionally opening or shutting it on somebody would not likely be considered occupying the vehicle, even though it involves physical contact with the vehicle.[29]

Sufficient Proximity and Vehicle Orientation

Other courts are more liberal in applying the definition of "occupying." They do not require the person to be in physical contact with the vehicle. Instead, the person needs only to be in **sufficient geographic proximity** to the vehicle. Circumstances included in this standard could include a person filling the gas tank of the car, a person fixing a flat tire,[30] or a person standing next to a car waiting for the driver to unlock the door. These examples illustrate another point that courts consider—the orientation of the person to the vehicle. A person waiting for the car door to open is obviously oriented toward the vehicle. Consider, on the other hand, a pedestrian who did not know the driver had been standing on the sidewalk next to where the vehicle was parked, facing away from the vehicle. Just by happenstance the pedestrian was within geographic proximity to the car. Courts would not consider this to be sufficient proximity because the pedestrian was not "vehicle oriented."[31] The relationship of the pedestrian to the vehicle was too tenuous for even the most liberal courts to consider the person as "occupying" the vehicle.

Some states completely disregard the policy definition of "occupying," reasoning that it is against public policy to apply a restrictive definition that legislatures did not intend when they created the coverage mandate. One court even found coverage for people (not named insureds) struck by an uninsured motorist while walking down the road after their vehicle had broken down. The court reasoned that it was sufficient that the people had previously been occupants of the vehicle.[32]

> The PAP expressly states that it covers the named insured or "family members" who are pedestrians. In the case cited above, the passengers were covered, too, based on their prior occupancy of the insured vehicle, not on policy wording covering them as pedestrians under the insured's policy.

CLAIM REPRESENTATIVE SOLUTIONS

Determining Whether a Person Is an "Occupant"

Claim representatives should understand the importance of investigating the facts leading up to and surrounding an incident. Specifically, they should investigate the following:

1. What activity was the person engaged in at the time of the injury?
2. Was this activity vehicle oriented?
3. Was the person in physical contact with the vehicle or just within close proximity to it?
4. Specifically, how close was the person to the vehicle?

After the facts have been thoroughly established, the claim representative can then apply the facts to the way the jurisdiction interprets coverage.

Bodily Injury

Both the PAP and the Business Auto Coverage Form define the term "bodily injury." The definitions are similar. The PAP defines the term as follows:

> "Bodily injury" means bodily harm, sickness or disease, including death that results.

The Business Auto Coverage Form defines the term slightly differently:

> "Bodily injury" means bodily injury, sickness or disease sustained by a person including death resulting from any of these.

Although the two have subtle differences, most of the issues that courts consider are the same, but the term "harm" found in the PAP is potentially broader than "injury." It might be hard to imagine a sickness or an illness that could result from an auto accident, but the key phrase is "resulting from." This would include the triggering of diseases such as pneumonia, asthma, reflex dystrophy syndrome, and heart attacks. Relating these to the auto accident could require extensive medical investigation.

If a physical injury causes the emotional distress, then the claim for the emotional distress would be covered. But what if the claim is solely for a nonphysical injury? For example, consider the case of a husband who is standing next to his wife when a vehicle zooms by, barely missing him but striking her. Can he make a bodily injury claim for the emotional distress of seeing his wife injured?

Emotional Injury Claims Without Any Physical Injury

Courts are more likely to recognize an **emotional injury** claim if the person witnessed the horror firsthand or was in close enough proximity to be in reasonable fear for his or her own safety. Courts are also more likely to consider the claim a "bodily injury" when there is a consequential physical-injury component to it.[33]

Is an Emotional Injury a Bodily Injury?

The majority of courts would state that a purely emotional injury is not bodily injury[34] but is instead an injury to the psyche.[35] A significant number of states (currently about twelve)[36] supports the minority view that emotional distress is "bodily injury" within the definition of the PAP. The reasoning courts in these states use is that the definition includes "harm" and "sickness and disease," significantly broadening the term "bodily injury."[37]

The most troublesome states for insureds are those that recognize emotional injury claims but do not consider them to be covered "bodily injury." In these jurisdictions, the insured is legally liable for causing emotional injury damages, but the damages are not covered under the insurance policy.[38] These damages may be covered by an umbrella policy that covers "personal injury" rather than "bodily injury." However, the adjuster is cautioned to read the definitions to determine if a purely emotional injury is defined as a personal injury within the policy. The compensability and coverage of purely emotional-distress claims are complicated, and claim representatives should bring these claims to the attention of claim managers when they encounter them.

CLAIM REPRESENTATIVE SOLUTIONS

Coverage Determination for Emotional Injuries

The determination of coverage for emotional injury claims is two pronged. First, the claim representative must determine whether the emotional distress claim is recognized by the courts as a legal cause of action. Second, the claim representative must establish whether the emotional distress is considered a "bodily injury" as covered by the policy.

Some questions claim representatives must investigate and resolve in determining whether a person has a recognizable claim are:

- Do the courts in the given jurisdiction recognize emotional (purely nonphysical) injury claims as compensable?
- Do the courts in the given jurisdiction consider purely nonphysical injury claims to be "bodily injury?"
- Did the person witness the injury to a spouse or child?
- Was the person who witnessed the accident also within the "zone of danger?"
- Did the emotional injury lead to a physical injury (for example, high blood pressure, fatigue, sleeplessness, nausea, diarrhea, or ulcers)?

Employees

In the Business Auto Coverage Form, coverage is often based on whether a person was an employee of the named insured. But who is an employee? Does this definition include people who are hired to fill short-term needs? Would it include independent contractors or workers leased from another company? The definitions section of the Business Auto Coverage Form (1997 edition CA 00 01 07 97) defines "employee" as follows:

> E. "Employee" includes a "leased worker". "Employee" does not include a "temporary worker".
>
> H. "Leased worker" means a person leased to you by a labor leasing firm under an agreement between you and the labor leasing firm, to perform duties related to the conduct of your business. "Leased worker" does not include a "temporary worker".
>
> N. "Temporary worker" means a person who is furnished to you for a finite time period to support or supplement your workforce in special work situations such as "employee" absences, temporary skill shortages and seasonal workloads.

These definitions, which are also found in commercial general liability (CGL) policies, clarify that "leased workers" are the same as regular employees but temporary workers are not. Businesses often contract with other companies specializing in leasing drivers. These drivers are covered in the same manner as an insured's regular employees.

This definition does not address the thornier issue of whether the worker who is not a "leased worker" or "temporary worker" is a regular employee. Independent contractors who are not leased from other companies might still be considered employees of the policyholder, depending on the nature of their employment relationship. Many employers call workers "independent contractors" to avoid taxes, withholdings, and workers compensation benefits. The label "independent contractor" does not make a worker an independent contractor. Instead, the extent of control exercised by the employer, the length of employment with the business, the manner of compensation, whether the employer provides the person with tools to do the job, and other issues determine the status of a worker as an employee or independent contractor. These details must be investigated in determining whether a person is an employee of an insured and covered under the policy.

CLAIM REPRESENTATIVE SOLUTIONS

Employee vs. Independent Contractor

Courts use the following factors (not necessarily listed in order of importance) in determining whether a worker is an employee or an independent contractor. The Internal Revenue Service (IRS) uses similar criteria for making its determination (the descriptive names used by the IRS are in parentheses):

1. The degree of control an employer has over the details of work (Instructions)

2. The need for special skills of an independent contractor versus the skills commonly found in employees working for the employer

3. The extent to which the employer provides the tools, material, and equipment (Significant investment)

4. The place of work (Work done on employer's premises)

5. The method of compensation (Payments)

6. The degree of integration of services into the business operation

7. Training requirements

8. The duration of the relationship (Continuing relationship)

9. What kind of time constraints exist? (Full-time requirements/Set hours of work)

10. Does the worker make services available to the public or mainly to the one employer? (Working for more than one firm)

11. Does the employer have the right to fire the worker?

12. Does the worker have the right to quit?

13. Does the worker have the right to hire subordinates? (Hiring assistants)

14. Does the worker deliver personal service, or can the worker substitute another person to perform the job? (Services rendered personally)

15. What type of reporting requirements exist between the worker and employer?

16. Who controls the sequence of tasks that must be performed?

17. Does the employer pay the worker's business and travel expenses?

18. Can the worker realize a profit or a loss?

LIABILITY COVERAGE INSURING AGREEMENT

Both the PAP and the Business Auto Coverage Form have liability insuring agreements. These insuring agreements have several provisions that are frequently the subject of litigation. One reason that provisions in the liability coverage section are subject to dispute is that auto liability insurance is now required in all states for persons owning autos.[39] In addition, forty-one states have laws requiring proof of insurance for every person who registers a motor vehicle.[40] As mentioned earlier, whenever a state requires coverage, insurance companies are not permitted to have coverage that is more restrictive than what the law states. Courts often cite public policy reasons for disregarding or liberalizing policy wording that contradicts statutory wording or even legislative intent.

An excerpt from the PAP liability insuring agreement reads as follows:

PART A—LIABILITY COVERAGE

INSURING AGREEMENT

A. We will pay damages for "bodily injury" or "property damage" for which any "insured" becomes legally responsible because of an auto accident. Damages include prejudgment interest awarded against the "insured".

The insuring agreement goes on further to define who is an "insured."

B.　"Insured" as used in this Part means:

1. You or any "family member" for the ownership, maintenance or use of any auto or "trailer".

2. Any person using "your covered auto".

3. For "your covered auto", any person or organization but only with respect to legal responsibility for acts or omissions of a person for whom coverage is afforded under this Part.

4. For any auto or "trailer", other than "your covered auto", any other person or organization but only with respect to legal responsibility for acts or omissions of you or any "family member" for whom coverage is afforded under this Part. This Provision (B.4.) applies only if the person or organization does not own or hire the auto or "trailer".

The following questions may be encountered by claim representatives handling personal auto liability claims:

- Can a person be legally liable to his or her spouse?

- Can one insured make a bodily injury claim against another?

- What is an auto?

- If an injured party does not have to pay medical expenses because he or she has health insurance, can he or she still claim these expenses as damages?

- What constitutes use of an auto?

Co-Owner and Co-Insured Liability

Nearly all states now permit spouses to sue each other.[41] Some insurers do not expect their policies to cover the liability of one spouse to another; however, in states that permit intrafamily claims, the policy might not exclude these claims. Thus, if the husband runs his car into his wife's car, the liability section of the policy determines whether this **co-owner liability** is covered. Many courts would not consider the wife's car to be in the care, custody, or control of the husband in this circumstance; therefore, there might be no policy exclusion (in the standard ISO policy) that specifically addresses this type of property damage claim. Furthermore, although collision coverage is the appropriate coverage to pay for this type of situation, some insureds do not carry collision coverage or have high deductibles and seek coverage under the liability section. Modern lifestyles complicate the scenario somewhat because spouses sometimes have their own cars, paid for out of their own checking account or using their own credit. Other states take the position that the spouses are co-owners (known by the legal term "tenant" in common ownership) and each has a one-half interest in the automobile. Consequently, the other spouse could be entitled to collect for one-half of the damage.[42]

The legal right of husbands and wives, or children and parents, to sue each other is a relatively new but growing liability exposure. Because courts had not historically allowed intrafamily lawsuits, insurers had no need to include wording that precluded coverage. However, as more courts permitted these claims, insurers began to add exclusionary endorsements or wording (known as household exclusions) that preclude coverage for intrafamily claims. A large and growing number of states consider any such limitation to be against public policy and therefore not valid (or valid over the minimum amount of liability coverage required by law).[43] Claim representatives should consult with claim management if they are unsure how a particular state handles these liability and coverage issues.

What Is an Auto?

The liability section of the PAP provides coverage for "any auto" but states:

> B. We do not provide Liability Coverage for the ownership, maintenance or use of:
>
> 1. Any vehicle which:
>   a. Has fewer than four wheels; or
>   b. Is designed mainly for use off public roads.
>
>   This Exclusion (B.1.) does not apply:
>   a. While such vehicle is being used by an "insured" in a medical emergency;
>   b. To any "trailer"; or
>   c. To any non-owned golf cart.

The definition of "auto" clearly would not cover a motorcycle designed for use on public roads or an off-road all-terrain vehicle. However, some courts have held that an auto could be a modified vehicle that was used off public roads if the vehicle could be licensed for road use with only slight cosmetic changes.[44]

Some state statutes define motor vehicles to include golf carts, motorcycles, and mopeds even though they are obviously not intended to be covered based on policy wording. Interestingly, the 1998 edition of the PAP provides coverage for "any non-owned golfcart" through an exception to the exclusion. This change occurred after a surprising amount of litigation on that issue. The issue of what an auto is surfaces in uninsured or underinsured motorist claims, too.

CLAIM REPRESENTATIVE SOLUTIONS

What Is an "Auto"?

Important investigative questions for determining what is an "auto" include:

- Information about the extent of modification

- How the vehicle is used

- Whether it is used exclusively off public roads or is sometimes used illegally on public roads

Most of the coverage disputes, however, relate to contradictions between statutory definitions of automobiles or motor vehicles that are broader than the policy provisions. Claim representatives should consult with claim management regarding the need to attain statutory definitions of automobiles.

What Does "Use" of the Auto Mean?

Sometimes incidents occur when the insured auto is only loosely connected to the injury or damages. Some courts have reasoned that injuries resulting from shooting at deer from a car are too far removed from the **use of the auto** and not "due to" the use of the auto. Giving someone a sexually transmitted disease, although not intentional, would probably not be considered "use" of the auto if the location of the transmission was the auto. The following real-life claim demonstrates how "use" of the auto has been determined by the courts.

> A pedestrian was injured by a dog that was inside the insured auto. The dog bit the pedestrian as he was walking past the auto. The court ruled that the automobile use was not causally connected to the dog bite because the auto was not functioning as a vehicle at the time of the incident.[45]

No clear pattern has emerged from the states regarding what constitutes the use of an auto when the auto is not being operated at the time of the accident or when it is not operated in a normal manner. However, courts have stated that "the mere use of a vehicle in some way connected to the events giving rise to the injury is insufficient to establish coverage. There must be a causal connection between the use of the vehicle and the injury."[46] Just because the auto was the place of the incident does not mean that there is a causal connection to the injury. As one court explained, "The automobile is so much a part of American life that there are few activities in which the use of an automobile does not play a part somewhere in the chain of events. Clearly the parties to an automobile liability policy do not contemplate a general liability insurance contract."[47]

For this reason, claim representatives must do a complete investigation into the details of the incident, determine how significant the vehicle was in causing the injury based on the circumstances, and consult with claim management for guidance.

The Duty To Defend

The second part of the PAP liability insuring agreement provides insureds with a defense. The PAP reads as follows:

> We will settle or defend, as we consider appropriate, any claim or suit asking for these damages. In addition to our limit of liability, we will pay all defense costs we incur. Our duty to settle or defend ends when our limit of liability for this coverage has been exhausted by payment of judgments or settlements. We have no duty to defend any suit or settle any claim for "bodily injury" or "property damage" not covered under this policy.

The insurer's expenditures for defense costs do not reduce the coverage limits available to insureds under a PAP.

Two questions related to the insurer's duty to defend are:

- Does the insurance company have a duty to defend a policyholder for a claim that might not be covered? If so, what circumstances trigger the duty to defend an insured?

- When does the duty to defend end?

Whole books have been written addressing that first question. As a general rule, the **duty to defend** is broader than the duty to pay damages. If the allegations against the insured are fraudulent or potentially outside the coverage provided, the insurer is still ordinarily obliged to defend the insured. Under such circumstances the defense may be provided under a reservation of rights, and sometimes the defense is terminated after the facts have been gathered if they prove the circumstances are outside the policy coverage. For this reason, companies are sometimes required to provide insureds with legal defense for lawsuits involving circumstances that might not be covered. For example, assume the insured receives a lawsuit from a plaintiff alleging the insured intentionally rammed the insured vehicle into the side of the plaintiff's vehicle. The plaintiff alleges that the insured was overcome with "road rage" because the plaintiff would not permit the insured to merge into his lane of traffic. The policy potentially excludes coverage for this. However, the insurance company would most likely owe a duty to defend the insured if the insured disagreed with the plaintiff's assertion that the damage was intentional, at least until the facts could be shown to prove the plaintiff's assertions. These can be challenging claims that require investigative skills and a great deal of caution.

When does the duty to defend end? The wording of the insuring agreement has been changed to help clarify this issue. The wording in the 1994 edition was as follows:

> Our duty to settle or defend ends when our limit of liability for this coverage has been exhausted.

Many insurers saw this as a clear-cut provision indicating that once the limits have been paid, the duty ends. However, many courts did not permit the insurance company to pay just the limits and then walk away from the suit, leaving the insured responsible for the legal defense costs if the plaintiff still wanted to pursue the rest of the damages from the insured. Now the wording in the policy is as follows:[48]

> Our duty to settle or defend ends when our limit of liability for this coverage has been exhausted by *payment of judgments or settlements* [emphasis added].

The current Business Auto Coverage Form[49] has the same wording. The intent of this change was to clarify that an insurer cannot offer or tender its limits, and be relieved of its duty to defend an insured, before a settlement amount has been agreed upon or before a judgment has been reached.

Before tendering limits in the hope of closing a claim, claim representatives should check to see how the duty to defend provision is worded. If the wording is not explicit, claim representatives should consult with claim management or legal counsel to determine how courts in their jurisdiction address this issue.

EXCLUSIONS IN THE LIABILITY COVERAGE

Exclusions restrict coverage. For this reason, courts will interpret exclusionary language very narrowly. Exclusions sometimes contravene state statutes requiring certain types of coverages such as liability or uninsured motorists. States will, in these cases, consider public policy issues when analyzing the exclusion.

Intentional Injury

Intentional injuries are normally excluded. Insurers have invoked the intentional injury exclusion in a wide variety of situations involving autos. Assault and battery with a car, rape or sexual molestation in an auto, and discharging firearms from an auto are activities for which people have sought coverage. In addition to defending coverage on the basis of intentional injuries, insurers have also claimed that these activities are never covered in the insuring agreement because they do not involve the "use" of the auto (an issue previously discussed).

The most complicated aspect of enforcing the intentional injury provision is the investigation that must delve into and establish the motivation of the person committing the act. Courts will generally find in favor of insurers if they truly believe the injury was intentional, but this belief must be supported by a comprehensive, well-organized investigation of the insured's activities. Insureds are often less than helpful in assisting with investigations in such situations. Claim representatives who encounter claims involving potentially intentional injuries must take thorough, probing statements from the insured to determine the truth.

Another complicating factor is that courts are sometimes willing to cover claims when the act that caused the injury or property was intended, but the resulting consequence of the act was not intended. For example, the insured's intent might have been to bump another vehicle's bumper to force the other driver to let the insured into a line of traffic. If the other vehicle subsequently careened over the edge of a cliff because of the contact, some courts might not consider the result intentional even though the act that caused it was. The age of the driver might also be a factor in assessing whether injuries were intentionally inflicted. Youthful operators sometimes drive in reckless ways that adults would expect to lead to an injury. Young drivers sometimes do not have this foresight.

Care, Custody, or Control

Both the PAP and the Business Auto Coverage Form have exclusions for "property damage" to property in the care, custody, or control of the insured. (The wording of the exclusion in the two policies varies slightly.) Because of the relatively small dollar amounts involved in property damage claims, this issue is not intensely litigated. However, it is often the subject of controversy in claims because, unlike most auto claims, claims that fall within this exclusion often involve autos or other property owned by parties whom the insured knows personally. The PAP excludes the following type of "property damage":

A.3. For "property damage" to property:

a. Rented to;

b. Used by; or

c. In the care of;

that "insured".

This Exclusion (A.3.) does not apply to "property damage" to a residence or private garage.

CLAIM REPRESENTATIVE SOLUTIONS

Investigating Intentional Injuries

When encountering claims that involve potentially intentional injuries, claim representatives should:

1. Reserve the company's rights through a reservation of rights letter.

2. Take detailed statements from the insured, claimant, and witnesses to try to establish the insured's mindset at the time of the incident. This should be performed as soon as possible after an incident. Claim representatives should keep in mind that even when the insured's subjective intent is different from what actually occurs, coverage might not apply, especially if what occurs was reasonably foreseeable by an ordinary person. As part of the investigation of the insured's intent, claim representatives should determine whether the insured was under the influence of drugs or alcohol, or suffering from a mental illness at the time of the incident, because some courts look at these factors in determining "intent."

3. Determine whether the incident involved the "use" of an auto by assessing how important the auto's role was in the incident.

4. Consider how the courts in the given jurisdiction have defined the word "accident." The courts may not consider intentional acts to be the requirement of being unexpected or unforeseeable.

This wording varies somewhat from the traditional care, custody, or control wording, but the purpose of the exclusion is similar. If an insured was moving a friend's sofa and chairs in the back of an insured's pickup truck and accidentally ran off the road, sending the furniture into a ditch, the furniture damage would not be covered. If an insured, Jack, borrows his friend Sam's car and backs it into a tree, the damage to Sam's car would not be covered under the liability coverage of Jack's (or Sam's) auto policy (although it would be covered under Jack's physical damage coverage if Jack carries collision coverage and Sam does not). Insureds are understandably sympathetic to their friends and will attempt to seek coverage under their own policy, especially if a friend's vehicle is not insured for "collision damage."

Five states have laws requiring insurance companies to pay for damage to rental cars under the liability section of the policy.[50] This requirement invalidates the care, custody, or control exclusion for damage to those vehicles. A few states have also passed legislation requiring the individual driver's liability coverage to apply to damage to a vehicle owned by a dealership that occurs while the vehicle is being test-driven by an insured.[51]

Business Use of a Personal Auto

The PAP is intended to cover loss exposures related to the personal rather than commercial use of an insured automobile. The loss exposures from many business activities, such as driving taxis, are higher than what the average person would experience in using an automobile for personal use. For this reason, the PAP has several business-related exclusions. However, the PAP does permit incidental business use of personal autos and addresses this through an exception to the business exclusions. Claim representatives handling the claims involving the business use of autos that are insured under a PAP should answer the following three questions:

- Is there an exclusion that eliminates coverage for the activity?
- Is there an exception to the exclusion that allows coverage for the activity?
- Was there any material misrepresentation of the use of the auto on the insured's application for PAP coverage?

Business Exclusions

Four liability coverage exclusions (exclusions 4 through 7) deal with business-related losses. Each of the exclusions has an exception [italic emphasis added] that gives back coverage in some circumstances:

4. For "bodily injury" to an employee of that "insured" during the course of employment. This Exclusion (A.4.) *does not apply to "bodily injury" to a domestic employee unless workers' compensation benefits are required or available for that domestic employee.*

5. For that "insured's" liability arising out of the ownership or operation of a vehicle while it is being used as a public or livery conveyance. *This Exclusion (A.5.) does not apply to a share-the-expense car pool.*

6. While employed or otherwise engaged in the "business" of:
   a. Selling;
   b. Repairing;
   c. Servicing;
   d. Storing; or
   e. Parking;

   vehicles designed for use mainly on public highways. This includes road testing and delivery. *This Exclusion (A.6.) does not apply to the ownership, maintenance or use of "your covered auto" by:*
   a. *You;*
   b. *Any "family member"; or*

   c. *Any partner, agent or employee of you or any "family member".*

7. Maintaining or using any vehicle while that "insured" is employed or otherwise engaged in any "business" (other than farming or ranching) not described in Exclusion A.6.

   This Exclusion (A.7.) does not apply to the maintenance or use of a:

   a. *Private passenger auto;*

   b. *Pickup or van; or*

   c. *"Trailer" used with a vehicle described in a. or b. above.*

Exclusion 4 eliminates coverage for injuries to employees of insureds. The PAP is not intended to cover workers compensation losses.

Exclusion 5 eliminates coverage for a vehicle while used as a "public or livery conveyance." This exclusion applies to situations in which the insured uses the insured vehicle to make a profit as a taxi transporting the public or as a livery delivering objects. However, two issues might arise:

- Would this exclusion apply to an insured who transports people on a limited basis?

- Would this exclusion apply to an insured who delivers pizzas part time?

In cases involving the transportation of people, courts will examine the profit motive, the regularity of the activity, and whether the amount paid to the vehicle's owner is voluntary. If, for example, an insured, for a set fee, picked up neighborhood children each day in the insured's van and transported the children to daycare centers, courts would probably consider this arrangement to be public conveyance.[52]

Coverage for insureds delivering pizzas is less certain. This issue has been extensively litigated, and with a few exceptions courts have been loathe to deny coverage. The courts have used various reasons for permitting coverage. The state supreme court of New York ruled that this provision could not be enforced to deny coverage for the occasional delivery of pizzas.[53] Some states ruled that delivering pizzas for an hourly wage was not the same as delivering pizzas for a fee.[54] In addition to the difficulty in determining how to apply the policy wording to a given situation, some courts have stated that "business use" exclusions violate the public policy of providing coverage to injured parties under state-mandated requirements.[55]

Exceptions to Business Use

Claim representatives should be mindful that Exclusion 7 allows an exception for the business use of a "private passenger auto or van owned by an insured." This exception gives back coverage to most PAP insureds because private passenger autos and vans represent most of the vehicles insured under the PAP. So when a PAP insured uses a car (as opposed to a truck) to run errands for business purposes, coverage applies. The following case illustrates the court's interpretation of an exception to this business exclusion:

   At the time of the accident, a son was using his mother's car, with her permission, as a pizza delivery vehicle. The insurer denied coverage because the vehicle was being used for business at the time of the accident. The court stated that the policy wording did not support the denial and further determined that a policy exclusion for business use conflicted with the statutory mandate of compulsory insurance and was therefore against public policy. Coverage would have to be given to the son.[56]

Even in cases that are more clearly not covered because of the business use exclusion, claim representatives should know the relevant state's position on the enforcement of the business use exclusions before denying coverage.

Material Misrepresentations

The general rule is that a **material misrepresentation** or omission made in an application for insurance coverage will void the insurer's obligations under the policy.[57] A misstated or omitted fact is deemed material if it could reasonably be considered as affecting an insurer's decision to enter into the insurance contract with the insured, the insurer's evaluation of the degree or character of the risk, or the calculation of the premium.[58] Insurers have sometimes prevailed when they have established that the insured made a material misrepresentation of the use of the auto when he or she completed the application for coverage. In such cases, insurers are permitted to void the policy, which effectively eliminates coverage, even if no exclusion would expressly eliminate coverage.

> Even if the insured's employer has a commercial auto policy that covers the employee while using his or her own car on behalf of the employer, the PAP will provide primary coverage for the insured, and the employer's policy will provide excess. This is based on standard policy wording.

In most cases involving the business use of a personal auto, insureds do not intentionally misrepresent their activities or the activities of their children. For example, an insured who uses his or her own car to travel extensively on business trips each day, but who stated on his or her application that the car is used only to commute fewer than ten miles to work, has potentially misrepresented the use of the vehicle. This misrepresentation would be considered a material misrepresentation if (1) it was done intentionally with the intent to deceive and (2) the difference in the actual business use and the use claimed on the application would have affected the insurer's decision to accept the insured or the amount of premium to charge for coverage. Material misrepresentation is also something to consider in an investigation of fraud.

Unauthorized Use of an Insured Vehicle

Coverage is not provided under the PAP or Business Auto Coverage Form for unauthorized users of insured vehicles. This issue has been addressed in different ways. The Business Auto Coverage Form defines an insured driver as "anyone else while using with your permission a covered auto you own, hire or borrow." The PAP gives coverage to "anyone using a covered auto" but then excludes unauthorized users. The policy excludes coverage as follows:

8. Using a vehicle without a reasonable belief that that "insured" is entitled to do so.

CLAIM REPRESENTATIVE SOLUTIONS

Investigating Material Misrepresentations

In investigating the issue of material misrepresentation, claim representatives should consider the following:

1. Was the insured using the vehicle for business purposes at the time the application was completed?

2. Is the wording on the application regarding business use clear enough for an ordinary, reasonable person to understand?

3. Were any follow-up calls made to the insured to confirm the information given on the application?

4. Is the business use significant enough that an ordinary, reasonable person would consider it to be business?

5. Would it have made a difference in the amount of premium charged if the insured had admitted to using the vehicle for business use?

The "without a reasonable belief" wording is somewhat different from "without permission" (which was the intent found in older ISO policies and in some non-ISO auto policies).

Under the PAP wording, even if the owner had not expressly given permission, courts sometimes rule that a person had "implied" permission. Courts have used the argument that the situation was such that the owner would have given the person permission if he or she had asked. An example of implied permission might be a man who, while visiting his sister during Christmas vacation, takes his sister's car to the store to buy groceries for the Christmas dinner. The "reasonable belief" wording would seem to include this situation as well. Although claim representatives should take the statement of insureds and drivers in these situations, they are likely to hear the user claim that he or she had a reasonable belief to use the vehicle. Courts apply an objective (though somewhat flexible) standard to determine what is "reasonable." The typical standard would be whether an ordinary, reasonable person would think he or she was entitled to use the vehicle under the circumstances presented. The job of the claim representative in these situations is to investigate the facts that would address the issue of whether an ordinary person would consider the belief to be reasonable. The most common controversial situation that occurs with this exclusion involves unauthorized use by insureds' underage, unlicensed children.

Underage, Unlicensed Drivers

The issue of unlicensed, minor drivers is likely to become less of an issue with the new 1998 wording of the PAP than it was under older edition wording.

In 1998, ISO changed the policy wording to reads as follows:

8. Using a vehicle without a reasonable belief that that "insured" is entitled to do so. This Exclusion (A.8.) does not apply to a "family member" using "your covered auto" which is owned by you.

The exception to the exclusion clarifies that the exclusion should not apply to "family members." Underage drivers who are "family members" would be covered because they do not need permission in order to be covered. However, claim representatives should be cautious in assuming that their own company has adopted this PAP version. Insurers that do not use ISO policies, but rather have their own policies, may not have wording that expressly gives coverage to underage drivers. Claim representatives working for these companies must continue to investigate the issue of whether minors have reasonable belief.

Cars Owned or Available for the Regular Use of Insureds

When insureds are involved in accidents with vehicles that are not one of "your covered autos" as defined in the policy, claim representatives should consider whether PAP exclusions B.2. and B.3. for vehicles furnished or available for regular use apply to the claim. These exclusions are intended to prevent two or more vehicles, which are used more or less interchangeably, from being covered under a policy whose premium is based primarily on risks arising from the operation of one vehicle. Without these exclusions, the insurance premium would not properly reflect the additional loss exposure for insureds using multiple cars. Courts have been reluctant to dismiss the importance of these exclusions and have favored the insurers' argument that permitting owners to obtain coverage for multiple vehicles by paying a premium for only one car would have wide-reaching effects and unacceptable social consequences. The exclusions read as follows:

> B. We do not provide Liability Coverage for the ownership, maintenance or use of:....
>
>   2. Any vehicle, other than "your covered auto", which is:
>   a. Owned by you; or
>   b. Furnished or available for your regular use.
>   3. Any vehicle, other than "your covered auto", which is:
>   a. Owned by any "family member"; or
>   b. Furnished or available for the regular use of any "family member".
>
>   However, this Exclusion (B.3.) does not apply to you while you are maintaining or "occupying" any vehicle which is:
>   a. Owned by a "family member"; or
>   b. Furnished or available for the regular use of a "family member".

Exhibit 2-1 shows a decision tree that can be used to help analyze the coverage situation. Analyzing the exclusions in this manner can help claim representatives isolate the specific coverage issues that should be investigated. Two challenging aspects of this coverage are determining whether the insured owned the other vehicle involved in the accident and whether the vehicle was furnished or available for the insured's regular use.

Consider Karl, who is the named insured under a PAP. Karl lives with his wife, Mary, and their son, Fred. Fred's friend Tom leaves Fred his car to look after while Tom goes into the military service in a foreign country. Tom gives

EXHIBIT 2-1

Decision Tree for Exclusions B.2. and B.3. of the PAP—The Use of Cars Owned or Available for the Regular Use of Insureds

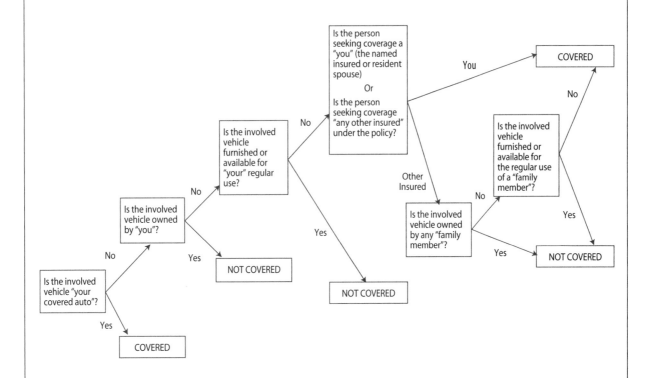

Definitions

"You and Your"

Throughout this policy, "you" and "your" refer to:

1. The "named insured" shown in the Declarations; and
2. The spouse if a resident of the same household.

If the spouse ceases to be a resident of the same household during the policy period or prior to the inception of this policy, the spouse will be considered "you" and "your" under this policy but only until the earlier of:

1. The end of 90 days following the spouse's change of residency;
2. The effective date of another policy listing the spouse as a named insured; or
3. The end of the policy period.

"Family member"

"Family member" means a person related to you by blood, marriage or adoption who is a resident of your household. This includes a ward or foster child.

"Your covered auto"

"Your covered auto" means:

1. Any vehicle shown in the Declarations.
2. A "newly acquired auto".
3. Any "trailer" you own.
4. Any auto or "trailer" you do not own while used as a temporary substitute for any other vehicle described in this definition which is out of normal use because of its:
   a. Breakdown;
   b. Repair;
   c. Servicing;
   d. Loss; or
   e. Destruction.

This Provision (J.4) does not apply to Coverage For Damage To Your Auto.

Fred permission to use his car as part of the agreement for taking custody of it. Following the decision tree presented, the vehicle is not a "your covered auto," nor is it owned by "you" (Karl or Mary). It is not furnished or available for "your" (Karl or Mary's) regular use. The person seeking coverage, Fred, is a "family member" who is not defined as a "you." The vehicle is not owned by Fred. Coverage would be provided only if Tom's car was not furnished and available for Fred's regular use. After analyzing this situation, the claim representative would need to determine whether the vehicle was furnished or available for Fred's regular use.

What does it mean for an auto to be "furnished and available for regular use"? In making this determination, courts look at how steadily, or how often, the vehicle is available to an insured and at what restrictions were placed on the use of the vehicle.[59] These are not the sole definitive criteria, but they are factors that courts consider. In the case involving Fred, the court would consider the agreement Fred had with Tom. If, for example, he had unrestricted use of the vehicle for the time Tom was doing military service (for several months), then a court would most likely rule that the vehicle was available for Fred's regular use. The exclusion would likely apply even if Fred used the car only occasionally because Fred had the opportunity to use the car anytime. The issue of what constitutes regular use must also be analyzed because having a vehicle available for occasional or casual use is not excluded.

The following real case decisions identify some of the factors that courts consider in determining whether a vehicle has been used regularly:

> In a claim involving the use of a nonowned car, the insured had to seek permission and obtain the keys from the owner each time the insured used the car. Also, the insured used the car only six or eight times during a nine-month period. The court ruled that this was not regular use.[60]

> The mother of the named insured lived with the family. The mother owned her own car, but she did not drive. She had others drive her where she needed to go. The mother's vehicle was kept at the insured's house, but it needed repairs. After the repairs were made, months later, the insured was involved in an accident while test-driving it. The mother had given permission to use the vehicle for that purpose. The vehicle had been operable for only fifteen days of the entire time it was stored at the insured's house. The court ruled that this vehicle was not furnished or available for the regular use of the insured, despite the length of time it was stored at the insured's house.[61]

> The named insured's employer leased a vehicle that the named insured drove. The named insured received the car and kept it at home for two months. He had unrestricted use of the car (including for personal use). The court ruled that this vehicle was furnished and available for regular use.[62]

> Over a two-year period, the named insured's employer had furnished the named insured with one of its vehicles on about ten different occasions. During the year of the accident, the insured had used the company vehicle seven or eight times for periods ranging from thirty minutes to a few hours. The insured returned the car to the employer's motor pool after

using it. She had no free access to a fleet vehicle. The court ruled that the insured did not have regular use of the employer's car.[63]

In a slightly different situation, an insured had regular access to and use of company pool cars. The court ruled that the exclusion applied even though the access was not to a particular pool car. The court considered it regular use as long as the insured had regular access to some pool car.[64]

The named insured's use of a rental car for three consecutive weeks while vacationing in Florida did not constitute "regular" use of the car.[65]

CLAIM REPRESENTATIVE SOLUTIONS

Determining Insured's "Regular" Use of Vehicle

Claim representatives must first analyze the coverage situation. If there is an issue of ownership, then the claim representatives should check vehicle registration addresses, personal property taxes, and other vehicle-related documents, in addition to taking a detailed statement from the insured.

A detailed statement would also be required in determining whether the insured's use of a vehicle was regular or occasional. The statements should examine the factors used to determine regular use, such as the restrictions placed on the use of the vehicle, the number of times the vehicle had been used before the accident, and the duration of prior use. Statements from other family members and the owner of the other vehicle are also useful.

Exclusionary Endorsements

Some exclusions are added as endorsements. The ISO PP 03 26 Liability Coverage Exclusion endorsement, which is included with the PAP in several states, excludes liability coverage for bodily injury to "you" or any "family member" and prevents insurance from paying in states that permit one insured family member to collect bodily injury damages from another insured family member. For example, a husband injured as a passenger while his wife was driving would not be able to collect under the liability coverage if this endorsement were attached. Although this was once a more common endorsement or policy provision, it is now one that has been disallowed or significantly restricted by several courts ruling that it is against public policy to have such an endorsement, especially in states that mandate liability and/or uninsured motorists coverage. At the time this was written, this endorsement was disapproved in thirty-six states.

The named driver exclusion is another common example of an exclusionary endorsement. Where permitted by law, some companies may exclude coverage for a specifically named driver who has access to the car, but because of a history of accidents or previous dangerous driving habits is considered to be an unacceptable risk. Instead of eliminating coverage for the entire family, the company specifically identifies this driver and excludes him or her, typically with a signed endorsement. Eliminating the one driver permits other family members to continue having coverage (at an affordable rate) rather than losing coverage altogether or being placed in a high-risk plan. Historically, many courts and state legislatures did not support these exclusions because they did not protect innocent victims, whereas forcing the entire family into a high-risk plan (at higher rates) that covers the risky driver was seen as a better alternative. This endorsement fell out of favor with insurers because courts would not support them. This exclusionary endorsement is now being revived partially in response to insurance regulators who want to help consumers find insurance and to keep rates affordable. Insurers are hoping that with regulatory support for offering this endorsement, they will be able to enforce it.

LIMIT OF LIABILITY FOR THE LIABILITY COVERAGE

Another section of auto policies that falls into controversy is the Limit of Liability provision. This provision reads as follows:

LIMIT OF LIABILITY

A. The limit of liability shown in the Declarations for each person for Bodily Injury Liability is our maximum limit of liability for all damages, including damages for care, loss of services or death, arising out of "bodily injury" sustained by any one person in any one auto accident. Subject to this limit for each person, the limit of liability shown in the Declarations for each accident for Bodily Injury Liability is our maximum limit of liability for all damages for "bodily injury" resulting from any one auto accident.

The limit of liability shown in the Declarations for each accident for Property Damage Liability is our maximum limit of liability for all "property damage" resulting from any one auto accident.

This is the most we will pay regardless of the number of:

1. "Insureds";

2. Claims made;

3. Vehicles or premiums shown in the Declarations; or

4. Vehicles involved in the auto accident.

B. No one will be entitled to receive duplicate payments for the same elements of loss under this coverage and:

1. Part B or Part C of this policy; or

2. Any Underinsured Motorists Coverage provided by this policy.

The issue of stacking is also encountered in cases involving automobile *uninsured* motorists coverage. But courts are more likely to allow stacking in uninsured motorist claims.

The second paragraph of provision A is intended to prevent "stacking" liability limits. Courts have not traditionally permitted insureds to add together (stack) the limits for liability for all insured vehicles and come up with a larger combined limit. The policy wording does not allow this, and although the issue has been litigated occasionally, courts will not permit insureds to stack the liability limits, except in unusual circumstances.[66] Stacking is explained in detail in the discussion of limits of liability under uninsured motorists coverage.

Two issues that claim representatives should be aware of under this limit of liability provision relate to the "each person" limit and to application of "duplicate payments for the same elements of loss."

Per Person Limit

The per person limit is sometimes challenged when more than one impact occurs. If, for example, an insured collides with another car and comes to a stop and then accidentally backs into a third car, courts have consistently considered these impacts to be one accident, subject to one policy limit, because the proximate cause of the impacts is the negligence of the first accident.

The "per person" limit is disputed in cases involving "derivative" claims such as loss of consortium claims and emotional injury claims. The issue is whether these derivative claims are separate claims that trigger additional per person limits. Derivative claims are discussed in the next section.

Many policies have a "per person" limit of liability as well as a total limit of liability. A policy limit expressed as $100,000/$300,000/$50,000 would have a "per person" bodily injury limit of $100,000. The insurer is responsible for up to $100,000 for the bodily injury claim of any one person, but no more than $300,000 for all bodily injury claims for any given accident. The last number, $50,000, is the limit of liability for property damage.

Derivative Claims Versus Separate Injury Claims

Derivative claims are claims that are derived from the injured person's claim. Two common controversies involve loss of consortium claims and pure emotional injury claims based on seeing a family member killed. Courts are divided on whether these types of claims are separately compensable or are derived claims that can be based only on the injured party's loss.

Loss of Consortium Claims

Courts are divided on whether to consider these derivative claims as separate claims with separate per person limits.[67] When a married person is injured, his or her spouse can claim a loss of companionship and services that would have normally been provided by the injured spouse. Consortium has been succinctly expressed as "sex, service, and society."[68] Some states have permitted consortium-type claims for the loss of parents or children based on the loss of companionship.[69] A consortium claim is a **derivative claim**—that is to say a claim that is derived from the injured person's claim. Most courts do not consider it to be a separate claim. Some courts do not even consider it to be a "bodily injury" claim because the injury involved has occurred to a relationship.[70]

Some insurance companies have policies that specifically include "loss of services" in the definition of "bodily injury." In those kinds of policies, the claims are separate, and the claimant is entitled to make claim under an additional per person limit.[71] If, for example, the policy is $100,000/$300,000/$50,000, then a husband who suffered serious injuries might be entitled to $100,000 and the wife would be entitled to an additional amount up to the $100,000 limit.

Pure Emotional Injury Claims

Other derivative cases involve emotional distress claims based on witnessing a family member's physical injury. As mentioned earlier, not all states consider this emotional trauma to be compensable. For those states that do consider it compensable, some may consider it a separate injury.

APPLICATION OF LIMITS TO AN EMOTIONAL INJURY CLAIM

Phil caused an auto accident involving another car. A man and his wife were in the other car. The wife was killed, and the man suffered an emotional injury from witnessing the death of his wife. Phil has injury liability coverage of $25,000/$50,000. Phil's insurer pays the $25,000 limit to the estate of the deceased woman. The man makes a claim for an additional $25,000 for his emotional injury.

Question: Assuming that the damages for the husband's emotional injury equal or exceed $25,000, how much does Phil's insurer owe?

Answer: First, the insurer must determine whether purely emotional injury claims are compensable. In this case, the state considers them to be so. Next, the insurer must determine whether the compensable emotional injury claim is a "bodily injury." In this state, case law has ruled that it is. Finally, the insurer must determine whether the emotional injury claim is considered a separately compensable claim by the husband or a claim based only on the wife's loss. In this state, they are considered separate. Based on all of these laws, the insurer owes an additional $25,000.[72]

Duplicate Payments (Offsets)

The last paragraph of the Limit of Liability provision deals with "duplicate payments" and reads as follows:

> B. No one will be entitled to receive duplicate payments for the same elements of loss under this coverage and:
> 1. Part A or Part C of this policy; or
> 2. Any Underinsured Motorists Coverage provided by this policy.

This provision is intended to prevent claimants from receiving duplicate payments under liability coverage, medical payments coverage, and uninsured motorists coverage. These "offsets" are often challenged. The "offset" for amounts paid under the uninsured motorists coverage is easy to implement and is not usually an issue for the courts. However, the offset for medical payments coverage is not so simple and is subject to legal wrangling. The following case examples illustrate the problems that claim representatives face in enforcing this provision. The second example is intentionally less clear, but it is the kind of situation claim representatives face.

Further complicating the issue, is the fact that courts in some states find that the offset violates public policy or the reasonable expectations of the insured.

Courts in states that have mandatory liability for uninsured motorists coverage argue that it is against public policy to deduct optional coverage payments (such as medical payments) from required coverage payments (such as liability or uninsured motorists), especially if insureds are paying a separate, additional amount for these coverages.[73] Claim representatives should consult with claim management before making decisions about this issue, especially when faced with claims approaching the policy limits.

CASE EXAMPLE—OFFSET FOR DUPLICATE PAYMENT

An insured, Martha, has a limit of liability for the liability coverage of $100,000, and she carries $5,000 medical payments coverage. Her passenger, Vicki, sustains bodily injury damages of $100,000. Because Vicki was a passenger, she is also entitled to Martha's $5,000 medical payments coverage.

Question: Should the company pay $100,000 or $95,000 ($100,000 less the $5,000 paid under medical payments)? The situation would be clearer if the claimant's damages exceeded $105,000, because even if the $5,000 is considered "duplicate" and deducted from the damages owed, the bodily injury policy limit of $100,000 remains. Is it possible to uniformly tell the difference between an injury that deserves $100,000 in general damages and one that deserves $95,000 in general damages? Consider the following case.

CASE EXAMPLE—DUPLICATE PAYMENTS?

The insured driver is involved in an auto accident with another vehicle. The claimant was a passenger in the insured's auto at the time of the accident. The insured has a PAP with a $100,000 limit for liability coverage and a $5,000 limit for medical payments coverage. The claimant incurs $20,000 in medical expenses, and his total claim including general damages is between $60,000 and $70,000. The company pays the claimant his $5,000, the limit of the medical payments coverage. The liability investigation continues and concludes that the insured is 90 percent at fault for the accident. The insurance company then owes the claimant somewhere between $54,000 and $63,000 under the liability coverage. The claimant seeks the additional 10 percent from the driver of the other vehicle. The insured's liability claim under the insured's policy is settled for $58,000.

Question: Was the settlement reduced by the $5,000 paid under the medical payments coverage? Many readers may have difficulty answering this because the answer is "yes" if the claim representative says it was or "no" if the claim representative says it was not. The reason for this confusion is because with the variability in damage awards given by courts, the best that a claim representative can establish is a range of settlement figures, not a precise amount. The claim representative should certainly use the "no duplicate payment" wording as a talking point in negotiation, but often it is impossible to tell how much if any of the offset was actually applied.

Out-of-State Coverage Limits

The purpose of the out-of-state coverage provision is to provide insureds traveling through other states with enough coverage to meet the financial responsibility or similar laws of the state they are traveling in at the time of an accident. This provision applies if the other state's requirements are higher than the limits of the insured's policy. This provision is easy to implement. Claim representatives need only determine whether the limits of the other state are higher. In 1999, the various state financial responsibility limits ranged from $10,000/$20,000/$5,000 in Mississippi to $50,000/$100,000/$25,000 in Alaska. Additional wording in this provision agrees to interpret the policy to provide at least the required minimum amounts and types of coverage for the following:

> A. If the state or province has:…
>> 2. A compulsory insurance or similar law requiring a nonresident to maintain insurance whenever the nonresident uses a vehicle in that state or province, your policy will provide at least the required minimum amount and types of coverage.

The policy makes clear that it covers any compulsory insurance required by nonresidents, but sometimes there is a disagreement over whether a state's no-fault statute requires the insured nonresident to have no-fault coverage. The argument against providing no-fault coverage is that the wording hinges on "compulsory insurance or similar state law." Some state laws are designed only to protect residents of the state, not to provide additional benefits to nonresidents, and they do not expressly require nonresidents to have the benefits.[74] This argument has less merit in states that require no-fault benefits for "any motor vehicle operator or occupant of a motor vehicle."

The no-fault benefit issue is not so troublesome with the Business Auto Coverage Form because its liability coverage section specifically provides out-of-state no-fault coverage by stating that it will "provide the minimum amounts and types of other coverages, such as no-fault, required of out-of-state vehicles by the jurisdiction where the covered auto is being used."

OTHER INSURANCE

Sometimes more than one auto insurance policy applies to a vehicle. This commonly occurs when an insured borrows another person's vehicle. Often in this situation two auto insurance policies apply, one covering the insured driver and another policy covering the owner of the vehicle.

Both the PAP and Business Auto Coverage Form have similar "Other Insurance" provisions. The PAP provision reads as follows:

> OTHER INSURANCE
>
> If there is other applicable liability insurance we will pay only our share of the loss. Our share is the proportion that our limit of liability bears to the total of all applicable limits. However, any insurance we provide for a vehicle you do not own shall be excess over any other collectible insurance.

According to this wording, if an insured is driving someone else's vehicle, then the insured's own coverage would apply but on an excess basis. This is known as the excess clause. The primary responsibility for payment rests with the insurance company that provides coverage on the nonowned vehicle the insured was driving. In other words, the primary insurance follows the car. Most states apply the Other Insurance provision according to the wording of the excess clause. However, some states apply the Other Insurance provision differently.

CLAIM REPRESENTATIVE SOLUTIONS

Claims Occurring in Other States

If an insured who has minimum limits is involved in a serious accident in another state, claim representatives should determine whether the other state's minimum limits exceed those of the insured's. For claims that occur in no-fault states, claim representatives should obtain copies of the no-fault statutes to determine the applicable coverage in those states. The wording can also help determine which coverage is primary in cases in which an insured has medical payments coverage and is traveling in a state that requires automobile operators to have no-fault medical payments coverage.[75]

State Laws Contrary to the Policy Wording

Courts in some states have resolved coverage overlaps differently from the way the policy stipulates. These laws contravene the policy wording for basically two reasons.[76] The first reason is that courts have used public policy issues to override the stated policy wording. The public policy arguments vary. Some have been as arbitrary as saying that the contribution by pro rata is too difficult to calculate. The second main reason for ruling against the policy wording is because a state statute contradicts the wording. Some state statutes are so comprehensive that they even spell out how overlapping insurance should be resolved. The state's idea of how to resolve this sometimes differs from the way the policy reads.

The two ways states have applied coverage contrary to the policy wording are (1) making the operator's insurance primary rather than excess and (2) apportioning the loss either through contribution by equal shares or through pro rata contribution. Usually, statutory wording that completely contradicts the policy and makes the operator's policy primary over the owner's policy is found in no-fault states.[77] More commonly, policy conflicts should be resolved through apportionment. As mentioned earlier, apportionment can be by equal shares or on a pro rata basis.

Contribution by Equal Shares

The **contribution by equal shares** method provides that each policy contribute the same amount. For example, with a $10,000 loss, each policy would contribute $5,000. Each contributes until the lower limit policy is exhausted.

Courts often use the term **mutually repugnant** to describe the conflict between two insurance clauses that cancel each other out.

States that apply this method may just invalidate the policy wording because they find it too difficult to understand (ambiguous), or they may find that it contravenes public policy. One superior court ruled that the policy wording was "an enigma of which policy should be given effect over the other and the court abandons its search for the mythical primary insurer and insists that both insurers share the loss."[78] Several courts have washed their hands of trying to make a determination as to which policy is primary. These courts consider the disputes over competing clauses (mutually repugnant clauses) to be "contests between insurance companies to see who will pay last." In such cases, courts typically rule that the wording for both policies is null and void and force both policies to be primary and share equally in the loss.[79]

Other states just see it as a general violation of public policy to allow one insurer not to pay. They believe that because insurance is required and because the driver paid for liability insurance for covered losses, each policy must share equally in the loss.[80]

Pro Rata Contribution

Historically, when Other Insurance provisions conflicted and required the two policies to contribute, they shared in the loss on a pro rata basis, with apportionment made up to the limit of liability of the policy.[81] The apportionment of losses on a pro rata basis is equitable to insurers because it forces larger limit policies (that most likely have higher premium charges) to contribute more than smaller limit policies.[82] **Pro rata contribution** has its origin in the policy language of the following Other Insurance provision, which states, "Our share is the proportion that our limit of liability bears to the total of all applicable limits." The math involved in apportioning losses on a pro rata basis is more complicated than under the equal shares method, because it requires multiplication by fractions. It is perhaps an indictment of our education system that at least one court has used the reason of math illiteracy for applying the equal shares method over the pro rata approach.[83] The following is an example of how pro rata contribution works:

> The insured has a Personal Auto Policy with a $100,000 single limit of liability for liability coverage. The vehicle the insured is driving has a commercial policy with a $400,000 limit of liability for liability coverage. The insured is involved in an accident that injures a third party who has $50,000 in damages. The state requires the two policies to contribute on a pro rata basis. In this case the PAP would owe ($100,000/$500,000) × $50,000 or $10,000. The commercial policy would owe ($400,000/$500,000) × $50,000 or $40,000.

If each policy had contributed on an equal shares basis, then the PAP and the commercial policy would have owed $25,000 each.

Claim representatives must be aware of the states that have laws contrary to policy wording before they handle any claim with the potential for involving more than one carrier. This must be determined at the beginning of the investigation because states may not permit insurers to go to other insurers seeking contribution after they have settled a loss.[84] Claim representatives should involve other insurers from the beginning and place them on notice, in writing (preferably using registered or certified mail), of their potential for contribution.

Applying the Other Insurance Provision to Dealer or Repair Shop Autos

Recently, several states have passed legislation making personal automobile insurance of the driver of nonowned autos primary if the driver is test-driving a dealership's car or is borrowing or renting a car provided by an auto-repair facility while the driver's own car is being repaired.[85] In rare situations, some states have even required the liability coverage to apply to the physical damage of the vehicle being driven even though this is contrary to the care, custody, or control exclusion of the liability section of the policy.[86]

CLAIM REPRESENTATIVE SOLUTIONS

Applying Statutes to Rental Car Coverage

If claim representatives know, or suspect, that a statute applies, they should answer five questions:

1. Was the car used by the insured being test-driven and owned by a dealership?

2. Was the car used by the insured owned by a repair facility?

3. Was the car being used because the insured's car was being serviced or repaired?

4. Does the statute make the insured's policy primary for renting cars from just the repair facility, or does it also include rental car companies?

5. Does the law make the liability section of the insured's policy pay for the damage to the vehicle being driven?

Insureds Driving Rental Cars

When an insured is involved in an auto accident while driving a rental car, truck, or motor home, does the insured's own PAP become the primary liability insurance, or is the rental company's liability insurance primary?

What about damage to the rented vehicle? Does the insured's PAP cover damage to the rented vehicle, or is the damage the responsibility of the rental company?

What effect does the rental contract have on either of these questions?

What effect does state law have on these questions?

These are commonly asked questions for claims dealing with insureds who are involved in accidents while driving rental cars. Not surprisingly, the answers to these questions vary by state.

Effect of State Laws on Which Policy Is Primary[87]

The determination of which policy is primary is often made by state statutes or state case law. Ten states have statutes or case law that makes the insured driver's PAP primary. Another ten states have statutes or case law that makes the rental company's liability policy primary; at least two of these base their decisions on the state no-fault law. One state's statutes make the rental company's insurance primary unless the rental company is self-insured, in which case the law makes the insured's PAP primary.

Many of these laws exempting rental companies from primary liability require the rental company to expressly state in the contract that it is secondary. Some states require this to be printed on the front page of the rental agreement.

Conduct of the Insured

The conduct of the insured driver can affect whether the PAP is primary or secondary. If, for example, the accident was caused because the insured was intoxicated or under the influence of drugs, then most rental car agreements would void coverage. PAP policies do not typically have such exclusions. Also, if the insured driver gave the rented vehicle to a person not authorized by the rental company to drive, then the agreement may not apply. This law varies from state to state. The majority rule, however, is that to be an authorized driver, a person must have the permission of the vehicle owner (the rental car company).

Vicarious Liability

Eight states have statutes that make the titled owner of every vehicle responsible for damage done by the vehicle regardless of fault; thus the rental car companies, as owners, are responsible for damages and injuries caused by people who rent their vehicles.

Which State's Law Applies

The general rule is that the law of the state where the loss occurred applies. However, if the vehicle was rented in a state with an unlimited vicarious liability law, and the loss occurred in another (non-vicarious) state, attorneys for the injured parties have occasionally been successful in applying the law of the state where the vehicle was rented.

States With No Statute or Case Law

More than thirty jurisdictions still have no case law or statute determining the order of payment in rental vehicle cases. Most of the rented vehicle accidents pit the PAP's excess other car coverage against the rental company's contract wording. Some rental car agreements have what courts refer to as "escape clauses." Rental car companies insert these **escape clauses** to avoid providing coverage if other insurance is available. An example of the wording of an escape clause is:

> If there is no other valid and collectible insurance, whether primary, excess or contingent, available to the renter sufficient to meet minimum

financial responsibility law requirements then the rental car agency shall provide protection.[88]

The very name that courts have given this clause shows their disdain for this type of provision. A number of courts view the escape clause as void either because it provides no insurance at all (sometimes even when the renter specifically paid the rental car agency for liability insurance coverage) or because the clause is inconsistent with statutes mandating insurance coverage on vehicles. If the state voids the escape clause and the excess clause of the insured's auto policy is honored, the rental agency's insurer would be primary.

Some states consider the escape clause found in the rental agreement and the excess clause in the auto policy to be "mutually repugnant."[89] In these cases, the state would require the same apportionment, either contribution by equal shares or pro rata, as it does with mutually repugnant excess clauses found in insurance policies.

Supplemental Liability Insurance

In the past ten years, rental companies have been selling supplemental liability insurance that typically (with the exception of one state) covers losses exceeding statutory limits up to the limits of the supplemental policy, usually $1 million. In the one state that is the exception, Texas, supplemental liability insurance policies must cover first dollar damage. Basic liability insurance covering at least statutory limits is included in the daily rental rate of the rented vehicle. These supplemental coverages go by the acronyms of LIS, SLI, Million Dollar Package, and other names. The existence of these supplemental coverages is significant in that some courts are now finding against insureds who refused to purchase the supplemental coverage. The courts reason that the insured driver was offered the opportunity to purchase liability insurance through the rental car company that would have covered this loss on a primary basis. Because the insured refused to make that purchase, some courts seem more willing to make the insured's PAP primarily responsible.

Rented Vehicles That Are Substitutes or Replacement Vehicles

Some states make the insured's PAP primary if the rental unit replaced the insured's vehicle while it was being serviced or after it had been stolen.

Damage to the Rented Vehicle

An accident in a rented car will almost always involve damage to the rented vehicle. If the damage was the insured's fault, the rental company may have a claim against the insured's PAP, if the PAP covered comprehensive and collision losses.

- Damage Waivers. Nearly every rental company offers its customers an opportunity to purchase a damage waiver, in which the rental company waives its right to recover from the customer all or a portion of damage to the rented vehicle. However, all waivers have exclusions, such as driving while intoxicated, that can void the waiver and leave the insured with full responsibility. And a court in one state has declared that unless the exclusions are noted on the face of the rental agreement, the waiver covers all damage to a rented vehicle. Three states require that for a rental company to recover damages to a rented vehicle, the rental company must first have offered the insured the opportunity to purchase a damage waiver.

- Damage Waiver Laws. Thirty-two states have enacted laws regulating the sale of damage waivers. Although most deal with disclosure, some deal with the issue of partial damage waivers. In some states, a damage waiver must cover all damage to the rented vehicle. In others, damage waivers may exclude a portion of the damages. Claim representatives should read the rental contract carefully and compare it with the law to determine whether the waiver is in compliance. If not, the insured can, in most cases, rescind the rental agreement and escape liability altogether.

Special Vehicle Rental Laws

In the past two decades, more than thirty states have enacted statutes that regulate the rental company's conduct at the time the rental transaction is entered into. The regulations cover damage waivers, disclosures of one sort or another that must be made in the rental contract or on signs in the rental office, price of damage waiver, advertising, what categories of damages can be recovered for injury to a rented vehicle, loss of use, recovery of administrative fees, definitions of authorized drivers, liability for theft and vandalism, and other elements of the claim.

The penalty for violation of these laws is almost always rescission of the rental contract. If the contract is rescinded, the insured can escape liability for injury to third parties, property damage, and collision damage to the rented vehicle. Even the largest rental car companies sometimes fail to comply with these special laws, which apply to light trucks and motor homes in all but one state. Especially for serious claims, claim representatives should determine whether the rental car contract was legally compliant with rental contract laws.

Vehicles "Loaned" to the Insured by an Auto Dealer or a Service Shop

The standard form ISO dealer garage policy makes the dealer's coverage primary. However, many states have overridden this rule by statute and case law, making the insured's PAP responsible for losses occurring while the insured was driving the "loaner." A few state courts have determined that these loaners are in fact "rentals" and subject to the laws applying to rental cars, which may make the PAP coverage primary.

Self-Insured Rental Car Companies

Self-insured rental car companies argue that the "Other Insurance" provision that would make them primary does not apply to them because they do not have "insurance" on the vehicle.[90] States that do not accept this argument reason that self-insureds are required by law to provide at least minimum liability limits and should therefore, at the very least, share equally in the loss up to the amount of the minimum limits required under the state's financial responsibility law.

Other states reason that self-insurance is a "functional equivalent of insurance"; therefore, the limit of liability for the rental car company is the amount the company provides to meet state commerce department requirements.[91]

CLAIM REPRESENTATIVE SOLUTIONS

Investigating Rental Car Coverage

For claims involving vehicles rented by insureds, claim representatives should:

A. Determine whether the state where the loss occurred has a case or statute that definitively decides which policy is primary.

B. If there is no statute making the insured secondary, continue as below:

1. Read the rental agreement carefully—especially the insurance section. Many rental agreement forms, even those of large companies, promise to provide primary insurance. Where a promise of primary liability is made by the rental company, its policy will be primary no matter where the loss occurred—even in a state with a statute declaring rental company liability secondary. In addition, compare the rental agreement form with the vehicle rental laws of the state in which the vehicle was rented. If it does not comply, the insured may escape liability.

2. Read all applicable insurance policies carefully. The insured's policy may exclude coverage for rented cars in its "other car" coverage, or it may exclude the type of vehicle that was rented. Furthermore, the rental company's liability policy may provide primary coverage even when the rental agreement offers only secondary coverage. Finally, rental companies carry two policies. The first provides liability coverage for the renter. The second covers liability of the rental company. If the rental company was at fault, such as by renting an unsafe vehicle, the second policy may come into play.

MEDICAL PAYMENTS COVERAGE INSURING AGREEMENT

The second part of the PAP covers medical payments. The insuring agreement reads as follows:

PART B—MEDICAL PAYMENTS COVERAGE
INSURING AGREEMENT

A. We will pay reasonable expenses incurred for necessary medical and funeral services because of "bodily injury":

1. Caused by accident; and

2. Sustained by an "insured".

We will pay only those expenses incurred for services rendered within 3 years from the date of the accident.

B. "Insured" as used in this Part means:
1. You or any "family member":
a. While "occupying"; or
b. As a pedestrian when struck by;

A motor vehicle designed for use mainly on public roads or a trailer of any type.
2. Any other person while "occupying" "your covered auto".

Medical payments coverage is not included in the basic Business Auto Coverage Form, but it can be added by endorsement. The wording is similar to that found in the PAP. Auto medical payments is probably not as popular with businesses because employees who sustain injuries arising out of and in the course of their employment are usually covered by workers compensation, and they are not entitled to duplicate compensation because of the following exclusion:

> We do not provide Medical Payments Coverage for any "insured" for "bodily injury":
>
> 4. Occurring during the course of employment if workers' compensation benefits are required or available for the "bodily injury".

This exclusion applies only while the insured is in the course of employment. If, for example, the insured is in a company car and is driving to a park on a Sunday afternoon to have a family picnic, this exclusion would not apply.

Two common coverage issues claim representatives encounter that are related to this insuring agreement involve the definitions of "family member" and what it means to "occupy" a vehicle. Those issues were explained earlier in the definitions section of this chapter. Determining whether a medical expense is reasonable or necessary is sometimes difficult, but the issues deal more with the medical investigation and injury and treatment evaluation than with pure coverage concerns. According to most policies, the medical services must be rendered within three years. Therefore, recommended future treatments, although acknowledged within three years, are not "rendered" as required by the policy.[92]

Many people are unaware that the medical payments coverage applies to insureds struck by vehicles while they are pedestrians. One question that often arises is whether the term "pedestrian" extends to insureds while riding on bicycles. Insurance Services Office issued a clarification stating that the term "pedestrian" could include an insured riding a bicycle.[93] Many insurers also take the position that this includes people on rollerblades, skateboards, and even on horseback. The PAP does, however, exclude coverage for occupants of any motorized vehicles with fewer than four wheels (such as motorcycles). Interestingly, the Business Auto Coverage Form includes motorcycles as "autos" and, contrary to the PAP, people occupying motorcycles are covered under the business form.

Coverage in No-Fault States

Accidents occurring in no-fault states make the medical payments coverage determination more complicated. As mentioned earlier in the Out-of-State

Coverage section, no-fault personal injury benefits often extend to people involved in accidents in no-fault states even if a person does not reside in a no-fault state. One of the personal injury protection (PIP) benefits provided in no-fault states is for medical expenses. Claim representatives must then determine how to coordinate the medical payments coverage with the PIP benefit. Determining coverage can become especially complicated when the insured is a passenger in another person's vehicle. Determining which policy should respond has an outcome that varies widely by state. Claim representatives should seek assistance from claim management or legal counsel to help make this determination.

Other Insurance

Although disputes do arise, most of the issues discussed earlier regarding other insurance in the liability section do not apply to the medical payments section because medical payments coverage is not typically a required coverage under state financial responsibility laws (except in no-fault states). However, public policy issues arise when applying the offset provision against payments made under a mandated coverage such as liability or uninsured motorists.

Subrogation

The General Provisions of the auto policy permit the insurance company to recover payments from responsible parties. This provision is discussed later in this chapter in more detail. Some states do not permit subrogation of medical payments,[94] and some other states permit it only in limited situations. Whether payments are made under PIP versus medical payments is also a factor affecting subrogation.[95]

UNINSURED MOTORISTS COVERAGE INSURING AGREEMENT

Although all fifty states have some type of financial responsibility laws requiring motor vehicle owners to carry a minimum amount of liability insurance, and forty states have compulsory insurance laws requiring proof of insurance at the time the vehicle is registered, fourteen out of every 100 drivers are uninsured.[96]

Uninsured Motorists (UM) Coverage is designed to meet the problem of bodily injury caused by an uninsured motorist. About half of the states have financial responsibility laws requiring uninsured motorists coverage. Although the PAP includes such coverage, the Business Auto Coverage Form does not include it in the basic policy, but it can be added by endorsement when required by state law or as an optional coverage for insureds. The wording for this form is similar to the PAP but varies widely by state. The PAP uninsured motorists insuring agreement reads in part:

> PART C—UNINSURED MOTORISTS COVERAGE INSURING AGREEMENT
>
> A. We will pay compensatory damages which an "insured" is legally entitled to recover from the owner or operator of an "uninsured motor vehicle" because of "bodily injury":

1. Sustained by an "insured"; and
2. Caused by an accident.

    The owner's or operator's liability for these damages must arise out of the ownership, maintenance or use of the "uninsured motor vehicle".

    Any judgment for damages arising out of a suit brought without our written consent is not binding on us.

B. "Insured" as used in this Part means:

1. You or any "family member".
2. Any other person "occupying" "your covered auto".
3. Any person for damages that person is entitled to recover because of "bodily injury" to which this coverage applies sustained by a person described in 1. or 2. above.

The coverage applies to named insureds and "family members" as well as those "occupying" covered autos. The damages must be for bodily injury "caused by an accident" by the operator of an "uninsured motor vehicle." Some questions encountered by claim representatives handling UM claims are as follows:

- Are drive-by shooting "accidents" caused by the operation of an uninsured motor vehicle?

- Are assaults occurring in or upon a vehicle covered by the uninsured motorists coverage?

- If an exclusion applies to liability coverage for the operation of a vehicle, is the vehicle then "uninsured"?

The answers to these questions vary by jurisdiction and by how courts apply the following two criteria to a given set of circumstances:

1.   An accident caused by the operation of an uninsured motor vehicle.
2.   A vehicle that meets the definition of an "uninsured motorist."

Accidents and Operation of a Vehicle

Shootings from passing cars, physical assaults on insureds, and intentional collisions are examples of situations in which victims might seek to recover for injuries under no-fault laws or medical payments coverage, as well as uninsured motorists coverage. Most courts would consider these intentional incidents to be accidental from the perspective of an innocent victim, but courts are not in agreement over whether these are caused by the *operation or use* of an uninsured motor vehicle. As mentioned earlier in this chapter, use of an automobile means more than just operation of a vehicle. Courts have applied the same reasoning in ruling that insurance should not apply to claims resulting from shootings from cars because shooting a gun from a moving vehicle was not considered an activity that arose out of the operation or use of the vehicle. However, in some circumstances, the use of the vehicle *is* an important part of the incident. In these cases, courts have reasoned that the vehicle was an active accessory to the assault and therefore coverage should be afforded.[97] The following cases illustrate the kinds of facts that courts consider and explain the reasoning courts used in finding coverage. The reasoning courts use can be applied to other intentional acts with circumstances involving a vehicle, such as claims involving persons injured by objects thrown from cars.

> A girl driving her father's car was shot in the back by an assailant in a second vehicle. The assailant fled, and the victim sought coverage under her father's uninsured motorists coverage. The insurer denied coverage on the basis that the shooting was not related to the operation of the vehicle and could have occurred anywhere. The court reasoned that because the assailant counted on the speed of the vehicle to pursue his victim and to make a successful escape, the vehicle was an active accessory to the assault.[98]

> A woman driving down a highway was blocked by three vehicles and was shot by an assailant in one of the vehicles. The court decided that the woman's uninsured motorists coverage applied because the vehicles restricted her movements, and this was enough of a causal connection to the injury to trigger coverage.[99]

> A man driving his car was involved in an accident with another vehicle. A verbal altercation followed the accident, and the driver of the second vehicle pulled out a gun and killed the man. The court held for coverage, ruling that the initial collision occurred as a result of the use of the vehicle and had it not been for that initial accident, the fatal assault would not have occurred.[100]

The following contrasting cases present factual situations in which courts have not held for coverage:

> A woman was riding as a passenger in a car when she was shot by an assailant in another car. The court declined to afford coverage, reasoning that it was not enough that the vehicle facilitated her injury but it must actually *cause* her injury. The court further stated that the cause of her injuries was the independent, voluntary, and deliberate act of a criminal using the uninsured vehicle as a gun platform, not as a car.[101]

> A woman was riding in a car when she was passed by a vehicle occupied by two men in fast pursuit of a third vehicle. The men sprayed the third vehicle with bullets from an automatic weapon. One of the bullets struck the woman. The court denied coverage to the woman, stating that no evidence linked the bullet wound to the use of an automobile. The court admitted that it would have found coverage if evidence had been shown that the speed, trajectory, or movement of the uninsured vehicle somehow caused the bullet to go astray.[102]

> A man sitting in his car at a red light was shot by the passenger of an uninsured vehicle that had pulled up behind him. The court ruled that the uninsured motorists coverage did not apply because damages are owed only when the insured is legally entitled to recover from the owner or operator of an "uninsured motor vehicle." The owner/operator of the vehicle was not liable for the unexpected actions of his passenger.[103]

> One court refused to provide coverage for a drive-by shooting because a drive-by shooting is not a risk the parties to the insurance contract would reasonably interpret as insurable and to find coverage would be to expand coverage beyond the parties' reasonable expectations.[104]

Cases involving physical assaults that are not related at all to another vehicle are even less likely to be considered an accident or to be based on the operation of a vehicle. The following cases illustrate this point:

> A man was stabbed by unknown assailants while exiting his car. The court ruled that the uninsured motorists coverage would not apply because the man's injuries were caused by the stabbing and not the use of the auto even if he was alighting from the auto.[105]

> The insured and another man became involved in an altercation over driving etiquette. They stopped their cars, and the other man got out of his car and punched the insured in the nose while the insured was still seated in the car. The court ruled that the incident was not an accident and was not related to the operation of a vehicle even though the argument related to the insured's driving behavior.[106]

> An insured was abducted by a man who forced her into his car, sexually assaulted her, and then murdered her. The court ruled that UM coverage would not apply because the incident was not an accident, and because the murderer's actions were an intervening cause that broke the connection between the use of his auto and her injuries.[107]

Despite the variability in court decisions, some general guidelines have emerged. Courts look at the significance of the role of the vehicle in these incidents. The more significant the role of the uninsured vehicle, the more likely the courts will find UM coverage. A loose connection between the injuries and the incident will not usually trigger coverage.

The Definition of an Uninsured Motor Vehicle

As part of the investigation into whether an "accident" was caused by the "operation" of a vehicle, claim representatives must establish that the other unidentified vehicle actually existed and caused the damages.

The PAP defines an "uninsured motor vehicle" as follows:

> C. "Uninsured motor vehicle" means a land motor vehicle or trailer of any type:
>
> 1. To which no bodily injury liability bond or policy applies at the time of the accident.
>
> 2. To which a bodily injury liability bond or policy applies at the time of the accident. In this case its limit for bodily injury liability must be less than the minimum limit for bodily injury liability specified by the financial responsibility law of the state in which "your covered auto" is principally garaged.
>
> 3. Which is a hit-and-run vehicle whose operator or owner cannot be identified and which hits:
>
>   a. You or any "family member";
>
>   b. A vehicle which you or any "family member" are "occupying"; or
>
>   c. "Your covered auto".
>
> 4. To which a bodily injury liability bond or policy applies at the time of the accident but the bonding or insuring company:
>
>   a. Denies coverage; or

b. Is or becomes insolvent.

However, "uninsured motor vehicle" does not include any vehicle or equipment:

1. Owned by or furnished or available for the regular use of you or any "family member".

2. Owned or operated by a self-insurer under any applicable motor vehicle law, except a self-insurer which is or becomes insolvent.

3. Owned by any governmental unit or agency.

4. Operated on rails or crawler treads.

5. Designed mainly for use off public roads while not on public roads.

6. While located for use as a residence or premises.

What is an uninsured motor vehicle?

• If an unidentified vehicle runs an insured vehicle off the road, is this unidentified vehicle an "uninsured motor vehicle"?

• If a rock falls from a passing truck and injures an insured, is the truck considered an "uninsured motor vehicle"?

The answer to the first question hinges on whether the unidentified vehicle is a **hit-and-run vehicle,** because the policy covers "a hit-and-run vehicle whose operator or owner cannot be identified." Again the answer varies by state. Courts refer to these unidentified vehicles as "phantom" vehicles. The term "phantom" reflects the suspicion that many courts have for claims involving these vehicles.

"Phantom" Vehicles

The negligence of the driver of a **phantom vehicle**, an unidentified vehicle that leaves no physical evidence of contact with the insured vehicle, is difficult to assess because there is little evidence other than the insured's own testimony. This situation creates a moral hazard. For example, if an insured falls asleep at the wheel, runs off the road, and is injured, he has no coverage for the injuries except medical payments (if that coverage was purchased). However, if the person is run off the road by a phantom vehicle and this is considered an uninsured motor vehicle, then he might be able to collect medical expenses, wage loss, and pain and suffering damages. Thus, the potential for recovering more money might induce some insureds to falsely claim they were forced off the road instead of revealing the truth that they simply fell asleep or accidentally drove off the road.

But does the phantom vehicle trigger coverage? This depends on whether the jurisdiction requires physical contact and, if not, what type of evidence is required to prove the negligence of the phantom vehicle's driver.

Physical Contact Requirement

The plain, ordinary meaning of "hit-and-run" implies physical contact. In fact, more than forty states require physical contact to trigger the UM coverage. However, almost half of the states requiring physical contact permit an exception if there is competent, **corroborative evidence** that supports the existence of a hit-and-run vehicle.[108] What constitutes competent, corroborative evidence varies by jurisdiction. For example, some of the states that have uninsured motorists statutes requiring vehicle owners to purchase uninsured motorists coverage define "uninsured motorist" to mean a vehicle that makes physical contact with the insured. Some state statutes are even stricter and do not provide coverage if the at-fault hit-and-run driver cannot be identified. Other states have physical contact requirements based not on statute but on common-law interpretation of the coverage.[109]

CASE APPLICATION

Phantom Vehicle

Consider the claim of Sam. While returning home on a two-lane highway, Sam (insured under a PAP) is seriously injured when he runs into a guardrail located on a sharp turn. Sam says that he was run off the road by another vehicle.

Is Sam's claim covered as uninsured motorist damage?

In Sam's case, what would claim representatives investigate?

The claim representative handling Sam's UM claim determined from the police report that the accident occurred at 3:00 A.M. According to his statement, Sam had departed from a tavern where he had spent the previous six hours before the accident. The police report indicated that Sam was traveling at a high rate of speed (at least 60 m.p.h.) when he hit the guardrail. The posted speed limit was 35 m.p.h. Because of the seriousness of the injuries and the potential exposure (Sam had $500,000 in uninsured motorists coverage), the claim representative hired a forensic investigator to perform an accident reconstruction. This expert determined that no other vehicle made contact with Sam's vehicle. The claim representative requested a signed medical authorization form from Sam and ordered the blood test results from the emergency room where Sam was taken. The results indicated that Sam's blood alcohol level was .20 (twice the legal limit). Because there was no physical contact and no corroborative evidence supporting that another vehicle caused the accident, the claim representative denied Sam's uninsured motorists claim.

The Search for Corroborative Evidence Test

An Ohio Supreme Court ruling reflected the position of about half the states when it said, "Public policy prohibits insurance policy provisions which require physical contact as an unequivocal prerequisite to recovery under the uninsured motorists coverage."[110] States supporting this view will allow a claim to go forward if there is other evidence, such as independent third-party testimony or other physical evidence, to establish the negligence of the unidentified motorist. Such evidence normally requires the statements of disinterested parties as minimum corroborative evidence. Other states make exceptions to the physical contact requirement only when there is other physical evidence. These states require that corroborative evidence include some physical evidence, such as contact with other vehicles or property.[111] In Sam's case, there was no corroborative evidence to support his allegations that another vehicle caused his accident. The evidence pointed to Sam as being solely responsible for the accident.

Sometimes uninsured motorist claims can be paid when there is strong support-ing evidence that another vehicle was involved and caused the damages. These claims have physical evidence to support the insured's allegations of another vehicle. The following actual cases describe circumstances in which coverage has been found because they met the "physical contact" requirement:

> A passenger in an insured vehicle was struck and killed by the tire and rim of an unidentified vehicle. The court ruled that coverage should apply because the tire and rim were parts of the car and the passenger's fatality was proximately caused by the accident.[112]

> An occupant in an insured vehicle was struck by a rock that fell from an unidentified dump truck. The court ruled that an object from the uniden-tified vehicle was sufficient to meet the contact requirement.[113]

The following demonstrates how courts might shift the burden of proof to insurers in denying coverage involving unexplained accidents.

> A man was struck in the head by a large rock that crashed through his windshield. The man did not see where the object came from, but the location of the incident and the six-pound weight of the rock made it unlikely to have been thrown by a person. The man used the theory of res ipsa loquitur ("the thing speaks for itself") to argue that the injury was due to the negligence of some unidentified vehicle. The court felt that because of the size of the rock, it had to have come from one of two places—the back of a truck in the oncoming lane of traffic or from between the dual wheels of a large truck. The court reasoned that in any case, the truck driver would have been negligent either in failing to properly cover a load or in failing to avoid a large rock. Coverage was granted.[114]

When shootings were addressed earlier, the issue of causation was discussed as a policy defense. Another potential policy defense relates to physical contact. Bullets might not be considered "physical contact with another motor vehicle" but instead contact with a projectile originating from another vehicle. This could make a difference in states having the physical contact requirement.

One point that should be considered is the amount of time between when a car part detaches and when it strikes the insured. A part that is detached and later causes an accident is less likely to trigger coverage, as illustrated by the following decisions:

> An insured was injured in a single-car accident when the insured struck a tire and wheel lying in the middle of the road. The court ruled against coverage because no physical contact with a motor vehicle had oc-curred.[115] Similarly, a court ruled against coverage when an insured vehicle ran over a metal license plate in the road[116] and when an insured slid on oil spilled by an unidentified vehicle.[117]

> In perhaps the most intellectually creative case, an insured argued that the oncoming headlights and sound of a horn from an unidentified vehicle made "molecular contact" with the insured. Notwithstanding the correct-ness of the physics, the court ruled that physical contact must be more substantial than just light and sound energy.[118]

States that have no physical contact requirement are the most challenging for claim representatives. Some protection against fraud is offered by the provisions. An examination under oath (EUO) is formal testimony of a person. The testimony is recorded by a court reporter. It is similar to a deposition except that a deposition occurs after a suit has been filed. Questioning under an EUO can sometimes be broader than under a deposition.

No Requirement for Contact To Trigger UM Coverage

As mentioned earlier, forty states have physical contact requirements, but many of these permit exceptions. Some other states have no physical contact requirement and consider it to be against public policy to require any physical contact. Exhibit 2-2 is a bulletin from the South Dakota Division of Insurance requiring companies to drop any policy wording suggesting that physical contact be required in order to trigger coverage. This bulletin shows how an Insurance Department can have a role in clarifying and enforcing coverage.

Arbitration of Uninsured Motorist Claims

The PAP and Business Auto Coverage Form UM endorsement often contain provisions requiring insureds and insurers to settle their monetary disputes through arbitration.[119] The purpose of the provision is to provide an efficient, inexpensive method for settlement when the two parties cannot agree on the amount of compensation. The **arbitration clause** in the PAP reads as follows:

ARBITRATION

A. If we and an "insured" do not agree:

1. Whether that "insured" is legally entitled to recover damages; or

2. As to the amount of damages which are recoverable by that "insured"; from the owner or operator of an "uninsured motor vehicle", then the matter may be arbitrated. However, disputes concerning coverage under this Part may not be arbitrated.
Both parties must agree to arbitration. If so agreed, each party will select an arbitrator. The two arbitrators will select a third. If they cannot agree within 30 days, either may request that selection be made by a judge of a court having jurisdiction.

B. Each party will:

1. Pay the expenses it incurs; and

2. Bear the expenses of the third arbitrator equally.

C. Unless both parties agree otherwise, arbitration will take place in the county in which the "insured" lives. Local rules of law as to procedure and evidence will apply. A decision agreed to by two of the arbitrators will be binding as to:

1. Whether the "insured" is legally entitled to recover damages; and

2. The amount of damages. This applies only if the amount does not exceed the minimum limit for bodily injury liability specified by the financial responsibility law of the state in which "your covered auto" is principally garaged. If the amount exceeds that limit, either party may demand the right to a trial. This demand must be made within 60 days of the arbitrators' decision. If this demand is not made, the amount of damages agreed to by the arbitrators will be binding.

EXHIBIT 2-2

Bulletin From the South Dakota Division of Insurance

DEPARTMENT OF
COMMERCE AND REGULATION

BANKING
COMMERCIAL
INSPECTION
HIGHWAY PATROL
HIGHWAY SAFETY
HUMAN RIGHTS
INSURANCE
SECURITIES

Location: 910 E. Sioux • Mailing Address: c/o 500 E. Capitol
Pierre, South Dakota 57501-5070

Department Secretary: 605/773-3177 or 773-3178 Fax: 605/773-3018
Division of Insurance: 605/773-3563 Fax: 605/773-5369

BULLETIN 96-2

TO: All auto insurers

FROM: Darla L. Lyon, Director, S.D. Division of Insurance

DATE: April 18, 1996

RE: Uninsured motorists coverage—SDCL 58-11-9

It has come to the attention of the South Dakota Division of Insurance that some uninsured motorist policy provisions contain references to physical contact requirements in regard to hit-and-run situations in order for coverage to be effective. It is the position of the Division that under uninsured motorists coverage, as set forth in SDCL 58-11-9, references in policies to physical contact requirements such as "hitting," etc., may no longer be used.

This position is based on a South Dakota court case, *Clark v. Regent Ins. Co., et. al.*, 270 N.W.2d 26 (S.D. 1978), which holds that physical contact may not be required for uninsured motorists coverages. This case has never been overturned or modified by subsequent case law or statute and therefore has full legal force and effect.

Be advised that if your company's policy language requires physical contact in a hit-and-run case to trigger the uninsured motorists coverage, that language is null and void. No future filings containing a requirement of physical contact as pertains to hit-and-run coverage under uninsured motorist will be approved.

This is a typical uninsured motorists coverage arbitration clause. Notice that it applies to any "insured," not necessarily the named insured; therefore, beneficiaries who did not purchase the policy are still bound to its terms. This clause does not permit arbitration of "disputes concerning coverage." However, it does permit arbitration over whether the "insured" is "legally entitled to recover damages" or disputes over "the amount of damages recoverable."

> ### CLAIM REPRESENTATIVE SOLUTIONS
>
> ### Investigating Phantom Vehicles
>
> When insureds allege that a "phantom" vehicle caused their accident, claim representatives should determine whether the state requires physical contact in order to make an uninsured claim. If the state requires physical contact as a prerequisite for coverage, then that should be a central part of the investigation.
>
> If the state permits coverage for phantom vehicles, then the claim representative must search for corroborative evidence to support the insured's allegations.
>
> Detailed statements are obviously essential in assessing the liability of the driver of a phantom vehicle. Even if the phantom vehicle exists, the driver of the uninsured (or unidentified) vehicle must be liable for the accident in order for the insured to collect. Claim representatives are also expected to make every effort to identify the responsible party when there is a hit-and-run vehicle involved rather than to just pay the uninsured motorist claim because it is more convenient than trying to identify the responsible party. This is especially true when the phantom vehicle had some identifiable markings, such as a company name on its side. Claim representatives should provide information about the unidentified vehicle to assist the police in their search.

The following questions might be appropriate issues for arbitration, depending on the state:

- Did a phantom "hit-and-run" vehicle actually exist and cause the insured to have an accident?[120]
- Is it permissible to stack policy limits for uninsured motorists coverage?[121]
- Did the insured commit fraud in procuring the uninsured motorists coverage?
- Was the insured "occupying" the vehicle at the time of the accident?
- Was the insured a resident of the named insured's household?[122]

Courts disagree over what constitutes "disputes concerning coverage" (which are not appropriate for arbitration) and what constitutes disputes over what the insured is "legally entitled to recover" (which are appropriate for arbitration). Other issues that vary by state include the following:

- Whether the arbitration decision is binding
- Whether arbitration is mandatory
- Whether a trial can be requested when arbitration awards exceed the minimum limit for bodily injury liability specified by the financial responsibility law of the state

In Pennsylvania, for example, courts have stated that "there is no limit to jurisdiction of arbitrators over what issues may be submitted"[123] and "public policy favors arbitration because it rids claims of the tedious process of litigation."[124] Courts in other states have taken the position that arbitration deprives parties of their right to settle disputes in court and is therefore contrary to public policy.[125]

One reason that such variation exists is that some states have uninsured motorists statutes that address arbitration specifically. In these states, the statutes define the circumstances under which arbitration is permitted and the binding nature of arbitration decisions. For example, in Washington, a statute indicates that once parties agree to submit their disputes to arbitration, then the statute rather than the policy wording governs the rights of the participants in arbitration. The statute states that decisions by arbitrators are valid and enforceable without the right of appeal (except for fraudulent conduct of arbitrators) regardless of what the policy says. This means, for example, that the insurance company would not be entitled to a trial even though the policy specified that it would have that right when the award exceeds the minimum financial policy limits.[126]

Other states have similar statutes that govern the rights of parties who submit disputes to arbitration. The Connecticut uninsured motorists statute also mandates that policies with uninsured motorists coverage provide an arbitration clause in the policy. Furthermore, arbitration is appropriate for settling coverage disputes, including issues such as whether the insured gave prompt notice to the insurance carrier or whether a person was a resident of the insured's household.[127] The policy states that if the award is greater than the amount of the state's financial responsibility laws, then either party may demand a trial rather than accept the arbitrator's decision. If, for example, the state's financial responsibility law requires $30,000 uninsured motorists coverage, then any arbitration award greater than that amount is not binding. Some states have disallowed this part of the provision because they believe it provides an unfair advantage to the insurance company by providing an "escape hatch" for an unfavorable award, which contravenes public policy.[128]

Do the parties have to accept arbitration? Are the parties bound by the arbitration decision? Historically, courts did not look favorably on any agreement that limited a party's access to the courts. However, over the years as court dockets have become backlogged, states have modified their view with respect to arbitration. Many states have enacted statutes permitting binding arbitration. Despite this trend, a few states hold that arbitration provisions are not enforceable.[129]

LIMIT OF LIABILITY—UNINSURED MOTORISTS COVERAGE

Undoubtedly the most important and controversial uninsured motorists coverage issue involves the application of the limit of liability provision. It is the subject of a great deal of litigation.

CLAIM REPRESENTATIVE SOLUTIONS

Laws Affecting Arbitration Clause

Claim representatives should understand that the laws affecting the arbitration clause vary by state. Claim representatives who are familiar with the way arbitration works in one state should not assume it works the same in others. Before incurring the time and expense of arbitration, claim representatives should consider (1) what coverage issues are arbitrable and (2) whether the arbitrator's decision is binding. Once the claim representative agrees to arbitrate the claim, he or she may not be able to stop the process and proceed to trial.[130] Conversely, once a lawsuit has been filed, the insurer may be unable to invoke the arbitration clause to avoid litigation.[131] Some companies will enter into arbitration even if the results are not binding as a way of demonstrating that they have made a good faith effort to settle the claim without litigation.

The uninsured motorists limit of liability section for the PAP reads as follows:

LIMIT OF LIABILITY

A. The limit of liability shown in the Declarations for each person for Uninsured Motorists Coverage is our maximum limit of liability for all damages, including damages for care, loss of services or death, arising out of "bodily injury" sustained by any one person in any one accident. Subject to this limit for each person, the limit of liability shown in the Declarations for each accident for Uninsured Motorists Coverage is our maximum limit of liability for all damages for "bodily injury" resulting from any one accident.

This is the most we will pay regardless of the number of:

1. "Insureds";

2. Claims made;

3. Vehicles or premiums shown in the Declarations; or

4. Vehicles involved in the accident.

B. No one will be entitled to receive duplicate payments for the same elements of loss under this coverage and:

1. Part A. or Part B. of this policy; or

2. Any Underinsured Motorists Coverage provided by this policy.

C. We will not make a duplicate payment under this coverage for any element of loss for which payment has been made by or on behalf of persons or organizations who may be legally responsible.

D. We will not pay for any element of loss if a person is entitled to receive payment for the same element of loss under any of the following or similar law:

1. Workers' compensation law; or

2. Disability benefits law.

The most common contradiction of policy wording occurs when courts permit insureds to stack the limits of liability. **Stacking** means that insureds who have more than one vehicle may add the limits of liability together to obtain a higher limit. For example, stacking would permit a person who owns two cars with $50,000 uninsured motorists coverage on each to add the two limits and recover up to $100,000. This is in direct contradiction to the policy wording described above.

Why are courts more willing to allow stacking with uninsured motorists coverage limits than with liability coverage limits?

Courts view uninsured motorists coverage differently than the liability insurance coverage. One court explained the difference by stating, "We must not confuse uninsured motorists coverage protection as insuring to a particular motor vehicle as in the case of automobile liability insurance. It [uninsured motorists coverage] is bodily injury insurance which protects against such injury inflicted by a negligent uninsured motorist."[132] This difference between insuring the vehicle for its operation and insuring the individual for injury sets the stage for stacking policy limits for the uninsured motorists coverage.

Intra means "within," and *inter* means "between." The Internet allows communication between people in different companies. An intranet is for people within the same company. Intrapolicy stacking is for vehicles on the same policy, while interpolicy stacking refers to vehicles on separate auto policies.

Stacking

Stacking has been, and continues to be, litigated in many jurisdictions with varying results. In 1999, seventeen states permitted stacking of uninsured motorists coverage.[133] Claim representatives should check with claim management to determine whether stacking applies in the jurisdictions where they are assigned uninsured motorists claims.

Stacking can be interpolicy or intrapolicy. Stacking might be permitted in some states when insureds are covered under multiple auto policies (interpolicy stacking)[134] but may not be covered under a single policy that covers multiple vehicles (intrapolicy stacking). Intrapolicy stacking is less common and is permitted in only eleven states, compared to interpolicy stacking, which at the time this was written was permitted in seventeen states. A common example of intrapolicy stacking is a family that has three different autos on the same policy. An example of interpolicy stacking could be when a daughter who lives at her parents' home has a separate policy from her parents but with the same insurance company. Collecting the limits from both policies would be interpolicy stacking.

Another situation sometimes occurs when an insured is injured by an uninsured motorist while occupying another unrelated person's car. Collecting the limits from the two policies involved is often permitted because many courts do not consider this to be stacking. The following case explains how this can occur:

> An Iowa statute prohibits stacking of uninsured motorists coverage under two insurance policies that have antistacking provisions (which are common in almost all auto policies). The court distinguished between the concept of stacking, which concerns whether more than one coverage should apply to the insured, and "Other Insurance" provisions, which address the rules of responsibility between different insurance companies.[135]

Reasons for Permitting Stacking

Public policy is a reason courts have allowed stacking in states that mandate the coverage. The courts of some states have found that it violates public policy to prohibit stacking of coverages that are mandated by the state's financial responsibility laws.[136]

The court cases cite basically three issues in permitting stacking:

1. The coverage is required by state law, and policy language cannot reduce coverage from that provided by the statute.
2. The insured pays a separate premium for each vehicle. (This reason is often referred to as the premium rule.)
3. The coverage is intended to apply to an insured's injury rather than to legal responsibility related to a particular vehicle (as with liability coverage).

The **premium rule** allows the insured to add together separate uninsured motorists coverage amounts, on separate vehicles, for which separate premiums have been paid.[137] The following case illustrates this rule:

> The insured paid separate premiums for coverage on two separate vehicles. The insured was billed in one lump amount, but the premium was, in fact, $24 higher than the premium for a single vehicle. The court disregarded the policy's clear limitation against stacking coverage and allowed the insured to add the $10,000 coverage from the second vehicle.

Even states that permit intrapolicy stacking are inclined to permit stacking only in circumstances in which the injured party paid premiums for uninsured motorists coverage on multiple vehicles. Courts are less inclined to permit occupants, other than the named insured and family members, of an insured vehicle to stack all of the coverages purchased by the named insured. For example, a nonfamily member passenger in an insured car is not likely to be allowed to stack the coverage from the insured's two other cars, even if the insured would be permitted to do so.[138] Also, employees are not typically allowed to stack all of the uninsured motorists coverages for a fleet of vehicles purchased by their employer.[139] As one court noted, injured employees could have millions of dollars of coverage, something not reasonably contemplated by the insurer.[140]

ISO continues to make policy changes to address court interpretations of policy wording regarding stacking. As with other policy provisions, claim representatives should always check to make sure that the court ruling allowing stacking of limits was based on the current policy wording or at least has some general reason (such as public policy) that mutes or contravenes the policy wording.

Duplicate Payments

As with the other insuring agreements, the uninsured motorists coverage states that no one is entitled to coverage for duplicate payments for the same elements of loss under the medical payments or liability sections of the policy. Again, as with the liability coverage section, the issue arises regarding the enforceability of the medical payments coverage offset.

Offset for Medical Payments

A majority of states permit medical payments offset. However, a number of states consider the offset provision to be invalid. The states that do not permit an offset cite two familiar arguments, the premium rule and public policy, as reasons insureds who paid separate premiums for each coverage should be entitled to coverage under each section up to the limit of liability.[141] "A policy provision that undertakes to reduce the amount payable under the uninsured motorists coverage is repugnant to the mandate of uninsured motorist laws" is how one court explained its position.[142] These courts are unwilling to enforce a provision that attempts to reduce the uninsured motorists coverage, and attempts to do so are labeled as "unjust violations of public policy."[143] Claim representatives must always ensure that no law prohibits them from enforcing the offset provision.

CASE EXAMPLE—MEDICAL PAYMENTS OFFSET

Cynthia was injured by an uninsured motorist while driving her father's car. The father's car had uninsured motorists coverage and $2,000 medical payments coverage. Cynthia incurred $1,706 in medical expenses. The insurance company paid Cynthia $5,500 (including the $1,706 in medical expenses) for her uninsured motorist claim, and Cynthia signed a release for that amount. Cynthia asked for an additional $1,706 for payment under the medical payments section of the policy. The company refused to pay based on the offset provisions contained in the policy. Cynthia sued. The trial court found in favor of the insurance company, and the appeals court affirmed the decision. The case was subsequently appealed and transferred to the state's supreme court. The supreme court ruled in favor of Cynthia because the provision had the effect of placing her in a worse position than if she had been able to collect from the tortfeasor (wrongdoer), because if she had received compensation from the tortfeasor, she would have been able to collect damages of $5,500 plus $1,706 from her own medical payments coverage. To prevent her from doing the same with her own uninsured motorists coverage defeated the purpose of the statute and the uninsured motorists coverage provision because it failed to provide protection equivalent to what the insured would have legally been entitled to recover from the tortfeasor.[144]

Workers Compensation

Both the PAP and commercial auto policies exclude coverage for obligations owed under workers compensation laws from UM as well as medical payments coverage. The PAP UM exclusion reads as follows:

> We will not pay for any element of loss if a person is entitled to receive payment for the same element of loss under any of the following or similar law:
>
> 1. Workers' compensation law; or
> 2. Disability benefits law.

The commercial auto policy wording for uninsured motorists coverage varies by state, but most states have wording that prevents recovery for workers compensation benefits under the uninsured motorists coverage.

If an insured is injured by an uninsured motorist while in the course of employment, can the insured collect uninsured motorists coverage? The insured would seek workers compensation benefits through the employer but could collect damages that exceed the amount paid under workers compensation under the uninsured motorists coverage or for expenses not covered by workers compensation.

State workers compensation statutes often permit employers or their insurers to seek reimbursement for workers compensation payments from the responsible parties.

If an insured employee is injured by an uninsured motorist during the course of employment and collects workers compensation, could the insured's employer or its workers compensation carrier then subrogate against the insured's PAP insurer under the uninsured motorists coverage? The coverage expressly states that it does not intend directly or indirectly to benefit any insurer or self-insured under any workers compensation law. Moreover, the law has not viewed the uninsured motorist insurer as a responsible party as intended in the workers compensation statute.

Other Insurance

The same issues that apply with the Other Insurance provision in the liability section of the policy also apply to uninsured motorists coverage. As with liability insurance, the Other Insurance provision does not always work as intended. Some states require pro rata contribution or contribution by equal shares.[145] Because state financial responsibility statutes address uninsured motorists, some state statutes are so specific as to address how insurance proceeds (and claim expenses) should be apportioned. An example is shown in Exhibit 2-3.

EXHIBIT 2-3

Pennsylvania Financial Responsibility Statute

(a) General rule. Where multiple policies apply, payment shall be made in the following order of priority:

   (1) A policy covering a motor vehicle occupied by the injured person at the time of the accident.

   (2) A policy covering a motor vehicle not involved in the accident with respect to which the injured person is an insured.

(b) Multiple sources of equal priority.—The insurer against whom a claim is asserted first under the priorities set forth in subsection (a) shall process and pay the claim as if wholly responsible. The insurer is thereafter entitled to recover contribution pro rata from any other insurer for the benefits paid and the costs of processing the claim.

When insureds have the potential for other sources of recovery such as from passengers in covered autos (or when insureds are passengers in vehicles owned by others), claim representatives must clarify how the state apportions insurance proceeds before issuing uninsured motorist payments.

UNDERINSURED MOTORISTS COVERAGE

The Underinsured Motorists (UIM) Coverage is the newest automobile insurance coverage offered by insurance companies. It is now required in about fifteen states.[146]

Underinsured motorists is by far the most controversial, and many would say most confusing, coverage. Each state has a thicket of cases that address various underinsured motorists coverage issues. The issues are too numerous and too policy- and state-specific to summarize. Some of the issues encountered with uninsured motorists coverage, such as stacking, offsets, contribution of other insurance, and arbitration, also apply with the underinsured motorists coverage. Claim representatives are cautioned against generally applying court decisions related to uninsured motorists to underinsured motorists cases. The courts (even in the same jurisdiction) do not always come to the same conclusion, especially in states where underinsured motorists coverage is optional but uninsured motorists coverage is mandated.

The major point of contention with the underinsured motorists coverage is the definition of an underinsured motor vehicle, which triggers coverage. An "underinsured motor vehicle" is defined in two different ways. One definition looks at the inadequacy of the tortfeasor's liability insurance in paying the amount of damages suffered by an insured (damages trigger). The other way looks strictly at the limits of the liability insurance carried by the other motorist and compares them to a preselected amount chosen by the insured (limits trigger). Currently, twenty-two states support the "damages trigger," and the rest apply the "limits trigger."

The **damages trigger** defines an underinsured motor vehicle as one that does not have adequate insurance to cover the amount of damages suffered by an injured insured. Under this trigger, a motorist with $1 million in liability insurance coverage could be considered "underinsured" if the insured suffered damages in excess of that amount. Under the more conservative **limits trigger,** the other vehicle is considered "underinsured" only if it has less liability insurance than the amount of underinsured motorists coverage selected by the insured. If, for example, the other driver had $50,000 liability insurance and the insured purchased $50,000 underinsured motorists coverage, then there would be no claim because the vehicle is not considered "underinsured." This holds true even if the insured suffered in excess of $1 million in damages because states using the "limits" trigger do not even consider the extent of the injury claim. The amount of damages has no bearing on whether the other vehicle is considered underinsured.[147]

Besides the issue of the definition of underinsured motor vehicle, claim representatives are likely to encounter the following questions:

- Does the other party have to pay his or her insurance limit in order for the insured to make an underinsured motorist claim?
- Can the insured's insurance company subrogate against the underinsured motorist after paying the claim?

Because of the complexity of this coverage, many large law firms have published material explaining how local jurisdictions address the various issues of this coverage. A claim representative should seek material on how this coverage applies in his or her own jurisdiction.

DUTIES OF THE INSURED AFTER AN ACCIDENT OR A LOSS

Both the PAP and the Business Auto Coverage Form have a section describing the duties that an insured must perform after an accident or a loss. The Business Auto Coverage Form goes into more detail as to what actions are expected of an insured. The insurer may not be obligated to provide coverage unless there is full compliance with these duties. Additional duties are imposed if the insured is seeking protection under the uninsured motorists coverage. Claim representatives should familiarize themselves with these duties because they can be valuable tools in fighting fraudulent claims.

In general, courts require full compliance with these duties as long as they do not unfairly restrict coverage.[148] However, the details of compliance are often the subject of litigation, especially regarding the duties to "cooperate" and act "promptly."

Cooperation

The willingness to cooperate varies widely by insured. Some courts will not enforce this duty unless the insurance company provides clear statements of how it expects the insured to cooperate, documents the requests in writing, and makes the requests consistently (for example, once each month) and persistently (for example, up until the time the insurance company files suit to seek a coverage defense).[149]

Prompt Notice Versus Late Notice

Prompt notification is mentioned twice in the policy. The insured must provide:

1. Prompt notification to the insurance company about the accident.
2. Prompt notification to the police of a hit-and-run driver.

What is prompt notification? Within one day? One week? One month? Does it matter if the insured is hospitalized and unable to call? These are some questions claim representatives encounter. The answers vary by state.

The purpose of a notice provision is to allow the insurance company to:

- Determine its rights and liabilities.
- Investigate the claim.
- Protect against fraudulent claims.
- Secure early settlements.

An insurer should have the right to assess coverage in a timely fashion and determine its obligations at the earliest possible time. Insurers should be able to investigate the claim as soon as possible. When notice is delayed, memories fade, the opportunity to examine the physical surroundings and take pictures is lost, the ability to find and speak to witnesses is hampered, and the ability to secure an early settlement and avoid litigation becomes more difficult.[150]

GENERAL PROVISIONS

This section presents provisions and conditions that apply to both the PAP and Business Auto Coverage Form, which have general provisions. The two most likely provisions to cause controversy for claim representatives are the fraud provision and the subrogation provision.

Fraud

The wording of the fraud provision varies enough between the PAP and the Business Auto Coverage Form to warrant examining each of the provisions and comparing their differences. The PAP fraud provision reads:

> FRAUD
>
> We do not provide coverage for any "insured" who has made fraudulent statements or engaged in fraudulent conduct in connection with any accident or loss for which coverage is sought under this policy.

The business auto concealment, misrepresentation or fraud provision reads:

> Concealment, Misrepresentation Or Fraud
>
> This Coverage Form is void in any case of fraud by you at any time as it relates to this Coverage Form. It is also void if you or any other "insured", at any time, intentionally conceal or misrepresent a material fact concerning:
>
> a. This Coverage Form;
> b. The covered "auto";
> c. Your interest in the covered "auto"; or
> d. A claim under this coverage form.

In both of these auto policies, the civil penalty for fraud is loss of coverage for the *entire* claim. If, for example, an insured is injured by an uninsured motorist and seeks coverage under the medical payments and uninsured motorists coverage and fraudulently presents a fabricated medical bill for $300, the entire claim for medical payments and uninsured motorists coverages could be voided, even if the rest of the bills and damages are legitimate. However, some courts are reluctant to deny coverage for the entire claim and often pressure insurance companies to pay the legitimate part of the claim.

The PAP does not provide coverage if the insured engages in "fraudulent conduct" or makes "fraudulent statements." This wording is potentially broader than the terms used in the Business Auto Coverage Form, which uses the more legal, well-defined terms of intentional concealment and material misrepresentation. **Concealment** by an insured is withholding or hiding information that the insurance company is entitled to know. A material misrepresentation by an insured is a false statement the insured makes about an important point that the insurance company relies on. Both of these misdeeds would probably fall under the wording of "fraudulent conduct" or "fraudulent statements." However, a deliberate lie by an insured that he paid $9,000 for a car when he paid only $8,900 might be considered a "fraudulent statement" but not a material misrepresentation because the $100 difference might not be considered important. For this reason, some courts have required that fraudulent statements must also be sufficiently substantial in order for coverage to be denied.

Another fine legal point involving misrepresentations relates to how courts view misrepresentations discovered before a payment is made. A minority of courts will not consider the lie to be a material misrepresentation if the company discovered the false information before making payment, arguing that the company did not rely on the statement. This reliance argument is one that claim representatives are likely to hear from attorneys representing policyholders or claimants anytime fraud is discovered. Most courts will not accept this argument because it does not penalize insureds who make material misrepresentations and it encourages fraud.

Subrogation

The wording for the PAP clause that addresses subrogation (the insurer's right to recover payment) is as follows:

OUR RIGHT TO RECOVER PAYMENT

A. If we make a payment under this policy and the person to or for whom payment was made has a right to recover damages from another we shall be subrogated to that right. That person shall do:

1. Whatever is necessary to enable us to exercise our rights; and

2. Nothing after loss to prejudice them.

   However, our rights in this Paragraph (A.) do not apply under Part D, against any person using "your covered auto" with a reasonable belief that that person is entitled to do so.

B. If we make a payment under this policy and the person to or for whom payment is made recovers damages from another, that person shall:

1. Hold in trust for us the proceeds of the recovery; and

2. Reimburse us to the extent of our payment.

The wording under the Business Auto Coverage Form is similar but does not have the additional wording requiring the insured to hold in trust proceeds received or reimburse the company for payments received. Courts do not always permit insurance companies to seek recovery for payments made under the medical payments, uninsured motorists, or underinsured motorists coverage.

Recovery of Medical Payments

The law, in general, does not permit injured parties to assign their injury claims to others. Courts realize that if this were permitted, a market would then develop whereby injured parties would sell their claims to the highest bidder. Some courts take the position that subrogation for amounts paid under the medical payments coverage is tantamount to an assignment of a personal injury claim and should therefore not be permitted.[151] Many states that permit subrogation take the position that medical expenses are only part of an injury claim and therefore subrogation of medical payments is not the same as assigning a personal injury claim.

Recovery of Uninsured/Underinsured Motorists Payments

Because uninsured and underinsured motorists coverages are comprehensive and include medical expenses, wage loss, and general damages such as pain and suffering, they truly constitute a person's entire injury claim. Therefore, states that do not permit assignments of third-party claims would not normally permit subrogation. However, the uninsured motorists statutes in many states permit subrogation. For this reason, subrogation is typically permitted in states that have statutory wording addressing the issue of subrogation.[152] Barring statutory wording, states will normally follow the court's decision on medical payments subrogation.

CONCLUSION

Naturally, people feel anxiety anytime they learn that things work differently from the way they understood them to work. After reading this chapter, claim representatives might feel that they cannot deny a claim or rely on any policy wording because the courts will find coverage and the insurer will be sued for bad faith. As mentioned earlier, most policy provisions apply as stated or at least have consistent interpretation within a given jurisdiction. Claim representatives do not commit bad faith just by failing to anticipate that a court would disallow a policy provision. Insurers can, however, be subject to bad faith claims if their claim representatives fail to consider previous court decisions that have construed policy provisions differently from the way the claim representative interprets the provision. Claim representatives should be fair and open to the possibility that coverage could be interpreted differently from the way they read it.

One of the main purposes of this chapter is to alert claim representatives to policy provisions that are commonly litigated or have the potential for misinterpretation. This should help to avoid needless litigation and improve customer service. If claim representatives are unsure of how the courts in their jurisdiction address a policy provision, they should consult with claim management personnel or legal counsel before denying a claim about which they have doubts.

CHAPTER NOTES

1. National Aviation Underwriters v. Altus Flying Service, 555 F.2d 778, 782 (10th Cir. 1977).
2. Standard Venetian Blind Co. and Sheldon Morris v. American Empire Insurance Co., Supreme 503 Pa. 300, 469 A.2d, 563 (1986).
3. Tonkovic v. State Farm Mutual Auto Ins. Co., 513 Pa. 445, 521 A2d. 920 (1987).
4. Bowler v. Fidelity and Casualty of New York, 53 N.J. 313, 250 A.2d 580 (1969).
5. Hayes v. American Standard Ins. Co., 847 S.W.2d 150, 152, 153, 154 (Mo. Ct. App. 1993).
6. Government Emp. Ins. Co. v. Dennis, 645 P.2d 672, 675 (Utah 1982).
7. Government Emp. Ins. Co. v. Dennis, 645 P.2d 672, 676 (Utah 1982).
8. Remington v. Aetna Cas. and Sur. Co., 646 A.2d 266, 271 (Conn. App. Ct. 1994).
9. National General Insurance v. Sherouse 882 P.2d 1207 (Wash. Ct. App. 1994) and Countryside Casualty Company v. McCormick, 722 SW 2d. 655 (1993).
10. Government Employees Ins. Co. v. Allstate Insurance Co., 369 S.E.2d 181 (Va. 1988).
11. Lawrence v. New Hampshire Insurance Co., 616 A.2d 806 (Conn. App. Ct. 1992).
12. Allstate Insurance Co. v. Barnes, 896 S.W.2d 565 (Tenn. Ct. App. 1995).
13. State Farm Fire & Casualty Co. v. Davidson, 896 S.W.2d 565 (Tenn. Ct. App. 1995).
14. Pierce v. Aetna Casualty and Surety. Co., 627 P.2d 152, 154 (Wash Ct. App. 1981).
15. Friedman v. Alliance Ins. Co., 240 Kan. 229, 237, 729 P.2d. 1160 (1986).
16. Phelps v. State Farm Mutual Automobile Insurance Co., 426 S.E.2d 484 (Va. 1993).
17. Trezza v. State Farm Mutual Automobile Insurance Co., 519 So. 2d 649 (Fla. Dist. Ct. App. 1988).
18. Concord Group Insurance Cos. v. Sleeper, 600 A.2d 445 (N.H. 1991).
19. National General Insurance v. Sherouse, 882 P.2d 1207 (Wash. Ct. App. 1994).
20. Arents v. General Accident Insurance Co., 655 A.2d 936 (N.J. Super. Ct. App. Div. 1995).
21. Hicks v. Automobile Club Insurance Assn., 473 N.W.2d 704 (Mich. Ct. App. 1991).
22. Countryside Casualty. Co. v. McCormick, 722 S.W.2d 655 (Mo. Ct. App. 1987).
23. Barricelli v. American Universal Insurance Co., 583 A.2d 1270 (R.I. 1990).

24. Pierce v. Aetna Casualty Insurance Co., 627 P.2d 152 (Wash. Ct. App. 1981).

25. Government Emp. Ins. Co. v. Dennis, 645 P.2d 672, 674 (Utah 1982).

26. Etter v. Travelers Ins. Cos., 657 N.E.2d 298, 300 (Ohio Ct. App. 1995).

27. Putkamer v. Transamerica Ins. Co., 563 N.W. 2d 683 (Mich. 1997).

28. Rohlman v. Hawkeye-Security Insurance Co., 526 N.W.2d 183 (Mich. Ct. App. 1993).

29. Steuben Contracting Inc. v. Employers Insurance of Wausau, 975 F.Supp. 479 (NY 1997).

30. Wickhum v. Equity Fire and Casualty Co., 889 P.2d 1258 (Okla. Ct. App. 1994). See also: Tata v. Nichols, 848 S.W.2d 649, 653-54 (Tenn. 1993) (plaintiff who was under the hood of another's car attaching jumper cables was "upon" the car for purposes of uninsured motorists coverage); Martinez v. Great Am. Ins. Co., 499 So. 2d 364, 366 (La. Ct. App. 1986), reviewed in part on other grounds, 503 So. 2d 1005, 1006 (La. 1987) (wrecker driver who had hooked up disabled truck to his wrecker and was standing between them to operate lift mechanism was "occupying" truck for purposes of uninsured motorists coverage); Pope v. Stolis, 712 S.W.2d 434 (Mo. Ct. App. 1986) (plaintiff leaning over engine compartment of neighbor's car reaching to attach jumper cables, with stomach and knees touching the car, was "upon" the car and therefore "occupying" it for purposes of uninsured motorists coverage).

31. Allied Mutual Ins. Co. v. Western National Mutual. Ins. Co., 552 N.W.2d 561, 562 (Minn. 1996).

32. Dawes v. First Ins. Co. of Hawaii, Ltd. 883 P.2d 38 (Haw. 1994).

33. Kufalt v. Hart, 636 F. Supp. 309 (N.D. Ill. 1986).

34. Gerald Boston, David Kline, and Jeffrey Brown, *Emotional Injuries Law and Practice* (Eagan, Minn.: West Group, 1999), pp. 16-1–6-11.

35. Garvis v. Employers Mutual Casualty Co., 497 N.W. 2d 254 (Minn. 1993).

36. Barry Ostrager and Thomas Newman, *Handbook of Insurance Coverage Disputes*, 9th ed. (New York: Aspen Publishers, 1998), pp. 305-310.

37. Lavanant v. General Accident Insurance Co., 79, N.Y. 2d 623, 584 N.Y. 2d 744, 595 N.E. 2d 819 (1992). See also: NPS Corp. v. Insurance Co. of North America, 213 N.J. Super. 547, 517 A.2d. 1211 (1986); California Mutual Ins. Co. v. Robertson, 213 Cal App. 3rd 1172, 262 Cal. Rptr. 173(1989) and Boston, Kline, and Brown, pp. 16-4–6-10.

38. Bernard v. Cordle, 687 N.E. 2d 3 (Ohio 1996).

39. A.M. Best Company, *Best's Directory of Recommended Insurance Attorneys and Adjusters* (Oldwick, N.J.: A.M. Best Company, 1999), pp. 24-25T.

40. The National Underwriter Company, *FC&S Bulletins*, 1999, p. D.1.

41. *Best's Directory of Recommended Insurance Attorneys and Adjusters*, pp. 28-29T.

42. Poetz v. Klamberg, 781 S.W. 2d 253 (Mo. App. 1989).

43. Halpin v. American Family, 823 S.W.2d 479, *483. See also: Insurance Statutes, of Coverage Exclusion for Injury to or Death of Insured's Family of Household Members, 52 A.L.R.4th 18 (1987); Jordan v. Aetna Casualty & Surety Company, 264 S.C. 294, 214 S.E.2d 818 (1975); Nationwide v. Seeman, 702 A. 2d 915 (DE 1997); Farmers Insurance Exchange v. Dotson, 913 P. 2d 27 (Co 1996); Smalls v. State Farm Mutual Automobile Ins. Co., 678 A. 2d 32 (D.C. App. 1996).

44. For coverage: Economy Fire and Casualty Co. v. Stevens, 273 S.E. 2d 649 (1981). Against coverage: Atkinson v. Allstate Insurance Company, 354 S.E. 2d. 866 (1987).

45. Keppler v. American Family Mutual Insurance Co., 588 N.W. 2d 105 (Iowa 1999).

46. American National Property and Casualty Co. v. Julie Rayburn, B125033, November 8, 1999 (CA App. 2d).

47. Truck Ins. Exch. v. Webb, 256 Cal. App. 2d at p. 145 (1999).

48. Insurance Services Office, Inc., clarified this issue with this wording in the 1998 edition.

49. Insurance Services Office, Inc., 1997, Business Auto Coverage Form.

50. Maureen C. McLendon, *Commercial Auto Insurance*, vol. 1 (Dallas: International Risk Management Institute, Inc., 1995), pp. III.K20-K23.

51. Missouri Revised Statutes 379.201.

52. Johnson v. Allstate Insurance Co., 505 So. 2d 362 (Ala. 1987).

53. American Motorists v. Travelers Insurance, 604 N.Y.S.2d 475 (N.Y. Sup. Ct. 1993).

54. United Services Automobile Association v. Couch, 643 S.W.2d 668 (Tenn. Ct. App. 1982); Progressive Casualty Ins. Co. v. Metcalf, 501 N.W.2d 690 (Minn. Ct. App. 1993); Pizza Hut v. West General Ins. Co., 816 S.W.2d 638 (Ark. Ct. App. 1991).

55. Stanton v. Nationwide Mutual Ins. Co., 623 N.E. 2d 1197 (Ohio 1993); Liberty Mutual Insurance Co., 623 N.E. 2d 536 (NY 1993).

56. Stanfel v. Shelton, 563 So. 2d 410 (La. Ct. App. 1990).

57. Christiana General Ins. Corp. v. Great American Ins. Co., 979 F. 2d 268 (2d Cir. 1992).

58. Nappier v. Allstate Ins. Co., 961 F. 2d 168 (11th Cir. 1992); American Home Assurance Co. v. Fremont Indemnity Co., 745 F. Supp. 974 (S.D.N.Y. 1990).

59. Zaragoza v. West Bend Mutual Ins. Co., 546 NW 2d 510 (Iowa 1996).

60. Hughes v. State Farm Ins. Co., 236 N.W. 2d 870 (1976).

61. Shelter Mutual Ins. Co. v. Tucker (1988 Tenn), 864 F2d 413.

62. Lemoine v. Herrmann (1990 La App. 4th Cir), 559 So. 2d 898.

63. United States Sugar Co. v. Nationwide Mutual Ins. Co. (1985 Fla App D2) 475 So. 2d 1350, 10 FLW 2287.

64. Galvin v. Amica Mutual Ins. Co., 417 N.E. 2d 34 (1981).

65. Factory Mutual Ins. Co. v. Continental Casualty Co. (CA5 Fla), 267 F2d 818 (1959).

66. First National Insurance Co. of America v. Charles Clark et al. (Missouri Supreme Ct. No. 11032, 1994).

67. Davis v. Foley, 457, S.E. 2d 532 (W.V. 1995).

68. Whittlesey v. Miller, 572 S.W. 2d. 665 (Tex. 1978).

69. Gerald Boston, David Kline, Jeffrey Brown, pp. 6-28–6-30.

70. Vue v. State Farm Ins. Co., 568 N.W. 2d 527 (Minn. 1997).

71. Valliere v. Allstate Ins. Co., 324 Md. 139, 596 A 2d. 636 (1991); Allstate Ins. Co. v. Handengard, 70 Or. App. 262, 688 P. 2d. 1387 (1984); and Tate v. Allstate Ins. Co., No. 1951906, 1997 WL 155277 (Ala. 1997).

72. Anthem Casualty Insurance Co. v. Miller, Pa. Superior Court, 1999 107 (May 1999).

73. Webb v. State Farm Mutual Ins. Co., 479, S.W. 2d 148 (Mo. App. 1972); Wilson v. American Standard Ins. Co. 792 S.W. 2d 669 (Mo. App. 1990); Kuda v. American Family Mutual Ins. Co. 790 S.W. 2d 464 (Mo. Banc 1990).

74. The National Underwriter Company, *F.C.& S. Bulletins* (Cincinnati: The National Underwriter Company, 1999), pp. Personal Auto A.3-9–3-10.

75. State Farm Mutual Ins. Co. v. Baker, 14 Kan App. 2d 641, 797 P.2d 168 (1990) and K.S.A. 40-3110 (a).

76. *Couch on Insurance*, 2d 62:71 Rev. 1983 et seq. and 8 A Appleman, *Insurance Law and Practice*, 4901 (rev. 1981).

77. Bukulmez v. Hertz Corp., 710 P. 2d 1117, 1120 (CO 1985).

78. Hoffmaster v. Harleysville Ins. Co., 441 Pa. Super. 490 657 A.2d 1274 (1995) and Lamb-Weston, Inc. v. Oregon Auto Ins. Co., 341 P.2d 110 (OR 1989).

79. Continental Cas. Co. v. Weekes, 74 So. 2d 367, 369 (Fla. 1954). See also Cosmopolitan Mutual Insurance Co. v. Continental Cas. Co., 28 N.J. 554, 147 A.2d 529, 534 (1959); Lamb-Weston, Inc. v. Oregon Auto Ins. Co., 219 Or. 110, 341 P. 2d 110 (1959).

80. Allstate v. Avis, 947 P. 2d 341 (CO. 1997).

81. *Couch on Insurance* 2d 62:71 (Rev. 1983).

82. Rader v. Johnson, 910 S.W. 2d 280 (Mo. App. 1995).

83. Allstate Ins. Co. v. Frank B. Hall Co., 770 P. 2d at 1347; Universal Underwriters, 657 P. 2d 581; Carriers Ins. Co. v. Policyholders Ins. Co., 404 A. 2d 216, 221-22 (Me. 1979).

84. State Farm Ins. Co. v. MFA Ins., 671 S.W.2d 276 (Mo. Supreme Ct. 1989).

85. Insurance Services Offices, Inc., "ISO Circular-Summary of Personal Auto Laws, Regulations and Court Decisions," March 9, 1999, pp. 4-5.

86. Missouri Statute section 379.201 and Missouri Insurance Department Bulletin 93-05.

87. Information from this section on state laws affecting rental car coverage comes from a CD-ROM entitled "Claims Involving Rented Vehicles," used with permission by Law Publishers, LLC, 1819 Pennsylvania Avenue, NW, Washington, DC 20006, www.rentalclaims.com, March 2001.

88. Alamo Rent-A-Car, Inc. v. State Farm Mutual Automobile Ins. Co. and Valley Forge Ins. Co. No. 28806 Supreme Court of Nevada.

89. State Farm Automobile Ins. Co. v. Budget Rent-A-Car of Missouri, Inc. (Mo. Appeals 1994). See also Avis Rent-A-Car System, Inc. v. Allstate Ins. Co. 937 P. 2d 802 (Co. App. 1996).

90. Alamo-Rent-A-Car, Inc. v. State Farm Mutual Ins. Co. and Valley Forge Ins. Co. No. 28806 Supreme Court of Nevada, 1998.

91. McClain, et al. v. Begley et al., 465 N.W. 2d 680 (Minn. 1991).

92. Czarnecki v. American Indemnity Co., 131 S.E. 2d 347 (N.C. 1963).

93. The National Underwriter Company, *F.C.& S. Bulletins* (Cincinnati: The National Underwriter Company, 1999), pp. Personal Auto A.4-2–4-3.

94. Travelers Indemnity Company v. Chumbley (394 S.W. 2d 418, MO App. 1965).

95. State Farm Mutual Ins. Co. v. Baker: 14 Kan. App.2d 641, 797 P.2d 168 (1990).

96. Insurance Research Council, *Uninsured Motorists* (Malvern, Pa.: Insurance Research Council, 1999), p. 2.

97. State Farm Automobile Ins. Co. v. Davis, 937 P.2d 1415 (9th Cir. 1991).

98. Wausau Underwriters Insurance Co. v. Howser, 422 S.E.2d 106 (S.C. 1992).

99. Cung La v. State Farm Automobile Ins. Co., 830 P.2d 1007 (Colo. 1992).

100. Abercrombie v. Georgia Farm Bureau Mutual Insurance Co., 454 S.E.2d 813 (Ga. Ct. App. 1995).

101. Ruiz v. Farmers Ins. Co. of Arizona, 865 P.2d 762 (Ariz. 1993).

102. Taylor v. Phoenix Ins. Co., 622 So. 2d 506 (Fla. Dist. Ct. App. 1993).

103. State Farm Mutual Automobile Ins. Co. v. Spotten, 610 N.E.2d 299 (Ind. Ct. App. 1993).

104. State Farm Mutual Ins. Co. v. Blystra, 883 F. Supp. 583 (D.N.M 1995).

105. State Farm Automobile Insurance Co. v. Fernandez, 9 Cir, 767 F. 2d 1299 (Hawaii 1985).

106. Wieneke v. Home Mutual Insurance Co., MN App, 397 NW 2d 597 (MN 1986).

107. Edwards v. State Farm Mutual Automobile Ins. Co., 399 NW 2d 95 (MN App. 1986).

108. McLendon, p. IV.D.30.

109. McNeil v. Hicks, 459 S.E.2d 47 (N.C. Ct. App. 1995). See also Illinois Statute 215 ILCS 5/143a Illinois Rev. Stat. 1987, ch 73 par. 755 a(2) (I); Scanlan et al. v. Maryland Casualty Ins. Co., Ill. Appeals Ct. Second District. No. 2-89-1289.

110. Girgis v. State Farm Mutual Automobile Ins. Co., 662 N.E.2d 280 (Ohio 1996).

111. Rogers v. Schuman-Mann Supply Co., 397 S.E.2d 463 (Ga. Ct. App. 1990). See also Motor Vehicle Accident Indemnification Corp. v. Eisenberg, 218 N.E.2d 524 (N.Y. 1996).

112. Allstate Insurance Co. v. Killakey 580 N.E.2d 399 (N.Y. 1991).

113. Oanh Thi Pham v. Allstate Insurance Co., 254 Cal. Rptr. 152 (Cal. Ct. App. 1988).

114. Keith Kruger, *Missouri Insurance Law Update*, July 1995, Buchanan County Circuit Court Case No. CV394-624CC.

115. State Farm Fire and Casualty Co. v. Guest, 417 S.E.2d 419 (Ga. Ct. App. 1992).

116. Eagle Insurance Co. v. Watanabe, 567 N.Y.S.2d 34 (N.Y. App. Div. 1991).

117. Kern v. Nevada Insurance Guaranty Assn., 856 P.2d 1390 (Nev. 1993).

118. Miller v. United States Fidelity and Guaranty Ins. Co. 738 P.2d 425 (Idaho Ct. App. 1987).

119. Cameron Mutual Insurance v. Madden, 533 S.W.2d 538 (Mo. Supreme Ct. 1976).

120. McLendon, pp. IV.D.34–35.

121. Moomaw v. State Farm Mut. Auto. Ins. Co., 379 F.Supp. 697 (S.D.W.Va.1974); Cunningham v. Insurance Co. of N. America, 213. Va. 72, 189 S.E.2d 832 (1972); Blakeslee v. Farm Bureau Mut. Ins. Co. of Mich., 388 Mich. 464, 201

N.W.2d 786 (1972); Citizens Mut. Ins. Co. v. Turner, 53 Mich. App. 616, 220 N.W.2d 203 (1974).

122. Mortgensen v. Heritage Mutual Ins. Co., 590 N.W. 2d (Iowa 1999).

123. Tucker v. Government Employees Ins. Co., 288 So. 2d 238 (Fla. 1973); Great Central Ins. Co. v. Edge, 292 Ala 613, 298 So. 2d 607 (1974); Cameron Mutual Insurance v. Madden, 533 S.W.2d 538 (Mo. Supreme Ct. 1976).

124. Gordon R. Broom & Thomas Scott Stewart, *A Look at Uninsured and Underinsured Motorist Issues*, THE BRIEF, Summer 1997, p. 36.

125. Cano v. Travelers Insurance (Mo. Banc. 1983). See also Chilberg v. Rose, 903 P.2d 1377 (Mont. 1995).

126. Linderer v. Royal Globe, 597 S.W. 2d 656 (Mo. App. 1980).

127. Mancini v. Utica Mutual Ins. Co., 653 A.2d 727 (R.I. 1995).

128. Van Tassel v. Horace Mann Insurance Co., 207 N.W.2d 348 (Minn. 1973).

129. Webb v. State Farm Mutual Automobile Ins. Co., 479 S.W.2d 148 (Mo. Ct. App. 1972).

130. Shearer v. Motorist Mutual Ins. Co., 371 N.E.2d 210 (Ohio 1978); Bertolami v. Merchants Mutual Ins. Co., 414 A.2d 1281 (N.H. 1981).

131. Kuda v. American Family Mutual, 790 S.W.2d 464 (Mo. 1990).

132. Midwest Mutual Insurance Co. v. Aetna Casualty, 565 S.W. 2d 711(Mo. App. 1978).

133. A. S. Klein, Annotation, *Uninsured Motorist Endorsement: Validity and Enforceability of Provision for Binding Arbitration, and Waiver Thereof*, 24 A.L.R.3d 1325, 1327 (1995).

134. Ohio Casualty Ins. Co. v. Benson (1981), 87 NJ, 432 A2d 905; Gerdes v. Travelers Insurance Co. (1981), 109 Misc 2d 816,440 NYS2d 976; Protective Ins. Co. v. Palma (1987) (Fla App 3d), 507 So. 2d 649, 12 FLW 1022.

135. Haegle v. Pennsylvania General Ins. Co. (1984), 330 Pa Super 481, 479 A2d 1005 and Cabus v. Dairyland Ins. Co. (1982 Colo. App), 656 P2d 54.

136. Windrim v. Nationwide Mutual Ins. Co. (1992), 412 Pa Super 155, 602 A2d 1356.

137. Lamar v. Colonial Penn Ins. Co. (1990), 396 Pa Super 527, 578 A2d 1337.

138. Federal Kemper Ins. Co. v. Reager (1992, ED Pa) 810 F Supp 150.

139. Barnhart v. Civil Services Employees Co., 398 P.2d 873 (Utah 1965). See also Alsbach v. Bader, 616 S.W. 2d 147 (Mo. App. 1981).

140. Petersen v. United Services Auto Assn., 91 Wash App. 212, 955 P.2d 852 (Div. 3 1998).

141. Connecticut General Statutes 38-175 c, d; and Stevens v. Hartford Accident & Indemnity Co. (1995), 39 Conn App. 429,664 A2d 826.

142. Parker v. American Family Ins. Co., 296 Ill App. 3d 110, 230 Ill. Dec. 580, 694 N.E. 2d 211 (3d Dist 1998).

143. A. S. Klein at 1328-29.

144. Arner v. Liberty Mutual Ins. Co. (1996, App. Div, 2d Dept.) 649 NYS2d 185.

145. Peterman v. State Farm Mutual Auto Ins. Co., 961 P.2d 487 (Colo 1998).

146. McLendon, p. IV.D.2.

147. McLendon, p. IV.D.31.

148. Billings v. State Farm Mutual Auto Ins. Co., 741 S.W. 2d 886. See also Girard v. State Farm Mutual Ins., 737 S.W. 2d 254 and Friend v. State Farm Mutual Auto Ins., 746 S.W. 2d 420.

149. American Guaranty & Liability Ins. Company v. Chandler Manufacturing Company, Inc.

150. Appleman, *Insurance Law and Practice*, 4731 (1981).

151. Jones v. Aetna Casualty & Surety Co., 497 S.W. 2d 809 (Mo. App. 1973) and Travelers Indemnity Co. v. Chumbley 394 S.W. 2d 418 (Mo. App. 1965); Peller v. Liberty Mutual Fire Ins. Co., 220 Cal.App.2d 610, 34 Cal.Rptr. 41. See Fifield Manor v. Finston, 54 Cal.2d 632, 7 Cal.Rptr. 377, 380-383, 354 P.2d 1073, 1076-1079, 78 A.L.R.2d 813, 818-821; City of Richmond v. Hanes, 203 Va. 102, 122 S.W.2d 895.

152. Kroeker v. State Farm Mutual Ins. Co., 466 S.W. 2d 105 (Mo. App. 1971).

Coverage Issues With Homeowners and Commercial Liability Policies

Coverage Issues With Homeowners and Commercial Liability Policies

This chapter describes common coverage issues and practical concerns encountered by claim representatives in handling commercial general liability (CGL) claims and homeowners liability claims. Several issues discussed in Chapter 2 on auto policies, including coverage for emotional injuries, coverage for punitive damages, complications related to the investigation of intentional acts, and determination of the insurer's duty to defend, are also concerns under homeowners and commercial liability policies. One major difference among homeowners, commercial liability, and auto policies is that the former two have little state statutory wording to contravene policy wording. This is because states do not require business owners or homeowners to purchase liability insurance for the properties they own, deterring the public policy argument that sways many auto policy coverage interpretations. Despite this disentanglement from statutory wording, numerous coverage issues still surface in homeowners and commercial liability policies.

Commercial operations generally have more severe loss exposures than do homeowners. Commercial losses are often challenging even for experienced claim representatives, regardless of the coverage issues. With respect to coverage, commercial policies have a wide variety of features not found in homeowners policies. One feature found in many commercial policies is the deductible for liability claims. For example, commercial policy insureds might have an occurrence deductible for every product liability loss. Personal lines insurance, such as homeowners coverage, usually has deductibles for first-party losses only, not for third-party liability claims.

The policy wording examined in this chapter is based on Insurance Services Office (ISO) 1998 version of the Commercial General Liability Coverage Form (CG 00 01 0798) and the 2000 version of the Homeowners Section II—Liability Coverages. This chapter begins with a discussion of common issues in the homeowners and CGL policies, namely:

- The definition of "occurrence"
- The definition of "property damage"

- The duty to defend insureds
- Coverage for punitive damages

The chapter continues with a presentation of basic homeowners liability coverage, followed by a presentation of coverage issues involving the CGL policy.

COVERAGE ISSUES COMMON TO THE CGL AND HOMEOWNERS POLICIES

A person looking for controversial coverage issues common to both the CGL and the homeowners policy needs to look no further than the insuring agreement of each. Coverage A of the CGL policy covers liability for bodily injury and property damage. The CGL Coverage A insuring agreement reads in part as follows:

> COVERAGE A—BODILY INJURY AND PROPERTY DAMAGE LIABILITY
>
> 1. Insuring Agreement
>
>   a. We will pay those sums that the insured becomes legally obligated to pay as damages because of "bodily injury" or "property damage" to which this insurance applies....
>
>   b. This insurance applies to "bodily injury" and "property damage" only if:
>
>   (1) the "bodily injury" or "property damage" is caused by an "occurrence"....

The insuring agreement of the Homeowners Section II–Liability Coverages reads in part as follows:

> COVERAGE E—Personal Liability
>
> If a claim is made or a suit is brought against an "insured" for damages because of "bodily injury" or "property damage" caused by an "occurrence" to which this coverage applies, we will:
>
> 1. Pay up to our limit of liability for the damages for which the "insured" is legally liable....

Common to both insuring agreements are the terms "bodily injury," "property damage," and "occurrence." Each of these terms is defined in both the CGL and homeowners policies, but applying the definition of the terms to specific claim circumstances is often challenging and varies by jurisdiction. The controversy related to the term "bodily injury" was described in the previous chapter on auto coverage issues. The following sections deal with the coverage disputes surrounding the terms "occurrence" and "property damage." Because of the comprehensive coverage provided by both the CGL and the homeowners liability section, insurers must sometimes defend insureds from unusual claims that are potentially not covered. Determining the insurer's duty to defend the insured is another area of intense debate and litigation. This subject is presented in the first part of the chapter. A brief explanation of coverage for punitive damages is provided as well.

"Occurrence"

What is meant by an "occurrence"?

The definitions found in the homeowners policy and the CGL policy are substantially the same. The CGL defines **"occurrence"** as follows:

> "Occurrence" means an accident, including continuous or repeated exposure to substantially the same general harmful conditions.

The homeowners policy defines it as follows:

> "Occurrence" means an accident, including continuous or repeated exposure to substantially the same general harmful conditions, which results, during the policy period, in:
>
> a. "Bodily injury"; or
> b. "Property damage."

In an occurrence policy, any occurrence must take place during the policy period (setting aside the territory issue) in order to be covered. Under this type of policy, it is irrelevant whether the resulting claim is brought after the policy expires, as long as the damage-causing event happens during the policy period. Although the types of liability claims arising out of commercial activities differ from those arising out of homeowners' activities, courts use similar reasoning in determining what constitutes an occurrence and whether an incident is one occurrence or more.

Claim representatives often encounter claims that require them to answer the following questions:

- What constitutes an occurrence?
- How is the number of occurrences determined?
- When does an occurrence take place?

Claim representatives should be aware that homeowners insurers with the ISO 2000 form have additional defenses for certain types of claims under the new intentional injury exclusion wording and potentially under the sexual molestation exclusion. These exclusions are discussed later in the chapter.

What Constitutes an Occurrence?

Claim representatives sometimes face the challenge of determining whether a problem even meets the definition of an occurrence. For example, an insured installs a heating/cooling system that does not work properly, and the company that purchased the system loses employee productivity and incurs costs for portable heaters and fans. Is this an occurrence?

This commercial liability question gets to the heart of the meaning of an occurrence. Courts would not likely consider this to be an occurrence because the circumstance of the building becoming too hot and too cold was not an accidental event and because the damages do not include any loss of use of the building or even any loss of value to the property.

The issue of what constitutes an occurrence arises in homeowners claims as well.

- Would the death of a neighbor resulting from gunplay by an insured's twelve-year-old son be considered an occurrence?
- If an insured tackled a guest but did not intend to injure the guest, is the incident an occurrence?
- If an insured's minor son molests a minor girl on five occasions, is this an occurrence? If so, how many occurrences?

An occurrence must be accidental (fortuitous rather than intended), and damages from such an incident must be unexpected. In making such a determination, courts place significance on the age of the insured. For example, in the case of the twelve-year-old involved in a gunplay accident, most courts would consider any injuries to be unexpected from the twelve-year-old's perspective and would therefore consider the incident an occurrence. On the other hand, when an adult insured intentionally tackles a guest but claims that he did not intend or expect to injure the guest, courts would be less sympathetic. Most adults could reasonably foresee that an injury could result from such activity. For that reason, most courts would likely consider injuries sustained by a guest whom an insured tackled *not* to be an occurrence.[1]

The last question, regarding whether molestation of a minor by an insured minor constitutes an occurrence, is a complicated one. If an insured is sued for negligent supervision of a minor son who molests another minor, then it could be considered an occurrence because it was not expected from the parents' perspective. The fact that the molestation took place on several occasions would not necessarily mean that these were all separate occurrences. Using the number of causes approach, described below, multiple molestations by the same person could be considered to be caused by the same general harmful conditions.[2]

Determining the Number of Occurrences

The following are examples of questions claim representatives have encountered in commercial liability claims:

1. If an insured's snow removal operation damages 100 different customers' doors in a four-hour time period, is this just one occurrence?
2. If an insured sold a defective plumbing system to several customers and these plumbing systems failed several years later, is this one occurrence or one for each customer's system that failed?

These questions regarding the number of occurrences are important, because the number of occurrences affects the limit of liability and insureds who have "per occurrence" deductibles. Some courts would consider the situation described in Question 1, involving the insured's snow removal operators, to be one occurrence.[3] This is probably a minority view, but it is made possible because most courts use the number of *causes* approach rather than the number of resulting claims approach.[4] If all of the claims were traceable to the inexperience of one driver or the defect of one of the insured's pieces of snow removal equipment, then the ruling of one occurrence is consistent with the number of causes approach that many courts take.

The following reasoning of one court reflects how most courts determine the number of occurrences:

Given the definition of "occurrence," it is more reasonable to evaluate an occurrence as the cause of property damage rather than as the property damage itself. In other words, analysis should focus on "the underlying circumstances which resulted in the claim for damages" (instead of the number of items damaged).[5]

Determining the number of causes can be challenging. If, for example, the plumbing problem had not been related to the labor but instead to a defective pipe, courts would likely consider the multiple claims to be only one occurrence. A majority of courts would probably consider the claims to be just one occurrence because one identifiable cause (the defective pipe) would have created all the claims.[6] The following are examples of situations that have been determined to be only one occurrence:

- An insured's defective forklift causes damage to several appliances over a year, and the cause of all the claims is the undetected defect in the forklift. The court determined that this could be one occurrence.[7]

- A distributor sold defective vinyl siding to twenty-six different customers who presented more than 1,400 claims. The court ruled that the multiple sales were a single occurrence, stating that the intention of the policy was not to gauge coverage on the basis of individual incidents, but rather in the underlying circumstances that resulted in the claims for damages.[8]

- The insured sold a defective compound used in the manufacture of tiles, paint, shoes, and floor mats. The compound generated a noxious odor in the various products. The court found that all the claims resulting from this compound were only one occurrence, even though they involved different products and the claims were made over several years.[9]

The issue of determining the number of occurrences also arises in homeowners claims. The following question has been encountered in homeowners claims:

If the insured homeowner is responsible for the death of two people involved in the same accident, would this be considered one occurrence or two?

The current wording in the definition explicitly states that an occurrence includes "continuous or repeated exposure to substantially the same general harmful conditions." This strengthens the argument that courts will look at the number of general causes (harmful conditions) rather than the number of claims generated by the cause or condition. With this in mind, it is easy to see how a court could rule that if an insured caused an accident that killed two people at the same time, it would be just one occurrence.[10] Unlike in the auto policy, homeowners liability is not separated into a per-person limit but instead has one *per occurrence* limit.

Determining When an Occurrence Takes Place

The following commercial claim questions illustrate the problem in determining *when* an occurrence took place.

- The insured contractor builds a defective roof, but the roof does not collapse for several years. Does the "occurrence" trigger apply when the contractor built the defective roof or when the roof collapsed?
- A respirator made by an insured fails to keep out harmful substances, causing a person to be exposed to the substance each week. The person does not become sick from the substance for several years. Did the occurrence take place each week throughout the years as the harmful substance accumulated in the person's body or when the person finally became sick?

The first question posed above relating to the collapsed roof requires a determination of when the occurrence took place. The second question is similar, except that it involves a "bodily injury" claim instead of a "property damage" claim. Damage or injury claims occurring over a period of time are known as progressive damage claims. Courts have historically taken several different approaches in deciding these questions, and disagreements continue.[11] The approaches courts use vary by jurisdiction and are based on the following rules:

- Exposure rule
- Manifestation rule

Under the **exposure rule,** only the policy in force at the time that the person or property was exposed to the damage-producing element must cover the claim. Coverage under the exposure rule is triggered even if the "property damage" or "bodily injury" (the product defect or the internal injury to a person) could not have been detected at that time. In some cases, courts have ruled that coverage is triggered only at the time of installation, based on the exposure rule.

In cases involving defective product installations, some courts have used the exposure rule to say that the occurrence took place as soon as the product was installed into the structure or integrated into the system.[12]

In the question involving the respirator, a court using the exposure rule would state that the occurrence took place as soon as the person was exposed to the harmful substance that was not filtered out by the respirator.

The competing approach to the exposure rule is the manifestation rule. According to the **manifestation rule,** the occurrence takes place at the time the injury or property damage is discovered (manifests itself). Courts favoring this rule point out that it is often difficult, if not impossible, to determine exactly when "bodily injury" or "property damage" begins.

Some courts favor a "double trigger" and make both the policy in force at the time of first exposure and the policy in force at the time of manifestation pay. Finally, some courts take the approach that the beginning policy (initial exposure), the end policy (manifestation), *and* all policies in between must pay. This is known as a continuous trigger.

What difference does it make which rule the courts use, if the insurer has to pay? It can make a difference as to *which* insurer has to pay, if the insured has changed insurance carriers. It also affects policy limits if, for example, the courts permit double triggers on more than one policy and potentially on more than one limit of liability. (Whether all of these policies can be stacked or whether they are just apportioned is another controversial issue.) It also affects the application of the statute of limitation. Claims are permitted to be made only within a specified time period from the date of the occurrence. Courts using the exposure rule have dismissed lawsuits because the statute of limitation had expired by the time the plaintiff discovered the problem and filed suit. Thus recovery for the claim was barred under the exposure rule of occurrence.[13]

Exhibit 3-1 summarizes the different questions and court rulings related to an occurrence.

EXHIBIT 3-1

Questions Related to the Interpretation of "Occurrence"

Question	Issue	Court Interpretation
What constitutes an occurrence?	Expected or intentional losses may not meet the definition of occurrence.	Most courts still take the position that an incident must be accidental and have the element of fortuity in order to be considered an occurrence.
How many occurrences are generated by an insured's single act of negligence when multiple parties are injured?	An insured produces one defective product that injures several people at different times. An insured's actions cause harm to several different parties.	Most courts will look at the number of causes, not the number of parties making claims. A defective product that injures multiple parties over a period of time would constitute one cause.
If an injury is suffered but not discovered until much later, when did the occurrence take place?	Claimants exposed to harmful substances may not be aware of the problem for years until they are diagnosed with a disease. A building has inherent problems that are not discovered until years later when it begins to collapse.	Courts may apply the exposure rule, the manifestation rule, a double trigger (both rules), or a continuous trigger (time from initial exposure through date of manifestation).

Property Damage

Coverage issues related to the meaning of bodily injury were discussed in Chapter 2. Although some litigation occurs over the definition of property damage in homeowners policies, the definition of property damage is more commonly disputed in CGL policies because of the severity and variety of property damage losses arising from commercial operations. The CGL policy mentions property damage forty-eight times and defines **property damage** as follows:

> "Property damage" means:

> a. Physical injury to tangible property, including all resulting loss of use of that property. All such loss of use shall be deemed to occur at the time of the physical injury that caused it; or

> b. Loss of use of tangible property that is not physically injured. All such loss of use shall be deemed to occur at the time of the "occurrence" that caused it.

The homeowners policy contains the following simpler definition:

> "Property damage" means:

> Physical injury to, destruction of, or loss of use of tangible property.

Both definitions include consequential damages from physical injury to property. If, for example, a business's building is damaged by an insured and the business's operations are affected, the loss of income would be included within the CGL policy's first definition of property damage. Under the second prong of the definition, property damage can occur even if there is no physical injury. The following examples illustrate property damage claims that are intended to be covered:

> The insured contractor, engaged in road repairs, damages a gas main, requiring that the gas be shut off. As a result of the interruption of the gas service, a factory served by a gas line leading from this main had to be temporarily shut down. The "loss of use" claim would be covered even though none of the tangible property of the factory had been damaged.

> An insured's crane buckles and blocks the entrance to a building. The claim for the loss of use of the building (tangible property) would be covered.

Would the following claims meet the definition of "property damage"?

- An insured's operations cause another party to lose computer data. Is this considered "physical injury to tangible property"?

- If an insured installed material that is later considered to be hazardous and rendered a building dangerous to occupants, would the cost to remove and replace the material be covered as "property damage"?

There is no agreement as to whether computer data are tangible property. Under the ordinary meaning of the term, they would not be tangible because the data could not be touched by the human hand.[14] Others consider this definition to be archaic and too restrictive in an era when so much information that used to be in paper form is now stored electronically, and they propose a new view of property damage. Proponents for this view contrast electronic data, which they believe should be covered because the data were or could be converted to paper form with a printer, with the completely intangible ideas forming the basis of intellectual property such as copyrights (which are clearly not covered).[15]

The second question, involving material making the building dangerous, provides an example of a situation that has in some cases triggered coverage, or at least a duty to defend. In one case, an insured installed asbestos in a building and rendered the building dangerous. The court found that the costs to remove the asbestos and repair the building were covered under property damage and also met the definition of an occurrence because the insured did not foresee or expect any injury to be sustained by placing the material in the building. Courts have found defects that pose serious health risks and require the evacuation of the building to be property damage.[16]

Even if these claims are accepted as occurrences and property damage, exclusions may preclude coverage. Exclusions to the CGL Coverage A and Homeowners Section II are covered later in this chapter.

Duty To Defend Against a Suit

Both the insuring agreement of Section II of the homeowners policy and the insuring agreement under the CGL express the insurer's right and duty to defend the insured against any suit seeking damages for bodily injury or property damage to which the insurance applies. The duty to defend is controversial under both homeowner and CGL claims, because the types of claims vary widely and may not have always been contemplated by the insurers. The CGL policy defines the word "suit" to include informal civil proceedings and arbitration proceedings as well as formal lawsuits.

Courts have consistently held that the insurer's duty to defend is broader than its duty to pay damages. Even if a suit is later found to be groundless, false, or fraudulent, the insurer must defend an insured whenever the plaintiff alleges facts that could conceivably fall within the coverage of the policy.

When does the duty to defend end? According the insuring agreement wording found in both the CGL policy and the homeowners 2000 version, defense coverage applies until the policy limits are "exhausted by judgment or settlement." This should prevent insurers from paying the limits and walking away from the claim without a settlement that protects the insured from further liability. The issues of insurance coverage and the duty to defend are described in more detail in Chapter 4.

Punitive Damages

Applying the rule of common usage of an undefined term would probably lead claim representatives to believe that punitive damages are covered because the policy does not exclude them and most insureds would consider punitive damages to be covered damages. **Punitive damages** provide an

Punitive damages are awarded in addition to compensatory damages when the defendant acted with recklessness, malice, or deceit. These should not be confused with general damages, such as pain and suffering, which are considered compensatory damages. Other examples of compensatory damages are medical expenses, wage loss, and property repair costs.

example of how public policy sometimes works in favor of insurers. The purpose of punitive damages is to punish the wrongdoer for his or her malicious acts or acts of gross negligence. Consider a case in which children at a daycare center were repeatedly molested by a daycare worker who was a convicted rapist. The daycare management failed to supervise the person, failed to do a background check on the person, and ignored complaints by parents. Because of the degree of care required of the daycare center to ensure the protection of children and because of the complete lack of such care in this case, a court might find gross negligence that could lead to an award of punitive damages against the daycare center (in addition to compensatory damages for the children for their emotional injury claims).

Who pays for punitive damages? Forcing insurance policies to pay for punitive damages defeats the purpose of punitive damages, which is to punish the wrongdoer. Despite this, about half the states consider punitive damages to be covered by insurance.[17] Also, insurance companies are responsible for additional *general* damages (to cover emotional injuries such as pain and suffering) awarded against an insured for "aggravating circumstances," such as drunk driving or speeding. These are claims for circumstances that indicate behavior beyond ordinary negligence but that do not meet the threshold of punitive damages. Such awards are commonly claimed because additional general damages are usually covered.[18] The answer to the question that opened this paragraph is that punitive damages are potentially covered, and general damages with a punitive aspect to them are definitely covered.

Some insurance companies further clarify the issue with endorsements that expressly exclude punitive damages. Other companies address this on their application forms with wording such as, "This application for insurance does not include a request for coverage against punitive damages."

Despite all of the reasons to prevent covering punitive damages, some states do require insurers to pay for punitive damages.[19] The states permitting punitive damages based their decisions on one or more of the following reasons:

- The policy language is ambiguous, and ambiguities should be construed in favor of the insured.
- Punitive damages are reasonably expected to be covered.
- The danger of bankruptcy outweighs the public policy issue.
- The policy wording does not support denying coverage for these damages.

HOMEOWNERS SECTION II—LIABILITY COVERAGES

When people think of the homeowners policy, they typically think of a policy that insures against fire, wind or water damage, and theft of personal property. The ISO homeowners policy combines these first-party Section I coverages with third-party Section II coverages for liability. People think of Section II of the policy as covering claims made by people who slip and fall while at the insured's premises. Although slip-and-fall claims are covered under the homeowners policy, homeowners liability coverage is much broader and potentially covers a wide variety of claims. The following examples of claims illustrate how broad the homeowners liability coverage can be:

- While playing in a recreational softball league, an insured knocks down and injures an opposing player. The player sues the insured for playing too aggressively.

- After shopping at a supermarket, an insured carelessly discards a shopping cart in the parking lot. The shopping cart rolls into and damages the side of an expensive car.

The homeowners policy Section II would respond to each of the preceding claims against an insured.

Section II of the homeowners policy consists of two coverages. Coverage E is personal liability insurance protecting insureds against liability for both property damage and bodily injury claims. Coverage F is medical payments insurance. Both coverages are provided automatically as part of the ISO homeowners policy package. Section II also has a provision for "additional coverages," including claim expenses, first-aid expenses, damage to the property of others, and loss assessment.

Section II Coverage E—The Personal Liability Insuring Agreement

The insuring agreement for Coverage E—Personal Liability reads as follows:

> COVERAGE E—Personal Liability
>
> If a claim is made or a suit is brought against an "insured" for damages because of "bodily injury" or "property damage" caused by an "occurrence" to which this coverage applies, we will:
>
> 1. Pay up to our limit of liability for the damages for which the "insured" is legally liable. Damages include prejudgment interest awarded against the "insured"; and
>
> 2. Provide a defense at our expense by counsel of our choice, even if the suit is groundless, false or fraudulent. We may investigate and settle any claim or suit that we decide is appropriate. Our duty to settle or defend ends when our limit of liability for the "occurrence" has been exhausted by payment of a judgement or settlement.

Claim representatives analyzing coverage under homeowners and CGL liability policies must first determine whether the given claim falls within the insuring agreement. In addition to confirming that a claim occurred within the defined policy period, claim representatives normally consider the following four requirements:

1. Whether an "insured" had a legal obligation to pay damages
2. Whether the damages were "bodily injury" or "property damage"
3. Whether the damages were caused by an "occurrence"
4. Whether the damages took place within a covered territory

These requirements should be analyzed even before determining whether an exclusion applies, because if the claim does not fall within the insuring agreement, then it is not covered.

To meet the first requirement, an insured must be legally liable to pay monetary damages. In homeowners claims, legal obligations typically arise from torts committed by insureds. Torts are civil wrongs that require an insured to pay money to the claimant. Torts, and other ways that insureds can become legally liable, will be discussed in detail in Chapter 5.

The issue of what constitutes a bodily injury was discussed in Chapter 2. Issues related to the definitions of property damage and occurrence are addressed later in this chapter in the section examining CGL coverage definitions.

Section II Coverage F—The Medical Payments to Others Insuring Agreement

The Coverage F—Medical Payments to Others insuring agreement is more limited in its scope than the automobile medical payments coverage and Coverage E—Personal Liability because it applies only to "others." Claim representatives accustomed to dealing with personal auto coverages sometimes find this insuring agreement confusing because, unlike the medical payments coverage provision found in personal auto policies, the homeowners medical payments coverage does not provide coverage for insureds or regular residents of the insured's household. The issue of who is a "regular resident" sometimes causes coverage disputes. Similar to the auto medical payments coverage, the homeowners medical payments coverage does not require the insured to be liable for the coverage to apply.

> Coverage F applies:
> 1. To a person on the "insured location" with the permission of an "insured"; or
> 2. To a person off the "insured location," if the "bodily injury":
>   a. Arises out of a condition on the "insured location" or the ways immediately adjoining;
>   b. Is caused by the activities of an "insured";
>   c. Is caused by a "residence employee" in the course of the "residence employee's" employment by an "insured"; or
>   d. Is caused by an animal owned by or in the care of an "insured."

Situation 1 covers persons on the "insured location" with the permission of the insured. Claim representatives must consider the circumstances of persons on the insured's premises because permission does not have to be expressly stated by the insured. For example, acquaintances of an insured would most likely have implied permission to visit an insured without an invitation. This same implied permission would apply to people delivering packages or even salespeople. Trespassers, people without any legitimate purpose to be on the insured's property, would not be covered under Coverage F.

A second set of circumstances for claims occurring *away* from the insured location can be covered under Coverage F if the circumstances meet any one of the four criteria "a" through "d" listed below:

a. Circumstances involving claims arising out of the insured location. This would include pedestrians injured on sidewalks adjoining the insured's property or neighbors injured by an insured's tree blown over by the wind.

b. Injuries caused by activities of the insured. This would include accidentally knocking someone down at a skating rink.

c. Injuries caused by residence employees while in the course of employment also trigger medical payments coverage. Injuries to another person caused by a residence employee while running an errand for the insured would also be covered.

d. Injuries caused by an animal owned by or in the care of an insured are also covered even if occurring off the insured's premises. An insured whose dog bites a neighbor's child while the insured is walking the dog in a park would have medical payments coverage for injuries to the child.

Section II Coverages E and F can cover a wide variety of claims both on and away from the insured's residence premises.

HOMEOWNERS SECTION II—EXCLUSIONS

Twelve exclusions apply to both Coverage E—Personal Liability and Coverage F—Medical Payments to Others. An additional six exclusions apply only to Coverage E, and another four apply only to Coverage F. The following section describes the bodily injury and property damage exposures that are excluded for both Coverages E and F. The exclusions involving the most litigation are the intentional acts exclusion and the business pursuits exclusion; therefore, they are covered in greater detail. Exhibit 3-2 summarizes the exclusions found in the homeowners liability sections.

Motor Vehicles, Watercraft, Aircraft, and Hovercraft Liability Exclusions

Section II Coverages E and F exclude liability arising out of motor vehicle liability, watercraft liability, aircraft liability, and hovercraft liability. The exclusions are comprehensive and include the ownership, maintenance, use, loading or unloading, and negligent entrustment of these vehicles. This exclusion applies to claims of negligent supervision or negligent entrustment by an insured. In the past, if an insured loaned his or her car to a drunk driver who caused an accident, some courts considered this negligent entrustment to be a separate act from using or operating the motor vehicle. These courts found coverage for negligent entrustment, ruling that the motor vehicle exclusion did not apply because the cause of the accident was not the operation of the auto but instead the negligence of the insured in letting an intoxicated person drive. Recent policies specifically exclude negligent entrustment. The homeowners 2000 policy has an extensive revision of coverage that attempts to clarify the vehicle exclusion. Some of the standard exceptions still exist, such as for the following:

The ISO definition of **"motor vehicle"** is a self-propelled land or amphibious vehicle or any trailer or semitrailer that is being carried on, towed by, or hitched for towing to such a vehicle.

- Vehicles in dead storage on the insured's location
- Vehicles used to service the insured's residence, such as riding lawn mowers
- Vehicles used to assist handicapped people

EXHIBIT 3-2

Section II—Homeowners Exclusions

I.   Exclusions applying to both Coverage E and Coverage F
- Motor Vehicle Liability
- Watercraft Liability
- Aircraft Liability
- Hovercraft Liability
- Expected or Intended Injury
- Business
- Professional Services
- Insured's Premises Not an Insured Location
- War
- Communicable Disease
- Sexual Molestation, Corporal Punishment, or Physical or Mental Abuse
- Controlled Substances

II. Exclusions applying only to Coverage E—Personal Liability
- Loss Assessment and Contractual Liability
- Property Damage to Property Owned by an Insured
- Property Damage to Property Rented to, Occupied or Used by, or in the Care of an Insured
- Bodily Injury to Persons Eligible for Other Benefits
- Nuclear Liability
- Bodily Injury to an Insured

III. Exclusions applying only to Coverage F—Medical Payments to Others
- Residence Employees Off the Insured Location and Not Arising Out of or in the Course of Employment
- Persons Eligible to Receive Other Specified Benefits (such as workers compensation)
- Nuclear Exposures
- Regular Household Residents (who are not resident employees)

Limited coverage applies to recreational vehicles used on the insured's premises; to low-power, nonowned watercraft; and to model or hobby aircraft.

One major exception to the motor vehicle exclusion allows for coverage for motorized golf carts. The golf carts exception is somewhat lengthy. Claim representatives should read it any time a claim arises involving a golf cart.

What if an auto was only incidentally related to the accident caused by an insured? The previous chapter on auto coverage issues described situations when courts have concluded that the auto "use" was not the cause of the accident because the auto was only incidentally involved. For example, when a person shoots a gun from a car, the gun caused the injury, not the car. In such cases, courts have ruled that the *auto* insurance policy did not apply. If the auto policy does not apply, would it then be possible for an insured's homeowners coverage to apply? Consider the following cases:

While in a car, an insured lit a firecracker that injured passengers. The court considered the auto to be incidental to the accident.[20]

An insured accidentally discharged a firearm inside a pickup truck, injuring passengers. The court ruled that the accident was independent and not auto related.[21]

Most courts hold that the auto exclusion does not apply if the motor vehicle is just the site of an incident that could have occurred without the involvement of the auto.[22] The same concept would hold true with claims incidentally related to watercraft, aircraft, or hovercraft.

Expected or Intended Injury Exclusion

As mentioned earlier in this chapter, intentional injuries or damages are typically excluded from coverage under liability policies, but application of the exclusion to a given set of facts can often be difficult. The exclusion in the homeowners policy reads as follows:

> Coverages E and F do not apply to the following:
>
> 1. "Bodily injury" or "property damage" which is expected or intended by an "insured" even if the resulting "bodily injury" or "property damage":
>   a. Is of a different kind, quality or degree than initially expected or intended; or
>   b. Is sustained by a different person, entity, real or personal property, than initially expected or intended.
>
> However, this exclusion 5.1 does not apply to "bodily injury" resulting from the use of reasonable force by an "insured" to protect persons or property.

Because exclusions are interpreted narrowly, the burden is on the insurance carrier to prove that a particular exclusion applies.[23] Courts also realize that in many cases the only way that an innocent victim can be compensated is through insurance, because many perpetrators have inadequate personal financial assets to compensate the victims.

What does **"expected results"** mean? Some courts take the position that expected result and intended result are identical. Other courts state that expected is the opposite of accidental. Finally, a third interpretation is that an expected result is one that was "reasonably foreseeable." Such interpretations are more likely to exclude coverage because they broaden the application of the exclusion.[24] An "intended" result would occur exactly as the person causing it desired.

Courts are split as to what standard (subjective or objective) they should use for determining whether the injury or property damage involved **expected results.** The subjective standard looks mainly at what the insured intended and expected. The more objective standard is based on what a *reasonable* person would expect from a particular act. Many courts use the objective standard because of the impractical nature of relying solely on the insured's after-the-fact testimony regarding his or her intent. Other courts find the objective standard too restrictive because it potentially excludes negligent acts of insureds that have foreseeable harm. As the United States Court of Appeals stated, "to exclude all losses or damages which might in some way have been expected by the insured, could expand the field of exclusion until virtually no recovery could be had on insurance."[25]

Unintended Consequences

An age-old debate has raged over coverage for intentional acts that cause **unintended consequences.** The following cases illustrate claims involving intentional acts with unintended consequences. These coverage decisions were based on policy wording that was not as explicit as that found in the homeowners 2000 edition.

> An insured's teenage son and his friend exchanged insults with another group of teenagers. The son went home, returned with his BB gun, and shot the gun "in the general direction of the group" in an attempt to scare the other teenagers. One of the other teenagers was shot in the eye, causing him to lose the eye. The court was convinced that the intent of the insured's son was only to scare and not hurt the boy and therefore awarded coverage.[26]

> An insured struck a man who he believed to be an intruder in his home. Later he found out that the man was his brother-in-law who was helping the insured's wife move her belongings. The court ruled that the exclusion should not apply if the insured mistook the man for a burglar.[27]

The classic example of a case of unintended consequences is with an insured who punches another person, breaking his nose and causing him to fall back and fracture his skull. Coverage would not apply to the broken nose, but under previous policy wording, some jurisdictions would permit coverage for the fractured skull because that injury was unintended. This interpretation may no longer be valid with the homeowners 2000 policy wording, which seems to clarify that unintended consequences of intentional acts are also excluded by adding that the exclusion applies even if the injury or damage is (1) of a different kind, quality, or degree than initially expected or intended; or (2) sustained by a different person, entity, or real or personal property than initially expected or intended.

With the homeowners 2000 edition, the interpretation favored by conservative jurisdictions should become the prevailing interpretation, leading to less coverage for intentional acts.

The following cases illustrate that a voluntary act might not preclude coverage if the results are unintended or unexpected. One important point is the element of intent. Consider the following case:

> While extremely intoxicated, the insured was involved in a fistfight. Police officers attempted to subdue the insured. A scuffle ensued with the

police officers, and when the insured grabbed the belt of one of the officers, the officer fell and sustained injuries. The court ruled that the insurer owed the insured a defense against injury claims because the focus of coverage determination should be on whether the insured intended the injuries, not on whether grabbing the police officer's belt was intentional. The court also stated that, because of the insured's intoxicated state, he might not even have had the capacity to form intent.[28]

As illustrated in this case, intent depends on a person's state of mind, and that state of mind can be altered by drugs or alcohol. Because alcohol or drug intoxication impairs a person's judgment, several jurisdictions have taken the position that people in an intoxicated state do not have the capacity to form intent, and therefore the intentional acts exclusion cannot apply. The same reasoning holds for people who suffer from mental illnesses that affect their judgment. This is sometimes difficult for insurers to accept. One lesson that can be learned from these cases is that claim representatives must be able to set aside moral judgment when evaluating coverage.

The following case illustrates that the definition of "occurrence" should also be considered in evaluating coverage for any intentional acts.

An insured struck a man in the face with his fist. The man left the scene without any apparent serious injury. Several hours later, the man lapsed into a coma and died. The court ruled that this was not covered because the insured's act was deliberate and therefore not even an "occurrence."[29]

This case points out the importance of considering the definition of occurrence as a defense in claims involving deliberate acts. The element of accident is still applicable to occurrences. Deliberate acts by their nature are not accidents. What distinguishes this case from others that have been covered is that there was no intervening act or event. The victim did not fall down, and his head injury was not worsened by something other than the strike to the head inflicted by the insured. Having a different outcome than what the insured expected does not always trigger coverage.

The exception to this intentional injury exclusion permits insureds to use reasonable force to protect persons or the insured's property. Judicial interpretation of what constitutes reasonable force will vary by state, but an insured should not assume that he is covered if he shoots intruders in his home or trespassers on his property.

The ISO Homeowners 3—Special Form defines **"occurrence"** as an accident, including continuous or repeated exposure to substantially the same generally harmful conditions, which results, during the policy period, in:

a.   "Bodily injury"; or

b.   "Property damage."

CLAIM REPRESENTATIVE SOLUTIONS

Intentional Injuries

When encountering claims that involve potentially intentional injuries, claim representatives should:

1. Read the intentional injuries exclusion that applies at the time of the incident. Does the policy specifically exclude consequences that are greater in severity than expected by the insured? As mentioned earlier, the homeowners 2000 policy excludes a greater number of circumstances than previous policies did.

2. As with all coverage questions, reserve the company's rights through a reservation of rights letter.

3. As soon as possible after an incident, take detailed statements from the insured, claimant, and witnesses to try to establish the mindset of the insured at the time of the incident. Even when the insured's subjective intent is different from the outcome, coverage might not apply, especially if the outcome is reasonably foreseeable by an ordinary person. As part of the investigation of the insured's intent, claim representatives should determine whether the insured was under the influence of drugs or alcohol or suffering from a mental illness at the time of the incident.

4. Assess whether the injury or property damage was worsened by some intervening act after the insured's intentional act.

5. Determine whether the definition of "occurrence" might also be a viable coverage defense given the circumstances of the claim.

Parental Liability for Intentional Acts of Their Children

The following case illustrates one final and important issue related to the application of the intentional damages exclusion.

> The insured's fifteen-year-old son and his friend vandalized a school building. The school board brought an action against the insured for vicarious liability. The state has a statute that imposes liability on parents or guardians of any minor who damages school property. The insurer denied coverage, arguing that this was an intentional act and the damage was not an "occurrence" because of the deliberate nature of the vandalism. The court ruled that the damage was not intended from the perspective of the parents and therefore coverage should apply.[30]

Nearly every state has a statute holding parents and guardians liable (to some extent) for property damage caused by minor children. The issue of vicarious **parental liability** surfaces in a wide variety of claims ranging from sexual molestation to vandalism.

Vicarious liability is indirect legal responsibility that occurs when one party is held liable for the actions of another party. For example, state statutes might require parents to be responsible for the property damage caused by their children up to a specified dollar amount.

ISO recently changed the intentional damages exclusion wording to read as follows:

Coverage E—Personal Liability and Coverage F—Medical Payments to Others do not apply to bodily injury or property damage... "which is expected or intended by *an* insured...."

Before this change, the wording read that these types of damages were excluded if they were expected or intended by "*the* insured." Changing from "the" to "an" may seem inconsequential, but it is a potentially significant change that could affect courts' interpretation of this policy exclusion.

> One reason that some courts favored providing coverage under the old homeowners policy wording was because of the **Severability of Insurance** provision found in Section II Conditions, which reads as follows:
>
> > **Severability of Insurance.** This insurance applies separately to each "insured." This condition will not increase our limit of liability for any one "occurrence."
>
> The severability of insurance provision entitles each insured to a separate insurance contract with the insurer and allows coverage to apply to each insured independently of how coverage applies to another insured. This is an example of how a policy condition can affect the interpretation of liability coverage. Courts used this provision to argue that although the intentional injury or damage of one insured was excluded, claims made against another insured (such as a parent) as a result of the intentional damages, such as vandalism, by a separate insured (for example a teenage son) would be covered. This is especially true when an excluded act of one insured is imputed to another insured who, by some other theory of negligence, has remotely or unknowingly contributed to the injury or damage.
>
> ISO did not change the wording of this condition, so it is uncertain whether courts will continue to apply this condition to interpret coverage in favor of the insured. Policy conditions are discussed later in this chapter.

The homeowners 2000 wording appears to eliminate coverage for the statutory vicarious liability of parents for the intentional damage caused by teenage family members, because the exclusion applies even if any insured (such as the teenage insured) intended the bodily injury or property damage.[31] The wording also appears to eliminate coverage for claims of negligent supervision made against the parents for intentional damages caused by teenagers.

As with all claims, claim representatives must take detailed statements and thoroughly investigate claims involving intentional acts. If insureds are liable either vicariously through statutes or through their own negligent supervision or entrustment, then a careful analysis of coverage is required. Claim representatives must apply the facts to the policy wording and withhold moral judgments about the insured's character or the nature of the act committed. Claim representatives may need to seek management guidance or legal counsel in determining coverage for claims involving acts of deliberate harm.

Business Exclusion

The homeowners policy is not intended to cover most business exposures for the same reason that personal auto policies are not intended to cover commercial auto exposures. Business liability coverage is not essential to most purchasers of the homeowners policy, and business liability coverage normally requires special underwriting and rating. The homeowners policy contains a business exclusion that has been heavily litigated over the years. More litigation is expected as more people are telecommuting and working from their homes (as many as fourteen million people currently telecommute).[32] Some business loss exposures can be covered by adding an endorsement to the homeowners policy.

A common question is whether the business exclusion applies to the babysitting or lawn mowing activities of an insured's child. Recent changes in the policy wording clarify some of the circumstances of coverage for teenagers. The following is the business exclusions wording (boldface emphasis added):

Coverages E and F do not apply to the following:

a. "Bodily injury" or "property damage" arising out of or in connection with a "business" conducted from an "insured location" or engaged in by an insured, whether or not the "business" is owned or operated by an "insured" or employs an insured. This exclusion **E.2.** applies but is not limited to an act or omission, regardless of its nature or circumstance, involving a service or duty rendered, promised, owed, or implied to be provided because of the nature of the "business".

b. This exclusion E.2. does not apply to:

    (1)   The rental or holding for rental of an "insured location":

        (a)   On an occasional basis if used only as a residence;

        (b)   In part for use only as a residence, unless a single family unit is intended for use by the occupying family to lodge more than two roomers or boarders; or

        (c)   In part, as an office, school, studio or private garage; and

    (2)   An "insured" under the age of 21 years involved in a part-time or occasional, self-employed "business" with no employees.

The second exception in the business exclusion is new to the homeowners policy and attempts to address some of the coverage disputes that have arisen over coverage for the business pursuits of an insured's teenage son or daughter.

What is a "business" activity? Are all money-making activities "business" activities? The term "business" as defined in the homeowners policy includes "a trade, profession or occupation." The cases that are litigated involve hobbies or activities that provide insureds with revenue but that might not be considered an occupation of the insured.

In establishing whether an activity is a **business activity**, courts have looked at two major elements: continuity of activities and a profit motive. The first element looks at the regularity and duration of the employment or business activity. Was the activity performed twice a week for one year or a few times a year without any planned schedule? The second element examines the purpose of the activity and the insured's intent. Does the person make money from the activity? Is the activity intended to be a means of livelihood for the insured? Consider a foster parent who receives money from the state for taking care of foster children. The expenses incurred by the household in caring for the child would greatly exceed the allowance from the state. In this situation, there would be no profit motive and therefore no business.[33] But losing money does not mean that the insured is not engaged in a business pursuit. If, for instance, the insured sold cosmetics at home but did not make a profit from the pursuit, it would still be considered a business because the *motive* was to make money.

The most common cases challenging the business exclusion involve babysitting. Insureds might mistakenly believe that babysitting a child for one or two days a week would not be considered a business activity, but this is not correct. If, for instance, an insured took in four or five children all day long, every weekday for two years, this would satisfy both the continuity element and the profit motive element. Unfortunately, not all claims are this clear-cut. Consider the following case.

APPLICATIONS

Business Exclusion to Babysitting

The insured's fifteen-year-old daughter was employed to babysit two children while she was on summer break from school. The girl watched the two children for ten hours on Mondays, Wednesdays, and every other Friday. Her duties were to watch the children, prepare their meals, bathe and dress the children, and perform light housekeeping duties. For this she was paid $2.00 per hour (well below minimum wage).

One day the girl placed the younger child in the bathtub, turned on the water, and left the water running. When the girl returned, she discovered that the water was very hot. She removed the child from the tub, but the child had already sustained second- and third-degree burns over her body. A claim was made against the insured's daughter for the injuries. The insurer denied coverage based on the business exclusion.

The court ruled that the babysitting activities of the insured's teenage daughter did not satisfy the profit-motive element and thus was not a "business pursuit" within the meaning of the business exclusion of the insured's homeowners insurance policy. In spite of the fact that it appeared that she babysat for money and not out of friendship or charity, the court ruled in her favor because:

1. Her babysitting was not a significant source of income, insofar as her hourly wage was well below minimum wage;
2. She was not licensed as a daycare provider;
3. She did not advertise;
4. Babysitting did not take place in her house; and
5. She was a full-time student on summer break.[34]

The babysitting claim in this case involved an older policy edition. Under the new 2000 edition policy wording, the insured (who was under twenty-one years of age) would have had to prove only that the babysitting job was "part-time or occasional." Many of the cases involving the business exclusion were based on old policy wording that permitted coverage for incidental business activities. The old wording allowed coverage for more situations. For this reason, some of the prior court decisions on business pursuits involving minors might no longer be useful in assessing how a court would interpret the new provision.

Renting property, as a business pursuit, is specifically addressed in the business exclusion. Section II coverage excludes rental income if the insured rents to others all or part of the "insured location." Three exceptions to this exclusion are allowed for common rental situations:

1. Rental on an occasional basis
2. Renting rooms to no more than two people
3. Rental for use as an office, school, studio, or private garage

Exhibit 3-3 summarizes some of the important questions and issues related to a homeowner's business pursuits.

Professional Services Exclusion

Liability related to the insured's rendering or failure to render professional services is excluded. For example, an architect might be liable for a loss resulting from improper drawings provided to a client. Even if this caused "property damage," the claim would not be covered. These exposures are handled through professional liability policies.

"Insured's Premises Not an Insured Location" Exclusion

A loss that arises out of premises that are not an "insured location" is not covered. Types of locations not covered include:

1. Other premises owned by an insured
2. Other premises rented by an insured
3. Other premises rented to others by an insured

The purpose of this exclusion is to prevent an insured from purchasing just one homeowners policy to cover all other premises he or she owns or rents.

War

This exclusion eliminates liability coverage for any loss that results from war in its various forms.

Communicable Disease

This is one of the more recent exclusions included to the homeowners policy. It excludes any loss that results from the transmission of a communicable disease by an insured. The wording was added to exclude a growing number of claims for negligent transmission of sexually transmitted diseases; however, the exclusion for communicable diseases is much broader than just for sexually transmitted diseases.

If a child contracts a disease like chicken pox or measles from an insured, would this exclusion apply?

If an insured makes food for a picnic that gives other people salmonella, would the exclusion apply?

EXHIBIT 3-3

Questions Related to Homeowners Coverage for Business Pursuits

Questions	Issue	Court View
Are the named insured's activities such as lawn mowing, babysitting, house painting, fundraising, and foster care excluded under the homeowners policy?	Does the insured have a profit motive? Is it a consistent activity? Does the insured advertise or obtain licenses to do the activity?	Courts will consider the nature of the activity. If the motive for doing the activity is profit and the activity is performed regularly, courts will likely consider it to be a business pursuit.
Are the insured's children covered if they do odd jobs such as lawn mowing, babysitting, and painting?	The homeowners 2000 policy expressly permits part-time, occasional, self-employed work by an insured's child who is younger than 21.	Courts have historically applied the business exclusion narrowly for insureds' children, even when the policy was vague regarding excepting their activities from the exclusion.
Does an insured need to profit from an activity for that activity to be considered business?	Insureds receive money for charitable acts. Self-employed insureds lose money on in-home businesses.	If the intent is not profit but philanthropy, the activity is not business. On the other hand, an insured can lose money on a job that the courts would consider a business because the insured's intent was to make a profit.
Does coverage apply when the insured rents part of his or her residence?	Policies usually permit renting the insured's residence on an occasional basis or renting part of the insured's residence.	
Is there coverage for professional activities if they are performed at the insured's residence?	Professional activities are specifically excluded by the policy.	

To answer these questions, claim representatives would need to know the definition of **communicable disease.** Because the term is not defined in the policy, courts would look to its common usage. A standard English dictionary defines "communicable illness" as an infectious illness and "an infectious illness can be passed from one person to another, especially through the air you breathe."[35] This is an extremely broad definition that covers a wide variety of illnesses.

A more scientific definition is found in the *Dictionary of Epidemiology*. It reads as follows:

> Communicable disease (Synonym: infectious disease). An illness due to a specific infectious agent or its toxic products that arises through transmission of that agent or its products from an infected person, animal, or reservoir to a susceptible host, either directly or indirectly through an intermediate plant or animal host, vector or the inanimate environment.[36]

Based on this definition, a communicable disease is one that can be spread either directly from person to person or indirectly through a vector. Examples of vectors include mosquitoes (which carry malaria), water, or food that carries typhoid and salmonella. Thus, under this definition, a host of diseases—such as chicken pox, measles, mumps, typhoid fever, and even salmonella—could be considered communicable diseases.

A distinction is often made between communicable and contagious diseases. The term "contagious disease" is not well defined. A contagion is the transmission of infection by direct contact, droplet spread, or contaminated fomites.[37] Some people use the term to mean an infectious disease that can only be transmitted from one person to another person directly (without a vector). Thus, measles and chicken pox would be both "contagious" and communicable; however, malaria is communicable but not contagious. Based on this application of the term, "contagious" would be a subset of communicable diseases rather than a different type of disease altogether.

Before the communicable disease exclusion, courts historically favored providing coverage for claims involving salmonella food poisoning. Courts might continue to permit coverage for this by narrowing the communicable disease exclusion to only those diseases transmitted directly.

Sexual Molestation, Corporal Punishment, or Physical or Mental Abuse

This recently developed exclusion is designed to preclude coverage for any loss that arises out of sexual molestation, corporal punishment, or physical or mental abuse. Before this exclusion was added to the homeowners policy, insurers had to rely on the following three defenses:

1. It was against public policy to cover these actions.
2. The injury resulting from these acts was intentional and was therefore excluded.
3. These injuries were expected from deliberate acts and did not meet the definition of an occurrence.

Despite these coverage defenses, some courts still found coverage, so this additional exclusion was added.

Coverage is clearly not permitted in cases when adults sexually molested children, even if the claim is presented as being negligence or as causing unintended harm, because courts consistently held that the sexual molestation of a child by an adult infers the intent to harm and is therefore not covered. Coverage determination becomes more uncertain when the molestation is by one child against another. In this child-to-child situation, courts have not found the injuries to be intentional and have ruled that public policy favored compensating victims.[38]

To date, there has not been enough litigation on this exclusion to assess how courts will interpret it.

Controlled Substances

Section II excludes any loss that results from the use, sale, manufacture, delivery, transfer, or possession of a **controlled substance** (such as cocaine, marijuana, and narcotic drugs). Coverage would not be provided for an insured who gives drugs to a guest who, in turn, ingests the drugs and dies of an overdose. Before the controlled substances exclusion was adopted, many courts found coverage for overdose claims because the consequences were not intentional and many courts did not feel strongly enough to preclude coverage based on public policy issues.

The policy excludes any controlled substance as defined by the Federal Food and Drug Law. Controlled substances are not limited to the drugs mentioned specifically in the exclusion. Many prescription drugs, such as Tylenol with codeine, are also controlled substances.

> Claim representatives can obtain a schedule of controlled substances by contacting the Drug Enforcement Agency (DEA) or by accessing the DEA Web site at www.usdoj.gov/dea/pubs/csa.html. The American Academy of Nurse Practitioners has a concise list of the drug schedule at aanp.org/schedule.htm.

The exception to the controlled substance exclusion is for the "legitimate use" of prescription drugs. Claim representatives must determine (1) whether the prescription drugs involved were controlled substances and (2) whether they were used for legitimate purposes.

The controlled substance exclusion does not exclude all drug-overdose claims. Common tragedies involving teenagers overdosing from "huffing" butane or model airplane glue or abusing other substances that are not controlled substances would not fall within this exclusion and are therefore covered unless a court believes that it would be against public policy to permit insurance to cover such claims.

Exclusions Only for Personal Liability—Coverage E

The following list of exclusions applies only to Section II—Coverage E—Personal Liability and not to the medical payments coverage section:

- Loss assessment
- Contractual liability
- Damage to property owned by an insured
- Property damage to property rented to, occupied or used by, or in the care of an insured
- Bodily injury to persons eligible for other benefits
- Nuclear liability
- Bodily injury to an insured

Loss Assessment

The homeowners policy excludes Coverage E—Personal Liability for liability assessments charged to the policyholder. Homeowners who belong to an association of property owners can incur these loss assessments. Consider a claimant who fell from a defective deck of the homeowners association's club house and the claimant sustained permanent brain damage and was awarded a multimillion dollar verdict. This award exceeded the association's insurance policy limit, and according to the association's bylaws, each member of the association could be assessed for a percentage of the excess amount. This percentage assessment would not be covered.

> A limited amount of coverage ($1,000) for this type of loss is provided under the Additional Coverage section of the policy. This section is described later in this chapter.

Contractual Liability

The homeowners policy excludes Coverage E for liability assumed under a contract an insured entered into. However, the homeowners policy does have the following two exceptions to this exclusion:

1. Liability assumed under written contracts relating to the ownership, maintenance, or use of an insured location
2. Liability assumed under written contracts before an occurrence

These exceptions do not supercede exclusions found elsewhere in the policy.

The intent of these exemptions is to make liability coverage apply under written contracts having to do with the insured's normal activities associated with homeownership. Examples of contracts exempted could be leases, repair contracts, or construction contracts. For example, as part of a repair agreement, an insured signs a contract with a roofer that states that the homeowner will provide a defense and pay any damages on behalf of the roofer (a hold harmless and indemnity agreement). If during the repairs the roofer drops a bundle of shingles on the insured's neighbor, Coverage E would apply to the claim under this exception. Coverage would apply (and liability could be found) even though the insured was not personally negligent in any manner.

Damage to Property Owned by an Insured

Section II of the homeowners policy is intended to apply to third-party claims against insureds. The Section II exclusion applies even if one insured damages the property of another insured. This exclusion clarifies that Coverage E does not apply to property damage one insured caused to the property of another.

The insured's property is covered under Section I of the policy for specified causes of loss.

Property Damage to Property Rented to, Occupied or Used by, or in the Care of an Insured

This is the omnipresent "care, custody or control" exclusion. It applies to places, dwellings, or rooms rented to an insured. It would also apply, for instance, when an insured borrows his neighbor's riding lawn mower and accidentally crashes it into a tree.

The exception to this exclusion is for property damage caused by fire, smoke, or explosion. If an insured accidentally sets a hotel room on fire, then the property damage would be covered by this exception.

> Section II—Additional Coverages discussed later in this chapter has a section devoted to damage to the property of others. It provides minimal coverage for property damaged while in the care of the insured.

Bodily Injury to Persons Eligible for Other Benefits

Coverage E excludes bodily injury to any person who is eligible to receive workers compensation benefits or benefits based on occupational or nonoccupational disability laws. In some states, domestic workers are not covered by workers compensation laws. In those states, the insured's homeowners policy might provide coverage for employers liability claims under the coverage for "residence employees" in some circumstances.

Nuclear Liability

Homeowners liability Coverage E excludes liability for nuclear occurrences. The intent of the exclusion is to limit the insurance industry's overall liability for nuclear occurrences to the coverage provided by specialty nuclear energy policies.

Bodily Injury to an Insured

Coverage E does not apply to bodily injury to the named insured, any resident relatives, or any other residents under the age of twenty-one and in the care of either of the aforementioned residents. This exclusion became necessary as many states began to allow husbands and wives or parents and children to sue each other. Traditionally, these suits were not allowed because courts felt that they threatened family harmony. Today, many states recognize that family members can be liable for negligent acts resulting in injuries to other family members. As this occurred, the "family member" exclusion was added to personal lines liability policies.

As mentioned in the previous chapter on auto policy coverage, this "family member" exclusion has not been upheld in a majority of states. Many courts have ruled that this exclusion contravenes public policy in auto policies because automobile insurance is a mandated coverage. However, the public policy argument has not been accepted with homeowners policies because state statutes do not require the purchase of homeowners policies. Consequently, the "family member" exclusion in the homeowners policy has generally been upheld by courts.[39]

Exclusions Applicable Only to Coverage F

Four exclusions apply solely to Coverage F—Medical Payments to Others. These exclusions read as follows:

> Coverage F does not apply to "bodily injury":
> 1. To a "residence employee" if the "bodily injury":
>   a. Occurs off the "insured location"; and
>   b. Does not arise out of or in the course of the "residence employee's" employment by an "insured"
> 2. To any person eligible to receive benefits voluntarily provided or required to be provided under any:
>   a. Workers' compensation law;
>   b. Non-occupational disability law; or
>   c. Occupational disease law;
> 3. From any:
>   a. Nuclear reaction;
>   b. Nuclear radiation; or
>   c. Radioactive contamination;
> All whether controlled or uncontrolled or however caused; or
>   d. Any consequence of any of these; or
> 4. To any person other than a "residence employee" of an "insured", regularly residing on any part of the "insured location".

The Coverage F exclusion that is most likely to lead to a coverage dispute is Exclusion 4 because determining whether a person is "regularly residing" with the insured can be challenging.

HOMEOWNERS SECTION II—ADDITIONAL COVERAGES

In addition to the personal liability and medical payments coverages, four coverages come under the general heading of **Additional Coverages in Section II** of the homeowners policy: (1) claim expenses, (2) first-aid expenses, (3) damage to the property of others, and (4) loss assessment. Although some of these are limited in dollar amount, all apply in *addition* to the other policy limits.

Claim Expenses

In addition to any claim administration or defense cost that insurers must provide because of the Section II insuring agreement, the homeowners policy also pays for the following claim expenses:

1. Expenses we incur and costs taxed against an "insured" in any suit we defend;
2. Premiums on bonds required in a suit we defend, but not for bond amounts more than the Coverage E limit of liability. We need not apply for or furnish any bond;
3. Reasonable expenses incurred by an "insured" at our request, including actual loss of earnings (but not loss of other income) up to $250 per day, for assisting us in the investigation or defense of a claim or suit; and
4. Interest on the entire judgment which accrues after entry of the judgment and before we pay or tender or deposit in court that part of the judgment which does not exceed the limit of liability that applies.

Claim expenses are seldom encountered by insureds, but this coverage is helpful to insureds on those rare occasions when those expenses are incurred. Interest expenses on judgments described in Item 4 can be substantial.

First-Aid Expenses

The homeowners policy will cover any expenses incurred by an insured for first aid rendered to others for bodily injury covered by this policy. This is the only coverage that permits the insured to voluntarily pay the expenses of others without invalidating coverage. This coverage does not apply to first aid given to an insured.

Damage to the Property of Others

Claim representatives frequently encounter claims payable under **Damage to Property of Others** coverage, which can be thought of as the "good neighbor" coverage provision. For example, if an insured borrowed and wrecked a neighbor's riding lawn mower, this additional coverage provision would allow for payment up to $500 for damage to the neighbor's property. The insured does not even have to be liable for the damage in order for this coverage to apply. This coverage also permits payment for property damage caused by young children (younger than thirteen years old) even if the damage was caused intentionally.

Loss Assessment

A limit of $1,000 is available to pay for loss assessments against individual homeowners belonging to a corporation or an association of homeowners. The loss assessment must be the result of a bodily injury or property damage claim made against the homeowners' corporation or association. This might result from a claim that was not covered by insurance or had damages in excess of the association's insurance limits. This type of claim is excluded under Coverage E, but this additional coverage would allow a limited payment of up to $1,000.

CONDITIONS APPLYING TO LIABILITY COVERAGES

Eight conditions apply to the Section II—Liability section of the homeowners policy.

APPLICATIONS

Section II—Additional Coverage—Damage to Property of Others

The insured borrows a bike from a friend. It is a racing bike with a replacement cost of $1,600 and an actual cash value of $1,400 (figuring depreciation). Despite the insured's efforts in locking the bike on her porch, the bike was stolen.

Question: How would Section II—Liability Coverage apply to this loss?

Answer: First, under the main Section II coverage part, an exclusion would apply because the property was in the care of an insured. However, the Section II—Additional Coverage for damage to the property of others would provide limited payment despite the fact that the insured was not negligent. The insured does not have to be liable in order for this additional coverage to apply. This coverage is limited to $500, which is $1,100 short of the replacement cost for the bike. But there may be more coverage elsewhere in the policy.

Question: Wouldn't a theft be covered under Section I of the homeowners policy, therefore obviating the need to apply Section II coverage?

Answer: Section I provides coverage for property loss to the insured's dwelling and contents and extends to the property of others while it is stored on the insured's premises. The homeowners Section I coverage for contents items would cover theft losses because theft is a Section I covered peril (cause of loss). However, unless the insured has a *personal property* replacement cost endorsement (not to be confused with replacement cost endorsement for the house itself), the policy would allow for the actual cash value ($1,400) of the racing bike minus the policy deductible. Assuming that the insured had a $250 deductible, the owner of the bike could collect $1,150 under Section I coverage. This leaves a difference of $450 from the full replacement cost.

Question: Could this $450 difference then be made up by application of the Section II additional coverage provision?

Answer: The policy reads as follows:

> **Damage to Property of Others.**
>
> We will pay, at replacement cost, up to $500 per "occurrence" for "property damage" to property of others caused by an "insured."
>
> We will not pay for "property damage":
>
> a.   To the extent of any amount recoverable under Section I of this policy...;

This coverage applies without deductible and at replacement cost; therefore, the insurer could pay the $450 difference to the owner based on this additional coverage provision. This example illustrates how Section I and Section II of the homeowners policy intersect. It also shows how a simple claim for a theft of a bicycle can be challenging. It demonstrates why even claim representatives who handle only liability claims need to have a working understanding of first-party coverages such as those found in the homeowners Section I.

Limits of Liability

The limit of liability condition states that the amount shown under Coverage E—Personal Liability on the declarations page is the total limit of liability that the insurer will pay for a liability claim resulting from any one "occurrence." As mentioned previously, courts sometimes disagree over the definition of "occurrence." If, for example, an insured sprays pesticides twice each week over several months, and the pesticides cause a bodily injury or property damage to a neighbor, then most courts would consider this to be one occurrence and subject to one limit of liability. Courts might consider claims involving multiple claimants to be less clear.

Coverage F—Medical Payments limit of liability is paid on a per-person basis for bodily injury due to one accident.

Severability of Interests

The severability of interests condition states that the insurance applies separately to each insured. Sometimes this condition is not applied in a way that insureds might expect. Courts are often reluctant to provide coverage to an innocent or a noninvolved insured when one insured has obviously committed an act that is excluded. The following case illustrates this point:

The named insured's wife ran a daycare center out of the insured home. One of the children was bitten by a dog owned by the insured's son, who lived at the insured residence. The claim against the wife was not covered because it fell under the "business pursuits" exclusion. A separate suit was filed against the named insured and his son for negligence in harboring a dangerous dog. The son and the father sought coverage, stating that the severability clause should provide coverage because they were not involved in the daycare business run by the wife. The court denied coverage, reasoning that the child would not have been exposed to the dog had it not been for the daycare business from which all insureds benefited.[40]

Despite challenges, courts continue to use this condition to help interpret coverage when a claim is made against more than one insured.

Duties After Occurrence

Claim representatives should be familiar with the duties insureds have after an occurrence takes place. The homeowners 2000 edition expresses the need to *cooperate* with the insurer and firmly states that failure to comply with these duties can be grounds for coverage denial if the failure to comply is prejudicial to the insurer. The prior wording only *implied* that cooperation with the insurer was required, while the new wording explicitly states it.

Exhibit 3-4 lists six types of general duties and two types of duties applicable to Section II—Homeowners Liability and Coverage F—Medical Payments to Others.

EXHIBIT 3-4

Coverage Conditions Section II—Homeowners Liability

Duties After "Occurrence"

In case of an "occurrence," you or another "insured" will perform the following duties that apply. We have no duty to provide coverage under this policy if your failure to comply with the following duties is prejudicial to us. You will help us by seeing that these duties are performed:

1. Give written notice to us or our agent as soon as is practical, which sets forth:
   a. The identity of the policy and the "named insured" shown in the Declarations;
   b. Reasonably available information on the time, place and circumstances of the "occurrence"; and
   c. Names and addresses of any claimants and witnesses;

2. Cooperate with us in the investigation, settlement, or defense of any claim or suit;

3. Promptly forward to us every notice, demand, summons or other process relating to "occurrence";

4. At our request, help us:
   a. To make settlement;
   b. To enforce any right of contribution or indemnity against any person or organization who may be liable to an "insured";
   c. With the conduct of suits and attend hearings and trials; and
   d. To secure and give evidence and obtain the attendance of witnesses;

5. With respect to C. Damage to Property of Others Section II—Additional Coverages, submit to us within 60 days after the loss, a sworn statement of loss and show the damaged property, if in an "insured's" control;

6. No "insured" shall, except at such "insured's" own cost, voluntarily make payment, assume obligation or incur expense other than for first aid to others at the time of the "bodily injury."

D. Duties Of An Injured Person—Coverage F—Medical Payments To Others.

1. The injured person or someone acting for the injured person will:
   a. Give us written proof of claim, under oath if required, as soon as is practical; and
   b. Authorize us to obtain copies of medical reports and records.

2. The injured person will submit to a physical exam by a doctor of our choice when and as often as we reasonably require.

Failure to comply with these duties can lead to coverage denials.

Condition E confirms that payments under Coverage F are not to be considered admissions of liability because payments are owed even when an insured is not negligent. The policy reads:

> **E. Payment Of Claim—Coverage F—Medical Payments To Others.**
>   Payment under this coverage is not an admission of liability by an "insured" or us.

Suit Against the Insurance Company

No legal action can be brought against the insurance company unless the insured has complied with the policy provisions. Furthermore, no legal action can be taken against the insurer until the insured's liability for a claim has been determined either by a settlement or an award.

Finally, Condition F provides that no other party has the right to join the insured in a legal action against the insurer. This last item attempts to prevent a claimant from joining an insured and filing a joint legal action against the insurance company. Some states permit insureds to assign to claimants their legal rights to sue the insurance company in exchange for an agreement by the claimant not to collect from the insured for any damages not covered by the insurance policy. This situation leads to an adversarial relationship between the insured and insurer and allows the possibility of collusion between the insured and claimant. A condition common to Sections I and II addresses the issue of assignments of this policy and states the assignments will not be permitted without the insurance company's permission. The application of this provision may vary by state and by insurer.

Bankruptcy of an Insured

If an insured is insolvent or bankrupt, the insured might be free of liability for any judgment. This condition states that even though the insured might be free of legal obligations to pay the claimant, the insurer must still defend or pay the claim.

Other Insurance

This condition recognizes the possibility that an insured might be covered by other insurance. A non-named insured, such as someone taking care of the named insured's dog, might meet the definition of an "insured" under the named insured's policy and also have his or her own homeowners policy. Some named insureds also have personal umbrella or excess liability policies in addition to a homeowners policy. This condition states that the homeowners policy is excess over other collectible insurance except for insurance written specifically to cover excess liability.

Policy Period

This provision states that the bodily injury or property damage must occur within the policy period.

Concealment and Fraud

The homeowners policy also has the standard condition that precludes coverage for concealment or fraud. Before the homeowners 2000 edition, this condition was found in the conditions common to Section I and Section II. The 2000 policy reads as follows:

> J.   Concealment or Fraud
>
> We do not provide coverage to an "insured" who, whether before or after a loss, has:
>
> > 1. Intentionally concealed or misrepresented any material fact or circumstance;
> > 2. Engaged in fraudulent conduct; or
> > 3. Made false statements; relating to this insurance.

Summary of Homeowners Policy

The homeowners policy provides coverage for a wide variety of liability claims. These claims need not always occur on or even arise out of the insured's premises. Claim representatives should be cautious in denying coverage because many unusual claims can be covered under the Homeowners Section II Liability Coverage. Exclusions involving intentional acts and business pursuits, among others, can be challenging and require thorough investigations. The CGL has similar exclusions but has many more related to business exposures.

OVERVIEW OF THE CGL FORM[41]

The foundation for most commercial liability insurance programs is commercial general liability insurance. Subject to its exclusions and conditions, this insurance covers a wide range of liability loss exposures that most organizations face. These loss exposures fall under the following general categories:

- Premises and operations liability
- Products and completed operations liability
- Liability for various personal or advertising offenses

The policy form most commonly used to provide this insurance is the Commercial General Liability (CGL) Coverage Form filed by Insurance Services Office (ISO). This chapter examines the 1998 edition of the CGL form. Some insurers use independently filed CGL policies. The American Association of Insurance Services (AAIS) files comparable forms on behalf of its member insurers. The two versions of the CGL form are the occurrence version (CG 00 01) and the claims-made version (CG 00 02). They differ only with respect to the event that must take place in order for a claim to be covered under that policy.

This chapter describes coverage issues related to the "occurrence" form. Apart from their different coverage triggers and a few related provisions, the two versions of the CGL coverage form are the same, containing the following sections:

- Coverage A—Bodily Injury and Property Damage Liability
- Coverage B—Personal and Advertising Injury Liability
- Coverage C—Medical Payments
- Supplementary Payments
- Who Is an Insured
- Limits of Insurance
- Conditions
- Definitions

This chapter focuses on common coverage issues and practical claim concerns on Coverages A and B. A summary of Coverage C, without an extensive discussion of coverage issues, is also included.

COVERAGE A—BODILY INJURY AND PROPERTY DAMAGE LIABILITY

The Coverage A insuring agreement expresses two promises: one to pay damages on behalf of the insured and another to defend the insured against claims or suits seeking damages. The same agreement, because it covers bodily injury and property damage claims occurring under so many different circumstances, can also be viewed as providing the following "coverages":

- Premises and operations liability coverage
- Contractual liability coverage
- Fire legal liability coverage
- Products and completed operations liability coverage

For many years, these different coverages were provided individually in separate forms or endorsements. Although they are now combined under Coverage A of the CGL policy, describing Coverage A in terms of these coverages is helpful both for learning the scope of Coverage A and for making CGL coverage understandable to policyholders.

Premises and Operations Liability Coverage

Premises and operations liability coverage is the most basic component of general liability insurance. The CGL separates premises-operations and products-completed operations coverage. Before the CGL separation approach became widely accepted, many liability forms covered only premises and operations liability.

For purposes of this discussion, premises and operations liability coverage can be loosely defined as all coverage provided by Coverage A except for products and completed operations, contractual liability, and fire legal liability. Basically, the premises and operations coverage encompasses bodily injury or property damage caused by either of the following:

- Accidents occurring at any premises owned, rented, or used by the named insured.

- Accidents occurring away from such premises, but only if they arise out of the named insured's ongoing (as opposed to completed) operations.

Some examples of premises and operations liability claims are:

- A customer twisted her ankle on a loose carpet at the named insured's premises. She later made claim against the named insured for her medical expenses resulting from the injury.

- A passerby was severely injured by a bulldozer negligently operated by an employee of the named insured. The passerby later sued the named insured for medical expenses, wage loss, and pain and suffering resulting from his injuries.

- A building and its contents were damaged by water when a plumbing contractor working in the building negligently disconnected a water supply line. The building owner sued the insured plumbing contractor for the cost of restoring the damaged property.

In addition to the restrictions imposed by the insuring agreement, several exclusions define the scope of premises and operations liability coverage. These exclusions and the application issues involving these exclusions are explained later in this chapter.

Contractual Liability Coverage

Although the CGL has an exclusion for contractual liability under Coverage A, exceptions to this exclusion provide for some limited contractual liability coverage. Contractual liability coverage covers liability that the insured has assumed under an "insured contract" as defined in the policy. This is an example of how an exception to an exclusion can serve as an insuring agreement. Contractual liability coverage and an explanation of the "insured contract" are found later in the section on Coverage A exclusions.

Fire Legal Liability (Damage to Rented Property) Coverage

Another aspect of CGL coverage that is included in coverage for damage to property rented but that is often regarded as a distinct coverage is fire legal liability coverage. This coverage is expressed as an exception to exclusions. It states that: "Exclusions **c.** through **n.** [see list under CGL Coverage A exclusions for details] do not apply to damage by fire to premises rented to you or temporarily occupied by you with permission of the owner. A separate limit of insurance applies to this coverage as described in Section III—Limits Of

Insurance." This exception provides coverage for liability for fire damage to premises rented to the named insured or temporarily occupied by the named insured with the owner's permission.

Fewer exclusions apply to fire legal liability claims than to other types of premises or operations claims. Only exclusion "a" (expected or intended injury) and exclusion "b" (contractual liability) apply to fire legal liability coverage. Most notably, the exclusion of property damage to property rented to or occupied by the named insured does not apply to fire liability coverage. Thus, if the insured becomes legally liable for fire damage to premises rented to the insured, the policy will pay up to the "fire damage limit" for that occurrence. The limit for fire legal liability coverage is ordinarily lower than the each-occurrence limit of Coverage A. The application of limits is covered later in this chapter in the section on Coverage A Limits of Liability.

The "damage to premises rented to you" coverage complements fire legal liability coverage. This covers the insured's liability for property damage (other than fire damage) to premises (including their contents) rented to the named insured for a week or less. Fire legal liability is not subject to this one-week limit.

Products and Completed Operations

Products and completed operations liability coverage is another component of Coverage A of the CGL policy. It can also be purchased as a stand-alone coverage in the ISO Products/Completed Operations Liability Coverage Form (CG 00 37 or CG 00 38). The coverage responds to claims for bodily injury or property damage arising out of the named insured's products or completed operations.

Both the CGL form and the separate products/completed operations form contain a precise definition of the **"products/completed operations hazard."** This coverage responds to bodily injury or property damage claims occurring away from premises the insured owns or rents and arising out of the insured's "product" or "work." "Your product" and "your work" are described later in this chapter.

The definition of the completed operations hazard contains various provisions to clarify when work would be considered completed and when it would not be considered completed.

Several of the Coverage A exclusions might apply to a products or completed operations claim, but four exclusions are particularly unique to these exposures:

- Damage to your product
- Damage to your work
- Damage to impaired property or property not physically injured
- Recall of products, work, or impaired property

These exclusions are aimed at precluding coverage for the cost of repairing or replacing faulty products and work of the insured, or even withdrawing them from the market. Products and completed operations liability coverage is intended to cover bodily injury or property damage that results from failure of a product or completed work, not to cover the faulty product or work itself. These specific exclusions are discussed in the following section on Coverage A exclusions.

COVERAGE A EXCLUSIONS

Coverage A of the CGL restricts coverage with fourteen exclusions. These exclusions are identified by lowercase letters "a" through "n" and are described as follows:

Exclusions

This insurance does not apply to:

a. Expected Or Intended Injury

b. Contractual Liability

c. Liquor Liability

d. Workers' Compensation And Similar Laws

e. Employer's Liability

f. Pollution

g. Aircraft, Auto Or Watercraft

h. Mobile Equipment

i. War

j. Damage To Property

k. Damage To Your Product

l. Damage To Your Work

m. Damage To Impaired Property Or Property Not Physically Injured

n. Recall Of Products, Work Or Impaired Property

Many of these exclusions have complicated applications or coverage issues that will be explained.

Expected or Intended Injury

The expected or intended injury exclusion eliminates coverage for the following:

"Bodily injury" or "property damage" expected or intended from the standpoint of the insured. This exclusion does not apply to "bodily injury" resulting from the use of reasonable force to protect persons or property.

With auto and homeowners claims, claim representatives must perform a detailed investigation of the facts in order to form a reasonable supposition about the insured's mindset at the time of the event.

What if a person commits an act intentionally but claims that the results of the act were unintended? This is the issue facing claim representatives anytime the intended injury exclusion is invoked under a liability policy. The 1998 CGL intended injury exclusion differs from that found in the 2000 homeowners policy in that the CGL exclusion does not specifically state that unintended consequences are not covered. Like the homeowners policy, the

CGL does clarify that coverage would be permitted for intentional injuries if the purpose of the act was to protect people or property. An example of this exception to the exclusion as it might be encountered in a commercial operation is security guards who take action to stop people from robbing a store. If the robbers are injured by the security guards, this exception would permit coverage to apply. Even without this exception, some courts have ruled that the act of self-defense should not fall within this exclusion. Exhibit 3-5 summarizes some of the important aspects to consider regarding expected or intended injuries as they apply to the homeowners and CGL policies.

Contractual Liability

The contractual liability exclusion eliminates coverage for bodily injury or property damage for which the insured is obligated to pay damages by reason of the assumption of liability in a contract or an agreement. However, the exclusion contains two exceptions.

The first exception is that the exclusion does not apply to liability that the insured would have in the absence of the contract or agreement. For example, assume that the named insured is a tenant in an office building. A visitor to the tenant's premises was injured as the result of a dangerous condition on the tenant's premises. The injured visitor then brought a negligence action against the tenant and won damages. This is an example of something that was obviously intended to be covered by the CGL policy. This exception clarifies that the insurer is still obligated even if there happens to be a contract that also makes the insured liable. In theory, this first exception does not create any additional obligation for the insurer.

The second exception exposes the insurer to additional liability for certain types of contractual liability. Specifically, the exclusion does not apply to liability assumed under an "insured contract" as defined in the policy. This is another example of how an exception to an exclusion can act as an insuring agreement. For example, the tenant's CGL policy will cover claims if the tenant-insured had agreed to hold the landlord harmless from any claim for injury occurring on the tenant's premises. The keys to this exception are that the tenant-insured assumed liability:

1. Under an "insured contract" and
2. Before the accident occurred.

What is an "insured contract"?

The following section identifies "insured contracts" covered under this second exception.

Insured Contracts

The CGL definition of "insured contract" defines the scope of contractual liability coverage. An **insured contract** is any of the following:

*   A lease of premises
*   A sidetrack agreement

EXHIBIT 3-5

Questions and Issues Related to Expected or Intended Injury Claims Under Homeowners or CGL Policies

Questions	Issues or Examples	Court Opinion(s)
Are unintended consequences of deliberate acts excluded?	The insured shoots into the air to scare people, but some people are struck by bullets. The insured deliberately pushes someone, who falls down and sustains a serious head injury.	The 2000 homeowners exclusion is more restrictive than wording found in previous homeowners policies and the wording found in the CGL 1998 edition. For claims made under the 2000 homeowners policy, courts will most likely apply a more conservative interpretation and exclude injuries that are more serious than initially expected by the insured. The 1998 CGL wording is not as restrictive and may leave room for courts to cover more unintended consequences. Both the homeowners and CGL policies under current editions now provide coverage for the use of reasonable force to protect persons or property. An insured's ability to form intent is also a factor. Courts have ruled that insane persons, or even heavily intoxicated persons, are unable to form intent because they didn't know what they were doing. Coverage has been provided in such cases under both homeowners and CGL policies.
How do courts determine a person's intent?	The insured states that he or she did not intend to cause the injuries, or the extent of injuries, suffered by the claimant.	Courts have taken two views: (1) the subjective standard based on what the insured expressed as the intent and (2) the objective standard based on what an "ordinary, reasonable person" would have expected. Courts will likely apply the objective standard to homeowners 2000 claims but apply the subjective standard to CGL claims.
What does the term "expected" mean?	If an exuberant insured tackles a guest who suffers injuries as a result of the tackle, is the injury "expected"?	For homeowners and CGL policies, the minority of courts take the view that damages must be intended in order to be "expected." Most courts apply the exclusion if it can be shown that the injury or damage was reasonably foreseeable.
Are insureds covered if they are vicariously liable for intentional injuries?	An insured's teenage son vandalizes a school. A state law holds parents liable in such situations. An employee deliberately harms a third party without the knowledge of the insured business owners.	Historically, courts favored providing coverage to parents. The policy wording in the past did not clearly preclude coverage. The homeowners 2000 coverage clarifies and excludes all intentional damage claims committed by any insured. Courts have not yet ruled on this new wording. Courts have clearly favored covering vicarious liability claims to businesses insured under CGL policies.

- An easement or a license agreement
- An obligation, as required by ordinance, to indemnify a municipality
- An elevator maintenance agreement
- That part of any other contract pertaining to the named insured's business under which the named insured assumes the tort liability of another party to pay for bodily injury or property damage to a third person or organization

The contract can be either oral or written; however, as noted above, the injury or damage must occur after the contract was executed. An insured cannot make its insurer liable after the fact. The CGL covers liability for damages assumed under an "insured contract" as long as liability is assumed before the injury occurs. The most common "insured contracts" that claim representatives encounter are lease agreements.

Lease Agreements

Landlords commonly require a tenant to sign a lease before permitting the tenant to occupy the property. Leases specify not only conditions dealing with rental or lease financing arrangements but also the respective responsibilities of landlords and tenants. For example, a tenant may agree to hold the landlord harmless for any bodily injury or property damage arising out of the leased premises. Hold harmless and indemnity agreements are common in leases and should always be investigated in any claim involving premises with a tenant/landlord. Lease agreements are not consistent. Some agreements hold the landlord harmless while others hold the tenant harmless. Claim representatives must read the agreement to determine which party is liable.

A **hold harmless agreement** is a contractual arrangement whereby one party assumes the liability for claims and relieves the other party of responsibility. An **indemnity against liability agreement** gives one party a right to compensation from the other party for claims specified by the contract. A **hold harmless and indemnity agreement** is a common contractual provision found in leases.

Because a lease of premises is an "insured contract," the bodily injury or property damage liability the tenant assumes under the lease would be covered under the tenant's CGL policy. However, any agreement by a tenant to indemnify a landlord for *fire* damage to rented premises is not an "insured contract" because this exposure is already covered under the policy's fire legal liability coverage.

Defense Costs Assumed Under an Insured Contract

Under hold harmless and indemnity agreements, the indemnitor (party that must pay based on the agreement) may assume liability not only for damages paid to the claimant, but also for defense costs incurred by the indemnitee (the party benefiting from the agreement). Beginning with the 1996 edition of the CGL, the policy form clarifies this issue, stating that, for purposes of contractual liability coverage, the term "damages" includes reasonable attorney fees and necessary litigation expenses incurred by the indemnitee.

Liquor Liability

The liquor liability exclusion is aimed at insureds in the business of manufacturing, distributing, selling, serving, or furnishing alcoholic beverages. The exclusion eliminates coverage for bodily injury or property damage for which any insured may be held liable because of any of the following:

1. Causing or contributing to the intoxication of any person
2. Furnishing alcoholic beverages to a person under legal drinking age or under the influence of alcohol
3. Violating any statute, ordinance, or regulation relating to the sale, gift, distribution, or use of alcoholic beverages

The laws mentioned in 3 above, which apply in varying degrees in many states, are sometimes referred to as dram shop acts or alcoholic beverage control acts. The application and scope of these laws vary by state, but their general purpose is to give claimants injured by intoxicated persons the legal recourse to sue and collect damages from the establishments that served the person. Most dram shop laws hold the establishments liable if they served alcohol to obviously intoxicated patrons or to minors. Some states have common-law decisions that create liability even when a statute may not apply. These liquor liability laws are discussed in more detail in Chapter 6.

The exclusion applies only if the *named* insured is "in the business of manufacturing, distributing, selling, serving or furnishing alcoholic beverages." Determining whether an organization is in the alcoholic beverage business is not always easy. If the insured is in the alcoholic beverage business and wishes to insure the excluded exposure, the insured must usually buy separate liquor liability insurance.

Workers Compensation and Similar Laws

The CGL policy excludes coverage for any obligation for which the insured may be held liable under any workers compensation, disability benefits, unemployment compensation, or similar law. The purpose of the exclusion is to avoid a duplication of coverage between the CGL policy and other policies designed to provide specific employee protection.

Employers Liability

Some employees are not protected by workers compensation or similar laws. Such employees, if injured on the job, can make a claim against the employer to recover damages for their injuries. Because such claims can be covered in the employers liability section of the standard workers compensation policy, the CGL form contains a broad exclusion intended to eliminate CGL coverage for any employee suits that would be covered under employers liability insurance.

The exclusion applies to bodily injury to an employee of any insured arising out of and in the course of (1) employment by the insured or (2) the performance of duties related to the conduct of the insured's business. The policy defines the word "employee" to include "leased workers" (persons leased to the named insured to perform duties related to the conduct of the named insured's work). However, "employee" does not include temporary workers who have been furnished to the named insured to substitute for permanent employees on leave or to meet seasonal or short-term needs.

Pollution

The pollution exclusion is by far the most complicated and prone to litigation. Even the definition of a pollutant generates disputes:

> Pollutants means any solid, liquid, gaseous or thermal irritant or contaminant, including smoke, vapor, soot, fumes, acids, alkalis, chemicals and waste. Waste includes materials to be recycled, reconditioned or reclaimed.

This is a very broad definition and could be seen as excluding a host of items such as paints, hand cleaners, and lubricating oils that may or may not have been intended to be excluded. The CGL pollution exclusion eliminates coverage for most claims for bodily injury or property damage resulting from the release of pollutants. Although the exclusion is commonly referred to as the "absolute pollution exclusion," it is not, in fact, absolute because it does not bar coverage for pollution in all instances.

The exclusion contains three explicit exceptions:

1. For bodily injury or property damage caused by heat, smoke, or fumes emanating from a hostile fire at the insured's premises or at a site where the insured (or its contractor or subcontractor) is working

2. For bodily injury or property damage resulting from the escape of lubricants or fuels needed to perform normal functions of mobile equipment

3. For bodily injury caused by smoke, fumes, vapor, or soot from equipment used to heat a building, if the bodily injury is sustained within that building

Environmental liability laws are complicated even without overlaying coverage issues. Under the federal government's Comprehensive Environmental Response, Compensation and Liability Act (CERCLA) (also known as the Superfund law), the government has broad rights to seek cleanup funds from owners of hazardous waste sites even if the property owners were not the ones who polluted the site. Jurisdictions are split on whether a potentially responsible party (PRP) letter from the government triggers the duty to defend. Another issue is whether reimbursement of the government for cleanup costs would even be considered *damages* under the CGL policy. Currently, thirty-two states had cases allowing coverage for these costs, thirteen states did not allow coverage, and the rest were undecided.[42] This is just one of a host of complicated issues involving the pollution exclusion.

Because the application of this exclusion is complex, claim representatives who do not specialize in pollution or environmental liability can easily become overwhelmed in trying to determine whether coverage exists for a pollution claim. A typical claim representative should know three things about the CGL pollution exclusion:

1. Courts have interpreted the exclusion in ways that insurers did not expect, and coverage may exist for claims that might appear to be excluded.

2. The wording of the exclusion continues to evolve in response to changing court decisions.

3. The exclusion is complicated, and claim representatives may need to consult with claim management or legal counsel.

CLAIM REPRESENTATIVE SOLUTIONS

Pollution Liability Coverage

Because the policy wording regarding pollution exclusions has changed so much and so frequently, claim representatives must ensure that they are applying the proper policy wording to a given claim. Related to this, claim representatives should conduct a detailed investigation to determine when the pollution occurred. The following are some questions claim representatives should answer when faced with pollution claims:

- What theory of occurrence (manifestation versus exposure) triggers coverage for the jurisdiction in question?

- Do older liability policies apply to the claim?

- How did the policy wording of the older policies differ from the wording of the current policy? Do the differences affect coverage?

- If the claim was presented by a PRP letter, does the jurisdiction in question recognize this as a "suit" that triggers the duty to defend?

As with all coverage issues, investigations should be performed under a reservation of rights.

Aircraft, Auto, or Watercraft

Liability arising out of the ownership, maintenance, or use of aircraft, automobiles, and watercraft is mainly excluded from CGL coverage. These exposures are normally insured under separate aircraft, auto, or marine policies. Exceptions to this exclusion exist for auto and watercraft, and claim representatives are likely to encounter situations involving autos that fall within the exceptions.

The CGL covers liability arising out of the parking of an auto on or "on the ways next to" premises owned or rented by the named insured. However, the auto must not be owned by or rented or loaned to any insured. For example, the insured owns a restaurant and provides valet parking service. While parking a patron's car, a restaurant employee struck and injured another patron in the insured's parking lot. The bodily injury would be covered. Any damage to the vehicle, however, would not be covered because of the "damage to property" exclusion, discussed later in this chapter.

"Auto" Versus "Mobile Equipment"

Although the words "aircraft" and "watercraft" are not defined in the CGL policy, the word "auto" is defined. Thus, the scope of the auto exclusion depends on the meaning of "auto." The policy definition of "auto" is as follows:

"Auto" means a land motor vehicle, trailer, or semitrailer designed for travel on public roads, including any attached machinery or equipment. But "auto" does not include "mobile equipment."

Because mobile equipment is not auto, it is important to read the policy definition of **mobile equipment,** which is much longer than the "auto" definition. This definition is shown in Exhibit 3-6.

Generally speaking, the CGL covers liability arising out of the ownership, maintenance, or use of mobile equipment (because mobile equipment is not an "auto").

EXHIBIT 3-6

Mobile Equipment Definition

"Mobile equipment" means any of the following types of land vehicles, including any attached machinery or equipment:

a. Bulldozers, farm machinery, forklifts and other vehicles designed for use principally off public roads;

b. Vehicles maintained for use solely on or next to premises you own or rent;

c. Vehicles that travel on crawler treads;

d. Vehicles, whether self-propelled or not, maintained primarily to provide mobility to permanently mounted:

   (1) Power cranes, shovels, loaders, diggers or drills; or

   (2) Road construction or resurfacing equipment such as graders, scrapers or rollers;

e. Vehicles not described in a., b., c. or d. above that are not self-propelled and are maintained primarily to provide mobility to permanently attached equipment of the following types:

   (1) Air compressors, pumps and generators, including spraying, welding, building cleaning, geophysical exploration, lighting and well servicing equipment; or

   (2) Cherry pickers and similar devices used to raise or lower workers;

f. Vehicles not described in a., b., c. or d. above maintained primarily for purposes other than the transportation of persons or cargo.

   However, self-propelled vehicles with the following types of permanently attached equipment are not "mobile equipment" but will be considered "autos":

   (1) Equipment designed primarily for:

      (a) Snow removal;

      (b) Road maintenance, but not construction or resurfacing; or

      (c) Street cleaning;

   (2) Cherry pickers and similar devices mounted on automobile or truck chassis and used to raise or lower workers; and

   (3) Air compressors, pumps and generators, including spraying, welding, building cleaning, geophysical exploration, lighting and well servicing equipment.

Continued on next page.

> The CGL auto exclusion states that operation of the equipment *attached* to the types of vehicles listed in f (2) and (3) is covered under the CGL. For example, assume that a cherry picker attached to a truck was being used by a tree service to trim trees alongside a road. If a worker elevated on the cherry picker accidentally dropped a tree limb onto a car passing below, the car owner's claim would be covered under the tree service's CGL. The CGL, however, would not apply if the truck collided with another vehicle on the way to another job site. Auto insurance is needed to cover the over-the-road exposure.

Negligent Entrustment

Negligent entrustment (with auto liability) occurs when the owner or other person in control of the auto entrusts the vehicle to one who is unskilled or otherwise incompetent to operate the vehicle. Examples include giving the car keys to unlicensed or intoxicated drivers.

The aircraft, auto, and watercraft exclusion applies not only to ownership, maintenance, or use but also to "entrustment to others of any aircraft, auto or watercraft." The reference to *entrustment* is intended to preclude any attempt to circumvent the exclusion by maintaining that liability did not arise from the ownership, maintenance, or use of the vehicle but arose instead because of the insured's *negligent entrustment* of the vehicle to another party. Such attempts to circumvent the exclusion have been made with regard to rental autos when the plaintiff sued the auto owner because the owner entrusted the auto to a person who was not competent to operate it.

Loading and Unloading

The ISO Business Auto Coverage Form and the CGL were designed to eliminate overlapping coverage. For that reason, it is useful to consider the wording of the two policies together. The Business Auto Coverage Form excludes coverage for the following activities involving "handling of property" (loading and unloading):

7. Handling Of Property

   "Bodily injury" or "property damage" resulting from the handling of property:

   a. Before it is moved from the place where it is accepted by the "insured" for movement into or onto the covered "auto"; or

   b. After it is moved from the covered "auto" to the place where it is finally delivered by the "insured".

8. Movement Of Property By Mechanical Device

   "Bodily injury" or "property damage" resulting from the movement of property by a mechanical device (other than a hand truck) unless the device is attached to the covered "auto".

Although these exclusions do not use the words "loading and unloading," they effectively define the scope of coverage for this type of activity. Business auto coverage applies while the insured is engaged in the process of handling cargo from the time it is picked up until it is "finally" set down or, for loading, from the moment it is physically "accepted," lifted, taken to, and placed in or on the vehicle.

In contrast to the coverage provided under the Business Auto Coverage Form described above, the CGL specifically addresses loading onto or unloading from autos, aircraft, or watercraft. The CGL exclusion for the use of auto, aircraft, or watercraft applies to the use of these while loading and unloading.

How does the CGL define loading and unloading? It is essentially the obverse of the exclusion found in the Business Auto Coverage Form. The CGL definition of **"loading and unloading"** reads as follows:

> 11. "Loading or unloading" means the handling of property:
>
>   **a.** After it is moved from the place where it is accepted for move-ment into or onto an aircraft, watercraft or "auto";
>
>   **b.** While it is in or on an aircraft, watercraft or "auto"; or
>
>   **c.** While it is being moved from an aircraft, watercraft or "auto" to the place where it is finally delivered;
>
> but "loading or unloading" does not include the movement of property by means of a mechanical device, other than a hand truck, that is not attached to the aircraft, watercraft or "auto".

The above definition describes activities *not covered* by the CGL. Whereas the Business Auto Coverage form provides (by exception) coverage if the movement was by means of a mechanical device *attached* to the auto, the CGL would allow coverage for movement by mechanical device *not* attached to the auto, such as with a forklift.

The primary issue then becomes whether the property in question has been accepted by the insured for delivery or whether the insured has finally delivered the property. Determining these timing issues can be challenging. Consider the following questions and how they would need to be answered in a claim investigation:

- What is meant, for example, by the phrase "before it is moved from the place where it is accepted by the 'insured' for movement into or onto the covered 'auto'" or the phrase "finally delivered"?
- If an item is taken off the back of a truck and set on the sidewalk at the address of the delivery, then picked up again and taken inside a building, does coverage extend until the item is "finally" accepted by the consignee within the building?

The following cases illustrate how coverage applies and why it is important to conduct a thorough investigation into the specific activities of the parties involved. These cases illustrate the importance of a detailed investigation. It is not sufficient for claim representatives to deny or accept coverage just because the insured states that the accident occurred while loading or unloading an auto. Coverage determination requires investigation of the specific details of activities the employees performed at the time of the occurrence.

APPLICATIONS

Loading/Unloading Claims

Case 1

An insured under a CGL policy operates a warehouse. The insured's warehouse employees move items from the warehouse to the loading dock located just outside the warehouse doors. From the loading dock, items are picked up and placed on trucks by operators of independent trucking companies.

Question: If a third party is injured by a warehouse employee while moving the item from the warehouse to the loading dock to be put on a truck, does the business auto policy or the CGL policy apply to this claim?

Answer: The warehouse operator's CGL would apply.

Question: If a person (perhaps a passerby) is injured while the truck driver is moving the item off the dock onto the truck, which policy applies?

Answer: If the item had been "accepted" by the trucking company, then their business auto policy would apply.

Question: What is "acceptance"? The policy does not define this term. If, for example, the driver and the warehouse employee exchanged paperwork regarding the item, but the insured's warehouse employee moved the item from the dock to the truck, would the CGL provide coverage?

Answer: The answer to this question would be decided based on the details of the investigation. If the item had not been accepted, then the warehouse insurers would still provide coverage.

Case 2

A carpet company that has both a business auto and a CGL policy contracts to deliver and install carpeting in a customer's premises. Upon arrival, some employees of the carpet company remove a long roll of carpeting and carry it into the premises. While entering the door they accidentally strike the customer in the head, causing an injury. The coverage would fall under the business auto policy rather than the CGL. Even if carpet company employees unloaded the carpet at the street, set it on the sidewalk, and picked it up again, the business auto form would still apply because the carpet is not "finally delivered" until it is inside the premises where it is to be installed.[43]

Case 3

A trucker delivered a load of gravel that was dumped at a place where it was to be spread, then left for another load. A subcontractor's employee accidentally drove into the pile of gravel and was injured. The business auto and CGL insurers both contributed to the settlement and then went to court to determine which insurer was ultimately responsible. The auto insurer argued that it had no exposure because the unloading of the gravel had been completed; the CGL insurer argued that the loss arose from the "unloading" and was therefore excluded by its policy. The court ruled that the loss did not arise out of unloading of the gravel because the delivery had been completed; therefore, the CGL insurer was responsible for the claim.[44]

Mobile Equipment

As discussed above, the CGL definition of "auto" specifically does not include "mobile equipment." Thus, the CGL covers the ownership, maintenance, or use of mobile equipment in most circumstances. However, the CGL contains an exclusion that eliminates coverage for mobile equipment in two situations:

1. *When bodily injury or property damage arises out of the transportation of mobile equipment by an auto owned, operated, rented, or loaned to any insured.*
2. *When the bodily injury or property damage arises out of "the use of mobile equipment in, or while in practice for, or while being prepared for, any prearranged racing, speed, demolition, or stunting activity."*

War

This exclusion eliminates coverage for most liability arising from war. It reads as follows:

> "Bodily injury" or "property damage" due to war, whether or not declared, or any act or condition incident to war. War includes civil war, insurrection, rebellion or revolution. This exclusion applies only to liability assumed under a contract or agreement.

Damage to Property

The name of this exclusion might be misleading because the CGL covers property damage occurring under a wide variety of circumstances. The exclusion contains six subparts, which detail the scope of this exclusion. These six subparts are abbreviated below.

1. The named insured's own property
2. Premises sold, given away, or abandoned
3. Loaned property
4. Property in the care, custody, or control of the insured
5. Property being worked on
6. Faulty work

The damage to property exclusion is mainly concerned with property damage that occurs while the insured has possession of the damaged property or is working on it. These are excluded by subparts 3, 4 and 5.

The CGL policy also excludes damage to property loaned to the named insured. Although property loaned to the insured is usually also in the insured's care, custody, or control at the time of an occurrence, the separate exclusion of loaned property eliminates coverage for such property even if the insurer cannot establish that the loaned property was in the insured's care, custody, or control at the time of the occurrence.

Subpart 4 excludes damage to personal property in the care, custody, or control of the insured. (Personal property includes all property other than the land and property attached to the land, such as buildings.) A common example of personal property in the care, custody, or control of the insured is property of customers being worked on or stored by the named insured.

Repair shops, dry cleaners, carpet cleaners, miniwarehouses, kennels, furniture refinishers, photo developers, and fur storage facilities are just a few of the many types of businesses that take care, custody, or control of customers' property. Such businesses are generally held liable for any damage to customers' property that results from their negligence, but the CGL does not cover this. Instead, these businesses must purchase first-party property insurance coverage.

Subpart 5 of the property damage exclusion eliminates coverage for damage to "that particular part" of real property on which the named insured or the named insured's contractors or subcontractors are performing operations, if the property damage arises out of those operations.

The reference to "that particular part" is important. No coverage applies to "that particular part" of real property damaged while work is being performed on it. But, by inference, coverage does apply for damage to any other part of the property besides "that particular part," as long as it is not otherwise excluded. Moreover, the exclusion applies only to real property. Real property includes land and all property attached to it, such as buildings and fixtures. Thus, the exclusion does not apply to personal property, which includes all property other than real property.

APPLICATIONS

Exclusion Limited to "That Particular Part"

A general contractor was constructing a steel-frame building. While employees of the general contractor were positioning steel columns and beams with a crane, a beam being hoisted by the crane slipped and fell as a result of the crane operator's negligence. The falling beam struck and damaged other steel components that had already been erected. The beam that fell was bent so badly that it could only be sold for scrap.

Question: Assuming that the general contractor was legally liable for the property damage, what coverage would the general contractor's CGL provide for this claim?

Answer: Most courts would take the position that the general contractor's CGL policy would cover the property damage caused by the beam that fell. The property damaged by the beam was not "that particular part" of real property being worked on at the time of the accident. The policy would not cover the damage to the fallen beam, since it was personal property in the insured's care, custody, or control. (The dropped beam could not be excluded as "that particular part" of real property, since the beam was not attached to the building when the accident occurred and therefore not real property.)

Damage to Your Product

Although several of the Coverage A exclusions might be involved in a products or completed operations claim, four exclusions are particularly important. These exclusions are titled as follows:

- Damage to your product
- Damage to your work
- Damage to impaired property or property not physically injured
- Recall of products, work, or impaired property

These exclusions are aimed at precluding coverage for the cost of repairing or replacing faulty products and work of the insured, or even withdrawing them from the market. Products and completed operations liability coverage is intended to cover bodily injury or property damage that results from failure of a product or completed work, not to cover the faulty product or work itself.

The "damage to **your product**" exclusion eliminates coverage for property damage to "your product" arising out of it or any part of it. The exclusion applies regardless of whether the product is physically damaged or merely rendered useless. The purpose of this exclusion is to prevent the insurer from having to pay for the repair or replacement of a product that was incorrectly designed or defectively produced. However, the exclusion does not eliminate coverage for bodily injury or property damage caused by the insured's product, only damage to the product itself.

Damage to Your Work

The "damage to your work" exclusion is similar to the "damage to your product" exclusion, except it applies to operations. This exclusion applies only to property damage included in the "products/completed operations hazard," which is defined in the CGL policy.

> "**Your work**" means:
> a. Work or operations performed by you or on your behalf; and
> b. Materials, parts or equipment furnished in connection with such work or operations.
>
> "Your work" includes:
> a. Warranties or representations made at any time with respect to the fitness, quality, durability, performance or use of "your work"; and
> b. The providing of or failure to provide warnings or instructions.

The "damage to your work" exclusion eliminates coverage for property damage to "your work" arising out of that work or any part of it. The basic purpose of the exclusion is to prevent the insurer from having to pay for replacing, repairing, or otherwise redoing faulty work of the named insured.

When a subcontractor performs some aspects of the named insured's work, coverage may apply to damage to "your work." The exclusion does not apply if the damaged work or the work out of which the damage arises was performed on the named insured's behalf by a subcontractor.

Damage to Impaired Property or Property Not Physically Injured

In many cases, the named insured's product or work is a component of a larger product or a structure. One purpose of this exclusion is to eliminate coverage for costs associated with tangible property that cannot be used because it incorporates the insured's product or work. The beginning of the exclusion eliminates coverage for the following:

> "Property damage" to "impaired property" or property that has not been physically injured, arising out of....

APPLICATIONS

"Damage to Your Work" Exclusion—Case 1

John, a sole proprietor engaged in the sign installation business, erected a sign on a tall steel tower at a service station. John provided both the sign and the tower. A few weeks later, wind blew down the sign and tower. They fell on the service station's building and injured a mechanic. An investigation revealed that the sign and tower were blown down because John had failed to secure them properly.

The service station owner sued John for destruction of the sign and tower, damage to the building, and resulting business interruption (loss of use). The mechanic sued John for medical expenses, income loss, and pain and suffering.

Question: What damages would John's CGL cover?

Answer: John's CGL would cover all damages claimed except the cost of replacing the sign and tower, which were "your work."

Impaired property has a lengthy definition, but the following illustration provides one example of when the exclusion for impaired property would apply. In the context of *products*, bearings manufactured by the named insured may be components of engines assembled by another manufacturer. If the named insured's bearings are defective, the engine manufacturer could incur substantial expenses in correcting the problem and would probably make a claim for damages against the bearing manufacturer. The impaired property exclusion applies only if the property can be restored to use by the repair, replacement, adjustment, or removal of "your product" or "your work." In the situation described above, the engines containing defective bearings would be excluded as being "impaired property." By excluding "impaired property," the insurer avoids paying claims when the only thing wrong with the property is the presence of the insured's defective component. The impaired property exclusion applies in other circumstances as well.

The impaired property exclusion contains an important exception: The exclusion does not apply to the loss of use of property arising out of *sudden and accidental physical injury* to "your product" or "your work" after it has been put to its intended use. In the previous example, the damage to the engine would be covered if the bearings caused the engine to seize. However, it would not cover the expense of preemptive repairs before a failure. This is similar to the following exclusion.

This exclusion has had an uneven history of court rulings. It is a lengthy, wordy exclusion that many courts have struggled to understand and apply in conjunction with other controversial provisions in the policy, such as definitions of "occurrence" and "property damage."[45]

Recall of Products, Work, or Impaired Property

When a product is discovered to be defective and capable of causing injury, governmental authorities may require the seller or manufacturer to *recall* (withdraw) the product from the market. In many cases, manufacturers voluntarily withdraw their products or notify consumers to bring the product to an authorized agent of the manufacturer for inspection, adjustment, or repair. Recalls may occur when the product is only suspected of being defective or dangerous.

The costs of recalling products can be severe. After seven persons in the Chicago area died from taking cyanide-contaminated extra-strength Tylenol in 1982, Johnson and Johnson spent about $150 million to recall the product from the market and stop further production.

CGL Limits of Liability

The amount the insurer is obligated to pay for damages under Coverage A is subject to various limits of insurance. Defense costs are payable *in addition to the limits of insurance*. However, the insurer's duty to defend ends when the applicable limit of insurance has been used up in paying damages for judgments or settlements. Claim representatives should be familiar with

1. The each-occurrence limit and
2. The two aggregate limits of the CGL.

The **each-occurrence limit** is the most the insurer will pay in any one occurrence for all damages under Coverage A plus all medical expenses under Coverage C. Since Coverage C (medical payments) is usually subject to a relatively low limit (such as $5,000 per person), the each-occurrence limit is principally concerned with limiting damages under Coverage A. A typical each-occurrence limit is $1 million per occurrence. Additional insurance for each occurrence is commonly provided through an excess or umbrella liability policy.

The CGL policy also has two aggregate limits. An aggregate limit caps the total amount that the insurer will pay under the policy for a given policy period. To illustrate, say that a policy has an each-occurrence limit of $1 million and an aggregate limit of $2 million. This means that the insurer will pay up to $1 million for each covered occurrence, but after payments for two or more occurrences total $2 million the insurer will no longer have an obligation to pay claims or defend against suits. An excess or umbrella liability policy is often in place to provide coverage if an aggregate limit is exhausted.

The **general aggregate limit** of the CGL policy is the most that the insurer will pay for the sum of the following:

- Damages under Coverage A, except those that arise out of the "products-completed operations hazard"
- Damages under Coverage B
- Medical expenses under Coverage C

The **products-completed operations aggregate limit** is the most the insurer will pay under Coverage A for damages arising out of the "products-completed operations hazard."

- *Products-completed operations aggregate limit (per policy)*: the most the insurer will pay under Coverage A for damages within the products-completed operations hazard.
- *Each-occurrence limit*: the most the insurer will pay for damages under Coverage A and medical expenses under Coverage C for any one occurrence. This each-occurrence limit applies to products-completed operations claims as well.
- *Personal and advertising injury limit*: the most the insurer will pay under Coverage B for damages because of personal injury and advertising injury sustained by any one person or organization.
- *Damage to premises rented to insured*: the most the insurer will pay under Coverage A for damage resulting from any one fire covered by fire legal liability coverage.
- *Medical expense limit*: the most the insurer will pay under Coverage C to any one person.
- *The general aggregate limit (per policy)*: the most the insurer will pay for the sum of (1) damages under Coverage A other than damages within the products-completed operations hazard, (2) damages under Coverage B, and (3) medical expenses under Coverage C.

The limits of insurance included in the CGL policy are reviewed below and illustrated in Exhibit 3-7.

APPLICATIONS

Aggregate and Each-Occurrence Limits

Moray Manufacturing Corporation has a CGL policy with these limits:

General aggregate	$1,000,000
Each occurrence	$500,000
Products-completed operations aggregate	$1,000,000
Each occurrence	$500,000
Personal and advertising injury	$ 500,000
Medical payments	$5,000

Moray is having a bad year for liability claims. The following amounts were paid as damages for seven different occurrences or offenses.

Damages	Type of Occurrence or Offense
1. $350,000	Premises/operations
2. $500,000	Products
3. $600,000	Personal/advertising injury
4. $300,000	Personal/advertising injury
5. $200,000	Products
6. $400,000	Products
7. $3,000	Medical payments

Question: How much would Moray's CGL insurer pay for each occurrence or offense listed above? Assume that the claims were paid in the order listed above and that no other claims were received during the same policy period.

Answers:

1. The insurer would pay $350,000. This payment reduces the general aggregate limit to $650,000.

2. The insurer would pay $500,000. This payment reduces the products-completed operations aggregate to $500,000.

3. In accordance with the personal and advertising injury limit, the insurer would pay $500,000 of the $600,000 judgment. This payment reduces the general aggregate to $150,000.

4. The insurer would pay only $150,000 of the $300,000 judgment, because $150,000 is all that remains of the general aggregate limit.

5. The insurer would pay $200,000. This payment reduces the products-completed operations limit to $300,000.

6. The insurer would pay $300,000 of the $400,000 products claim. This is all that is left of the products-completed operations aggregate limit.

7. The insurer would pay none of the medical payments claim. Medical payments coverage is subject to the general aggregate limit, which was exhausted by earlier claims.

APPLICATIONS

Each-Occurrence, Fire Damage, and Medical Expense Limits

A gas explosion caused a fire to break out at Discount Appliance Store. Several customers were injured, and the store building, which Discount leases, was damaged by the fire. Discount's CGL policy had an each-occurrence limit of $500,000, a damage to premises rented limit of $100,000, and a medical expense limit of $5,000. The following claims were made against Discount as a result of the fire:

1. Three customers who were treated at a hospital emergency room for smoke inhalation asked Discount to pay their medical bills of $1,000 each. Discount's insurer paid these expenses under the medical payments coverage.

Continued on next page.

2. A fourth customer sued Discount for $1 million. Disputing the amount of damages, the insurer contested the claim in court and incurred $25,000 in defense costs. The customer received a judgment for $200,000 in damages.

3. The landlord demanded that Discount pay for the $125,000 in fire damage to the landlord's building.

4. A fifth customer sued Discount for a large sum. Again, the insurer defended, at a cost of $10,000. The customer won a $300,000 judgment against Discount.

Question: How much will the insurer pay for claims 2, 3, and 4 above? Assume that the claims were paid in the order shown above and that no other claims had been paid during that policy period.

Answers:

Claim 2: The insurer would pay $200,000 in damages and $25,000 in defense costs. Only the $200,000 paid in damages would reduce the each-occurrence limit.

Claim 3: In accordance with the fire damage limit, the insurer would pay only $100,000 of the $125,000 fire legal liability claim.

Claim 4: The insurer would pay only $197,000 of the $300,000 damages awarded, because the each-occurrence limit had been reduced to $197,000 by the payments for claims 1, 2, and 3. The insurer would also pay the $10,000 in defense costs, since defense costs are payable in addition to policy limits. However, the insurer would have no further obligation to defend against or settle any further claims arising out of the fire, because the insurer had paid damages equal to the each-occurrence limit.

EXHIBIT 3-7

Illustration of CGL Limits of Insurance

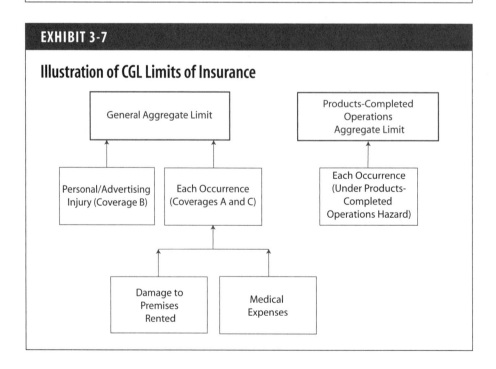

COVERAGE B—PERSONAL AND ADVERTISING INJURY LIABILITY

The CGL policy automatically includes **personal and advertising injury liability coverage** as Coverage B. The CGL policy defines "personal and advertising injury" as including many intentional offenses. This coverage encompasses a wide variety of claims and activities that result in neither "bodily injury" nor "property damage." The all-important definition of "personal and advertising injury" and the exclusions related to Coverage B are discussed below.

Coverage B—Coverage Offenses and Practical Concerns

Coverage B of the CGL policy relates to claims of "personal and advertising injury." Before 1998, personal injury and advertising injury were considered two different injuries with differing exclusions. Claim representatives must be careful to check which policy edition date the insured has, because pre-1998 versions have significantly different wording. The 1998 edition of the CGL combines personal injury and advertising injury into the following definition that provides a broad coverage:

> **"Personal and advertising injury"** means injury, including consequential "bodily injury", arising out of one or more of the following offenses:
>
> a. False arrest, detention or imprisonment;
>
> b. Malicious prosecution;
>
> c. The wrongful eviction from, wrongful entry into, or invasion of the right of private occupancy of a room, dwelling or premises that a person occupies, committed by or on behalf of its owner, landlord or lessor;
>
> d. Oral or written publication of material that slanders or libels a person or organization or disparages a person's or organization's goods, products or services;
>
> e. Oral or written publication of material that violates a person's right of privacy;
>
> f. The use of another's advertising idea in your "advertisement"; or
>
> g. Infringing upon another's copyright, trade dress or slogan in your "advertisement".

To understand the definition of "personal and advertising injury," claim representatives should understand the nature of the offenses itemized.

It is important to keep in mind that some of the issues regarding the definition of occurrence that apply to Coverage A bodily injury and property damage claims do not necessarily apply to Coverage B claims. The 1998 version of the CGL no longer includes the term occurrence in the Coverage B insuring agreement. Coverage B offenses under the definition of "personal and advertising injury" might not always be occurrences. For example, false imprisonment or slander (offenses expressly mentioned in this coverage) could in some situations lack the element of fortuity (happening by accident) and therefore fall outside the typical definition of occurrence. Perhaps the most important coverage provided is the duty to defend against the sometimes dubious offenses alleged against an insured.

Coverage B—Exclusions

The broad, all-encompassing scope of the Coverage B insuring agreement appears to give coverage to a wide variety of actions that would traditionally be considered "uninsurable" because they lack fortuity. The offenses are in many cases intentional, and the consequences are foreseeable. The Coverage B exclusions restrict coverage for blatantly intentional acts and bring back an element of fortuity to the coverage. They also define the circumstances when coverage applies. The 1998 CGL has the following ten exclusions for Coverage B:

> **Exclusions**
>
> This insurance does not apply to:
>
> a. "Personal and advertising injury":
>
>   (1) Caused by or at the direction of the insured with the knowledge that the act would violate the rights of another and would inflict "personal and advertising injury";
>
>   (2) Arising out of oral or written publication of material, if done by or at the direction of the insured with knowledge of its falsity;
>
>   (3) Arising out of oral or written publication of material whose first publication took place before the beginning of the policy period;
>
>   (4) Arising out of a criminal act committed by or at the direction of any insured;
>
>   (5) For which the insured has assumed liability in a contract or agreement. This exclusion does not apply to liability for damages that the insured would have in the absence of the contract or agreement;
>
>   (6) Arising out of a breach of contract, except an implied contract to use another's advertising idea in your "advertisement";
>
>   (7) Arising out of the failure of goods, products or services to conform with any statement of quality or performance made in your "advertisement";
>
>   (8) Arising out of the wrong description of the price of goods, products or services stated in your "advertisement";
>
>   (9) Committed by an insured whose business is advertising, broadcasting, publishing or telecasting. However, this exclusion does not apply to Paragraphs 14.a., b. and c. of "personal and advertising injury" under the Definitions Section; or
>
>   (10) Arising out of the actual, alleged or threatened discharge, dispersal, seepage, migration, release or escape of "pollutants" at any time....

The first two exclusions explain that Coverage B does not apply if the insured had knowledge that the act would inflict a personal injury or in the case of defamation had knowledge that the information stated was false. Establishing that an insured knew something was false can be extremely difficult. An important distinction in these two exclusions is the use of the term "the insured" rather than the term "any insured." This leaves open the potential for coverage to apply for the liability of a company (under principal-agency law) if an insured's employee commits the offense. The third exclusion eliminates coverage for offenses taking place before the policy began.

The fourth exclusion eliminates coverage for violations of criminal laws "by or at the direction of *any* insured." This exclusion eliminates coverage for criminal violations "by or at the direction of *any* insured." This is a revised exclusion and is much more restrictive than the wording of other exclusions in this coverage. Determining whether any insured has violated a criminal code can be tricky and requires claim representatives to obtain legal assistance. Numerous state criminal laws overlap with civil wrongs covered as personal or advertising injury. The following are examples of offenses that would be excluded because they are criminal violations.

Examples of offenses that are criminal violations in some states.[46]

- In Iowa, it is a criminal violation to act to prevent a discharged employee from obtaining employment (such as providing defamatory information to prospective employers).[47]

- In Michigan, it is a criminal violation to falsely accuse another person of a crime or a degrading act.[48]

- In California, slander is a criminal violation.[49]

- California has criminal codes for wrongful detention of a person[50]

Exclusions five through eight are somewhat self-explanatory. The ninth exclusion is somewhat complex because of disputes as to whether a company is "in the business of advertising, broadcasting, publishing, or telecasting" because these activities might be incidental to the insured's business. The tenth exclusion clarifies that Coverage B, as with Coverage A, is not intended to cover pollution.

COVERAGE C—MEDICAL PAYMENTS

The CGL policy, like the homeowners policy, provides medical payments coverage, which pays regardless of whether the insured is legally liable. The coverage is frequently included in liability policies as a way of providing a modest amount of coverage for settling minor injury cases without having to make a determination of liability. In that sense, the coverage is viewed as a means of making prompt settlements, satisfying potential liability claimants, and avoiding possibly larger liability claims. When medical payments coverage is not wanted, it can be excluded by endorsement. The medical payments coverage has a specified limit of liability ($5,000 is common for commercial policies).

SUMMARY

The homeowners policy Section II provides insureds coverage for personal liability claims.

Claim representatives handling claims under either the homeowners policy or the CGL coverage form encounter complicated issues related to intentional injuries, the definitions of "bodily injury" and "property damage," and the determination of what constitutes an "occurrence." Both policies have a broad duty to defend the insured that requires insurers to provide a legal defense against lawsuits alleging a wide variety of offenses, many of which may ultimately not be covered.

Coverage A of the CGL covers claims from four different sources:

1. Premises liability
2. Contractual liability
3. Fire legal liability (damage to property rented to the insured)
4. Products and completed operations liability

Claims resulting from any of these must meet the definition of an "occurrence," which has different interpretations according to the jurisdiction of the claim. The differing interpretations affect how claim representatives apply coverage. The CGL excludes coverage for auto liability but includes claims arising out of the operation of "mobile equipment." The CGL dovetails with the business auto coverage form for activities related to "loading and unloading" an auto. Specific details must be investigated in order to determine which policy would apply. Each of the Coverage A exclusions has particular coverage issues and practical concerns that claim representatives must understand.

Coverage B covers claims arising out of "personal and advertising injury." Many of the offenses are of an intentional nature, but coverage is excluded if the insured had "knowledge that the act would violate the rights of another" and would inflict "personal and advertising injury." This creates a great challenge for claim representatives, who must determine whether this exclusion applies. The exclusion for criminal acts might require familiarity with criminal law and advice from legal counsel to help assess coverage. Claim representatives handling claims under a CGL will encounter many unique circumstances and must become accustomed to investigating and applying coverage to unfamiliar situations.

This chapter was not intended to cover or summarize all of the policy provisions. Claim representatives should always refer to the specific policy wording if they have questions about how the policy applies to a given claim. The purpose of this chapter is to provide a basic understanding of homeowners liability and commercial general liability coverages, to alert claim representatives to some areas of coverage dispute, and to provide suggestions on how to deal with some of the more complicated policy provisions. Because of the complicated nature of liability claims, claim representatives should not be afraid to ask for expert or claim management assistance in handling these types of claims.

CHAPTER NOTES

1. Gilman v. State Farm Fire & Casualty Co., 526 N.W. 2d 378 (MN. App. 1995).

2. State Farm Fire & Casualty v. Elizabeth N. 9 Cal App 4th 1234, 12 Cal Rptr 2d 327 (1992).

3. Unigard Ins. Co. v. United States Fidelity & Guaranty Co., 111 Idaho 891. 728 P. 2d 780 (1986).

4. Barry Ostrager and Thomas Newman, *Handbook of Insurance Coverage Disputes*, 9th ed. (New York: Aspen Publishers Inc., 1998), p. 417.

5. Cargill, Inc. v. Liberty Mutual Ins. Co., 488 F. Supp. 49 (D. Minn. 1979).

6. Ostrager and Newman, p. 408.

7. Elston-Richards Storage Co. v. Indemnity Ins. Co., 194 F. Supp. 673 (MI 1961).

8. Champion International Corp. v. Continental Casualty Co., 546 F. 2d. 502 (2d Cir Ct. 1976).

9. Union Carbide Corp. v. Travelers Indemnity Co., 399 F. Supp. 12 (W.D. Pa. 1975).

10. Lantier v. Aetna Casualty & Surety Co., 614 So. 2d 1346 (La. App. 1993).

11. "Trigger of Coverage—A Policyholders Perspective," *Insurance Litigation Reporter*, June 1994, pp. 268-272.

12. Eljer Manufacturing, Inc. v. Liberty Mutual Ins. Co., 972 F. 2d 805 (7th Cir. 1992).

13. MRI Broadway Rental, Inc. v. United States Mineral Products Co., 681 N.Y. S. 2d 783 (1990).

14. Michael J. Brady, Kevin W. Alexander, and Michael D. Moorehead, "Lost or Damaged Computer Data: Property Damage or Intangible Information under the Commercial General Liability Policy?", *Federal Insurance and Corporate Counsel Quarterly*, Fall 1995, p. 111.

15. Donald S. Malecki, *Malecki on Insurance* (Cincinnati, Ohio: Malecki Communications Company, April 1997), p. 5, and also Ostrager and Newman, p. 314.

16. U.S. Fidelity & Guaranty Co. v. Wilkin Insulation Co. (1989), 193 Ill. App. 3d 1087, 140 Ill. Dec. 907, 550 N.E.2d 1032; Marathon Plastics, Inc. v. International Insurance Co. (1987), 161 Ill. App.3d 452, 112 Ill. Dec. 816, 514 N.E.2d 479; W.E. O'Neil Construction Co. v. National Union Fire Insurance Co. (N.D.Ill. 1989), 721 F.Supp. 984; Elco Industries, Inc. v. Liberty Mutual Insurance Co. (1980), 90 Ill. App.3d 1106, 46 Ill. Dec. 319, 414 N.E.2d 41.

17. Ostrager and Newman (9th ed., 1998), pp. 765-771.

18. Moreland v. Columbia Insurance Company (Mo. App. 1993).

19. Lanceford v. Peachtree Casualty Insurance Co., No A97A1533, WL 795266 (Ga. App. 1997).

20. Richard Knox Mutual Ins. Co. v. Kallen, 376 F. 2d 360, 364 (6th Cir. 1967) and Wirth v. Maryland Casualty Co., 368 F. Supp. 789, 792 (W.D. KY 1973) and Allstate Ins. Co. v. Watts, 811 S.W. 2d 883, 887-88 (Tenn. 1991).

21. Nationwide Ins. Co. v. Auto-Owners Mutual Ins. Co., 37 Ohio App. 3d 199, 2020, 525 N.E. 2d 508 (1987).

22. Arnold P. Anderson, *For the Defense* (Chicago, Ill.: Defense Research Institute, April 1999), p. 22.

23. Steelman v. Holford, 765 S.W. 2d 372 (Mo. App. S.D. 1989).

24. Quincy Mutual Fire Insurance Company v. Abernathy et al., 469 N.E. 2d 797 (1990).

25. City of Johnstown, N.Y. v. Bankers Standard Ins. Co., 877 F. 2d 1146, 1150 (2nd Cir. 1989).

26. Physicians Insurance Co. of Ohio v. Swanson, 569 N.E. 2d 906 (1988).

27. Curtain v. Aldrich, 589 S.W. 2d 61 (Mo. App. W.D. 1979).

28. Safeco Insurance Co. v. Dotts, 685 P. 2d 632 (1984).

29. Safeco Insurance Co. v. Dotts, 685 P. 2d 632 (1984).

30. Property Casualty Co. of MCA v. Conway 1997 WL 29252 (N.J. Jan. 28, 1997).

31. The Catholic Diocese of Dodge City v. Raymer, Hammeke et al. v. Farmers Insurance Co., 825 P.2d. 1144 (1992).

32. World Wide Web: http://www.att.com/press/0797/970702.bsa.html, Telecommute America, American Internet Users Survey, December 1999.

33. Stuart v. American States Insurance Co., 953 P. 2d 462 (1998).

34. AMCO Insurance Co. v. Beck et al., 929 P.2d 162 (1996).

35. *Longman Dictionary of Contemporary English*, 3d ed. (Essex, England: Longman Group Ltd., 1995).

36. *Dictionary of Epidemiology*, 3d ed., ed. John M. Last, (Oxford, England: Oxford University Press, 1995). The same definition is also given in *Control of Communicable Diseases Manual*, ed. Abram S. Berenson (Washington, D.C: American Public Health Association, 16th ed., 1995).

37. *Dictionary of Epidemiology*.

38. Country Mutual Ins. Co. v. Gagan, 698 N.E. 2d 271 (1998).

39. Hahn v. Berkshire Mutual Ins. Co., 547 N.E. 2d 1144 (Mass. Ct. of Apps. 1990). See also Neil v. Allstate Ins. Co., 549 A. 2d 1304 (PA. Sup. Ct. 1988).

40. American Family Mutual Ins. Co. v. Moore et al., and Dennis et al., 912 S.W. 2d 531 (Mo. App. 1995).

41. Portions of this section on the commercial general liability (CGL) policy are adapted from Donald S. Malecki and Arthur L. Flitner, *Commercial Liability Insurance and Risk Management*, 4th ed., vol I (Malvern, Pa.: American Institute for CPCU, 1998), pp. 71-142.

42. Ostrager and Newman, 10th ed., pp. 598-609.

43. Ken Brownlee, *Casualty Claims Practice* (Clark Boardman Callahan, Thomas Legal Publishing Inc., 1995), p. 22:12.

44. Home State County Mutl. Ins. Co. v. Acceptance Ins. Co., 958 SW 2d 263 (1997).

45. Serigne v. Wildey, 612 So. 2d 155 (La. App. 5th Cir. 1992).

46. Malecki, p. 4.

47. Iowa Codes Annotated (Sec. 730.1).

48. Michigan Compiled Laws Annotated (Sec. 750.370).

49. California Codes Annotated (Sec. 258).

50. California Codes Annotated (Sec. 236).

Avoiding and Handling Coverage Disputes

Avoiding and Handling Coverage Disputes

Coverage issues that claim representatives encounter in auto and other liability claims, such as those described in Chapters 2 and 3, can result in coverage disputes. Many common mistakes that contribute to these disputes are detailed in this chapter, as well as some solutions to help claim representatives avoid these mistakes when making coverage decisions. Discussions will focus on issues such as how to protect coverage defenses before investigating a claim and while defending a lawsuit, when and how to use negotiation or arbitration to resolve coverage disputes, how to properly deny coverage, and when to use declaratory judgment actions to resolve coverage disputes.

MISTAKES IN COVERAGE DECISIONS

Claim representatives should make every effort to avoid mistakes in coverage decisions. These mistakes are costly not only in terms of increased bad faith awards, increased litigation costs, and loss of customer satisfaction when coverage is wrongfully denied, but also in increased loss ratios when coverage is improperly provided. Some common coverage-decision mistakes that should be avoided include:

- Failing to read and/or understand applicable policy provisions
- Making a coverage decision without knowing all of the facts of the claim
- Failing to take into account state-by-state differences in coverage interpretation
- Assuming policy wording is clear and unambiguous
- Basing coverage decisions on emotional reactions
- Improperly or inadequately explaining coverage
- Overcommitting to a coverage position

The following sections provide examples of these mistakes and suggestions for avoiding them.

Failing To Read and/or Understand Policy Provisions

Insurance policies contain numerous and sometimes complex provisions. Many policy insuring agreements, conditions, and exclusions have exceptions that qualify how coverage applies. Busy claim representatives who are familiar with a policy in general terms might not know or recall all of the details of the various provisions; therefore, they apply coverage based on how they think the policy reads rather than how it actually reads. This is a dangerous practice.

> **Example:** A claim representative receives a loss involving an insured vehicle used for business purposes at the time of the accident. He tells the insured, "This is excluded under that PAP business exclusion." The insured calls her agent, who realizes the claim representative's error and informs the claim representative's supervisor. The supervisor points out that the claim representative had overlooked the exception to the exclusion for private passenger vehicles and had wrongfully denied the claim (as discussed in Chapter 2).
>
> **Solution:** Claim representatives must base the coverage decision on what the policy says, not on what they think it says. Even the most experienced claim representatives are unlikely to have memorized every word of the entire policy. Claim representatives, even experienced ones, should review policy wording before making a coverage decision if they have even the slightest doubt. The consequences of being wrong make the risk of not referring to the policy too great.

Making a Decision Without All of the Facts

Coverage decisions are based on the application of facts to policy provisions. Claim representatives can make poor coverage decisions if they fail to gather all the facts before making their decisions.

> **Example:** A claim representative receives a call from an insured who wants to know whether uninsured motorists coverage applies to his teenage son who has been injured as a passenger in an uninsured car belonging to a neighbor. The claim representative responds, "Sure, that's covered because your son is covered as a family member and he doesn't even have to be in your insured car." The man is happy and submits his son's medical bills to the claim representative for payment. The claim representative later discovers that the son resides solely with his mother, not the insured, and that the son and a friend had stolen the car. Not only was the son not a covered family member, but also his illegal use of the car was specifically excluded.
>
> **Solution:** Obtain a detailed account of the facts before committing to coverage. If the details initially provided by the insured are not sufficient to make a coverage decision, the claim representative may need to reserve the insurer's right to apply coverage defenses and then conduct a more extensive investigation. Reservation of rights will be discussed later in the chapter.

Failing To Consider Jurisdictional Differences

Claim representatives who handle claims in different states should recognize the coverage provisions that commonly have varying interpretations and should ask claim management or legal counsel for information regarding any differences in coverage interpretation.

For example, one policy term that jurisdictions differ on is "uninsured motor vehicle," especially as it applies to hit-and-run vehicles. Courts sometimes refer to unidentified vehicles as "phantom" vehicles. The PAP states that an uninsured motor vehicle includes a hit-and-run vehicle whose operator or owner cannot be identified and which hits:

    a. You or any "family member";

    b. A vehicle that you or any "family member" are "occupying"; or

    c. "Your covered auto."

The PAP definition leaves room for variation in interpretation. Consider whether the vehicle in the following events would be considered a hit-and-run vehicle:

- An unidentified vehicle runs an insured vehicle off the road without actually making contact with the insured vehicle.

- A rock falls from an unidentified passing truck, injuring an insured.

- An insured is shot by a motorist in an unidentified vehicle.

Uninsured Motorists (UM) Coverage in each of these cases depends on how the state involved interprets the term "hit-and-run vehicle." The ordinary meaning of "hit-and-run" implies physical contact. In fact, more than forty states require physical contact to trigger UM Coverage. However, almost half of the states requiring physical contact permit an exception if *competent, corroborative evidence* supports the existence of a hit-and-run vehicle.[1] What constitutes competent, corroborative evidence varies by jurisdiction. Some state statutes do not provide coverage if the hit-and-run vehicle is a "phantom" vehicle and the driver cannot be identified. In such cases, the statute precludes coverage even though the standard policy wording clearly does not require identification of the driver.

Other states have physical contact requirements based on common law interpretation of the coverage rather than on statute.[2] For example, an Ohio Supreme Court ruling reflected the position of about half of the states when it said, "Public policy prohibits insurance policy provisions which require physical contact as an unequivocal prerequisite to recovery under the uninsured motorists coverage."[3] States supporting this view will allow a claim to proceed if corroborative evidence, such as independent third-party testimony or physical evidence, establishes the negligence of the unidentified motorist. Testimony normally must be from disinterested parties. Some states make exceptions to the physical contact requirement only when physical evidence, such as contact with other vehicles or property, establishes negligence.[4]

Assuming Clear and Unambiguous Policy Wording

A claim representative who has read an insurance provision may not believe anyone could possibly have an understanding of the provision that differs from his or her own. What these claim representatives sometimes fail to consider is that they often have an extensive technical vocabulary and a perspective on coverage interpretation that differs from those of most policyholders. Sometimes this difference can be overcome by thoroughly explaining a provision to a policyholder. At other times, this difference cannot be overcome because the policyholder's interpretation is as valid as that of the claim representative.

> **Example:** A claim representative trained to look at the precise meaning of words in a policy may look at the Personal Auto Policy (PAP) medical payments provision covering insureds who are pedestrians and apply the coverage only when a person is walking. A policyholder might think that pedestrian means anyone who is not on or in a motor vehicle. Insurance Services Offices, the author of the PAP, believes that this latter interpretation is possible.
>
> **Solution:** Claim representatives must be open to the possibility that some policy wording is subject to different interpretations. Claim representatives should analyze viable alternative coverage interpretations that policyholders raise and should inform claim management of these interpretations.

Basing a Coverage Decision on Emotional Reactions

Claim representatives must separate their personal feelings about a claim or an insured from the coverage decision.

> **Example:** A claim representative received a loss notice based on a call from an insured's girlfriend, who claimed that the insured smashed her hand in the car door during a dispute. The claim representative called the insured, who referred the claim representative to the attorney who was handling his criminal defense against charges of assault and battery. The following exchange took place:
>
> **Claim Representative:** We received a claim from a victim of your client Bob Smith. Mr. Smith happens to have an auto policy with our company.
>
> **Attorney:** Well, I think it's premature to say who the victim is, but my client is looking to your company to pay for his defense.
>
> **Claim Representative:** We don't pay for criminal defenses.
>
> **Attorney:** He's asking for a defense of the injury claim by the woman who got her hand caught in Mr. Smith's car door.
>
> **Claim Representative:** I already talked to the woman, and she said Mr. Smith slammed the door on her hand.
>
> **Attorney:** That's just a boldfaced lie.

Claim Representative: Intentional acts are excluded. Besides, it's been over a week now since this occurred. The first report of this came from the victim.

Attorney: (Loudly) This wasn't intentional, and one week doesn't make any difference!

Claim Representative: Sure it does, and besides, this isn't something insurance should even cover. This isn't an auto claim.

Attorney: So you aren't going to provide any coverage for your insured on this?

Claim Representative: No way!

The claim representative denied coverage prematurely based on an emotional response to the facts of the claim. The claim representative may also be misinterpreting the exclusion because he tells the lawyer that the exclusion applies to "intentional acts" when in reality it applies to intentional injuries. The distinction could mean the difference between having and not having coverage.

Solution: Claim representatives should gather all the information about an incident before analyzing whether coverage would apply. Sometimes coverage applies to situations that do not seem as if they should be covered. This frequently occurs when an insured is seeking a defense for intentional acts with seemingly intentional injuries. Because of the long-standing principle that the duty to defend is broader than the duty to indemnify, the determination of coverage can be contentious.

Claim representatives sometimes encounter insureds who are unpleasant, obnoxious, or unsavory. Sometimes insureds make unusual claims, such as for damages from drive-by shootings, that may not have been contemplated by the policy writers. The coverage decision should be based on the application of facts to the policy wording and not based on the personality of the insured or the insured's attorney. Nor should the coverage decision be based on the claim representative's own opinion of whether insurance, in general, should apply to such acts.

Improperly or Inadequately Explaining Coverage

In today's claim environment, claim representatives are busy and policyholders are difficult to reach by phone. These factors contribute to poor coverage explanations, often made through brief voice-mail messages left by claim representatives who have been unsuccessful in making person-to-person contact with the insured. These messages usually are not detailed enough to properly explain the coverage.

Example: The named insured borrowed a friend's uninsured car to run an errand. The insured backed into a telephone pole, damaging the pole and the back bumper of the friend's car. The damage to the car is excluded under

Continued on next page.

the PAP as "property damage" to property used by or in the care of an "insured." This is an exclusion found in nearly all liability policies. The claim representative left a hasty message on the insured's answering machine stating, "Your policy covers the damage to the telephone pole, and we will work that out with the utility company. If they send you a bill, forward it to our claim office. The damage to the car you were driving isn't covered." This message failed to explain why all of the damages were not covered. If this was the only explanation the insured received, the insured would probably think the decision was arbitrary and unfounded. Such a brief coverage explanation would probably not satisfy most state unfair claim practices acts, which require insurers to state the specific policy exclusion.

Solution: Follow up all oral conversations with letters or e-mails to the insured. Most states require coverage denials to be in writing. When insureds have only minor property losses with no accompanying injury claims, some insurance companies take the position that a conversation with the insured is adequate as long as the insured understands and agrees with the reasoning for the coverage decision. Claim representatives should provide full coverage explanations to insureds. Inadequate coverage explanations lead to dissatisfied customers, complaints, and ultimately more time spent on the claim than if the coverage had been properly explained initially.

Overcommitting to a Coverage Position

Often claim representatives or even claim management personnel overcommit to their initial coverage position and have difficulty changing the position. This can occur when they take an initial coverage position on a high-profile claim or authorize the expenditure of many resources to help establish support for their own coverage opinion. The investigation of arson or fraud cases requires extensive and costly investigation by arson specialists, private investigators, and other experts. Some claim representatives and claim managers believe that once they have spent a great deal of money on investigations, they should deny coverage. This can lead to poor coverage decisions.

Example 1: While at a meeting with insurance company executives, Sarah Schwartz, a claim manager, gives an initial report on a potentially large loss involving a claimant who suffered a spinal cord injury from the insured's use of an unlicensed, rarely used pickup truck stored on the insured's farm. Sarah reports that although the facts are still being investigated and legal counsel is researching prior case law, she is "absolutely confident that the facts and the law will support a coverage denial, and the only real exposure is the legal costs to defend the coverage position." Later, when the facts are more fully developed, the coverage position seems less certain. The legal research indicates that courts are divided on whether coverage applies. Sarah does not want to lose face and dreads returning to the executives with this less-favorable scenario. At the next executive meeting, Sarah reports the facts and case law that support her initial coverage position and hopes the outcome of the trial matches her position.

Example 2: Bob Miles, a claim manager, reviews the facts of a case and tells the claim representative handling the claim that this claim looks fraudulent. Bob authorizes an extensive surveillance of the insured, who is making a claim for benefits under the personal injury protection (PIP) coverage. The surveillance shows that the insured is involved in unusual activities but does not convincingly show that the insured is committing fraud. Bob feels that he should make a coverage denial based on fraud because the company has spent so much money on surveillance.

Solution: Claim personnel should avoid making statements that would be difficult to rescind if they prove to be incorrect. If they do publicly commit to a position that proves to be unsupported, they should not allow their fear of losing respect to force them to make a bad coverage decision.

"Loss of face" is a common obstacle to good decision making. Decisions take place in a social context in which the decision maker cares about the audience's opinion. For a claim representative, this audience includes the insured, the claimant, a claim manager, claim auditors, and other claim representatives. "Face saving" means protecting a person's self-worth, dignity, sense of honor, and his or her desire to look fair and competent to others. Loss of face is the reason claim representatives sometimes find it difficult to reverse their own decisions. Claim representatives desire the reputation of being competent, reasonable, consistent decision makers, and they might feel that a reversal would threaten that reputation. Therefore, claim representatives should not commit too soon or too much to a coverage decision that could change.

Claim representatives should also keep in mind face-saving issues as they relate to the decisions of claim managers, insureds, and claimants.

Coverage investigations frequently do not prove what claim personnel suspect. Claim representatives should perform investigations to learn the truth, not to support preconceived notions. The cost of the investigation should not influence a coverage decision. Bad faith awards, loss of customer goodwill, and costs to defend the bad decision are far more costly than a good investigation preceding the decision.

In summary, claim representatives can avoid many coverage disputes by:

- Reading the exact coverage wording and not relying on memory.
- Obtaining all necessary facts of the claim before applying coverage.
- Being aware that different states and jurisdictions may have varying coverage interpretations.
- Keeping an open mind on how others might interpret policy wording.
- Explaining coverages properly and adequately.
- Holding judgment and statements about a coverage decision until all pertinent issues have been resolved.
- Separating personal beliefs and emotions from the coverage decisions, which should stand on their own merits.

INVESTIGATION UNDER A RESERVATION OF RIGHTS

Sometimes coverage issues cannot be decided when the loss is reported because additional facts must be gathered. In some cases, the first notice of loss is a lawsuit filed against the insured for a claim that might not be covered. In these situations, the insurance company may choose to investigate the claim or defend the lawsuit under a reservation of rights. Such reservations preserve the right to deny coverage later if circumstances warrant denial. Before conducting the investigation or defending the lawsuit, claim representatives must ensure that the company's rights to deny or limit a claim are reserved by advising the insured of a potential coverage issue. Failure to do this could **waive** policy rights and cause the insurer to be **estopped** from later denying or limiting the claim after the investigation is completed. Claim representatives reserve the insurer's rights by sending the insured a reservation of rights letter or by obtaining a signed nonwaiver agreement from the insured.

Waiver is the relinquishment or refusal to accept a right. In practice, a party is required to take advantage of that party's rights at a proper time, and neglecting to do so will be considered a waiver. If, for example, the policy requires an insured to submit a proof of loss form within sixty days after a loss, but the insurance company does not provide the insured with this form to complete, then the insurance company has waived its right to require the form. Waiver can also be intentional. If the insurance company representative knew the company had a right to require the insured to perform a duty under the terms of the policy (such as give a statement), then the claim representative can voluntarily or intentionally give up that right (although it would not normally be good practice to do so).

Estoppel is a bar that precludes someone from asserting a right. In insurance, estoppel normally means that the insurance company is barred from denying coverage. This term is an example of the slowly disappearing tendency of the legal profession to speak in legalese. Estoppel simply means stopped from or not allowed to assert a right. If a claim representative tells the insured to have her car repaired and the insured does so, then the claim representative would be estopped from denying the claim later. In this example, the claim representative's act of telling the insured to have her car repaired waived the insurer's right to deny coverage and led to the insurer's being estopped from later denying coverage. The insured made repairs relying on the claim representative's affirmation of coverage. This reliance would be detrimental to the insured if the insurer later tried to deny coverage because the insured had already authorized, and perhaps paid for, repairs. **Detrimental reliance** is an element required to invoke estoppel.

Reservation of Rights Letters and Nonwaiver Agreements

Reservation of rights letters and **nonwaiver agreements** are written notices advising the insured that the insurance company is investigating coverage issues surrounding a claim and that the insurer is reserving the right to deny coverage if such a denial could be supported by the facts gathered in an investigation. These written notices are used when doubt exists as to whether a claim is covered and the insurer needs time to gather facts to make a decision. The purpose of reservation of rights letters and nonwaiver agreements is to help the insurer avoid waiving rights and being estopped from denying coverage later. Reservation of rights letters are written by insurers and sent to insureds. A nonwaiver agreement is essentially a reservation of rights that the insured has assented to and signed.

Rights should be reserved promptly after a coverage issue has been discovered.[5] Reservation of rights letters or nonwaiver agreements should be clear and unambiguous.[6] Most states require that a reservation of rights letter, or nonwaiver agreement, inform the insured of all potential issues known to the insurer at the time it is written. These documents should not be tricky or cryptic.[7] Instead they should be clear and simply stated. Normally insurers advise only insureds of potential coverage problems through reservation of rights letters, but a minority of states require insurers to advise third-party claimants as well. This requirement is common in states that have statutes permitting third parties to sue insurers directly (in lieu of actions against the insured).

The Content of Reservation of Rights Letters

Most insurers believe that reservation of rights letters should mention every conceivable reason the insured may not ultimately be entitled to coverage. Generally, courts will not permit insurers to later assert additional policy defenses they knew or should have known about when the letter was written.[8] Courts may require an explicit explanation of policy provisions that apply rather than a mere recitation of potential provisions.[9]

A reservation of rights letter should include the following elements.[10]

- Identification of the named insured and the person seeking coverage, *3* policy period, policy number, and limits
- Acknowledgment of receipt of the loss notice or lawsuit *1*
- Description of the claim *2*
- A statement advising the insured to inform the carrier of any other policies that might apply to the claim
- A reference to each policy provision that might preclude coverage, with an explanation of why such a provision may result in a coverage denial
- A description of information needed from the insured
- A statement that the reservation of rights letter is not a denial of coverage and that the insurer is still investigating
- A statement that any actions taken by the insurer will not constitute a *5* waiver of rights or admission of coverage
- A reservation of the right to add to or modify the insurer's coverage *4* position later based on additional coverage issues discovered during the investigation

A majority of courts require that the reservation of rights letter be "received by the insured" to be effective. Consequently, many insurers send reservation of rights letters by certified or registered mail. Other insurers require only that the claim representative be able to prove that the letter was sent to the insured by file documentation. Some insurers send the letter by both certified and regular mail because some insureds will not go to the post office to sign for the certified mail (which is how most certified mail is delivered).

Exhibit 4-1 shows an example of a reservation of rights letter for an uninsured motorist claim.

EXHIBIT 4-1

Sample Reservation of Rights Letter

Certified Mail

Personal and confidential letter for Franklin Smith

July 9, 2001

Franklin E. Smith

727 West Oak

Springfield, PA 19803

Re:	Policy No. PAP 3982342
Insured:	Franklin and Doris Smith
Date of Loss:	January 1, 2001

Claim identification information

Dear Mr. Smith:

Acknowledgment of receipt of loss and brief description of loss

On July 1, 2001, we received notice of a loss that was reported to have taken place on Route 3 in West Festus, Pennsylvania, on January 1, 2001, involving an uninsured motorist. As a result of this loss, you have requested coverage for a claim involving your 1998 Ford Pickup with $100,000 uninsured motorists coverage limit.

We read the following policy provision:

PART E—DUTIES AFTER AN ACCIDENT OR LOSS

We have no duty to provide coverage under this policy unless there has been full compliance with the following duties:

A. We must be notified promptly of how, when, and where the accident or loss happened. Notice should also include the names and addresses of any injured persons and of any witnesses.

B. A person seeking any coverage must:

Citation of all of the insured's duties

1. Cooperate with us in the investigation, settlement, or defense of any claim or suit.

2. Promptly send us copies of any notices or legal papers received in connection with the accident or loss.

3. Submit, as often as we reasonably require:

     a. To physical exams by physicians we select. We will pay for these exams.

     b. To examination under oath and subscribe the same.

    4. Authorize us to obtain:

     a. Medical reports; and

     b. Other pertinent records.

    5. Submit a proof of loss when required by us.

  C. A person seeking Uninsured Motorists Coverage must also:

    1. Promptly notify the police if a hit-and-run driver is involved.

    2. Promptly send us copies of the legal papers if a suit is brought.

Citation of specific reasons coverage may not apply

A question exists as to whether coverage applies to this loss. The following are known reasons coverage may not apply:

1. The loss was not promptly reported to us. This is a policy violation as stated in Duty A above.

2. The loss reportedly involved a hit-and-run driver. Our preliminary investigation indicates that the police were not promptly notified of this accident. This is a policy violation as stated in Duty C.1 above.

3. A question also exists as to whether the loss was caused by a "hit-and-run" vehicle.

Statement that claim is not being denied but instead is being investigated with the understanding that it could be denied later

Conglomerate Insurance is not at this time denying coverage but is investigating this loss. We are alerting you that no act of any company representative while investigating, negotiating settlement, or defending a lawsuit will be considered a waiver of rights.

Statement expressly reserving the insurer's rights and requesting information from the insured to help determine coverage

Conglomerate Insurance expressly reserves the right to deny coverage if the facts indicate that policy coverage does not apply to this loss. There may be other reasons, not stated above, that coverage does not apply. Conglomerate Insurance reserves the right to change its coverage position based on the actions of the outcome of the investigation and does not waive the right to deny coverage for any valid reason.

For our mutual benefit, we will strictly comply with all policy provisions and require that you comply with all policy provisions, including cooperating with and assisting us in the investigation of this loss. We ask you to provide any information regarding the above three stated coverage questions, other information regarding the circumstance of this loss, and information regarding any other insurance that might apply to this loss.

We regret any inconvenience that compliance with your policy provisions may cause you, and with your cooperation, we will resolve this coverage issue as soon as possible.

Sincerely,

Jennifer Jones
610-993-2583, ext. 4994
JJONES@ConglomerateIns.com

In the sample reservation of rights letter, the claim representative cited all of the insured's duties even though not all of the duties were violated. The purpose of doing this is to remind insureds of the need for their cooperation in the claim. In this case, the claim representative mentioned the specific policy provisions that might apply. Most courts require reservation of rights letters to be specific rather than just stating that rights are reserved for "any good and sufficient reasons."[11] Claim representatives should also include any insurer-specific wording. The wording of the sample letter has less "legalese" than many traditional reservation of rights letters. This is to balance the need for meeting legal requirements with the need to communicate to the insured in a nonthreatening and understandable manner. Reservation of rights letters for third-party claims involving lawsuits are discussed in the following section on the duty to defend.

THE DUTY TO DEFEND AND COVERAGE DISPUTES

As described in Chapters 2 and 3, one important coverage that insurers provide is payment for legal counsel to defend an insured against covered liability claims. An insurer's decision regarding its duty to defend is one of the most important decisions an insurer must make. Entire books have been written addressing the insurer's duty to defend an insured when coverage questions exist. Although most liability policies state that the insurer has no duty to defend against claims that are not covered by the policy, the general principle is that the duty to defend is broader than the duty to indemnify. This leads to insurers defending against lawsuits involving damages or occurrences that are not covered under the policy. An increasing number of courts have upheld that an insurer has a duty to defend where the policy language gives the insured a reasonable expectation that the insurer will provide a defense.[12] Courts will resolve any doubts in favor of the insured in determining whether the policy requires the insurer to defend against a claim.

The financial consequences of the duty to defend can be quite significant because, without it, insureds could incur defense costs of thousands, and even hundreds of thousands, of dollars. The high potential costs of providing a defense increase the likelihood of coverage disputes. With respect to the duty to defend, claim representatives should consider the following:

- Whether the claimed event triggered the duty to defend
- How to defend a lawsuit without losing the right to deny coverage later
- The need to appoint separate legal counsel to the insured

The Duty To Defend and the Insurance Policy

Insuring agreements of liability policies provide coverage for defense costs associated with defending insureds from lawsuits. In general, the duty to defend is triggered by a civil action (a lawsuit) against the insured. If the civil action is based on allegations of negligence or some other covered offenses, the duty to defend is normally triggered. The following section discusses this issue in more detail. The PAP insuring agreement, for example, reads in part as follows:

> We will settle or defend, as we consider appropriate, any claim or suit asking for these damages. In addition to our limit of liability, we will pay all defense costs we incur. Our duty to settle or defend ends when our limit of liability for this coverage has been exhausted by payment of

judgments or settlements. We have no duty to defend any suit or settle any claim for "bodily injury" or "property damage" not covered under this policy.

A key point is that the limit of liability listed in the policy is for damages only. The insurer's expenditures for defense costs are covered but do not reduce the limits available to insureds under a PAP. The same is true of most homeowners policies and commercial general liability (CGL) policies. Although rare, some liability policies, such as professional liability policies, include the defense costs within the limit of liability or have a separate limit applicable to defense costs.

Events That Trigger the Duty To Defend

In some circumstances, actions other than a lawsuit may trigger the duty to defend. The CGL Coverage Form defines the word "suit" to include informal civil proceedings and arbitration proceedings, as well as formal lawsuits.

In addition to civil lawsuits, other actions such as administrative proceedings may, in some states, also be considered "suits." An example of an administrative action that might trigger the duty to defend is a letter from the Environmental Protection Agency advising an insured that the insured is a potentially responsible party (PRP) for cleaning up a hazardous waste site. Such letters are known as PRP letters. Some courts have considered these letters to be "suits."[13] However, other courts have not accepted these letters as triggering coverage, arguing that a suit requires judicial involvement and that therefore these letters are not suits.[14] Most courts do not make such a fine distinction and look instead to whether the proceedings will potentially have serious financial consequences for the insured.[15]

The Duty To Defend and the Allegations of the Lawsuit

In determining whether the insurer has a duty to defend, courts generally base their findings solely on the allegations expressed in the complaint or petition of the plaintiff. If the allegations stated in the lawsuit fall within what is covered under the policy, regardless of what the true facts might be, then the insurer must defend the insured. In states that accept this rule, plaintiff lawyers representing third parties will "**plead into coverage**" by artfully wording their complaints. The insurer must then provide a defense based on the wording of the lawsuit complaint if the state does not permit insurers to use extrinsic facts (facts outside the complaint) to overcome the allegations of the complaint. This leads to insurers defending unusual claims. Consider the following example of how a plaintiff's lawyer turned a murder into a negligence claim that the court determined to be covered.

Example: Pleading Into Coverage

Michael was covered under a homeowners policy. Michael was found guilty of murdering Tom. Tom's estate filed suit against Michael for wrongful death. The suit contained the following allegations against Michael:

1. Michael intentionally shot and killed Tom.

2. Michael negligently harmed Tom.

Continued on next page.

> 3.   Michael negligently assessed the need for self-defense against Tom.
>
> The first allegation is not covered, but the second two might be. Michael's testimony in the criminal case established that he intentionally shot Tom. The court determined that Michael's insurer owed a duty to defend. In this case, the state, Illinois, had established that a defense was owed even where there was no bonafide dispute and the pleadings were based on unsupported allegations.[16] Many other jurisdictions do not accept the rule of looking *only* at the allegations found in the complaint.

Regardless of the pleadings, an insurance carrier is permitted to deny a claim if it does not insure the defendant, and insurers are entitled to bring facts outside the complaint. Insurers are permitted to do this to prove that (1) the insured had not paid premiums to keep the policy in force,[17] (2) the policy was not in effect at the time of the loss, or (3) the location of the loss was not covered.[18]

The trend is to require the insurer to examine the allegations of the suit and defend the insured not only against claims alleged in the lawsuit but also against claims that could reasonably be asserted based on the allegations of the lawsuit. For example, if the lawsuit alleged that the insured intentionally invaded the privacy of a person by disclosing personal medical information, the possibility exists that the motive of the insured was not intentional but accidental disclosure of the medical information. The insurer cannot deny the duty to defend because the insured's version of the event might indicate a lack of intent. Insurers can only deny the duty to defend when any possible claims are clearly outside the scope of coverage.[19] These courts require insurers to look **"beyond the four corners of the complaint"** and to consider the facts, the reasonable expectations of the plaintiff, or both of these factors. One court explained its reasoning as follows:

> The defendant cannot construct a formal fortress of the third party's pleadings and retreat behind its walls. The pleadings are malleable, changeable, and amendable. To restrict the defense obligation of the insurer to the precise language of the pleadings would not only ignore the thrust of the cases but would create an anomaly for the insured.[20]

Requiring insurers to look beyond the "four corners" of the complaint normally broadens the insurers' duty to defend, because most courts that accept this rule require insurers to look outside the allegations of the complaint only if it might benefit the insured to do so.[21] A small number of states allow insurers to bring in facts outside the complaint for purposes of proving that the allegations of the complaint are not true.

Defense Under a Reservation of Rights

In addition to investigating a claim under a reservation of rights, insurers sometimes defend the insured against lawsuits under a reservation of rights. The purpose here is to defend the insured while the investigation into coverage is taking place. Given the costs of litigation today, it could be a huge financial burden for an insured to hire a lawyer and incur legal costs while the insurance company is investigating the coverage. The general rule is that if a carrier assumes the defense of its insured *without* notifying the insured of potential coverage issues, then the insurer is not allowed to raise coverage issues later.

The elements of the reservation of rights letter described earlier would also be included in a letter advising the insured of the insurer's intent to defend the lawsuit under a reservation of rights. For third-party lawsuits, the reservation of rights letter to the insured normally includes these additional items:

1. A statement about the separate legal counsel hired to defend the insured. (The details of this statement, and who selects this separate legal counsel, vary according to state law.)
2. A statement advising the insured of the potential for a judgment in excess of the policy limit (if this is even remotely possible) and the insured's responsibility for any award in excess of the limits. Accompanying this is a statement about the insured's right to hire a lawyer, at the insured's own expense, to review excess exposures and address any coverage issues.

Ordinarily, a defense under a reservation of rights permits the insurer to withdraw from the defense of a claim if the insurer proves a coverage defense; however, some states may require a formal declaratory judgment action before withdrawal. (Declaratory judgment actions are legal actions discussed later in this chapter.)

The insurer has a duty to investigate the underlying claim thoroughly even though it may not provide coverage. The insurer must inform the insured of all information relevant to the insured's defense, including a realistic and periodic assessment of the insured's chances to win or lose the pending lawsuit. An example of good communication would be advising insureds of all settlement offers presented to the claimant.[22] This keeps the insured advised of the insurer's efforts and gives the insured an opportunity to provide feedback.

Requirement of Separate Legal Counsel

Once a coverage issue has been discovered, a conflict of interest arises between the insured and insurer. The insurer may seek legal counsel to determine whether coverage can be denied. The insurer may also be required to appoint legal counsel for an insured who is being sued by a third party. The insurance company is not permitted to assign the same lawyer to handle both the defense of the insured against the lawsuit of a third party and the investigation of coverage for the insurance company. Such a situation could result in the insured not confiding facts to his or her own attorney for fear that it might affect coverage, or in the lawyer postponing the defense of the liability claim until the coverage issue has been resolved. This lack of attorney-client communication could cause delays in defense efforts and weaken the defense, possibly leading to higher awards against the insured.

The rule commonly applied to this conflict is expressed in the following court decision:

> A conflict of interest between the insurer and insured does not relieve the insurer of its obligation to defend the insured. When there is a conflict, the insurer must either provide an independent attorney to represent the insured or pay the costs incurred by the insured in hiring counsel of the insured's own choice.[23]

A majority of states permit the insurance company to choose the lawyer for the insured. The lawyer chosen must be competent in handling the type of case assigned. In California and several other states, the insured may choose his or her own legal counsel, and the insurer must pay all reasonable attorney fees.[24] The insurance company has the right to require that the attorney selected by the insured be competent to handle the lawsuit.

NEGOTIATION OF COVERAGE ISSUES

It is rare for most insurance claim representatives to negotiate insurance coverage. Most claim representatives normally negotiate damages only, not coverage. Consider, for example, an insured making a claim for uninsured motorists coverage. If coverage exists, a claim representative would assess the insured's bodily injury claim by looking at the medical and wage loss information and present the insured with what the claim representative believes is a fair settlement. If the insured disagrees, the claim representative would negotiate the amount of the settlement based on the insured's damages. This differs from negotiating the application of uninsured motorists coverage with the insured. If the claim representative questions whether the insured was even struck by an uninsured motorist, he or she would not negotiate this point. Most insurers would take the position that uninsured motorists coverage either exists in full or not at all. The reason for taking this "all or nothing" approach is that the legal and business complications surrounding coverage negotiations make such an approach challenging, risky, and even foolish.

The following example illustrates the potential risk involved in coverage negotiations.

Example: Risks of Coverage Negotiation

Sam is a claim representative with Car Mutual. Judy Jackson, an insured with Car Mutual, made a claim for an automobile accident involving the use of a roommate's car. Sam called Judy's roommate, Kim, who told him that Judy didn't really have permission to use the car on the night of the accident because Kim had not yet purchased insurance for it. Judy disputed Kim's version of the conversation and stated that she had permission and that the only reason Kim was upset now was because Judy had had an accident. After gathering facts about the claim, Sam told Judy that this coverage is a "toss up" and a court could rule either way, for or against coverage, because the facts on permission were disputed. "Kim didn't have her own insurance at the time of the accident, so we'd be on the hook if you had permission. For

---

that reason, I'm willing to pay a little to conclude this, but I just can't pay the whole amount," Sam said.

Sam offered to pay for half the property damage caused by Judy. Sam explained that this was a compromise for "questionable" coverage. Judy declined the offer and filed suit not only for the amount of coverage but also for bad faith damages. The suit alleged that Sam admitted the coverage was questionable and that he had acted in bad faith by not agreeing to pay the claim in full.

This example shows what might happen if a claim representative tries to negotiate coverage. In the preceding example, a court could rule that coverage should apply because even the insurer admitted it was possibly covered (based on Sam's own admission). Because a well-established principle is that the insured should be given the benefit of the doubt, a realistic possibility exists in many states for a bad faith award against Car Mutual.

Coverage negotiations are complex and require a great deal of finesse. In addition to the legal complexities involving the tacit admission that the policy is unclear, other factors such as the size of the potential loss, the nature of the dispute, the relationship between the insured (or the broker) and the insurance carrier, and even the personalities of the representatives or insureds can affect negotiations. For these reasons, insurers normally permit only high-level claim management personnel, in-house legal counsel, or outside legal counsel to negotiate coverage.

Settlements of coverage are complex legal matters that usually require an attorney's assistance. Simply obtaining a release from a policyholder on a coverage issue usually requires a lawyer's services because standard preprinted releases of liability do not settle disputed coverage. Some issues to consider when obtaining a release from a policyholder are:

- The confidentiality of the settlement agreement
- The wording and scope of the settlement agreement
- The specific parties bound by the agreement
- The need to buy back the insured's policy

A **policy buy-back** is a complicated legal maneuver whereby the insurer purchases back the policy from the insured in exchange for an agreed-upon amount of money. Several legal reasons exist for doing this, but these reasons are beyond the scope of this course.

Even if an insurer does not believe that coverage should apply to a claim, the insurer might see a benefit in settling with one particular policyholder but wish to avoid opening a floodgate to claims from other insureds. Confidentiality agreements and policy buy-backs are used in these circumstances. Acquisitions and mergers of insurance carriers and corporate insureds must also be considered in drafting the release agreement so that all potential insurers are released from future liability.

ARBITRATION OF COVERAGE ISSUES

Arbitration is another option that is sometimes used to resolve coverage issues. Arbitration requires a third party to resolve the dispute. In response to an escalation of coverage disputes and increases in the costs to litigate coverage issues, insurers have added to some policies, such as the CGL policy, endorsements that permit insureds and insurers to resolve coverage disputes through arbitration. Arbitration can be binding, meaning that the parties cannot appeal the decision to the courts, or nonbinding, meaning that either party can appeal the decision to the courts. Exhibit 4-2 shows an amendatory coverage endorsement for binding arbitration. Exhibit 4-3 shows an endorsement for nonbinding arbitration.

EXHIBIT 4-2

Endorsement for Binding Arbitration for the CGL Form

COMMERCIAL GENERAL LIABILITY

CG 24 02 11 94

THIS ENDORSEMENT CHANGES THE POLICY. PLEASE READ IT CAREFULLY.

BINDING ARBITRATION

This endorsement modifies insurance provided under the following:

COMMERCIAL GENERAL LIABILITY COVERAGE PART
LIQUOR LIABILITY COVERAGE PART
OWNERS AND CONTRACTORS PROTECTIVE LIABILITY COVERAGE PART
POLLUTION LIABILITY COVERAGE PART
PRODUCTS/COMPLETED OPERATIONS LIABILITY COVERAGE PART
RAILROAD PROTECTIVE LIABILITY COVERAGE PART
UNDERGROUND STORAGE TANK POLICY

If we and the insured do not agree whether coverage is provided under this Coverage Part for a claim made against the insured, then either party may make a written demand for arbitration.

When this demand is made, each party will select an arbitrator. The two arbitrators will select a third. If they cannot agree within 30 days, either may request that selection be made by a judge of a court having jurisdiction. Each party will:

1.   Pay the expenses it incurs; and

2.   Bear the expenses of the third arbitrator equally.

Unless both parties agree otherwise, arbitration will take place in the county or parish in which the address shown in the Declarations is located. Local rules of law as to procedure and evidence will apply. A decision agreed to by two of the arbitrators will be binding.

Uninsured motorists coverage has a provision for arbitration, but binding arbitration is not legally enforceable in every state even when the policy states that insureds must submit to arbitration. As litigation has increased, more states have recognized the benefits of arbitration and have begun to enforce policy provisions requiring arbitration.

EXHIBIT 4-3

Endorsement for Nonbinding Arbitration for the CGL Form

COMMERCIAL GENERAL LIABILITY
CG 24 01 11 94

THIS ENDORSEMENT CHANGES THE POLICY. PLEASE READ IT CAREFULLY.
NONBINDING ARBITRATION

This endorsement modifies insurance provided under the following:

COMMERCIAL GENERAL LIABILITY COVERAGE PART
LIQUOR LIABILITY COVERAGE PART
OWNERS AND CONTRACTORS PROTECTIVE LIABILITY COVERAGE PART
POLLUTION LIABILITY COVERAGE PART
PRODUCTS/COMPLETED OPERATIONS LIABILITY COVERAGE PART
RAILROAD PROTECTIVE LIABILITY COVERAGE PART
UNDERGROUND STORAGE TANK POLICY

If we and the insured do not agree whether coverage is provided under this Coverage Part for a claim made against the insured, then either party may make a written demand for arbitration.

When this demand is made, each party will select an arbitrator. The two arbitrators will select a third. If they cannot agree within 30 days, either may request that selection be made by a judge of a court having jurisdiction. Each party will:

1. Pay the expenses it incurs; and

2. Bear the expenses of the third arbitrator equally.

Unless both parties agree otherwise, arbitration will take place in the county or parish in which the address shown in the Declarations is located. Local rules of law as to procedure and evidence will apply. Any decision agreed to by the arbitrators may be appealed to a court of competent jurisdictions.

Arbitration frequently results in some monetary award because arbitrators tend to split the difference between what each party claims. Some insurers find it frustrating to pay awards for claims when the insurer believes that no coverage applies. This does not mean that arbitration necessarily works to the disadvantage of insurers, because the amount of the award can be less than the cost that the insurer would have incurred to defend its coverage position. Insurers have found that arbitration awards are often more predictable than jury verdicts and, for that reason, prefer arbitration to court. Policyholders' attorneys sometimes assert that arbitrators do not see ambiguities in wording in the same way as insureds because arbitrators are skilled professionals who are familiar with insurance policy wording. If one of the parties entered arbitration as a way to gain enlightenment on how to proceed on similar coverage issues, that party might be frustrated because arbitrators do not always explain their decision making. Despite the imperfections of arbitration, more and more parties are turning to it to help resolve policy disputes.

Binding Arbitration as Valid and Enforceable

Courts that uphold the arbitration provision do so based on the general principles of contract law and the changing legal environment. The judicial view of arbitration has gradually changed from disapproval to eager acceptance as court dockets have swelled from increased litigation. These courts do not believe that arbitration reduces the level of uninsured motorists coverage established by statute. Instead, they take the view that the common law right to a trial by jury is not absolute but subject to exception (waiver) and that arbitration is a valid waiver.[25]

Binding Arbitration as Void and Unenforceable

Jurisdictions that do not enforce the uninsured motorist arbitration provision have two main reasons for doing so:[26]

1. Binding arbitration is contrary to public policy because it denies parties access to the courts.

2. Binding arbitration is contrary to the state's uninsured motorist statutes.

States do not want to limit a person's access to the courts unless the person has expressly and voluntarily given up that right. Some courts believe that the insurance contract and this provision are too complex and that insureds are unable to understand such a formidable document to make an informed decision to give up their right to a trial.[27] With rare exceptions, even courts that accept binding arbitration will not permit a minor to be bound by arbitration.

COVERAGE DENIALS

After claim representatives have completed a thorough investigation, analyzed the facts and coverage, and concluded that coverage does not apply, they then issue a coverage denial. Denials take one of two forms: (1) a general denial reserving all policy defenses or (2) a denial based on specific coverage defenses, clearly setting forth all of the known defenses.

The general denial invites litigation and is at risk of rejection by courts because it does not adequately explain the coverage decision. Most insurers prefer to expressly cite all applicable coverage provisions when making a denial. The following court decision explains the rationale for requiring insurers to specifically list the reasons for the denial in the denial letter:

> The grounds for denial should be set out [in the denial letter] so a policy-holder knows what the [coverage] defenses will be and can adequately prepare to address those defenses. If other defenses can be raised later, an insurance company can make it impossible for an insured to know what the real [coverage] defense reason is and thus mislead the insured into not investigating that [coverage issue]. When the insured learns of the [coverage] defense it may be too late for a proper investigation.[28]

The risk of being more specific in the denial is that the insurer may forfeit the right to raise any other policy defenses later. A few states do not permit insurers to raise additional coverage issues not set forth in the denial letter. Most states take the position that other defenses can be raised as long as the insured was not prejudiced by the denial. Unfortunately, proving that the insured was not prejudiced can be difficult and costly. A few states take the position that a court cannot extend coverage as a penalty for the insurer issuing a denial.[29] Claim representatives should not rely on this position but should attempt to list all reasons for denying coverage that are known at the time of the denial.

On claims denied on the basis of arson and fraud, it is considered prudent to mark "personal and confidential" on the outside of the denial letter's envelope. Insureds have alleged that the insurance company defamed them by not maintaining confidential communications. For this reason, some companies do not send denial letters to the insured's agent. Although only a few courts have awarded recovery for defamation of character resulting from pernicious wording in denial letters, the litigation potential for these claims is enough of a threat to warrant taking this extra precaution.[30]

Denials and Unfair Claim Practices Acts

Some states' unfair claim practices laws have statutory wording that specifies how denials should be made. All states require that denials be prompt, timely, and fair, but some states set time periods (usually thirty days) to either accept or deny a claim or to provide a detailed explanation of why the insurer needs more time to make a decision. Many of the state statutes require an explanation for a denial of coverage. The following is an example of one state's wording:

> In the case of claims denials or offers of a compromise settlement, a failure to promptly provide a reasonable and accurate explanation of the basis for such actions . . . [is] an improper claims practice . . . .[31]

Other state statutes require the insurer to "clearly inform the claimant of the insurer's position regarding any disputed matter"[32] or "promptly provide a reasonable explanation of the basis relied on in the insurance policy, in relation to the facts or applicable law, for the denial of a claim . . . ."[33]

Policy Violations

Even claims that fall within the insuring agreement and are not specifically excluded may not be covered because the insured violated policy conditions. Besides fraud, the two most common policy violations leading to coverage disputes are late reporting of losses and failure to cooperate with the insurance company.

The insured has a duty to promptly notify the insurance company of a loss. The purpose of a notice provision is to allow the insurance company to:

1. Determine its rights and liabilities
2. Investigate the claim
3. Protect against fraudulent claims
4. Secure early settlements

An insurer should have the right to investigate coverage and determine its obligations in a timely fashion. When notice is delayed, memories fade and important details are forgotten, the opportunity to examine the physical surroundings and take pictures is lost, the ability to find and speak to witnesses is hampered, and the ability to secure an early settlement and avoid litigation becomes more difficult.

Some courts look solely at whether the notice was unreasonably late and unexcused. The interpretation of what is unreasonable and unexcused varies by state. A legitimate excuse might exist when a person is physically unable to make notice because of injuries sustained in the accident. Many courts examine whether the late notice **prejudiced** (adversely affected) the insurance company. What does it mean to be prejudiced by late notice?

> The terms "in a timely fashion" and "a reasonable delay" and similar wording found in policies are imprecise and are often the subject of dispute.

Claim representatives should consider the following in determining whether the company was prejudiced by late notice:

- Was information lost because of the late notice?
- Was evidence lost, altered, missing, or destroyed because of the late notice?
- Did damages increase because of the late notice?
- Was the opportunity to settle lost because of the late notice?
- Was the ability to defend an insured lost?

Failure to cooperate is another policy violation that can lead to coverage disputes. Failure to cooperate often occurs in complicated losses that require extensive, time-consuming record gathering on the part of the insured. Insurers should consistently and continually seek cooperation from uncooperative insureds until coverage is denied or the claim is transferred to legal counsel for litigation.

Claim representatives should not assume that because the insured reported the claim late or failed to cooperate that they can respond in kind. For example, if an insured is two months late in reporting a claim, courts will not excuse insurers who delay the claim disposition for an additional two months.[34]

DECLARATORY JUDGMENT ACTIONS

As used in most insurance coverage claims, a **declaratory judgment action ("dec action")** is a lawsuit seeking a judicial determination of whether policy coverage applies to a claim. Insurers normally file declaratory judgment actions to determine whether a claim falls within the insuring agreement, meets the definition of a policy term, or falls within an exclusion. However, declaratory judgment actions have also been used to determine whether and to what extent an insured has complied with a duty owed under the policy (such as prompt notice or cooperation). Exhibit 4-4 shows the different uses of declaratory judgment actions in insurance claims.

EXHIBIT 4-4

Questions Resolved by Declaratory Judgment Actions

Common Questions About Whether Coverage Applies	Common Questions About the Rights and Duties Under a Policy
Does a particular exclusion apply?	Has the insured violated any policy conditions?
Do the damages claimed fall within the definition of "bodily injury" or "property damage"?	Is the insured required to provide additional financial information in order to meet the policy requirements?
Do other insurance policies apply?	Is the insured required to submit to more than one examination under oath?
Is a vehicle an "uninsured motor vehicle"?	
When did the event take place?	Is a second named insured (e.g., a spouse) required to submit to a separate examination under oath?
What are the limits of liability?	Is the insured required to permit the insurer to reinvestigate the premises?
Does a policy violation preclude coverage?	

A declaratory judgment action does not address the issues of fault or monetary damages. A court will not render "advisory opinions" on coverage but instead will require that there be an actual case in dispute. A declaratory judgment action that focuses litigation strictly on the coverage issue may help to avoid costly litigation that involves the defense and investigation of all liability and damages facts of a claim.

To avoid bad faith claims, insurers sometimes use declaratory judgment actions as an alternative to coverage denials. States that accept this doctrine as a way of avoiding bad faith permit filing a declaratory judgment action as long as a reasonable coverage question exists.[35]

If the underlying issues of a tort claim can be separated, courts will often permit declaratory judgments.[36] In some cases, the facts and the coverage are too closely intertwined to be separated. Examples of such cases involve the determination of whether a driver was a "hit-and-run" driver as described in the uninsured motorists coverage section. Another example is determining whether the insured committed an intentional injury (which is excluded). In these cases, courts would generally defer the decision to the court assigned to the underlying tort case. Declaratory judgment actions do not determine fault. An insurer could not, for example, file a declaratory judgment action to determine whether an uninsured motorist was liable for an accident. These types of questions are based on facts that must be resolved through liability lawsuits.

SUMMARY

Claim representatives need to be aware of the common coverage-decision mistakes, such as:

- Failing to read or understand the policy before making a coverage decision
- Making a coverage decision without knowing all the relevant facts
- Failing to consider state or jurisdictional differences in coverage interpretation
- Assuming the policy wording is clear and unambiguous
- Making a coverage decision based on an emotional reaction to the insured
- Improperly or inadequately explaining a coverage decision
- Overcommitting to a particular coverage position

Too many coverage disputes are left unresolved because of the need to save face, because of personality conflicts with policyholders, or because of an inability to effectively communicate with the insured. For these reasons, claim representatives handling coverage disputes must possess strong interpersonal skills. They must be open-minded and conscientious people who avoid errors but are willing to admit mistakes.

Claim representatives must know when and how to write a proper reservation of rights letter to guard against waiver and estoppel. Sometimes, an insurer must defend an insured under a reservation of rights. The duty to defend is broader than the duty to pay damages, and this duty is one that claim representatives often encounter when presented with lawsuits involving questionable claims that are potentially covered. The duty to defend is triggered by different events, depending on the jurisdiction. In all jurisdictions, though, the allegation made against the insured in the lawsuit must be considered. Questionable claims are defended under a reservation of rights and require the insurer to appoint separate legal counsel for insureds and use their own legal counsel for assessing the coverage. The same attorney cannot be used for both.

Negotiating coverage is risky and complex and usually involves the assistance of legal counsel. Arbitration, both binding and nonbinding, is becoming an increasingly popular alternative to litigation. Declaratory judgment actions are sometimes used to resolve coverage disputes, especially on serious claims.

Coverage denials must comply with unfair claim practices acts and can be based on exclusions or coverage violations. The reason for the denial should be well-explained and understandable to the insured.

In making coverage decisions, claim representatives should not fear bad faith allegations, but they should respect the seriousness of the exposures that bad-faith lawsuits carry. Because coverage denials can have devastating consequences to insureds, claim representatives must thoroughly investigate the facts, document their decisions, and effectively communicate their coverage decisions to insureds. Claim representatives should follow internal company guidelines on handling coverage disputes. Some companies require that all coverage denials be issued by supervisory or other management personnel. Claim representatives should be aware of the methods for avoiding litigation but also be able to determine what claims would be good candidates for declaratory judgment actions.

CHAPTER NOTES

1. Maureen C. McLendon, *Commercial Auto Insurance*, vol. 1 (Dallas: International Risk Management Institute, Inc., 1995), p. IV.D.30.

2. McNeil v. Hicks, 459 S.E.2d 47 (N.C. Ct. App. 1995). See also Illinois Statute 215 ILCS 5/143a Illinois Rev. Stat. 1987, ch. 73 par. 755 a(2) (I) and Scanlan et al. v. Maryland Casualty Ins. Co. Ill. Appeals Ct. Second District. No. 2–89–1289.

3. Girgis v. State Farm Mutual Automobile Ins. Co., 662 N.E.2d 280 (Ohio 1996).

4. Rogers v. Schuman-Mann Supply Co., 397 S.E.2d 463 (Ga. Ct. App. 1990). See also Motor Vehicle Accident Indemnification Corp. v. Eisenberg, 218 N.E.2d 524 (N.Y. 1996).

5. Firemans Insurance Co. v. Burch, 442 S.W. 2d 331 (Tex. 1968).

6. Allstate Insurance Co. v. Browning, 598 F. Supp. 421 (Ore. 1983).

7. Allen v. Atlantic National Ins. Co., 214 N.E. 2d 28 (Mass. 1966).

8. American & Foreign Ins. Co. v. Church Schools in the Diocese of Va., 645 F. Supp. 628 (Va., 1986).

9. Transamerican Ins. Group v. Beem, 652 F.2d 663 (6th Cir. 1981).

10. Adapted from Robert N. Kelly, "The Opening Act-Notice, Investigation, and Reservation of Rights," *Litigating the Coverage Claim* (Chicago: American Bar Association, 1992), pp. 21–22.

11. Fellows v. Mauser, 302 F. Supp. 929 (D. Vt. 1969), and Duke v. Hoch, 468 F. 2d 973 (5th Cir. Fla. 1972).

12. Barry Ostrager and Thomas Newman, *Handbook of Insurance Coverage Disputes*, 9th ed. (New York: Aspen Publishers, 1998), p. 157.

13. Ostrager and Newman, pp. 559–561.

14. Aetna Casualty & Surety Co. v. Gulf Resources & Chemical Corp., 709 F.Supp. 958, 960 (Idaho 1989).

15. Ray Industries v. Liberty Mutual Ins. Co., 728 F. Supp. 1310 (Mich. 1989).

16. American Family Mutual Insurance Co. v. Savickas, No. 1–98–4428, 1–97–0026, 1998 WL 729898 (Ill. App.).

17. Bituminous Casualty Corp. v. Fulkerson, 212 Ill App. 3d 556 N.E. 2d 256 (1991).

18. Saylin v. California Guarantee Assn., 179 Cal. App. 3d 256, 224 Cal. Rptr. 493 (1986), and Fire Ins. Exchange v. Jiminez, 184 Cal. App. 3d 437, 229 Cal. Rptr. 83 (1986).

19. Lee Russ and Tom Segalla, *Couch on Insurance*, 3D, Lawdesk Series (West Grove Publishing, 1999), 2d para 51:48, at 489.

20. Russ and Segalla, pp. 161-203.

21. Gray v. Zurich Ins. Co., 65 Cal. 2d 263, 278, 54 Cal Rptr. 104, 419 P. 2d 168 (1966).

22. Tank v. State Farm Fire and Casualty Co., 715 P. 2d 113 (Wash. 1986).

23. American Motorists Ins. Co. v. Trance Co., 544 F. Supp. 669, 686 aff'd 718 F. 2d 842 (7th Cir. 1983).

24. San Diego Navy Federal Credit Union v. Cumis Insurance Society, 162 Cal. App. 3d 358 (Ca. 1984) and American Law Reports 4th 932.

25. Graham v. State Farm Mutual Automobile Ins. Co., 565 A.2d 908 (Del. 1989). See also United States Arbitration Act.

26. A. S. Klein, Annotation, *Uninsured Motorist Endorsement: Validity And Enforceability Of Provision For Binding Arbitration, And Waiver Thereof*, 24 A.L.R.3d 1325, 1327 (1995).

27. Barnhart v. Civil Services Employees Co., 398 P.2d 873 (Utah, 1965). See also Alsbach v. Bader, 616 S.W. 2d 147 (Mo. App. 1981).

28. Shelter Mutual Ins. Co. v. Crouch, 714 S.W. 2d 827, 828 (Mo. App. 1986).

29. Servidone Cont. Corp. v. Security Ins. Co., 488 N.Y. S. 2d 139, 142 (N.Y. 1985).

30. Moore & Assoc. v. Metropolitan Life Ins. Co., 604 S.W. 2d 487 (Texas App. 1980), and Sullivan v. Metropolitan Casualty Ins. Co. v. State of New York, 256 F. 726 (5th Cit. 1919).

31. Missouri Rev. Statutes 375.1007 (12).

32. New York Ins. Law 2601 (e) (4).

33. California Ins. Comm. 790.03 (h) (13).

34. Prudential Property and Casualty v. Persaud, 682 N.Y. S. 2d 412 (App. Div. 2d Dept.).

35. State Farm Fire and Casualty Co. v. Poomaihealani, 667 F. Supp. 705 (1987).

36. Brohawn v. Transamerica Ins Co., 276 Md. 396, 347 A.2d 842 (1975).

Determining Legal Liability

Determining Legal Liability*

Chapters 2 through 4 dealt with coverage issues in liability claims. Determining coverage is followed by the need to assess liability. Given a set of facts, a claim representative should be able to identify the potential liability exposures facing an insured. After reading this chapter and the next, students should have a basic understanding of the different ways in which insureds can become liable and also the defenses available to insureds for liability claims. The investigative tools and activities needed to assess liability are discussed in the next chapter. In most uses, claim professionals need not be lawyers to make liability decisions, but some complicated claims may require assistance from legal counsel.

Much of the civil law (the noncriminal law) in the United States is known as common law. **Common law** is judge-made law evolving from decisions on individual cases. Once common law has been adopted by the higher courts of a state, such as the state supreme court or the state appeals courts, all lower trial courts must follow that law in subsequent similar cases. This is the principle of **stare decisis** (to stand by things decided). Judges in trial courts have the discretion to determine whether the case at hand is similar enough to a previously decided case to invoke the principle of stare decisis. Common law can, and does, change over time.

Statutory law consists of written enactments by federal (Congress) or state legislative bodies or by other government officials. **Statutory law** is specifically embodied as written law known as statutes. Common law and statutory law must be considered together when assessing liability. A lawsuit based on statutory law must be interpreted by the courts. These two forms of law, common law and legislation, determine liability for most claims.

This chapter explains how liability is determined based on tort law. Detailed discussions of automobile, premises, and product liability are found in Chapters 11, 12, and 13.

---

*This chapter is adapted with permission from the reference source *Casualty Claim Practices*, 4th ed., 1995, written by Ken Brownlee, CPCU, and Patrick Magarick, J.D., LL.M., published by Clark, Boardman, Callahan, a division of West Group Publishing, St. Paul, Minn.

TORTS

A more detailed definition of a tort is a wrongful act or omission, arising in the course of social relationships, other than contracts, which violates a person's legally protected right, and for which the law provides a remedy in the form of an action for damages.[1]

The term **"tort"** means a civil wrong for which the victim can receive some form of compensation. A person or an entity committing a tort is a **tortfeasor**. Torts fall into three broad categories:

- Negligence
- Intentional torts
- Strict liability

Other laws and legal principles such as the rescue doctrine, joint and several liability, and *res ipsa loquitur* affect the determination of negligence. These concepts are described in detail following the sections covering the elements of negligence and the various types of negligence.

Civil tort law differs from criminal law in that a crime is an offense against society, while a tort is an offense against an individual or a group of individuals. The purpose in prosecuting a crime is to punish the offender, while the purpose of a tort action is to compensate the victim. Many acts can be both a crime and a tort. For example, the act of killing someone could be murder (a crime) and also wrongful death (a tort). An intoxicated driver who is involved in an auto accident could face both criminal charges for driving while intoxicated and a tort lawsuit by the injured parties for negligent operation of the auto.

Civil tort law differs from civil contract law in that the parties involved in tort law do not voluntarily enter into a specific agreement (as they do under contract law). For example, in contract law, the parties knowingly assume certain duties or obligations to each other. An insurance policy is an example of a contract in which the duties are specifically expressed. The insurance company must pay claims that are covered under the terms of the policy, and the insured must comply with specific duties in making a claim. In contrast, tort law duties are imposed by a general standard of conduct.

How is the standard of conduct specified in tort law? The common characteristic of all tort claims is that tortfeasors should be held liable for unreasonable conduct and their victims should receive compensation if this conduct caused injuries. The standard of what constitutes unreasonable conduct can be established by common law (court decisions) or statutory law (legislation). Determining whether conduct is tortious (unreasonable conduct based on established standards) is challenging, and most of this chapter deals with helping students understand how liability is determined in tort law. This discussion begins with the most common category of torts, negligence. Most claims that insurance claim representatives encounter involve negligence.

Negligence

Negligence involves conduct that creates an unreasonable risk of harm to another. Negligence has the following four elements:

1. Duty owed to others

2. Breach of the duty owed

3. Proximate causation

4. Damages

If any one of these elements does not exist in a given case, then there is no negligence. Claim representatives must examine each of these four elements in determining liability based on negligence. These elements are described below.

Determination of the Duty Owed and to Whom It Is Owed

Assessing the duty owed is the first step in determining negligence. As mentioned earlier, the duty owed may arise from common law or from statutes. Common-law duties can be general or specific. Examples of specific duties might be storing hazardous materials or complying with traffic regulations. Acting according to the standard of what an ordinary, reasonable person would do under similar circumstances is a general duty. A man who walks down a crowded street carrying a plate glass window over his head would have a duty to be very careful not to hit others with the window. This duty exists even if there is no specific law requiring this particular behavior.

To be deemed negligent, a person must first have a duty to exercise a level of care to protect others from harm. The level of care can vary depending on the circumstances. The chapters on auto liability, premises liability, and product liability will give examples of the duty owed in differing situations.

Determination of the Breach of Duty Owed

A person seeking damages must demonstrate not only the first element of negligence, that a duty was owed (and the degree of that duty), but also the second element, a breach of the duty owed. That is to say, the conduct of the insured fell below the standard of care owed to the claimant (in other words, a violation or breach of the duty owed). Claim representatives must use considerable judgment in assessing this element and base decisions on a detailed and thorough investigation. In an auto accident, the injured party would have to prove not only that the defendant owed a duty to drive the auto in a safe manner (which would be easy to establish) but also that the defendant breached this duty by failing to drive the vehicle in a safe manner (which would be more difficult to establish).

Determination of Causation (Proximate Cause)

Another necessary element of negligence is evidence that the breach of duty owed by one party caused the damages claimed by the other. Duties owed are often breached, but if those breaches do not cause damage (either directly or indirectly), then there is no liability. Courts look for an unbroken chain of events in determining whether an act is the **proximate cause** of a claimant's damages.

The question of causation often depends on whether the consequences are reasonably **foreseeable**. An adult might reasonably foresee that small children left unattended in a yard near a busy road might become excited and run into traffic or that an unrestrained dog with vicious tendencies might attack a person.

If a manufacturer produces a toaster that is defective and causes a house fire, the damages to the house would be reasonably foreseeable as a consequence of manufacturing the defective toaster. However, if as a result of the fire, the fire department is called to the scene and, en route to the scene, the fire truck hits a pedestrian, the defective toaster is not the proximate cause of the injury to the pedestrian. The injury to the pedestrian would not be the natural, probable result of making a defective toaster.

One landmark case dealing with causation involved a railroad worker who attempted to assist a man trying to board a train. The railroad worker accidentally knocked a package out of the passenger's arm. Unknown to the railroad worker, the package contained fireworks, which exploded when they fell. The shock of the explosion caused some parts of a structure to fall onto a woman waiting at the other end of the train platform. The court ruled that the railroad worker's act was not the proximate cause of the woman's injuries, and therefore he was not negligent because it was not reasonably foreseeable that his act would cause such an injury.[2] The injury was not a natural, probable consequence of the railroad worker's assisting a passenger onto a train.

In another well-known case, a court found a life insurance company liable for the death of a child because it negligently issued a life insurance policy on the child. The insurance company issued the policy to an aunt of the child who had no insurable interest in her nephew's life. The aunt poisoned the child, and the father sued the insurer for negligence in issuing the policy to the aunt. The court found the insurer liable, stating that the insurer should have foreseen that there is a risk of harm in issuing a policy on the life of a person when the policyholder has no insurable interest in the life of the insured.[3] Therefore the proximate cause of the child's death was the insurance company's issuance of a life policy to a person without an insurable interest.

People are responsible for the reasonably foreseeable consequences of their own acts. When the act of another comes between the original wrongful act and the resulting injury, then there might not be an unbroken chain of events leading to the damages. An intervening cause is anything that occurs after the defendant's breach of a duty that contributes to the victim's damages. This defense is discussed in detail later in this chapter. In the case of the life insurance policy on the child, described above, some other courts might conceivably have considered the aunt's actions as an intervening cause that would have absolved the insurer of liability.

Determination That Damages Resulted

For negligence to be proved, a fourth element is necessary: damages. Some type of compensable loss must result from the breach of duty. Every day, people commit acts that cause someone else unnecessary inconvenience. A customer service representative misinforms a customer; a cashier rings up the wrong price; or a manager makes a decision that causes others to do needless, redundant work. No matter how "negligent" these acts might appear, the inconvenience caused would not, in and of itself, normally cause actionable damage.

A common example of a liability claim that meets all three elements of negligence except for compensable damages involves the common "no damage" auto accident. While sitting in traffic, a driver becomes distracted and allows his car to roll into the car waiting in front of him. The bumpers of both cars absorb the impact, and there is no damage. The driver had a duty to operate the vehicle safely, and he breached that duty when he allowed his car to roll into the other, proximately causing the impact. However, if the impact did not cause any damage, then there is no liability. This type of claim is often controversial because some opportunistic victims have been known to exaggerate, or even fabricate, damages in these situations to create liability.

Furthermore, a person's actions may be "negligent," but because of the circumstances, no *additional* damages result beyond original damages not caused by the person. For example, a doctor performs surgery on a patient seriously wounded by a gunshot. The patient dies two hours after the operation as a result of the wounds. The doctor might have accidentally left a sponge in the person. However, if the patient's injury was so severe that he or she would have died from the gunshot wound anyway, the surgeon's negligence would not be considered the legal cause of the death. Therefore, the surgeon would not be liable for breach of the duty owed because this was not the proximate cause.

Methods for determining negligence in auto, premises, and product liability claims are covered later in the chapters devoted to those areas.

Negligent Entrustment

The doctrine of **negligent entrustment** presumes that people are aware that others might be likely to engage in negligent acts. A person who permits children to play with matches and gasoline should realize that the children might injure themselves or others. Similarly, a person who lends a car to a reckless or an incompetent person should reasonably foresee that the car could become a deadly weapon. These are examples of negligent entrustment. Negligent entrustment is alleged most commonly with vehicle owners who lend their vehicles to others and with employers who hire people without properly checking their backgrounds. Parents who entrust children with dangerous instruments such as weapons or automobiles can also become liable.

Negligence Per Se

Violation of a statute creates a presumption of negligence as a matter of law. For instance, a traffic ordinance mandating a fifteen-mile-per-hour speed limit in a school crossing establishes a duty to drive at this limit. A violation of this ordinance would be a breach of the duty. Such a breach would likely be considered **negligence per se,** which means negligence is presumed against the violator.

Courts have occasionally held that some facts indicate negligence as a matter of law. These cases usually involve circumstances in which the degree of care used was obviously inadequate under the circumstances. In rare instances, courts have found an absolute duty to comply with a statute and have refused to accept even reasonable excuses for the behavior. For example, a shop owner who sells a gun to a minor would likely be liable even if he could show that he sold the gun with the good faith belief that the minor was an adult.

A violation of an ordinance (even a local one) can establish negligence per se. For example, if an owner of a dog that bites a person violated a municipal "leash law" requiring the dog to be fenced in or on a leash, this would likely be considered negligence per se.

The purpose of the statute used to allege negligence per se should relate to a duty owed to the class of person injured. Consider the following case:

A farmer was sued by a motorist for allowing weeds to grow in a ditch that obstructed the motorist's view of traffic at an intersection. A local statute made it a criminal offense to "ship, sell or grow noxious weeds." The purpose of the statute was to protect farmers and ranchers from infestations of noxious weeds. Because the purpose of the statute was not designed to protect travelers on roadways, the court reasoned that the motorist could not claim negligence per se because the motorist was not in the class of persons intended to be protected by the statute.[4]

The motorist in this case would still have been able to allege that the farmer was negligent for failing to keep the grass from obstructing the view of motorists, but without being able to use negligence per se, it would be much more difficult to prove that there was a duty owed and that it had been breached by the farm owner in allowing the weeds to grow.

For negligence per se to be used, the violation of the law must be related to the breach of duty owed and must be the proximate cause of the damages. For example, if a person was injured by a vehicle owner who violated a state law requiring autos to be registered, then the failure to register the vehicle would not be considered negligence per se because its violation did not contribute to the accident. The failure to register was not the proximate cause.

> **Gross negligence** implies a failure to exercise even slight care. The act or omission must be of an exaggerated or aggravated nature. This type of willful and wanton conduct is almost indistinguishable from intentional harm in some jurisdictions. Gross negligence implies such disregard for the safety of others as to be unreasonable. It falls just short of deliberate and intentional action. The difference between gross and ordinary negligence is not well defined, but it is important for claim representatives to recognize aggravating circumstances that could affect damage awards. "Aggravating circumstances" are discussed in Chapter 8.

Claim representatives use the same general principles in determining negligence for auto, premises, and product liability claims. In each case a duty owed must be breached by the actions of the insured, and the claimant must incur damages proximately caused by the insured's actions. Claim representatives must also apply the principles of foreseeability and intervening causes. The differing aspects of negligence among auto, premises, and product claims are covered in the chapters devoted to those respective topics.

OTHER LAWS AND LEGAL PRINCIPLES AFFECTING NEGLIGENCE

Various legal doctrines affect the application of tort law. Examples of such doctrines include the rescue doctrine, joint and several liability, and *res ipsa loquitur*.

Rescue Doctrine

Under the **rescue doctrine**, the party causing an accident can be liable to any people involved in rescue efforts as a result of the accident. For example, a "good Samaritan" motorist is injured while aiding the driver of a car that negligently struck a bridge. The negligent driver could be liable for any injuries suffered by the good Samaritan. The rationale is that the motorist rescuing the driver would not have been in that dangerous situation had it not been for the driver's own negligence. This doctrine applies to serious or life-threatening situations in which a person of good conscience would feel obligated to help.[5]

In one case, a mother, seeing her pregnant daughter's car rear-ended, walked between her daughter's and the defendant's cars and was knocked down when a third car collided with the defendant's car. The driver causing the initial accident was also liable to the mother.[6] Some states do not permit police or firefighters to invoke the rescue doctrine because it is an essential part of their job to act as rescuers.

Under related good Samaritan laws, a negligent party may not be able to sue a rescuer. For example, a negligent driver is thrown onto the pavement. A rescuer stops and carries the person away from the traveled part of the roadway. While moving the negligent driver, the rescuer injures the driver's neck, causing the person to become paralyzed. Under a good Samaritan law, the rescuer perhaps could not be sued by the injured party for causing the neck injury. The situations covered by these good Samaritan laws vary by state. Some states still permit the first party to sue the good Samaritan rescuer if the rescuer acts in a negligent fashion. If, in the previous example, the negligent driver was already lying in a fairly safe location, out of traffic and off the traveled portion of the road, then moving the person might be considered negligent.

Joint and Several Liability

Joint tortfeasors are parties that act together in committing a civil wrong or parties whose independent acts unite to cause a single injury that cannot be easily apportioned among the wrongdoers. Acts of joint tortfeasors can occur at the same time (concurrently) or in sequence (successively).

Concurrent Joint Tortfeasors

When the independent, negligent acts of two or more parties combine to produce a single injury, the parties are concurrent joint tortfeasors. For example, Ann and Bert both cause an accident at the same time, and their combined negligence caused damages to Cathy. If the damages caused by Ann cannot easily be separated from those caused by Bert, then Ann and Bert are concurrent joint tortfeasors. As joint tortfeasors, they are jointly and severally liable for any injuries and damages suffered by Cathy.

What does joint and several liability mean to a claimant?

Perhaps this concept would be easier to understand if courts referred to it as joint and *separate* liability. Under the doctrine of joint and several liability, joint tortfeasors can be held *separately* responsible for the *entire* amount of a claimant's damages. This gives the claimant the advantage of choosing the tortfeasor (typically the one who has the "deeper pocket"). The claimant can receive only one satisfaction (payment of the amount of damages suffered) but can choose which tortfeasor to pursue for the entire claim. This often happens when one party is uninsured.

Not all claims involving two vehicles that cause an accident are joint tortfeasor claims. For example, assume Mary has completely stopped her car behind Lee's at a safe distance when Mary is struck by Paul and collided into Lee's auto. In this case, Mary is not negligent and is therefore not a tortfeasor; instead, she is a second victim of Paul's negligence. The only relationship she has to the third vehicle is that her car made contact with the claimant's.

Some legal observers argue that joint and several liability favors claimants too much because it allows them to "bring in" (legally join as defendants) parties who are remotely connected to an accident. For example, a pedestrian standing in a phone booth near a road is struck by an auto whose intoxicated driver was speeding. If the driver of the auto is uninsured, the pedestrian might try to bring in the owner of the telephone booth for placing the phone booth in an area that could be struck by an errant vehicle. Under the principle of joint and several liability, the claimant would need only to prove that the owner of the telephone booth was 1 percent at fault. If that could be established, then the owner of the telephone booth could be forced to pay the *entire* claim. Some states have modified the principle of joint and several liability to prevent such situations. Such modifications may apply only in limited circumstances. Claim representatives may need to seek guidance from legal counsel.

Successive Joint Tortfeasors

When the negligent acts of two or more parties do not combine to produce a single event (such as an auto accident) but do combine to produce the injury, the parties are **successive joint tortfeasors.** Damages caused by successive joint tortfeasors are often divisible and therefore require the claimant to seek payment from each tortfeasor individually.

For example, Dan's auto strikes Ethan's in the rear. Ethan pulls off to the side of the road to discuss the event with Dan. While they are talking, another driver, Fran, strikes Ethan and his car. The general rule is that each successive joint tortfeasor is individually responsible for the effects of his or her own act. In this case, the damage to Ethan and his auto might be divisible between Dan and Fran.

Res Ipsa Loquitur ("The Thing Speaks for Itself")

In some cases, the circumstances of an occurrence are such that negligence is presumed to have occurred and is attributed to the defendant even if there is no proof of a specific act of negligence by that defendant. The application of *res ipsa loquitur* (Latin for "the thing speaks for itself") gives the injured party a legal advantage. To invoke this doctrine, three elements must be present:

1. The instrumentality (tools or objects) that caused the accident must be in the defendant's exclusive control.

2. The accident must be one that did not happen in the ordinary course of events if those who have control exercise proper care.

3. The accident must not have been due to any negligence on the injured party's (the claimant's) part.

For example, a roofing contractor is performing work on the roof of a building, and a large bundle of roofing material falls from the roof of the two-story building and strikes a pedestrian on the sidewalk below. The pedestrian could invoke the doctrine of *res ipsa loquitur*. The pedestrian would need to establish that the roofing contractor had control of the roofing material, that roofing material does not normally fall off a roof unless there is negligence, and that the pedestrian did not contribute to the accident through his or her own negligence. In this case, it appears that all three elements of the doctrine would be present and the pedestrian could successfully invoke the doctrine of *res ipsa loquitur* to establish negligence on the part of the roofing contractor.

The doctrine of *res ipsa loquitur* has been applied in numerous situations, such as actions against the operators of autos and aircraft, actions against tenants in fire losses, claims against beauty shop operators for patrons' hair loss, claims against building owners for falling elevators, and claims against manufacturers of defective products.

NEGLIGENCE AND OTHER TORT DEFENSES

A thorough investigation and evaluation of the facts may reveal a number of defenses available to the tortfeasor. The defenses that should first be considered are those developed in the initial evaluation of the elements of negligence, such as:

1. The defendant did not owe a duty to the claimant,

2. The defendant did not breach the duty owed, and

3. The duty breached was not the proximate cause of the claimant's damages because the damages were not foreseeable or they were caused by a third party's act or a natural force.

These are basic defenses but are too often overlooked.

Claim representatives must also investigate other defenses as well, such as statutory defenses, negligence on the part of the claimant, assumption of risk, failure to heed a warning, or failure to take advantage of "the last clear chance" to avoid an accident. The following subsections are devoted to the defenses a defendant might have in tort actions commonly encountered in liability claim work.

Unforeseeability

As previously stated, one basis for negligence is the defendant's failure to act as an ordinarily prudent person would. Such a hypothetical person who cannot foresee a danger cannot be expected to take any action to avoid it. Responsibility is limited to situations in which an ordinarily prudent person could foresee danger under similar circumstances.

Because foreseeability comes in many gradations, it is difficult to establish a guideline that applies to all claims. Claim representatives often have difficulty determining foreseeability. The following hypothetical cases illustrate situations when the need for "greater care" was not foreseeable.

A store's customer falls on the sidewalk outside the store after tripping over a "quarter-sized piece of dried gum." Case law in the state holds that a premises owner can be held liable only when some condition poses an unreasonable degree of risk to others. Such a small defect in the premises' condition would not put a reasonably prudent premises owner on notice that a dangerous condition existed on the sidewalk.

The driver of an auto has a latent (undetected) problem with his heart. One day while driving, he unexpectedly suffers a heart attack. The car careens out of control and strikes another car in the oncoming lane of traffic. Because the driver had no knowledge of the heart condition, he could not foresee the heart attack and the accident following it. This case also raises the possibility of the defense of intervening cause, discussed in the following section.

Intervening Cause

As explained in the section on proximate cause, an **intervening cause** is a new and independent force that breaks the chain of connection between the original act of negligence by the defendant and the ultimate injury or damage to the claimant. An intervening cause is anything that occurs after the defendant's breach of a duty that contributes to the victim's damages. Such intervening cause may be sufficient to avoid liability on the part of the defendant for his or her original negligence. An intervening cause is an act or an event that causes the claimant's injury or damage. The timing of the act or event is *after* the defendant's original act of negligence.

For example, a truck driver drives over the speed limit on a snow-covered interstate highway. He loses control and jackknifes the tractor-trailer, which ends up blocking all the lanes of the highway. This accident causes traffic to back up for miles. Thirty minutes after this accident and three miles away from the original scene of the accident, another driver fails to notice that traffic has stopped and runs into the rear of a third car that is stopped. Although the original truck accident caused the traffic problems, the second driver's negligence is the intervening cause of the damages to the third car stopped on the interstate. Even though this type of accident might reasonably be a foreseeable consequence of blocking traffic, the driver of the tractor-trailer would not be liable because the damage to the stopped cars would be due solely to the intervening act of the second driver's negligence. The time and distance from the original accident are too far removed to make the trucker's accident the proximate cause of the damage to the stopped cars.

Act of God

An act of God (force of nature) may be the primary or intervening cause of an accident, and many jurisdictions accept this as a defense that relieves the defendant from liability. However, courts have, for the most part, held that for this rule to apply, the defendant must not have acted or failed to act in a way that contributed to the disastrous result. Forces such as tornadoes, floods, earthquakes, or similar upheavals are beyond human control. If, for example, a tornado lifted an automobile off the auto owner's driveway and dropped it onto a neighbor's house, the auto owner would not be liable for the damage to the neighbor's house. However, people who drive on roads made icy by an "act of God" (an ice storm) must nevertheless maintain control of their vehicles.

Contributory Negligence

The doctrine of contributory negligence originated in the English common law decision in Butterfield v. Forrester,[7] in which the court stated, "One person being at fault will not dispense with another's using ordinary care for himself."[8] The doctrine bars recovery by the claimant when the claimant's own negligence contributes to the accident and the resulting injury or damage to the claimant.

Contributory negligence requires that a claimant's own negligence contribute to the claimant's injuries. Contributory negligence bars recovery even when the claimant suffered injuries as a result of the chain of circumstances set in motion by the defendant's original negligence. Theoretically, the percentage of negligence with which the claimant can be charged is immaterial. According to the contributory negligence cases, even a slight degree of negligence on the part of a claimant would preclude compensation. Today, only a few states still permit contributory negligence because the doctrine is considered too harsh.[9] At the time of this writing, only five jurisdictions still allowed contributory negligence as a complete defense.[10] The harshness of the law also encourages exceptions that still exist in some states. When contributory negligence was the prevalent doctrine, a major exception was for acts that were willful and wanton. Such acts went beyond the scope of mere negligence when they were committed knowingly, intentionally, or in reckless disregard for the safety of others.

Comparative Negligence

Most states have now adopted comparative negligence laws in various forms. With **comparative negligence,** a court weighs the defendant's negligence against the claimant's negligence. If both parties caused an injury, then a percentage of negligence is attributed to each. Some states have "pure" comparative laws, while others have adopted a modified form of the law.

"Pure" Form of Comparative Negligence

Pure comparative negligence means that damages are apportioned according to the degree of negligence that each of the parties has in the accident. No matter how great the degree of the claimant's own negligence, as long as it is not 100 percent, a claimant may still recover for an amount discounted by his or her own negligence.[11] Under pure comparative negligence, a claimant who is 90 percent at fault for an accident can still collect 10 percent of his or her damages from the defendant.

"Modified" Form of Comparative Negligence

Modified comparative negligence excludes recovery by the claimant in circumstances in which the claimant's negligence was the major cause of the accident. Two thresholds of modified comparative negligence exist: 50 percent and 51 percent.

1. Under the "50 percent rule," recovery is permitted only if the negligence of the claimant is less than 50 percent
2. Under the "51 percent rule," recovery is permitted only if the claimant's negligence is no more than that of the defendant (50 percent or less).

Making decisions on whether a person is 50 or 51 percent at fault is challenging for courts.[12]

The following example compares pure comparative laws to contributory laws and to modified comparative law. These laws are discussed in more detail in Chapter 11 on auto liability.

EXAMPLE

Comparison of Pure Comparative Negligence to Contributory Negligence and Modified Comparative Negligence

Pam and Tom are involved in an auto accident. Pam is 10 percent at fault, and Tom is 90 percent at fault. Pam, who was not hurt in the accident, sustained $5,000 in damages to her car. Tom sustained serious injuries and damages totaling $60,000 for his luxury automobile.

Under Contributory Negligence:
Pam collects nothing from Tom.
Tom collects nothing from Pam.

Under Pure Comparative Negligence:
Pam recovers from Tom ($5,000 × 90%) = $4,500
Tom recovers from Pam ($60,000 × 10%) = $6,000

Under Modified Negligence (50 Percent Rule):
Pam collects $4,500.
Tom collects nothing because he is more than 50 percent at fault.

"Slight" Form of Comparative Negligence

The third and least common form of comparative negligence is known as "slight" negligence and is used in only two states. In slight comparative negligence, the claimant can recover if his or her fault was only "slight." The recovery is still reduced by the claimant's percentage of negligence. If the jury finds the claimant to be more than slightly negligent, then no recovery is permitted at all.[13]

Immunity

Immunity is a complete defense to a tort claim and is granted only to certain parties. Fewer immunities are permitted by law today because insurance has made many of the original reasons for the immunities obsolete. Parties historically granted immunity are governments, public officials charities, spouses, and parents.

Governmental (Sovereign) Immunity

The principle that a governmental entity is immune from tort liability for its employees' wrongful acts and omissions is known as **governmental immunity** (sometimes referred to as **sovereign immunity**). Governmental immunity can apply to the acts of federal, state, or local governments or to the acts of public officials such as judges or legislators.

Under the Federal Tort Claims Act (FTCA), the government can be sued for monetary damages "for loss of property or personal injury or death caused by the negligent act or omission of an employee of the federal government, under circumstances where the United States, if it were a private person, would be liable to the claimant."[14] Thousands of claims are made against the United States each year, many of them for auto accidents.

Some states have statutes similar to the FTCA in that they waive their immunity under certain circumstances. Many of these states also have set damage caps that limit how much a party can collect for a claim against the government. One million dollars is a common limit. Waivers of immunity vary widely by state, but two circumstances under which waivers occur are (1) when damages are caused by auto accidents and (2) when a problem has been reported to the government, but the government has failed to take measures to correct it.

> Many state statutes that waive immunity require claimants to file a written notice within a designated period of time. This requirement is important for claim representatives to know if they are pursuing contribution or subrogation against government entities.

Local municipalities, including police and fire departments, school districts, and public hospitals, have also enjoyed at least partial immunity. The key issue arising with local governments is whether the function performed is governmental or proprietary. In general, local governments are immune from liability for their governmental activities but may be sued for proprietary functions.

A **proprietary function** is one performed by the government that could just as easily be performed by a private entity. Operating gas and water utilities and casinos, maintaining public streets, and performing snow-removal operations are examples of activities sometimes conducted by governments that could be performed by private companies as well.

Planning where streets and bridges should be built is a function that only the government can perform because of the political nature of the activity. This would be a government function, and the government entity could claim immunity from any liability stemming from designing and planning the streets or bridges. However, a government could contract the construction of the streets and bridges to a private company. This would be a proprietary function, and therefore immunity would not be a viable defense for liability stemming from it. Even when local governments perform governmental functions, state laws may waive immunity under certain circumstances and up to specified damage amounts. Exhibit 5-1 summarizes how one state applies municipal governmental immunity.[15]

Claim representatives should check state statutes for claims potentially involving government entities.

Interestingly, acts performed by private entities that resemble governmental acts—such as community policing—are not immune from liability. Privatization of public safety is an increasingly common phenomenon. For example, many urban colleges have private police forces whose size rivals that of local public law enforcement. There are now around two million hired guards in the United States. This is twice the number in place in 1980. These security guards do not have immunity from liability for acts performed in the line of duty.[16] The immunity of police officers and firefighters is covered in the following section.

Official Immunity

As a general rule, police officers and firefighters have official immunity while performing discretionary acts within the scope of their duties. If the police receive two calls at the same time, they must choose, based on the information presented, which call to respond to first. If they make a mistake in setting priorities, they cannot be held liable for it, even if it was obvious from the information provided that they misprioritized the calls and it could be proved that they made a mistake in deciding the order in which to respond to the calls.

The preceding example illustrates a **discretionary act**. Discretionary acts require that judgment and reason be applied to the circumstances. They differ from **ministerial acts**, which are basically routine tasks performed in a pre-scribed manner, in obedience to a specific mandate, and without exercising personal judgment or opinion. Many public employees have immunity for their discretionary acts but not for ministerial acts. Distinguishing between the two can be difficult. In one case, an explosion occurred as part of a fertilizer exportation program run by the government. The court held that planning the way the fertilizer should be bagged, labeled, and transported required judgment and was therefore a discretionary act covered by immunity. However, the actions of the lower-level employees in carrying out these plans (in bagging, labeling, and transporting the fertilizer) were ministerial acts and therefore not immune from liability.[17]

EXHIBIT 5-1

Summary of Governmental Immunity in Pennsylvania Municipalities

Limitations on Liability

A political subdivision or an employee of a political subdivision can be liable only under the following situations:

- Harm caused by any self-propelled or motor vehicle operating in air, land, or sea, including by rail.

- Damage to property of others in care, custody, or control of the subdivision.

- Harm caused by real estate in possession of subdivision except if claimant intentionally trespasses on land or if harm is caused by real estate fixtures such as trees, lights, or utility fixtures owned by subdivision but located on property of another over which subdivision has a right of way.

- Harm caused by dangerous conditions of traffic controls, street lights, or trees in care, custody, or control of subdivision, provided subdivision should have found out about danger in time to take precautions.

- Harm caused by dangerous condition of utilities owned by subdivision but running across property of another, provided subdivision should have discovered danger in time to take precautions.

- Harm caused by dangerous condition of streets owned by subdivision and sidewalks within rights of way of streets owned by subdivision, provided subdivision should have discovered danger in time to take precautions.

- Harm caused by domesticated, but not wild, animals in care, custody, or control of subdivision.

Defenses

- Subdivision not liable for act of employee unless act is within scope of office or duties of employee.

- Subdivision not liable for act of employee if employee is guilty of fraud, criminal conduct, willful misconduct, or actual malice.

- All those defenses ordinarily available in any type of case, such as comparative negligence and assumptions of risk.

- Conduct was authorized or required by law, or employee in good faith reasonably believed the conduct was authorized or required by law.*

- Conduct was within the policymaking discretion granted to the employee by law.*

- The governing body or chief executive officer has absolute immunity.*

Are not available if conduct was a criminal act, actual fraud, willful misconduct, or actual malice.

Examples of acts some courts deemed discretionary and thus "cloaked in" (covered by) official immunity include the following:

- Intermingling of patients and employees in a state-run mental-health hospital;[18]
- Supervising and maintaining a 911 emergency number system;[19]
- Designing policies and standards for prisons;[20]
- Maintaining a swimming area in a public park; and[21]
- Inspecting daycare centers.[22]

Public officials also have immunity for their wrongful acts and omissions. A public official's immunity is separate from governmental immunity. The public duty doctrine holds that a public official may not be held liable for the breach of a duty owed to the general public. Judges and legislatures, as well as other public officials, receive complete immunity as long as they act within the scope of their duties. This official immunity is broad.

> Although immunity for public officials is broad, these officials still commonly have public official liability insurance to protect them from claims alleging that they abused their authority and acted outside the scope of their immunity.

The purpose of this immunity is to allow public officials to carry out their duties without fear of being sued. Few competent people would choose to seek public office if they felt they would be sued constantly for their decisions. If, for example, a judge makes an error in allowing evidence against a party in a lawsuit, that party cannot sue the judge for the error even if the party has to incur additional legal expenses to file an appeal.

Charitable Immunity

In the past, charitable organizations, including educational and religious organizations, received immunity under common law. The purpose of this immunity was to prevent tort claims against them and to help continue their existence. Most states have abolished charitable immunity. Some states have allowed liability when liability insurance is available but have denied liability when payments must be made from the charities' trust funds, reasoning that the funds were donated for charitable purposes and could not be diverted to pay judgments from tort claims.

Family Member Immunity

Historically, children could not sue their parents, and husbands and wives could not sue each other. The basis for family immunity was to preserve family harmony. Family member immunity has been discontinued, especially with auto liability claims, because of the existence of mandatory auto liability insurance. The purpose for preserving immunity seems obsolete to some courts when insurance is available to pay for injuries to a family member. In situations in which insurance is not readily available, some courts have maintained family member immunity.

Because of a trend toward limiting or abolishing parental immunity, especially for motor vehicle accidents, claim representatives often find it difficult to determine whether a particular jurisdiction will continue to hold to the doctrine. Several states still hold to the doctrine of parental immunity in non-auto accidents in which mere negligence is involved, but they make exceptions when a child is emancipated or suffers sexual abuse.

Claim representatives should consider parental liability when an insured is involved in a claim with a minor and should investigate the circumstances to determine whether the minor's parents were negligent in their supervision of the child. Consider a claim in which a mother negligently failed to supervise her three-year-old son, who ran into traffic and was struck by the insured defendant. If the state does not have parental immunity, the mother could be brought into the claim as a third party responsible for the injury to the child; i.e., the defendant could sue and seek contribution from the mother.

Interspousal immunity arose out of the concept that a husband and wife were one entity and could not therefore sue each other. The majority of states have abolished interspousal immunity, rejecting the notion of the unity of husband and wife as well as the argument that lawsuits create family discord. No immunities exist for siblings or other family members.

Assumption of Risk

One who voluntarily enters a dangerous situation, with full knowledge of that danger, is deemed to have assumed the risk of possible injury, thus relieving the defendant of liability. Assumption of risk is commonly applied in cases of sports activities in which the claimant is either a participant or spectator, although it may be applied in many other circumstances. The assumption of risk defense has been used in claims in which the claimant decided to ride in a car driven by an obviously intoxicated person.

The following are two essential elements of assumption of risk:

1. Knowledge and understanding of the risk involved, and
2. Voluntary assumption of the risk.

In recent years, many courts have combined assumption of risk with comparative negligence. Courts held that because contributory negligence was abolished as a complete defense, the doctrine of assumption of risk should no longer be available as a complete bar to recovery.[23] These courts argued that the facts used to show an assumption of risk could be used in a comparative negligence defense to illustrate the claimant's negligence and thus reduce the amount of damages owed to the claimant. Adoption of comparative negligence has increasingly led to the demise of the assumption of risk defense, but some states still continue to permit its use.[24] Indeed, assumption of risk can apply in circumstances in which no negligence exists, such as in some sports activities. For example, a person engaged in downhill skiing assumes the risk of falling and being injured, yet the choice to ski is not itself negligent.

Statute of Limitation

Another defense that completely bars recovery is statutes of limitation (or statutes of repose for warranty cases). A **statute of limitation** is a law that limits the time during which a claimant can file a lawsuit. No one can bring a lawsuit after that time has expired. The purpose of the statute is to protect persons from having to defend against "stale" lawsuits. Over time, memories fade, witnesses move, and evidence is lost. Statutes for tort claims typically range from two to five years depending on the state. Most states have different limitations for tort claims and breach of contract claims. Uninsured or underinsured motorist claims may have longer statutes of limitation because these claims are based on insurance contracts.

Breach of warranty claims (discussed later in this text under product liability claims) are another example of an area in which the injured party may have a different statute of limitation than the one based on tort law.

In tort claims, the statute of limitation begins running when the cause of action "accrues." Most courts hold that accrual occurs when the accident took place, not necessarily when it was first reported to the defendant. If an injury results from an auto accident occurring on March 1, 1995, and the state has a five-year statute of limitation on auto injuries, then the statute would run until March 1, 2000. This statute of limitation bars recovery even if the claimant did not make a claim until much later or if the injury became more serious over time.

A problem arises when the injury is unknown even to the claimant—for example, if a person has an operation and the surgeon leaves a sponge inside his or her body. Say that this patient does not know the cause of any complications from the surgery for two years. If the state has a two-year statute of limitation on medical malpractice, the claim would be barred unless exceptions could be made to the statute. To mitigate this problem, many states have created the **discovery doctrine**, which provides that the statute does not begin to run until an injury is discovered or should have been discovered. Some states have applied this rule to construction defects that are not discovered until years later. Claim representatives should know the statutes of limitation for the states where they handle claims and should consult with claim management or legal counsel if they have questions. This defense would also apply to intentional torts and strict liability claims.

INTENTIONAL TORTS

Intentional torts differ from negligence in that they are not fortuitous (not accidental). Instead, they result from deliberate actions. The first intentional torts presented in this section are expressly covered offenses under the commercial general liability (CGL) policy Coverage B—Personal and Advertising Injury Liability. Although the purpose of this chapter is not to describe coverage issues, it is important for claim representatives to understand that some "intentional torts" are still potentially covered even if the intentional torts are not expressly stated in the policy. Legitimate disagreements occur over whether the perpetrator intended the damages. Some intentional torts, such as assault, battery, and even defamation, are also crimes. Exhibit 5-2 below, compares crimes to intentional torts. The following is a list of intentional torts described in this chapter

- False arrest, imprisonment, or detention
- Malicious prosecution
- Wrongful eviction
- Defamation or disparagement
- Invasion of privacy
- Breach of confidentiality
- Copyright or trademark infringement
- Interference with business relationships
- Assault and battery
- Intentional infliction of emotional distress
- Conversion
- Trespass

EXHIBIT 5-2

Comparison of Intentional Torts to Crimes

	Intentional Torts	**Crimes**
Legal Basis	Civil law—mainly common law	Criminal statutes
Action of Parties Involved	A person injured files a lawsuit against the wrongdoer.	The state or federal prosecutor files charges against the wrongdoer.
Burden of Proof	Plaintiff must prove case with preponderance of evidence. (The weight of evidence must favor plaintiff.)	State (or other prosecuting authority) must prove defendant guilty beyond a reasonable doubt.
Damages (Punishment)	Out-of-pocket expenses, general damages, punitive damages.	Fines, imprisonment, probation, community service execution.

False Arrest, Imprisonment, or Detention

False arrest or imprisonment is the intentional, unprivileged detaining of a person without his or her consent. It need not be a physical restraint. Neither ill will nor malice is required to constitute this tort.[25] A show of apparent authority or the apparent threat of physical force is all that is usually necessary. False arrest or detention is often alleged by persons arrested or detained for suspected shoplifting. If, for example, a security guard restrains a person suspected of shoplifting, it is not uncommon for the suspected shoplifter to make a counterclaim for false arrest, detention, or imprisonment.

Retail outlets using security guards are a common target for this type of claim. False arrest complaints are often made in conjunction with other allegations such as assault, battery, defamation, false imprisonment, and intentional or negligent infliction of emotional distress. Claim representatives should carefully check their claim databases when these types of claims are alleged because some claimants have a history of making these claims whenever they are accused of shoplifting.

Malicious Prosecution

Generally, four components must be met in order to prove malicious prosecution.

1. The defendant (party who filed the original criminal charges) filed charges for a criminal prosecution against the claimant,
2. The case was resolved in favor of the claimant (the party accused),
3. The defendant was motivated by malice in filing charges against the claimant, and
4. The defendant filed charges without probable cause.

Juries tend to be sympathetic to people who have been accused wrongfully.

The following is a hypothetical case example illustrating malicious prosecution.

Case Example—Malicious Prosecution

A homeless man loiters on or around the premises of a pharmacy. He occasionally enters the store to buy items. The insured pharmacy is annoyed by his presence and complains to the police that the man was stealing cigarettes. The police and the pharmacy have no proof of such an offense other than that he had a new pack in his pocket, which he claimed to have purchased at another store. The police pursue the case, it goes to trial, and the man is found innocent of the crime. The homeless man's court-appointed lawyer shows that the charges against the man were motivated strictly by the fact that he was homeless and perceived by the pharmacy as bad for business. He then became a claimant and filed suit against the pharmacy for malicious prosecution.

One defense available in most states is "reasonable cause." Claimants cannot successfully sue for malicious prosecution if the defendant can prove "reasonable grounds" for believing that a wrongdoing was committed. In this case, many courts would not find the pharmacy's charges against the homeless man to be based on "reasonable grounds," and the pharmacy would therefore be at risk for an adverse verdict on the malicious prosecution.

Wrongful Eviction

Evicting a tenant recklessly and unjustly would be an example of wrongful eviction. However, a tenant-landlord relationship does not have to exist for this tort to occur. A property owner or tenant who wrongfully evicts unruly patrons or guests might also be guilty of wrongful eviction. The following case illustrates how broad the term "eviction" can be.

Because he was African-American, a man was denied the right to play at a country club hosting a school tournament. The Court of Appeals held that the failure of the country club to allow the man, a member of the local high-school tennis team, to play in the high-school tennis match at the club constituted "eviction." The fact that the "eviction" was based on race made it wrongful eviction.[26]

Defamation and Disparagement

Defamation is an intentionally false communication that injures another person's reputation or exposes the person to hatred or contempt by the community.[27] Written defamation is called **libel**, while oral defamation is known as **slander**. Disparagement is a term traditionally used to refer to false statements about another's goods or services.[28] **Disparagement** (of reputation) is communication of false statements about the business practices of a person or company that damage the company in the public's eye. The three common elements of defamation, whether libel or slander, are as follows:

1. A false statement tending to hold the person or organization up to public disgrace

2. Publication of the statement

3. Damages

If the owner of a garage runs an advertisement on the radio accusing another garage owner of padding repair bills and the accusation is untrue, then the business lost by the second garage owner would be damages for which he or she could sue the other owner. "Publication" need not be to the entire community to be defamation.

The following case illustrates defamation as libel and disparagement:

An advertising manager for *Playboy* magazine wrote a letter to eleven of the magazine's advertisers alleging that a competitor, *Penthouse* magazine, had failed to meet circulation guarantees it had made to its advertisers. *Penthouse* sued *Playboy* for libel and other related torts.[29]

Courts debate the issue of damages for defamation claims because sometimes it is difficult to prove how a slanderous remark or libelous writing causes harm. Some types of defamation are actionable without proving damages. Slander affecting a person's business or trade, such as calling a lawyer a "crook," is an example of this type of offense.[30]

A common situation in which defamation is alleged involves a terminated employee. This is especially true if the termination is mishandled and false or unsupported comments are made about the departing employee.[31]

Truth is a defense to defamation. Defendants can escape liability by proving that the statement they made was true. Determining the truthfulness of such statements is one of the tasks of the claim representative handling the investigation of defamation claims. However, making true but damaging statements does not prevent a claimant from filing suit. In such a situation, the insurer would owe the defendant a duty to defend against the lawsuit. It is wise to encourage insureds not to make damaging statements even if the statements can be proved true.

Invasion of Privacy and Breach of Confidentiality

The right of privacy is the right of an individual to be left alone to live a life of seclusion, free of unwarranted publicity. A wrongful invasion of that right may give rise to a tort claim.

Invasion of privacy can also include publishing information about another person's private affairs that causes shame or humiliation. For example, sharing private medical records indicating that a person suffers from an illness, without that person's permission, would be an example of invasion of privacy. Publicizing that a person who is not a public figure has a sexually transmitted disease would probably be considered unreasonable and not a matter of legitimate public interest. Public figures such as politicians, entertainers, and athletes have great difficulty asserting claims for invasion of privacy because their personal lives are considered legitimate matters of public interest.

Another aspect of privacy involves physical or electronic intrusion on a person's privacy. Examples include interference with personal mail or telephone conversations, trespassing into a person's home, photographing a person in the privacy of his or her home without the person's consent, and electronically eavesdropping on a person's private conversation.

Liability claim investigations that are overly aggressive or clumsily performed run the risk of triggering an invasion of privacy claim. Examples of activities that might be considered invasions of privacy include:

- Publishing private medical information about an insured or a claimant,
- Obtrusive surveillance and photography of a claimant in the seclusion of the claimant's home,
- Wiretapping telephone lines,
- Electronically monitoring a claimant's cellular telephone calls,
- Secretly recording conversations that a claimant has with his or her family, and
- Harassing a claimant with requests for interviews at all hours of the day and night.

Breach of confidentiality, which is the misuse of confidential information, can also be considered a tort, similar to invasion of privacy. The following case examples illustrate breaches of the duty of confidentiality.

Claim representatives are sometimes frustrated by hospitals and doctors who are reluctant to release medical histories. The reason for this reluctance is that healthcare providers can become liable if they release information that is beyond the scope of the authorization.

CASE EXAMPLES—BREACH OF CONFIDENTIALITY

Case 1

A hospital turned over to a law firm thousands of patient registration forms containing detailed information about their medical conditions, including diagnoses of alcohol and drug abuse, mental illness, and sexually transmitted diseases. The law firm was supposed to review the files and find potential Social Security claimants as a way to help the hospital collect unpaid medical bills from patients. The court ruled that such a broad disclosure of personal medical records by the hospital to the law firm violated the patients' privacy. To make matters worse, a disgruntled law firm employee sent copies of the registration forms to a local television station to "expose the breach of confidentiality" by the hospital. This employee's act constituted an invasion of privacy by the law firm. The state supreme court agreed to recognize an independent tort for the unauthorized, unprivileged disclosure to a third party of nonpublic medical information that a physician or hospital had gathered within the patient-physician relationship.[32]

Case 2

A patient signed an authorization for release of treatment information, allowing a mental-health center to transmit treatment information about the person to a third party. The mental-health center released a complete record of the patient's treatment, including past treatment for sexual addiction. The patient successfully sued the mental-health center for releasing this information because the treatment for sexual addiction preceded the time period covered by the authorization. The court held this release of information to be unauthorized.[33]

Copyright or Trademark Infringement

Copyrights and trademarks apply to intellectual property, and misappropriating this property is a tort. **Infringement of copyright** is the unauthorized use of copyrighted material (or use without permission of the copyright holder). The symbol © may be affixed to copies of a copyrighted work, but even works without this symbol are protected. The date of the copyrighted material usually appears next to this abbreviation (for example, © 1999 Insurance Institute of America). Copyrighted material can take the form of literature, music, pictures, graphics, sculptures, and audiovisual recordings. If, for example, a pharmaceutical company used the Beatles' song, "A Hard Day's Night" to advertise its sleep aid product without getting permission, the manufacturer would be committing copyright infringement.

Infringement of trademark or **service mark** is the unauthorized use or imitation of another's trademark or service mark. Trademarks are the distinctive emblems, marks, logos, mottoes, or slogans that a company affixes to its products to help promote the products. Service marks distinguish the company's services. Either the abbreviation ™ or ® is affixed to trademarks. Post-it® is an example of a trademark used by the 3M Corporation. The Institutes use the following service mark (logo):

Infringement of trade dress is another tort. Trade dress relates to the non-functional physical detail and design of a product or its packaging, which indicates or identifies the product's source and distinguishes it from the products of others. The brown packaging of plain M&Ms® and the yellow packaging of peanut M&Ms® are distinctive packaging that illustrate examples of trade dress. Trade dress includes color schemes, textures, sizes, designs, shapes, and placements of words, graphics, and decorations on a product or its packaging. A growing trade dress issue involves the look, color, and design of company Web sites. Trade dress elements, taken as a whole, are not essential to products' uses, nor do they affect the cost or quality of products even though certain particular elements of the trade dresses may be functional. Claim representatives handling commercial liability claims should be able to distinguish between infringement of trade dress and trademark. Trade dress is expressly covered under the 1998 commercial general liability (CGL) policy, but infringement of trademark is not.

Copyright and trademark infringement claims are becoming more prevalent because of the Internet. A click of a computer mouse can copy a company logo from the company's Web site. Whole texts, pictures, and works of art are found on the Internet and can easily be copied electronically. Many people have the misconception that material can be used without permission if it is available on the Internet. Legally, there is no distinction between copying a book or musical recording and copying material from the Internet.

Patent infringement is a related intellectual property tort. An inventor who holds a patent for an invention may enforce the right to exclude others from making, using, or selling the patent invention in an action for patented infringement. Patent infringement involves using or selling—without the owner's consent—any product, process, or apparatus of a legally protected item (one for which a patent may have been filed). A person may directly infringe a patent without knowing of the patent or intending to infringe it. Good faith is not a defense to a claim of direct infringement.

Interference With a Business Relationship

Infringement of copyrights, patents, and trademarks and defamation or disparagement of the company's reputation fall within the broad category of **business torts**. These torts involve the wrongful obstruction of the business rights of others. **Interference with business relations** is another example of a business tort.

One such example of this business tort is interference with making a contract. Companies have a right to form contracts with customers, suppliers, and employees as a normal part of business operations. This right is recognized as a property right, and the law opposes interference with it. Intentionally inducing a person or company from entering into a contract is an example of interference with the making of a contract. Claim representatives can expose themselves to allegations of tortious interference if they attempt in some way to keep insureds from entering into contracts with public adjusters or attorneys. Telling insureds that they are wasting their money by hiring public adjusters or attorneys would expose a claim representative to an allegation of interference with the business relations of these parties and insureds.

Interference with performance of the contract is another example of wrongful interference. One well-publicized case involving interference with contract performance is Texaco, Inc. v. Pennzoil.[34] In this case, Pennzoil agreed to purchase a part of Getty Oil for $110 per share and a Memorandum of Agreement was drafted. One month later, Texaco, knowing of the agreement, went to Getty and offered $125 per share to sell to Texaco. Getty agreed to do so, and Pennzoil sued Texaco for tortiously inducing Getty to break its agreement to sell shares to Pennzoil. The court awarded Pennzoil $9 billion.

The tort of interference with business relations can occur even without a contract. If, for example, the owner of Bob's Videos stations his employees outside Mary's Movies to induce customers not to shop at Mary's, Bob (the owner) could be accused of tortious interference with Mary's customer relations. Companies are not held liable for normal business efforts to attract customers to their own business—only when their aggressive efforts prevent specific customers of competitors from doing business are they held liable. For example, if Frank is test-driving a new car from Metro Motors, hears on the radio that Reliable Motors is offering free financing on cars, and decides to go to Reliable, Reliable cannot be held liable for tortious interference. Interference requires a *direct* attempt to *divert specific customers* from a business. Ads designed to attract customers and targeted to the general public at large are permissible. Some specific actions, such as union picket lines, are also permitted forms of "interference."

Assault and Battery

Assault and battery is a legal phrase commonly tied to criminal law, but assault and battery are also civil torts. An **"assault"** may be a physical or verbal (or even implied) threat of causing injury or death. The **"battery"** is the actual physical contact. Common defenses to such accusations include self-defense, defense of life or property, or even misinterpretation of the action claimed. Commonly, the issue that a claim representative must resolve is whether an expression of anger over something constitutes an "assault."

An example of an assault would be a security guard in a mall approaching a person suspected of shoplifting and shouting at the person, "I'm going to crack your head open, you little sneaky thief." Battery would occur if he followed through on this threat. But the term "battery" is broader than violent physical abuse. Battery has been construed to mean any unwanted physical touching of a person. Sexual harassment claims, for example, often allege battery because of the element of unwanted touching. Although in criminal cases the two charges are often made together, an assault (a bodily threat) can occur without battery, and battery can occur without an assault.

Intentional Infliction of Emotional Distress

Extreme and outrageous deliberate conduct that causes another party mental anguish is **intentional infliction of emotional distress**. The following are the elements of this tort:

1. The misconduct is intentional or reckless.

2. The misconduct is extreme or outrageous.

3. The misconduct leads to emotional distress (and damages).

4. The emotional distress must be severe.

First, the conduct must occur to deliberately inflict harm on a person who, in turn, suffers severe emotional distress. The emotional distress should be foreseeable from the type of harm inflicted. The second element requires the misconduct to be extreme or outrageous. *Outrageous conduct* goes beyond mere insults, indignities, threats, annoyances, or petty oppressions. An example of outrageous conduct would be fabricating a tragic story to watch the reaction of the listener for the teller's personal amusement. If, for example, a person lied to a mother and told her that her child's daycare had just been attacked by a gunman, the person telling this lie would be guilty of outrageous conduct.

Intentional infliction of emotional distress is alleged much more than it is successfully proved, such as in employment liability claims in which a supervisor insults and humiliates an employee. This tort is also alleged in bad faith lawsuits against insurance carriers for wrongful refusal to pay claims. Most courts would not view these examples as sufficiently meeting the criterion of being outrageous.

Conversion

Conversion is a tort involving physical property but not necessarily damage to that property. **Conversion** is usually the wrongful assumption of ownership over items of personal property. Burglary, robbery, and larceny are examples of wrongful possession of another's property, but conversion may be less sinister. Consider the following example:

A restaurant has valet parking, and the parking attendant takes possession of the car to park it. The attendant has the right to park the car at the attendant's discretion, but if, instead of parking the car, the attendant takes the car on a joy ride while the owner is dining at the restaurant, the parking attendant has committed conversion. The parking lot attendant had legal right of possession of the vehicle initially. However, this right of possession "converted" to an illegal possession when the attendant took the car for a joy ride. Conversion is sometimes alleged against garage owners who take customer cars left at their shop for repairs and use them for their own personal activities.

Trespass/Nuisance

Trespass is wrongfully entering (however briefly) the property of another person. Trespass must be physical, but it need not involve bodily entry; it can also be indirect. Throwing a brick at a neighbor's house would be a trespass even if the person who threw the brick never entered the neighbor's property. Bothering the neighbors with loud noises or bright lights would not be a trespass, but fumes or underground contaminants that migrate to another's property would be. A lawsuit may allege trespass (criminal, intentional, or civil) where the uninvited occupancy has caused some element of damage or has exposed the claimant to some related action. For example, parking an automobile over a railroad siding might be a trespass on the railroad's right-of-way, resulting in delay costs to the railroad. Another legal concept called nuisance is much broader and includes "noise pollution."

Nuisance

A precise definition of "nuisance" does not exist. This term can cover a host of wrongful acts. In its broadest meaning, a **nuisance** is a wrongful maintenance or use of property that results in some damage or injury. Keeping a quantity of dynamite in a dangerous place or manner is a nuisance. Noxious fumes, ringing of bells, and erecting dangerous structures can all be nuisances depending on the circumstances.

A property owner may be responsible for a nuisance—for creating it and for permitting it to remain. The owner may also be liable for taking possession of and ownership over property where a nuisance has been erected and knowingly permitting it to remain.

The two types of nuisance are public nuisance and private nuisance. A **public nuisance** exposes the general public to the possibility of injury. It is an interference with a right common to the general public. Maintenance of a hog farm close to a residential area is an example of a public nuisance because it exposes the general public to harm.

Playing loud music late at night is an example of a **private nuisance.** Another example would be a blasting operation that exposes neighboring landowners to fumes and noise. The blasting operation also could lead to a trespass claim if the dynamite caused particles to fall onto neighboring land.

The law permits some nuisances in some cases. For instance, the blowing of a loud train whistle when the train crosses a street intersection might ordinarily be considered objectionable but may be permitted by law because of its very useful purpose.

STRICT LIABILITY IN OTHER THAN PRODUCT LIABILITY CLAIMS

The doctrine of strict liability is often used with product liability (and will be discussed later in the chapter on product liability). But strict liability can also apply to areas other than products. Strict liability can be invoked in claims involving dangerous instrumentality, dangerous (ultrahazardous) activities, aircraft, and owning wild animals. Strict liability is imposed without a finding of negligence.

Dangerous Instrumentalities

When an obviously dangerous instrumentality is being used, stored, or transported, the highest degree of care is required. Thus, one who stores nitroglycerin, for instance, should use every precaution to avoid injury or damage to others arising from the explosion of the nitroglycerin. A similar example is the storage of inflammable gas or explosives in populated areas where the danger of a mishap is obvious. Crop-dusting chemicals are so dangerous that the highest degree of care is necessary to avoid injuring crops not involved in the dusting, animals, and human beings.

Abnormally Dangerous Activities

Other examples of situations that call for the highest degree of care involve dangerous activities. Strict liability applies to dangerous activities such as the erection or maintenance of dams; the drilling of oil wells, particularly off shore; some mining operations of a particularly dangerous nature; and other operations that are potentially very hazardous. The Restatement (Second) of Torts helps to define a dangerous activity.

The Restatement (Second) of Torts, 520, provides:

"In determining whether an activity is abnormally dangerous, the following factors are to be considered: (a) whether the activity involves a high degree of risk of some harm to the person, land or chattels of others; (b) whether the gravity of the harm which may result from it is likely to be great; (c) whether the risk cannot be eliminated by the exercise of reasonable care; (d) whether the activity is not a matter of common usage; (e) whether the activity is inappropriate to the place where it is carried on; and (f) the value of the activity to the community."[35]

Blasting operations are another example of a dangerous activity. People who use dynamite or other explosives in blasting operations do so at their own peril. In most jurisdictions, they are held absolutely responsible for damage or injury as a result of flying debris.

Wild Animals

Another area to which strict liability applies is the care and maintenance of wild animals. When an animal's dangerous propensities are known, or should have been known, the owner is strictly liable. Even in cases involving domestic animals, such as dogs, when the owner knew or should have known of the vicious propensities of the animal, courts will impose strict liability regardless of negligence. Proving "dangerous propensities" requires demonstrating that the animal's actions were foreseeable.[36] Most of the states holding owners strictly liable for animals do so by means of statutes rather than common law. Chapter 12 has a section on dog-bite claims and describes the criteria that some municipalities use to determine whether a dog is dangerous.

Aircraft

A number of states hold owners or lessees of aircraft strictly responsible for any damage that occurs resulting from any accident involving the aircraft. Because courts already require a greater degree of responsibility for aircraft than for ordinary vehicles, such state statutes are in the minority because they seem redundant.

SUMMARY

This chapter explains that torts fall into three categories:

- Negligence
- Intentional torts
- Strict liability

The four elements of negligence—(1) a duty owed, (2) a breach of the duty, (3) proximate causation, and (4) damages—must all be present for a party to be negligent. Conduct that breaks a specified law can create a presumption of negligence. This is known as negligence per se.

Intentional torts such as assault and battery are not commonly covered by insurance, but it can sometimes be difficult for claim representatives to establish that the resulting injury or damages to a claimant were intended by an insured. For that reason, claim representatives should understand how intentional torts can lead to liability. In addition, a few intentional torts are covered under commercial policies.

A number of defenses exist for people accused of committing a tort. Common defenses include the following:

- Unforeseeability
- Intervening cause
- Act of God
- Contributory or comparative negligence
- Immunity
- Assumption of risk
- Statute of limitations

This chapter described how one party, usually an insured, becomes liable to another party based on the insured's own conduct. The following chapter describes how one party can become liable for acts of another and how multiple parties can end up in the same claim or lawsuit.

CHAPTER NOTES

1. Henry Campbell Black, *Black's Law Dictionary*, 6th ed. (St. Paul: Minn.: West Publishing, 1990).
2. Palsgraf v. Long Island Rail Company, 162 N.E. 99 (N.Y. 1928).
3. Liberty National Life Insurance Company v. Weldon, 107 So. 2d 696 (Alabama 1965).
4. Hidalgo v. Cochise County, 13 Ariz. App. 27 (1970).
5. Lowrey v. Horvath, 689 S.W. 2nd 625 (Mo. 1985).

6. Hughes v. Polk, 634, 199 N.W. 2d 224 (Mich. App. 1972).

7. Butterfield v. Forrester, 11 East 60 (1809).

8. William L. Prosser, *Prosser & Keeton on Torts*, 5th ed. (1984), p. 65.

9. Ala.: Golden v. McCurry, 392 So. 2nd 815 (Ala. 1980) (court stated that any change should come from the legislature).

   Md.: Harrison v. Montgomery County Dept. of Education, 456 A. 2nd 894 (295 Md. 422, 1983).

   Tenn.: Gross v. Nashville Gas Co., 608 S. W. 2nd (Tenn. Ct. App. 1980).

10. Ala.: Allman v. Cox, 75 A. 2nd 110, 130 So. 2nd 194 (1961).

    D.C.: Robers v. Cox, 75 A. 2nd 776 (D.C. Mun. Ct. App. 1950).

    Md.: Gutterman v. Biggs, 249 Md. 421, 240 A. 2nd 260 (1968).

    N.C.: Miller v. Miller, 273 N.C. 228, 160 S.E. 2nd 65 (1968).

    Va.: Smith v. Virginia Electric & Power Co., 204 Va. 128, 129 S.E. 2nd 655 (1963).

11. Alas.: Kaatz v. State, 540 P. 2nd 1037 (Alaska 1975).

    Cal.: Li v. Yellow Cab Col., 13 Cal. 3rd 804, 119 Cal. Rptr. 858, 832 P. 2nd 1226, 40 Cal. Comp. Cas. (MB) 258, 78 A.L.R. 3rd 393 (1975).

    Fla.: Hoffman v. Jones, 280 So. 2nd 431, 78 A.L.R. 3rd 321 (Fla. 1973).

    Ill.: Alvis v. Ribar, 85 Ill. 2nd 1, 52 1, 52 Ill. Dec. 23, 421 N.E. 2nd 886 (1981); Coney v. J.L.G. Industries, Inc., 97 Ill. 2nd 104, 73 Ill. Dec. 337, 454 N.E. 2nd 197, Prod. Liab. Rep. (CCH), p. 9617 (1983).

    Iowa: Goetzman v. Wichern, 327 N.W. 2nd 742 (Iowa 1982).

    Kan.: Kennedy v. Sawyer, 228 Kan. 439, 618 P. 2nd 788, Prod. Lia. Rep. (CCH) p. 8810 (1980) (in product liability cases only).

    Ky.: Hilen v. Hays, 673 S.W. 2nd 713 (Ky. 1984)(because it is fairer, simple to administer, and more just).

    La.: By statute.

    Mich.: Placek v. Sterling Heights, 405 Mich. 638, 275 N.W. 2nd 511 (1979).

    Miss.: By statute.

    Mo.: Gustafson v. Benda, 661 S.W. 2nd 11 (Mo. 1983).

    Mont.: Trust Corp. of Montana v. Piper Aircraft Corp., 506 F. Supp. 1093, Prod. Liab. Rep. (CCH) p. 8939 (D. Mont. 1981) (products liability case).

    N.H.: Hanson v. N. H. Pre-Mix Concrete, 110 N.H. 377, 268 A. 2nd 841 (1970).

    N.Y.: By statute.

    N.D.: Day v. General Motors Corp., 345 N.W. 2nd 349, Prod. Liab. Rep. (CCH) p. 9923 (N.D. 1984) (in strict liability cases).

    R.I.: By statute.

    Texas: Duncan v. Cessna Aircraft Co., 665 S.W. 2nd 414, Prod. Liab. Rep. (CCH) p. 9774 (Texas 1984), remanded (July 11, 1984).

    Wash.: Lamborn v. Phillips Pacific Chemical Co., 89 Wash. 2nd 701, 575 P. 2nd 215 (1978).

    Calif.: Li v. Yellow Cab Co.

12. Ark.: Missouri P.R. Co. v. Star City Gravel Co., 452 F. Supp. 480 (E.D. Arkansas. 1984) Ark. 1978.

Ga.: Zayre of Georgia, Inc. v. Ray, 117 Ga. App. 396, 160 S.E. 2nd 648 (1968).

Idaho: Seppi v. Betty, 99 Idaho 186, 579 P. 2nd 683 (1978); Odenwalt v. Zaring, 102 Idaho 1, 624 P. 2nd 383 (1980).

Minn.: Marier v. Memorial Rescue Service, Inc., 296 Minn. 242, 207 N.W. 2nd 706 (1973).

N.J.: Van Horn v. William Blanchard Co., 173 N.J. Super 280, 414 A. 2nd 265 (1980).

S.C.: Langley v. Boyter, 284 S.C. 162, 325 S.E. 2nd 550 (Ct. App. 1984). Quashed on other grounds, 286 S.C. 85, 332 S.E. 2nd 100 (where court stated, "We hold the doctrine of contributory negligence as it has previously been applied in S.C. abrogated and replaced with the modified form of comparative negligence which permits recovery by a person who has been negligent in causing an accident, so long as his negligence is not greater than…that of the claimant.").

Vt.: Stannard v. Harris, 135 Vt. 544, 380 A. 2nd 101 (1977).

W.Va.: Bradley v. Appalachian Power Co., 163 W.Va. 332, 256 S.E. 2nd 879 (1979).

Wis.: Wisconsin Natural Gas Co. v. Ford, Bacon & Davis Constr. Corp., 96 Wis. 2nd 314, 291 N.W. 2nd 825 (1980); Reiter v. Dyken, 95 Wis. 2nd 461, 290 N.W. 2nd 510 (1980).

Wyo.: Board of County Comm'rs v. Ridenour, 623 P. 2nd 1174 (Wyo. 1981).

13. Neb.: Malcom v. Dox, 169 Neb. 539, 100 N.W. 2nd 538 (1960).

S.D.: Wilson v. Great N. Ry., 83 S.D. 207, 157 N.W. 2nd 19 (1968).

14. Federal Tort Claims Act (FTCA 28 U.S. C. para 1346 B).

15. Political Subdivision Tort Claims Act enacted into law by Pennsylvania state general assembly in 1978.

16. Milo Geyelin, "Hired Guards Assume More Police Duties as Privatization of Public Safety Spreads," *Wall Street Journal*, June 1, 1993 p. B1. See also Edward Felsenthal, and the case of Exeutive Security & Investigative Services Inc. of Totowa, New Jersey involving the town of Sussex, New Jersey, *Wall Street Journal*, June 24, 1993, p. B9.

17. Dalehite v. United States, 346 U.S. 15, 34-36 (1953).

18. Bates v. State of Missouri, 664 S.W. 2d 565 (Mo. App. 1983).

19. Rusticci v. Weidemeyer, 759 S.W. 2d 620 (Mo. App. 1984).

20. Kanawaga v. State of Missouri, 685 S.W. 2d 836–837 (Mo. App. 1985).

21. Cox v. Dept. Of Natural Resources, 699 S.W. 2d 443, 449 (Mo. App. 1985).

22. Jamierson v. Dale, 670 S.W. 2d 195, 196 (Mo. App. 1984).

23. This has most often been a factor in products liability suits brought under strict liability. Austin v. Raybestos-Manhattan, Inc. 471 A.2nd 280, Prod. Liab. Rep. (CCH) 9924 (Me. 1984).

Tex.: Duncan v. Cessna Aircraft Col, 665 S.W. 2d 414, Prod. Liab. Rep. (CCH) 9774 (Tex. 1984), remanded (July 11, 1984).

24. Tex.: Farley v. M M Cattle Col., 529 S.W. 2d 751 (Tex. 1975), concurring op. Withdrawn, substituted at 18 Tex. Sup. Ct. J. 453 (Tex.).

Wyo.: Barnette v. Doyle, 622 P. 2nd 1349 (Wyo. 1981); Brittain v. Booth, 601 P.2d 532 (Wyo. 1979).

Contra: Mont.: Zahrte v. Sturm, Ruger & Co., 203 Mont. 90, 661 P. 2d 17, Prod. Liab. Rep. (CCH) 9552 (1983) (comparative negligence principles apply to assumption of risk).

25. *Black's Law Dictionary*.

26. Insurance Company Of North America v. Forrest City Country Club 819 S.W. 2d 296 (Ct. App. Ark. 1991).

27. McGowen v. Prentice, La App. 341 So. 2d 55, 57 and also Wolfson v. Kirk, Fla. App., 273 So. 2d 744, 776 and Restatement, Second of Torts 559, 563.

28. *Black's Law Dictionary*.

29. Playboy Enterprises, Inc. v. St. Paul Fire and Marine Ins. Co. 769 F.2d 425 (Ill. 1985).

30. Donald Hirsch, *Casualty Claim Practice* (New York: Irwin McGraw-Hill, 1996), pp. 76–77.

31. Indiana Ins. Co. v. North Vermillion Community School Corp. No. 83A05-9406-CV240 (Ind. App., May 24, 1996).

32. Biddle v. Warren General Hospital 715 N.E. 2d 518 (Ohio 1999).

33. Hicks v. Talbott Recovery System Inc. 98-8821 (11th Cir. Nov. 22, 1999).

34. Texaco Inc. v. Pennzoil 729 S.W. 2d 768 (Tex. 1987).

35. S. Vandall, "Design Defects in Products Liability: Rethinking Negligence and Strict Liability," *Ohio State Law Journal*, vol. 43, no. 61, 1982.

36. Nelson v. Hall, 165 Cal. App. 3d 709, 211 Cal. Rptr. 668 (3d Dist. 1985).

Other Bases of Legal Liability

Vicarious Liability

Liquor Liability Laws

Environmental Impairment Liability

Class Actions and Mass Tort Litigation

Bailments

Contracts

Summary

Other Bases of Legal Liability

Chapter 5 described the various ways in which one party's conduct, like an insured's, could create liability to another claimant. This chapter describes how the conduct of others can "impute" liability to a separate party, making both parties liable to a claimant. This situation, known as vicarious liability, occurs in relationships that hold one party legally responsible for the conduct of another. Examples of such relationships include a parent's liability for the conduct of his or her child, a principal's liability for work performed by an agent, one partner's responsibility for what another partner does, or even a drinking establishment's liability for the conduct of one of its patrons.

This chapter also explains how one party's conduct can lead to multiple claims, which is especially common in environmental liability claims.

Finally, this chapter concludes by explaining how parties become liable under contract law. Contractual liability is less common in personal lines claims but occurs frequently in commercial liability.

VICARIOUS LIABILITY

In its broadest sense, **vicarious liability** arises when one person is responsible for another person's actions. This type of liability typically involves a superior (such as an employer or a parent) being held liable for the wrongful conduct of subordinates (such as employees or children) or associates (such as business partners). Both statutes and common-law doctrines sometimes create vicarious liability. In some states, owners of autos are held liable for the negligence of drivers who borrow their cars. What these claims have in common is that one party has vicarious liability for the conduct of another party because of some relationship between the two parties.

Vicarious liability is distinguishable from negligent supervision or negligent entrustment claims, which are not technically forms of vicarious liability. Claims of negligent supervision or negligent entrustment involve negligence on the part of a parent, an employer, or an owner of an auto, whereas vicarious liability exists even if the responsible party was not personally negligent.

Vicarious liability applies in situations involving agents, business partners, parents, and even independent contractors in some situations.

Agency

People can be held responsible when others act for them at their request or with their consent. Examples are an employee performing work for an employer or a friend running an errand for the sole benefit of another friend. A person who performs work on behalf of another is known as an **agent**. Agents are not necessarily *insurance* agents, although insurance agents are agents of the companies for which they work. The person or organization for whom an agent works is called a **principal**.

Legal doctrine holds that a principal is vicariously liable for the acts of its agent as long as the agent is acting within the scope of the work requested by the principal (also known as the scope of the agency).

Determining whether an agent is acting within the scope of the agency's work at the time of an accident involves a number of factors, including whether the conduct was of the type the agent was hired to perform, whether it occurred within the authorized time and space limits of the agency relationship, and whether it was motivated even in part by an intent or a purpose of serving the principal. The definition of a principal-agent relationship is broader than that of an employee-employer relationship. An employer-employee relationship involves wages for work, but this wage factor is not required for a principal-agent relationship to exist.

An agency may be created orally, in writing, expressly, or by implication or estoppel. An agent and a principal, or an employer and employee, may be sued individually or jointly. A principal or an employer against whom liability has been determined and who did not contribute to or condone the wrongful act might, in theory, sue the agent or employee for the recovery of any judgment rendered against the principal or employer, although this is seldom pursued.

A court uses the same reasoning to determine whether an agent or employee is negligent as it would use in other negligence cases. First, some legal duty must be owed to the claimant that has been breached by some lack of reasonable care by the agent, and this violation must have caused the claimant damages.

Sub-Agency

A **sub-agency** exists when an agent transfers the agency duties, in part or in whole, to another party. Ordinarily, one cannot delegate discretionary duties requiring judgment. However, unless specifically forbidden to do so, an agent may delegate agency duties in any of the following circumstances:

1. When the principal specifically authorizes the delegation
2. When the act is unlawful for the agent but not the sub-agent
3. When the act to be performed is purely mechanical
4. When it is customary in the industry to delegate the act

Temporary or Special Employee

In some instances, an employer may loan, hire, or direct a regular worker to do work for a different employer for a temporary period or to do a specific job. In such cases, the responsibility for the employee's negligence may then rest with the temporary employer rather than the general employer.

Liability depends on control, as in all agency questions, and all of the facts concerning control would have to be gathered. An important factor in determining control is in whose business the employee was engaged at the time of the incident, although this alone is usually not enough. The elements of control are discussed later in the section on independent contractors.

Deviation From Agent's Duties

No uniform guidelines exist for determining a principal's responsibility for the negligence of his or her agent or employee when the agent or employee deviates significantly from the authority granted by the principal. To determine whether there has been any deviation from the scope of the authority granted, it is necessary to learn the limits of the principal's authority. As previously stated, such authority may be either expressed or implied. It may be restricted by instructions not to do certain things, or it may consist of directives to do certain things. Performing an errand for someone else is an example of an agent's duty. Driving off course to do a personal errand or to go shopping or drinking at a tavern could be considered a significant deviation.

Partnerships and Joint Enterprises

A **partnership** is a business enterprise involving two or more persons who agree to share their time, efforts, skills, money, or other resources with the understanding that each will share in the profits or losses of the enterprise. Each partner is an agent of the partnership. The legal obligations one of the partners incurs are also incurred by the enterprise as a whole. The partners are joint and severally liable, which means that a person could choose to sue just one partner or all of them. Partnerships may have employees as well as partners. The partnership can be held vicariously liable for the acts of employees in the same way as can any other employer.

Independent Contractors

An independent contractor is another type of agent but is different from an employee. An owner of property, generally speaking, is not liable for the negligence of an independent contractor with whom the owner has arranged to perform some work. However, it is immaterial what the individual calls himself or herself because the circumstances indicate whether that individual is an employee or an independent contractor. Generally speaking, determination of status depends on control of the operation. If the principal maintains some control over the method of work or means of operation, the situation is usually one of an employer-employee relationship and not one involving an independent contractor.

Recall from Chapter 2, some of the general factors (but by no means all of them) that are usually necessary to determine an employment relationship include the following:

1. How was the worker hired? Was a definite salary set by the hour, day, or week, or was there a lump-sum price agreement?
2. Was there any limitation on hiring?
3. Who pays Social Security, unemployment, or other taxes?
4. Who owned the tools and supplied the materials?
5. Who directed the work?
6. Who hired and paid additional help? Who had the authority to fire them?

The number of factors that might apply makes determination difficult, but the idea of control over the details of the worker's job is central to every court's analysis.

Even when a clear independent contractor relationship exists, property owners or other persons who hire an independent contractor can be held responsible for the independent contractor's acts. The following are examples of such situations:

1. The work that the independent contractor is required to do is illegal.
2. The work constitutes a public nuisance.
3. By statute the owner must make certain repairs.
4. The property owner has agreed to become legally liable for damages caused by the independent contractor.
5. The work to be done is inherently dangerous, such as blasting operations or building demolition. (The topic of inherently dangerous activities is covered later in the chapter in the discussion on strict liability.)
6. The work cannot be delegated as a matter of law.
7. The owner has failed to use reasonable care in the selection of the independent contractor.
8. There is interference on the part of the property owner resulting in injury to a third party.

The last two items are separate from the idea of vicarious liability for an independent contractor's act because the cause of action is based on the negligence of the *owner* (for interfering or for improperly hiring the contractor). A more lengthy discussion of employee versus independent contractor is covered in the AIC 34 textbook *Principles of Workers Compensation*.

Parental Liability

Parental responsibility for their children's tortious acts is another recent development of legislative rather than common law. Under common law, a parent was not liable for a child's torts. Although almost all states have enacted statutes and many cities and towns have passed ordinances concerning tortious acts of children, there is little uniformity in these statutes and ordinances. Most of them invoke parental liability only for a child's deliberate acts, known legally as "willful and wanton" acts. In addition, the amount for which the parent may become liable is usually limited and can be as small as several hundred dollars or as great as $5,000. Detractors argue that such statutes are unfair to parents and unlikely to curb juvenile delinquency. Generally speaking, courts have upheld the constitutionality of such statutes as long as the amount of the parent's liability for a child's act is limited.

Liability of Minor Children

Courts have generally held that children younger than a certain age cannot, in most instances, be liable for their torts. Negligence presumes a capacity for exercising due care. In terms of negligence, the standard of care required of a child should be, and usually is, that which is ordinarily shown by the average child of similar age and mentality under similar circumstances.

In most jurisdictions, there is a legal presumption that a child younger than seven years of age cannot appreciate the harm he or she might cause. Some states have lowered the age at which a child may be held comparatively liable to age five. Application of negligence laws to younger children usually involves situations in which a court is asked to assess *comparative* negligence against a child for his or her not recognizing traffic dangers. Some defendants have successfully argued that children younger than seven are capable of understanding the dangers of running into a busy street.

Typically, when a child is older than seven, courts base negligence on the standard of conduct for a child of like age and mentality. The age after which a child can be held liable for his or her acts varies. Historically, children between the ages of seven and fourteen could be found negligent, but the burden of proving negligence is on the person making the claim against the child. Most courts would now consider teenagers to be capable of exercising due care and of understanding the danger that their negligent conduct might create for others. A teenager operating a vehicle would be bound to the same standard as an adult.

When the act of a child is illegal and the benefit thereof accepted or instigated by the parent, the parent can be liable. For example, if the child stole or robbed something of value from someone and the parent accepted it knowing of the theft, the parent would also be responsible for the child's tortious act.

Negligent Entrustment and Negligent Parental Supervision

As mentioned earlier, the rules of agency might apply so that parents could, with the usual agency exceptions, be held liable for their children's tortious acts. Moreover, parents can also be held liable for their own negligence related to the tortious acts of their children.

Under common law, several circumstances create parental liability for children's wrongful behavior. Following are four circumstances that could lead to liability under the theory of negligent parental supervision or negligent entrustment:

1. A parent acquiesced to, encouraged, or ratified the tortious act of a child.
2. A parent knowingly entrusted a dangerous instrumentality to a child who did not have the mental capacity or maturity to realize the dangers involved in its use.
3. The act of a child was illegal and the benefit thereof accepted or instigated by the parent.
4. A child previously exhibited vicious propensities that were known, or should have been known, to the parent, and the parent took no responsible precautions to avoid harm to others.

In the first situation, a parent might tell his or her unlicensed child to drive to the store and buy something. In such a case, the parent has encouraged and condoned the child's negligent act. This would constitute negligent entrustment of an auto to a child. An example of negligent supervision is a parent sitting idly by and watching (or encouraging) his or her child physically abuse another child.

An example of the second circumstance described above is a parent who gives a child a loaded gun. Even if the gun were not directly entrusted to a child, placing it or another dangerous instrumentality where a child could reach it would be enough to justify placing liability on the parent. An air rifle or a chain saw in the hands of a young child are other obviously dangerous instrumentalities. However, an object that could be lethal if used outside its intended purpose may not, in and of itself, be considered a dangerous instrumentality. Such objects could, for instance, be a hard baseball or a bat, a hammer or heavy wrench, or a similar object.

When a child previously exhibited vicious propensities that were known, or should have been known, to the parent, and the parent took no responsible precautions to avoid harm to others, the parent can be liable. For example, parents have a responsibility to protect others from their children who have severe mental or behavioral problems that may cause them to pose threats to others.

LIQUOR LIABILITY LAWS

When claimants are injured by intoxicated persons, claim representatives should investigate the possibility of liability on the part of the establishment that served the drinks to the defendant(s). Many jurisdictions now permit recovery based on "dram shop" statutes, a violation of liquor control statutes, or common-law negligence.

Dram Shop and Liquor Control Statutes

Dram Shop:

Taverns and other establishments that dispensed alcoholic beverages were historically known as dram shops. This antiquated name now exists mainly in legal terminology.

Today, all states have liquor control laws, and most have some form of a Dram Shop Act. **Dram shop acts** are statutes holding establishments that serve alcoholic beverages responsible for harm resulting from serving patrons alcohol in violation of statutes. In most states, it is a violation of the statute to serve (1) anyone who is visibly intoxicated or (2) a minor. The acts apply to owners or lessees of the property, bar, restaurant, or liquor store.

Most of the dram shop statutes make establishments liable for serving liquor to persons who are known to be intoxicated. The definition of "intoxicated," which triggers liquor liability, varies by state. One court defined it as follows:

> An abnormal mental or physical condition due to the influence of imbibing intoxicating liquors; a visible excitation of the passions and impairment of judgment, or a derangement or impairment of physical functions and energies. This may be reflected in the intoxicated person's walk or conversation, his common sense actions, or his lack of willpower.[1]

Note that this law does not impose absolute liability against drinking establishments for *any* person drinking but instead only for those who are visibly intoxicated.

The majority of these acts do not protect the intoxicated person but are instead designed to protect innocent parties from the actions of intoxicated persons. One state's law specifically allows a wife or child to bring an action based on the sale of liquor to the husband or father. In one case,[2] a dependent of an intoxicated patron successfully sued a tavern after the patron died as a result of alcohol poisoning. The patron had been served additional drinks even after the patron was obviously drunk.

Even states that do not have dram shop statutes have ordinances or regulations under their liquor control statutes. Such liquor control laws are criminal laws, but violating them has been construed in courts as negligence per se.

To help protect innocent parties, many states require, as a prerequisite to obtaining a license to sell liquor, an applicant to furnish a bond or an insurance policy to pay for injuries or damage resulting from a violation of the liquor provisions of the statute.

Employer Hosts/Company Parties

Most of the state dram shop laws do not apply to employers serving alcohol to employees, but employers can still become liable based on negligence and principal-agency liability. In determining liability, courts often make a distinction between social hosts (friends and family members) and employer hosts because the employer-employee relationship implies some benefit to the employer-host even though the employer does not sell drinks for profit. Employers may be vicariously liable for injuries caused by and to intoxicated employees when an employee becomes intoxicated while participating in an event that benefits the employer.[3]

Although it may be true that an employer gets no immediate short-term profit from serving liquor made available to employees without charge, there might be a benefit in establishing or keeping good employer-employee relationships. The same argument is used when an employee entertains a customer or a boss in his or her home. These situations benefit the employer and form a principal-agency relationship that makes the employer liable for the acts of an employee who is acting on behalf of the employer at a social event.

Social Hosts and Manufacturers

Liquor law liability can provide grounds for bringing co-defendants such as manufacturers or social hosts into an action. Consider the following case:

> Morris and others were injured when their car was struck by a vehicle driven by an intoxicated eighteen-year-old who had just left a high-school graduation party in Texas.
>
> Suit was brought against the graduate, his hosts, and the manufacturers of the beer consumed. The thrust of the action was that liability exists where there is a duty to warn the beer-consuming public of the dangers of consuming beer and then operating a motor vehicle while intoxicated. The trial court dismissed the manufacturers and the Court of Appeals affirmed, paraphrasing other cases that held that beer, in its regular form, is not a product defectively designed or marketed. The court concluded that Texas law does not impose a duty to warn of widely known risks and that the ordinary consumer surely understands that over-consumption of an alcoholic beverage may impair skills and judgment necessary to drive an automobile. The appellate court also agreed with the trial court that brewers could not be prosecuted for placing their product in a marketplace where it was easily accessible to minors, as they had no way of ascertaining a purchaser's age.[4] The social hosts of the event eventually settled with the claimants.

When liquor is served by a host at a social gathering, the law is more lenient to the host than it is to a "seller" of alcoholic drinks. As a general rule, social hosts are not held to the same degree of responsibility for acts of their guests as are those serving liquor for a profit.[5] However, in at least one case (a landmark decision in New Jersey), a social host who served alcoholic drinks to an obviously intoxicated guest and who knew that the person would soon be driving, was held liable for the resulting injury caused by the guest's drunken driving.[6] Courts usually come down much harder on hosts who serve liquor to minors. Some jurisdictions have limited recovery to situations in which the guest is a minor or an incompetent person.[7] A minority of jurisdictions hold that dram shop statutes' liability is broad enough to include social hosts. Most claims are brought based on violations of statutes specifically addressing liquor liability of those who *sell* alcoholic beverages.

The alcohol manufacturer is not usually brought into suits involving liquor liability unless it is a claim involving a serious injury or a fatality. One court found a manufacturer partially liable for the death of a college student who died of alcohol poisoning. The distiller of the tequila that the eighteen-year-old student consumed was found to be 67 percent liable for failing to warn of the risk involved in drinking too much alcohol by providing a label explaining the danger.[8] Most suits against manufacturers have been unsuccessful.

Common-Law Defenses to Liquor Liability

Most courts no longer recognize common-law defenses such as contributory negligence, comparative negligence, and assumption of risk for cases involving liquor liability.[9] One exception to this is for the **noninnocent participant** described in the case of Barrett v. Campbell.[10]

> The claimant had participated in purchasing "rounds" of drinks. He was later injured as a passenger in a car driven by one of the other drinking participants, who was intoxicated. The court held that the claimant passenger was not an "innocent party" under the Michigan Dram Shop Act and therefore was not entitled to recover against the seller of the alcoholic beverages.

Non-Auto Cases

Very few courts have extended dram shop liability beyond the limits of automobile injury. However, in the New Jersey case of Finney v. Ren-Bar, Inc.,[11] the appellate court made a noteworthy decision. A minor who worked as an assistant to a disc jockey caused damage as a result of a negligently started fire.

On the night of the accident, the minor was observed imbibing quite a few alcoholic drinks in a tavern after he finished working. He then went home and started to prepare a meal. After turning the stove burner on high under a pot of oil, he went into the living room and fell asleep. While he was sleeping, the overheated oil caused a fire. In a suit brought against the tavern, the jury found that the tavern that served the liquor to the minor was 75 percent responsible for the fire and subsequent damage. In affirming the judgment, the appellate court rejected the argument that liability for serving liquor to a minor was limited to motor vehicle accidents. It pointed out that it was foreseeable that an intoxicated minor could cause harm other than that related to the use of a motor vehicle.

ENVIRONMENTAL IMPAIRMENT LIABILITY

As an industrialized country, the United States produces tons of potential pollutants as products and byproducts of normal industrial activity. Discovery of the long-term effects of carcinogens, dangerous chemicals, and the disposal of hazardous wastes and the dangers of asbestos and polyurethane found in homes, workplaces, and schools have led to new laws regulating the use and disposal of these substances. Individual and class actions have been brought for the removal of lead paint, polyurethane, and asbestos from schools, other public buildings, and homes as a result of injury and damage from these pollutants.

Air, water, and ground can suffer from pollution. The Environmental Protection Agency (EPA) regulates each of these types of pollution.

Air Pollution

Any form of smoke, vapor, soot, or fumes or any combination of these that causes property damage or bodily injury could be considered air pollution. Airborne particles of any substance, including hazardous materials such as asbestos, are pollutants. Viral or bacterial agents in building heating, ventilation, and air conditioning systems have been considered pollutants when they cause illnesses. Legionnaire's disease, for example, is believed to be caused by bacterial growths in air conditioning systems.

Fumes from certain building materials, paints, and carpet often cause illness or allergic reactions in certain persons exposed to the fumes, leading to claims. Many individuals may also suffer reactions to chemicals commonly used in buildings to kill insects, molds, and rodents. Building owners and operators may face claims from tenants or employees for **"sick building syndrome" (SBS)** illnesses or allergic reactions to chemicals in the buildings. Causes of SBS involve a complex combination of building design, construction materials, and maintenance, as well as fungal and biochemical factors. Simply stated, SBS results when sealed, energy-conserving structures recycle contaminated air.[12]

Indoor air quality may well be one of the least understood, most serious health problems facing industrial nations. The Environmental Protection Agency states that poor indoor air quality is one of the top five environmental health risks of our time. Doctors who treat patients for sick-building-syndrome claims have reported caseload increases of 40 percent in the past decade. One source estimates the cost of sick-building illnesses to be $58 billion per year in the United States alone.[13]

The most common sign of SBS is a high incidence of complaints of general malaise, including headache; lethargy; dry, irritated eyes; congested nose; irritated throat; and coughs. These symptoms typically appear after working in the building for a couple of hours and then improve after leaving the building for a time. Investigating environmental liability claims is complex not only because of the technical nature of the claims but also because these claims often generate highly charged emotional responses that have social and political implications. These claims are costly because the causes are not always apparent and numerous experts are often required.

Multiple chemical sensitivity (MCS) is an ecological illness, often related to sick buildings, that eludes diagnosis because the symptoms are so diverse. Allergies to synthetic fabrics, perfumes, plastics, solvents, and other pollutants that may not affect less-sensitive people can trigger life-threatening reactions in MCS sufferers. High levels of formaldehyde in cabinets or synthetic carpets have been known to trigger such sensitivities.

Water Pollution

Water pollution involves harmful substances being introduced into any body of water. It has been traced to sources many miles from the place where it was released, and long-term exposure to minute quantities may cause harm. Water pollution can also arise suddenly from spillage resulting from either a catastrophic event in a pollution source or from loss while in transit, such as from the overturning or rupturing of a truck, ship, or railcar. One of the better-known water pollution cases involved the class action against polluters who dumped chemicals into the Love Canal near Niagara Falls, New York. Residents along the canal sustained illnesses from the contaminants in the water. Another famous case appeared in the book and movie *A Civil Action*, based on water contamination claims by residents in Woburn, Massachusetts.

Ground Contamination

Ground pollution can arise in a number of ways. Certain dumping and mining operations result in hazardous material contamination that can remain in the soil for hundreds of years. Spillage from buildings and storage tanks and during transit can also contaminate the ground, as can rupture or spillage from a pipeline, conveyor, or another fixed form of transport. Fires in industrial locations commonly cause ground contamination as materials such as petroleum products break down and hazardous materials that are usually stored in safe locations are released.

Underground pollution often results from a **leaking underground storage tank (LUST)**. Operators of underground storage tanks must keep records showing the amounts of substances placed in the tanks, amounts removed, and amounts replaced. When a shortage is discovered, a leak may be the cause. Such leaks tend to permeate many levels of soil and rock. The rule is that all of the pollutant must be removed, either by pumping from a series of wells dug to remove the pollution or by digging out the contaminated soil and rock. The contaminants may have migrated downward and outward for many years.

LUST losses are commonly associated with gasoline tanks placed at gas stations that might have either leaked while the station was in operation or have been abandoned with gasoline still in them. These events have resulted in a number of class actions by neighboring property owners alleging damage resulting from the contamination.[14]

Pollution Liability—Legal Bases of Recovery

Pollution liability arises out of common-law theories such as negligence, nuisance, and trespass and from statutory enactments.

Negligence

As in any negligence action, the claimant must prove that the defendant owed a duty to use care to avoid injury or damage but did not act like an ordinary prudent person under similar circumstances. As in all suits, there must be causal connection between the wrongdoing and the injury or damage.

Statutory Enactments

Municipal, state, and federal laws address pollution liability. Some federal laws that specifically address pollution are the Clean Air Act, the Clean Water Act, the Resource Conservation and Recovery Act, and the comprehensive Superfund law. The **Comprehensive Environmental Response, Compensation, and Liability Act (CERCLA),** popularly known as the **Superfund** law, was enacted in 1980. It was not the first major federal environmental law, but it has had the greatest effect on insurance claims. Under this law, the Environmental Protection Agency must discover and clean up dangerous waste sites. The EPA must consider whether a site has released hazardous substances or whether such a release appears imminent. The EPA must create a list of hazardous waste sites and establish a priority for dealing with them. It can order potentially responsible parties (PRPs) to eliminate contaminants and to clean up the sites.

The following are "potentially responsible parties" by Superfund definition:

1. The current property owner
2. The owner of the facility/property when the hazardous waste was deposited
3. Any person who contracted or arranged for disposal of the hazardous waste
4. Any person who accepted the hazardous waste for transportation or disposal

Past owners are liable only if hazardous waste was disposed of on the property during their ownership. Current owners are liable for all existing contamination as soon as they take title to the land. The statute does not require that the "potentially responsible party" be negligent in disposing of its waste. The courts have deemed CERCLA to impose absolute liability. The EPA does not have to prove negligence in order for the PRP to be liable.

If these PRPs do not clean up the sites, the EPA can take remedial measures to protect public health and welfare and to pay for these efforts out of Superfund.

One advantage for plaintiffs using CERCLA law over common-law remedies is that under common law, plaintiffs must sue to start a legal action, whereas under CERCLA, the EPA may initiate enforcement any time there is a "release, or threatened release" of a hazardous substance. The EPA will also do the expensive testing that may be required to prove contamination. If individual injuries are slight and the hazardous waste affects large numbers of people, individuals are unlikely to file lawsuits, but the EPA would take action. Designing and monitoring cleanup efforts is easier under Superfund laws because the outcome of litigation is more predictable. Because Superfund is a federal law, it is more uniform than the myriad forms of state laws on pollution liability.

The EPA may impose liability for cleanup costs retroactively against those who deposited hazardous waste before the statute became law on December 11, 1980. Because of the magnitude of the cleanup problem, both in cost and technical skill, there has been and will continue to be great emphasis on the recovery of costs from responsible parties, as well as encouragement of private cleanup efforts.

Nuisance

Unlike negligence claims, nuisance claims are based on an intentional act, even if the harm itself was not intended. Using the nuisance theory of liability in pollution claims has become more popular as public attitudes have changed the way juries view the dangers of hazardous waste. Historically, plaintiffs rarely prevailed because they could not prove that the hazardous waste sites posed a risk that outweighed the economic gain from the polluting activity. Today, society places a greater value on the unimpeded use and enjoyment of land and is more cynical about the economic benefits derived from hazardous waste contamination of the land. Some plaintiffs prefer filing actions under nuisance rather than under Superfund law because they can recover more in damages, which means higher potential jury awards. Nuisance claims can also be made for contamination by petroleum byproducts or from the application of fertilizers, while the Superfund law exempts these activities from its definition of "release of harmful substances."

Trespass

Black's Law Dictionary defines "trespass" as the commission of a wrongful act or the doing of a lawful act in a wrongful manner so as to injure the person or property of another. It has also been defined as an invasion of one's interest in the possession of land. Trespass includes pollution of water or directly onto the land itself.[15]

As in nuisance cases, liability under the theory of trespass is based on intentional invasion. The fact that the resulting harm from the intentional invasion was unintended is immaterial to liability. The advantage of bringing an action in trespass, as with nuisance, is that it is not necessary to prove that negligence caused the injury or damage. It is the defendant's wrongful conduct that determines liability. In actions based on trespass, defendants frequently are liable for the indirect or reasonably unforeseeable consequences of acts occurring while trespassing.

Continuing trespass may result from a failure to remove a hazardous condition created by the defendant or by continuing invasions; for instance, as in the seepage of gasoline or contaminated water onto the claimant's property.

Defenses to Pollution Liability Claims

Although defenses are more limited under current pollution laws than in the past, viable defenses still exist. The available defenses vary by jurisdiction. Under the negligence theory used to assert pollution liability, a defendant would have the ordinary defenses to negligence such as intervening cause or no proximate cause. When a claimant has contributed to the injury or damage by failing to take appropriate remedial action or when he or she has acted in a manner likely to invite or provoke the injury or damage, such actions would either mitigate damages or destroy the claimant's right of action based on comparative or contributory liability laws.

Only a few defenses can be effective against the absolute liability standard imposed by the Superfund law. Acts of war or acts of God are valid defenses if appropriate. Proving to the EPA that a defendant does not meet one of the four criteria of a "potentially responsible party" can also eliminate CERCLA liability.

The 1986 amendments to the Superfund law created an **innocent landowner defense**, which applies to an owner who purchased a contaminated site without knowledge of the problem and after an appropriate investigation into the prior use of the site. Ignorance of a problem is not the same as innocence. Investigation into prior use must be made. Recently the EPA agreed to make those who remediate "brownfields" exempt from Superfund liability. A **"brownfield"** is idle or abandoned property tainted by known or suspected environmental contamination. Often, such property is also subject to various state pollution laws.

A defense made to a nuisance claim is that the operation complained of was in the neighborhood long before the claimant came to be there. Zoning ordinances also have been used in defense of common-law pollution claims. Where local zoning ordinances permit businesses and manufacturing plants of a certain type—and in some cases invite such plants into the area—with full knowledge of the possibility of pollution, this defense may be a valid one.

When people's health is involved, courts have recognized the rights of the victims to use and enjoy land free from contamination as being superior to the rights of trade and economic benefits. The rights of trade usually yield to the primary rights of the victims. However, courts have considered the economic argument when no health issue is involved. The main question is whether the inconvenience created by the business's pollution is greater than the benefits that the people in the area will derive from the presence of the business. Courts look at the firm's ability to generate products and jobs.

Especially for pollution liability claims, claim representatives must perform a complete investigation of the physical facts. Because coverage is often uncertain in pollution claims, claim representatives should perform their investigations under a reservation of rights.

The following section deals with class-action lawsuits and mass tort litigation. Environmental liability claims are sometimes the subject of these types of legal action.

CLASS ACTIONS AND MASS TORT LITIGATION

Shell Oil sold plastic material that other companies used to manufacture plumbing systems. They were advertised as less expensive and more durable than copper pipe systems. But new homes across the United States that had those plumbing systems sprouted leaks, and numerous suits were filed against Shell.[16]

Insurance companies had a standard practice of rounding premiums to the nearest dollar. In 25 percent of the policies, the rounding up occurred twice, charging each of these customers an extra two dollars each year. A lawyer filed suit on behalf of the policyholders.[17]

Most lawsuits concern disputes between individuals or organizations and other individuals or organizations, but some, like the ones described above, involve multiple parties. Occasionally, a wrongdoer injures more than one person. In cases in which all of the injured parties have nearly identical injuries and the same cause of action against the wrongdoer, a single lawsuit filed on behalf of all the plaintiffs against the wrongdoer might be more efficient than lawsuits filed by each party individually. With a small number of parties, one lawyer might be able to represent all of the plaintiffs, but this might not work for one million different claimants, such as when stockholders sue a company for fraud or when thousands of customers sue a life insurance company for systematically overcharging them. In such situations, a legal procedure permits one person, or a small group of people, to file suit on behalf of all of the injured members of a group. This legal procedure is known as a **class action**.

Class actions have been allowed when there are common questions of law or fact that can be tried in one suit, reducing burdensome multiple litigation. Class actions historically involved claims in which the amount of damages in each claim was so small that it did not warrant individual suits.[18]

Traditionally, class actions have seldom involved torts because each of the people injured in tort claims has different injuries or liability issues. However, courts have recently begun to "certify" dissimilar tort victim members of a group. A class-action lawsuit that involves injured people whose liability claim against the wrongdoer is based on tort law (rather than contract law) is known as **mass tort litigation**. Historically, courts believed that tort actions had too many variables for them to be included in class actions, but this appears to have changed in recent product liability and pollution actions as well as other mass tort actions. Recently, mass tort litigation has involved claims related to cigarettes, asbestos, birth control pills and devices, various drugs such as Fen-Phen, tampons, and pollutants. In insurance, consumers have lodged class-action lawsuits against insurers for their use of aftermarket auto parts in auto repairs and for the misuse of managed-care techniques.

Today, a case involving numerous plaintiffs presenting identical liability questions can be tried as a class action, with each party submitting separate proof of damages. In June 2000, a Miami jury gave the largest punitive damage award in U.S. history, ordering the tobacco industry to pay about $145 billion to hundreds of thousands of Florida smokers suffering from diseases caused by cigarettes. The case was filed in 1994 on behalf of the entire class of Florida smokers injured by cigarettes, estimated to number between 300,000 and 700,000. It was the first class-action lawsuit on behalf of sick smokers to come to trial.

Legal Basis for Filing Class Actions in Tort Claims

Class actions provide access to the courts for a large group of persons who are interested in a single issue or action. One or more of them may sue or be sued as a representative of the class.

If a driver drove through a red light and struck a vehicle that in turn struck two more vehicles, injuring the three drivers and several passengers, could these injured individuals form a class and file suit collectively against the driver who didn't stop at the red light? The rule is that when a court must decide separate substantial questions before it can determine whether a person is a member of a class, a class action is not appropriate.[19] The type of claim described above would not be appropriate for a class action because the parties would likely have different injuries and possibly different liability allegations against the driver, and there are too few parties to combine claims.

Class actions are filed under Federal Rule of Civil Procedure 23 and are permitted in federal courts and in most state courts. The following criteria are considered in applying this rule to lawsuits:

For a lawsuit to become a class action, the trial court must certify the lawsuit as a class action.[20] The following four rules must all be met for a court to certify a class action:

1. "Numerosity"—To satisfy this rule, people constituting a class must be so numerous that it would be impractical to bring all of them separately into court.

2. "Commonality"—There must be an ascertainable class with a well-defined common interest in the questions of law and fact affecting the parties.

3. "Typicality"—The claims or defenses of the representative parties must be typical of all the class members.

4. "Adequacy of representation"—The named parties must fairly and adequately protect the interests of unnamed class members.[21]

Additional factors that are also considered include:

• The extent to which individual class members would have interests in controlling the prosecution of their claims in a separate action;

• The extent and nature of any litigation already commenced;

• The desirability of concentrating the litigation in one forum; and

• The difficulties to be encountered in the management of a class proceeding.

The court need not know the identity of all potential members to permit a class action to proceed. Where proof of membership is simple and obvious, the fact that a member's identity is not known should not prevent certification of a class action.[22]

BAILMENTS

A **bailment** exists when one person delivers property to another to be held for some special purpose. The purpose may be the safekeeping of the property or the performance of work on the property, such as cleaning, repairing, or restoring. The parties to the bailment are the **bailor**, who owns or lawfully possesses the property before the bailment, and the **bailee**, who receives the property to perform a service.

Kinds of Bailments

A bailee becomes liable to a bailor when the bailee is negligent. What constitutes negligence depends of the circumstances of the bailment. Bailments are usually divided into three classes (types). The duty owed by the bailee to the bailor varies according to the type of bailment; therefore, negligence is assessed differently under different circumstances. The three types of bailments are as follows:

1. *Bailments for the sole benefit of the bailor.* These bailments are known as "gratuitous bailments." An example of this type of bailment is a person's request of a neighbor to keep meat in the neighbor's freezer compartment. In a bailment of this type, the only duty that the bailee owes to the bailor is one of slight care.

2. *Bailments for the sole benefit of the bailee.* An example of this type of bailment is borrowing a lawn mower from a neighbor without compensation of any kind. Because the bailment is for the sole benefit of the bailee, the bailee must exercise the greatest degree of care to avoid liability for any damage to the property.

3. *Bailments for the mutual benefit of both parties.* This is the situation when an object of any kind is rented or hired for a fee. It is the type of bailment most often encountered in casualty claim work. The bailee must exercise an ordinary degree of care.

It is easier to determine the type of bailment than to determine the extent of care owed. What constitutes slight, ordinary, and high degrees of care depends on the circumstances of the claim. The main difference between an ordinary and a high degree of care is that a bailee could become liable for failing to take action when a high degree of care is owed.

Consider the following examples. Linda asks Karen permission to leave her car in front of Karen's house instead of in Linda's apartment-complex parking lot while Linda is on vacation. Linda gives Karen the keys to her car. This is a bailment for the bailor's (Linda) benefit, and Karen would owe only a slight degree of care. Karen could not be held liable for damage to Linda's car from theft or collision caused by another party. Karen would not be expected to check that the car was locked. Karen could be liable if she did something to damage Linda's car, such as allowing her children to play on it or scratching the paint with her lawn mower.

On the other hand, if Karen asked Linda whether she could borrow Linda's car for her own use, this would be a bailment for the bailee's (Karen) benefit. Karen would owe a high degree of care and would be expected to lock the car and park it in a safe place. She might be liable for having parked it on the street rather than in her driveway if a third party collided with it. Some courts might even hold her responsible for damage caused by a tree limb felled by a windstorm if Karen failed to move the car into the garage once she learned of the impending storm. When a high degree of care is owed, the bailee can be liable for acts of omission (failure to take action).

License Versus Bailment

Claim representatives must distinguish between a license and a bailment when investigating claims for vehicles damaged in parking lots. A license, in this context, means the right to use a space. For example, purchasing a theater ticket entitles the holder to a seat. In a license (either expressed or implied), the sole intent of the parties is to allow use of an area for storing an object; however, with bailment, the control of the object is vested in the bailee, and this requires greater responsibility.

> Claim representatives who handle liability claims involving garagekeepers, parking lot owners, and warehouses are especially likely to encounter claims involving bailment and must know the concepts of bailment law to investigate and settle the claims.

Distinguishing between a bailment and a license depends on the degree of control exercised by the bailee. If an object has been placed in the possession of another person with the intent that that person have complete control over it while it is in his or her possession, then the situation can be considered a bailment. Most courts have declared garage owners to be bailees, whereas, in some instances, parking lot owners would be considered bailees, depending on the extent of their control of the parking lot. If the parking lot attendant is given keys to the automobiles with the understanding that the automobiles can be moved at will, then the situation would likely be considered a bailment (even though the cars could be moved only within a restricted area). On the other hand, if the car's owner parks his or her car in a parking lot space and then walks away, the situation is more likely to be considered a license. In situations involving a license, the owner may issue a printed ticket exempting himself from liability or at least limiting liability. For cases in which the facts indicate a license only, courts will usually affirm such a contract.

Acts of Employees

Typically, when an employee acts within the scope of employment, the employer is directly responsible for the employee's acts. Even when a bailee's employee acts outside the scope of authority, most jurisdictions still hold the bailee liable. Some courts will not hold the bailee liable unless the bailee was guilty of negligently hiring the employee or knew of the employee's previous careless or larcenous tendencies.

Defenses and Limitations on Bailee Liability

Bailees are not strictly liable for everything that happens to bailed property while it is in their care. The same negligence defenses are available to bailees as to any other individual accused of negligence. Comparative and contributory negligence laws, specific laws addressing unique bailment situations, and written disclaimers still provide some defenses and limitations to liability.

Contributory and Comparative Negligence

Contributory negligence by a bailor or bailor's agent is usually a good defense in an action brought against the bailee for the bailee's negligence. For instance, should a bailor or bailee's agent leave an automobile with the keys in it on the parking lot of a garage without informing the garage (bailee), such an act might constitute contributory negligence and free the bailee of responsibility. Many jurisdictions have enacted legislation to this effect.

Laws of Particular Bailments

Some types of bailments are specifically addressed by laws. Examples include innkeepers, storekeepers, restaurateurs, and common carriers.

Innkeepers (hotels and motels) have been held strictly liable for guests' property. If items are stolen from a hotel or motel room, the business will be held liable for them. Most states now have laws that limit the amount of liability for which innkeepers are responsible. Innkeepers usually offer safes for storing valuable items, and guests' failure to use these safes can also limit guests' recovery ($500 is a typical maximum amount). Innkeepers are relieved of liability for acts of God, acts of war, or losses due to the negligence of guests.

Storekeepers are sometimes custodians of customers' property. For example, a clothing store is ordinarily responsible for the clothes a customer takes off and puts down temporarily while trying on new clothes.

Restaurateurs, in most jurisdictions, are not liable for the loss of a customer's coat or hat when hooks or clothes racks have been provided close to a customer's seat, particularly when a notice is posted disavowing responsibility. When a checkroom is available, however, the restaurateur accepts responsibility, even when no fee has been paid.

Common carriers offer to transport goods and passengers for the general public. They operate by truck, rail car, and/or aircraft. Common carriers are usually liable for the loss of or damage to goods in their custody except for losses resulting from acts of God, acts of war, acts of public authorities, inherent vice, or neglect by the person or organization that ships the goods. Contract carriers operate under a specific contract with a shipper. Liability depends on the terms of the contract.

Disclaimers

When bailment exists, courts have declared almost without exception that the bailee may not *exempt* itself from *all* liability with a disclaimer. However, courts commonly permit bailees to *limit* their liability with disclaimers, especially if they were not negligent in causing a loss. Courts generally look at one or two justifications to invalidate a disclaimer. One reason for invalidating a disclaimer is lack of notice. Most courts follow the rule that the bailee must prove that the bailor knew about the disclaimer. If a dry cleaner has a barely visible sign that reads: "Not responsible for stolen articles," the sign may not be considered sufficient to disclaim liability by the bailee (dry cleaner). Notices printed on the back of receipts are a common source of controversy. Normally the bailee must prove that the bailor was aware of the notice before it can rely on the limitation of the wording.[23] A clearly written, unambiguous notice would normally be valid. The following case illustrates a situation in which the language on a receipt was deemed sufficient.

A man brought in eighteen rolls of film featuring his family vacation in Europe to a photo developer. He was given a receipt for each roll of film. The developer lost or exposed fourteen of the eighteen rolls. The man sued the photo developer for $10,000. The following language was printed on the back of each receipt: "If any film or print is damaged or lost by us, even though by negligence, it will be replaced with an equivalent amount of Kodak film and processing, and except for such replacement, the handling of such film or prints by us for any purpose is without liability." The man did not read this note, and he admitted that he was aware that the developer gave printed receipts to customers limiting liability because of his experience as a lawyer and an amateur photographer. The court ruled the man's experience and awareness of the receipt wording were sufficient to make the disclaimer valid and limit his recovery.[24]

CONTRACTS

Every day, businesses and individuals form contracts. A contract may be as simple as the sale of a garden hose or as complex as the sale or lease of computer equipment with lengthy service agreements. Contracts establish the responsibilities of each party involved in the contract. Individuals and businesses can become liable based on the provisions described in these contracts or, in the case of implied warranties, based on the provisions that can be inferred from the contract.

Insurance policies are contracts between policyholders and insurance carriers. Many insurance coverage issues are based on and resolved by applying the principles of contract law. In making coverage decisions, claim representatives need to understand some basic principles of contracts. The following section describes the nature and enforceability of contracts.

A party that fails to comply with the terms of a contract is said to have breached the contract. Although **breach of a contract** is not a tort and does not usually involve negligence law, claim representatives occasionally encounter the law of contracts as it applies to liens, property rights, and warranties both expressed and implied and to hold harmless agreements, which are contracts that establish the responsibilities of one party to a third party not involved in the contract.

Contrary to what many people in claims believe, contractual liability may be covered under liability policies. The exclusions for contractual liability found in many liability policies allow for certain types of contracts, and some liability policies do not exclude contractual liability at all. For these reasons, claim representatives need to understand contracts.

Contractual Liability and the Nature of Contracts

To assess whether an agreement between two parties is subject to contract law, claim representatives must first determine whether the agreement was indeed a contract.

A contract is basically an enforceable promise. For a contract to be enforceable, the following basic requirements must be met:

1. Agreement—A "meeting of minds" must occur between the parties to a contract. This means that one party makes an offer that the other party accepts. Courts will look objectively at whether both parties actually had "a meeting of minds."

2. Consideration—Each party gives up something of value. Commonly, one party exchanges money for the other party's promise to perform some activity. Giving up the right to sue (signing a release) in exchange for a specified sum of money is another example of consideration claimants commonly give in settling liability claims.

3. Competent parties—The parties must have the legal ability to enter into contracts. A contracting party who is not of legal age, sane, or sober does not have the capacity to enter a contract and in certain circumstances has the right to disaffirm or cancel a contract.

4. Legality of purpose—The objective of the contract must be legal and not opposed to public policy. To be enforceable, a contract must not be made to induce acts of a criminal nature, and engaging in such a contract is a crime.

The first aspect of a contract, agreement, is based on two elements: an offer by one party and acceptance by the other. In contract law, an **offer** is a proposal in which one party (the offeror) promises to give something in return for a promise or an act by the other party (**the offeree**). Once an offer has been made, the offeree (party to whom the offer is made) has the power to form a contract by accepting the offer. The offer can be terminated in one of three ways:

• The offeror (party making the offer) can revoke the offer before the offeree accepts it.

• The offeree can reject the offer.

• The offer can be terminated by passage of a reasonable time period.

Acceptance is the offeree's agreement to the terms of the offer. Acceptance must mirror the original offer, or else it is considered a rejection with a counteroffer. For example, if a person offers to sell his or her car to another party for $5,000 and the offeree says, "I'll pay you $5,000 if you throw in a new set of tires," then it is not an acceptance but instead a rejection of the original offer with a counteroffer.

Two basic principles of contract law are:

1. Ordinarily, the law of the jurisdiction specified in the contract is applicable, all else being equal.

2. If the contract is silent as to the applicable law, the governing law is ordinarily that of the place where the contract was made.

Contracts may be **express contracts** that explicitly state the terms and intentions of the agreement or **implied contracts**, whose intentions and terms are indicated by the actions of the parties to the contract and the surrounding circumstances. If a woman drives her car into a repair facility and tells the owner, "Fix my car" and the garage owner agrees to do so, an implied contract is formed. The garage owner has agreed to use reasonable means to repair the car, and the woman has agreed to pay a reasonable price for the services. Of course, a good business practice would be for the garage owner to form with the woman an express contract that states the estimated cost of repairs to avoid controversy over the interpretation and enforcement of the implied contract.

Parol Evidence Rule

For written contracts, the general rule is that parties must abide by the written terms of the contract. After the written contract has been formed and signed, a party may not normally come back later and complain that the terms written in the contract are not what was discussed. In other words, the party cannot present oral testimony that contradicts the written wording of the contract. Such oral testimony is known as **parol evidence**. Parol evidence may be allowed to alter a written contract only in the following circumstances:

1. When the meaning of the written terms is ambiguous
2. To provide essential terms to a written contract that is not complete

Parol evidence can be used to show that a written contract is not valid or enforceable for the following reasons:

1. Conditions required to be met before the contract can be applied have not yet been met.
2. The agreement was illegal or fraudulent.
3. The agreement did not meet the requirements of a valid contract.

The following section discusses the validity and enforceability of contracts.

Validity and Enforceability of Contracts

A **valid contract** is one that meets all of the requirements for the formation of a contract. A valid contract is enforceable in court by either party to it. A **void contract** lacks one or more of the requirements of a contract and thus is not really a contract. A **voidable contract** can be rescinded (canceled) at the election of one or both of the parties to it. Contracts involving fraud or material misrepresentations are voidable. Insurance policies are contracts that are sometimes voidable. If, for example, an insured commits fraud or makes a material misrepresentation on the application when forming the insurance contract, then the contract may be voidable.

Minors can form contracts, but the contracts are voidable. For example, a minor could sign a release for an injury settlement or a contract to purchase a new car, but in either case, the contract can be voided by the minor whenever he or she chooses. For this reason, few contracts involving financial obligations are made solely with minors.

Some contracts are **unenforceable contracts**. A verbal contract to sell land could possess all of the elements of a contract but not be enforceable because the law requires real estate contracts to be in writing.

State laws exist to protect against false claims for payment from certain types of contracts. Contracts may be voided if one party intentionally lied to the other, the other party relied on this lie in forming the contract, and the other party suffered adverse consequences (damages) as a result of the lie. To help prevent parties from becoming involved in fraudulently formed contracts, most states require that contracts involving large amounts of money or real estate be in writing. The reasoning is that unscrupulous parties are less likely to commit fraud if the contract terms are expressly stated. These laws are known collectively as **Statutes of Fraud** because their goal is to protect against fraudulent claims. The extent to which these laws apply varies by state.

Contractual Concepts Applying to Insurance Policies

In general, an insurance policy is written and offered by an insurance company. The insured does not normally have an opportunity to change the wording of the insurance contract; typically, the insured must "take it or leave it." Such agreements are known as **contracts of adhesion**. Contracts of adhesion are also common in other business agreements, too, such as mortgage contracts and lease agreements. Any ambiguities in such contracts must be construed (interpreted) in favor of the party who did not write the contract. The rationale for this principle is that the party that wrote the contract had an opportunity to make the meaning clear. An ambiguity is an uncertainty or a vagueness of meaning. Sometimes the wording may have more than one possible meaning. In insurance policies, insuring agreements, exclusions, and limitations must be clearly expressed, otherwise courts will construe ambiguities in these provisions in favor of the insured.

Typically, contracts are assignable unless stated otherwise. In other words, the obligations and rights of one party can be assigned to another party. This assignment is commonly done with loans. One bank may assign a loan to another. Insurance contracts are not normally assignable by one insured to another without the approval of the insurance company. This is because insurance is a personal contract and one insured is not necessarily the same as another in terms of loss potential. Some states permit assignments of contracts by insureds to claimants if an award is rendered in excess of an insured's limit of liability. Any rights that the insured might have against the insurer are transferred to the claimant. Such assignments are rare.

Because a liability policy is a contract, policy provision interpretation is ordinarily subject to the law of the jurisdiction where the policy was purchased. This law might differ from the law of the jurisdiction where the accident occurred. Accordingly, when policy interpretation is required in a claim or suit based on the insured's alleged wrongdoing, jurisdiction can become a difficult issue, especially because, in recent years, many exceptions have been made to the general principles governing insurance policies.

Hold Harmless Agreements

A **hold harmless agreement** is a common contractual provision by which one party agrees to indemnify (make good or repay) another party in the event of a specified loss.

Hold harmless agreements are commonly found in leases that require a tenant to hold a landlord harmless from claims made by third parties who might be injured by the tenant's negligence. Through a hold harmless agreement, a tenant might agree to reimburse a landlord for any expenses incurred in defending or paying a lawsuit resulting from the tenant's customers' being injured on the landlord's premises.

Construction contracts also contain hold harmless agreements. For example, a construction contract might contain a hold harmless agreement in which the contractor (Lyle) agrees to indemnify and hold the owner (Tim) harmless for any liability that Tim may incur because of injuries to third persons arising out of the construction Lyle is performing. An injured party might sue Tim (the owner) or Lyle (the contractor) or both. By virtue of the hold harmless agreement, Lyle, the contractor, would ultimately bear the loss.

Hold harmless agreements might conflict with the underlying tort law principle that each person should be responsible for his or her own acts. Therefore, courts examine hold harmless agreements closely, especially when the relative bargaining power of one party is greater than the other's. In certain situations, particularly consumer-type contracts involving the sale or lease of a dwelling, state laws invalidate hold harmless agreements.[25]

Exculpatory Agreements

People frequently use **exculpatory agreements** (also called **exculpatory clauses**) in contracts to avoid liability for negligence. The participant in an activity signs a "release of liability" for activities specified in the contract. For example, Jim owns a dude ranch with horses that he allows tourists to ride around the surrounding area. Laurie pays Jim to ride a horse, and Jim has Laurie sign a contract releasing him from any liability associated with her riding the horse. Under the exculpatory clause of the contract, Laurie agrees not to sue Jim for any injuries she might sustain, even those resulting from Jim's negligence. The exculpatory clause relieves Jim of liability to Laurie. Courts view these agreements with skepticism but will usually uphold them in the following circumstances:

1. The exculpatory clause is not adverse to a public interest, nor is it against public policy. Agreements involving the use of dangerous instrumentalities such as explosives would be against public policy.
2. The party excused from liability is not under a duty to perform, such as a public utility or common carrier.
3. The parties had equal bargaining power, and the contract was conscionable.

Exculpatory agreements may excuse or limit liability expressly for negligent contract performance but are void for willful or wanton misconduct. Some state legislatures have enacted laws that limit or prohibit the use of exculpatory clauses in a variety of situations. The most common law is the prohibition of exculpatory clauses with minors.

The difference between hold harmless agreements and exculpatory agreements is that hold harmless agreements protect one party from a third party's claim (not a party to the agreement), while exculpatory clauses protect one party from the claims made by the other party involved in the agreement. For example, a recreational facility that has horseback riding might have a rider sign a hold harmless agreement to protect the facility from claims made by other people the rider might injure, and also an exculpatory clause to protect the facility from claims related to the rider's own injuries.

SUMMARY

Insureds can become vicariously liable for the acts of others. Parents can become liable for the acts of their children, principals for the acts of agents, and partners for the acts of other partners.

The criteria for establishing vicarious liability usually depend on the nature of the relationship and the extent of control one party has over another. The purpose and formality of the relationship, the duration of the relationship, and the extent that one party directs the other's work are all criteria that courts use in determining vicarious liability.

Environmental liability can be based on any number of theories, including negligence, trespass, nuisance, and strict liability. Environmental liability is one of the more common forms of liability that can lead to mass tort litigation and class-action lawsuits.

One party can become liable to another based on contracts. Contracts are not limited to formal, written agreements; they can also include less formal, verbal agreements. For a contract to be valid, competent parties must reach a mutual agreement regarding a matter that is not against the law, and each party must give something of value (known as consideration) to the other party.

Determining liability is a challenging job that requires a basic understanding of tort and contract law. Claim representatives must develop this legal foundation, but they should also learn when to ask for guidance from claim management or legal counsel.

CHAPTER NOTES

1. Sanders v. Officers Club of Connecticut, Inc., 196 Conn. 341, 493 A.2d 184 (1985).
2. Klingerman v. SOL Corp of Maine, 505A2d 474 (Me. 1986).
3. Chastain v. Litton Systems, Inc., 694 F. 2d 957 (4th Cir. N.C. 1982).
4. Morris v. Adolph Coors Co. 735 S.W. 2d 578 (1987).
5. DeLoach v. Mayer Electric Supply Co., 378 So. 2d 733 (Ala. 1979) and Keckonen v. Robles, 146 Ariz. 268, 705 P. 2d 945 (Ct. App. 1985) and Licer v. Quigle, 180 Conn. 252, 429A2d 855 (1980) and Bankston v. Brennan, 480 So. 2d 246 (Fla Dist. Ct. App. 4th Dist. 1985).
6. Kelly v. Gwinnell, 96 N.J. 538, 476 A.2d 1219 (1984) and Davis v. Sam Goody, Inc., 195 N.J. Super. 423, 480 A 2d 212 (1984).
7. Strand v. Cabrol, 37 Cal. 3d 720, 209 Cal. Rptr. 347, 691 P.2d 1013 (1984) also Charles v. Seigfried 191 Ill. Dec. 431, 623 N.E. 2d 1021 (Ill. App. 3d Dist. 1993).

8. Gabriella Stern, "Brown-Forman Found Liable in Death," *Wall Street Journal*, October 1, 1992, p. B8.

9. Sanders v. Officers Club of Conn. and Barrett v. Campbell, 131 Mich App. 552, 345 N.W. 2d 614 (1983).

10. Barrett v. Campbell, 131 Mich. App. 552, 345 N.W. 2d 614 (1983).

11. Finney v. Ren-Bar, Inc., 229 N.J. Super. 295, 551 A 2d 535 (1988).

12. Alan Hedge, a professor in Cornell University's Department of Design and Environmental Analysis as quoted in *Realty Times*, January 14, 1999, p. 1.

13. Michelle Conlin, "Is Your Office Killing You?", *BusinessWeek*, June 5, 2000, pp. 114–128.

14. Jareanvai v. Citgo Petroleum Corp. (DC Mass #96-11310BPS).

15. J. Beck, "The Defense of an Environmental Lawsuit Between Private Litigants," *Insurance Counsel Journal*, October 1976.

16. The class-action lawsuit named as defendants the companies that supplied raw materials used in the manufacture of polybutylene plumbing systems and components. Defendants include Shell Oil Company, Hoechst Celanese Corporation, f/k/a Celanese Corporation, d/b/a Celanese Specialty Operations, d/b/a Celanese Plastics Company, and E.I. DuPont de Nemours and Company. Garria Spencer et al., plaintiffs, v. Shell Oil Company et al., defendants. Civil Action No. CV 94-074, Alabama.

17. World Wide Web: http://www.insure.com/lawsuits/classaction.html.

18. Newman v. Tualatin Development Co., 287 Or. 47, 597 P.2d 800 (1979) (class action certified for negligence but not for warranty). See the following articles: Frazer, "Kinds of Class Action Cases," Okla. *City Univ. Law Rev.*, vol. 7, no. 1, Spring 1982; Hudson, "Mandatory Notice and Defendant Class Action: Resolving the Paradox of Identity Between Plaintiffs and Defendants," *Emory Law Journal*, vol. 40, no. 611 (1991); R. Rivkin & S. Silberfeld, "To Certify or Not to Certify: The Use of the Class Action in Mass Tort Litigation," *F.I.C. Quart.*, Winter 1983: Weber, "Class Actions in Environmental Cases," *Insurance Law Journal*, Oct. 1975.

19. Weaver v. Pasadena Tournament of Roses Assoc., 32 Cal. 2d 833, 198 P.2d 514 (1948).

20. Henry Campbell Black, *Black's Law Dictionary*, 6th ed. (St. Paul, Minn.: West Publishing, 1990).

21. Rivkin & Silberfeld.

22. Daar v. Yellow Cab Co., 67 Cal. 2d 695, 63 Cal. Rptr. 724, 433 P.2d 732 (1967).

23. Jethro Lieberman and George Siedel, *Business Law and the Legal Environment* (Orlando: Harbrace Jovanovich, Inc., 1988), p. 486.

24. Carr v. Hoosier Photo Supplies, Inc. 441 N.E. 2d 450 (S.Ct. Ind 1982).

25. James J. Lorimer; Harry F. Perlet, Jr.; Frederick G. Kempin, Jr.; and Frederick R. Hodosh, *The Legal Environment of Insurance*, 4th ed., vol. II (Malvern, Pa.: American Institute for Chartered Property Casualty Underwriters, Inc., 1993), p. 27.

Investigating Liability Claims

Investigating Liability Claims

I kept six honest serving men
they taught me all I knew
their names were What and Why and When
and How and Where and Who

—Rudyard Kipling

INTRODUCTION

Investigation is getting the facts. The claim representative must determine how, when, where, and why an accident happened so that a claim can be evaluated and settled or, in some instances, defended. This chapter covers the sources of information used in investigations, the rules of evidence related to those sources, and the practical considerations that make liability investigations more efficient and effective.

Chapter 1 stated that the job of the claim representative involves essentially three primary areas of claim handling: *coverage*, *liability*, and *damages*. Each of these areas requires an investigation and an evaluation. Based on the findings from the investigation and evaluation, the claim representative will conclude the claim either by payment, denial, compromise settlement, or litigation.

The right and duty of an insurance company to investigate claims are granted by the insurance policy itself.

Investigation must *precede* evaluation and negotiation, and it is concerned not only with liability but also with coverage and damages. Because coverage investigations were discussed in Chapters 1, 2, 3, and 4, most of this chapter focuses on the investigation of liability. However, claim representatives should make every effort to determine coverage before launching into a liability investigation. Without doing so first, claim representatives can waste time on a liability claim that is not covered and can, through their actions, waive an insurer's right to deny coverage. The concepts of waiver and estoppel, explained in previous chapters, apply when claim representatives gloss over potential coverage questions and proceed to the liability investigation without reserving the insurer's rights.

Coverage Versus Liability Questions

The difference between coverage and liability is one that many people, even those who work in the insurance industry, sometimes confuse. The liability of one party for the damages suffered by another is based on the law. A party can become liable based on any of a wide variety of legal principles, including negligence, vicarious liability, and contract law. Coverage, on the other hand, is based on the insurance policy wording, which is the contract the insurance company has with its insured.

An insured who becomes liable for damages to another party would owe compensation to the other party, but this compensation might not be paid by the insurance company if the situation or the damages claimed do not fall within those defined in the insurance policy. For example, an insured may have purchased a homeowners policy with liability coverage. If the insured becomes liable to a third party because of the insured's operation of a business in the insured's home, the claim may not be covered because of the business exclusion in the policy. The insured is still obligated to pay the third party, but his or her insurance company is not. Therefore, liability can exist without coverage.

Coverage can also exist without liability. Consider a person who is insured under an auto policy for liability coverage only. If the insured is stopped at a traffic light and is rear-ended by a third party, the insured is covered for the accident but is not liable. The third party is liable for damages, but the insured's insurance company would owe a duty to investigate and defend the insured if the third party alleged liability against the insured.

Recognizing Coverage Questions

It is worth repeating the typical situations in which coverage disputes require prompt investigative action on the insurer's part to assess coverage:

- Late notice of accident,
- An accident involving a car that is owned by an insured but is not listed in the policy,
- The date of the accident does not fall within the policy period,
- A question exists concerning whether an "insured" driver had a reasonable belief that he or she was entitled to use the car,
- Applicability of an exclusion,
- Failure to cooperate, or
- Fraud on the insured's part.

Whenever any of these situations has a bearing on a claim, the claim representative will need to conduct a detailed investigation of that particular issue. As explained earlier, claim representatives must reserve the insurance company's rights and be certain the insured knows that the insurance company is not committed to paying the claim until further coverage investigation has been undertaken.

Recognizing Liability Questions

The objective of a liability investigation is to determine who is legally liable or, put simply, who is at fault. Occasionally, this is readily apparent from the accident report, but ordinarily the claim representative will need to conduct an investigation.

As claim representatives review the accident report, they should analyze the accident and decide what specific information will be necessary to determine liability. The claim representative should make notes and outline what the proposed investigation will cover so that it can proceed in an orderly fashion. The scope and priority of investigations are covered later in this chapter. The need for setting investigative priorities and limiting the scope of the investigation will become apparent after reading the discussion on the various types of evidence available.

Claim representatives gather evidence in an effort to determine liability. The following sections describe the different types of evidence that might be obtained and the rules of evidence admissibility in court. Claim representatives should be aware of these rules of admissibility. Because inadmissible evidence has little effect on the liability determination by a court, the settlement value of a claim should be based on admissible evidence.

The investigative process involves inquiry, verification, and comparison of the information obtained. Claim representatives must not only obtain information but also *verify* and *compare* it through other available sources. For example, the insured's or claimant's statement should be checked against the police report and compared to statements made by any witnesses to the accident. Frequently, claim representatives will find it necessary to observe the place of an accident, especially in more serious or complex cases. In injury claims, claim representatives will gather medical documentation (with the necessary authorization from the claimant). Lost income can be verified by a wage or salary report from the employer (again, with the necessary authorization). Photographs are often needed to verify a loss or memorialize a physical condition of an accident scene at the time of the incident.

Claim representatives may need to investigate claims with the help of experts. For example, determining whether a person's injury was related to a car accident as opposed to a pre-existing condition may require a medical expert. Claim representatives may need to hire mechanics, construction experts, or engineers to determine whether the cause of a loss is related to an insured's activity.

As claim representatives conduct investigations, they must continually compare new information with that already obtained so that any conflicts may be immediately recognized. When newly acquired information contradicts older information, claim representatives must reexamine the new information and, in many cases, investigate further to resolve the conflict or at least determine which version of the facts is more credible.

Evidence and Rules of Evidence

Information used to assess liability and verify damages is acquired through various types of evidence. Evidence falls into several loosely defined categories: oral evidence, real evidence, demonstrative evidence, and documentary evidence. **Oral evidence** includes statements made by insureds, claimants, and witnesses, including expert witnesses. **Real evidence** generally refers to animate or inanimate physical and tangible items that are related to the original litigated occurrence.[1] It could include mechanical parts, weapons, scars on a person's body, and similar physical items directly related to the claim. In the broadest sense, real evidence is any item that is exhibited to a judge or jury and that could include demonstrative evidence. **Demonstrative evidence** includes tangible items that were constructed after the original occurrence to prove the facts presented by the litigants. These are visual aids designed to assist the judge and jury in understanding the facts. Such items could include:

- A timeline of events
- A diagram of an accident scene
- A map
- A model of a building
- Pictorial exhibits

Pictorial evidence preserves a visual image of physical facts such as skid marks, damage to a car, broken bones, and potholes in a parking lot. Pictorial evidence includes photographs, X-rays, videos, and similar items.[2]

Documentary evidence includes written items such as contracts, letters, instruction manuals, sales brochures, and other writings that can help to establish liability or damages.

For evidence to be admitted by a court to decide a case, it must be relevant, competent, and material (also known as consequential). For example, the fact that a woman had consumed four margaritas might not be relevant if she was injured while sitting idly in her car at a stop light when she was struck in the rear by another party. Even if the woman had been arrested for driving under the influence, her level of intoxication would not be relevant because it would not show how the accident occurred. **Relevant evidence** must prove that something is more or less likely to be true. The woman's intoxication would not likely help to prove that she contributed to the accident.

Material evidence (or consequential evidence) tends to establish a particular element of the claim that has legal significance. Consider a liability claim for a permanent total disability. The claimant would try to establish future wage loss and loss of other benefits of work such as life insurance and paid vacation days. The defense might argue for certain offsets—for example, money saved in the form of less wear-and-tear on the plaintiff's car and reduced wardrobe expense. These facts might be relevant but also so inconsequential as to be immaterial. In most cases, something immaterial is usually also irrelevant, and the two terms are commonly used together and interchangeably.

Competent evidence relates to the reliability of the source of the evidence and whether it is adequate to justify admission into court. Many competency problems involve witnesses giving testimony at trial regarding events that occurred many years ago. Their memory has faded to the point that their testimony might not be considered reliable. Physical evidence can also be challenged for competency if it was improperly stored, transported, or preserved. The court must be able to determine that the evidence exhibited is indeed the same evidence that related to the accident. To help establish the competence of real, physical evidence, claim representatives should document the chain of custody of the physical evidence. The importance of chain of custody is discussed later after the section on physical evidence.

Statement Taking

The first type of evidence that a claim representative normally gathers is oral evidence. Statements are the most common type of oral evidence claim representatives will use, and they are the essence of a liability claim investigation. A statement, as that term is used in claim handling, is a written or recorded account or declaration of the pertinent facts and circumstances of an accident as related by someone directly involved or by a witness. A sworn statement contains language attesting that the statement is true and is signed by the person giving the statement (referred to as the interviewee).

Statements are taken for several reasons. The basic purpose of a statement is to gather information so that the claim representative can make a proper decision with respect to disposition of the claim. A statement also enables the interviewee to later review and remember what was said at an earlier time, if that becomes necessary. Finally, a statement may be used to confront (or impeach the testimony of) an individual who previously gave a statement and later changed his or her version of the accident.

Well-done, comprehensive statements can help to reduce claim and litigation expenses. A comprehensive statement that intelligently covers the details of an accident can eliminate the need for defense counsel to take the interviewee's deposition and can enable legal counsel to know the pertinent facts so that no surprises will arise later on or at trial. A detailed statement also helps claim representatives and legal counsel to see whose testimony may hurt the insured's case. In short, good statements not only help to clarify matters of liability but also may be a factor in minimizing claim and legal expenses.

The key to statement taking, as in the investigation of a claim, is to answer the questions who, what, when, where, and why as they relate to the happening of the accident. Statement guides or outlines help to remind claim representatives to cover certain points, but good statement-taking requires active listening and critical thinking to lead to asking good follow-up questions.

The two kinds of statements claim representatives take are *written* statements and *recorded* statements. The purpose of this text is not necessarily to teach claim representatives how to take written or recorded statements but instead to (1) describe some of the practical issues regarding the value of statements in determining liability and (2) explain some of the rules of evidence related to statements. The AIC 33 textbook *The Claims Environment*[3] provides a more comprehensive explanation of statements. Appendices A and B at the end of this chapter give guidelines for taking written and recorded statements and list some common mistakes claim representatives make when taking statements.

Written Statements

A written statement is simply a statement written in longhand by the claim representative and, after it has been read and accepted, signed by the interviewee. Written statements are still used occasionally with serious injury claims or when claimants are represented by attorneys. Written statements allow time for reflection, and some claimant attorneys prefer them as a way of controlling what their clients attest to. They minimize allegations that the questions were leading or that the claim representative entrapped the claimant. Such allegations are sometimes made with respect to recorded statements. Written statements also give claim representatives one advantage over recorded statements in that they have more time to reflect and formulate follow-up questions that will help them obtain a more complete statement.

CASE EXAMPLE

Use of a Written Statement[4]

The following case study is a true example of how written statements can be used in court.

In a premises fall-down case, the claimant had signed a written statement to the effect that she did not know what caused her to fall on a stairway. The claim representative took a comprehensive statement and ruled out any debris or foreign objects that might have contributed to the fall. He also confirmed that the surface of the stairway was not slippery and that a sturdy railing was in the stairway. In addition, the claimant stated that the lighting was fine and that there were no witnesses to the accident. In effect, the claim representative had obtained a signed statement that ruled out any liability on the insured landlord's part. Consequently, the claim was denied. Soon after the denial, the claimant sued the insured. The insurer defended the case.

When the claimant testified at trial, she stated that the reason she fell was poor lighting and some unidentified, slippery substance on the stairway. On cross-examination, the defense attorney read her earlier signed statement into evidence. When asked whether this was the plaintiff's statement, she replied that she did not recall. The defense attorney, showing the plaintiff her signature, asked whether, in fact, that was her signature. Her reply was something to the effect that, yes, that was her signature but she did not remember ever giving such a statement or signing it.

The defense attorney then showed her the closing sentence, which read: "I have read the above two and a half pages and they are true." The attorney asked whether she had written that sentence, and she answered in the affirmative. Thus, the claimant was unsuccessful in implying that she was pressured into signing the statement without reading or accepting it. In short, her testimony was impeached by a good, complete statement, and this resulted in a verdict for the defendant.

Recorded Statements

Recorded statements are recorded on cassette tapes, writable compact discs, or some other type of digital storage, and they may be taken in person or by telephone. At one time, written statements were the norm in claims, but in the interests of increased efficiency and production, companies have turned almost exclusively to recorded statements. Because recorded statements can be obtained in minutes, as compared to the hour or so typically required to take a comprehensive written statement, using them can accelerate the claim process. Claim representatives who learn to take comprehensive recorded statements (in considerably less time than it would take to obtain a comparable written statement) have more time to spend on other facets of the claim or on other assignments. Most recorded statements are now conducted by telephone.

Special Situations Involving Statements

Some special situations may preclude statement-taking or require claim representatives to alter their statement-taking manner.

Statements Taken in a Hospital

Caution must be used with respect to taking statements from claimants who are hospitalized. Many jurisdictions have rules that preclude or restrict taking the statement of a hospitalized patient. The rationale is that the patient may be on medicine, in pain, or under stress from the accident. Claim representatives should be familiar with the rules in their states that may affect statement-taking with people in hospitals.

Statements of Minors

Statements may be taken from children provided they are literate and old enough to know the difference between right and wrong. Older children, in the middle or late teens, ordinarily require no special handling. Their statements may be taken in the same manner in which adults' statements are taken.[5]

With younger children, a parent should be present during the statement-taking process. The parent, along with the child, may be introduced in a recorded statement, and the claim representative should obtain the parent's permission to record the child's statement. If a written statement of the child is taken, the parent should witness the child's signature and the representative should obtain a separate statement from the parent noting that the parent was present during the child's statement and that the child's account of the accident was accurately recorded.

Statements of Illiterate People

When a statement is taken from an illiterate person, a recorded statement, if feasible under the circumstances, may be the best method of securing such an individual's account of the accident. In other situations, perhaps where the individual has difficulty speaking, the claim representative may elect to take a written statement. If a written statement is taken, a disinterested person will need to be present to read the statement to the interviewee.

A separate statement should then be obtained from the disinterested person to the effect that he or she read the statement to the interviewee and that the latter acknowledged it to be true and wrote his or her signature or some other appropriate mark accordingly.

Statements of Non-English Speakers

Immigration is changing the demographics of America. Immigration, mostly from Asian and Latin American countries, will account for most of the population growth in the United States in the next ten years. This means that claim representatives in many parts of the United States must be prepared to deal with claimants who speak little if any English.

In the case of someone who can neither *read, write, nor speak* English, it is necessary to find an interpreter. Professional interpreters for communicating by phone are available through commercial services.[6] The claim representative must direct his or her questions to the interviewee through the interpreter. The interpreter should speak and ask questions in the interviewee's native language and then translate his or her answers into English.

Upon completion of the statement, the interpreter should read and explain the statement to the interviewee so that the latter understands it. The interviewee should sign and then the representative should write a separate statement indicating that the interpreter translated the interviewee's statement and that the interviewee stated that it was true and signed it in the interpreter's presence. The separate statement of the interpreter should also note that the interpreter understood and translated both English and the interviewee's native language. The interpreter should then sign the separate statement. Recorded and written statements should be translated and transcribed by professionally certified interpreters and translators.

Negative Statements

Some situations require claim representatives to take statements from people who claim to have no knowledge of the accident. In serious accidents, statements should be secured from people who were near the accident scene. Even if they indicate that they did not see the accident and cannot comment specifically about the cause, a statement to that effect should be taken. Such a statement is referred to as a **negative statement**. Negative statements can be very important in the defense of a claim in which an individual suddenly decides, long after the accident, that he or she did witness the accident and agrees to furnish evidence unfavorable to the insured. If the claim representative had earlier obtained a negative statement from this "witness," the statement could be used either to discourage such later testimony from the witness or to refute it, if need be.

Admissibility of Statements and Other Oral Testimony

In determining the competence of testimony, the court must make two separate findings. First, it must determine that the witness was in a position to observe the subject matter of the testimony at the time the incident took place. Second, the court must determine that the witness has sufficient present memory (at the time of trial) of the events in question to be examined concerning them.

Suppose a witness saw a rear-end collision that occurred three years ago. The witness's testimony may be impeached because of the length of time that has transpired.

One way for claim representatives to overcome this competence issue is by taking prompt statements. If, for example, during the initial investigation, the witness gave a statement to the claim representative, the witness might review that statement before testifying at trial. If the statement had been taken promptly after the event, it would be difficult to refute.

Hearsay[7]

Hearsay is information that a witness testifying in court heard about from someone else and did not see or hear himself or herself. The following are concerns that courts have about hearsay, and they explain why hearsay is often inadmissible:

1. The potential inaccuracy in secondhand reporting of the witness's statement.
2. The original witness's statement is not made under oath, and the jury could not view the demeanor of the witness making that original statement.
3. The witness making the original statement may not be available to be cross-examined.

The **hearsay evidence rule** states that hearsay cannot be used in court because secondhand testimony is unreliable and because the person who made the original statement is often unavailable for cross-examination. Hearsay is not limited to oral statements. Statements in the form of letters, affidavits, declarations, diaries, memos, notes, and e-mails can all constitute hearsay.

Testimony during a hearing or trial is not hearsay unless the witness repeats something someone else said or wrote. However, a statement introduced to prove something other than its truth might not be excluded as hearsay. For example, testimony may be offered to show the speaker's state of mind.

Example: Dana and Bruce were fighting, and Dana shouted, "Bruce, you are a lousy husband!" Marla heard the argument and was asked to testify at Dana and Bruce's divorce trial. Marla was permitted to repeat the statement "Bruce, you are a lousy husband" because it was not introduced to prove that

Bruce was a lousy husband, but rather to show that Dana was angry. This is one way secondhand information gets admitted into court.

Another common way that hearsay is admitted is through **prior contradictory statements**. A witness's earlier out-of-court statement may be presented at a trial or hearing if it contradicts his or her in-court testimony. The reason it is admitted is because the prior contradictory statement is being used to cast doubt on the witness's credibility. Addressing witness credibility is a common way for hearsay to be admitted. For example, if a witness originally said that the claimant fell during a snowstorm, but later at trial testified that the claimant fell days after the storm, then the prior statement could be admitted to show that the court testimony might not be credible.

In addition to the prior contradictory statement exception, a great many other exceptions to the hearsay rule also exist. These exceptions are typically based on the belief that the circumstances in which the hearsay is given make the hearsay evidence more likely to be truthful and reliable. The following are some common exceptions to the hearsay evidence rule:

- Admissions against interest
- Spontaneous, excited utterances (*res gestae*)
- Statements made for the purpose of making a medical diagnosis
- Recorded recollection
- Business and financial records
- Public records
- Guilty pleas
- Previous convictions

Admissions against interest are statements against the personal, pecuniary, or proprietary interest of a witness. Reliability of such statements is based on the assumption that a witness is unlikely to make a statement against himself or herself unless true.

Spontaneous, excited utterances are statements made under stress during or immediately after a traumatic event. Because of the speed with which an event occurred, the witness would not have time for fabrication. If, for example, immediately after an accident, the driver gets out of the car and says, "I'm so sorry; I couldn't see the traffic light because the sun was in my eyes," then this statement is admissible under the excited utterance exception. (It would also be admissible under the admission against interest exception.) Not all excited utterances are used against the declarant (person making the statement). For example, if, immediately after a serious accident, witnesses heard an injured person make expressions of pain before he died, testimony by those witnesses could be used to show that the person suffered after the accident.

Similarly, **statements made to doctors for purposes of making medical diagnosis** are also admissible. The reliability of these statements is based on the belief that people will not lie to their doctor about their health because their statements affect diagnosis and treatment. This exception does not apply to statements regarding past physical conditions. For example, a statement, "My back was really sore after the accident," would not be admissible because it is not related to the current diagnosis. However, a statement to a doctor such as, "It hurts when I turn in this direction" would be admissible because it relates to the immediate examination and diagnosis.

Although recorded recollections are normally considered hearsay and not admissible, some **past recorded recollections** (recording in writing, with tapes, or electronically) are admissible if:

1. They were accurately prepared.
2. They were made by the witness soon after the event occurred.
3. The witness testifies in court to the two preceding items.

If, for example, shortly after an accident, an eyewitness goes home and accurately writes down a description of the accident, this written description (past recorded recollection) can be used later in court if the witness no longer recalls the events. As long as the witness testifies that he or she wrote the description soon after the accident, it is admissible. Of course, a witness's current recollections are also important, but these past recollections are helpful when the witness has forgotten some facts or when the witness's memory needs to be refreshed. If these recollections were written or recorded by someone other than the witness, then the witness must verify their accuracy and agree that the description was made while the memory of the event was still fresh. Reliability of this information is based on the assumption that recollections that are immediately written down and recorded by a witness are likely to be accurate.

Business or financial records are documents kept regularly in the ordinary course of operating a business. Trustworthiness is founded on the fact that businesses routinely rely on the accuracy of such records.

Public records come in many forms. They set forth the activities observed pursuant to legal duty or factual findings resulting from a legally authorized investigation. There is a presumption of accuracy in public records because officials have a duty to make proper entries. Police reports would fall into this category of exceptions. The *factual findings* reported by the investigative officer, such as skid marks, the position of the vehicles when the officer arrived, and the physical condition of occupants in a vehicle would all be admissible. The officer's *opinions, conclusions* about fault, and *evaluations* of injuries or damage would be admissible only if they are based on facts and not on other, less reliable sources of information such as a passenger's statement.

Although a police report as a whole might not be considered hearsay, the report might contain hearsay statements. Police officers may write in their report what witnesses and others say. This does not mean that the statements don't have value but that they, by themselves, are not admissible evidence. Claim representatives should not rely solely on a police officer's conclusions or recollections of what witnesses might have said. Instead, they should contact the witnesses listed on a police report and obtain their statements directly.

Guilty pleas are admissible for proving liability. Guilty pleas are also admissions against interest. Evidence that a person pled guilty to a traffic violation can be used to establish negligence. Courts recognize that some people plead guilty to avoid spending time and money, but the burden of explaining the plea is on the person pleading guilty.

Prior convictions are usually not admissible to establish liability. For example, evidence that a traffic court found a person guilty of speeding would be hearsay and inadmissible in a civil court case. Some prior *criminal* convictions are admissible, but only for the purpose of establishing the lack of *credibility* of a witness.

Statements of Insureds

In most liability policies, the liability insuring agreement specifically states that the company may investigate and settle any claim or suit as it considers appropriate. Furthermore, most liability policies contain the so-called cooperation clause found in the "Duties After an Accident or Loss" section of the policy. According to this section, a person seeking any coverage (an insured) must cooperate with the insurer in the investigation, settlement, or defense of any claim or suit. This cooperation includes providing statements to claim representatives as often as needed. In most claims, the insured is the first person the claim representative contacts.

Claimant Statements

Although the insured is under a contractual obligation to cooperate with the representative in the claim investigation, a claimant or third-party witness is not. Usually, the claim representative has only one opportunity to obtain a statement from a claimant or witness. The importance of obtaining an informative and comprehensive statement during that initial contact cannot be overemphasized. Claim representatives are advised to conduct the initial investigation as comprehensively as possible, almost as if the case were going to trial.

When it is considered necessary (as it is in most cases) to contact the claimant, such contact should be made promptly in an effort to gain the claimant's confidence and trust and thereby establish rapport. It is important that after an accident, the claimant receive some immediate assurance of the company's interest in and consideration of the claim. In addition, the sooner the claim representative contacts the claimant, the better the chance that the claim representative will get an accurate account of the accident.

In a sense, the investigation of a claim is a psychological process in which the claim representative plays a multifaceted role—that of provider of information, counselor and motivator. Occasionally, a claimant's response to the representative's initial contact may be guarded and uncooperative.

The claimant has no legal obligation to cooperate with the representative or to give a statement, and the claim representative cannot compel the claimant to cooperate. However, before paying a claim, the representative needs to obtain information that frequently only the claimant can provide. The claim representative should indicate to the claimant that before a decision can be made with respect to payment of the claim, the representative needs to obtain the claimant's version of the accident as well as specific information about the injuries sustained and the medical expenses incurred. In other words, if the claim is paid, the payment must be justified by sufficient information gathered during the investigation.

Statement Priority Considerations

It is important that a claimant be contacted immediately so that the claim representative can develop a rapport with him or her. But should the claim representative contact the insured first? What if the claim representative has difficulty connecting with the insured?

The *insured* probably should be contacted first when the liability situation is complicated or unclear. In such cases, the insured's detailed version of the accident is necessary before a reasonably clear picture can be formed of how the accident occurred. In addition, when a coverage question exists, the claim representative should contact the insured before the claimant to explain the reservation of rights before proceeding with the investigation with the claimant.

The claimant should be contacted immediately even without having gotten the insured's version of the accident if rapport is the overriding factor in a claim, such as when liability is clear and the claimant's injuries are serious. The claimant might be contacted first when injuries are minor and there is no real question of liability (where liability is clear or probable), such as when the insured admitted fault at the time the accident was reported.

Obtaining Information From the Claimant's Attorney

Claimants are often represented by attorneys, but that should not keep claim representatives from trying to obtain information about the claimant. Because claim representatives are not permitted by law to speak directly to claimants, many fail to ask the claimant's attorney for statements, assuming that they will not cooperate. However, attorneys may be willing to assist if they believe that their client could benefit from providing a statement. In such situations, attorneys may prefer written, in-person statements that they can control better than recorded statements.

Information about injuries and wage loss can often be obtained from the attorney without a formal statement from the claimant. Claim representatives can ask the attorney to indicate the nature of the injury and the amount of the special damages on a claim. Too often, if the attorney replies that he or she does not yet have any information, claim representatives drop the questioning, write in their files, "the attorney does not have any information yet," and move on to the next claim.

Because the attorney accepted the case in the first place, it usually means that he or she spoke directly with the claimant and has some knowledge of the nature and extent of the injuries. When an attorney replies that he or she does not have any injury information, the claim representative might reply in the following manner: "I realize that you may not have any details yet, but you can give me at least a general idea of the injury for my file, can't you? I mean, did your client break a bone, or are we talking about soft-tissue injuries here? Was there any hospitalization? Did Mr. Claimant lose any time from work? What kind of work does he do? What part of the body was injured? Can you tell me whom the claimant is being treated by?" Claim representatives should develop a more persistent approach to obtaining this information when talking with attorneys the first time. If the inquiry is made courteously, claim representatives should be successful in obtaining information about the claimant's injuries, which is needed for establishing appropriate reserves and properly directing the investigation.

Witness Statements

With respect to claim investigations, a witness is someone who has personal knowledge of the accident through direct observation. Usually, a **witness** is one who has seen or heard the accident and can furnish evidence regarding the cause of the accident and the damages sustained by the parties involved. A witness can also be called on to give evidence or testify in court regarding the accident. Insureds and claimants are technically witnesses, too; however, in typical claim usage, "witness" refers to a third party.

The term "witness" refers to an "ordinary" witness rather than expert witnesses. Expert witnesses possess a special skill, experience, or an educational degree that qualifies them to testify on matters relating to their particular area of expertise—for example, medical doctors, engineers, and scientists. Expert witnesses are discussed later in this chapter.

Witnesses are often the key to clarifying the liability situation in an accident. Generally, ordinary witnesses are limited to furnishing evidence about the facts of an accident as they observed it. They usually are not permitted to testify as to their opinions or conclusions. There are some exceptions, however. An ordinary witness may be allowed to express an opinion about such things as the speed of cars, the emotional state of another person, the drunk or sober condition of another, the identity of a person by his appearance or voice (e.g., telephone conversations), or the value of objects or services with which he or she is familiar.[8]

Promptness in contacting witnesses is essential to a good investigation. The claim representative needs to make contact with the witness when the recollection of the accident is still fresh in his or her mind. If contact is delayed, the witness may forget important aspects of the accident or become indifferent or resistant to helping with the claim.

Locating Witnesses

Identifying and locating witnesses are the claim representative's responsibilities. The insured will often be able to identify witnesses to the accident, and police reports often contain the names and addresses of witnesses.

In addition to the insured and the police report, people who were with the insured or claimant are usually good sources of information with respect to the cause of the accident and the nature and extent of the injuries sustained. For auto accidents, passengers may be able to furnish important information. In premises fall-down cases, any person who might have accompanied the claimant at the time of the accident may be a valuable source of information.

When a claim warrants the additional effort, a neighborhood canvass of the accident scene should be conducted. This ordinarily entails a personal building-to-building or house-to-house search near the accident scene for people who may have witnessed the accident or arrived on the scene immediately after it occurred.

In some cases, someone may have seen or heard of a person whose testimony could have a significant bearing on the claim. Not every witness has to be an "eyewitness." Information about injuries or comments made by the parties to an accident frequently can be valuable. Exhibit 7-1 lists common sources for helping to identify potential witnesses.

Classification of Witnesses

Witnesses are classified according to their *attitude* and *liability position* regarding the accident. Classifications include friendly, unfriendly, supporting, adverse, or hostile. Although somewhat arbitrary, these classifications can have strategic and legal implications.

A *friendly* witness is one who cooperates willingly with the claim representative in the investigation. The witness may simply feel an obligation to come forth and tell the truth as his or her civic responsibility, or he or she may be a friend of the insured or claimant who simply wants the truth to be told.

Although the witness may cooperate fully with the claim representative, his or her position on liability may not support the insured. Such a witness may be classified as a *friendly* adverse witness because of the person's position or viewpoint on liability. If the witness's position is favorable to the insured's interests, he or she would be considered a *supporting* witness.

An *unfriendly* witness is one who does not cooperate in the investigation of the claim. The person's resistance may stem from a desire to avoid getting involved, based on a dislike of insurance companies or even antisocial behavior. In the event that this witness's version of the accident, if one could be obtained, were favorable to the insured, the witness would be an unfriendly but supporting witness. Usually, such a witness will be of little help to the insured's case unless some cooperation can be obtained.

A **hostile** witness is one whose response to the insured is more than just unfriendly; it is also adverse, and usually a hostile witness displays an attitude of bias or prejudice. The witness may hold a personal dislike based on the insured's race or nationality, occupation or position in society, physical features, or personality.

EXHIBIT 7-1

Sources for Identifying Witnesses

1. The insured.

2. The police report.

3. The motor vehicle report filed by the adverse driver. (Some states make this information confidential.)

4. Service people who may have been in the vicinity of the accident, such as mail carriers, bus drivers, police officers, newspaper carriers, and so on. (This obviously requires some leg work. A representative can go to the scene of the accident at the approximate time it happened and may find such service people available. Many such people are in the vicinity of the accident scene every working day at about the same time, since their jobs entail making deliveries or pickups on a regularly scheduled basis.)

5. Tow truck operators who may have removed the cars from the scene. Tow truck operators are often listed on the police report.

6. Photographers with access to police radios who regularly take photos of serious accident scenes to make them available for a charge to attorneys and insurance companies. (Experienced claim representatives usually know where to locate these photographers.)

7. Newspaper accounts of the accident. Sometimes a reporter will include the names of witnesses in his or her newspaper report of the accident. (Newspaper photographers should also be checked for information about witnesses.)

8. Newspaper advertising for witnesses. If the case warrants, advertising in the newspaper for witnesses can sometimes be effective in locating them. "Witnesses" who come forth in response to such ads, however, must be closely scrutinized for motivation and integrity.

9. Neighborhood checks. Walking around the neighborhood near the scene looking for people who might have seen the incident occur.

The classification of hostile witness has legal implications for trial. Normally a lawyer cannot ask a friendly or cooperative witness leading questions. For example, an insured's lawyer could not put a friendly witness on the stand and ask questions such as, "Is it true that this person (the claimant) ran the red light?" Instead, the lawyer is permitted to ask the witness only what he or she observed. This is to prevent the witness's testimony from being reduced to just agreeing with the lawyer's own words. However, lawyers *are* permitted to ask leading questions of hostile witnesses. This is commonly performed in cross-examination (questioning of the opposing party's testimony), but if a witness who was initially thought to be cooperative turns hostile, then the lawyer can ask the judge to have the witness declared a hostile witness, which permits a change in the mode of questioning.

Practical Considerations With Witnesses

It is important that claim representatives ask the witness to identify someone who will always know where the witness can be located. In addition, the claim representative should obtain the witness's Social Security number, his or her employer's name and address, and the identity of relatives or close friends who live nearby. If it appears that a case is heading for trial and a problem arises in locating a witness, this kind of information will aid the claim representative or legal counsel.

Claim representatives must understand that a witness is under no legal obligation to cooperate or give a statement, but once a lawsuit has been instituted, a witness can be compelled to testify at trial by subpoena. The downside of compelling a witness to testify is that it runs the risk of alienating the witness, with the result that his or her testimony may be useless or, worse yet, detrimental to the insured's case.

Impeachment of a Witness's Testimony

Impeachment is the process of calling something into question. Impeaching the testimony of a witness means calling into question the reliability of the testimony.

This applies to the testimony of insureds and claimants as well as to third-party witnesses. Testimony is impeached or challenged based on subject-matter inaccuracies or inconsistencies, lack of competence of the person giving the testimony, or a character problem in the person giving testimony.

Competence of Person Giving Testimony

The competence of a witness is likely to be challenged in court. To qualify the competence of a witness, the lawyer calling the witness must establish that the witness had an opportunity to see what happened, did see what happened, and still recalls what he or she saw many months ago. The lawyer could use statements taken by the claim representative after the accident to assist the witness in recalling the events. This is true even if the signed statement itself is not admissible evidence. State and federal rules allow a witness's recollection of events to be refreshed using statements and depositions. After a witness is determined to be competent, testimony regarding what he or she saw, heard, and did is evidence that the court uses to determine the issue at trial. After the witness's direct testimony has been given, opposing lawyers have an opportunity to cross-examine the witness. This includes asking questions about the witness's competence to testify. For example, the lawyer might point out that memories fade over time and several months have passed since the event.

Character of Witness

The character of a witness may be impeached. Character impeachment involves proving that a witness is unworthy of belief. Sometimes criminal convictions are used to establish a lack of witness credibility. Other methods of impeachment include:

Bias: Evidence that a witness is biased or has an interest in the outcome of a suit or claim is admissible as evidence to raise doubts about the witness's credibility.

Prior inconsistent statements: A witness's credibility may be attacked by showing that, on a previous occasion, the witness made a statement that is inconsistent with a material portion of the present testimony.

Character for truthfulness or untruthfulness: Evidence referring to a witness's reputation for truthfulness or untruthfulness is admissible to attack or support the credibility of that witness.

Expert Testimony

Experts render a valuable service by establishing facts on controversial issues. Determining how an accident occurred, whether a product failure injured a person, whether an injury is related to an insured's accident, whether weather played a role in an accident, and to what extent a business lost income because of an interruption are all things that experts can help to determine. Examples of experts who may be used in claims are medical specialists, accident reconstruction experts, engineers, climatological experts, accountants, and others, depending on the nature of the claim.

Overall, using an expert can prove to be of great advantage. Caution must be exercised to use the expert under the proper circumstances, as the cost involved can be substantial.

Typically, defense counsel chooses the expert because they usually know the capabilities of most experts and know which ones present themselves well, which are best qualified, and which are likely to be available.

Medical Specialists

As discussed previously, the need for a medical specialist may occur frequently. As a general rule, it is wisest to delay the defense medical examination to permit healing to progress, which often results in a favorable prognosis.

Accident Reconstruction Expert

An accident reconstruction expert is needed in cases in which injuries are serious and liability cannot be conclusively determined by information otherwise available. By using physical facts such as the point of impact on a car, the type of road surface, the weather, skid marks, and the coming-to-rest point of the vehicles, the expert may be able to arrive scientifically and mathematically at an accurate conclusion regarding the speed and direction of all vehicles involved in a crash. This information can then be used to assess negligence or comparative negligence.

Forensic Chemists and Toxicologists

Product liability claims, particularly those that relate to ingested products, are often the subject for a chemist, who can determine the chemical content of the product and establish whether it was the cause of the injury. If, for example, foreign matter is found in food, a chemist could assess whether that foreign matter produced a toxic substance and caused the alleged injury.

Construction Engineers

Any number of claims may require the services of a construction engineer, from the aspects of both collision with an object and damage resulting from the negligence of a contractor. Sometimes construction fails and causes injury. For example, a walkway, bridge, or roof may collapse and injure people. The cause of such a collapse must be discovered in order to determine liability. Construction engineers can help with this assessment. They can analyze the damage and determine the liability, perhaps pointing to a subcontractor or defective building materials.

Automotive Engineers

Numerous claims are made alleging that defective automobile parts caused injuries or fatalities. The use of automotive engineers becomes an important element both in the pursuit and the defense of these claims. The defects may involve anything from tires to gearshifts to improper design. Extremely large verdicts have been awarded in some of these claims, with a great deal of accompanying publicity. Defense verdicts are also rendered but usually not with the same amount of media attention.

Climatological Experts

Climatologists have proved to be a valuable source of expertise in establishing the weather conditions when they are alleged to be involved in an accident. These experts can pinpoint conditions in any given area of concern and answer questions presented in the course of the claim, such as:

How long had the snow or ice been on an insured's parking lot when the accident happened? Did the insured have sufficient time to remove the snow or ice, or was it a general condition in the entire community? Was the wind that blew an insured's tree onto a neighbor's car an unusually strong one approaching hurricane speeds, or was it a mild breeze that just blew over a dead tree that the insured should have removed before it had a chance to blow over?

Answering these questions can help with liability assessments. Experts in this field acquire weather data from numerous sources throughout the local area, including amounts of rainfall and snowfall and other climatological conditions.

Accountants

The services of an accountant are usually required to assist in evaluating property losses resulting from fire, theft, or burglary of inventory or stock and in cases in which loss of income claims are made. On occasion, the need for this type of expert arises in liability claims as well. A car or truck may crash into a building housing a retail store or a factory, causing loss of merchandise or stock and closing the business until repairs have been made to the building. Such claims require an immediate investigation to determine liability and, if it is present, employing an accountant to accurately establish the value of the loss. Unless such an expert is retained, the liability insurer may risk having to pay for shortages, obsolescence, or other charges.

SCIENTIFIC EVIDENCE

Generally, scientific evidence refers to evidence that draws its convincing force from some principle of science, mathematics, or the like. Typically, experts present scientific evidence. Based on the 1993 Supreme Court decision Daubert v. Merrell Dow Pharmaceuticals, experts are permitted to offer their scientific opinions only after the trial judge has decided that the opinion:

1.   Is based on good scientific knowledge and
2.   Will assist the court in understanding the issue in question.

The judge acts as a gatekeeper to prevent highly speculative scientific opinion from reaching a jury. Sometimes a special hearing is required to determine whether an opinion should be admitted. Factors that a judge will consider are (1) whether the principles and methods used in obtaining the evidence have been tested and have gained general acceptance in the scientific community, (2) whether they have been published and subjected to peer review, and (3) whether the rate of error is acceptable. For instance, DNA evidence has been used to prove a defendant's innocence because DNA tests are considered reliable.

Voice Identification

In claims, it may sometimes be necessary to confirm that the person heard on a recorded statement is actually the person who is identified in the recording. Sometimes insureds or claimants will deny that they gave a voice recording or claim that the recording has been altered. In some such cases, scientific evidence may be required to determine the identity of the voice. Courts might rely on devices that are capable of producing graphic impressions of a person's voice (spectographic voice identification) to make this determination. This evidence would be admitted only if the method used to produce the graphic was generally accepted and certified by the Organization of Voice Examiners.[9] Claim professionals who need this type of evidence must ensure that the experts used are familiar with the rules of evidence.

Detection of Intoxication and Narcotics

Claim representatives sometimes encounter claims involving people who were allegedly intoxicated. Liability sometimes hinges on determining whether the insured or claimant had been under the influence of drugs or alcohol at the time of the accident. Breathalyzers can measure the level of a person's intoxication. Legislatures have given extensive attention to these devices and typically accept their results and the presumptions from their results. For example, a blood alcohol level of 0.05 percent (or less) raises the presumption that the person was not under the influence of alcohol. However, a finding of 0.10 percent would create the presumption of intoxication.

A drug called Nalline has been used to detect recent use of narcotics. When Nalline is administered, the person's pupils dilate if he or she has recently used narcotics. Courts have generally accepted Nalline tests.[10] Courts have also accepted urine and blood tests in establishing alcohol or narcotics use.[11]

Psychological Testimony

As the field of psychology advances, many of its principles have become scientifically accepted and used in trials. In one case, a defendant sought to introduce evidence that his "personality profile" was inconsistent with the crime of murder. The judge ruled that this evidence should be excluded and not heard by the jury because it was not reliable enough to prove the defendant's innocence (the error rate and the high risk of prejudicing a jury would outweigh any benefit from the evidence).[12] On the other hand, psychological testimony stating that a common characteristic of sexually abused children is that they recant their testimony shortly before trial has been considered admissible in liability claims involving sexual molestation. To make a proper liability decision, claim representatives should consult with legal counsel about the admissibility of psychological testimony proffered by the claimant because it is a continually evolving legal area.

DEMONSTRATIVE AND DOCUMENTARY EVIDENCE

As part of a liability investigation, claim representatives must gather documents such as police and weather reports, medical and financial records, and similar documentary evidence. For many claims, demonstrative evidence such as diagrams, photographs, and videos are required to properly evaluate and present liability issues to a judge or jury.

Police Reports

Police and highway patrol reports often contain a wealth of information about the vehicles involved, the parties involved, witnesses, and the observations of the police officer after he or she arrived on the scene. Many police reports have diagrams of the accident and show important physical facts such as skid marks or visual obstructions. Exhibit 7-2 shows an example of the typical information contained on a police report.

As mentioned earlier in the discussion on hearsay, a police report contains secondhand information or hearsay. Ordinarily, it contains basically what other people have told the police officer, unless the officer witnessed the accident. In cases in which an investigating officer is dispatched to the scene almost immediately after the accident occurred, his or her report regarding the position and condition of the cars in the street, location of debris, and conditions of the drivers and occupants may be particularly helpful.

On the positive side, the police report ordinarily contains the names and addresses of those involved in the accident as well as the names and addresses of any witnesses. It also includes information about claimed injuries, points of impact and vehicle damage, factors contributing to the accident, and any

EXHIBIT 7-2

Excerpt From Police Report

Police Report

Accident Date: 12-31-XX	Accident Time: 9:35 P.M.
Location: Route 21	High Ridge
Speed Limit: 35 mph	Weather Conditions: Rain

Probable Contributing Circumstances:

V1	V2	
☐	☐	Vehicle Detect
☒	☐	Speeding
☐	☐	Signal Violation
☐	☐	Improper Turn
☐	☐	Drinking
☐	☐	Drugs
☐	☐	Wrong Way
☐	☐	Failed To Yield
☐	☒	Improper Lane Use
☐	☐	Improper Passing
☐	☐	Following Too Closely
☒	☒	Inattention

C	Injury	Safety Devices
O	1. Fatal	1. None used
D	2. Disabling	2. Seat Belt
E	3. Evident - Not disabling	3. Air Bag
S	4. None apparent	4. Child Restraint

Name	Date of Birth	Injury	Safety Devices	Vehicle
Bill Johnson	4-1-75	3	1	1
Ed Smith	2-25-75	2	1	1
Unknown	—	—	—	2
Lisa Malchance	7-13-87	1	N/A	N/A
Eve Malchance	8-9-49	4	N/A	N/A

Diagram of Accident:

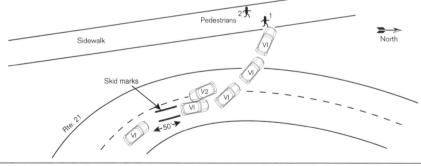

Officer's Statement:

Driver #1 (Bill Johnson) stated that he was traveling at around 45 mph, which driver admits to being "A little too fast," when he was met by an oncoming vehicle (Vehicle #2) in his lane of traffic. Driver #1 stated that he took evasive action but could not avoid the vehicle. He subsequently lost control of the vehicle and struck Pedestrian #1.

Passenger in Vehicle #1 (Ed Smith) stated that Driver #1 lost control of the vehicle after the impact with Vehicle #2 and then left the roadway and struck Pedestrian #1.

Pedestrian #2 (Eve Malchance) said that she was walking with her daughter (Pedestrian #1, Lisa Malchance) when she heard the accident and turned around to see Vehicle #1 heading for her daughter. She had no time to react before Vehicle #1 struck her daughter, killing her instantly.

Vehicle #2 left the scene of the accident and could not be identified.

traffic violations or arrests. In most cases, there is a sketch or diagram of the accident made by the investigating officer from information furnished by the drivers and witnesses, if any.

Some police officers, especially those in rural communities, are willing to talk with claim representatives about the accident. They can provide information about complaints alleged, attention given to injured persons, and accusations or comments made by the drivers that may shed important light on the case. Police in metropolitan areas may have less willingness or time to provide additional information.

Diagrams

Frequently, a diagram of the accident scene is helpful in forming a picture of how the accident happened. In more serious cases, claim representatives will want to personally inspect the accident scene as soon after the accident as possible.

A diagram can be an important part of a claim file. It should carefully document all permanent physical landmarks, traffic controls, signs, and so on to portray the scene as it appeared at the time of the accident. Accident investigation templates with sufficient symbols to draw a fairly detailed diagram are usually available from a variety of sources. Many companies supply their claim representatives with such templates or symbols for diagramming accidents.

Ideally, a diagram should be drawn to scale so that it will portray the accident scene as accurately as possible. It should also contain a legend or table showing the date, time, and location the diagram depicts; the date of the accident; the name of the representative who made the diagram (optional); and any other identifying marks that might be important, such as landmarks, obstructions, and so on.

The diagram also should indicate directions. For example, north is always at the top of the diagram. The names of the streets; the location of traffic controls; location of lights; the presence of any obstructions such as trees, shrubs, or other impediments; the presence of any hills or slopes, with some indication of the distances between these items, should also be included in the diagram. The points of impact of the cars involved or, if a fall-down case, the specific location of the fall should be shown as well. An example of a diagram is shown in Exhibit 7-3.

When statements are being taken in person, it is a good idea to request that the party being interviewed, whether an insured, a claimant, or a witness, make a diagram (usually before the statement) that can serve as a basis for discussion. The individual should be asked to sign or initial the diagram, and it should be made a part of the claim file along with the statement.

Photographs, Videos, and Films

When evidence that is material to a case must be preserved, such as skid marks, it is essential that photographs be taken promptly. It is advisable, in moderate to serious claims, to have professional photographs taken. Skid marks, for example, usually do not last for more than a few days, so time is limited. Of course, if professional photographs cannot be arranged or taken promptly, the representative should take his or her own photos of the scene. Skid marks or road factors such as broken pavement or potholes should be measured and described on a tab or tape and attached to the photographs. The location and nature of debris from an auto accident may also be of considerable value and should be photographed.

EXHIBIT 7-3

Diagram of Auto Accident[13]

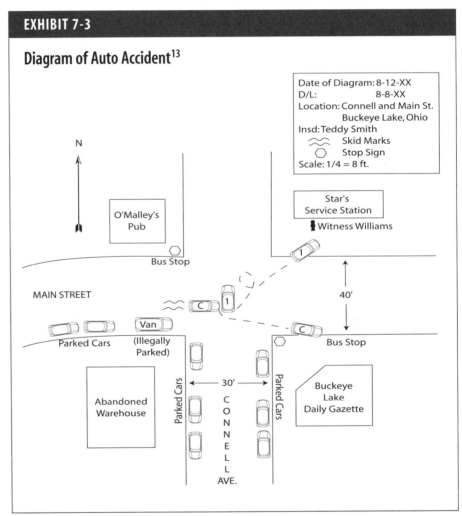

In serious cases, photos of the scene of the accident, regardless of whether any visible objects remain from the accident, can be valuable when a representative or supervisor is trying to formulate a picture of how the accident occurred. Of equal importance with respect to photos is the position of the cars at the accident scene. Photographs of the points of impact and damage to the vehicle(s) should be taken from several angles.

Photos should be identified with the date of the accident; the date, time, and place of the photograph; and the direction of the view. This information should be included in the tab that is attached to the photo.

As mentioned earlier, some photographers are linked to local police departments with two-way police radios and make a practice of photographing the scenes of serious accidents and selling the photos to interested parties such as insurance companies and attorneys. Because of the potential value of this kind of photograph, claim representatives should learn the identity and location of such photographers. It is also important to keep in mind that a newspaper photographer or a television cameraperson may have photographs or videotape that recorded the aftermath of a serious accident. Claim representatives can ask the media to review the photographs or videos. News media usually provide videos and photographs for a reasonable cost.

Finally, selecting a professional photographer should be done with some care. The criteria should be quality of the photography as well as the reliability and witness quality of the photographer. Would he or she make a good and credible witness?

Videos and films are sometimes used to establish the claimant's physical ability to perform certain activities. If a person who claims to be disabled because of a back injury is videotaped at a party doing the limbo, it can help to establish a lack of credibility in the claimant's allegations. Videos or films are usually taken without the claimant's knowledge by professional investigators the insurance company has hired, but occasionally they are taken by acquaintances of the claimant who find insurance fraud distasteful.

Videos or films that are taken by investigators doing activity checks must be made carefully so as not to invade the privacy of the claimant. Since the objective of an activity check is to obtain information about the claimant's injuries and current activities, the questions the claim representative asks of claimants must be confined to that subject. Claim representatives should hire only licensed, ethical investigators who would make a good impression on a jury.

To be useful in court, the video or film must clearly identify the claimant as the person engaging in the activity. The person taking the video or film must be able to establish the date, time, and place of the activity. To avoid the argument that the claimant was "just having a rare good day," it is sometimes necessary to show the claimant doing activities on more than one occasion.

Manuals and Instructional Materials

Items such as contracts, sales brochures, manuals, instructions, and internal memos are all potential documentary evidence. These writings must be authenticated (identified as the true documents) and relevant in order to be admitted as evidence. Courts prefer the original document over photocopies whenever a person wishes to prove the terms of a contested writing. Claim representatives should treat this documentary evidence with the same care and detail as real, physical evidence and be able to establish a chain of custody. The chain of custody issue is covered in detail later in this chapter in the section on real evidence.

Weather Reports

Weather can be a factor in automobile as well as premises fall-down claims. In such cases, weather reports should be obtained. They are particularly helpful in claims that are reported too late for the representative to be able to personally inspect the scene and preserve it with photographs. Some claims are reported months or even years after the accident occurred. A premises fall-down case in which it is alleged that an accumulation of snow and ice caused the claimant to fall is a good example of a claim in which weather reports can be useful. Claim representatives can secure weather reports for the days or weeks preceding an accident (even when the request for these reports is made long after the accident occurred). These reports indicate the extent and kind of precipitation that occurred in the area. Weather reports are available from any branch of the National Weather Service, from local airport authorities, or from independent meteorological organizations. The government's National Climatic Data Center (NCDC), located in Asheville, North Carolina, is the world's largest active archive of weather data. NCDC produces numerous climate publications, responds to data requests from all over the world, and operates the world's largest archive of weather data.[14]

Motor Vehicle Reports

Most states require that motorists in an auto accident involving property damage over a specified amount or any bodily injury complete an accident report to be filed with the state motor-vehicle department. The accessibility of these reports to insurance companies varies from state to state. In some states, the reports are confidential and cannot be obtained by insurers, while in other states, they can be obtained and are admissible as evidence against the particular motorist, should the motorist admit fault.

Traffic or Criminal Court Hearings

Although the evidence presented at traffic court hearings is generally not admissible in a subsequent civil trial, much valuable information can be gathered from the hearing. Ordinarily, there is considerable consistency between the evidence furnished in a traffic hearing and that furnished in a subsequent civil case.

At times, it is advisable for claim representatives to attend a traffic court hearing and to take notes and document the claim file as to what evidence was presented at the hearing. It is important to remember, however, that claim people should refrain from advising or representing insureds in a criminal matter. Advising or counseling an insured in this manner constitutes the practice of law. For this reason, the insured should be advised to refer any inquiries concerning the criminal case to his or her personal attorney.

The relationship between traffic court and civil court can become confusing for insureds. If an insured pleads guilty in traffic court, the guilty plea *can* be admitted as evidence that the insured was negligent, but evidence that a traffic court found an insured who pled not guilty to be guilty of the traffic infraction would not be admissible in a civil lawsuit against the insured.

Claim Database

Insurance Services Office, Inc. (ISO) has the property and casualty insurance industry's most comprehensive database, ISO ClaimSearch^{SM}, which was created as a tool for fighting insurance fraud. The ISO ClaimSearch is a single system that contains information on bodily injury, property, and vehicle claims and houses a database from the former Index and PILR systems and from the databases formerly administered by the National Insurance Crime Bureau (NICB).

This database contains records of bodily injury claims made against subscriber companies. When a subscriber company receives a bodily injury claim, information about the claimant—such as name and address, reported injuries, age, Social Security number, occupation, date and place of accident, treating doctor, and so on—is reported to the bureau. Any information about the claimant's previous claim activity is accessible to a subscriber company. As a result, subscriber companies gain information about the person's claim history, including previous injuries sustained, and this can alert companies to a "professional" claimant or an individual who attempts to make a living by presenting inflated, groundless, or fraudulent claims.

Newspaper Articles

Sometimes information can be obtained from the details presented in a newspaper article. The newspaper articles by themselves are probably not admissible evidence, but they may list information and names of witnesses that the claim representative can use in his or her investigation.

Medical Records

Claim representatives can learn much about a claimant's injury and/or disability through medical records. These include emergency room reports; physician bills and reports; and hospital records that contain nurses' notes, medicines taken, and the results of lab tests or X-rays. All of these convey vital information about the claimant's injury and help to establish the claimant's damages. A signed medical authorization from the claimant is necessary before medical records can be obtained.

Autopsy Report and Death Certificate

In cases in which death results from an accident or from a cause that is not readily apparent, an autopsy is usually performed on the deceased person. An **autopsy** is a scientifically detailed examination of the body of the deceased in an effort to determine the cause of death. Autopsy reports ordinarily can be obtained from the medical examiner's office upon payment of the required fee. Autopsy reports are particularly important in cases in which there is a possibility that the claimant's death may have been caused by a factor other than the accident, such as a heart attack or blackout, that preceded the accident.

A **death certificate** identifies the cause of death and any contributing factors and is valuable to claim people when knowledge or confirmation of the precise cause of death is necessary.

Toxicology reports may also be requested when the representative suspects the claimant might have been drinking before or at the time of the accident. Such reports will indicate whether alcohol or any other drugs or toxins were in the deceased's bloodstream at the time of death.

School Records

Information obtained from a claimant's school records can be significant in developing a profile of a minor claimant's physical and mental activities before and after the accident. Information about attendance, grades, athletic ability, and time off from school because of the accident can help to determine the seriousness of the claimant's injuries.

Income Tax Records

These records can be helpful in establishing what a person reported to the government as income. If a person is claiming wage loss, then income tax records, along with wage loss forms completed by the claimant's employer, are needed to verify the lost wages claim. Income tax records can provide an overall picture of the person's wages, which is important to know when a disability extends over several months or years. A claimant who derives most of his income from landscaping work in the summer may have an extensive wage loss claim for losses in the summer months, but it would be inaccurate to project these summer earnings through winter months when the claimant historically earned much less. A signed authorization from the claimant is required to obtain wage information.

Other Records

Other reports or records that are sometimes helpful or necessary for claim representatives to obtain include the following:

- *Military records*—For background information on the claimant. If discharge records are available, they also may be quite helpful.
- *Divorce proceedings*—When divorce is a factor in a claim, the record of the divorce proceeding is necessary to determine dependency information.
- *Health club record*—Used to determine whether the claimant continued to exercise during an alleged period of disability.
- *Credit card records*—Can establish where the claimant was and how the claimant spent money during the alleged period of disability. Sometimes these records will indicate claimant activities that are inconsistent with a given disability.
- *Telephone records*—Can indicate when an insurance agent or a claim representative was called. This can be important in coverage situations in which it is necessary to confirm that the insured called the insurer. For

example, if the insured alleges calling an agent to modify coverage on a given day, telephone records could establish whether such a call was made. For a coverage dispute based on late notice, telephone records could help to determine whether the insured called and reported the claim to the claim department months earlier as alleged.

- *Liens and bankruptcy records*—Are helpful in suspected fraud or arson claims because they help to answer questions about the financial condition of the insured and the motive for committing fraud or arson.

PHYSICAL (REAL) EVIDENCE

Physical or real evidence consists of items such as a malfunctioning toaster that started a fire, defective parts or machinery that caused injury, glass that shattered, and property damaged in an accident. This type of tangible, physical evidence must be competent and must be identified and authenticated through a well-documented chain of custody in order to be admissible at trial. For example, while inspecting a car shortly after an accident, a claim representative noticed a frayed piece of brake cable lying under the car. Recognizing the potential importance, the claim representative photographed the cable in its location, then placed it in an envelope. The claim representative sealed the envelope, wrote a description of the contents, including where and when it was collected, and gave the envelope to an engineering firm for analysis. The engineering firm sent the item and analysis to lawyers to be used at trial. This is an example of the chain of custody that must be documented and established to admit an item into evidence at trial. The first link, the claim representative taking possession of the cable, connects the brake cable to the vehicle involved in the accident. Failure to document the chain of custody can result in the evidence not being admitted.

Spoliation of Evidence

Spoliation is the failure to preserve property for another's use in pending or future litigation. Claim representatives should preserve evidence, especially when the physical evidence may be needed later by one side or the other for litigation or subrogation purposes.

Several state court decisions have held that spoliation occurs when "crucial" evidence is destroyed or altered. Examples of crucial evidence include a heater that exploded, a furnace that malfunctioned, a car that caught fire, or a crimping machine alleged to have caused an injury. In determining whether crucial evidence had been destroyed, an Alabama decision held that where a party saved a component part of a gas system but failed to preserve the entire system, evidence was spoliated. The reasoning behind these holdings is that if a product is the focus of an investigation, the entire product is crucial evidence.[15] The same logic applies to an entire automobile if the automobile is crucial evidence to establishing liability. For example, accident reconstruction experts (discussed in the next section) are sometimes asked to make determinations about the cause of an accident based on the damage to the vehicle. In such cases, claim representatives should forego selling the vehicle for salvage until all related claims have been concluded.

Claim representatives and their companies can be sued for failing to preserve crucial evidence. For that reason, claim representatives should err on the side of caution and store in a safe place any evidence that is likely to be used for litigation until the claim has been completely concluded.

ADMISSIBILITY OF OTHER TYPES OF EVIDENCE

Claim representatives are sometimes presented with other types of evidence, such as the habits of the insured or claimant or actions taken by an insured or a claimant after an accident has occurred.

Habit and Routine Practice

Evidence of the habits of a person, regardless of the presence of eyewitnesses, is relevant to prove the conduct of a person conformed with his or her routine practice.[16]

Consider a man who drives his car through a neighborhood to avoid traffic each day. Each day, he slows down but does not stop at the stop sign, and this conduct is observed by various residents in the area. If he later has an accident with the insured, and the insured alleges that the man "rolled through the stop sign," then evidence of his habit would be relevant to the claim. The insured's version could be supported by the testimony of others, even though they were not eyewitnesses to the accident with the insured. The man could refute the testimony, but it could still help establish that the insured's version is more credible.

Habit should be distinguished from character traits; such traits that are not habitual behavior are not admissible. For example, that a person is "punctual" or "clean" would not be admissible; these are generalizations. However, this same person's habit of arriving at 9:00 A.M. and parking in the same spot every day would be admissible if it had a bearing on a claim.

Subsequent Remedial Measures

Measures that are taken after an event that, if taken previously, would have made the event less likely to occur, are not admissible to prove negligence.[17] For example, if a man is attacked on the parking lot of a drinking establishment and the next night the establishment posts security guards in the parking lot, this subsequent measure could not be used to show that the establishment should have had security guards to start with. The same rule applies to a business that fixes the stairs where a person fell. The fact that it fixed the stairs would not be admissible to prove liability.

Privilege

Some evidence that one party gives to another is not admissible because of the relationship between the two parties. This evidence usually involves statements by one party to another. **Privilege**, as recognized by the law, allows a person to refuse to disclose and to prohibit others from disclosing certain confidential communications. It is based on the promotion of free communication on topics relevant to certain professional services or the establishment of areas of private communication and activity.

The most commonly encountered privilege is that of attorney-client. This privilege protects confidential communications made to a practicing attorney in his or her professional capacity and is necessary and proper to enable the attorney to perform the functions of his or her office. In order for the privilege to exist, the client must consult the attorney in a professional capacity and seek advice on a legal matter.

Another common privilege is that of physician-patient. This privilege protects confidential communications made to, or documents shared with, physicians, surgeons, or physician's assistants in their professional capacity to assist in the diagnosis and treatment of a patient. Without a medical authorization signed by the patient, doctors will refuse to release medical information and documents based upon this privilege. In addition, claim representatives should be aware of several other forms of privilege, such as husband-wife (marital), clergy-penitent, counselor-student, and journalist-informant.

SETTING THE SCOPE OF THE INVESTIGATION

It would not be practical to gather all the possible evidence on every single claim. How much evidence is necessary for a given claim? How extensive should the liability investigation be? The scope of a liability investigation depends on several factors, such as the following:

1. The existence of coverage questions
2. The potential damage exposure or the damages alleged
3. The nature and complexity of the accident or loss
4. The likely degree of liability
5. The insurance company's claim philosophy

Coverage Questions

The investigation of coverage issues is often extensive because the company must establish whether the facts of the accident fall within the terms of the policy, and this decision seldom occurs without taking detailed statements and examining the facts. Coverage denials based on insufficient investigations can lead to bad faith lawsuits.

Potential Damage Exposure

An auto accident involving several cars and serious injuries will require a prompt and thorough investigation because of the potential extent of damages. Even if liability is doubtful, the damage exposure would be enough to require an extensive investigation. On the other hand, a rear-end collision with no injuries may require a minimal investigation and may be handled rather routinely.

Accident Complexity

The complexity of the claim is another factor in determining how extensive an investigation is required. A premises fall-down case in a supermarket parking lot, where responsibility for maintenance and repairs may rest with an insured supermarket because of the wording of a lease between the supermarket and the landlord, might require a comprehensive investigation. Product liability claims typically require numerous hours of investigation, as do environmental liability claims, because of the difficulty of determining whether a product failure caused an injury or whether the insured's operations caused environmental damage. Experts are often needed to help determine accident causation on these types of claims.

Liability Assessment

An initial liability assessment will also determine the scope of an investigation. Because the discussion of the investigative process will repeatedly refer to the various categories of liability as they relate to the insured, it is necessary to explain these liability categories before proceeding. There are four categories of liability: clear, probable, doubtful, and questionable.

When an insured's liability is characterized as *clear*, it means that there is no question that the insured was entirely at fault for the accident and that the claim is one for settlement (assuming that coverage is in order). An example of a clear liability auto case is one in which the insured admits to colliding with the rear of the claimant's vehicle when there were no extenuating circumstances such as a sudden stop by the claimant.

A case of *probable* liability on the insured's part simply means that while it may not be a clear-cut case of liability, the insured was probably at fault for the accident. In other words, it is likely that, based on the facts, the insured would not prevail if the case were litigated. An example of a probable liability case might be an intersection accident in which the insured was facing a stop sign and did not come to a full stop, while the claimant was subject to no traffic controls. Although there may be some room to argue for the imposition of some contributory negligence on the claimant's part in such cases, the details and circumstances of the accident point convincingly to the insured's greater negligence. In a clear or probable liability case, the investigation needed to determine liability may be minimal. The coverage and damages aspects of the claim, however, may need to be extensively investigated.

When an insured's liability is viewed as *doubtful*, it means that in all likelihood the insured was not negligent or legally liable for the accident. The doubtful liability classification is sometimes used to describe a case in which the insured is virtually free from liability as well. When there is doubtful or no liability on the insured's part, a minimum of investigation may be necessary. But if the claim is one that is being pressed by the plaintiff and will need to be defended, a thorough investigation will be necessary and warranted so that a successful defense can be developed and presented at trial.

The final category, which creates the greatest challenge for claim representatives, is that of *questionable* liability. In a case of questionable liability, it is unclear which party bears primary responsibility for the accident. It may be a case in which each party is partly negligent for the mishap, and there may be a genuine question as to how the accident happened. Questionable liability claims may be defended, depending on the circumstances of the case and the laws of the particular jurisdiction, but more often than not, these cases are compromised.

A questionable liability claim will also require a thorough investigation of liability and damages. Whether the claim is denied or negotiated to a compromise, the claim representative will need to support his or her decision with a well-documented claim file.

Telephone Investigations

Today's fast-paced, efficiency-driven claims environment requires companies, independent adjusting firms, and third-party administrators to handle claims as cost effectively as possible. Telephone claim handling is appropriate because the majority of claims are minor in dollar amount and can be resolved rather routinely and with a minimum of investigative effort. Low or fixed dollar-amount, high-volume claims such as collision, comprehensive, or property damage, and even medical payments and minor bodily injury claims can be appropriately handled by telephone claim units.

Most companies that use telephone investigations as their primary method of investigation believe that considerable investigation can be accomplished using the telephone. Telephone claim representatives, for example, can secure telephone-recorded statements of insureds, claimants, and witnesses. They can obtain police and fire reports and, with proper authorization, can verify lost wages and medical and hospital expenses as well as obtain doctors' reports on claimants.

In addition to having claim representatives handle liability by phone, some companies give call center employees or insurance agents the authority to settle relatively minor, routine claims that require little or no investigation. These workers still need to know how to identify claims that should be passed on to the main claim handling personnel.

If the telephone units are handling anything more than routine claims, managers should be sure that claim representatives are properly trained and capable of handling the more complicated claims. Second, claim representatives should be taught to recognize early the potentially troublesome claims that are not suited for volume-oriented telephone claim handling but rather require the face-to-face personal contact and attention of an experienced field claim representative.

Obtaining Help From the Field

The kinds of claims that telephone units handle depend basically on company claim philosophy. Some companies limit the telephone claim units to minor property damage claims, assigning all bodily injury claims and moderate to severe property claims to field claim representatives. Other companies have their telephone units handling small to moderate bodily injury claims as well, including the negotiation and settlement of such claims. Still other companies operate almost exclusively with telephone claim representatives who handle virtually every type of claim and play a dual role. They spend most of their time in the office, but occasionally they do field investigations on more serious or complicated claims. Some telephone units assign limited work to independent claim adjusters as the need requires.

Setting Investigation Priorities

It is important that claim representatives conduct their investigations in a logical and orderly manner.

Whether the claim is assigned to an office telephone representative or a field claim representative, the accident report should be reviewed and checked carefully. This is true regardless of whether the representative begins the investigation in the field without any direction from his or her supervisor or receives the assignment directly from the supervisor with specific items of investigation being assigned. As the claim representative studies the accident report, he or she should make notes about any unusual circumstances or problems associated with the claim.

When reviewing accident reports, claim representatives should be thinking in terms of *coverage*, *liability*, and *damages*. Analyze what coverage is provided, what the liability situation is, and what damages are being claimed. As a claim representative gains more experience, the important points or unusual aspects of a claim will stand out in the representative's mind as he or she examines the loss report.

An investigation outline developed at the beginning stages of the claim can be helpful in the claim representative's conducting the investigation in an organized manner. The investigation should be planned and scheduled so that information or evidence that may be available for only a short time is obtained first. Damaged property, for example, must be inspected and perhaps photographed before repairs are made. Diagrams and photographs of the accident scene should be obtained promptly. This is especially true if weather conditions such as snow or ice were a factor in the claim. Usually, there is little value in, for example, taking photos in May or June of a premises fall-down case involving snow and ice that occurred in February. Although the photos will provide a general picture of the scene of the accident, they cannot possibly depict the scene as it was at the time of the accident.

Investigating the Injury and Damages

This chapter is not intended to describe the details of medical investigation. For a thorough explanation of this topic, consult the AIC 34 textbook, *Managing Bodily Injury Claims*.[18] The injuries reported should be carefully examined with a view toward determining precisely how they were caused. Once the investigation gets underway, the claim representative will attempt to determine the nature and extent of the injuries and confirm that a causal relationship exists between the accident and the injuries. Whenever it is discovered that the claimant previously sustained an injury similar to the current injury, the representative should secure a medical history from the claimant. This entails gathering specific information about prior injuries, treatment, lost time from work, and disability.

Reporting on Liability Claims

The purpose of conducting a liability investigation is to help assess liability and to have this information to use later to settle the claim. Claim representatives often have more than 100 files that they are working on at the same time, and they need to be able to quickly recall the information about each. Conducting a thorough investigation that uncovers important liability issues is of little use if these issues and important facts are forgotten or overlooked at the time of negotiations.

The reality is that claim representatives may have little time to review before entering negotiation on a claim that they investigated weeks or even months earlier. When a claim representative receives a call from an attorney, it is difficult for the claim representative to ask the attorney to call back later, knowing that it may be several days and numerous phone messages later before the claim representative can speak with the attorney again. Claim representatives cannot afford to rely solely on memory. The information they obtain in an investigation must be recorded in the claim file within a reasonable time and organized in a way so that it can be quickly recalled and used in settlement negotiations.

Other people also need to know what is happening in a case. Supervisors, managers, and sometimes defense attorneys find themselves in positions where they are compelled to make a decision in the claim representative's absence. The file must speak for itself and provide these people with sufficient information to make a proper decision. Furthermore, claim representatives may not always be available to answer questions about a claim. They may resign, get transferred, take a vacation, or become ill. Many claim units handle claims in teams, and each team member must have access to all important liability information.

Common captions in an initial report include:

1. Date, time, and place of accident,
2. Coverage information and coverage questions,
3. Accident description,
4. Insured's data,
5. Claimant's data,
6. Assessment of liability,
7. Injury and damages,
8. Subrogation possibilities, and
9. Recommendations for future handling.

Appendix C shows an example of a claim report on a somewhat complicated liability claim.

CONCLUSION

The liability investigation involves identifying witnesses, taking statements, and assessing evidence. Claim representatives must be familiar with the rules of evidence regarding statements and other evidence gathered as part of the liability investigation. To prevent overworking a simple claim or under investigating a complex one, claim representatives must establish a scope for the investigation. Many claims require only a few phone calls and an estimate of property damage. Other claims require detailed, comprehensive investigations in which claim representatives must gather information from numerous evidentiary sources and consult with experts about the evidence. Establishing an appropriate investigative scope requires good judgment that in many cases comes from experience. Claim representatives must report on their liability investigations in a concise, organized manner.

CHAPTER NOTES

1. Adapted from Graham Lilly, *An Introduction to the Law of Evidence*, 3d ed. (St. Paul, Minn.: West Publishing Company, 1996), p. 26.

2. Lilly, p. 592.

3. Doris Hoopes, *The Claims Environment*, 2d ed. (Malvern, Pa.: Insurance Institute of America, 2000).

4. Robert Prahl and Stephen Utrata, *Liability Claim Concepts and Practices* (Malvern, Pa.: Insurance Institute of America, 1985), pp. 255-256.

5. James H. Donaldson, *Casualty Claim Practice*, 3d ed. (Homewood, Ill.: Richard D. Irwin, Inc., 1976), p. 622.

6. Examples include Language Line Services at www.languageline.com; OnLine Interpreters, Inc., and Interpreting Services International, Inc.

7. This section adapted from Lectric Law Library's Legal Dictionary (www.lectlaw.com), November 2000.

8. Donaldson, p. 622.

9. United States v. Jones 24 F. 3d 1177, 1179-80 (9th Cir. 1994).

10. People v. Zavala, 239 Cal. App. 2d 732 (49 Cal. Rptr. 129 1966).

11. Spence v. Farrier, 807 F. 2d 753 (8th Cir. 1986).

12. Byrd v. State, 593 N.E. 2d 1183, 1184 (Ind. 1992).

13. Prahl and Utrata, p. 227.

14. World Wide Web: http://www.ncdc.noaa.gov/.

15. Alabama: Cincinnati Ins. Co. v. Synergy Gas, Inc., 585 Gas, Inc., 585 So. 2d 822 (Ala. 1991).

16. Federal Rule of Evidence, Article IV Rule 406.

17. Federal Rule of Evidence, Article IV Rule 407.

18. James R. Jones, *Managing Bodily Injury Claims* (Malvern, Pa.: Insurance Institute of America, 2000).

Appendix A—Recorded Statements

I. **Recorded Statement Guidelines**

1. All parties to the interview must be identified. Date and time of the interview and location of all parties at the time of the interview must be established. Identity of the interviewee should include his or her name, age, and address.

2. It must be clear in the recording that the interviewee was aware that a recording was being made and that it was done with his or her permission.

3. All proper names, unusual sounding locations, and any other words that may not be clear should be spelled out.

4. All interruptions must be explained. The machine should not be stopped after the recording begins unless there is a valid reason, and this reason must be explained in the recording itself.

5. Continuity of the recording is necessary. If recording with a cassette and a second cassette is necessary, or if the cassette must be turned over, the interruption of the recording must be explained both before and after changing or turning the cassette.

6. The interview must deal with all aspects of applicable and pertinent facts surrounding the loss or accident.

7. At the end of the interview, the interviewee must be given an opportunity to make additions or corrections, and an offer extending this opportunity must be part of the recording.

8. The interviewee must be asked whether the questions were understood and whether the answers given were true to the best of his or her knowledge.

9. The interviewee must again be made aware of the fact that the interview was recorded.

10. When the interview has been completed, the representative should play back the last few words to make sure the interview has been recorded.

II. **Instructions to the Interviewee**

Before the interview starts, the claim representative needs to explain the procedures:

1. The representative should tell the interviewee that this will be a question-and-answer type of interview.

2. The representative should let the interviewee know that he or she will be asked his or her age, marital status, occupation, employer, salary (if a claimant), and Social Security number. This is necessary in order to identify the person being interviewed.

3. The representative should not be afraid to ask the interviewee to speak up if the telephone reception is unclear or if the interviewee is speaking too quietly for the microphone to pick up the responses during the personal interview.

4. When a representative is about to conduct an in-person interview and a second person is present, the representative should ask that person not to interrupt the interview. The representative can explain that he or she will be glad to answer any questions after the recorded interview is completed. If the person does interrupt, the representative must identify the person and have the person state his or her relationship to the accident.

5. The representative should explain to the interviewee that he or she is interested only in the physical facts of the accident during the interview and that other, unrelated factors can be discussed after the interview. (Do not negotiate the claim during the recorded interview or discuss the insurance policy. The representative is interested only in the facts, just as he or she would be when writing a longhand statement.)

6. The interviewee should be asked whether he or she remembers:

    • The date and time of the accident

    • The names of his or her passengers, witnesses, and other parties and their addresses

    • The exact place of the accident—highway, stairs, intersection, city or county, and state

The representative should instruct the interviewee to have his or her Social Security number handy.

7. Even with a telephone-recorded interview, the representative should ask the interviewee to draw a sketch of the accident scene, because this will help the interviewee keep his or her thoughts in order.

8. Before recording a telephone interview, the representative should ask the interviewee not to hang up when the interview is completed so that the representative may make arrangements to visit the interviewee and inspect damages.

9. The representative should advise the interviewee that the recorder will be turned on and that he or she will make a short introduction of the interview.

III. Common Mistakes

Common mistakes claim representatives make when recording interviews include:

1. Don't refer to insurance during the interview. (If coverage is an issue, take a separate statement concerning the coverage question.)

2. Don't ask leading questions. Instead of asking, "You were in the left lane?" or "Were you in the left lane?" ask, "What lane were you in?" Or, instead of asking, "Did you slip on the ice?" ask, "What caused you to fall?"

3. Don't ask argumentative questions, which tend to create an adverse or a hostile environment.
4. Don't give your opinions.
5. Don't express excessive sympathy.
6. Don't invite a settlement demand during the interview.
7. Don't use legalistic words or phrases.

APPENDIX B—WRITTEN STATEMENTS[1]

I. **Format of a Written Statement**

In general terms, a statement comprises three parts: the *introduction*, the *body*, and the *closing*. The introduction will include items such as the date, time, and location of the statement; identification of the interviewee; and so on. The body will include accident data such as the date, time, and location of the accident; vehicle identification (if an auto accident); physical description of the scene; accident description; and injury information. The closing or conclusion will include a closing statement by the interviewee in which he or she states: "I have read the above ( ) pages and ( ) lines and they are true." Where required, there should be a brief acknowledgment by the interviewee that he or she has received a copy. The closing should also include the interviewee's signature, and the signature should be witnessed.

II. **Written Statement Captions**

1. *Identification of date, time, and location of the statement.*

2. *Identification of the interviewee.* The interviewee should be immediately identified. The identification should include age, address, telephone number, marital status, occupation, etc.

3. *Date, time, and location of the accident.*

4. *Vehicle identification.*

5. *Background or origin and destination of trip.* Include identity of any passengers, activity of driver and passengers before accident, and whether any drinking or drugs were involved.

6. *Physical description of scene.* Include weather and road conditions in detail.

7. *Accident and injury description.* Gauging precise distances is difficult. Asking in terms of car lengths might help.

8. *Events after the accident.* Accusations; conversations; witnesses; police; identity of ambulance, hospital, doctors, etc.; condition of vehicles, and so on.

9. *Conclusion.* As mentioned previously, it is important to have the interviewee read the statement and write, at the close of the statement, "I have read the above ( ) pages and ( ) lines and they are true." Then the representative should have the interviewee sign the statement.

10. *Signature.* The statement should be signed immediately below the closing sentence and on the right side of the page. The left side of that line is reserved for someone to witness the interviewee's signature, preferably a family member or neighbor. Each page of the statement should be signed and witnessed.

III. Rules for Taking Signed Statements

The following guidelines for taking signed statements are helpful in ensuring that the format and mechanics of the statement will be correct:

1. At the top right of the first page, note the date, time, and place the statement is being taken.

2. Number and date each consecutive page.

3. No margins should be used.

4. No paragraphs or indentations should be used.

5. No gaps should be left any place on any page.

6. No erasures should be made; all errors should be struck through, the correction should be inserted above it, and the interviewee should initial the correction.

7. No abbreviations (or shortcuts in writing) should be used.

8. Statements must be taken in ink or indelible pencil. (Ballpoint pens or typewriters are satisfactory.)

9. Use the language of the person being interviewed—if he or she uses slang, use slang in the statement.

10. Make the statement clear, concise, chronological, legible, and complete in every respect. A written statement should flow naturally and lead up to the happening of the accident step by step. In other words, the accident should not be presumed to have already occurred in the statement, but rather it should be worked up to in a natural step-by-step sequence (use a Statement Outline or Guide).

11. The interviewee should read the statement and certify, in his or her handwriting, that he or she has read and understands the statement. Example: "I have read the above two pages and eleven lines and state that they are true."

12. The interviewee should sign at the end of the statement and at the bottom of each page of the statement, and his or her signature should be witnessed.

APPENDIX NOTE

1. Robert Prahl and Stephen Utrata, *Liability Claim Concepts and Practices* (Malvern, Pa.: Insurance Institute of America, 1985), p. 251.

APPENDIX C—LIABILITY CLAIM REPORT[1]

EXHIBIT A-1

Claim Report

XYZ Insurance Co.

Casualty Report

Date: October 3, 20X0

Insured: Crawford Feedlot, Inc.

OPEN COMPANION CLAIMS

Symbol	Claimant's Name	Reserves
P1	Leo Ferrara	$5,000
P2	J. King, Inc.	$5,000
P3	J. King, Inc.	$5,000
P4	Larry Gower	$5,000
B5	Leo Ferrara (fatality)	$10,000
B6	Maria Ferrara	$10,000

Policy No.: 656 7837

Date of Loss/Claim: September 23, 20X0

First Report

ATTACHMENTS

1.   Diagram of accident scene

2.   Two photographs of the scene

3.   Police report

SOURCE & DATE OF ASSIGNMENT

This assignment was received from the Home Office on September 25, 20X0, by fax.

COVERAGE

The insured's policy has a general aggregate liability limit of $2 million and a $1 million per occurrence limit. The insured operation is a 30,000-head cattle feedlot near Montgomery, Okla.

DESCRIPTION OF SCENE

The accident occurred on Highway 61 near Montgomery, Okla. In the area where the accident occurred, Highway 61 is a two-lane blacktop roadway with shoulders. The stretch of highway on which the accident occurred is flat with no obstructions to visibility. The speed limit there is 65 mph. At the time of the accident, it was raining heavily, but night had not fallen yet.

DESCRIPTION OF ACCIDENT

During a rainstorm, about 100 head of cattle wandered approximately 70 yards from the insured's pasture to Highway 61. Based on how far they traveled and the time of the accident (about 7:15 P.M.), the cattle probably got loose at about 7 P.M. Our investigation reveals that an eastbound vehicle operated by Larry Gower stopped in the middle of the road because the cattle were on the highway. Two westbound vehicles also stopped in the middle of the road. The first westbound vehicle to stop was a pickup truck operated by Leo Ferrara. His wife, Maria Ferrara, was in the front passenger seat. The second westbound vehicle, which was pulling a goose neck trailer, was a pickup truck operated by Anthony Sewell. A third westbound vehicle driven by Gus Jones, who apparently did not see the two stopped vehicles because of the driving rain, struck the rear of the goose neck trailer, knocking it loose from Mr. Sewell's pickup truck and propelling it forward. The trailer then hit Mr. Ferrara's vehicle, driving it forward across the eastbound lane and off the road (see the diagram). Mr. Sewell's pickup was also pushed into the eastbound lane and hit the vehicle driven by Mr. Gower. The impact to Mr. Ferrara's vehicle was so violent that Mr. Ferrara was killed and Mrs. Ferrara was seriously injured.

The cattle were loose because they had forced themselves through a gate at the edge of the pasture. The gate has one lock, and the insured did not observe the gate to be open or the lock to be loose earlier in the day. According to the insured, the last time the gate was open was approximately three months ago. The insured guesses that the lock was not properly secured then, that it was merely stuck in what appeared to be a locked position without actually being locked. During the storm, the cattle pushed on the gate, which caused the lock to pop open and the gate to swing open, allowing the cattle to escape from the pasture.

The insured was not aware that the cattle were free until after the accident occurred. According to the insured, Jack Holman, the manager of the feedlot, drove past the pasture at approximately 6:50 P.M.; at that time, the gate was closed and the cattle were still in the pasture.

INSURED

On September 29, I obtained a recorded statement from Jack Holman. Mr. Holman resides at 854 Maple St., Montgomery, Okla., telephone (555) 633-3057. Mr. Holman said that he has been the manager of the feedlot for the past year and is responsible for the operation of the feedlot.

Mr. Holman confirmed the facts set forth above. He said that he was not aware of the cattle being loose until about 20 minutes after the accident occurred. With the help of other employees, Mr. Holman then rounded up the cattle and returned them to the pasture.

CLAIMANTS

- Leo and Maria Ferrara, 784 Wilson Blvd., Martinsville, Okla, 68768. Mr. Ferrara was operating his 1994 pickup at the time of the accident. As mentioned, Mr. Ferrara was killed in the accident, and his wife was seriously injured.

- Anthony Sewell, 23 N. Broad St., Montgomery, Okla., 68770. Mr. Sewell was driving a 1996 flatbed pickup, which was pulling a goose neck trailer. The vehicle that Mr. Sewell was driving is owned by J. King, Inc., an oil field maintenance company in the Montgomery, Okla., area.

- Lawrence J. Gower, RR 18, Box 4, Temple, Okla. Mr. Gower was operating a four-door 1997 sedan owned by Premium Distributors, Inc., of Oklahoma City, Okla., 68782.

- Gus Jones, 178 Columbus Court, Montgomery, Okla., 68770. Mr. Jones was operating a 1981 tractor truck also owned by J. King, Inc.

WITNESSES

The police report indicates that the insured's manager, Jack Holman, witnessed the accident. That is incorrect. According to Mr. Holman, he did not witness the accident. No witnesses other than the claimants have been identified.

POLICE REPORT

I obtained a copy of the Bolton County Sheriff's Department report on this accident and have enclosed it. The report confirms the facts as I have stated them, with the exception of identifying Mr. Holman as a witness. The Sheriff's Department did not, however, release the narrative portion of the police report to me. According to the Sheriff's Department, we can get a copy of the narrative report by filing a subpoena for the report.

CATTLE

Although the insured's cattle were on the highway at the time of the accident, none were struck by any of the vehicles involved.

PROPERTY DAMAGE

As a result of the accident, the vehicle driven by Mr. Ferrara was declared a total loss, as was the vehicle driven by Gus Jones. The trailer that Mr. Sewell's pickup was pulling was totaled in the accident, and the pickup itself also sustained some damage. The vehicle driven by Larry Gower was damaged but not totaled. Mr. Ferrara's vehicle has been transported to a salvage auction in Santa Fe, New Mexico. Mr. Gower's vehicle is being repaired in a body shop in Montgomery, Okla. The vehicle driven by Mr. Sewell is still being operated, and the vehicle driven by Mr. Jones is on the grounds of J. King, Inc., Montgomery, Okla.

ADVERSE CARRIERS

The insurance carrier for Leo Ferrara is ABC Insurance Company, policy number 67PHE122890-656734. The insurance carrier for J. King, Inc., is DEF Insurance Corp., policy numbers SEC-1750011 and SEC-17588456. The insurance carrier for Mr. Gower is the GHI Auto Insurance Company, policy number 20DPRI21513.

At this time, all parties have filed claims only with their own insurers.

INJURIES

As mentioned above, Mr. Ferrara was killed in the accident. Mrs. Ferrara was seriously injured and transported to the hospital. The extent of her injuries is still unknown. No one else was treated for injuries.

LIABILITY

Our insured's liability is still questionable. The insured was not aware that the cattle were loose until after the accident occurred, and Mr. Holman promptly returned the cattle to the pasture after he was notified that they had broken free. The problem with the lock was not discovered until after the cattle had been returned to the pasture.

PHOTOGRAPHS

I obtained 35 mm photographs of the accident scene, gate, and lock and of the 1981 tractor truck owned by J. King, Inc.

TO BE DONE

I will take statements from the insured and any employees to find out more about how the cattle got out and determine whether the insured had actual or constructive knowledge of the problem with the lock. The rest of the investigation will depend on a home office decision to contact other involved parties. (See Remarks section.)

REMARKS

I'd like to request that a decision be made about whether we should contact any of the adverse carriers as a result of this accident. From what we know at this point, the insured is not liable and the injuries are solely the result of Mr. Jones's failure to stop. Even if we do not contact the other parties, they might bring us in as a joint tortfeasor anyway.

Question: Should we contact the other parties and determine their position on liability and damages? Please inform me of recommendations for future actions.

Jeffrey M. Hart

Claim Representative

P.O. Box 1307

Ardmore, OK 68112

(555) 263-1884

APPENDIX NOTE

1. Michael J. Betz, *Writing at Work*, 2d ed. (Malvern, Pa.: Insurance Institute of America, 1999), pp. 227-231.

Evaluating and Valuing Liability Claims

Evaluating and Valuing Liability Claims

Previous chapters dealt with determining coverage and investigating and assessing liability. This chapter deals with how claim representatives set values on liability claims by determining the likely amounts owed.

Liability claims are valued based on a variety of objective and subjective factors. Liability evaluations contemplate all the facets of a claim that influence its value. These include, among other things, facts and circumstances of the accident, the applicable law, the nature and extent of the injuries, the measure of provable damages (both tangible and intangible), and the defenses available.

Although this text presents this evaluation phase as a separate phase, occurring sequentially after claim representatives have investigated liability, the reality is that initial damage valuations often occur concurrently with liability investigations. For example, as claim representatives interview insureds, claimants, and witnesses and gather facts that will help determine who was at fault, they also ask questions about the extent of property damage and injuries. It is common practice to ask claimants making injury claims to complete forms authorizing claim representatives to obtain medical documents and wage loss information even before liability has been determined. To wait until all of the facts have been gathered and a liability determination made would significantly slow the claim process and increase the time it takes to settle a claim.

Claim representatives gather information to support payments for damages. Liability claim damages include property damage, injuries, wage loss, death, and other compensable losses. After gathering liability and damage facts, claim representatives apply some method for establishing a claim value or a range of settlement amounts. Claim representatives may also need to analyze specific medical aspects of anatomy, injury diagnosis, impairments, and disabilities. However, that detail of analysis is beyond the scope of this text and is covered in the AIC 34 text *Managing Bodily Injury Claims*.[1]

This chapter explains the nature of liability claim evaluations and why setting dollar values on liability claims can be challenging. Most of this chapter is devoted to describing the numerous factors and variables that affect settlement valuations. Variables such as attorney representation and the personal characteristics of claimants, insureds, and witnesses influence how much will ultimately be paid. The last part of this chapter describes different methods for analyzing these factors in establishing dollar values.

A good settlement valuation accurately reflects four critical factors:

- The risk to the claimant of a defense verdict in favor of the insured
- The proportionate share of liability of an insured
- The numerous variables that affect a jury's likely award
- A reasonable estimate of damages the claimant is likely to be able to prove

Establishing claim settlement figures is not an exact science, but figures can be arrived at through a reasonable, uniform, systematic approach.

NATURE OF LIABILITY CLAIMS EVALUATIONS

People unfamiliar with liability claims may wrongly assume that liability claim settlement values can be calculated as simply as those in other areas of insurance. However, because of the underlying complexity and subjectivity of liability and damage assessments, settlement valuations can be quite complicated.

Liability comes in various degrees that are subjectively determined. Damages are composed of complex and subjective factors ranging from how much pain a claimant suffered as a result of a broken arm to how a local jury feels about "punishing" a large corporate defendant with a big jury award.

Claimants with similar injuries and medical expenses might receive significantly different settlements for a number of reasons. First, not all people respond in the same way to an injury. One back injury is not the same as another. A similar accident and injury can create different levels of pain and disability, depending on the claimant.

In addition, several factors affect expected jury awards that go beyond the facts of an accident or the impairment suffered by a claimant. What a jury might award on a given case ultimately affects the settlement value of the claim. Objective factors such as the age, gender, and occupation of the claimant and insured, and subjective factors such as the reputation of the claimant's attorney or the jury's perception of the claimant as being sympathetic or a complainer, all affect the settlement value of a claim.

One study at Brigham Young University presented a hypothetical case to nearly 700 personal injury lawyers. The lawyers were given exactly the same facts. Evaluations and ultimate "settlement values" varied from $18,000 to $95,000.[2]

The dual purpose of this chapter is to (1) describe many of the critical factors that influence jury awards and settlement values and (2) present methods for evaluating settlements in a logical, systematic way.

TRENDS AND PATTERNS IN LIABILITY AWARDS

With many high-verdict cases profiled in the media and plaintiff lawyers consistently insisting that claim representatives are "out of touch" or unfair in their settlement offers, it might be helpful to look at the real numbers and trends in settlements and jury awards.

Exhibit 8-1 shows the percentage distribution of settlements by dollar amount nationwide over seven years.[3]

EXHIBIT 8-1

Percentage Distribution of Settlement Amounts

Settlement Range	1993	1994	1995	1996	1997	1998	1999	Overall
$1 – $9,999	33%	34%	32%	31%	28%	22%	17%	30%
$10,000 – $24,999	21	23	21	20	18	16	13	20
$25,000 – $49,999	11	12	12	11	12	11	9	12
$50,000 – $74,999	6	6	6	6	6	7	7	6
$75,000 – $99,999	4	3	4	4	4	4	5	4
$100,000 – $249,999	10	9	9	11	12	15	16	11
$250,000 – $499,999	6	5	6	6	7	9	9	6
$500,000 – $749,999	3	2	3	3	4	5	7	3
$750,000 – $999,999	2	2	2	2	2	3	4	2
$1,000,000 – $2,499,999	3	3	4	4	4	6	10	4
$2,500,000+	1	1	2	2	3	3	5	2

The median (middle) *settlement* award nationwide increased from $20,000 in 1993 to $100,000 in 1999. Average (mean) settlements increased from $217,394 to $609,725 over the same time period.

Interestingly, during this same time period, *jury awards* remained stable. In 1993, 50 percent of all awards were less than $50,000, and in 1999, 51 percent of all awards were less than $50,000. However, the mean (average) award increased from $520,344 to $642,101 during the same time period. The main reason the mean award increased is the size and frequency of awards given for those in the top 10 percent and an increase in the middle-range claims between $100,000 and $250,000. The highest awards were given for medical malpractice, business liability, and product liability claims.[4]

The increase in settlement figures versus the stability of award figures reflects a concerted effort by the industry to settle more cases and avoid the high costs of litigation.

The mix of cases going to trial was also relatively stable. Auto personal injury and landowners liability still account for around 60 percent of all cases that go to trial. Overall, claimants win slightly more than half of the verdicts (56 percent in the 1990s) and are most successful in auto liability and business cases (around 65 percent wins).[5]

Although claims are normally settled for less than the amounts that juries would award on similar cases (for reasons that are explained later in this chapter), jury award trends affect settlements. Even when the "average" verdict remains stable, increases in the number of high verdicts affect the behavior of attorneys and potential litigants and the decision making of insurance claim personnel. High verdicts are often highly publicized and as the possibility of a high verdict increases, litigants and their attorneys may be more willing to reject settlements and "roll the dice" by taking the case to trial. Uncertainty leads insurers to offer more before trial to reduce the risk of a high verdict award. Trends toward increasing awards may also cause insurers to settle cases with high damage potential but little liability.

FACTORS AFFECTING LIABILITY AWARDS

As mentioned earlier, a wide variety of factors affects settlement values. The two most obvious factors are the extent of an insured's liability and the damages incurred. Claim representatives assess liability based on the law and legal factors affecting liability (covered in Chapters 5 and 6) and the facts of a given claim that are discovered during the liability investigation (covered in Chapter 7). Claim representatives must also evaluate damages. A large portion of this chapter is devoted to damage valuation. Once liability and damages have been determined, claim representatives can establish a settlement range by applying liability assessment to damages and weighing other factors that affect the claim value.

Evaluating Liability and Legal Factors

Claim representatives should first review all of the facts, then consider the theories of liability that might apply and all of the legal defenses that may be available to the insured. If some facts are still unclear, it may be necessary to hire an expert to help determine liability or damage issues. An accident reconstructionist might be needed on serious auto accident cases to help determine what the physical facts suggest about the speed and direction of the vehicles involved. After reviewing the facts, claim representatives should do the following:

1. Review and apply the relevant law. Most personal injury cases involve some form of negligent behavior based on common-law duties or statutes.

2. Determine the legal obligations and defenses that apply to the facts, such as comparative and contributory negligence. These are covered in Chapters 5, 11, 12, and 13.

3. Determine what choices, if any, the claimant might have in applying the law. Sometimes claimants may be able to "shop" for different venues.

4. Determine what category liability falls into—clear, probable, question-able, or doubtful. This will be a general assessment based on the facts and application of the law. These categories will help to establish liability percentage ranges.

5. Review the facts and determine whether other potentially liable parties have been overlooked. If so, claim representatives should consider contacting them and finding out their liability position and willingness to help settle the claim.

Determine the Applicable Choice(s) of Law

Throughout this text, examples are given of how laws vary significantly by jurisdiction. Jurisdictional differences affect coverage as well as liability. In a number of claims, the laws of more than one jurisdiction potentially apply. When this situation arises, courts must apply rules to decide which jurisdiction's laws should prevail.

The discussions about differences in laws in previous chapters of this text have referred to differences in substantive law. **Substantive law** creates, defines, and regulates the rights of the parties. Substantive law addresses the interpretation of coverages and liability issues, such as whether comparative or contributory negligence applies, whether there are caps on noneconomic damages, or whether a person can make a claim for purely emotional injuries. **Procedural law** prescribes the methods of enforcing the rights. For example, procedural law would state that a party has twenty days within which to answer a complaint (lawsuit).

In tort cases, as a general rule, the substantive rights are determined by the law in the place where the tort was committed. This generally holds true even if the lawsuit is filed in another jurisdiction. If, for example, a person from New York were on vacation in Florida and struck another person, who lived in Georgia, Florida's substantive law would still apply even if the lawsuit were filed in New York. In this situation, the procedural law of New York would apply.

Courts make one major exception to this general rule under the **significant contacts rule**. According to this rule, the substantive law of the state having more significant contacts to the parties could also apply, even when the tort occurred elsewhere. For example, if the resident of New York had harmed another resident of New York while vacationing in Florida and filed suit against the other New Yorker in New York, then New York would have more significant contacts to the case than Florida because both parties live in New York and the case was filed in New York. Thus, the substantive law of New York would apply. Many states do not accept this rule and continue to follow the general rule that substantive law is based on the place where the tort occurred.

The legal strategy of seeking jurisdictions that offer the most favorable substantive law is known as **forum shopping** (or jurisdiction shopping). Forum shopping occurs most frequently with corporate defendants because they do business and have agents, sales representatives, and business properties (contacts) in many locations. For example, a person from State A is injured by a truck in State B that is owned by Conglomerate Trucking. State A has more favorable laws to the claimant than State B. If Conglomerate has offices in both State A and State B, then using the significant contacts rule, the claimant could not only file the lawsuit in State A but also have the court apply the substantive law of State A. Conglomerate might challenge this by claiming that State A is an inappropriate forum, arguing that the distances to go to the trial are too far and too inconvenient for parties and witnesses involved. The court would have to decide the merits of this argument.

Another alternative that Conglomerate, or a similar defendant, might pursue is to have the case "removed" from the state court to a federal district court on the basis of **diversity of citizenship**. "Diversity of citizenship" in this context means that the parties are from different states. The federal court would accept the case only if it involved considerable damages. (Currently the amount must exceed $75,000, but this amount continues to increase.) Federal courts have different procedures, and the juries that sit on federal cases come from a broader geographic area, which can affect verdicts.

Claim representatives should keep in mind that claimants sometimes have a choice of jurisdiction, and they must consider how a jurisdiction's laws are likely to affect the value of the claim.

General Assessment of Liability

As mentioned in the previous chapter, liability can be clear, probable, questionable, or doubtful. *Clear* liability means that there is no question that the insured was entirely at fault. *Probable* liability simply means that while it may not be a clear-cut case of liability, the insured was probably at fault for the accident, and, based on the facts, the insured would not prevail if the case were litigated. In a case of *questionable* liability, it is unclear which party bears primary responsibility for the accident. It may be a case in which each party is partly negligent for the mishap, and a genuine question may exist as to how the accident happened. *Doubtful liability* means that in all likelihood, the insured was not negligent or legally liable for the accident.

An important point to remember is that claim representatives should not summarily dismiss (and deny) claims because liability is questionable or doubtful, because a compelling damages case sometimes saves a weak liability case from being dismissed by a judge. Once the case goes to trial for a jury to decide, the results can be unpredictable. A particularly sympathetic claimant with serious injuries may be given a substantial award even when liability is questionable or doubtful. For that reason, it is advisable for claim representatives to gather damage information even when the liability investigation favors the insured. The following sections deal with damage valuations.

Evaluating Damages in Tort Actions

Damages are awarded as compensation to a party for any loss or harm sustained because of the misconduct of another. In liability claims, the purpose of awarding damages is to make the injured party "whole" by returning the party to a pre-loss position. The law does this by giving the party the right to compensation for various types of damages.

Because most liability claims are based on tort actions, the damages presented in this chapter are those resulting from torts. Damages can also result from contractual obligations; these can, in some circumstances, be covered by liability insurance policies, but the vast majority of liability claims are based on negligence and other torts.

"Damages" is the term used to denote the amount awarded as compensation for the loss sustained. As mentioned in Chapter 1, damages that serve the purpose of compensating a party for a loss are called **compensatory damages.** Compensatory damages fall into two broad categories: "special" damages and "general" damages, as mentioned in Chapter 1.

Special damages or "specials" are out-of-pocket expenses that claimants incur as a result of a loss. Specials include items such as medical bills, prescription bills, lost wages, funeral expenses, costs to repair or replace damaged property, and impairment to earning capacity (for an individual or a business). Special damages are generally verifiable, either through receipts, verification with the entity that provided the medical or repair service, or calculations by technical experts.

General damages are the natural and necessary result of the wrongdoer's actions but have no fixed amount of loss. General damages are more difficult to measure than special damages because they are determined more subjectively. **General damages** include items such as the value of the claimant's pain and suffering, inconvenience, disfigurement, emotional distress, permanent injury, loss of enjoyment, loss of consortium, and other noneconomic intangible losses. Even though these elements of damage are difficult to measure, the law recognizes them. In fact, for bodily injury claims, general damages are often several times larger than the special damages. Many jurisdictions require juries to award general damages whenever special damages are awarded for bodily injury claims.[6]

The distinction between special and general damages is not just an academic categorization. In a lawsuit, special damages are supposed to be specifically identified in the complaint (lawsuit) in order to give the defendant an opportunity to verify them. General damages naturally flow from injuries and may not require the same specificity in the lawsuit.[7]

Punitive Damages

Some parties commit such outrageous misconduct that they must be punished. Punitive damages are awarded for this purpose. **Punitive damages** are sometimes called exemplary damages because they are intended to make an example of the defendant's wrongdoing. Punitive damages are typically awarded for intentional injury or gross negligence. In negligence cases, terms such as "reckless," "willful and wanton," or "with malice" are used to describe behavior justifying punitive damages. Many people confuse general compensatory damages such as pain and suffering with punitive damages. Punitive damages are in excess of compensatory damages.

Unlike compensatory damages, punitive damages may be based on the wealth and financial condition of the tortfeasor as well as on the circumstances of the incident.

Substantial punitive damage awards are given against corporate defendants because it requires more money to punish them. States vary as to the limit on punitive damages a court can award. Courts do not generally permit punitive damage awards so great that the company becomes bankrupt and unable to continue business. Some states limit punitive awards to some multiple of compensatory awards. For example, a million-dollar award for $2,000 in compensatory losses might be considered excessive, but a million-dollar award for $200,000 in compensatory losses would likely be allowed.

The following are examples of situations in which punitive damages might be awarded:

- An intoxicated driver of a motor vehicle drives through a crowd of children who are leaving school.
- A manufacturer of a defective product continues to sell the product after discovering that it could cause serious harm to users.
- An employer flagrantly violates safety standards and harms workers.

Punitive damages are rare. Even in a "liberal venue" such as Manhattan, New York, punitive damage awards are issued in fewer than 1 percent of cases.[8] Punitive damages are more common with product liability claims, in which claimants received punitive damages in 2.6 percent of the cases.[9] Perhaps the most infamous case involved the Ford Pinto. In this case, Ford's management knew of the defect with Pinto fuel tanks that made them vulnerable to explosions with rear impact, but they calculated that the cost of repairs (less than $50 per car) would be too expensive in total and decided to accept the risk. When people were injured by rear-impact explosions, a court awarded punitive damages and characterized Ford's management decision as "corporate malice." Ford appealed the size of the award—$3.5 million—but the court allowed the award to stand because it represented less than 0.005 percent of Ford's net worth, less than 3 percent of its annual net income, and only 1.4 times the amount of compensatory damages.[10]

Factors that courts consider in determining whether punitive damages should be awarded include the following:

- Nature of the offense
- Need to punish the wrongdoer
- Need to deter the wrongdoer from similar conduct in the future
- Need to deter others from similar conduct

As mentioned in Chapter 3, whether liability insurance provides coverage for punitive damages depends on the state. Several states refuse to permit insurance to cover punitive damages because to do so defeats the purpose of punishing the tortfeasor, but many states permit insurance coverage to apply to punitive damages.

Exhibit 8-2 illustrates various types of damage categories. The following section describes relevant issues related to how claim representatives evaluate the following types of damages:

- Property damage
- Bodily injury claims
- Emotional distress claims
- Death claims

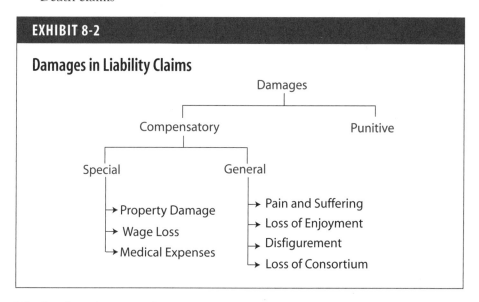

EXHIBIT 8-2

Damages in Liability Claims

The burden of proving damages rests with the claimant. Evidence must clearly demonstrate the actual damages were sustained. Juries are not required to imagine or speculate about evidence not presented. Claims for future losses, such as future medical expenses, must be proved with a reasonable degree of certainty.

Property Damage Claims

When personal property is damaged, the owner may recover for the reasonable cost to repair the property or replace it if it cannot be repaired economically. When the property must be replaced, the owner is entitled to the reasonable market value of the property before loss or destruction. Generally, the owner may also recover damages from the loss of use of the property for a reasonable time period. For example, a claimant could also claim the cost of renting a substitute car while his or her car is in the shop.

Under certain circumstances, a claimant may also recover the loss of profits from the use of the property. A damaged truck or tractor-trailer may cause the owner to lose revenue, especially if a substitute vehicle cannot be rented to make deliveries. Damage to a building may cost the owner to lose rent from tenants or sales from customers while the building is unable to be used. Some business interruption claims can be extensive, and claim representatives may need to hire accountants to help ascertain the loss.

A few jurisdictions permit **diminution in value** for property damaged and repaired. The reason for permitting this claim is that the owner is entitled to the difference between the value of the property before the accident and its value after the accident. Proponents of this damage theory argue that if after making repairs, the owner has still suffered a loss because the market value for a previously wrecked car is less than that of one that has not been wrecked, then the owner is entitled to be compensated for that diminution of value. For example, a claimant's car is repaired for $5,000. Because the car has been "wrecked," it now has a lower market value than it did before the accident, even though it has been repaired and the repairs are barely noticeable. On an open market, prospective buyers might discount the value of this car, thinking it might have potential problems. If after repairs, the market value of the car was $500 less than that of similar cars that had not been wrecked, then this would constitute a $500 diminution of value. Some jurisdictions would allow this diminution of value loss. A number of repair facilities have software that calculates diminution of value. This is a controversial issue on which claim representatives should seek guidance from claim management.

Bodily Injury Claim Valuation Factors

Claim representatives evaluating bodily injury should consider the following damage elements:

- The amount of medical expenses
- The type of injury
- The claimant's wage loss or loss of earning capacity because of the injury
- The pain and suffering resulting from the injury
- The extent of disability and impairment
- The claimant's loss of enjoyment from an injury
- Any disfigurement resulting from the injury
- Whether preexisting conditions contributed to the injury

Exhibit 8-3 shows a sample of how a judge might instruct a jury to evaluate an injury claim.

Most bodily injury liability claims are soft tissue injuries. This is especially true for auto liability claims, as nearly 75 percent of injury claims were for sprains or strains only.[11] More serious injuries usually lead to higher settlements. Exhibit 8-4 shows the percentage of injury types for liability claims over $75,000. Soft tissue injuries represent a minority of these more serious claims.[12]

Excessive jury awards for soft tissue injury claims are commonly appealed even when liability is clear. For example, an award of $100,000 for a claimant who experienced only discomfort from low-back and neck pain as a result of an auto accident might be deemed excessive, and therefore the award would be reduced.[13] In some cases when juries give clearly excessive awards, insurers may successfully negotiate lower amounts because neither side wants to incur more legal costs related to an appeal.

EXHIBIT 8-3

Sample Instructions a Judge Could Give to a Jury

"In determining the amount of damage, if any, suffered by the plaintiff as a proximate result of the accident in question, you will take into consideration the nature, extent, and duration of the injuries you believe from the evidence Plaintiff has sustained, and you will decide upon a sum of money sufficient to reasonably and fairly compensate Plaintiff for the following items:

The reasonable medical expenses Plaintiff has necessarily incurred as a result of the accident.

The medical expenses you believe the Plaintiff is reasonably certain to incur in the future as a result of the accident.

The physical and mental pain, suffering, anguish, and disability endured by the Plaintiff from the date of the accident to the present.

The physical and mental pain, suffering, anguish, and disability you believe Plaintiff is reasonably certain to experience in the future as a result of the accident."

EXHIBIT 8-4

Percentage of GL Claims Over $75,000 by Injury Type
Closed Claims of $75,000 or More
1995 Survey

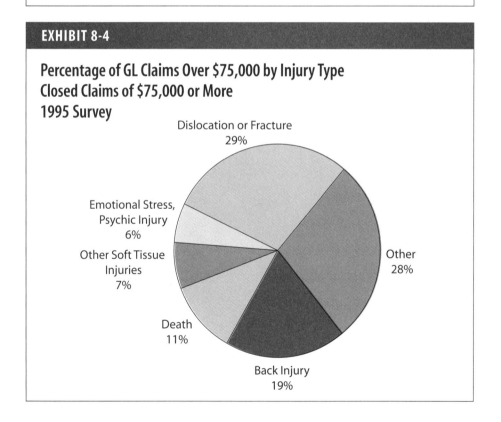

Medical Expenses

Both incurred and future doctor and hospital bills are examples of medical expenses that are compensable in bodily injury claims. Travel expenses incurred going to and from healthcare providers is also compensable. Medical expenses must be reasonable and necessary to be compensable. Claim representatives sometimes use independent medical reviewers to determine whether medical expenses are reasonable and necessary. Claim representatives need to be mindful of the potential for claimants to build up medical expenses, especially with soft tissue injury claims for claimants who are represented by attorneys.[14]

Future medical expenses are recoverable, too. These might include doctor fees, home nursing, physical therapy, and medical supplies and equipment. If these costs are substantial and expected to last for many years, an economist might be needed to help calculate the rate of inflation and the present value of these future medical expenses.

Exhibit 8-5 is an example of the kinds of medical expenses that might be incurred in connection with a serious accident requiring a trip to the emergency room, surgery, and a hospital stay.

EXHIBIT 8-5

Common Sources of Medical Expenses

Emergency Treatment Items
- Ambulance
- Emergency room
- Treating physician
- Radiologist
- Surgery Costs
  - Hospital fees
  - Operating surgeon
  - Consulting surgeon
  - Anesthesiologist

Hospitalization
- Hospital costs
- Room fees
- Medical supplies
- Treating physician
- Laboratory costs
- Radiology costs

After Hospital Discharge
- Treating physician
- Physical therapy
- Occupational therapy
- Psychological consulting
- Costs for temporary medical devices (crutches, wheelchair)
- Visiting nurse
- In-home nurse
- Supplemental nutritional needs
- Transportation to and from medical provider

Wage/Income Loss

Losses of wages, profits, or other compensation are items of special damages compensable in bodily injury claims. Wage and income losses usually refer to an actual economic loss due to an inability to perform a specific job because of an injury suffered. "Wage loss" is normally the term used to describe the claimant's loss of earnings from the time of injury until the time of recovery from the injury. It is usually based on the job the person was performing before the loss occurred. In contrast, loss of earning capacity claims are based on future estimated losses resulting from a permanent disability.

As a general rule, wage loss is calculated on a gross basis without deduction for taxes. However, this is not the rule in all jurisdictions, especially federal court cases, which normally allow an offset for taxes.[15]

Courts are skeptical about earnings and earnings projections for self-employed people when the net income is questionable or not readily calculable.

Pain and Suffering

In personal injury claims, pain and suffering are considered "natural and necessary" results of a claimant's bodily injury. Compensation for pain and suffering frequently constitutes the largest portion of awards for bodily injury claims. A claimant is entitled to recover for pain and suffering resulting from an injury caused by the tortfeasor. For claims that are not settled through negotiation, the conversion of this loss into a specific dollar amount is left to the court, which is usually a jury. Future as well as past pain and suffering are also compensable, particularly in cases in which a permanent injury is alleged.

Exhibit 8-6 shows the breakdown of general damages that are paid on auto bodily injury claims compared to special damages. The 2 to 1 ratio of pain and suffering damages to medical expenses is common in premises liability claims as well as auto claims.

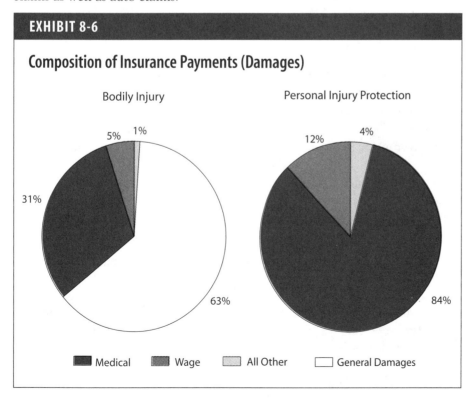

EXHIBIT 8-6

Composition of Insurance Payments (Damages)

Bodily Injury

Personal Injury Protection

Medical   Wage   All Other   General Damages

In valuing the general damages of bodily injury claims, claim representatives should answer the following questions:

1. What are the specific injuries, and what type of pain is associated with them?
2. Are they consistent with the accident?
3. Did symptoms (and pain) preexist?
4. Are other causes contributing to the pain?
5. Is pain acute (and temporary) or chronic (and long-term)?
6. What is the resulting disability, and how does it affect the claimant's daily activities and ability to work and enjoy life?
7. Do the claimant's age, occupation, and gender affect pain and suffering?

Although claim representatives often think of "pain and suffering" as one inseparable unit of damage, it helps to quantify pain and suffering by breaking it down into more elemental components. Pain and suffering is physical pain, mental suffering, and mental anguish.

When evaluating pain and suffering claims, claim representatives should consider the kinds of physical pain that might naturally arise from the injury. One kind of pain is that from the physical impact at the time of the accident. Smashing one's head against a windshield or falling down a flight of stairs causes immediate pain. The severity of this immediate pain affects the claim value. Pain associated with lingering aftereffects is also compensable. Some aftereffects, such as the healing process for serious burns or the "phantom pain" from an amputated limb, would be more severe and should be compensated more greatly than the aftereffects of a bruise or sprain. Physical pain can result from undergoing physical therapy, trigger-point injections, or painful diagnostic procedures such as myelography or discography (used to diagnose back injuries).

Mental suffering includes the fear, anxiety, depression, and anger related to a physical injury. Mental suffering, like physical pain, varies from one individual to the next, but some situations are more likely than others to generate mental suffering. A person who was rescued from a car that had careened into a river would likely suffer mentally from the thought of what might have happened had the rescuer not arrived in time. Mental suffering can result from not being able to support oneself financially, from anxiety over the possible long-term effects of an injury, or even from the thought of future medical treatments. Grief, despair, anger, and humiliation may all be considered forms of mental suffering.

Mental anguish, the unpleasant mental consequence resulting from an injury, is sometimes used to denote psychic injuries not directly related to physical pain. The horror of seeing one's scarred face in a mirror, the embarrassment of being unable to perform normal activities, and the grief over losing an appendage are examples of mental anguish. The distinctions between the different kinds of suffering are not as important for claim representatives to know as are the sources of suffering on a given claim.

Damages for pain and suffering can be proved by the testimony of medical providers; the individual's own testimony; and the testimony of employers, clergy, family members, or friends of the claimant. These parties are permitted to attest to the expressions of pain they observed. Obviously, the testimony of doctors and other disinterested parties would be given greater weight.

Because pain and suffering constitutes such a large part of the monetary damages for bodily injuries, the credibility of witnesses significantly affects awards. Juries give considerable weight to the nature of an injury, which influences the severity, intensity, and duration of the pain. The more juries understand the objective facts about the injury, the more weight they give to medical testimony rather than the subjective testimony of the claimant or other witnesses. Damages for future pain and suffering require medical evidence that would indicate the probability of future suffering.

Because these valuation factors are subjective and juries have wide discretion in evaluating and awarding general damages, liability claim representatives must become comfortable evaluating general damages with some degree of ambiguity.

Permanence of Impairments and Disabilities

Perhaps the greatest contributor to large money awards is a determination by a jury that the injury will cause an impairment that will remain with the plaintiff for the rest of the plaintiff's life. This impairment may affect the person's ability to function in the way he or she functioned before the injury.

The following are some issues to consider regarding permanent injuries:

1. Have job/family and recreation been changed for the worse as a result of this permanent injury?
2. Does chronic pain accompany the injury?
3. Does disability or disfigurement accompany the injury?
4. Has the person's personality been affected?

Usually the highest jury awards are given to people who suffer permanent, catastrophic injuries. The median award for paraplegia in 1996 was $7,650,000, which vastly exceeds even the median award for death claims.[16]

Claim representatives encountering claims involving permanent injuries must be careful not to underestimate the potential value of these losses. Usually experts should be brought in early to help evaluate the potential losses and suggest ways to contain the loss potential, such as through physical and vocational rehabilitation.

Loss of Enjoyment

Most jurisdictions treat loss of enjoyment as a compensable general damage, distinguishable from pain and suffering, although some components of loss of enjoyment duplicate the components of pain and suffering. Loss of enjoyment claims are based on the claimant's reduced capacity to enjoy certain activities. This includes the loss of physical and intellectual gratification and other lifestyle losses. The diminished capacity to enjoy sex, read a book, play golf, or even go for a walk are examples of loss of enjoyment that might be claimed under this category. The term "**hedonic damages**" is sometimes used interchangeably with loss of enjoyment damages.

Loss of enjoyment or hedonic damages have two components. These may help claim representatives to evaluate this kind of damage. The first component is a medically determined permanent impairment. Some impairments, such as loss of use of an appendage, may be presumed to cause a loss of enjoyment, and courts may require no further evidence. A permanent injury that causes an impairment to mental health, disfigurement, interference with work-related activities, interference with performing necessary daily activities, interference with being able to parent, interference with sexual relations, and shortening of life expectancy would likely be presumed to cause loss of enjoyment.

Some courts may take a more operational view of loss of enjoyment and look for more than evidence of a physical impairment, especially when the effect of the physical impairment may not be obvious. In such cases, the specific activities that the person enjoyed and performed before the loss would be compared to what the person can do and will likely be able to do in the future. This view of loss of enjoyment damages would require evidence of specific activities the person used to do but can no longer do. An example of such evidence might be testimony from the brother of a claimant, who testifies that he and the claimant played basketball every Saturday morning in the summer and now the claimant will no longer be able to do that.

The following are summaries of cases with loss of enjoyment claims:

> As a result of an auto accident, a woman suffered severe injuries to her hip and knee. The woman, who was athletic and liked to run, swim, dance, and bicycle, could no longer do these activities or even go for walks. She was awarded $1 million.[17]

> A woman who was injured suffered a loss of mobility, a loss of hearing, and an inability to cook everyday meals. Her infirmities prevented her from participating in social, civic, and church activities. She was awarded damages for her loss of enjoyment of these activities.[18]

Disfigurement

Some injuries cause permanent disfigurements. The reaction to a disfigurement varies by claimant. Even if the claimant does not suffer a great deal of physical pain, the emotional toll related to the disfigurement can be still be significant. In one case, a little girl was bitten by a dog. The girl testified that she did not suffer much and she did not appear to be embarrassed by the scarring on her face. However, the court determined that an award of only $1,000 was insufficient to compensate the girl because the jury should have considered the emotional reaction the girl will suffer as she becomes a young woman.[19]

A scar on the face of a fifteen-year-old girl would be viewed by a jury as more traumatic than one on a sixty-year-old man. Thus the age and gender of the claimant affect the value of the claim as much as the disfigurement itself.

Diminished Earning Capacity

Permanent injuries may cause impairments and disabilities that prevent claimants from working in the same capacity as they did before the loss occurred. **Diminished earning capacity** is the reduction in the capacity to work and earn money before and after an injury.[20]

Calculation of diminished earning capacity is not a simple task even for experts.

Following are some factors to consider in diminished earning capacity claims:

- Occupation and wages of claimant
- Age of claimant
- Expected work life of claimant
- Life expectancy of claimant
- Education and training
- Previous job history

Calculation of a person's diminished earning capacity is usually performed with the help of rehabilitation experts and economists. Union rules on seniority and expected promotions can also affect calculations. In one case, the claimant was injured while working for the railroad. The claimant was allowed to introduce evidence that the company's promotion system was based mainly on seniority and to project the likely promotions that the claimant would have received.[21]

Calculations of diminished earning capacity for minors or people just beginning their careers can be challenging. Pre-accident earnings may not be an accurate reflection of earning potential because a young person may not have established a clear vocational goal. Factors to consider in loss of earning capacity claims involving young people include the following:

1. The degree to which the person has an established vocational or career goal
2. The degree to which the person has the skills and abilities needed to be proficient in the desired vocation
3. The extent of training, education, and experience the person has
4. How the person compares to others who have the same vocation or vocational goals

To help establish earning potential for minors, a variety of evidence has been admitted, including the following:

- The activities the minor participated in at school
- Physical description of the minor
- The minor's scholastic ability based on grades and teacher and counselor evaluations (awards and honors also are helpful)
- The parents' intent and ability to send the minor to college (showing that the minor's siblings went to college would help to establish this)
- The parents' occupations
- Government statistics on income figures for different occupations

Because of the nature of evidence on these types of claims, the most recurrent and effective defense against them has been that the calculations and the assumptions required to make the calculations are too "speculative." No consistent rules exist concerning the admissibility of evidence for loss of earning capacity claims. The following summary of cases illustrates the nature of evidence that has been considered admissible and inadmissible in loss of earning capacity claims with minors:

> The claimant was injured while attending law school. A law school professor reviewed the claimant's academic records, interviewed the claimant, and reviewed medical reports about the claimant's injuries and then issued an opinion as to the claimant's likelihood of succeeding in law school and practicing law. The court ruled that this testimony was admissible.[22]

> A man en route to enlist in officer's candidate school claimed that his injuries prevented him from getting into officer's candidate school and deprived him of the officer's income he would have earned upon completion of the school. The court did *not* admit this because it was too speculative given that the claimant had not yet entered the school.[23]

In establishing the loss of earning capacity of minors, the parties are *not* held to the requirements of estimating these earnings with reasonable certainty, as they are in cases involving adults. The courts recognize that since the earning capacity of a minor is untried, the question of damages for such a loss must be left to the good judgment of the jury.[24]

Most reasonable evidence may be permitted, and Exhibit 8-7 lists some common tools used to assess the lost earning capacity for adults and minors.

EXHIBIT 8-7

Tools for Proving Lost Earning Capacity

- Income tax returns
- Payroll record
- Testimony of employer
- Awards and honors
- Testimony of co-workers
- School records
- Reports from treating physician
- Medical records showing preexisting conditions that might limit a person's abilities or shorten the person's work life
- Psychologist reports
- Vocational assessment expert testimony
- Demonstrative evidence (This could include videos of the workplace showing the physical demands of the job or photographs of a building showing areas that don't permit access for people with disabilities.)
- Claimant's own testimony
- Government statistics
- Economists' testimony

Loss of Consortium/Companionship

An injury that adversely affects any relationship the victim had with a spouse or family member is **loss of consortium**. Loss of consortium claims allege losses in love, companionship, services, and comfort from another person. Loss of consortium claims have been made by spouses, parents, children, and grandchildren, although claims by spouses are by far the most common. Some states do not permit loss of consortium claims by family members other than spouses.

Personal injury to (or death of) a spouse deprives both the injured person and his or her family of the society, services, and companionship experienced before the loss. Because loss of consortium is not based on any fixed, economic loss, it is considered a general damage. However, if substitute services are hired, then the associated expenses would be considered special damages and they would be indicated separately in a lawsuit. If, for example, a wife hired a maid to clean the house while her husband was impaired from an injury, then the cost would be part of the claimant's special damages. The loss of such services can be claimed even if the wife did not hire a maid; in such a case, a court would award this loss under the general damages category.

The loss of consortium claim is related to the loss suffered by the claimant. A spouse, for example, cannot have a large loss of consortium claim that is based on small damages to the claimant.

Preexisting Injuries

It is a well-established legal concept that a tortfeasor must "take claimants as they are." Tortfeasors are liable not only for damages resulting from direct and unique injuries inflicted in an accident but also for damages resulting from aggravation of a claimant's preexisting condition or predisposition to injury. An **"eggshell claimant"** is a term that liability claim representatives might hear, and it refers to a person who was in poor but functioning health at the time of the loss. After the loss, the person became severely disabled and dysfunctional. If proved that this last physical injury was "the straw that broke the camel's back," then the entire loss and disability is owed.[25]

Juries vary widely in the way they view these cases. Some juries have been hesitant to give awards for a complete disability when the claimant had a number of preexisting problems before the last loss occurred. Exhibit 8-8 shows an example of a judge's instruction to a jury regarding the issue of preexisting conditions.

Historically, one defense used in claims involving preexisting injuries was unforeseeability. Defendants argued that it was not foreseeable that, for example, a slight impact to the rear of a vehicle would cause an injury that was permanently disabling because the claimant was already in a fragile condition because of a preexisting medical problem. Recent case trends indicate that courts will hold defendants responsible for all injuries resulting directly from the wrongful act whether it is foreseeable or not.

The defendant can apportion the loss between the preexisting condition and the accident, but such calculations are difficult. The defendant has the burden of proving that damages should be apportioned between a preexisting injury and the one he or she caused.[26]

EXHIBIT 8-8

Sample Jury Instructions

"A person who has a condition or disability at the time of an injury is entitled to recover damages for any aggravation of such preexisting condition or disability proximately resulting from the injury. This is true even if the person's condition or disability made the plaintiff more susceptible to the possibility of ill effects than a normally healthy person would have been even if a normally healthy person would not have suffered any substantial injury. Where a preexisting condition or disability is so aggravated, the damages as to such condition or disability are limited to the additional injury caused by the aggravation. However, once the plaintiff has proved that this defendant has caused some injury, the burden of proving allocation of damages between this accident and plaintiff's preexisting condition is upon the defendant. If the defendant fails to meet his burden and the Jury finds that the harm is indivisible, then the defendant is liable for the entire condition or disability which resulted."[27]

Emotional Distress Claims

Pure mental injury claims are becoming more commonplace in liability claims. Post-traumatic stress disorder (PTSD) is one example of a mental injury claim that is alleged more frequently now than in the past. This psychological disorder is characterized by nightmares or re-experiencing the trauma of an incident when presented with certain stimuli associated with the original event. Authentic PTSDs result from unusually traumatic events such as being trapped inside a burning car. They are frequently, but not necessarily, associated with serious physical injuries.

As a general rule in tort law, claimants must show some kind of physical harm in order to make a claim for mental suffering. Pure mental suffering is not compensable in many jurisdictions. However, some jurisdictions now recognize pure emotional injury claims even when there is no underlying physical injury. If, for example, a person witnessed the horror firsthand or was in close enough proximity to some horror to be in fear for his or her own safety, then several states would allow recovery for pure emotional distress.

As mentioned in Chapter 2, liability insurance may not apply if coverages are limited to paying only for "bodily injury" because the majority of courts state that a purely emotional injury is not bodily injury[28] but is instead an injury to the psyche.[29]

Some of the following are issues that claim representatives must investigate and resolve in determining whether a person has a compensable emotional injury claim:

- Do the courts in the given jurisdiction recognize emotional (purely nonphysical) injury claims as compensable?

- Do the courts in the given jurisdiction consider purely nonphysical injury claims to be "bodily injury"?

- Did the person witness the injury to a spouse or child?

- Was the person who witnessed the accident also within the "zone of danger"?

- Did the emotional injury lead to a physical injury, for example, high blood pressure, fatigue, sleeplessness, nausea, diarrhea, or ulcers?

- How reasonable was the emotional reaction? (Would a substantial portion of society respond similarly?)

Death Cases

Claim representatives occasionally encounter claims involving fatalities. About 95,000 people each year die from accidental injuries.[30] Of this number, about half die because of motor vehicle accidents. It is especially important that commercial liability claim representatives understand how to evaluate death claims because most commercial policies have high limits of liability that can exceed the value of death claims. In personal lines liability insurance, the value of these death claims normally exceeds the limit of liability for insurance, thus the claim is concluded by paying the limit. As personal lines insurance liability limits increase and underinsured motorists coverage becomes more prevalent, personal lines liability claim representatives will need to become more familiar with how to evaluate death claims.

Death claims fall into two categories: survival claims and wrongful death actions. In most states, these two categories are separate and distinct. Claim representatives need to know the elements of each in order to evaluate the loss potential. Under common law, survivors have no rights to make claims for wrongful death or for a decedent's personal injuries. For this reason, states enacted statutes to permit survivors to collect for losses resulting from fatalities. The types of damages recoverable for death claims are governed by individual state statutes and court decisions interpreting these statutes. Consequently, the values of death claims can vary significantly from one state to the next. When evaluating death claims, claim representatives should obtain copies of pertinent survival and wrongful death statutes for the states in which the claims were made.

The legal term **decedent** is used in the following sections to describe the deceased claimant. In death claims, a personal representative of the decedent makes the claim. The personal representatives are usually spouses or other family members but can include other legally recognized parties such as the executors or administrators of the decedent's estate. The term **estate** is used in this chapter to denote the total of all types of property (including businesses, profits, savings accounts, stocks, and other financial assets) a person owned at the time of death. Dependents and other survivors can make claim to this property.

The value of death claims varies widely depending on the circumstances, but it has on average increased over the past decade. Nationwide, death cases in 1999 ranged from $11,700 to $285 million. The probability range of death cases was $467,000 to $2,652,500.*

---

* Jury Verdict Research, *Current Award Trends In Personal Injury* (Horsham, Pa.: LRP Publications, 2000).
"Probability range" is defined as the middle 50 percent, or 25 percent below the median up to 25 percent above.

Survival Actions

In a **survival action** (claim), the person representing the decedent makes claim for what the decedent would have recovered if he or she had lived. In essence, the person's claim "survives" even though the person died. The same elements of compensatory damages that were described earlier apply to survival actions. Generally, in a survival action, the personal representative of the decedent can make claim for medical expenses, loss of earnings, and pain and suffering the decedent incurred from the time of the accident until the time he or she died. As a general rule, survival actions are not permitted when a person dies instantaneously.

Some states limit survival actions to out-of-pocket expenses incurred for such items as medical expenses and wage loss. In states that include pain and suffering elements in their survival actions, the decedent must have been conscious of the pain and suffering before dying. If a person was seriously injured and lingered in a constant vegetative state before dying, then the states do not allow damages for pain and suffering because the person was not conscious.[31]

Some states include funeral expenses and future wage loss to the decedent's estate as part of the survival action;[32] however, most states would include these as wrongful death claims. A small number of states combine survival actions and wrongful death actions into one.[33]

Wrongful Death Actions

The general purpose of **wrongful death actions,** when initially enacted, was to provide survivors of the deceased with the same standard of living that would have been provided if the deceased had lived. Until the 1960s, the damages allowed under wrongful death actions were based on the **pecuniary loss,** which is the monetary economic loss to the survivors. About one dozen states still limit recovery to pecuniary losses. However, most states permit recovery for noneconomic losses such as the mental anguish of the survivor, loss of consortium, loss of counseling, and other subjective types of damages.[34] Even some of the states that hold to the more restrictive pecuniary loss rule have expanded the definition of pecuniary loss to include loss of companionship and society, loss of affection, and loss of parental care and guidance (and other items that have some economic value but are somewhat subjective).[35]

Every state permits the pecuniary loss element. Pecuniary loss is normally measured as the amount the decedent would have contributed to the survivors. This amount would break down into two categories: earning and household services. In effect, this amount is the net monetary contribution the deceased would have provided if he or she had lived.

To determine **earnings contribution,** claim representatives should not just figure the average annual earnings for a person and multiply that amount by the number of years the person would likely have worked. Even in states that permit only economic losses in wrongful death claims, the calculations can be complex and require several adjustments. Adjustments are made to reduce the future value of a stream of projected earnings back to a present value. These future earnings must be adjusted upward for inflation and expected wage increases, and deductions must be made for how much a person would have spent on himself or herself.

Determining the value of **household services** that the decedent would have provided requires extensive research. Exhibit 8-9 shows examples of household services that might be claimed in a wrongful death action. Each of these items has economic value that contributes to an estate. Because of the complexities of these calculations, claim representatives should consult with claim management and legal counsel as soon as possible to arrange for expert guidance in assessing wrongful death claims.

EXHIBIT 8-9

Examples of Skilled Work and Labor of Household Services Provided

Painting
Carpentry
Personal shopping assistance
Lawn care and landscaping
Daycare
Elder care
Cooking
Cleaning
Chauffeur services
Auto maintenance
Teaching/tutoring
Family counseling
Security and protection services

Many states have modified their statutes to permit claims for other damage elements such as loss of companionship, comfort, security, loss of parental guidance, counseling and academic tutoring, and mental anguish to survivors. Experts interview family members to assess the extent of these losses, which vary by family. Funeral expenses are also recoverable under most wrongful death statutes.

Claim representatives *must* check with the state statutes and court interpretations of those statutes to determine what elements are compensable in the state in which the action is filed. Exhibit 8-10 shows a comparison of how several states measure wrongful death claims and illustrates why it is advisable to consult legal counsel before evaluating the loss.

A number of books are available to explain the various complex computations in wrongful death cases, but most insurers would prefer to consult with experts.[36]

EXHIBIT 8-10

Comparison of Wrongful Death Statutes[37]

Alabama—Only punitive damages are recoverable. Loss of earnings, loss of consortium, and loss of contributions to the family are NOT recoverable. Damages incurred from the time of accident to the time of death are compensatory under wrongful death actions (rather than as a separate survival action).

Arizona—Juries shall award any damages to surviving parties that are "fair and just." This includes but is not limited to anguish, sorrow, mental suffering, and pecuniary losses.

California—Recovery is limited to "pecuniary loss," but this includes amounts to compensate survivors for damages such as loss of comfort, protection, companionship, and sexual relations. No recovery is permitted for mental suffering or grief.

Delaware—Juries may consider (1) the loss of expected monetary benefits that would have resulted if the decedent had lived, including the loss of inheritance and loss of earnings; (2) loss of parental, marital, and household services including child care; (3) funeral expenses up to $2,000; and (4) the mental anguish suffered by family members.

Florida—Extent of recovery depends on the survivor status. At minimum, a survivor is entitled to recover loss of support and services reduced to present value, and medical and funeral expenses paid by survivors. A surviving spouse is also entitled to collect for loss of companionship and protection and for mental pain and suffering. Surviving minor children may recover for loss of parental companionship and guidance and for mental pain and suffering.

Valuing Claims for the Death of Children

Assessing death claims with minor children is troublesome and highly subjective. Historically, the law did not place a high value on the deaths of older people or minor children because they had little economic production value. In fact, minor children are undisputedly a source of significant costs to parents. One study concluded that a middle-income family would spend about $335,000 on a child just until the age of seventeen.[38] This does not include costs for college. So if courts applied a pure economic loss standard, it would be difficult to justify an award for the loss of a child.

More states are now willing to look beyond the simple production value of minor children. As mentioned earlier, most states now have wrongful death statutes that permit recovery for noneconomic losses such as loss of companionship and mental anguish. Of these states, some have special provisions dealing with the loss of minor children.

In states that still hold to the economic loss rule, courts have considered the future economic value of children to aging parents. By permitting estimates of valuable services that children might provide to aging adults, such as long-term care, assisted-living facility care, transportation, and financial guidance, economic losses can be determined. Even including these valuable services, it is sometimes difficult to show that parents have sustained a true financial loss. Thus, many courts have permitted testimony on the loss of **intrinsic value of children.**

Plaintiff economists calculate this intrinsic value by starting with the assumption that parents are making a rational financial decision in having children and paying for their children's expenses. They argue that these expenses amount to an investment that parents will receive returns on later when the children are older and able to provide companionship and comfort. These economists reason that the money parents spend on children reflects the value they place on the children. Skeptics argue that these economic theories are nothing more than inventive strategies to get the case to trial and in front of a jury. Once the case is in the hands of a jury, damage awards might be based on the jury's somewhat subjective valuation of the loss.

Some states have dealt with the issue of economic versus noneconomic damages directly by enacting statutes that clearly specify that parents *can* recover for mental anguish and loss of companionship. For example, Florida specifically states that parents are entitled to recover for mental pain and suffering resulting from the loss of a minor child.[39]

Before evaluating wrongful death claims, claim representatives should consult with legal counsel or claim management and review the statutes and cases that define which parties are eligible to make claims and what types of damages are allowed.

Excessive Damages Award

Damage awards may be reduced if they are excessive. The judge has the discretion to reduce an award. This act is known as **remittitur.** Excessive awards sometimes occur as a result of a jury's prejudice or passion. The defendant must show that the size of the award was unwarranted. In some states, the standard is that the award "shocks the conscience." This is a difficult standard to meet; therefore, some courts have adopted a more objective standard of "deviating materially from other awards."[40]

One way in which defendants have shown that cases are excessive is by showing how the award exceeds the upper limit of similar cases without any explanation of why the circumstances in this case would require such an award.

Courts can also increase jury verdict awards. This action is called **additur.**

Collateral Source Rule

Many people injured in accidents have health insurance that covers their medical bills or disability insurance that covers their wage loss. If a claimant's medical expenses are paid by health insurance, should liability insurers then have to consider these expenses in determining damages? The answer is, it depends. A rule of evidence, known as the **collateral source rule,** bars the introduction of evidence that a claimant has other sources of recovery, and thus the defendant remains responsible for all damages, even those covered by insurance. Most states do not allow evidence of other sources to be admitted. However, a significant minority of states permit admitting other sources of income as evidence, and some states require that an offset be permitted to reduce the award by any amount that a claimant has received from collateral sources.[41] Elimination of the collateral source rule can have the effect of reducing the potential liability (or at least the amounts payable) of an insured by reducing the amount of damages the insured owes.

Mitigation of Damages

Claimants have a duty to mitigate, or contain, their own damages. The **mitigation of damages rule** requires claimants to take efforts to prevent damages that are avoidable. If, for example, a claimant received a small laceration as a result of the negligence of another person, then the claimant must make reasonable efforts to make sure the cut is promptly cleaned and treated so that it does not become infected. A claimant who failed to take these reasonable efforts would not later be able to recover for damages related to an infection, if the infection could have been prevented. The tortfeasor has the burden of proving that the resulting damages were preventable or avoidable.

This rule is normally applied to a claimant's conduct *after* an accident has occurred, but some states permit the rule to be applied to conduct *before* an accident if the claimant failed to take certain obvious safety precautions. The most common example is failure to use seat belts. Other states prefer to apply the mitigation of damages rule only to post-accident conduct, arguing that comparative or contributory fault is the appropriate pre-accident defense.

Attorney Representation

People often hire attorneys to represent them, especially when they have serious injury claims. When an attorney represents a claimant, the awards and settlements usually increase. Some reasons for this are that people represented are more likely to make frequent trips to chiropractors and to incur greater expenses such as for diagnostic evaluations. In one study of strains and sprains in auto claims, payments to claimants represented by attorneys averaged $4,122, compared to $1,447 for unrepresented claimants. However, unrepresented claimants netted more money after deducting for legal expenses, court costs, and higher expenses incurred.[42]

In assessing the claimant's attorney, claim representatives should consider the attorney's trial experience, the type and severity of cases that the attorney normally handles, the aggressiveness with which the attorney handles claims, and the attorney's reputation in the legal community. The value of the case will be determined by how the attorney is expected to present himself or herself in front of a jury.

An experienced, competent attorney is a better adversary to face than an inexperienced and/or incompetent attorney because the latter may not know how to evaluate a case. This means much time will be wasted preparing for a case that perhaps should have been settled.

Expert Witnesses

For claims involving hedonic damages, loss of earning capacity, or wrongful deaths, vocational rehabilitation experts and economists are often used. These experts are needed for the following reasons:

1. Juries understand that jobs and the economy are highly volatile and expect credible testimony from professionals who specialize in understanding the complexities of the job market and the economy.
2. Juries understand that physical disabilities are no longer as limiting as they once were and are more willing to accept expert testimony that people who suffer disabilities can switch careers and vocations and remain economically productive.
3. Many states have wrongful death statutes that require somewhat complicated present value calculations that are best done and presented by experts.

In addition to establishing how a given disability may affect future earnings, experts can also assess future expenses that the disabled person will likely incur. For example, they may be able to estimate future medical and equipment expenses, nursing and assisted-living costs, and household maintenance service expenses.

In serious claims such as those involving a loss of earning capacity, significant future expense claims, or wrongful death cases, experts should be consulted early rather than just before trial. Experts can help to guide claim representatives in investigating elements of damage and can give preliminary estimates that help to establish more accurate reserves. Starting early also gives the expert time to develop data to defend the insured.

Claim representatives (or claim management) should choose experts who have practical work experience as well as trial consulting experience in their areas of expertise. Experts whose sole source of income comes from testifying at trial may appear less credible. Credibility is also enhanced by educational credentials, licenses, and professional certifications and by authoring books and articles. Experts must have the ability to communicate complicated calculations to juries in simplified ways. Legal counsel should be able to assist in selecting experts.

Other Factors Influencing Jury Awards

A number of factors influence jury awards in addition to liability, damages, attorney representation, and expert witness considerations described earlier. These other factors fall roughly into three broad categories:

- Characteristics of the insured, claimant, and witnesses
- Aggravating or unusual circumstances of the loss
- The venue of the case

Characteristics of Insureds, Claimants, and Witnesses

Perhaps one of the most important characteristics is whether the insured or claimant is an individual versus a business or government entity. Awards against business and municipal defendants can be significantly higher than those against individuals under the same liability and damage facts. This especially holds true during economic downturns and when corporations are laying off workers.

The communication skills of the plaintiff and defendant affect jury awards. Parties who can convincingly state their case are likely to obtain more favorable verdicts. A claim representative's evaluation should take into account whether the person is believable, reasonable, and expected to give clear and concise answers. If a person appears to be overly nervous, belligerent, or hiding information, juries may discount his or her testimony.

Essentially, the personality and appearance of the parties can swing the balance on the value of the case. If a claim representative finds a client to be boorish, distasteful, or insincere, the chances are good that the jury will have the same impression.

Exhibit 8-11 shows a sample of the jury instructions that a judge might give to a jury before deliberations that sanction jury members and show the latitude that juries have in assessing the credibility of parties.

EXHIBIT 8-11

Sample Jury Instructions—Judge to Jury

"The weight of evidence is not necessarily determined by the number of witnesses testifying on either side. You should consider all the facts and circumstances in evidence to determine which of the witnesses are worthy of greater credence. You may find that the testimony of a smaller number of witnesses on one side is more credible than the testimony of a greater number of witnesses on the other side. The credibility or believability of witnesses should be determined by their manner upon the stand; their relationship to the parties; their fears, motives, interests, or feelings; their opportunity to have observed the matter to which they testified; the reasonableness of their statements; and the strength or weakness of their recollections. If you believe that a witness has lied about any material fact in the case, you may disregard the entire testimony of that witness or any portion of that testimony which is not proved by other evidence."[43]

Aggravating Circumstances

Aggravating circumstances can elicit emotional reactions in juries that influence liability and damage assessments. This section describes some of those circumstances. The list is practically endless, which is why claim representatives must use judgment in evaluating a claim.

When alcohol or drugs contribute to an accident, juries are more likely to feel the need to punish the wrongdoer by assessing liability and higher damage awards. They are less sympathetic to claimants who are injured while intoxicated or under the influence of drugs. Perpetrators of hit-and-run auto accidents are similarly "punished" by juries with high awards. Aggravating circumstances may result in punitive damages, but more commonly they result in higher compensatory awards.

Sometimes the claimant's actions reduce the sympathy juries might normally have for an injured party. Studies have shown that juries tend to be less sympathetic to motorcycle drivers, apparently believing that motorcycle riders assume the risk by choosing that form of transportation. Similarly, teenage drivers and older drivers have stereotypical reputations that may influence a jury. Pedestrians and elderly and pregnant claimants often engender greater sympathy and higher awards.

Particularly horrifying accidents, such as with dog bites to young children or near-death experiences, can create sympathy for the claimant and influence jury verdict awards.

The Venue

Exhibit 8-12 shows a comparison of median awards of compensatory damages for selected states. These may vary, but for the most part, they remain stable for state-to-state comparison purposes. The exhibit illustrates the importance of the **venue** (or location) of a case.

EXHIBIT 8-12

Comparison of Median Awards by State[44]

State	Median Award From 1993 Through 1999
Alabama	$25,000
Alaska	$140,000
California	$80,000
Florida	$67,218
Illinois	$58,170
Mississippi	$15,000
Nevada	$73,020
New York	$275,300
Oklahoma	$10,000
Pennsylvania	$87,500

Venues are influenced by factors such as the economic conditions of a community, the occupations of people who live there, the average income level of people in the community, the education level of people in the community, and general cultural values there. On average, urban areas award higher amounts than rural areas. Communities made up of people who have occupations with rigorous physical requirements tend to give lower damage awards, especially for soft tissue injuries. Communities with high levels of education and income may render more defendant verdicts but give higher awards for people who are seriously injured. These differences are why claimants engage in forum shopping.

METHODS FOR CALCULATING SETTLEMENT RANGES

Claim representatives may use one or more of the following techniques for evaluating the settlement range for a given claim:

- Individual case method
- Roundtable techniques
- Formula methods
- BATNAs
- Expert systems (computer evaluation)
- Settlement valuation templates

Individual Case Valuation Method

When the individual case method is used, the claim representative evaluates the settlement value based on all the circumstances of the claim and his or her experience in similar cases. All of the liability, damages, and miscellaneous factors are considered and used in establishing a claim value. Because of the numerous factors that must be analyzed and their subjective nature, the individual case valuation can yield settlement valuations that vary widely from one claim representative or attorney to another. For serious injuries, this is still the preferred technique for settlement valuation. Combining this method with the roundtable technique, an expert system evaluation, or a settlement valuation template can help to make the settlement range calculations more uniform.

Roundtable Technique

The roundtable technique involves having the claim file evaluated by two or more claim professionals, each suggesting a settlement range. Ideally, none should initially know the figures the others have selected. After the evaluation and a discussion, a consensus range may be reached, or an average of all the figures may be computed. Because this technique is time-consuming, it is not appropriate for minor claims. However, for serious or prolonged claims, it is a suitable method with which to value claims.

Formula Method

In the formula method, a mathematical formula is used to set reserves. For example, a formula might be based on the assumption that a certain ratio exists between the medical cost and the general damages. This is sometimes known as the "X Times Specials" method. For example, the value of a claim with $1,000 in medical expenses and a "3 times specials" formula would be $4,000 (calculated $1,000 for medical + $3,000 in general damages). The assumption behind this method is that medical expenses are somehow an indicator of pain and suffering. Experienced claim representatives would have little trouble seeing the fallacy of this assumption.

Despite its obvious faults, this method is still used widely with soft tissue injuries and other minor to moderate injury claims. Its advantages are simplicity and uniformity (which make it appear more fair). It can help to avoid the quagmire of more "rational" approaches and may result in an early, mutually agreeable settlement.

Best Alternative to Negotiated Agreement (BATNA)

The most an insurer would pay would be based on the insurer's **best alternative to a negotiated agreement (BATNA)**. If, after considering *all* of the facts, an insurer should do better than the lowest settlement demand of the claimant, the insurer should accept the alternative.

Normally, this alternative would be taking the case to trial. Using this alternative, a settlement should not exceed the combined value of the cost of litigating a case plus the highest probable award that a jury would give.

For example, if the costs to try a soft tissue injury claim are $10,000 and the highest probable award is $35,000, then a BATNA would be $45,000. Basically, the BATNA is a modified worst-case scenario. Some people use the BATNA as the highest figure in a settlement range. Others (more commonly) use a slightly lower figure, arguing that the BATNA does not reflect the claimant's desire to avoid litigation costs and the uncertainty of litigation.

Litigation may not always be the BATNA for insurers if they have other viable alternatives to conclude the case. For example, binding arbitration may be the remedy for resolving disputes with insureds. The same calculations would apply; the highest probable arbitration award combined with the cost of arbitration would provide the BATNA.

Perhaps the greatest value of the BATNA calculation is that it forces insurers to consider the financial consequences of not reaching a settlement. This is especially helpful in claims in which emotional issues have caused the parties to lose track of their ultimate goal—a settlement. Calculating a BATNA can be a wake-up call that motivates parties toward settlement.

Expert Systems

Artificial intelligence involves attempting to develop machines to emulate human abilities such as learning, reasoning, communicating, seeing, and hearing. An **expert system** is artificial intelligence designed to identify and simulate the thinking pattern of experts as it performs a given task. Expert systems are developed by knowledge engineers who interview experts. In the case of claim evaluation software, the expert system would, in theory, simulate the thought processes of experienced, knowledgeable claim professionals.

An expert bodily injury system can be calibrated to specific companies. During the installation process, senior, skilled bodily injury representatives evaluate hypothetical injury claims that are then input to help assess the claim value factors. Later, actual settlements are entered based on objective and subjective injuries.

A claims expert system normally contains the following components:

- A database of knowledge about particular types of claims
- Relevant facts, information, assumptions, and procedures for solving claim valuation problems
- User interface that allows the user to present questions or answer prompts to help develop values. For example, a claim representative might input into the system that the claimant suffered a fracture of the right ulna. The system might then respond with questions such as, "Did the fracture require surgery?", "Is the fracture in the person's dominant arm?", or "What are the physical demands of the person's job?"
- An "inference engine" that controls how the expert system searches the knowledge base and produces conclusions

After the data have been input, the expert system uses its reasoning to establish a settlement range for a given state or county.

The expert system assigns "severity points" to factors influencing the value of the case. Usually an individual company determines how these severity points translate into dollars. For example, a claim in a certain urban venue might be given severity points that would adjust the settlement up by 20 percent.

To illustrate, an expert system might be asked to evaluate a soft tissue injury. After basic injury information has been plugged in, the system might ask for additional information such as whether the injury is accompanied by spasms, loss of motion, headaches, or radiating pain. The system would ask for treatment length and frequency and the types of medicines prescribed. Based on the claim representative's response to these questions, the system would generate an evaluation based on certain benchmarks or medical guidelines. The system has the capacity to incorporate and decipher a large amount of information about an injury, including the value from one venue to another.

An expert system evaluation might read as follows: "A strain of the cervical spine with treatment of one week of active therapy every day, followed by one week of reduced therapy and discharge the third week. There was one prescription, short term. No loss of motion, no recorded spasms, and no limitation of activity. Based on the type of injury and the location of the claim, a reasonable settlement range would be $1,750 to $3,200."

Advantages of Expert Claim Evaluation Systems

An expert system can be a learning tool for a new claim representative and can give him or her an opportunity to evaluate a claim beyond the factors one supervisor or trainer uses. The system usually contains a reference feature that allows the user to find definitions of medical terms and treatment processes. Another aspect common to expert systems is a "flagging" feature that identifies areas that need further investigation. All of these features can help claim representatives to better understand a given injury and likely disability and can help them in medical investigations.

The expert system contains a database of information that applies to each injured person under review, including a database of similar claims. This gives a claim representative the ability to classify information based on criteria developed by a wide variety of professionals. The expert system helps in classifying, storing, and assembling enormous amounts of information to be applied to a given injury claim.

Another benefit of the expert system is that it provides consistent and objective evaluations. The system will apply the same criteria and ask relevant questions about each type of injury submitted. The advantage of assisted evaluation is that it adds new depth and encourages a more comprehensive review of the medical records under consideration than do some traditional approaches.

A final benefit to consider is that the technology is contemporaneous, portable, and able to be updated. The programming allows for new medical processes and treatments to be downloaded and considered in evaluating claims in a consistent way.

Disadvantages of Expert Claim Evaluation Systems

Some issues that make expert systems less attractive include the cost, the effect of technical errors, data manipulation, the misuse of the technology, and demonization. In addition, the software is relatively new and untested in some types of claims.

The work needed to create and maintain an expert system is formidable. Knowledge engineers conduct extensive interviews with claim experts to develop a system. The system must be tested by comparing the decisions it reaches to those reached by skilled claim professionals in numerous trial runs. It is constantly updated to reflect changes in the many factors that influence claim values. The time it takes to enter data into the system makes an expert system an expensive evaluation tool. Time, expense, and training in technology are required and drive up costs.

Important data can easily be input incorrectly or, more commonly, incompletely. Claim representatives might fail to include all treatments or symptoms. A fracture might accidentally be input as a strain, which would significantly affect the evaluation. Attention to detail and a willingness to spend appropriate time reviewing and entering information from a medical record are essential to an accurate evaluation. A busy claim representative might be tempted to just input the "basic facts."

A company might be tempted to manipulate the system's evaluation to help achieve "better results." If this occurs, the system is compromised and the entire valuation process can be distorted. Systematic exclusion of information that reduces value or misclassifying certain treatments can lead to unnecessary litigation and can potentially subject the company to institutional bad faith claims.

This technology is designed to be a tool, *not* a substitute for claim representative judgment. The system simply does not replace certain skills in assessing the uniqueness of an individual claimant. A number of circumstances—such as the characteristics of an insured or a claimant or aggravating circumstances of a claim—require human judgment. Perhaps the biggest problem with expert systems is that in order to pay for them, some insurers think they must lay off workers or use less experienced and consequently less knowledgeable and less skilled workers. This strategy works to the disadvantage of the insurer in the long run.

Finally, the credibility of the system is sometimes an issue. It is easy to demonize this technology because it involves using automation to assess the value of human pain and suffering. That generates resentment from numerous groups. Some claim representatives override all valuations at will without any explanation because they believe they can evaluate a claim better than the system can. This leads to the arbitrary decision making that the system was designed to help improve. Workers lose trust in the benefits of the technology if claim staff is reduced whenever a system is introduced to a company or a claim department within a company.

Evaluation technology does not work well and human experience is needed regarding knowledge of the law of torts, contracts, agency, products, law of evidence, principles of investigation, and negotiation skills.

Settlement Value Template[*]

As mentioned earlier, a good settlement valuation accurately reflects four critical factors:

- The risk to the claimant of a defense verdict in favor of the insured
- The proportionate share of liability of an insured in the event of an unfavorable verdict
- The numerous variables that affect a jury's likely award
- A reasonable estimate of damages the claimant is likely to be able to prove

A settlement value template that integrates these critical factors in a logical, systematic way can be a useful tool for establishing a settlement range. This section presents a ten-step process that begins with the "perfect" case and then adjusts the value to reflect the peculiarities of the claim. Among the factors to be considered, besides liability and damages, are differences in jurisdictions, the quality of opposing counsel, the characteristics of witnesses, and other intangibles. This template method has the advantage of using a systematic approach without the time or expense of an expert system.

Exhibit 8-13 provides a sample calculation using this template.

The following describes how to develop each of the ten different steps.

---

[*] This settlement template is adapted from one developed by Bradford Purcell with the law firm of Purcell & Wardrope, CHTD, Chicago, Ill.

EXHIBIT 8-13

Sample Settlement Template

Steps in calculating settlement range:

1. Probable verdict range for a "perfect" case.

$100,000 – $150,000

2. The chances of a defense verdict,
   against the claimant on the claim (zero liability).

   (6 out of 10) =   60%

3. Calculate the risk amount based on Line #2.

   Reduce award range amounts to reflect risk to claimant.

   $100,0000 – (.60 × $100,000) = $60,000

   $150,000 – (.60 × $150,000) = $90,000

4. Calculate the risk-modified award range.

   $100,000 – $60,000 = $40,000 low

   $150,000 – $90,000 = $60,000 high

   Risk-modified award range $40,000 – $60,000

5. Estimated percentage of fault of defendant.   50%

6. Liability adjusted verdict range
   (range times percentage of fault). $20,000 – $30,000

7. Percent increase or decrease based on case variables.

   Insured is corporate defendant.   + 15 %
   Plaintiff attorney is inexperienced.   – 5 %
   Venue is somewhat liberal.   + 10 %
   Claimant had been drinking.   –10 %
   Total percentage adjustment for variables   + 10 %

8. Variable adjusted verdict range

   ($20,000 × 1.1) = $22,000 low

   ($30,000 × 1.1) = $33,000 high

9. Estimated defense costs through trial   ($14,000).

10. No medical liens. Settlement is not likely to be problematic.

Claim representatives might consider using the Jury Verdict Research definition of probable verdict range. They define this as the middle 50 percent, which is the highest and lowest of the 25 percent of awards above and below the median award. Sometimes this information is available, but more commonly claim representatives will have to estimate this range based on their experience of past settlements or awards or, more accurately, a company's database of past settlements or awards.

Step 1. This step begins by establishing the probable verdict range for a "perfect" case. Determine a probable verdict range based on provable damages, *without considering liability or other variables* such as the characteristics of the insured or claimant or the venue of the case. These variables will be considered later in the calculation. This initial range is arrived at by considering both the economic (medicals, wages, and future expenses) and the noneconomic (pain and suffering, disfigurement, loss of consortium, and disability) damage elements. Estimate the lowest and the highest probable verdict awards *unadjusted* for other factors.

Commercial verdict reporting services or personal injury valuation handbooks are often used to supply award information. However, experienced claim representatives or lawyers may be able to make their own settlement/award estimates.

Companies have their own database of settlements and awards, and online settlement companies have begun gathering a database of values of claims that have been settled through their site. As their databases become populated, establishing probable settlement ranges might become easier.

The following are five factors to consider that have predicative value with similar cases:

- Factual similarity.
- Cases from the same jurisdiction.
- Number of verdicts rendered for the factually similar claim.
- Recentness of the similar cases. (Valuation must take into account inflationary factors.)
- Similarity of damages.

This unadjusted verdict range starts the calculation process. Enter this range on Line #1.

Step 2. Determine the likelihood of an adverse verdict against the insured. Consider the liability issues, the defenses, and evidence regarding the damages. Based on these factors, estimate the number of times out of ten that a court would rule against the insured. For example, a "doubtful liability" case might be only one time out of ten, while a "probable liability" case might be nine times out of ten. Convert this number to a percentage (one out of ten is 10 percent; nine out of ten is 90 percent). Enter this percentage on Line #2.

Step 3. Calculate the risk of loss amount for the high and low awards by multiplying the claimant's chance of getting zero (a defendant's verdict) determined in Line #2 by the estimated award amounts. The rationale behind this reduction is that a good settlement should reflect the uncertainty of litigation. If the claimant risks losing completely, then this risk of loss should be figured into the settlement value. Assume that the reasonable verdict range in Line #1 ranges from a low of $100,000 to a high of $150,000. Further assume that liability is questionable and the claimant would likely receive nothing at all (a defendant's verdict) six out of ten times. In such a case, the calculation for Line 3 would be (.60 × $100,000) or $60,0000 and (.60 × $150,000) or $90,000.

Step 4. Determine the risk-modified verdict range by reducing the high and low estimated award amounts to reflect the risk that the plaintiff is taking in going to court. The 60 percent risk should be reflected in the settlement, and the high and low estimates should be reduced by 60 percent. Example: The low figure would then be ($100,000 – $60,000) or $40,000, and the high figure would be ($150,000 – $90,000). The risk-adjusted verdict range would then be $40,000 to $60,000. Enter this on Line #4.

Step 5. Determine the likely percentage(s) of fault that would be assessed against the insured. For example, the claimant trips and falls in a parking lot, and the circumstances indicate that the insured is between 50 and 35 percent at fault. Enter the high end on Line #5.

Step 6. Determine the liability adjusted (and risk modified) verdict range. Using the percentage in Line 5 and the amounts in the Line 4 example, this would leave a liability adjusted verdict range of $20,000 to $30,000. This range now reflects the fault of the claimant (and other parties) and is the reasonable settlement range based on the insured's responsibility. This range is then adjusted for other variables in Step 7.

Step 7. Consider other variables that affect the likely verdict range and calculate the percentage increase or decrease. As mentioned earlier, the following are some variables to consider:

- The skill and reputation of the claimant's attorney (exceptionally skilled versus exceptionally ineffective)
- The sympathy of the claimant
- The ability of key witnesses in terms of characteristics and communication skills
- Aggravating circumstances
- Venue of the case
- Characteristics of the insured (individual versus corporate defendant)

One suggestion is to add plus or minus 5 percent to each of the variables that apply. For example, a poor defense witness would increase the settlement range by 5 percent. A poor claimant lawyer would decrease the award by 5 percent. However, some variables such as venue may require higher adjustments. Also, awards against corporate defendants can be 25 to 50 percent higher than awards against individuals for the same facts and damages. Assessing the weight of these various factors requires some experience.

Step 8. Add or subtract that percentage amount to the verdict range. This is the verdict variable range. Assume in the example that the variable percentage is +10 percent. Then the verdict variable range would now be $33,000 ($30,000 × 1.1) to $49,500 ($45,000 × 1.1).

Step 9. Determine the estimated cost of defending the case (attorney fees plus other costs) through trial. If defense costs exceed the high end of the reasonable settlement range, then the settlement threshold should be near the high end of the range. If the defense costs are less than the low end, then the settlement threshold should be near the lower end of the range.

Step 10. Determine whether the settlement is likely to be problematic. Add all the liens, such as hospital liens, physician liens, workers compensation, and attorney liens. If the total amount of these liens is greater than the highest figure in the settlement range, then the claim settlement is problematic. Unless other parties (other tortfeasors) are likely to contribute to the settlement, or unless the plaintiff has collateral sources (like health insurance) to pay off the liens, or unless the liens can be significantly lowered through negotiation with the provider, then the case will likely proceed to trial because the claimant would feel obligated to take his or her chances in court rather than walk away with nothing.

No matter what method or combination of methods claim representatives use, they should try to remain fair and consistent.

VALUATIONS AND LIABILITY CLAIM RESERVES

The various factors and variables described in this chapter can help claim representatives to establish accurate reserves. Accurate reserves are needed to help insurers stay financially solvent, to give investors and lenders an accurate picture of a company's liabilities, and to help in developing appropriate premium charges for insureds.

One challenge is that many of the variables and factors presented in this chapter that affect the value of claims are not known at the time the reserve is initially established. One vital task that claim representatives *must* perform is to update reserves as they learn about these factors. Probably one of the most common problems of even senior claim representatives is failing to periodically update reserves based on new facts. They may faithfully record the new facts in their reports and claim diary notes, but even today's expert systems do not yet have the capability of adjusting reserves automatically. Claim representatives should try to anticipate some factors when they set reserves, but reserve changes are going to have to be made on almost any serious injury claim.

Establishing a specific time period (such as ninety days) for re-evaluating reserves is a good practice. Using some of the settlement valuation methods described in this chapter can help make valuations more uniform and consistent. Wildly fluctuating reserves can make investors and creditors nervous and unwilling to place funds with a company. Expert evaluation systems can also help to reduce reserve variability.

CONCLUSION

Claim representatives who are evaluating and valuing liability claims have a complex job that requires them to consider a wide variety of factors that cause seemingly similar claims to have significantly different values. Because nearly every claim has some unique feature that a claim representative may not have encountered, flexibility and open-mindedness are key.

Structured, systematic methods help to ensure that claim representatives take a logical, objective approach to establishing liability claim values. These systematic methods help ensure uniformity, fairness, and thoroughness. Every company has its own settlement philosophy. Some companies prefer to avoid litigation at all costs, some rely heavily on expert systems, and others rely heavily on individual claim representative experience. Claim representatives should be aware of their company's claim philosophy when valuing and settling claims. No matter what approach is taken, the goal for all liability claims is a fair settlement, and the foundation for a fair settlement is a thorough, well-reasoned evaluation of all factors.

CHAPTER NOTES

1. James Jones and Junie Maggio, *Managing Bodily Injury Claims* (Malvern, Pa: Insurance Institute of America, 1999).

2. Lavinia Hall, *Negotiation Strategies for Mutual Gain* (Newbury Park, Calif.: Sage Publications, 1993), pp. 151–154.

3. Jury Verdict Research Series, *2000 Current Award Trends in Personal Injury* (Horsham, Pa.: LRP Publications, 2001), p. 9.

4. *2000 Current Award Trends in Personal Injury*, pp. 3–5.

5. Erik Moller, *Trends In Civil Jury Verdicts Since 1985* (Santa Monica, Calif.: RAND Corporation, 1996), pp. 3–7.

6. Del Carmon Alcaron v. Circe, 704 S.W. 2d 520 (Tex. Ct. App. 1986).

7. Jerome Nates, Clark Kimball, Diana Axelrod, and Richard Goldstein, *Damages in Tort Actions*, vol. I (New York: Lexis Publishing, 2000), pp. 3–25.

8. Moller, p. 33.

9. Moller, p. 34.

10. Grimshaw v. Ford Motor Co., 119 Cal. App. 3d 757, 174 Cal. Rptr. 348 (1981).

11. Insurance Research Council, *Sprains and Strains Resulting From Auto Accidents* (Malvern, Pa.: Insurance Research Council, 1999), p. 1.

12. Insurance Services Office, Inc., *Closed Claim Survey for Commercial General Liability 1995* (New York: ISO, 1996), p. 10.

13. Don v. Cruz, 131 Cal. App. 3d 695, 182 Cal. Rptr. 581 (1982).

14. *Sprains and Strains Resulting From Auto Accidents*, pp. 17–18. Claimants with attorneys have, on average, higher medical diagnostic expenses and a higher number of visits to chiropractors than claimants who are not represented. These expenses often exceed recommended medical guidelines.

15. Hoge v. Anderson, 106 S.E. 2d 121 (Va. App. 1958), Duplechin v. Pittsburgh Plate Glass C., 265 So. 2d 787 (La. Ct. App. 1972), Dempsey v. Thompson, 363 Mo. 339, 251 S.W. 2d 42 (1952). In support of tax offset is the case Floyd v. Fruit industries, 136 A 2d. 918 (Conn. 1957) and Federal Tort Claims Act 28 U.S.C. 2401.

16. *2000 Current Award Trends in Personal Injury*, p. 26.

17. Elkins v. Kassing, 599 F. Supp. 658 (E.D. Mo. 1984).

18. Dogan v. Hardy, 587 F. Supp. 967 (N.D. Miss. 1984).

19. Foster v. Pyner, 545 N.W. 2d 584 (Iowa App. 1996).

20. Nates, Kimball, Axelrod, and Goldstein, vol. II, pp. 101–105.

21. Jones v. St. Louis-San Francisco Railway Co., 333 Mo. 802, 63 S.W.2d 94 (1983).

22. Kenton v. Hyatt Hotels Corporation, 693 S.W. 2d 83 (Mo. Banc. 1985).

23. Thienes v. Harlin Fruit Company, 499 S.W. 2d 233 (Mo. App. S.D. 1973).

24. Newman v. St. Louis-San Francisco Railway Co., 369 S.W. 2d. 583 (Mo. 1963).

25. Abernathy v. Superior Hardwoods, Inc., 704 F. 2d 963 (7th Cir. 1983).

26. David v. DeLeon, 250 Neb. 109, 547 N.W. 2d 726 (1996).

27. Proposed Jury Instructions by the District Court, Clark County, Nevada, Case No.: A355336. Department No.: XV, Docket L. Genoveva Herbert, Plaintiff, v. Edward Benson; Stacey Benson: ATC/VANCOM, Inc., vols. I through V, inclusive.

28. Gerald Boston, David Kline, and Jeffrey Brown, *Emotional Injuries Law and Practice* (Eagan, Minn.: West Group, 1999), pp. 16-1 to 6-11.

29. Garvis v. Employers Mutual Casualty Co., 497 N.W. 2d 254 (Minn. 1993).

30. National Safety Council, *Accident Facts* (Itasca, Ill.: National Safety Council, 1999), pp.16–17.

31. Nates, Kimball, Axelrod, and Goldstein, vol. I, pp. 4–34.

32. Nates, Kimball, Axelrod, and Goldstein, vol. I, pp. 1–19

33. Connecticut, for example, includes damages for the conscious pain and suffering of the decedent and damages the decedent could have contributed if he or she had lived, in addition to more common wrongful death damages such as the amount the decedent would have earned and the loss of spousal consortium.

34. Morton Daller, *Tort Law Desk Reference 2000, A Fifty-State Compendium* (New York: Aspen Law and Business, 2000).

35. Thomas Ireland and Thomas Depperschmidt, *Assessing Family Loss in Wrongful Death Litigation* (Tucson, Ariz.: Lawyers and Judges Publishing, 1999), p. 286.

36. Comprehensive sources include Elizabeth King and James Smith, *Computing Economic Loss in Cases of Wrongful Death* (Santa Monica, Calif.: RAND Corporation, 1988). Several texts on the subjects of hedonic damage calculations, household service calculations, and valuing death claims with children are published by Lawyers and Judges Publishing in Tucson, Ariz.

37. Daller.

38. Thomas Ireland and John O. Ward, *Valuing Children in Litigation: Family and Individual Loss Assessment* (Tucson, Ariz.: Lawyers and Judges Publishing, 1995), p. 249.

39. Section 768.21 (8), Fla. Stat. (1997).

40. Gasperini v. Center for Humanities, 116 S. Ct. 2211 (1996).

41. Insurance Information Institute, *The Fact Book-1999 Property/Casualty Insurance Facts* (New York: Insurance Information Institute, 1999), pp. 59–61.

42. *Sprains and Strains Resulting From Auto Accidents* (Malvern, Pa.: Insurance Research Council, June 2000), pp. 16–18.

43. Proposed Jury Instructions by the District Court, Clark County, Nevada, Case No.: A355336. Department No.: XV, Docket L. Genoveva Herbert, Plaintiff, v. Edward Benson; Stacey Benson: ATC/VANCOM, Inc., vols. I through V, inclusive. p. 36.

44. *Current Award Trends in Personal Injury*, p. 36.

Settling Liability Claims

Settling Liability Claims

So far, this text has dealt with coverage and liability determination and damage evaluation. Once coverage, liability, and damages have been determined, claim representatives must try to reach a settlement with the claimant or the claimant's lawyer. Settling insurance claims is one of the most visible activities claim representatives perform. Investigating coverage and liability and evaluating damages are equally important, and the goal for these processes is normally to achieve a settlement. Many claim department performance measurements are based on the number of settlements, the length of time it takes claims to settle, average settlement amounts, and settlements as a percentage of premiums or expenses. Settling claims requires more interpersonal skills than assessing coverage, liability, and damages. For this reason, claim managers and claim trainers find that settling insurance claims is usually the most difficult aspect of claim handling to teach.

The traditional way to settle liability claims is through negotiation. This chapter goes beyond traditional negotiation techniques and addresses other settlement approaches, such as mediation and arbitration. However, many of the concepts and strategies for successful negotiation, such as preparation and communication, also apply to these alternative methods.

This chapter is divided into three main parts. The first part deals with alternative ways in which claim representatives might settle liability claims when conventional negotiation techniques have failed. The second part covers settlement agreements and some of the issues related to them, especially the different types of releases. The third part concludes the chapter by explaining how claim representatives may be able to recover some or all of the liability payments made.

ALTERNATIVE METHODS FOR SETTLING LIABILITY CLAIMS

The most common way to settle liability claims is through negotiated settlement. Because of the importance of negotiated settlements, it is worth summarizing the key elements of negotiation. Negotiation is a process whereby parties exchange information in order to reach an agreement. In liability claims, the agreement is for the insurer to pay the claimant a specified sum of money in exchange for the right to sue the insured. The process of negotiation has four major elements:

- Communication
- Preparation
- Evaluation
- Power

These elements also exist with alternative settlement techniques. The difference is the way in which these elements are employed and the fact that at least one other party is involved to assist the insurer in reaching an agreement.

Alternative ways for achieving settlement—such as through mediation, arbitration, mini-trials, and other methods—are known as **alternative dispute resolution (ADR)** methods. Traditionally, these methods have been thought of as an alternative to litigation and have been used frequently to reduce litigation costs once a lawsuit has been filed. Some courts have mandatory mediations to help reduce their trial dockets.

Because claim representatives need to work proactively, these methods should be regarded as alternative *settlement* methods with the emphasis on avoiding even the initial stages of litigation. The idea is for claim representatives to approach settlement with a wide variety of options that they are ready and willing to implement if an impasse occurs during traditional negotiation. By quickly and effectively offering alternative solutions, claim representatives may be able to avoid further settlement delays and lawsuits. In rare instances, ADR is used as the first choice for settlement, but the traditional method of obtaining mutually agreed-on settlements through negotiation should continue to be the most common, primary method for settling liability claims.

This chapter uses the terms litigation, arbitration, and mediation. Mediation and arbitration are covered in detail in this chapter, and litigation is covered in Chapter 10. In brief, litigation refers to the process of resolving disputes through lawsuits and the courts. Occasionally, this means going all the way to trial and having a judge or jury decide the case.

Arbitration is a method in which the disputants present their claims to an impartial third party who weighs the facts and evidence presented and makes a decision. The decision can be binding or nonbinding on the parties depending on the what they chose beforehand.

Mediation is basically negotiation that is facilitated by a neutral party. The following section deals with mediation, but many of the processes and activities discussed would also apply to other ADR methods.

Overview of Alternative Dispute Resolution (ADR)

Other than negotiation, the most common ADR techniques are mediation, arbitration, appraisals, mini-trials, summary jury trials, and pretrial settlement conferences. For several years, insurance companies and plaintiff attorneys have been successfully using alternative dispute resolution (ADR) methods to avoid the expense of trials.

Opposing parties in claims share a common objective: the timely and satisfactory resolution of those claims. Often, it is unnecessary to engage in litigation to attain that objective.

The majority of insurance disputes involve moderate sums and turn principally on issues of damages rather than liability. Such cases do not necessarily require judicial intervention. ADR provides a less adversarial, less time-consuming approach that can resolve cases more quickly than by going to trial. The result is that fewer lawsuits are filed, litigation and claim administration costs are lowered, and court dockets are reduced, permitting cases that raise significant legal issues quicker access to the courts.

ADR offers a wide range of cooperative and nonbinding approaches that do not require parties to give up their rights to a trial. Claim representatives need to be able to describe the benefits of ADR, explain the processes involved, and decide when to employ ADR methods. ADR must leave parties with the feeling that justice was served. This means that the ADR method must be legitimate and have a credible process for resolving disputes.

Benefits of ADR

The following are some advantages that both claimants and insurers find from using ADR:

Timeliness: An ADR process can be concluded within three to six months of the submission of a case. This compares most favorably to the delays often experienced by litigants in the civil court system. ADR can be initiated and concluded in a relatively short period of time (a matter of weeks rather than months or years). One study showed that it takes large liability claims (those over $75,000) an average of forty-five months to settle.[1] Decisions can be made more quickly with ADR. Court trials may require several days of testimony, whereas arbitration may last for only a few hours.

Cost-effectiveness: Compared to traditional litigation, the cost of an ADR process is modest. The cost to take a $50,000 claim to trial in 1999 was more than $20,000. In 1999, the insurance industry spent nearly $34 billion processing and defending claims. ADR frequently eliminates the need for costly items such as nonessential but extensive depositions, expert witnesses, and procedural motions.

Professionalism: A properly selected neutral party to the ADR will usually be a mutually selected former judge or attorney with significant experience either in mediating or litigating the type of case in question. The respect this person holds helps to facilitate an agreement.

Flexibility: The parties themselves select the procedure to be implemented. The wide range of choices includes mediation, binding and nonbinding arbitration, and other options. Procedures can be tailored to meet particular needs. ADR gives parties increased flexibility in presenting their cases and may not have the same procedural rules as required in court. Parties have the ability to choose the mediator or arbitrator, but they cannot choose the judge.

Efficiency: The ADR procedures are fewer and generally less formal than those with trials. ADR procedures are designed to quickly identify the critical disputed facts and issues and to ensure that required information is exchanged.

Informality: Most ADR procedures are informal and relax the rules of evidence and procedure. Usually, no record of the proceeding is made. The informality of the proceeding encourages disputants to better express themselves than they would in the atmosphere of a courtroom and also encourages insurance companies to have claim professionals participate in the hearings. These elements play a large role in the high percentage of settlements accomplished through ADR.

Predictability: The decisions arrived at through ADR are generally considered to be more predictable than jury verdicts. This is related to the fact that experienced professionals, mutually selected by the parties, serve as the neutral party. Their decisions and input are based on years of experience and are likely to be more predictable than those of a jury, which comprises people who normally have no experience in determining claim values.

Protects the rights of disputants: In many cases, parties do not have equal resources, influence, and knowledge. This can sometimes occur with claimants who must face insurers who have greater resources. Even with attorney representation, the resource issue is still a problem because litigation may be too costly. ADR can facilitate justice because it is a more accessible alternative.

Protects privacy and confidentiality of disputants: Arbitration and mediation can be private forums, while testimony in court is a public record. Confidentiality can be confirmed through signed agreements before entering arbitration or mediation.

ADR Service Providers

ADR service providers are often engaged to provide input on the selection of mediators. Some ADR providers are national, while others are regional or local. Some providers are nonprofit organizations; others operate for profit. ADR providers typically perform the following services:

- Review the referral made by the initiating party,
- Contact and encourage the other party(ies) to participate in the mediation,
- Submit a list of qualified mediators or arbitrators to help the parties in their selection, and
- Administer the proceedings or ensure that the proceedings are conducted.

It is good practice to exercise care in the selection of an ADR provider. Parties should interview the provider, obtain a client list, check references, and ascertain the provider's reputation. As a rule, insurers deal with providers on a case-by-case basis and monitor their performance. Insurers generally use a number of providers in different locations.

Mediation Overview

Mediation and arbitration are the ADR procedures used most commonly. When mediation is used, the parties themselves decide the outcome, and if mediation should fail, other options, including arbitration, remain open.

Mediation is a process in which an impartial intermediary, usually selected by the parties, assists them in settling the dispute. The process is private, voluntary, informal, and nonbinding. The mediator has no power to impose a settlement. Usually, the mediator will meet initially with all parties together and then with each party separately. The mediator will continue to meet with all parties separately to convey information from the other parties and to discuss the case. This process may continue for a specified time or until settlement is reached. The mediator will bring the parties together in order to summarize the process when settlement has been reached or time allotted has passed.

The role of the mediator depends on the desires of the parties and the attitude of the individual selected to mediate. Some mediators attempt to persuade parties to make concessions and may propose settlement terms. Other mediators are less involved in the merits of the claim and concentrate on assisting in the creation of an environment in which the parties can constructively communicate with each other and devise a mutually acceptable solution. The process is not adversarial in the same sense as litigation or arbitration (discussed later in this chapter); however, a skillful mediator will provide opportunities for advocacy as well as conciliation.

The primary advantage of mediation is that it enables the parties to decide the outcome while still benefiting from the advice and participation of a neutral third party. The mediator can contribute significantly by defusing the emotions that often accompany disputes and assisting the parties in focusing on their real interests and objectives.

Types of Cases Suitable for Mediation

Most routine cases in which the main disputes involve the amount of damages and the degree of comparative fault are suitable for mediation. This includes multi-party disputes.

The fact that they are initially far apart in their positions should not discourage parties from entering mediation, as it is common for mediation to bridge wide gaps. Mediation helps each party to more realistically evaluate the case. Mediation may bring parties closer to settlement even if the case does not settle at the conclusion of the mediation.

The following are examples of cases suitable for mediation:

- Claims that will cause companies to incur legal expenses that are greater than the expected settlement value of the case.
- Claims that are likely to settle before or without a trial, but for which negotiations up to this point have not been successful.
- Lawsuits filed in jurisdictions where crowded court dockets prevent a case from reaching trial for a long time.
- Complex claims that will require extensive discovery.

> Discovery is the exchange of all relevant information between the plaintiff and defendant before trial. Discovery is sanctioned by the court and proceeds according to the rules of the court.

- Claims involving multiple parties and in which extensive discovery will be required.
- Claims involving plaintiffs with unrealistic expectations, who could benefit from a face-to-face meeting.
- Claims involving information that one or more of the parties do not want revealed in a court.
- Claims involving a plaintiff attorney who does not normally practice in the area of law involved in litigation.
- Claims with potential values that exceed the insured's limit of liability.
- Claims involving highly emotional issues. The emotional impact of the claim on the claimant can be assessed in person, and it is better to know what this impact will be before going to trial.

Claims that are not appropriate for mediation, or that have less potential for success in mediation, are those involving coverage disputes, those in which one party is adamant that it gets its "day in court" no matter what the costs, or those involving fraud.

The Mediation Process

Either party can suggest mediation as a tool to assist in settlement negotiations. Mediation is voluntary; therefore, cooperation from all parties must exist for it to be successful. The mediation process involves the following steps:

1. Selecting the mediator
2. Preparing for mediation
3. Making opening statements
4. Presenting evidence
5. Negotiating (This may include caucusing, which means meeting privately with the mediator away from the other party.)
6. Concluding the mediation

Claim representatives and lawyers must address several issues related to mediation. Although these issues might be worked out in detail *after* the parties agree to enter mediation, it is probably wiser to answer these questions before agreeing to enter mediation because the answers could affect a party's willingness to go through with mediation. Following are some questions that are best answered before agreeing to mediation:

- How will the mediator be selected? If one side is adamant about using a particular mediator or ADR provider, then the other side needs to know that before agreeing to mediation.

- Is discovery required before mediation, and if so, when should it take place? If one party is unwilling to share discoverable information before mediation, then it may be better to wait until that information is produced rather than enter mediation without it.

- Who should be required to attend the mediation? Just the claim representative and claimant's lawyer, or also the claimant? Involve everyone in mediation whose decision is necessary for settlement. Personal attendance is strongly preferred, although telephone participation can be an acceptable substitute. Benefits can be gained from seeing in-person the claimant, the claimant's attorney, or witnesses, even if negotiations fail. Seeing how well they can present themselves may be useful information, and this should be a factor weighed into the decision of whether to mediate.

- What are the costs of mediation, and how should these costs be allocated between parties? Billing arrangements differ by provider. Most providers charge a modest administrative fee for mediation. With some, the fee is contingent on their securing agreement of all parties to participate. The mediator's fees can be on a per-case or per-hour basis and vary widely. It is considered desirable for all parties to make a financial commitment. The initiating party may agree to bear the administrative fee, but because sharing the mediator's fee reinforces his or her neutral status, the mediator's charges are usually shared equally. If the other side is unwilling to make any financial commitment, then mediation may be unproductive.

- What limitations or stipulations should be contained in the mediation agreement? Normally, limitations are set regarding disclosures made during mediation and it is determined whether a confidentiality agreement is required if a settlement is reached. Ensure that all parties understand the expectations for confidentiality before agreeing to mediate.

- How long should mediation last? This will affect costs and scheduling and give some indication of how interested the parties are in mediation. If one side is not willing to spend more than ninety minutes on a complex environmental liability claim, then they may not be ready to talk seriously about the issues.

Selecting the Mediator

The availability of credible, neutral mediators is crucial to the success of ADR. Some providers offer panels that often include retired judges; others offer their own employees as neutral mediators. When considering a provider, the prospective user should ask about the type of mediators whom the provider will make available.

Providers use a variety of procedures for the selection of a mediator. As a rule, the parties should not grant the provider the right of appointment, but should retain the right to approve candidates. A mediator, in particular, is most likely to succeed if selected by mutual agreement of the parties and if all parties have confidence in his or her impartiality and judgment. In addition, many areas offer listings of local attorneys and retired judges who are available to conduct mediations.

Preparing for Mediation

As with any negotiation, preparation is a critical success factor. The following activities should be performed in preparation for mediation after it has been scheduled:

Review the claim. Know the specific details and evidence of the claim. This familiarity will ease the presentation and make it more credible and effective. Organize the file so that the basic documents of the claim can be referred to easily to support arguments and to educate the mediator.

Use objective criteria. Find objective criteria to measure the appropriate damages and evaluate settlement offers/demands. Have support for that objective information available during mediation and ready to present. Objective information such as book values on automobiles and jury verdicts on injuries helps to give credibility to a settlement offer.

Determine BATNAs. Determine the best alternative to a negotiated agreement (BATNA) for each party. Realistically evaluate the likely outcome if the case is litigated. Some factors to consider are the cost to litigate the dispute (attorney fees, expert fees, insured's time, witnesses' time) and the effect on the parties if settlement is not reached (disruption of work and family activities and emotional impact).

Take the proceedings seriously. Treat mediation as if it is the final resolution method and resist the temptation to not prepare in advance or present the offer in a take-it-or-leave-it fashion just because mediation is nonbinding.

Empathize. Consider how the other party views the possibility of litigation and how the other party evaluates the likely outcome of litigation. What evidence or arguments might change that evaluation? Try to understand the concerns and interests of the other party and incorporate them into offers and arguments.

Bring it all. Bring all relevant information to the mediation, even if it has not yet been shared. A determination as to whether to use it can be made during the mediation.

Learn from the past. Consider whether there is anything to be learned from the negotiations or conversations that have already taken place that could be applied to the mediation. What barriers prevented reaching an agreement, and how might mediation overcome them?

Invent options. Do not become focused on the limited ways in which a demand has been presented. Consider responding with offers and options that might appeal to the other side. Would structured settlements, advance payments, or neutral experts help to facilitate a settlement? Take the focus off the money and instead think about addressing the real needs of the claimant. Unfortunately, many attorneys do not determine their clients' underlying needs. Bring a list of questions that might help to determine what those underlying needs and issues are, such as future medical expenses, future disability and possible need for job retraining, or loss of enjoyment.

Establish rules. Make sure all parties agree to mediation rules beforehand. Some ADR providers supply standard agreement forms that can be tailored to fit specific arrangements. Parties should be assured that the statements and concessions made during mediation will not be used against them later in court. Without this assurance, parties are likely just to engage in posturing that does not move settlement forward. Parties should obtain this assurance before mediation takes place.

Courts typically regard mediated negotiations of disputes as settlement negotiations, and therefore statements the parties make during mediation are not admissible in any subsequent trial. It is a good idea for participants to make this clear in the beginning. They can ensure that this admissibility issue is addressed by including provisions in their mediation agreements that specifically state, "If the parties to this mediation do not settle and litigation follows, statements made in the mediation will not be admissible or discoverable, and the mediator may not be called as a witness." It is good practice to get all agreements in writing. Bring a laptop computer with a prepared agreement that can be changed to meet the needs of the parties. ADR providers can supply a generic agreement form. Exhibit 9-1 shows common wording on a confidentiality agreement.

EXHIBIT 9-1

Confidentiality Agreement

We will achieve more open communication if we each:

Agree to treat the statements made during the mediation as confidential (except for necessary internal company reports to management)

Agree that all statements made in mediation shall be privileged against use at trial

Agree that notes taken by the parties and the mediator will be destroyed at the conclusion of the mediation session (with the exception of the final agreement or notes related to the final agreement if the agreement is to be drafted later)

Agree that the mediator will not be subpoenaed as a witness in related litigation if the mediation fails to produce a settlement

Making Effective Opening Statements in Mediation

The claim representative or defense attorney may make the opening state-ment. A professional, well-prepared opening statement is critical, as it sets the tone for the subsequent negotiation during mediation. The audience is the other side, particularly the decision maker. The goal during this presenta-tion is not only to persuade the mediator but also, more importantly, to persuade the other party that it is in the best interest of all parties to find agreeable settlement terms. Because emotional issues may exist, it may be difficult to be heard by the other parties, as they will filter the information through their own perspective. An effective opening presentation that incorporates the other side's interests can open the filters and permit the insurer's side to be understood. Try to make the opening statement a turning point in the dispute. Claim representatives should consider the following approaches to help facilitate successful mediation:

- Consider what can be said and done during the opening presentation to create the most favorable circumstances for negotiation. Remember that mediation is not to be an adversarial or formal court forum. Behaving like a prosecuting attorney in a high-profile criminal case is not likely to be a successful tactic. Avoid threats, exaggerations, and legal jargon.

- Think about how to phrase the opening statement to make it more likely that the other side will hear and be receptive to the insurer's viewpoint and interests. Open with courtesies addressed to those on the other side and express appreciation for their participation in the mediation. Empa-thize with the other side's position and express a commitment to work together to settle the dispute. Demonstrate appreciation for the other side's efforts, limitations, difficulties, and frustrations.

- Maintain eye contact with the other side and address the claimant and attorney, not just the mediator. This may be the only opportunity the other side has to hear the insurer's version of the facts and the law.

- Indicate a willingness to respond to clarifying questions from the other side either when they are posed or at the end of the opening presenta-tion.

- Highlight the points of agreement and disagreement and strike a balance between being persuasive and being conciliatory. Focus on the facts that promote an understanding of each party's issues and show a willingness to listen and make concessions.

- Depending on the nature of the dispute, review the possible alternatives each side will face if agreement is not reached at the mediation. This ensures that all parties have thought through the consequences of not settling.

Presenting the Evidence in Mediation

Claim representatives or legal counsel should use admissible evidence to support their positions. Often each party will present a brief summarizing its position and describing the evidence that will be presented. If a brief was submitted to the other side before the mediation, claim representatives or legal counsel can try to determine whether the decision maker has read it by asking questions about the important parts of it. They can then proceed to presenting evidence such as documents, physical evidence, diagrams, charts, videos, and demonstrations. Having consultants/witnesses available by telephone during mediation can enhance the value of the evidence presented.

Negotiating in Mediation

Several strategies related to mediation can help claim representatives to achieve a negotiated agreement. In general, claim representatives should try to separate the person from the problem and not allow personalities to deflect attention away from the issues. They should focus on the underlying interests, not just the monetary figures. Offers should be based on identifiable losses that may be addressed in some monetary form, while less definable concerns such as the need for an apology on a sincere expression of sympathy should be handled by interpersonal communications. Mediators and caucuses may help with this.

The following are examples of specific strategies that should be considered:

- Obtain a demand from the claimant before entering mediation. This establishes a base and highlights the differences that must be overcome.

- Leave some room to negotiate in mediation. Don't make the best offer before entering mediation and then enter mediation hoping to convince the other side of the merits of that offer. The other side's expectation is that claim representatives will move from their original position. If claim representatives do not, they will not likely settle, even if they have made a generous offer originally. Understanding and controlling expectations are important to achieving a successful settlement.

- Communicate in a conciliatory tone and remember the goal is to obtain a satisfactory resolution. Listen to the other side's evaluation to help find out where differences exist. Then address those differences in a way they can understand.

- Evaluate the other side's emotional need to "win." Many times they have an emotional need to win that overshadows the monetary needs. Use the joint sessions to evaluate the other side's needs. Sometimes parties are looking for an apology as much as a monetary settlement.

- Negotiate global values when an impasse is reached on sub-issues. Don't allow negotiations to get hung up over a minor disagreement if the parties are close to agreement on the overall value.

- Do not make consecutive offers, which is the usual rule of thumb in negotiation. "Don't bid against yourself" is the conventional wisdom. Consider consecutive offers when new information is revealed or to revive stalled negotiations.

- Use "what if" inquiries. (For example, would those on the opposing party agree to accept $5,000 now and $50,000 in five years when their injured teenage son enters college?) These options may have been invented in preparation for negotiations, but sometimes they can be explored with probing inquiries only during negotiation. Where appropriate, develop nonmonetary and nontraditional settlement options that further the interests of the parties.

Using Caucuses

Many mediation sessions have parties **caucus**. Caucuses are private meetings with the mediator away from the other party. Some advantages of having caucuses are that they:

- Permit the mediator to establish a more personal rapport with each side.
- Permit a party to vent emotionally to the mediator without alienating the other side.
- Allow a mediator to uncover—or a party to share—sensitive or confidential information that would cause the other side to reevaluate its position. When sharing information with the mediator in private caucus, be clear as to what can be relayed and what is to remain confidential.
- Give parties an opportunity to strategize with the mediator on what to disclose and how to do so. Also, the mediator can float hypotheticals and gauge reactions privately before sharing them with both sides in the joint meeting.
- Shield each side from unproductive encounters with the other side.
- Allow more frank discussions with the mediator regarding whether the offer or demand is realistic.
- Permit mediators to speak frankly about one party's behavior and how it may be counterproductive to the negotiations.
- Give each side a chance to do some "homework" while the other side is in caucus. This helps maintain interest in the negotiations. Homework can include brainstorming the next move, calculating the cost of proposed settlement options, calling the office for more information, reporting back to superiors, and getting more settlement authority.

Some possible risks related to caucuses are that they:

- May contribute to a feeling of secrecy and undercut the "joint problem-solving" feel of a mediation with only joint sessions.
- May encourage parties to polarize and disavow responsibility for their own dispute, placing the burden on the mediator to bridge the gap.
- May contribute to a feeling of mistrust as parties wonder what is being said behind their backs.
- May inhibit consensus building in multi-party negotiations by encouraging parties to strike side deals.

Mediators can minimize these risks by explaining why caucuses will be used.

Role of the Mediator

Experienced claim practitioners realize that the mediator can be an effective "tool" in the negotiation process to convey information and to sound out the other side on sensitive issues. A mediator acts as a referee to the parties in dispute, but in some cases, the mediator can even be used to assist in negotiating issues such as chiropractic and medical treatment fees. The **mediator** can be a useful resource in the following ways:

- As a negotiating partner to help claim representatives test different methods to respond to the other side's arguments.
- To test a party's position. The mediator can point out flaws in the arguments or issues.
- To help generate ideas. Mediators can be used as a sounding board to help develop offers, counteroffers, and nonmonetary options.
- To help break down communication barriers. Mediators can smooth over communication problems by helping parties restate their positions in less threatening ways that will be more likely to be received by the other side.
- As a process consultant who gives ideas on how to proceed through the mediation.
- To get parties past an impasse by dividing the issues into smaller parts.
- To clarify issues and facts. The mediator may learn that the parties are basing their positions on different information and facts and can address these differences by facilitating a complete exchange of information.
- To determine the barriers to settlement and suggest ways to remove them.
- To encourage the parties by showing them the progress they have made.
- Calling for breaks at opportune times.
- Allowing silence to force parties to communicate.
- Using humor to break the tension.
- To remind parties of the consequences of not settling. This may mean suggesting that the parties stop the mediation. The suggestion, combined with the knowledge of the consequences, may jar the parties into making progress.

Concluding the Mediation

As mentioned earlier, it is good practice to get all agreements in writing. A blank settlement agreement should be completed at the end of the mediation. Each party involved in the agreement should sign it. The mediator should reiterate the confidentiality provisions discussed earlier.

Criticism of Mediation

Sometimes mediation is unsuccessful. The following are some criticisms of mediation:

- It may add to the overall costs and waste time and energy if the parties are not serious about settlement.
- Parties involved may lack expertise.
- No guarantee exists of concluding the claim.

Telemediation

Telemediation is a low-cost alternative to face-to-face mediation. In **telemediation**, the mediator works with the parties in dispute to help them facilitate a negotiation over the phone. This form of mediation can work well in situations that have only a few issues in dispute. The telemediator could get both sides to specify exactly what they need and then force them to commit to concluding the claim once the needs have been met. The telemediator can act as the rational go-between for parties who may have become too emotionally entrenched in their positions. Some insurance departments use telemediators to resolve disputes between insureds and insurance companies.

Arbitration Overview

The preparation and presentation skills needed for mediation also apply to arbitration. Claim representatives must prepare their claims, and they or their legal counsel must present the facts and evidence. In **arbitration**, the two parties present their cases to an impartial third party—the arbitrator—who acts as a judge, weighing the facts of the case and making a decision based on the evidence presented. The advantage of arbitration over mediation is that someone (other than the insurer and the claimant) decides the case.

Arbitration can be binding or nonbinding. **Binding arbitration**, which might be required by state law, requires the parties to accept the arbitrator's decision. In **nonbinding arbitration**, neither party is forced to accept the arbitrator's decision. However, the decision provides the "winner" with leverage for future negotiations. This method of dispute resolution is cost-effective for all parties and relieves the courts of the burden of handling such disputes. Parties choose arbitration over mediation because they want to have assurance that a decision will be made and as a way to avoid the much more costly alternative of litigation.

Arbitration Variations

Arbitration is becoming increasingly more flexible and accommodating of the parties' needs. Arbitration can include modifications and can be customized for various situations. Examples include high-low agreements, "baseball" arbitration, arbitration-mediation, mediation-arbitration, and inter-company arbitration.

High-Low Agreements

Some disputants will enter into arbitration with **high-low agreements**. To give them a higher comfort level before entering arbitration, some parties will enter into a high-low agreement, which stipulates that no matter what the arbitrator decides, the insurer will not be out more than a specified amount and the claimant will not receive less than some other specified amount. For example, parties might enter into arbitration with a $30,000-$70,000 high-low agreement. The parties would still accept the arbitrator's award within that range, but if the arbitrator issues an award below $30,000, the claimant would receive the $30,000 minimum, and if the arbitrator awards a figure higher than $70,000, then the insurer would only be responsible for paying $70,000. This gives more predictability to arbitration. The arbitrator is unaware of the high-low agreement and bases his or her decision on the merits of the claim.

High-low agreements may be most suitable for claims involving serious damage but having little or no apparent liability. By setting the low limit, the claimant escapes the possibility of a "defense verdict," and by setting the cap, the insurer can limit its exposure at less than the full damages.

Baseball Arbitration

"Baseball" arbitration received its name from the approach taken to resolve salary disputes between professional baseball players and their team owners. After negotiating, each side presents its case to the arbitrator along with its monetary figure. The arbitrator weighs the facts and evidence presented and then must choose *one* of the two figures. The arbitrator is *not permitted to split the difference*. This approach forces parties to make their most realistic offer before entering arbitration. After making their final realistic offers, parties often find that their differences are relatively small and may conclude the negotiation without going forward with the arbitration. Some industry observers believe that this approach favors insurers who are under legal and ethical constraints to make realistic offers in spite of the demands made by a claimant or an attorney. As one author advises plaintiff lawyers, "Make your first demand high because it makes subsequent demands appear to be more reasonable."[2] Baseball arbitration has the potential to effect reasonable offers and demands and to help settle liability claims even before the arbitration decision is made.

Mediation-Arbitration

In **mediation-arbitration**, the parties agree in advance to engage in mediation to attempt to resolve their disputes, but if they fail to reach an agreement, they must proceed directly to arbitration where a decision is made by an impartial third party.

The third party can be either the mediator or someone who was not involved in the prior mediation. Maintaining the mediator and having the mediator act as arbitrator is the most efficient way because the parties do not have to present their cases again. The mediator, who is already familiar with the facts, may just ask for some clarification on a few points, review what has already been submitted, and then decide the award. The disadvantage to this is that some parties are reluctant to confide in the mediator during the mediation, knowing that he or she may become an arbitrator who decides the claim.

The disadvantage of using another third party as arbitrator is the time it takes to present the cases again. However, if the parties enter mediation knowing that they will have to incur additional time and money in presenting their case to an arbitrator, it may help to encourage an agreed settlement in the mediation phase. On the other hand, such a time and money commitment could keep them from entering into a mediation-arbitration agreement.

Arbitration-Mediation

In **arbitration-mediation**, the parties first present their cases to an arbitrator, who then decides the award that should be given. This amount is kept confidential, and the parties then proceed to mediation. Mediation can proceed fairly quickly because the parties have already heard the other side's presentation during arbitration. If the parties come to an agreement during mediation, then the amount that the arbitrator decided as an award is never revealed. If, on the other hand, the parties cannot resolve their dispute through mediation, the arbitrator sets the amount of the claimant's award.

Inter-Company Arbitration

Inter-company arbitration is used to settle disputes between insurance companies regarding the financial responsibility each has for a given claim. Generally, one insurer settles with or on behalf of the insured. The case is then submitted to an arbitration service to determine what each insurer owes. Inter-company arbitration is commonly handled by organizations such as Insurance Arbitration Forums, Inc., or the American Arbitration Association. Insurer trade associations also offer arbitration services and other forms of alternative dispute resolution to member companies.

Inter-company arbitration sometimes takes the form of **paper arbitration**. Each side writes its contentions and encloses supporting documentation for them. The supporting documentation may take the form of transcribed statements, photographs, estimates of damage, and even medical and wage-loss information for no-fault auto claims and workers compensation claims.

Mini-Trials

Mini-trials, which closely resemble full trials in the traditional legal system, involve representatives (usually lawyers) for two parties presenting an abbreviated version of their case to a "judge." A mini-trial enables parties to test the validity of their positions in a trial setting and continue negotiations. The mini-trial allows the parties to present evidence and arguments to a panel or an adviser. Parties can terminate the process at any time. Parties agree not to disclose in future litigation anything that occurs during the mini-trial. This helps to preserve their rights in litigation should negotiation fail subsequently.

The parties select an impartial adviser, often a retired judge, an executive, or an expert, and decide the role of the adviser. The adviser can act as a passive participant or as an arbitrator or a judge. The adviser has no authority to make a binding decision but can pose questions that test the validity of each case and offer an opinion on the outcome of a trial based on the evidence.

Before the mini-trial, parties can exchange information on their anticipated testimony and the documents that they would introduce as evidence. Information gathered might be given to the adviser. Witnesses and experts might testify during the mini-trial. Lawyers are allotted a limited time to present the cases, and normal rules of evidence are not followed. The main advantage of mini-trials is that claimants and insurers can learn the likely outcome of their cases without having to contend with delays in the legal system.

Neutral Expert Analysis

There are several instances in which damages might be able to be established with the help of a **neutral expert**. Some negotiations reach an impasse over a particular technical issue. The parties may have different assessments of damages because of this technical information. Consider a claim in which the insured caused a fire that damaged a claimant's computer system. The claimant believes that the entire system must be replaced, while the insured argues that the system can be repaired. By enlisting the assistance of a mutually acceptable neutral expert who is familiar with system repairs, the issue causing the impasse might be able to be resolved. Another example might be a neutral antique dealer who could be called in to establish the value of a claimant's collectible item.

Summary Jury Trials

Summary jury trials are often used when specific claim issues must be resolved. Claims involving single issues such as a question of coverage, a question of injury causation, or similar questions are common with summary jury trials. The trials offer a forum for deciding the merit of the case for court proceedings and assist in negotiations.

A summary jury trial is staged much like a regular jury trial, except that only a few witnesses present the case. "Mock jurors" are pulled from a pool of persons selected to serve as possible jurors in an actual court case. Evidence and witnesses' testimony might be presented in both oral and written format for the mock jurors. Lawyers summarize information for the sake of brevity. The proceedings might be videotaped for later study. The mock jurors decide the case based on the limited, though representative, presentation.

A summary jury trial can be concluded in a relatively short time, so legal costs are reduced significantly. Fewer witnesses mean less expense for witness fees. Although lawyers are still required, the amount of time required to develop the case and prepare for trial is considerably less. Summary jury trials can produce an effective settlement and provide control over legal expenses.

Pretrial Conferences

Even if a claimant has already filed a lawsuit, the presiding judge might try to avoid a trial. In a **pretrial conference**, the judge encourages the litigants to try one last time to resolve their differences before the formal trial begins. The judge's role is similar to a mediator's, but in an effort to resolve the dispute, he or she might subtly express his or her opinion on the litigants' positions and, by extension, the probable trial outcome.

Settlement Days

Some ADR firms host special **Settlement Days**, during which parties can come together to solve several disputes at the same place. Typically, a conference room in a large hotel will be provided for each insurer, and the lawyers representing claimants can go from room to room settling different claims. The advantage of Settlement Days is that lawyers and insurers can block off one period of time (usually one or two days) and make themselves available to negotiate person-to-person. Many find that this person-to-person negotiation helps to facilitate settlement, and this is a rare opportunity in today's claim environment because of the busy schedules of claim representatives and lawyers. Claim representatives and claimant lawyers usually plan to negotiate smaller, less complicated claims that can be settled in about one hour or less. This gives them a chance to settle several claims on the same day and maximize the advantage of having many parties together for this limited time period.

Online Settlement Forums

Recently a number of **online settlement forums**[3] have been developed to help facilitate negotiations. These services use the Internet to offer arbitration and dispute resolution services for claims. With the tremendous growth in Internet use and the increased confidence of consumers in online transactions, it is only natural that the Internet has become a tool for resolving disputes. Attorneys and software engineers have teamed up to convert the concepts of blind bidding and traditional third-party mediation into an Internet forum. Some online forums are new, strictly Internet companies, while other online dispute resolution forums have roots established in traditional ADR methods and techniques.

Blind bidding is a common feature of online ADR. Parties in online ADR make a series of offers and demands, and neither side sees the other's offers and demands. They are notified if they have overlapping figures. Most online settlement providers will settle the claim automatically when this occurs. Different forums have varying settlement formulas. For example, one forum automatically settles the claims by splitting the difference if the offer and demand are within 30 percent or $5,000 (whichever is less) of each other.

Parties are informed of the settlement rules before entering negotiations. In the past, one traditional strategy for mediators was to find out, in confidence, the best figures from each party to determine whether there was any overlap that offered potential for settlement. This Internet strategy is a similar but more automated approach.

The following are some of the advantages of online settlement forums:

1. They permit asynchronous negotiations. An increasing problem has been the difficulty that claim representatives and claimants, or lawyers representing claimants, have in reaching each other by telephone. Parties find themselves in a seemingly endless cycle of voice mail messages. Online forums give parties the opportunity to make offers and demands at their convenience.

2. Participants claim that online settlement forums are less threatening, especially for unrepresented claimants. Online settlement forums eliminate aggressive posturing, bullying, and face-saving, which often occur with person-to-person or telephone negotiations. This not only benefits claimants wanting to avoid the awkwardness and embarrassment of

negotiations, but also, many claim representatives who are inexperienced at negotiations find these forums to be less stressful than dealing with claimant lawyers. Many people are now more comfortable with online dialogues and disputes than with personal encounters.

3. Some parties may be less likely to make outrageous demands or "low ball" offers as a way of influencing the other side's expectations because neither side knows the other's offer or demand figures.

4. Most online services offer follow-up human dispute-resolution mediators who try to bring the parties together when they don't settle within the allotted number of rounds (typically, between three and five offers and demands are permitted, depending on the service).

5. Some of the online services offer a database that disputants can access to help evaluate the value of their claim. The data can be broken down by injury type and jurisdiction or region. This could prove invaluable for claimants wishing to settle claims on their own without attorney repre-sentation. Less attorney involvement means that cases settle sooner, which is a benefit to claimants and insurers.

Virtual courts are also available on the Internet. With one such forum,[4] plaintiffs can register and file their complaint electronically. After filing the complaint, the plaintiff receives a docket number and is issued "Trial Books." The information submitted in the books includes the plaintiff's arguments and evidence including audio, video, or other data. Court documents cannot contain first and last names or racial, religious, or ethnic identification. The defendant is then notified of the case and is given an opportunity to respond in similar fashion.

Jury panels are selected by Web site applications in which potential jurors complete a simple profile. If an applicant's profile matches that required for a specific case, the applicant is sent a series of questions relating to the case at hand. If the parties like the applicant's answers, he or she will be selected for the jury.

The judgments of the jury may not be binding unless both sides agree to be bound. Past participants have accepted the vast majority of the decisions. The typical disputes submitted to the Internet courthouse are personal injury claims, but the service also has handled family disputes and sexual harass-ment claims. Attorneys have also used this service to perform mock jury trials for larger cases. The process is free. The site's creators hope to make money by licensing site content and by marketing their list of jurors to law firms that want to arrange their own mock trials.

Automated online settlement forums differ from standard e-mail negotiations in that the parties do not argue the merits of the case but instead only offer monetary figures. Automation can mean losing valuable information that would be communicated in typical exchanges. Information about what is motivating a party's offer or demand can sometimes help to structure negotia-tions and lead to mutually satisfactory agreements. But settlement also means that parties have less of an opportunity for their e-mail messages to degener-ate into unpleasant exchanges (known as flaming), which is all too common with e-mail. These unpleasant exchanges (which do not seem to occur with such frequency or intensity with in-person or even telephone encounters) can lead to personal grudges that make settlement impossible.

Some potential challenges for online ADR involve security, accessibility to the Internet, venue and choice of law issues, and contract enforceability.

Technology has been used for years to help evaluate claims; now it can help facilitate settlements. As more people become familiar with using online services, online settlements are likely to become more popular, especially if some of these challenging issues can be resolved.

Structured Settlements

A **structured settlement** is a method of resolving a claim that gives the claimant some payment immediately but defers much of the payment into the future. The future payment is usually disbursed over a period of time rather than in one lump sum. A liability insurer normally arranges a structured settlement by purchasing an annuity from a life insurance company and naming the claimant as "beneficiary" so that the claimant will receive periodic payments for a set number of years. The advantage to the claimant is that the interest earned on these annuities is tax-free, whereas if the claimant invests the lump-sum payment, interest on those investments is taxable. The advantage to the insurer is that the additional tax-free income may make the settlement more attractive to the claimant. This tax-free feature may be enough to help parties overcome an impasse, because the claimant receives more money in total than with a lump-sum payment.

Structured settlements are useful for addressing the following claimant needs:

- Ongoing regular medical treatments
- Adequate income to replace wages that can no longer be earned
- Ongoing household help
- Occupational therapy and rehabilitation
- Educational needs for children
- Lump-sum needs on an occasional basis for medical equipment replacement
- Payment of legal fees on a lump-sum or an extended basis
- Trusts, endowments, or annuities to take care of dependents or contingencies that may arise

Factors to consider in determining the amount and terms of a structured settlement are:

1. The life expectancy of the claimant
2. The likely cost of future medical expenses including rehabilitation, physical therapy, future surgeries, nursing home costs, home services, prosthetic devices, wheelchairs, and other equipment.
3. Cost of reasonable monthly living expenses, including mortgages, taxes, maintenance, food, clothing, and similar items.

4. Cost of dependents' needs
5. Legal fees
6. Lump sums for special contingencies[5]

SETTLEMENT AGREEMENTS

Once all parties have agreed to a settlement figure, they must conclude the settlement with the appropriate agreement. A **settlement agreement** is an oral or a written agreement by which parties compromise a disputed matter. In most claims, settlement agreements are in writing and involve some type of release document. Settlement agreements are contracts, and the principles of contract law apply to them. For a settlement agreement to be valid, there must be offer, acceptance, and consideration. The parties to the settlement agreement must have the legal capacity and authority to settle. Claimants must have the mental capacity to understand the nature and effect of the agreement. Authority is sometimes an issue that surfaces in liability claims. For example, an attorney must have the authority to bind his or her client to an agreement.

General Release of All Claims

A settlement agreement in a liability claim is called a release. A **release** is normally a written document that stipulates the terms of the settlement agreement.

Consideration by the insurer is usually some monetary amount. For some retailers settling claims with customers, consideration might be free merchandise (free movie tickets or free food coupons are sometimes used to "settle" minor claims). The claimant's consideration is giving up the right to sue. Claim representatives should make sure that all claimants' spouses, children, and parents and third parties who have liens (such as a hospital) release their rights.

Key elements of a general release are the following:

• Names and addresses of parties involved (claimant and insured)

• Date of the accident

• Amount of the settlement

• Statement that the release applies to all claims related to this accident that the claimant now has or will have in the future, whether they are known or unknown

• Statement that parties understand and agree to the terms of the release

• Signatures are required on written releases. This includes signatures of claimants, with date signed. With larger losses, signatures of witnesses and a notary may be required.

Some companies permit recorded, oral settlement agreements for smaller claims. These are usually for property-damage-only claims, and the claim representative simply tape-records the claimant's agreement terms in a telephone statement.

Issues With Releases

Claim representatives encounter several issues related to releases, such as the enforceability of releases, who must sign the release, and which *unnamed* parties might also be released.

Enforceability

Releases are legally enforceable contracts. Courts rarely set aside (allow parties to get out of) releases as long as the elements of a valid contract exist. Courts have been fairly consistent about not setting aside releases for claimants who want to sue later after having signed a release.

A few exceptions have occurred. Some releases have been set aside when signed shortly after the claimant suffered a serious injury, especially when the claimant did not have a clear prognosis of the injury. Claim representatives are encouraged to pay claims as soon as possible; however, it is inappropriate to obtain a release from a claimant before the claimant or claim representative has had a chance to thoroughly evaluate the claim. This is known as "indecent haste," and courts have set aside releases on the basis that undue advantage was taken of the claimant.[6] Some states have enacted statutes prescribing waiting periods for contracts, including releases. Some laws give claimants up to thirty days after an accident—if treatment is ongoing—before a bodily injury settlement can be concluded.[7] Releases obtained before the waiting period ended will not be considered valid. Releases have also been set aside when taken in a hospital from a claimant who was still emotionally upset and on medicine. Not all states have waiting periods, but good judgment should be exercised before obtaining a release from an injured claimant shortly after an accident. Exhibit 9-2 is an excerpt of one state's law regarding releases for automobile damage.

EXHIBIT 9-2

Regulation on Release for Damage to Motor Vehicle

North Carolina insurance regulation T11:04 .0421 HANDLING OF LOSS AND CLAIM PAYMENTS (4): If a release or full payment of claim is executed by an insured or claimant, involving a repair to a motor vehicle, prior to or at the time of the repair, it shall not bar the right of the claimant to promptly assert a claim for property damages unknown to either the claimant or to the insurance carrier prior to the repair of the vehicle or a claim for diminished value, directly caused by the accident which could not be determined or known until after the repair or attempted repair of the motor vehicle. Claims asserted within 30 days after repair for diminished value and 30 days after discovery of unknown damage shall be considered promptly asserted.

Releases With Husbands and Wives

For claims involving injuries to married persons and property owned by a married person, the husband and wife should *both* sign the release. This is done because the noninjured spouse has a potential claim for consortium that must also be extinguished or, in the case of damaged property, may have property interests even when not a title owner. Normally, jurisdictions permit issuing one lump-sum settlement for the claimant *and* spouse's claim. Having both parties sign the release also prevents one of the parties from coming back and asserting a claim for his or her "share" in the loss.

Releases Involving Liability of Principals (Respondeat Superior)

In most jurisdictions, a general release of the principal will also release unnamed agents or employees involved in the act. By the same token, a general release form will release unnamed principals. Courts permit this because the damages are not separate but are instead based on vicarious liability. If an employee injures a person, the employer may be responsible but only to the extent the employee caused damages. This is true for other claims involving vicarious liability. A general release could, in many states, release these parties even if they are not specifically named.[8] Nevertheless, it is good practice to include the names of all parties who will be released by a general release form.

Joint Tortfeasors

One traditional principle was that a release of one party constituted a release of all parties in situations involving joint tortfeasors. The "release-of-one rule" no longer applies in most states. Statutes or court case rulings preclude the unintended release of nonsettling joint tortfeasors.[9] A common principle of these laws is that the release will apply only to the parties listed on the release form.[10] (As mentioned earlier, this should not be confused with the release of other parties such as employers, parents, and partners who may have vicarious liability.)

One way to address the issue of joint tortfeasors is with a **covenant not to sue**. This is an agreement that states that in exchange for a specified sum of money, the claimant will not sue one of the joint tortfeasors. The agreement specifically leaves open the right of the claimant to sue the other tortfeasor. Claimants sometimes prefer this because it gives them some money with which to prepare for litigation against the other tortfeasor. Claim representatives should consult with management before entering into such an agreement, because they may have unforeseen legal ramifications.

Special Releases and Settlement Situations

Releases involved with minor claimants, partnerships, corporations, and death claims may have complicating issues that claim representatives need to consider.

Releases by and on Behalf of Minors

A person who has not attained the full legal age is known as a **minor** (also referred to by the legal term "infant" in some states). Legal age is eighteen years old in most states. A minor cannot effectively release legal liability for personal injury or property damage. Contracts formed by minors are voidable by the minors. Therefore, a release by a minor would provide an insured with little legal protection.

For personal injuries to minors, a parent or legal guardian must assume the responsibility for medical expenses incurred. The parents have an independent right of claim for their expenses and for their loss of services provided by the minor. Consequently, for claims involving minors, claim representatives must conclude two independent claims: one with the parents or legal guardians and one with the minor child. Sometimes, a child who is younger than eighteen may be married or emancipated (living independently) from parents. In such situations, the parents may have no claim of their own. The minor child is still unable to effect a release on his or her own behalf.

The two most common ways to conclude claims involving minors are through:

1. Parent-guardian release and indemnity agreements, or
2. Court-approved settlements (friendly suits).

Parent-Guardian Release and Indemnity Agreement

For less serious claims involving minors, a **parent-guardian release and indemnity agreement** (sometimes known just as a "PG release") may be used to settle the claims of the parent and the child. These are usually claims that involve a relatively small dollar amount. The main factor to consider is whether the injury has realistic potential for permanency. Claims involving even moderate amounts of money are sometimes settled using parent-guardian release and indemnity agreements if there is little chance of a permanent injury. A soft tissue back or neck injury would normally be a good candidate for this type of release. Under this type of agreement, the minor can still pursue the claim when he or she reaches legal age, but the insurer is given credit for the amounts paid to the parents on behalf of the child. The effect of the release is to bind the parents for their claim, but in reality they cannot extinguish the claims of the minor child. The indemnity agreement states that the claimant's parents must indemnify the insured (or insurer) for the amount paid to them on behalf of the minor, if the minor decides to make a claim after he or she reaches the legal age. The enforceability of the indemnity agreement part of this release is open to question, but in practice, parents do not sign these releases unless they are confident that there will be no future claims. Exhibit 9-3 shows an example of a parent-guardian release and indemnity agreement.

Court-Approved Settlements (Friendly Suits)

The only way to effectively release the claim of a minor is through a **court-approved settlement.** Each state has its own procedures for court-approved settlements, but each side is normally represented by a lawyer. In some cases, the insurer may even pay for the minor claimant's lawyer, who still must act on behalf of and in the best interest of the minor. The court will review all of the details of the settlement and then determine whether it is in the best interest of the minor (infant). The court may deny settlement approval or accept it. If it accepts the settlement, it will issue a judgment approving the

---

EXHIBIT 9-3

Parents-Guardian Release and Indemnity Agreement

FOR AND IN CONSIDERATION of the payment to me/us of the sum

of _____(Settlement Amount)_____Dollars _____

The receipt of which is hereby acknowledged, I/we, the undersigned, father and mother and/or guardian of

(Minor claimant)_____ a minor, do

forever release, acquit, discharge and covenant to hold harmless_____(Insured)_____

_____

heirs, successors and assigns of and from any and all actions, causes of action, claims, demands, damages, costs, loss of services, expenses and compensation, on account of, or in any way growing out of any and all known and unknown personal injuries and property damage which we may now or hereafter have as the parents and/or guardian of said minor, and also all claims or rights of action for damages which the said minor has or may hereafter have, either before or after he has reached his/her majority, resulting or to result from a certain accident which occurred on or about the_____day of _____20_____at or near _____(Place of accident)_____ .

I/we further promise to bind myself/ourselves jointly and severally, my/our heirs, administrators and executors to repay to the said _____(insured)_____ heirs, successors and assigns any sum of money, except the sum above mentioned that he/she/they may hereafter be compelled to pay on behalf of said minor because of the said accident.

It is further understood and agreed that this settlement is the compromise of a doubtful and disputed claim, and that this payment is not to be construed as an admission of liability on the part of _____ (Insured)_____ by whom liability is expressly denied.

I/we further state that I/we have carefully read the foregoing release and know the contents thereof, and I/we sign the same as my/our own free act.

WITNESS _____ hand and seal this_____day of _____20 _____ .

In presence of_____ .

CAUTION: READ BEFORE SIGNING.

Witness _____

STATE OF_____   SS _____

COUNTY OF_____

On this _____day of _____ , 20 _____, before me appeared to me personally known, and who acknowledged the execution of the foregoing instrument as _____ free act and deed, for the consideration set forth therein.

My Commission Expires

_____   Notary Public

---

settlement terms and amount. In claims involving a large sum of money, a trustee may be appointed and ordered to invest the money on behalf of the child until the child reaches the legal age. Court-approved settlements should be used when the claim involves large sums of money or when the injuries are of a potentially permanent nature. Some insurers have procedures that require management personnel to approve all injury claims with minors before settlement to determine whether they should be concluded with a parent-guardian release or with a court-approved settlement. The decision will normally be based on the following:

1. The duration of likely disability
2. The nature and severity of the injury
3. The amount of the special damages involved
4. The integrity and condition of the family and the minor's relationship with parents

Releases by Partnerships or Corporations

For companies that are sole proprietorships, the claim representative need only settle with the owner and have the owner execute the release. When settling with corporations, claim representatives must make sure they include the correct corporate name on the release, and it should be signed by an authorized officer of the corporation. For partnerships, either party should be able to sign the release. Claim representatives should confirm that the individual is a working partner and authorized to bind the partnership.

Releases in Death Claims

Requirements for settlement of fatal injury claims vary widely across the United States. In some states, the administrator or executor for the decedent's estate can sign a binding release, while in other states only the legal heirs of the decedent can effectively release their own claims. Legal counsel should be consulted in drafting releases for wrongful death and survival claims.

Uninsured Motorist Release

Typically, with uninsured motorist (UM) claims, the insurer pays the insured and then seeks recovery from the tortfeasor through subrogation. However, the insured's settlement with the UM carrier does not release the tortfeasor from liability, especially when the uninsured motorist claim payment does not make the insured "whole" (sufficiently compensate the insured's loss).[11] Exhibit 9-4 shows a standard **uninsured motorist release.** These releases do the following:

- Deduct the UM payment from any liability payment made to the individual.
- Protect the company's subrogation rights against the tortfeasor.
- Require the insured to cooperate with the insurer in pursuing subrogation.
- Require the insured to hold in trust and give to the company any funds the insured receives from the responsible parties.

Insureds cannot settle with the claimant and then turn around and collect for the same elements of loss from their uninsured motorist carrier.

EXHIBIT 9-4

Uninsured Motorist Release and Trust Agreement

UNINSURED MOTORISTS COVERAGE

KNOW ALL MEN BY THESE PRESENTS; that for and in consideration of the payment to _(NAME)_ of _(AMOUNT)_ Dollars $ _(NUMERIC)_ by _(COMPANY)_ hereinafter called the Company, the receipt of which I do hereby fully and forever release and discharge the Company from any and all claims and demands, actions and causes of action, which I may have against the Company under the Protection Against Uninsured Motorists Coverage of Policy No. _(POLICY #),_ because of personal injuries, both known and unknown, including future developments thereof, costs, loss of service and companionship, consortium, expense and compensation, resulting or to result from that certain accident on or about the _(DAY)_ day of _(MONTH)_ , _200X (YEAR)_ , at or near _(LOCATION)_.

I have not, without the written consent of the Company, made any settlement with or prosecuted to judgment any action against any person or organization who may be legally liable for bodily injury on account of which the Company is making this payment.

I agree that this settlement is in full compromise of a doubtful and disputed claim both as to question of liability and as to the nature, extent and permanency of such injuries and damages, and that the payment is not to be construed as an admission of liability.

I further agree that in consideration of this payment:

(a) any amount which I may be entitled to recover from any person who is an insured under the bodily injury liability coverage of said policy shall be reduced by the amount of this payment;

(b) that the Company shall be entitled to the extent of this payment to the proceeds of any settlement or judgment that may result from the exercise of any rights of recovery I may have against any person or organization legally responsible for the bodily injury because of which this payment is made.

(c) that I shall hold in trust for the benefit of the Company all rights of recovery which I shall have against such other person or organization because of the damages which are the subject of claim made under the Protection Against Uninsured Motorists Coverage;

(d) that I shall do whatever is proper to secure and shall do nothing after loss to prejudice such rights;

(e) that if requested in writing by the Company, I shall take, through any representative designated by the Company, such action as may be necessary or appropriate to recover such payment as damages from such other person or organization, such action to be taken in my name; in the event of a recovery, the Company shall be reimbursed out of such recovery for expenses, costs and attorneys' fees incurred by it in connection therewith;

(f) that I shall execute and deliver to the Company such instruments and papers as may be appropriate to secure my rights and obligations and those of the Company established by this provision.

I FURTHER STATE THAT I HAVE CAREFULLY READ THE FOREGOING RELEASE AND TRUST AGREEMENT AND KNOW THE CONTENTS THEREOF, AND I SIGN THE SAME AS MY OWN FREE ACT.

Signed this _____ day of _____ at _____

_____

Signature

Policyholder Releases

Policyholder releases are an unusual kind of release and should be used only with management approval. They are used when an insured or a claimant is paid for a claim when coverage is doubtful. Settlement may be made to avoid litigation. Policyholder releases are used in liability claim situations when an insurer makes a payment to a third party on behalf of the insured for a claim that may not be covered. These are complicated releases that require input from legal counsel.

Nuisance Settlements

In claim situations in which liability is doubtful and the amount claimed is relatively small, claim representatives must decide whether to deny liability or try to settle the claim. If liability is denied, the company incurs additional legal and administrative costs in defending the claim. The insured's time may also be taken up in depositions and phone calls. In such situations, the company sometimes applies a pure cost/benefit analysis to the claim and will try to settle the claim for some nominal amount as long as the cost to settle does not exceed the cost to defend it. This nominal settlement cost is known as **nuisance settlement**.

The advantages of paying nuisance claims are the following:

- Reduces legal costs of defending the claim
- Reduces administrative costs of keeping the file open
- Eliminates uncertainty of litigation from aberrant court awards
- Eliminates the uncertainty of the insured, who may be worried about a pending claim

Some arguments against paying nuisance claims include:

- Paying nuisance claims encourages future nuisance claims.
- Paying claims that do not have merit is unethical.
- Paying nuisance claims can cause insureds' premiums to increase without good cause.

Most companies have a philosophy on handling nuisance claims, and claim representatives must make sure they understand their own company's philosophy.

First-Call Settlements

Frequently, a claim can be settled during the initial meeting with the claimant. However, unless claim representatives consciously look for such opportunities, they may not be recognized. The ideal case for a **first-call settlement** is a clear or probable liability case in which the claimant has sustained minor or less serious injuries. But even questionable liability cases are sometimes appropriate for first-call settlements. Moderate or serious injury claims are not appropriate for first-call settlements.

The field representative is in a particularly good position to make first-call settlements because he or she can personally observe the claimant, see the effects of the injuries, and sense whether the claimant will be receptive to settlement on a first-call basis. This is not to say that first-call settlements cannot be made by telephone claim representatives in their initial telephone conversations with the claimant. The field representative, however, can be especially persuasive because he or she can often give the claimant a draft or check immediately and secure the necessary release.

Experience shows that claim settlements do not get any less expensive with time. Frequently, the best settlement is an early settlement. It must be kept in mind, however, that not all cases lend themselves to settlement on a first-call basis. In some instances, pressing for an early settlement might be tactless and insensitive. The representative must gain the experience and develop the judgment to be able to recognize situations in which a first-call settlement is warranted and the claimant is receptive to a settlement on that basis.

"Drop Draft" Settlements

Sometimes efforts to settle relatively minor claims reach an impasse, but the claimant does not seem to be pursuing the claim. In such situations, the claim representative might consider issuing a "drop draft" instead of holding the claim open for months or even years. A **"drop draft"** is just a payment for the amount the claim representative believes is owed. The drop draft is accompanied by a release with a letter explaining that the amount enclosed is what the claim representative determined was owed. If the claimant agrees, then he or she returns the signed release and the claim is closed. The instrument used to make payment is a draft that states that the funds will be made available only once a signed released has been received. The theory is that once the claimant sees the draft, he or she will sign it and conclude the claim.

Advance Payments[12]

An **advance payment** is a partial payment of the claimant's claim that is issued without obtaining a signed release. Sometimes claim representatives may encounter situations in which advance payments help to facilitate a mutually agreeable settlement at a later time. Some claimants do not have the financial resources or health and disability insurance to pay their medical bills or to go for an extended period of time without earning wages.

Insurers have found that issuing advance payments helps to relieve the claimant's financial anxiety, which helps develop rapport and trust with the claim representative. This helps later when the claim must be settled in its entirety. It also helps the claimant get better medical attention, which can reduce the length of time the claimant is out of work and reduce the possibility or extent of a permanent injury. Because insurers obtain the medical records for the medical bills they are paying on behalf of the claimant, they can better determine the loss exposure and reserve the claim more accurately. Advance payments have a social value in that they might keep the claimant from having to file bankruptcy or seek welfare relief. Concerns that advance payments help to finance lawsuits, result in overtreatment, or discourage early settlement have for the most part been unfounded. These concerns can normally be addressed by carefully selecting which claims are appropriate for advance payments.

Guidelines for Issuing Advance Payments

Insurers apply some guidelines (which vary by company) for determining good candidates for advance payments. The following are general guidelines describing appropriate claim circumstances for issuing advance payments:

- The insured's liability should be apparent.
- The claimant's injury should be obvious or undisputed and unlikely to resolve within a matter of days.
- The claimant should be willing to cooperate in helping the claim representative obtain medical and wage loss information for evaluating damages.
- Insurers should set a time limit for issuing advance payments.
- Insurers should have an amount limit and should pay only for reasonable and necessary expenses.
- Insurers should make clear that all payments will be credited against any future settlement amount or court award.

To avoid misunderstandings, the claim representative should address these issues by having the claimant sign an advance payment receipt for each advance payment received. See Exhibit 9-5 for an example.

EXHIBIT 9-5

Receipt for Advance Payment

This is NOT a release or an admission of liability by any party.

This is to acknowledge receipt of $_____ paid on behalf of _____ to be credited to the total amount of any final settlement or judgment in my/our favor for alleged damages resulting from an accident on _____ 200___ at _____.

I/we authorize the above sum to be distributed to the following parties:

_____.

Date _____

Claimant_____

Spouse _____

Witness_____

The receipt should stipulate the terms of the payment and should expressly state that the advance payments are not an admission of liability and that the insurer will get credit for all of the advance payments made. Courts favor the use of advance payments, and insurers have found courts to rule favorably for them in the rare cases when claimants have tried to take advantage of the advance payments by using them to build up their claim with questionable medical treatment. Some claimants have tried to introduce the advance payments as evidence of liability.

Claim representatives may issue advance payments directly to medical providers in order to satisfy liens (discussed later in this chapter). The claimant should sign an agreement stating that this advance payment will be credited against any future settlement or award.

Claim representatives must be careful about issuing advance payments when the statute of limitation is close to expiring. In such situations, the insurer must notify the claimant that the statute is about to run (expire) or advise the claimant in writing that the statute of limitation will be waived. This should be done only with management approval.

Liens

In liability claims, a **lien** is a charge that can be assessed against the settlement or award received by a claimant. The lien is based on services rendered to the claimant. Doctors, hospitals, workers compensation carriers, and lawyers commonly assert liens against settlements. Some liens arise from common law, and others are imposed by statutes.

Whenever an insurer knows a lien exists, the claim representative must make sure that the lien is satisfied. The easiest way to do this is to include the names of the parties asserting liens on the check issued to the claimant when a settlement is made. For example, consider a claim by John Prosser. John incurs medical expenses at Memorial Hospital for emergency room treatment. Memorial Hospital sends a lien and copy of its bill to the claim representative handling John's claim—in this case, Mary Smith. John is represented by a lawyer, Hank Jones, who submitted a lien letter to Mary when he advised her that he was representing John. Mary agrees to settle the claim for $3,000.

How must Mary conclude this?

Mary must write the check to John Prosser, Hank Jones, and Memorial Hospital to cover the attorney's lien and the hospital lien. Sometimes a separate check can be issued for the exact amount owed to the medical provider if that amount is known for certain. This amount would be deducted from the total settlement. The risk in doing this is that the amount issued to the provider may not be the final amount owed. Most claimants and their lawyers prefer to have one check issued. They can then satisfy the lien with payments from the claimant's own personal health insurance or try to negotiate the amount of the lien with the medical provider. In either case, they would prefer one check.

In most situations, insurers are responsible for paying liens *if* they have been formally notified of the lien. Liens that have been formally communicated to insurers are known as **"perfected" (recorded) liens**. In the preceding illustration, if Memorial Hospital had not submitted a lien before a settlement was made, then the insurer could not be held responsible for paying the lien. This would not excuse the claimant from paying the hospital. The exception to this rule is when the claimant receives medical payments from the government under Medicare coverage.

Medicare is by statute the secondary payor of claimants covered under workers compensation laws, auto or liability coverages, or no-fault laws, meaning these other types of insurance must pay bills to which they apply before Medicare owes anything. The federal statute provides that Medicare be reimbursed for its payments. If the claimant (beneficiary) does not reimburse Medicare within sixty days, then the insurer (or other third-party payor) must reimburse the government even if the insurer has already paid the claimant. If the government is forced to sue for its reimbursement, the statute provides that it is entitled to *double* the amount of its lien.[13]

The government can collect **Medicare liens** if the circumstances were such that the insurer *should have known* that Medicare was involved, such as with a claim involving an elderly person. Claim representatives should contact Medicare if they have questions. Medicare staff have been trained to handle claims involving third-party payors such as auto or liability insurance carriers. Exhibit 9-6 describes an internal memo issued to Medicare employees. This exhibit illustrates that Medicare will aggressively pursue companies that fail to include Medicare liens in their settlements. Insurers that do not recognize these liens are likely to end up paying medical expenses twice—once to claimants and again to Medicare. The agency responsible for Medicare is the Health Care Financing Administration (HCFA).

RECOVERING LIABILITY CLAIM PAYMENTS

Insurers may be able to recover some or all of the amounts paid on a liability claim through contribution, indemnity, subrogation, and salvage, or through coordination of insurance benefits.

Contribution

As mentioned earlier in the chapter on determining liability, more than one party may be responsible for a claim. In a study of serious injury liability claims, it was found that 22 percent of the claims had two parties responsible for the claimant's injuries, and 26 percent had more than two responsible parties.[14] In such situations, the law may entitle one tortfeasor to collect from other tortfeasors amounts paid to the claimant for damages owed by the other tortfeasor. Normally, the preferred method is for each tortfeasor to pay the claimant for his or her percentage of the claimant's damages. Unfortunately, tortfeasors do not always agree on what percentage that should be. The claimant can become frustrated by such a situation and file suit against both parties. To avoid litigation, one tortfeasor's insurer may take the lead and settle the claimant's entire loss amount and then seek **contribution** from the other tortfeasor's insurer for the amount owed by the tortfeasor that it insures.

Inter-company arbitration may be one way of settling this type of dispute. Claim representatives should seek management or legal counsel's approval before settling the entire claim on behalf of other tortfeasors because if the release is not drafted properly or the other tortfeasors are not given sufficient notice of the insurer's intent to settle all the claims, then the insurer might be precluded from recovery.

EXHIBIT 9-6

Internal HCFA Memo to Medicare Staff

MEDICARE SECONDARY PAYER
ALERT !!

The following two (2) issues should be read by all staff involved with Medicare Secondary Payer (MSP) decisions. Please ensure that your staff are aware of the following issues.

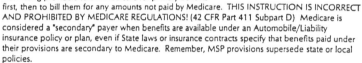

Automobile Insurance/Liability Insurance

We are very grateful to those providers who alerted us to the fact that some Automobile/Liability insurers are instructing providers to bill Medicare for primary benefits first, then to bill them for any amounts not paid by Medicare. THIS INSTRUCTION IS INCORRECT AND PROHIBITED BY MEDICARE REGULATIONS! (42 CFR Part 411 Subpart D) Medicare is considered a "secondary" payer when benefits are available under an Automobile/Liability insurance policy or plan, even if State laws or insurance contracts specify that benefits paid under their provisions are secondary to Medicare. Remember, MSP provisions supersede state or local policies.

Medicare regulations require that you obtain all information on possible MSP situations. You must ask the patient (or their representative) for the information contained on the MSP Questionnaire (refer to your training manuals) upon admission to your service, especially if the beneficiary's injury or illness resulted from an accident for which another payer is liable. When another insurer is liable, you must bill that carrier for primary benefits. If the liability carrier denies the claim on the basis that they consider Medicare the "primary" payer, please send a copy of the claim, the carrier's denial notice, and any other relevant information to us. We will work with you to educate the carrier on their responsibilities.

Please note that you and the beneficiary (or their representative) are responsible for taking any and all actions necessary to obtain payment from the Automobile/Liability carriers. Medicare will not make payment until all benefits available have been exhausted (documented proof will be required in all cases). However, under certain circumstances (outlined in your manual), conditional or secondary benefits may be payable.

Extension of Timely Filing for Certain MSP Claims
Affected by National Medicare Care, Inc. V. Shalala

On April 24, 1995, HCFA clarified its construction of the Omnibus Budget Reconciliation Act of 1993 provision amending the Medicare Secondary Payer (MSP) End Stage Renal Disease (ESRD) provision. We issued this clarification to you in our June 2, 1995 Medicare Memo and advised you that Medicare has extended until December 31, 1995 the timely filing period for claims for services provided between August 10 and September 30, 1993, when Medicare was not previously billed. National Medicare Care, Inc. challenged the clarification in the referenced case and subsequently, the Court enjoined the Secretary from enforcing the clarified policy with respect to claims for services provided between August 10, 1993 and April 24, 1995.

Indemnity

Indemnity is based on an agreement whereby one party agrees to secure another against an anticipated loss or damage. Hold harmless agreements are probably the most common type of contractual indemnity obligation. A hold harmless agreement is a provision in a contract signifying a commitment by one party to indemnify (make good or repay) another party in the event of a specified loss. A provision in a lease that requires a tenant to indemnify a landlord for damages is one example. Product liability claims frequently involve indemnity claims by retailers against manufacturers because of sales agreements between the retailer and manufacturer. Claim representatives need to consider potential indemnity contracts when investigating and settling liability claims. If an insurer provides liability coverage to a party that should be indemnified by another, the claim representative for that insurer should pursue indemnity.

Subrogation

After a settlement has been made on an insured's claim, insurers may seek recovery of their payments from parties responsible for their insured's damages. This is known as **subrogation**. Because in recent years property-liability insurance companies' premium income has been flat, recoveries from subrogation have become more important. Some larger companies collect more than $1 million each year in subrogation. A typical insurance company would have to write more than 10,000 new accounts to achieve the same financial result.

If an insurer pays its insured, the insurer is then subrogated to the rights of the insured and can sue the responsible party to recover its losses. This right is based on common law as well as on insurance contract wording.

Subrogation allows an insurer to make claim, and if necessary institute a suit, against the responsible party, in the name of the insured, to collect amounts the insurer paid to the insured. Subrogation is common in automobile collision and uninsured motorist claims but can also apply to other liability claims. Under most insurance policies (especially auto policies), the insured is not permitted to take any action that would jeopardize the insurer's recovery. The insured is required to cooperate with the insurer in recovering loss payments, and if the responsible third party pays the insured, the insured must hold in trust those funds; the insured is not permitted to collect twice for the same elements of loss.

Self-insured employers have the same rights as insurance carriers when they pay workers compensation claims for employees injured by third parties. In workers compensation, subrogation rights are created as a matter of law, usually by a specific provision in the compensation statute.

Claim practitioners pursuing subrogation should be aware of state bankruptcy law exemptions that may affect recovery. Some bankruptcy laws allow individuals to discharge all of their debts, including judgments on lawsuits, against parties who go through bankruptcy. One state makes an exception for individuals who injure others while driving under the influence of alcohol.[15] Some states require individuals to sell their homes and cars to pay off their debts, while others let debtors keep their primary homes and cars. One common feature of bankruptcy law is that creditors (including companies seeking subrogation) can no longer call or attempt to collect their money once the debts have been discharged.

Subrogation Process

The subrogation process involves:

- Identifying potentially responsible parties
- Placing these parties on notice
- Investigating third-party liability issues
- Collecting subrogation payments from legally responsible parties

To subrogate successfully, the claim representative must analyze the accident to determine whether there are any potentially responsible parties. Vehicular accidents, accidents involving a product, or slip-and-fall claims occurring on the property of someone other than the insured all offer the potential for subrogation.

The Subrogation Notice

Once subrogation opportunities have been identified, the claim representative should send out a **subrogation notice letter** to the party responsible for the damages. This letter should include the following information:

- The full identity of the insurer/claim representative
- A brief description of the loss
- The fact that insurance benefits are being paid
- The assertion of a compensation lien
- The amount of the lien
- Whether this is a final lien or an ongoing amount
- A request for a response
- The name of the responsible party's liability insurer

The claim representative sending out such a letter may need to follow up for a response; sometimes these letters are ignored or not accorded the same weight as a lawyer's letter of representation. The claim representative must place the subrogation notice letter in a diary for follow-up to ensure that the potential tortfeasor has contacted his or her insurer. The initial goal when pursuing subrogation is to identify and involve the third party's insurer.

The Subrogation Specialist

Because claim representatives are so busy with more pressing claims, subrogation claims sometimes do not get the attention they deserve. For this reason, many companies use subrogation specialists who handle only subrogation claims in a centralized subrogation unit. Studies have proven that this is a better way to obtain high levels of subrogation recoveries than having claim representatives handle subrogation on the liability claims they originally dealt with.[16]

The following are some advantages of a centralized subrogation unit:

1. *Enables coordination of outside services*

    Subrogation often requires the services of collection agencies, skip-tracers (to help locate responsible parties), and attorneys. Their fees vary widely.

A specialty subrogation unit can better determine the competitive price of these services than can many liability claim representatives. Because of the volume of cases handled there, the subrogation unit could better negotiate a contract price for these services.

2. *Benefits from a closer proximity to the home office or litigation unit*

   On product liability cases or cases involving complicated legal issues, it is often helpful to consult with the litigation unit. It could assist the subrogation unit in determining the viability of a subrogation claim, drafting installment agreements, and selecting attorneys and expert witnesses familiar with the issues involved. Being in close geographic proximity to the legal department is still an advantage in claim operations.

3. *Provides accountability of results*

   If subrogation duties are divided between the field and the home office, there is an inherent difficulty in determining who is responsible for the subrogation results. A centralized subrogation unit allows for the identification of successful and unsuccessful subrogation practices, which in turn allows for the improvement of performance.

4. *Reduces conflicting priorities*

   Liability claim representatives are confronted with claimants and insureds who have total losses, serious injuries, people threatening litigation, people who are looking for advice on their insurance coverages, and many other situations that demand their immediate attention. Even the most conscientious claim representative is likely to place subrogation at a lower priority than other liability claims. By the time the claim representative returns to the subrogation file, the issues have usually become stale, requiring an additional review. Another risk is that the statute of limitation may have run while the subrogation efforts were pending, precluding any recovery at all.

Subrogation results and best practices are likely to be emphasized even more in the future. Subrogation returns are easily quantifiable and comparable. The visibility and comparability of returns make them more likely to receive management attention.

Salvage

Salvage is damaged property that is turned over to the insurance company after the total value of the property has been paid on a claim. The most common example is salvage on a claimant's automobile. Salvage may also exist on products and merchandise damaged beyond repair by an insured's actions. Although the property may be considered a total loss for claim settlement purposes, it may still have some value and, if so, can be sold to recover part of the claim payment.

Coordination of Insurance Benefits

Another source of recovery that may be available is through other liability insurance that applies to the same loss or through nonliability sources of insurance.

An insured could be covered under more than one liability insurance policy, and in such cases, the recovery of the payments may be possible. As explained in the earlier chapters related to insurance coverage issues, such situations require the claim representative to determine how the Other Insurance provision applies. Based on policy wording, case law, or legislation, one of three possibilities occurs.

1. One policy is primary over the other.
2. The policies share equally in the loss (up to their limit of liability).
3. The policies share proportionally in the loss based on their limits of liability.

In other claims, the claimant may have other nonliability insurance sources of recovery, known as collateral sources. As explained in Chapter 7, **collateral sources** are sources *outside* the liability insurance system that reimburse claimants for all or some of their medical expenses, wage loss, or disability. Examples include healthcare insurance, no-fault auto insurance, and workers compensation. One study indicated that 73 percent of claimants paid under general liability policies and 55 percent paid under auto liability policies had at least one other collateral source.[17]

If a claimant's medical expenses are paid by health insurance, should auto insurers then have to consider these expenses in determining damages? It depends on state law. Based on the collateral source rule, most states do not allow evidence of other sources to be admitted. However, a significant minority of states permit admitting other sources of income as evidence, and some states require that an offset be permitted to reduce the award by any amount that a claimant has received from collateral sources.[18] This modification of the collateral source rule can have the effect of reducing the potential liability (or at least the amounts payable) of the insured by reducing the amount of damages owed by the insured.

SUMMARY

The most common way for resolving claim damage disputes is through a negotiated agreement. However, claim representatives must be informed and able to use a variety of alternative settlement methods including mediation and the various forms of arbitration. Litigation should not be the next natural choice if the parties involved reach an impasse in negotiations. Claim representatives must be able to identify which cases are suitable for mediation or arbitration, and they should be able to implement approaches that facilitate successful settlements. The importance of selecting and conducting the appropriate alternative settlement method is growing as the costs of not settling increase. Claim representatives should be able to describe the advantages and disadvantages of the various alternative settlement methods.

Claim representatives must conclude the claim with the most appropriate form of settlement agreement for the situation. Structured settlements can also help facilitate agreements and overcome settlement barriers, and parent-guardian releases can help conclude less serious claims involving minors.

Nonroutine claims, such as those involving multiple parties and/or serious injury claims with minors, require special settlement agreements.

Recovering liability claim payments through contribution, indemnity, subrogation, or salvage is becoming an increasingly specialized and important part of liability claim handling. Insurers should be able to identify successful practices for subrogation units, and claim representatives working in these units should be able to describe the legal and tactical approaches that enhance claim recovery.

CHAPTER NOTES

1. ISO Data, Inc., *Closed Claim Survey of Commercial General Liability Results* (New York: Insurance Services Offices, Inc., 1996), p. 25.

2. Susan B. Meek, M.D., J.D., *Alternative Dispute Resolution* (Tucson, Ariz.: Lawyers and Judges Publishing Company, Inc., 1996), p. 48.

3. At the time this was written, the leading online settlement site was Cybersettle.com, which had resolved more than 2,000 claims amounting to $30 million. Other forums used by insurers, claimants, and lawyers include ClicknSettle.com; SettleOnline.com, and MyClaim.com. Some of these have competing patents pending.

4. World Wide Web: www.i-courthouse.com (December 2000).

5. Ken Brownlee and Patrick Magarick, *Casualty Claim Practices*, 4th ed. (St. Paul, Minn.: Clark, Boardman, Callahan, a division of West Group Publishing, 1995), p. 17:40.

6. Wise v. Prescott, 244 La 157, 151 So. 2d 356 (1963).

7. Colorado State Statute Section 13-21-301, entitled Settlements, Releases and Statements.

8. Sampay v. Morton Salt Co., 388 So. 2d 62 (La. Ct. App. 1980).

9. Willis v. Total Health Care, 125 Mich. App. 612, 337 N.W. 2d 20 (1983).

10. Moore v. Bentrup, 840 S.W. 2d. (Mo. Ct. App. 1992).

11. Peltzman v. Beachner (Mo. Court of App. W.D. Non 49444, 1995).

12. Brownlee and Magarick, p. 17:26.

13. 42 USCA 1395y and 42 CFR 411.37.

14. ISO Data Inc., *Closed Claim Survey of Commercial General Liability Payments* (Insurance Services Offices, Inc., 1996), p. 17.

15. Chapter 7 Bankruptcy Law in Delaware.

16. Rodd Zolkos, "Ward Identifies What Makes Some Insurers a Cut Above," *Business Insurance*, August 21, 2000, p. 3. (This article was based on Ward Financial Group Best Practices study.)

17. ISO Data Inc., p. 18.

18. Insurance Information Institute, *The Fact Book—1999 Property/Casualty Insurance Facts* (New York: Insurance Information Institute, 1999), pp. 59–61.

Managing Litigation

Managing Litigation

Chapters 1 through 9 covered the role of the claim representative and the various activities that liability claim representatives perform, such as determining coverage, investigating and evaluating liability and damages, and settling claims. Most claims are concluded without a lawsuit being filed by the claimant. However, a significant number of claims end up in litigation, and claim representatives need to know how to handle them.

A **lawsuit** is an action in court initiated by one party to recover whatever that party believes is owed from the allegedly responsible party. The party bringing the lawsuit is the **plaintiff**, and the party allegedly responsible is the **defendant**. A lawsuit can have multiple plaintiffs and defendants.

Insurers are involved with two types of lawsuits. In a liability case, an insurer provides a defense for an insured when a claim is made against that insured. The other type of lawsuit occurs when the insurer decides that no coverage exists for a particular claim and the insured sues the insurer to provide coverage. This chapter deals with lawsuits (litigation) involving claims against insureds.

The exact tasks that claim representatives perform on litigated files vary by company, but all claim representatives need to understand the costs of litigation, the basic role that they have in controlling those costs, the phases of litigation, and the terminology commonly used in litigation. Claim representatives are an integral part of and should be familiar with the litigation process. They make decisions about what to investigate, what to document, and how to settle claims that can affect the likelihood of a lawsuit being filed and also the likely outcome of a lawsuit.

The purpose of this chapter is twofold:

1. To help claim representatives understand their role in the litigation process, and
2. To describe current litigation management techniques that have proven effective in controlling litigation costs.

The following sections describe some of the litigation costs that create the impetus for better litigation management. **Litigation management** is an ongoing process intended to control legal expenses while maintaining high-quality legal services.

Claim representatives must have a broad understanding of the lawsuit, the parties involved, and the strategies that each takes. Sometimes plaintiff attorneys make demands literally on the steps of the courthouse before a trial is scheduled to begin. Claim representatives must be able to make quick, well-reasoned decisions on cases involving substantial sums of money. To handle claims in litigation, claim representatives have to be informed on various subjects—such as money and finance, medicine, law, and time management—in addition to having investigative skills and "people" skills.

COSTS OF LITIGATION

In recent years, the rate of inflation in the national economy has been rather low. A benign 2 to 3 percent annual inflation rate—along with low interest rates—is good for the economy and favorable for the consumer of goods and services. In contrast, the cost of litigation has continued to rise. The following section explains the reasons for these rising costs and the need to control them through effective litigation management.

A trend in the early 1990s of increasing numbers of lawsuits being filed and the rising costs of defending those cases caused companies to take aggressive approaches to litigation management. An article written at that time summarized some of the data that generated the impetus for litigation management.

> [C]osts associated with the U.S. tort system have grown nearly four times faster than the U.S. economy. In 1991, the U.S. tort system cost 132.2 billion dollars—385 times its cost in 1933. Of this $132.2 billion, defense costs accounted for 18 percent or $23.7 billion. Considering that the gross national product has only increased a hundred-fold since 1933, such growth is spectacular.[2]

It is difficult to deny that, in absolute terms, litigation costs and indemnity costs continue to escalate.

Most insurers that write liability insurance spend more money on defense lawyers than on claim department staff salaries and independent adjusting expenses combined. Defense lawyers commonly charge more than $150 per hour and considerably more in urban areas. Pretrial preparation for an auto accident case could cost several thousand dollars. A trial could cost thousands more. Complex cases can involve hundreds of thousands of dollars in legal expenses. In addition to bearing financial costs, parties to lawsuits endure enormous emotional strain and demands on their time. The experience of litigation can be very unpleasant. For some, the monetary award does not compensate for the emotional cost of the trial process.

Society incurs substantial direct costs from litigation. Courts are expensive to operate, requiring maintenance and operation of courthouses and salaries for court personnel and judges. Society incurs indirect costs from litigation as well. Resources used for litigation are unavailable for other social benefits, such as subsidizing healthcare or better education. Ways need to be found to control litigation, litigation costs, and claim administration so that more of the total cost of the tort system goes to victims rather than lawyers or insurers.

THE ROLE OF THE CLAIM REPRESENTATIVE IN LITIGATED CASES

The general functions of the claim representative are to assess coverage and to investigate, negotiate, and evaluate claims. Some insurers expect claim representatives to help prepare claims for trial. The representative must also keep the claim file up to date so that it reflects all of the actions the claim representative has taken and indicates the status of the claim, whether it be in a preliminary, an investigating, or a negotiating stage.

At companies that use *outside* legal counsel (as opposed to in-house counsel), it is the duty of the claim representative to assess coverage, investigate liability and damages, evaluate the claim, and attempt to conclude the claim by negotiation, alternative dispute resolution methods, or claim denial. Having legal counsel perform these tasks is not only too expensive but also, in many cases, inappropriate.

The first step claim representatives must take is handling any coverage issues.

Handling Coverage Issues

Sometimes it is difficult, at the early stages of investigation, to make a coverage determination because the information available may be quite limited or because the first notice of the claim was the lawsuit. If this is so, the insurer may issue a reservation of rights or seek to enter into a nonwaiver agreement with the insured. The idea is to inform, or attain the assent of, the insured about the insurer's intent to continue to handle the claim without waiving any of its rights under the policy. Usually coverage is determined before a lawsuit is filed against an insured.

However, in some claims, coverage is still uncertain at the time the claimant sues the insured. This can occur either because (1) the claimant has filed suit quickly against the insured without leaving time for the insurer to conduct a coverage investigation, (2) because the alleged circumstances and facts of the incident may be outside what the policy covers (such as intentional acts of defamation, or assault and battery), or (3) because the alleged damages are not covered (such as with pollution damage or purely emotional injury damages).

Except in the most extreme circumstances, insurers will be reluctant to flatly deny coverage. As countless judicial decisions have declared, the duty to defend is broader than the duty to pay.[3] The insurer may have a duty to defend the insured—which it breaches at its peril—even if it subsequently turns out that the insurer is not obligated to pay out its policy proceeds. As explained in Chapter 4, the typical liability insurance policy obligates the insurer to defend an action against the insured "even if any of the allegations of the complaint are groundless, false, or fraudulent." A duty to defend arises if the complaint alleges facts that, if proved true, would obligate the insurer to indemnify the insured against the damages recovered by the claimant. The duty to defend, as a general rule, is determined by whatever allegation is stated in the lawsuit.

If the insurer decides to defend the insured under a reservation of rights, then the claim representative must draft and send a letter to the insured on a timely basis (usually by registered mail). It should be sent as soon as possible and before legal counsel takes action on behalf of the insured. It should state facts on which the insurer will rely in any subsequent denial of coverage, and it should refer specifically to the policy provisions on which the insurer will rely. The letter also should invite the insured to discuss the matter with his or her own personal attorney and to ask of the claim representative any questions that he or she may have.

Independent Legal Counsel

A defense lawyer cannot ethically represent both insurer and insured where their interests conflict, nor can a defense lawyer represent an insured client while undertaking to advise the insurer on an issue of that client's insurance coverage. In recent years, we have seen a drastic increase in courts' requiring that an insured be represented by independent counsel in situations involving real or potential conflicts of interest. The most common situation is the retention of independent counsel (sometimes called *Cumis* counsel)[4] in cases in which an insurer has reserved its right to deny coverage. Such independent counsel is retained at the expense of the insurer and selected by either the insurer or the insured, depending on the law of the jurisdiction. The retention of a second defense attorney obviously increases defense costs. In addition, an attorney retained on a one-time basis as independent counsel may be motivated to charge a higher rate and may lack the motivation to provide the efficient, cost-effective service that an insurer should be entitled to expect from counsel representing insureds on an ongoing basis. The claim representative should exercise vigilance in the selection of independent counsel (if the insurer has a role in selection) and should be aware that use of independent counsel can have a serious effect on litigation costs.

Performing a Case Evaluation

As a prerequisite to effective litigation management, the claim representative is expected to gather a sufficient amount of evidence concerning liability, the amount of damages claimed, and the specific details—consisting, for example, of out-of-pocket expenses, the claimed loss of earning capacity, and the injuries sustained or the property damage involved. He or she will then make some approximation of the value of the claim, or the lack thereof. Most insurers prefer to communicate these case evaluations to the attorney, realizing that the attorney may disagree with the evaluation or raise factors that have not been considered. It also helps insurers to assess the potential for an **excess verdict** and bad faith exposure.

It is important for the claim representative to assess each case objectively. Emotion should not shape the decision to try a case. From the outset, the claim representative must be looking for the most cost-effective way to resolve a claim. The costs of litigation must be weighed against the benefit an insurer might hope to gain from a defense verdict. A defense verdict that carries a $20,000 price tag for attorneys' fees and other litigation costs may be a hollow victory if the case could have been settled at an early stage for many thousands of dollars less.

Even after a case has been assigned to defense counsel, the claim representative will monitor discovery, may conduct additional investigation, and will assess damages. These efforts will not only pay dividends in enhancing defense counsel's trial preparation, but will also highlight possible opportunities to settle the case. Claim representatives handle a large volume of claims, only a small percentage of which go to trial. This enables an experienced claim representative to be well acquainted with different types of claims, their varying degrees of seriousness, and their settlement values. Even if a claim is not ripe for settlement, the claim representative must be on the lookout for opportunities to use alternative methods of dispute resolution to settle claims in creative ways. Such methods (discussed in the previous chapter) may include early neutral evaluation, mediation, nonbinding arbitration, nonbinding summary jury trials, "minitrials," and assisted negotiation involving a neutral third party.

Even if a case seems destined for trial and cannot be resolved by alternatives to trial, the claim representative should always keep in mind that most claims settle and that plaintiffs' attorneys' caseload is a volume business that is founded on negotiated settlements of most claims. The claim representative has many opportunities to become familiar with the characteristics and practices of plaintiffs' attorneys and to share his or her experience with defense counsel. The claim representative must beware of the rhetoric that sometime inflames the relationship between plaintiffs' counsel and defense counsel. Attacks and hardball antics are unlikely to lead to the cost-effective resolution of claims. The defense side can be firm but, at the same time, cooperative and courteous. An atmosphere should be cultivated in which each side can seek extensions of deadlines in order to, for example, evaluate issues and conduct additional investigation. A few telephone calls, made in a spirit of cooperation and mutual respect, may accomplish far more (with less expense) than an exchange of legal maneuvers.

Assessing Excess and Bad Faith Exposure

Another role that the claim representative, and usually the claim supervisor, has is to assess the case submitted for **excess exposure**, that is to say, the exposure of the insured's personal assets because of the potential of a jury award that might exceed the insured's limit of liability. The claim representative should make sure that the defense lawyer states at the beginning of the

An **excess verdict** is a jury award that exceeds the insured's limit of liability and exposes the insured's personal assets.

assignment his or her valuation of the claim to make sure that the attorney's valuation is in line with what the claim representative had established as a claim value.

Neither defense counsel nor the claim representative should link or relate the value of the claim to the policy limits. Settlement is ultimately the responsibility of the insurance company, but if the insurer fails to settle a claim, the case continues to trial, and a verdict award is issued against the insured for an amount higher than the insured's policy limits, then the insured is likely to allege bad faith against the insurer. This is true especially if the insurer was given an opportunity by the plaintiff to settle for the policy limits but declined to do so.

The insured should be kept informed of the claim representative's and the defense lawyer's thinking (supported by facts in the file) about liability, the plaintiff's injury, and damages. The insured's interest should be protected by keeping the insured advised and by seeking the insured's point of view. Allegations of bad faith are more difficult to prove when the insurer acts cautiously and reasonably throughout the claim process.

One test, set forth by a court, that many states follow is found in the case of Crisci v. Security Insurance Co.[5] The court decided that in determining whether an insurer has given proper consideration to the interests of the insured, the test is whether a prudent insurer without policy limits would have accepted a settlement offer. Claim representatives and defense counsel should ask themselves the question, "If the insurer were responsible for the entire amount of any jury verdict award, then what would we offer?" This question helps to ensure that the evaluation is not dependent on the insured's limits of liability. In other words, insurers should not rely on their insured's liability limits to protect them after making unreasonably low offers.

Conducting an Investigation

Claim representatives should try to reduce discovery costs (the cost of legal counsel's investigations after a suit has been filed) by having completed a thorough investigation before the lawsuit is filed. This is a costly and major component of litigation, and a poorly investigated claim file will be expensive for a law firm to investigate because the company is paying lawyer rates for work its claim representatives could have done.

Ideally, all relevant witnesses should have been identified and statements obtained before a suit is filed. Usually, the claim representative has developed secondary evidence in the form of police reports and statements from witnesses who were present at the scene and has examined and recorded the physical facts. These physical facts may include skid marks, debris and other evidence of the accident, and the extent of the damage to the vehicles and the injuries sustained by the persons involved.

Claim representatives may need to continue an investigation after a suit has been filed. Whenever possible, they should perform the investigation rather than the lawyer.

Choosing Legal Counsel

Depending on the company, defense counsel will be selected by claim management, a litigation specialist, in-house legal counsel, or claim representatives or through a combined effort of several people. At the least, claim representatives are typically asked to give feedback on the performance and customer service of attorneys. Insurers normally select law firms rather than specific lawyers. After they have worked with a law firm for a while, they may discover that they prefer certain lawyers who have particular expertise and request them to handle specific types of cases.

Careful selection of outside legal counsel can lead to improved service, reduced friction between claim representatives and defense counsel, lower legal costs, better results, and a more rewarding professional relationship. Insurers should realize that law firms are not any better than insurers at hiring and evaluating employees, and, in fact, they may not be as good at training as most insurers. Insurers should not permit serious cases to be the training ground for inexperienced lawyers.

On serious cases, claim representatives should know who at the law firm will be handling the case and determine whether the lawyer's experience is with the legal matter at hand. Insurers should understand that law firms are likely to experience turnover and may have to switch lawyers from one case to another. Although insurers should accept that this is going to happen (ideally not too frequently), the cost of getting another lawyer up to speed on the legal issues of a case should be borne by the law firm, not the insurer.

Insurers should prepare a list of questions before interviewing partners at a law firm and do their homework before meeting with law firm partners in person. Exhibit 10-1 provides a list of specific considerations to keep in mind when selecting legal counsel.

Customer Service Considerations for Legal Counsel

When choosing legal counsel, insurers should look for basic qualifications and also a firm's willingness and ability to meet the service needs of insurers and insureds. Insurers should select defense counsel that is familiar with the business of insurance. Defense counsel must also be able to meet insurer expectations on service needs such as promptly returning telephone calls and answering correspondence, providing timely periodic reports, taking time to make time and cost entries as they are incurred, contacting the claims person in advance whenever changed circumstances necessitate revising the estimate of fees and costs in a particular case, teamwork, and helping claim representatives stay abreast of legal changes by providing newsletters and seminars.

Insurers' emphasis on customer service is sometimes not shared by some long-time defense lawyers, who see legal competence as the only relevant qualification and do not believe in the new emphasis on customer service.[6] In the 1980s, long-time claim representatives had similar concerns when asked to perform more customer service activities. These claim representatives felt that they should be rated only on how well they understood insurance coverages and investigated, evaluated, and negotiated claims. Eventually they learned to integrate both customer service and technical aspects. The same is expected of defense attorneys.

EXHIBIT 10-1

Considerations When Selecting Legal Counsel

- Who are the firm's other clients? Are they similar to your company?
- What are the credentials of the lawyers in the firm?
- What are the lawyers' ratings? (Some organizations do formal ratings of lawyers.)
- What reputation does the firm have with other claim professionals?
- Does your company need legal defense nationwide? (In rural locations it is sometimes advisable to have local attorneys defend insureds to overcome the "big city lawyer" image.)
- What types of claims are being made against insureds, and what kind of lawyers are needed to handle them?
- Have attorneys in the firm written books or articles?
- Does the firm send out newsletters about recent cases and changes in the law?
- Do attorneys in the firm offer educational seminars to help keep claim representatives abreast of the numerous legal changes in the claim environment?
- Does the firm have appropriate technology to meet business needs?
- Who at the firm will be responsible for the account, and which attorneys will handle the files? (And what are their experience levels?)
- What is average case load per attorney?
- What is the personnel turnover rate?
- How many lawyers have left the firm in the past twelve months?
- What is the average supervisory span of control?
- What are the firm's hourly rates? (Note that this is only one criterion; it should *not* be the deciding criterion, and it probably deserves its place last on this list.)

Insurers should avoid law firms that:
- Seem too busy to perform needed work on cases.
- Guarantee outcomes.
- Are vague about fees and costs.
- Refuse to accept an agreement specifying billing procedures.
- Refuse to give references. (Some insurers ask for the name of a former client to get a more balanced perspective.)

Often, what distinguishes one firm from another is customer service. Nothing is wrong with placing customer service at the top of a claim representative's list for defense counsel, especially when customer service includes service to the insured as well as the insurer. Most firms have learned that they must practice law by convincing insurers that their services are cost-effective and valuable to the client/customer. A competent and observant defense lawyer will be responsive to his client's objectives and expectations.

Technological Considerations

Although law firms may not have the latest technology, if they don't at least have the same electronic capabilities as the insurer, then numerous opportunities for process-time reduction are lost. The following technological abilities may help with better litigation management and provide customer service:

- Compatible software formats to exchange data
- Project management systems
- Time tracking and billing software that the insurer can access
- E-mail
- Groupware for sharing case files and status reports

Computerized legal research has been available for a number of years as a kind of sophisticated, electronic extension of traditional research among the books in a law library. But the true revolution today is taking place on the Internet, where legal resources are growing at a phenomenal rate. Case law, statutes, regulations, and myriad other legal resources are increasingly available.

Yet the Internet's greatest effect on the law may be to change the nature of legal research. The Internet revolutionizes the process of finding information and customizing it for the needs of the defense lawyer or claim representative. Each of these partners on the defense team ought to know how to navigate, search, and save his or her research as a permanent internal resource and how to transfer research results to the other. The Internet—with its legal research sites and search engines—is a great equalizer. It can enable a claim representative to conduct state-of-the-art legal research. It can enable a small, innovative law firm to compete effectively with larger, less nimble law firms in providing cost-effective defense. Intelligent use of electronic resources, and the capability of sharing research results with the insurer client, ought to be taken into account when selecting counsel. The implications of technology for an efficient legal effort are profound. The "electronic working file" can increase exponentially the speed of communication and data exchange between counsel and claim representative, reducing paperwork and minimizing the amount of lawyer time spent writing periodic case evaluations.

Technology can be a wonderful tool, but its use is fraught with peril. Electronic mail encourages extemporaneous and candid communications. Users may be tempted to make remarks about an insured or opposing counsel that could be construed as invading privacy or defaming him or her. In addition, many people may have access to an electronic communication, and inadvertent disclosure and misdirected e-mail may lead to waiver of attorney-client privilege.

Firm Size

Small firms may be able to give immediate and extra attention. Smaller insurers may prefer small firms, because even a small insurance company can have influence over a smaller law firm, and this influence can give the company an advantage. Small firms may also be more willing to provide high-touch customer service and to offer customized litigation management, such as flexible billing arrangements. The disadvantage of small firms is that they can be quickly overwhelmed on larger cases that require extensive research and discovery. Some smaller firms specialize in certain areas of the law, which may be helpful. Large firms have a bigger pool of experts; better computer research facilities; and greater nonlawyer assistance, including paralegals, nurses, economists, and engineers. Many large firms offer "one-stop shopping" for all legal needs.

The Claim Representative's Relationship With Legal Counsel

Many different individuals are involved in claim resolution. Each claim representative will report to his or her supervisor, who may in turn be responsible to a litigation manager, who will need to have a broad overview of the claims being processed and an understanding of company policy and philosophy regarding claim handling. Other individuals who will become involved in handling certain claims include in-house counsel (often referred to as "staff counsel") and outside counsel.

Insurers (who pay the bulk of the system's costs) have been trying to squeeze the excess costs out of the litigation system. The relationship between some insurers and defense lawyers has soured over the past few years. Claim representatives need to understand the relationship problems with lawyers and the potential problems they might cause in trying to control litigation or even in providing service to the insured. The following excerpts from a defense attorney publication illustrate the strained and changing relationship between insurers and defense attorneys:

> Faced with unrelenting increases in lawsuit defense expenditures, a number of insurers have implemented aggressive litigation management techniques. Unfortunately, these changes have often been presented to outside counsel in the form of a mandate. And, as with any unilaterally mandated changes, implementation of them has been defensively and negatively perceived as little more than a heavy-handed attempt to restructure the attorney-insurer relationship to the detriment (both financial and otherwise) of the attorney, if not also the policy-holder client.[7]

One leading defense attorney noted that conversations among lawyers constantly turn to the lack of appreciation for the value of the defense lawyer and wrote the following:

> Many lawyers have given decades of their lives to trying cases for insurance companies, uncovering fraud, inflated claims, lost evidence, and that last piece of the truth which must be told. Yet, each defense lawyer has a story about a client who has been disloyal: a client who for the sake of a few dollars has abandoned a 20-year relationship; an otherwise satisfied client who is "shopping" its work searching for lower prices; a client who simply does not care any more about investigating, fighting, and winning. Not all insurance carriers and corporations are like this. There are just as many stories of companies standing tall next to their lawyers in the toughest of times. Yet, the economic pressures of the business world seem to be overwhelming the professional world of the defense lawyer.[8]

It is in this climate that insurance carriers are trying to control litigation costs. Insurers and their outside defense counsel must mend their sometimes dysfunctional relationship and become part of the team dedicated to controlling those costs. The lawyer and the claim representative should work together, each capitalizing on the specific skills and training of the other, with the claim representative directing their joint efforts toward the resolution of claims. This is essential in order for insurers to meet their expressed promise, and duty, to insureds to settle and defend claims properly.

Most of the following discussion will deal with the cooperative relationship between the claim representative and counsel, with the focus on prompt and responsible resolution of insurance claims. It should be understood, however, that the claim representative often will need to seek authorization and/or advice from, and report to, other members of the claims "team."

The Tripartite Relationship

The three points of the "defense triangle" are the insurer, the insured, and defense counsel. This is sometimes called the **"tripartite relationship."** The claim representative and defense counsel have obligations to protect the interests of the insured and to balance them with the interests of the insurer. Defense counsel has a legal and professional obligation to represent the interests of his or her insured client. Traditionally, the law has recognized that the insurer, as well as the insured, has a stake in the outcome of litigation and that both the insurer and the insured can be considered clients of defense counsel. The following excerpt summarizes the prevailing view of one organization of legal scholars:

> A lawyer's professional conduct on behalf of a client may be directed by someone other than the client, when the direction does not interfere with the independent professional judgment of the lawyer, is reasonable in scope and character (such as reflected obligations borne by the person directing the lawyer), and the client consents to the direction.[9]

The bottom line is that both the claim representative and defense counsel represent the insured. In the vast majority of cases, the interests of the insured and of the insurer run on a parallel track. Each wants to see the claim resolved, with a reasonable payment made to dispose of the claim if it is meritorious. The claim representative and defense counsel can and should work—as members of a team with complementary skills—toward an equitable resolution of the claim. Again, in the great majority of cases, a resolution will be reached that is fair and equitable for all parties.

To manage litigation and its costs effectively, insurers and defense counsel must work at building a team. Each must communicate with the other constantly and candidly about working toward common goals. The two sides need to clearly and unambiguously communicate their respective expectations about procedures, how litigation activities should be shared and coordinated, how and when lawyers should report, and how cost and billing issues should be addressed. Of critical importance is the shared accountability for results (such as lower costs and greater volume of settlements).

Periodic Case Evaluations

The claim representative is entitled to receive periodic case evaluations from defense counsel. Generally, the defense attorney is expected to provide a case evaluation every sixty or ninety days, including the overall status of the case. Between periodic reports, defense counsel should call the claim representative about significant developments, especially if new information becomes available that may shed light on exposure or prospects of settlement. It should go without saying that the defense partners ought to keep in touch by telephone.

Modern technology offers an alternative to composing long letters regarding the status of a case. Computer interfacing between the defense lawyer's and the claim representative's offices may allow the claim representative to directly access the legal file and the status of the case at any time. When appropriate, the claim representative also may be able to review pleadings and motions electronically before they are filed—another time-saver when compared with transmission by mail or even by fax.

It is not unusual for the value of a claim to change once depositions have been taken, or other types of discovery turn up important evidence (such as that the insured is no longer certain that he had a green light or the claimant had a number of preexisting medical problems before an accident). It is the claim representative's responsibility to reevaluate the settlement value of the claim as new facts are learned. Defense counsel can help with this evaluation.

Settling the Case

Ultimately, the insurer, and usually the claim representative, has the responsibility of settling the case. Frequently, legal counsel is given a settlement range because counsel is usually in more frequent contact with the plaintiff's attorney once a suit has been filed. For values above the settlement authorization, the attorney will consult with the claim representative, who will make recommendations to the claim management, supporting the request to increase settlement authority with evidence of the injuries, details of the expenses claimed, and an evaluation of the applicable law. The claim representative or attorney will then proceed as instructed, whether the instructions are directed toward further investigation, denial of the claim, or further negotiation of a settlement within the limits authorized.

Commonly, the plaintiff attorney will make a demand immediately before trial, or even during trial (after important testimony has been given), that the claim representative should respond to. Claim representatives should prepare for this by obtaining settlement authority from claim management and having quick access to a phone to call a claim manager if during the trial something happens to affect the value of the case. Deciding not to offer any more, or to maintain a claim denial, is also the responsibility of the claim representative.

THE CLAIM REPRESENTATIVE'S ROLE IN EACH STAGE OF LITIGATION

Litigation has several stages, beginning with the lawsuit and continuing until the case has been concluded, either through settlement, verdict award, or some post-verdict action. Exhibit 10-2 identifies the various stages of litigation. The Appendix of this chapter describes the parts of each phase in greater detail. The four phases of litigation are as follows:

1. The **pleadings**
2. **Pretrial motions** and **discovery**
3. **Pretrial conferences** and trials
4. **Post-trial actions**

In addition, claim representatives should be aware of court reforms designed to improve the efficiency of the civil justice system.

The Pleadings—Summons and Complaint, Answer

A lawsuit is begun by the service of a summons to the defendant. A **summons** is a writ issued by the clerk of the court and directed to the sheriff or another proper officer requiring the sheriff to notify the person named that an action has been commenced against him or her and to appear on a day named to answer the complaint in that action. The purpose of the summons is twofold. The court does not have jurisdiction of the defendant unless and until the summons has been served. Its second purpose is to notify the defendant of the action.

According to the generally applicable state statute, the summons must be served by a sheriff or another proper officer to the individual named. This is done by delivering a copy of the summons and complaint to the defendant personally, by leaving a copy of it at the defendant's house or usual place of abode with a person of suitable age and discretion residing there, or by delivering a copy of the summons and **complaint** to an agent of a corporation.

A **complaint** lists the allegations of what the defendant has done to harm the plaintiff.

All liability policies contain the following type of condition with respect to the action the insured must take when a lawsuit is served on him or her: "If claim is made or suit is brought against the insured, he shall *immediately* forward to the company every demand, notice, summons, or other process received by him or his representative." The purpose of this type of condition is to give the company adequate opportunity to perform its obligations under the insurance contract. The lawsuit papers must be forwarded to the company at once. Failure on the part of the insured to comply strictly with this condition may release the company from its obligations under the contract if the time to answer the lawsuit is exceeded and a default judgment (a judgment giving the plaintiff what was requested in the suit because the defendant failed to respond) is rendered against the insured. In some states, it is extremely difficult to have a default judgment set aside without conclusive evidence of a meritorious defense being offered in support of the application. In others, setting aside a default judgment is not so serious a situation, but in any case, it requires more legal work than would be necessary if the case were handled expeditiously.

EXHIBIT 10-2

Activities Involved in the Phases of Litigation

1. The Pleadings
    *   Summons and complaint
    *   Answer
2. Pretrial Motions and Discovery
    Pretrial motions
    *   Motion to dismiss
    *   Motion *in limine*
    *   Motion for summary judgment
    Discovery
    *   Depositions
    *   Interrogatories
    *   Requests for production of documents
    *   Requests for admissions
3. Pretrial Conferences and Trials
    *   Compulsory arbitration
    *   Settlement conferences in judge's chambers before trial
    *   Pretrial conference
    *   Jury selection
    *   *Voir dire*
    *   Opening statements
    *   Introduction of evidence (including testimony)
    *   Bench conferences
    *   Motion for directed verdict
    *   Closing statements
    *   Jury instructions
    *   Jury deliberations and verdict
4. Post-Trial Actions
    *   Motion of judgment *n.o.v.*
    *   Motion to reduce damage award or increase damage award
    *   Appeals to higher courts
    *   Enforcement of judgments
    *   Polling jurors

When the summons and complaint are received by the company—whether delivered by the insured personally, by mail, or by the insured's agent—the claim representative's first duty is to ascertain the date and the manner of service. The date on the summons merely indicates the date on which the clerk issued the process, not when it was served—the sheriff may have had the papers in his or her office for a week before service was effected. Claim representatives should ask the insured on which date he or she received it, whether it was served personally (rather than by mail), and who received the lawsuit papers.

The defendant generally has twenty days, exclusive of the day of service, within which to appear and answer. The insured does not have to appear in court within that time period, but the insured's attorney needs to file a timely response.

If the case is not likely to be settled soon, then the papers should be transmitted to defense counsel as soon as possible. The more time counsel has to prepare an answer and consider the defenses available, the better the defense will be.

If the case may be settled soon, then the claim representative may want to obtain an extension. In most circumstances, the plaintiff's attorney, on request, will agree to extend the twenty days for an additional period of time. In most jurisdictions, this can be done by having the plaintiff's attorney send a letter to the company, on the attorney's stationery, extending the time within which the defendant must respond. The claim representative will have to be familiar with the rules of court in the particular jurisdiction as to the periods of time that can be extended. Local defense counsel should be consulted about the procedures to be followed in these matters. At most companies, claim management has established guidelines for when and for how long an extension can be filed. In any case, extending the time helps to reduce legal costs and may provide a chance to explore opportunities for settlement or alternatives to litigation.

As mentioned earlier, legal counsel files an answer (formal legal response). The **answer** is a pleading that responds to the plaintiff's demand by either denying the allegations in the plaintiff's complaint or confessing to them. The defendant's arguments should prevent or reduce recovery on the facts alleged by the plaintiff. The complaint is the statement of the claim by the claimant, and the answer is the statement of the defendant's defense. The answer may deny some allegations of the complaint and may admit others.

Transmitting Case Information to Legal Counsel

When a suit is filed, the claim representative must promptly transmit the claim file to legal counsel. The claim file should be well organized. To help legal counsel understand the case and develop an answer to the lawsuit, companies use a cover letter to transmit case information.

A decision is no better than the information on which it is based. Therefore, the claim representative has a duty to transmit complete and accurate information to defense counsel about a given claim. The reports to the attorney should be clear and as brief as they can be but should contain all of the available information and evidence. In making the reports, the claim representative should confine the information transmitted in the file to the facts as supported by the available evidence. The claim representative should refrain from communicating unnecessary characterizations or opinions concerning the claimant or any other persons involved in the claim. He or she should be especially wary of making statements that are or could be seen as derogatory, demeaning, or suggestive of bias or an unwillingness to deal with the claimant fairly and in good faith. In many instances, others see company files such as when they are subpoenaed in court proceedings or reviewed by insurance examiners from various states. The reports should reflect the fairness and impartiality with which both the company and the claim representative view the evidence. Nothing should be in the file that could possibly form a basis for an action against either the company or the claim representative for defamation or bad faith.

Exhibit 10-3 shows an example of a case transmittal letter. As a general rule, case transmittal letters contain the following information:

- Identifying information such as the insured's name and address, claim number, and suit style [names of defendant(s) and plaintiff(s)]
- Basic coverage information
- Relevant facts to help legal counsel obtain a quick understanding of the claim
- Description of known and alleged damages
- Description of the investigation that has already taken place
- Description of the claim representative's evaluation of the claim
- Clear explanation to legal counsel of what the claim representative will do and what the insurer expects from legal counsel

Some insurers also use this letter to give settlement authority to legal counsel. The claim representative should be specific and state something to the effect of, "Here is the range we believe the case should settle for, and you have authority to settle the claim within this range (list relevant amounts). If you have thoughts on our evaluation, please let us know." Insurers should not give vague instructions such as "Handle as warranted" or "You should do whatever is necessary to prevent this from going to trial." Insurers that fail to give specific instructions should not be surprised if legal counsel acts in a manner they disagree with. In addition to the transmittal letter and the file material, claim representatives should send defense counsel an initial evaluation form (see Exhibit 10-4), which the attorney should complete and return promptly. This information can help the claim representative to establish the value of the claim.

Making Counterclaims

During the course of investigation of the claim, or after a lawsuit has been received, it may become apparent to the claim representative and defense counsel that the insured has a potential **counterclaim** against the plaintiff for the damages the plaintiff caused to the defendant. The defense lawyer should inform the insured about the potential counterclaim and advise him or her to seek independent counsel.

EXHIBIT 10-3

Example of Case Transmittal Letter

(DATE)

(INSIDE ADDRESS)

Re: Insured: (INSURED)

      Policy #:   (Claim No./Policy No.)

      Date of Loss: (D/L)

      Suit Styled: (SUIT STYLED)

      Date suit is filed and date by which suit must be answered

Dear (SALUTATION):

This will transmit the above styled lawsuit and supporting file material that we previously discussed.

Coverage

(IDENTIFY THE POLICY, COVERAGES, AND LIMITS OF LIABILITY. BRIEFLY DISCUSS ANY COVERAGE QUESTIONS OR STATE THAT THERE ARE NO COVERAGE ISSUES.)

Identification of Plaintiffs and Defendants

(REVIEW THE RELATIONSHIPS OF ALL PARTIES TO THE LITIGATION AND IDENTIFY ANY ADDITIONAL PARTIES TO BE JOINED.)

Insured Defendant

(SPECIFY THE DEFENDANT(S) FOR WHOM WE OWE A DEFENSE. IF THE DEFENDANT IS OTHER THAN THE NAMED INSURED, EXPLAIN THE BASIS FOR COVERAGE AND DEFENSE. ALSO IDENTIFY NOT COVERED ITEMS, E.G., PUNITIVE DAMAGES, IF ANY.)

Facts

(BRIEFLY REVIEW THE FACTS OF THE CLAIM, INCLUDING PHYSICAL EVIDENCE, OFFICIAL RECORDS, WITNESSES' VERSIONS, AND THE ASSERTED POSITIONS OF THE PLAINTIFFS AND DEFENDANTS.)

Damages

(OUTLINE THE CLAIMED DAMAGES AND OUR ASSESSMENT OF THE ACCEPTABLE RANGE OF DAMAGES.)

Current Evaluation

(DISCUSS OUR EVALUATION OF LIABILITY AND DAMAGES, INCLUDING POTENTIAL CLAIMS FOR INDEMNITY OR CONTRIBUTION. "WE HAVE OFFERED _____.")

What We Will Do

(LIST ADDITIONAL ACTIVITIES PLANNED. INCLUDE ADDITIONAL INVESTIGATION TO BE OBTAINED AND A TIMETABLE FOR DISPOSITION. WE WILL NEGOTIATE WITH PLAINTIFF'S COUNSEL.)

What Defense Counsel Should Do

(IN ADDITION TO FILING AN APPEARANCE AND ANSWER, LIST THE ITEMS OF REQUESTED DISCOVERY. INCLUDE A CLOSING ON THE ORDER OF: "PLEASE ACKNOWLEDGE ASSIGNMENT TO US AND THE DEFENDANT. YOU NEED COMMENT TO US FURTHER ONLY IN AREAS WHERE YOU DISAGREE WITH OUR POSTURE.")

Sincerely,

(Claim representative)

EXHIBIT 10-4

Initial Attorney Evaluation

(To be completed and returned to company within thirty days after assignment of file.)

Re: Plaintiff(s):

       Defendant(s):

       Date of Loss:

       Claim No:

The following preliminary information is necessary in order for us to properly evaluate the above file. We recognize that discovery is just underway and that all information necessary for a full evaluation is not available to you at this point. Notwithstanding this, please answer as many questions below as possible. We understand that revisions in your responses may be necessary later.

1.   The Attorneys

    a.   Please identify the attorney or firm representing Plaintiff in this case:

    b.   Are you familiar with that attorney's or firm's abilities as trial counsel? If so, please give your opinion as to those abilities (excellent, good, or average):

    c.   Are you aware of any past litigation involving Plaintiff's attorney or firm that would be relevant as to the abilities of Plaintiff's attorney or firm as trial counsel? If so, please elaborate:

    d.   Please identify the attorney within your firm who will be responsible for handling this file:

2.   The Venue

    a.   Please identify and describe the role that the venue where this case is now pending will have in terms of the probable outcome of the case.

    b.   From the perspective of the insured(s), is this a favorable venue, and why or why not?

    c.   Is a more favorable venue available to the insured(s)? If so, please elaborate and state the steps you have taken or will take to get the case transferred or removed to that venue.

    d.   If the trial judge is known, please comment on his or her anticipated influence or effect on the probable outcome of this case.

3.   The Applicable Law

    a.   Is anything unique or unusual about the applicable law of this jurisdiction that could significantly affect the outcome of this case? If so, please elaborate:

    b.   Based solely on what you presently know about the case, is there any exposure for punitive or exemplary damages? If so, please elaborate:

4.   Preliminary Comments as to Exposure

    a.   Please state your present opinion as to the potential liability and range of verdict.

    b.   Are you aware of similar cases in this venue or area that would be relevant to an evaluation of this case? If so, please elaborate:

    c.   Is there anything about this case, not mentioned above, that makes the exposure unusually high? If so, please elaborate:

Date:

                                                 (Signature)

Sometimes the defense lawyer, with the informed consent of the insured, seeks to prosecute the counterclaim. This can create a conflict of interest. If there is an opportunity to settle, the defense lawyer may have to sacrifice the insured's interest in the counterclaim in order to negotiate a settlement. Or, defense counsel may risk jeopardizing the settlement if he or she tries to protect the insured's counterclaim during settlement negotiations. Defense attorneys who file counterclaims on behalf of insureds should seek permission from the insurance carrier, which may grant permission if the likelihood of a conflict is slim.

Pretrial Motions and Discovery

Generally speaking, a party to an action may take the testimony of any person, including the opposing party, by deposition or by written interrogatories for the purpose of **discovery**, for use as evidence in the action, or for both purposes. A person may be examined regarding any matter (except attorney-client communications) that is relevant to the subject of the pending action. This may include questions regarding the existence and location of relevant documents or other tangible things and the identity and location of prospective witnesses. One party may require the other party to disclose the names and addresses of proposed expert witnesses on whom the party will rely.

Depositions consist of taking the witness's testimony under oath, before a notary or another person authorized to administer oaths, with a question-and-answer record being taken by a court reporter. **Interrogatories**, on the other hand, consist of the submission of written questions to the witness and the return of them with the answers. This procedure is usually used when the oral deposition is deemed unnecessary, either because of the cost or because written interrogatories will serve the same purpose.

Depositions are costly undertakings because they include the services of the court reporter and the transcription of the testimony taken, as well as the services of counsel. If the same result can be obtained by written interrogatories, which are served on the adverse party by mail and returned by the same means, the procedure is less costly. Claim representatives should ask legal counsel about the necessity of depositions. Depending on the nature of the case, depositions of witnesses may not be necessary if the claim representative has already obtained a good recorded statement.

The answers given in depositions or interrogatories often open avenues of investigation. If possible, the additional investigation can be performed by the claim representative. Depositions will also disclose the extent of the injuries claimed and the special damages. Specific questions can be designed for special cases and can be added to the interrogatories or asked at the time the deposition is taken. In some states, the rules of discovery permit an inquiry into and disclosure of insurance and the policy limits, even though such evidence is not admissible in the trial of the case. The rationale of these rules is that when the plaintiff knows the exact extent of the insurance coverage, there is a greater likelihood of settlement than when the plaintiff is uninformed and cannot know that his or her demand exceeds the policy limits.

Discovery is the process during which each party to a lawsuit tries to learn relevant information about the other party's case through formal rules of procedure.

Discovery proceedings include medical examinations of the claimant, and the defendant may compel the plaintiff to submit to a medical examination, which may include the taking of X-rays, blood samples, and other tests when appropriate. These are all matters of evidence to which the defendant is entitled before trial.

Liberal discovery rules have the potential for **discovery abuse**, particularly with regard to demands for document production. For example, some plaintiffs' attorneys attempt to bury the defendant in broad discovery requests that ask for every document in the possession or knowledge of the defendant. If the defendant fails to produce every item, it creates a "discovery fraud" issue that becomes the centerpiece of the plaintiff's presentation to the jury.[10] Procedural rules and sanctions exist to control such abuse of discovery, but judges sometimes are reluctant to enforce the rules firmly or to impose appropriate sanctions on attorneys and litigants. Discovery abuse wastes time, creates needless expense, and is often used to coerce settlements.

A **motion** is an application to the court, made by counsel, for a ruling or an order. There are many kinds of motions depending on the ruling sought. They may be made before, during, or after trial. Before trial, the defendant may make a motion, for example, to compel the plaintiff to answer interrogatories—where the plaintiff has either failed or neglected to do so when the proper demand was made. If the motion is granted, the court will issue an order directed to the plaintiff to answer the interrogatories. Making a motion is known as a "move." For instance, a party may *move* to have a case dismissed.

A **subpoena** (Latin *sub*, under; *poena*, penalty) is a writ (document) issued by either the clerk of the court or the attorney as an officer of the court and is directed to the witness, requiring him or her to appear and give testimony before a particular court or magistrate at a particular time. It is personally served to a person, either by the sheriff or another officer so authorized or, in some jurisdictions, by any person over the age of twenty-one. The subpoena states on its face that, for failure to attend and testify, the person will be held in contempt and subject to penalties. Payment must be tendered to the witness, covering his or her expenses in coming to and going from the court. This is usually fixed by the court in an amount applicable to all cases, with payment for additional mileage allowed when the witness has to travel some distance.

A "straight" subpoena calls for the presence of the witness and nothing more, while a "records" subpoena requires a witness to bring records or other items that he or she has in his or her possession or control and produce them at the trial. The most common use of this type of subpoena is to obtain hospital records of the claimant, by serving the custodian of the records and having him or her appear and identify the records. It is also used to compel the attending physician to appear and bring along all office records, records of tests, X-ray plates, and other information in his or her possession relating to the treatment of the patient.

Understanding motions and discovery proceedings can help claim representatives to understand and estimate the costs of litigation and to ask questions of legal counsel that may help control litigation costs without harming the quality of the insured's defense. Pretrial proceedings, including motions and discovery proceedings, are labor intensive and time-consuming. Understanding the kinds of information needed for a trial can also help claim representatives to better prepare claim files with complete investigations before litigation. Thorough investigation of a claim can forestall the need for formal discovery and can help legal counsel focus motions and discovery on the areas that are most likely to help the insured.

Claim representatives can perform many of the tasks that would otherwise require the work of a lawyer. For example, they can take statements of witnesses and identify and obtain medical and hospital records. They can review statements and records to determine whether they will suffice or whether a deposition of an examining physician is needed. They can recommend to defense counsel whether to depose the plaintiff's expert or to rely on cross-examination at trial. Cases of clear liability and/or relatively small exposure may require few if any depositions and few requests for documents or other discovery devices. The claim representative and defense counsel should work as a team to determine whether a deposition is essential to the defense of a case and should be able to agree to dispense with unnecessary depositions or other discovery.

It is not necessary (and probably not possible) for a claim representative to attend every deposition taken in every case for which he or she is responsible. But the claim representative should attend key depositions in significant cases. Part of a claim representative's continuing education should include attendance at enough depositions to help him or her to understand the importance of a good statement and see what happens at a deposition; why *some* depositions are necessary; how the necessary depositions fit into the plan for defense of the case; what kind of job the lawyers are doing; and how much lawyer and witness time is consumed by depositions (which will aid in understanding why discovery is costly).

Lawyers representing each party will ask for **requests for admissions**. The purpose of these requests is to help reduce the scope of the dispute by coming up with an agreed-on set of facts. The defense attorney may forward these requests to the claim representative for review. In insurance, facts usually "admitted" by the parties before trial include their names and addresses, dates of certain incidents, and other facts that are not in dispute but would otherwise need to be proved at trial. Sometimes lawyers are tempted to refuse to admit any facts. This results in the other side having to prove trivial details and draws out the litigation unnecessarily. Claim representatives and defense counsel should work together to devise a suitable case strategy. Generally, facts that are true should be admitted.

Pretrial Conferences and Trials

As the case has developed, the claim representative and the attorney working as a team have been constantly sifting and winnowing data, re-evaluating the claim in light of changing circumstances, and exchanging views on objectives for the disposition of the claim. The relationship and the spirit of cooperation should not change at the time of pretrial conference, during jury selection, or during trial. The claim representative should attend and be alert to what is going on during these processes, armed with adequate settlement authority from his or her supervisor. The following knowledge can help a claim representative determine whether to settle or try a case:

- The settlement value or potential jury verdict value of similar claims;
- The practices and predilections of the trial judge;
- Plaintiff counsel's level of preparation, as well as his or her willingness and ability to try the case to a verdict;
- The makeup of jury panels and the general characteristics of jurors in the community; and,
- The strengths and weaknesses of defense counsel.

Even when the point of no return seems to have been reached and the case is going to go to trial, emotion and ill will should not be allowed to carry the case through trial. The claim representative should draw on his or her experience to find creative and cost-effective ways to settle the case or, if necessary, to consult with and advise the defense lawyer who must try the case. The claim representative should have a clear understanding of trial strategy and tactics and should be comfortable with what the defense lawyer is trying to achieve.

Leading up to trial, the claim representative (in addition to constantly analyzing the case for settlement possibilities) will follow up with witnesses and ensure their timely attendance at trial and (with defense counsel) will thoroughly review the file to ensure that all investigation is complete and that everything is in order. Despite their heavy case workloads, claim representatives should attend their insureds' trials if at all possible. In addition to taking advantage of an incomparable opportunity to advance his or her professional knowledge, the claim representative can assist at trial. He or she can provide information that defense counsel may need at a moment's notice or help with a recalcitrant witness. Claim representatives should remain in the background and not be an obtrusive presence that might detract from defense counsel's efforts. Of course, as discussed above, a settlement opportunity may present itself at any moment during a trial to an observant claim representative.

During the trial, the attorney for the defendant may move to dismiss the complaint. If this motion is granted, it ends the trial right at that point. This action is known as a **directed verdict.** A directed verdict ends the case before deliberations begin because the plaintiff failed to provide enough evidence to support the allegations in the lawsuit.

Post-Verdict Activity

If a case is tried to a favorable verdict, the claim representative and the defense lawyer must discuss whatever post-trial motions are necessary for proper entry and enforcement of the judgment. If the trial results in an adverse verdict, the defense team must consider post-trial motions for **judgment notwithstanding** the verdict (referred to as **judgment *n.o.v.***) or for a new trial. A judgment *n.o.v.* motion asks the judge to rule in favor of one party even though the verdict favored the other party. This motion is granted only if the weight of the evidence was clearly in favor of the losing party, which sometimes happens in cases involving juries sympathizing with a plaintiff despite the facts. Sometimes a motion for a directed verdict is required before a judge can grant a judgment *n.o.v.*

Whatever the result, any opportunities that are available in the jurisdiction to poll the jury or interview jurors should be employed. This will aid in understanding how jurors perceived counsel, the plaintiff, the insured defendant, and the witnesses. This information can provide wonderful feedback on what worked in a case and what did not. Exhibit 10-5 provides a list of some probing questions to ask jurors after they have rendered a decision.

EXHIBIT 10-5

Suggested Questions for Juror Interviews

1. What did you view as the most important evidence?

2. Was there any type of evidence that you would like to have seen that you did not see?

3. When did you make up your mind—after opening statements, after closing of the plaintiff's case, after closing of the defendant's case, or after closing arguments?

4. What was your reaction to the following witnesses who gave testimony?

5. Reaction to all attorneys for both plaintiff and defendant.

6. Reaction to judge.

7. What did you think about the lawyers' conduct of the trial: length, use of exhibits, blowups, etc.?

8. Was there anything else that you would like to have known that neither side provided?

9. Did you have a clear understanding of the jury instructions and jury verdict form?

10. If damages were awarded, how did you arrive at this damage number?

11. Was it made clear during the trial that the burden of proof was on the plaintiff?

Obviously, such information will be useful in handling future claims, but it will also assist in the immediate decision of whether to appeal.

Either a losing party or a winning party can appeal a verdict to a higher court. However, an appeals court cannot overturn a judgment solely because it would have determined the facts differently. Appellate courts usually limit their opinions to a review of the application of law to the facts decided by the jury. Appeals courts hear no new evidence from witnesses. The distinction between the facts and the law, which the appeals court can interpret, can be subtle. For example, if a motorist was found to have driven thirty-five miles per hour in a twenty-five mile-per-hour zone by a trial court, an appellate court could not dispute that fact if the finding was reasonable. However, the appellate court could determine whether the judge correctly stated the law of negligence as it applied to the fact that the motorist was speeding. Although the standards under which a case can be appealed are beyond the scope of this chapter, certain basic principles apply to all appeals.

An **appeal** based on evidentiary matters is the most common form of appeal. During a trial, a judge rules on many matters, particularly those concerning the admissibility of evidence. An appeal might be based on the admission or exclusion of a piece of evidence that the appealing party's lawyers believe would have altered the outcome of the trial. For example, defense lawyers might argue that reputation evidence should have been allowed against the plaintiff to show that he or she is not a truthful person.

An appeal might be based on the instructions that the judge gave to the jury. A judge's error in stating the law is grounds for an appeal because the jury uses these instructions to apply the law to the facts. For example, if a judge misstated the law of negligence, lawyers might have grounds for a successful appeal.

Defense counsel and the claim representative should conduct a thorough review of the case to determine whether an appeal is called for. The analysis should include the following factors:

- The expense of an appeal, including appeal bonds and legal fees, and the time spent by the claim representative that will detract from his or her attention to other claim files,
- The likelihood of a successful appeal in light of the law of the jurisdiction,
- The strength of the defense case, and
- The views of the appellate judiciary and the potential for setting favorable or unfavorable appellate precedents.

Whether or not a case is appealed, a case "autopsy" is a good (if sometimes painful) learning tool for the claim representative and defense counsel. This analysis can aid in understanding what issues presented problems during the course of the trial, what went right and what went wrong, and what lessons can be applied to future cases. The claim representative and counsel can use this opportunity to address such issues as communications, cost-effectiveness, timeliness of various measures that were taken, and the overall results. This process could help to strengthen the claim representative/defense counsel relationship in connection with future claims.

Court Reform

Court administration reform (or **court reform** for short), particularly docket management, has greatly increased the efficiency of the administration of justice in recent years. Although judges are often criticized, it cannot be denied that they have taken a major and an active role in urging settlement on the parties to lawsuits. **Mandatory settlement conferences**, now required in most states, occur before the case becomes too involved. Parties must meet in front of the judge, who tries to obtain a settlement. Some detractors feel that the settlements are the product of coercion by judges—but without question, they do encourage settlement and reduce the number of litigated cases. As described in Chapter 9, compulsory arbitration of cases involving lower amounts of damage has also helped to reduce litigation. Proactive efforts to settle cases and move cases ahead to trial have resulted in increased efficiency in the courts.

Pretrial conferences help to ensure that cases are prepared for trial and that the trial will be conducted efficiently. Another purpose of pretrial conferences is to help parties reach an agreement before going to trial.

One problem is that not all judges are skilled at conducting settlement and pretrial conferences. The role of a judge in such conferences is considerably different from the judge's role on the bench at trial. His or her function at the conferences is not to rule and order, but to seek agreement and compromise by adversaries. Thus, the settlement/pretrial judge must act in large measure as a mediator, conciliator, and catalyst. Even-handed but persistent persuasiveness is required. Heavy-handedness and pessimism are to be avoided.

The overall benefit to the justice system from settlement and pretrial conferences can be enhanced by increasing the skills of the judges who conduct the conferences. To this end, one of the principal focuses of continuing judicial education ought to be settlement and pretrial skill development.

A second problem affecting the efficiency of settlement and pretrial conferences is the state of preparedness of attorney participants. Effective conferences require diligent effort on the part of counsel as well as the court. Unless counsel is thoroughly familiar with his or her case at the time of the conference, little good can be accomplished even with a highly skilled judge presiding. Unfortunately, some courts fail to require that pretrial conferences be attended by the attorneys who will try the case. In these courts, there often develops the practice of sending junior associates to attend pretrial conferences—and the associate frequently has no authority to enter into compromises or make stipulations. This practice renders futile any effort towards settlement or serious trial preparation and should not be tolerated.

For many years, court congestion and delay have been endemic in many jurisdictions. In times past, the attorneys generally scheduled cases. Relying on lawyers to set their own trial dates was responsible for much court delay. In recent years, the situation has improved, as a result of legislation, re-vamped court rules, and assumption of administrative responsibility by the court. Status conferences or scheduling conferences—called by judges—serve to inform the judge of the status of the litigation and to establish deadlines for such matters as discovery, bringing in additional parties, and motions for summary judgment. Status conferences are best suited for cases that are somewhat complicated and therefore may require considerable hands-on supervision by the court. For relatively uncomplicated cases, pretrial procedural deadlines (imposed by statute or rule) provide a less expensive caseflow management device. Such a statute or rule may provide that every case is deemed ready for trial within a specified period of time after the case is filed, unless a party moves that the court (for causes shown) establish a different schedule for the case.

Probably the greatest threat to effective judicial control of caseflow is the availability of the "easy" continuance, that is, the continuance (or postponement of a trial) granted almost as a matter of course on request of counsel. Even the soundest managerial system for caseflow management cannot be expected to produce prompt disposition of litigation if relief from court-imposed or statutory deadlines for pretrial proceedings or trial dates is readily available to counsel even without a showing of good cause. Indeed, to the extent that continuances may be obtained easily, effective judicial control over caseflow is weakened or destroyed.

In recent years, court systems across the United States have made great progress in enhancing effective judicial control of caseflow management. In many jurisdictions, the lapse of time from the filing of a lawsuit to the trial of a case has been reduced by about 25 to 30 percent. For example, in Cook County, Illinois (the Chicago area), the waiting time for trial dropped from six years in the late 1980s to four years in 1994.

LITIGATION MANAGEMENT TECHNIQUES

Insurers should not lose track of the big picture when performing litigation management. Litigation costs represent a much smaller percentage of loss than payments for damages. The largest part of the insurer's loss payments goes to paying the claimant's damages. On average, payments to legal counsel run around 10 percent of loss payouts, while damages represent 90 percent. This ratio should be kept in mind when contemplating any litigation management technique.

Some insurers have opted to pay higher hourly rates and retain top-flight attorneys for two main reasons. First, they believe that the reputation of hiring only top trial lawyers will keep plaintiff attorneys from filing frivolous suits and will help insurers obtain lower settlements because plaintiff attorneys will not want to face them in court. A second reason for using higher-priced lawyers is that the higher rates reflect greater efficiency in the work they do. Some associates with half the hourly rate may overwork a case (many times unintentionally) because they have not learned what must be done immediately and what can be put off until later. One insurer claimed to save $50 million in one year by using more expensive lawyers to defend and settle cases. The general counsel for the insurer stated, "The best lawyers are expensive, but the second-best are *very* expensive."[11]

The difficulty with this approach is that legal fees may dramatically increase, while the savings resulting from lawsuit deterrence and lower settlement payments are more difficult to quantify. The goal of litigation management should still be reducing the overall costs to the company.

Benefits of Good Litigation Management

Insurers, law firms, and insureds benefit from good litigation management.

Benefits to insurers include the following:

- Reduced and more consistent and predictable legal fees
- Better case assignment to appropriate legal experts
- Better relationship with legal counsel
- Reduced administrative costs and processes because of better understanding of the roles of all parties and clear direction and authority

The defense firm also benefits from good litigation management. It benefits in the following ways:

- Higher volume of work by making the client's work easier
- Less administrative expense
- Less friction with clients
- Development of legal expertise

Insureds also benefit through better customer service (e.g., reduced time away from work and family that occurs with litigation) and lower premiums from insurers that are better controlling expenses and losses.

Ten Principles of Good Litigation Management

Litigation management techniques vary by company, and some are more effective than others. The following general principles of good litigation management should apply universally:

1. Avoid litigation through effective negotiation or alternative dispute resolution.
2. Select appropriate legal counsel.
3. Work with legal counsel as a team.
4. Establish attorney/law firm performance measures and track performance.
5. Establish litigation guidelines.
6. Establish litigation case plans and budgets.
7. Perform legal audits.
8. Develop alternative billing arrangements.
9. Understand attorney needs and make sure attorneys understand company needs.
10. Do not permit unethical practices and avoid conflicts of interest.

The first three items were discussed previously. Disposing claims in the least expensive, shortest time possible is still the primary objective, and without question, negotiation is the best litigation management technique. This is not just an academic point to remember, but a claim philosophy that must be practiced throughout the claim operation.

General litigation guidelines are necessary to help lawyers understand and meet the overall expectations of their clients. Audits of some type are required to ensure compliance with guidelines, but the nature and extent of audits should be considered carefully because of some potential adverse consequences (which are discussed in later sections). Like claim representatives' and claim departments' performance, lawyers' and law firms' performance should be measured and tracked over time. Alternatives to hourly billing should be considered to help reduce administrative costs in monitoring hourly bills and to encourage law firms to better control their expenses.

Establish Performance Metrics (Quantifiable Measures)

Companies should establish measurable performance criteria that help them attain the results they want. By establishing criteria, they can help law firms to understand what they are trying to accomplish and track performance from one period to the next. **Performance metrics** vary by company, but the following are commonly used:

- Average costs per case
- Average hours per case
- Ratio of attorney to nonattorney (usually paralegal) costs
- Win/loss ratio at trials
- Ratio of cases that settle to those that go to trial
- Ratio of closed files to open files (may indicate whether opportunities to resolve cases are being missed)
- Early case estimates compared to ultimate payout of settlement/award and legal fees.

Gather Performance Data on Litigated Cases

Once performance metrics have been established, data should be collected to determine how a law firm performed. The ability to capture legal information varies greatly by insurer. For this reason, a number of insurers establish measurements based on the information they capture. This is known as management by visible numbers. In general, this approach is less effective than establishing performance standards first and then finding ways to capture the information, because some of the most visible data may not be good indicators of performance. But visible data, readily available, are usually better than no data at all. Generally, the more information, the better. The following information could be helpful in assessing legal defense needs and making law firm comparisons:

- How much money did the company spend on outside legal counsel last year?
- How much was spent on each type of claim (e.g., auto BI, premises slip-and-fall, product liability)
- How much money was spent at each law firm?
- What was the average settlement per type of claim?

- What was the average outside counsel fee per type of claim?
- What were budgeted versus actual figures?
- How much did law firms charge for specific tasks such as depositions, discovery, research, motion practice, trial preparation, secretarial services, meals, and travel?

Insurers that do not capture this level of detail will have to make certain assumptions and estimates in comparing law firms and in establishing litigation management strategies.

Establish Litigation Guidelines

Litigation guidelines should exist to develop clear, up-front understandings between the insurer and legal counsel about what the insurer expects of counsel. The guidelines enable the lawyer to make informed decisions regarding the necessity and benefits of performing certain services. These guidelines should create no more of an obstacle to a lawyer's performance than would the risk of nonpayment for services performed in the absence of any guidelines. In other words, litigation guidelines should not prevent lawyers from doing their job. They may, however, require them to explain why they want to perform certain tasks.

Companies often set guidelines. Examples include the following:

1. Preliminary workup of a case may be authorized to be performed at the lawyer's discretion. This workup might include reviewing the summons and complaint, appearance, investigative material, answers, demand for answers to interrogatories, requests of admissions, and refiling of cross-complaints. Beyond this, authorization would be required.

2. In general, lawyers should not engage in investigative or lengthy and repeated interviews that could be properly conducted by claim representatives. Authorization would be required to deviate from this practice.

3. Legal research requirements should be reported promptly to the insurer, with an explanation of the reasons any research necessitates more hours.

4. Firms should have interim billing.

5. Lawyers should provide *brief* narrative reports covering the highlights of depositions regarding liability and damages. Copies of depositions are not usually required.

6. Single copies of reports and other documents should be sent to the individual in charge of the file at the insurer. The insurer will make copies for claim management if required. (The cost of law firms making copies can become substantial, especially when compared to the cost of insurers making their own copies.)

7. Case plans and budgets are required on all cases.

Insurers' guidelines help to reduce litigation costs because they limit what defense counsel can do without permission. Unfortunately, lawyers may construe such insurance company initiatives as interference with their professional obligations and as attacks on their professional integrity.

If the guidelines are implemented with a heavy emphasis on cost cutting without considering the effect on the insured client, they can evoke negative reactions from the defense lawyer (as described by one defense lawyer in the following paragraph):

> ...an emphasis on economy can produce a reduction in competent representation and detract from a lawyer's obligation of independent judgment. The focus of concern today is guidelines that restrict the ability of defense counsel to perform basic, essential functions unless prior approval has been obtained. Such guidelines often mechanically limit the time or expense that can be devoted to a task, initially removing the ability of the lawyer to make the decision.[12]

This sentiment is fairly widespread and it behooves claim representatives to be aware of it and work to counter it by treating lawyers with respect, by making only reasonable demands, and by deferring to defense counsel on legal matters when they provide a reasonable explanation for deviating from established guidelines.

Claim representatives need to understand the ethical duties lawyers have to the insured client. The American Bar Association Model Rule 1.8 states that where a lawyer accepts compensation for representing a client from another (such as an insurer), there can be "no interference with the lawyer's independence of professional judgment or with the client-lawyer relationship." What constitutes "interference" is subject to debate, but good personal rapport and mutual respect can go a long way in reducing friction over litigation guidelines.

Case Litigation Plan

Establishing a case litigation plan can reduce litigation costs and foster better attorney-claim representative relationships. Claim representatives should work with defense counsel in establishing a discovery plan. The plan may be modified later if complications arise, but establishing the scope of the discovery and a schedule at the beginning is an efficient, cost-effective way of conducting it.

In many situations, medical records may suffice, precluding the need for a doctor's deposition. The claim representative can assist in securing the medical records. Whether it is necessary to depose a plaintiff's doctor or a plaintiff's expert or whether cross-examination at trial will suffice are questions that an experienced, competent claim representative should be able to address. If the liability exposure of a case is modest, or if liability is clear, it is probable that few (if any) depositions need to be taken.

The claim representative/defense counsel relationship should never deteriorate to a point at which defense counsel flatly insists on taking numerous depositions and the claim representative refuses to allow any. If defense counsel is convinced of the need for a deposition, he or she should be able to explain why it is necessary to provide the insured client with a professional defense and how it fits into the overall defense and discovery plan. As members of a team, they should each understand the discovery and litigation process and what is necessary for a particular case; as a team, they should develop and stick to a defense plan and budget.

Each party's willingness to provide input and feedback helps in evaluating cases. Candor is an essential part of the relationship. If the insurer feels that the litigation plan is too expensive and complicated, this concern should be voiced at the outset.

Three important elements of a litigation plan for a case involve (1) setting case objectives, (2) evaluating case factors, and (3) establishing a case budget.

Case objectives might include establishing the scope of discovery and agreeing on what should and should not be offered to settle the case. Case factors to consider in an evaluation may include the following:

- The uniqueness of the case (does the case break new territory on legal issues regarding liability or damages?)
- The publicity the case might bring
- Is the claimant willing and able to spend a substantial amount of money? (If the other side is determined to take the case to trial and has the resources to do so, then the efforts to control litigation costs will be more challenging because the plaintiff can influence what is challenged, what is admitted, the number and length of depositions, and how many documents will be reviewed. For this reason, assessing the plaintiff's motives and aggressiveness is needed in order to establish an accurate case budget.)

Perhaps the most fundamental, and effective, litigation management technique is the **case budget**. Even if a law firm and a client agree that a simple, straightforward hourly fee is appropriate, a detailed budgeting process, including a discovery plan, a pretrial motion plan, and a trial plan can still be performed. Most defense attorneys are comfortable working within a litigation budget, as long as they can make reasonable adjustments to that budget as needs change during the course of litigation. In establishing a case budget, claim representatives and attorneys should consider the likely activities that will take place during the various stages of litigation. For example, in the initial phase, attorneys will need to check their client's (insured's) version of the accident, prepare court documents, check the opponent's facts, and make a discovery plan.

After evaluating the various factors of the case, time can be estimated for partners, associates, and legal assistants related to the following activities:

- Case review (time to review facts, talk to the insured, review documents submitted)
- Legal research
- Initial pleadings (answer to complaint, cross- or counterclaims)
- Discovery (both offensive and defensive interrogatories and document demands, depositions, document production)
- Expert witnesses
- Motions
- Settlement and negotiation conferences and drafting settlement agreements

Travel time, court reporters, and reproduction costs for transcribed depositions can also be estimated. Normally initial case budgets do not include estimates related to trial activities because most cases settle before even having to prepare for trial. However, once a trial appears to be impending, those costs should be estimated in a second budget. This second case budget can not only help control litigation costs, but it can also serve as a catalyst to re-evaluate the amount offered. This second budget would include items such as pretrial conferences, compulsory settlement meetings, and trial preparation. Trial costs will vary depending on whether the trial involves a jury or only a judge who is deciding the case.

Companies should set a billing threshold for the case (expressed either in billing time or dollars), which serves as a reminder to check on the status of the case (perhaps a threshold that would likely be exceeded in ninety days). If the threshold (say, for example, $5,000) is exceeded early on, then the case budget may be inadequate. If this threshold amount is not exceeded after several months, then the case may not be getting adequate attention.

Legal Bill Guidelines and Bill Audits

Companies establish billing guidelines to help them keep track of what legal services are being rendered and the amounts that are being billed for those services. Insurers want to be billed only for time for services rendered by lawyers. They do not want to see clerical and secretarial time, spent on routine functions, billed as legal fees. They do not want to pay as much for the tenth rendition of oft-repeated services as they paid for the first rendition, and they do not want to receive bills for a lawyer's overhead expenses, such as utilities costs. To identify and get a handle on potential billing problems, many insurers have instituted billing guidelines, and some are requiring the use of specific billing software.

Previous sections featured discussion of insurers' efforts to control litigation costs through litigation management and emphasizing efficient use of legal services. A great deal can be accomplished along these lines if claim representatives and defense lawyers are infused with a spirit of balance and fairness. Billing guidelines and audits are difficult matters. Billing guidelines (or mandates) are closely coupled with audits in the minds of some defense lawyers, and they are difficult for these lawyers to accept. Outside third-party audits, in particular, are red flags waved in front of a lawyer's eyes.

Lawyers complain that requirements to provide detailed information to third-party auditors could potentially violate their confidentiality with their client (the insured) and may waive their attorney-client privilege, which protects communications between an attorney and his or her client from being discovered by the opposing side.

They also complain that billing guidelines may affect their ability to take measures that they consider necessary to fully represent the insured client.

Insurers should make sure their legal counsel understands that if any question is raised, defense counsel need only explain why certain tasks are necessary, and permission will be granted readily. In reality, though, many lawyers balk at constantly having to explain and justify to claim representatives the way they practice law, out of fear that too many requests to perform certain tasks will lead to a company's looking elsewhere for defense work.

Standards for Billing Practices

Law firms historically accounted for their time and expenses and reduced them to simple single-page statements, usually with a few brief paragraphs describing what was done followed by one lump-sum bill amount. Unscrutinized billing practices in the past resulted in billing abuses.[13] As insurance companies began to require more accountability, law firms began to prepare more detailed and itemized statements showing individual tasks performed by specific lawyers, paralegals, and other support personnel.

Suggested billing standards include the following:

- Have written billing guidelines.
- Have lawyers list insured and plaintiff names and claim or file number on the bill.
- Have activities billed by the tenth of the hour.
- Insist on detailed, itemized billings including a breakdown of work performed. This would include items such as:
  - The task performed
  - How long each task took (in tenths of an hour)
  - The name of the lawyer or paralegal who performed the task
  - Itemization of expenses (photocopy work, mileage, photographs, tolls including all receipts)

The following are examples of billing practices that have fallen into disfavor with insurers:

- Billing clients for lawyers' mistakes
- Paying for the education of new associates
- Billing for full work on work that was recycled from another client

Regarding this last practice, the American Bar Association issued an opinion that states that a lawyer who spends four hours on three clients has not earned twelve billable hours. Any savings should be passed along to the client.[14] This is common with travel time to one location at which the lawyer also services another client. Exhibit 10-6 provides a list of practices that are potential indicators of billing abuse.

Third-Party Bill Auditors

A rapidly expanding niche of the legal world is occupied by **third-party auditors**, entrepreneurs who claim the ability to accurately analyze lawyers' bills and help insurers cut the fat from those bills. Many of these auditors are former claim representatives or practicing lawyers. Many of them use proprietary software to aid in their analysis of legal bills, seeking to ensure efficiency and consistent results. The employment of such auditors by insurers has accelerated rapidly since about 1995. The use of third-party audits is troublesome in the eyes of defense attorneys. A leader of the defense bar recently cataloged some of the practical problems he has noted in regard to third-party audits:

> Some of the practical problems and common complaints of defense
> counsel include: (1) form over substance—the outside auditor is looking

---

EXHIBIT 10-6

Potential Indicators of Billing Abuse[15]

- Overuse of internal conferencing within the law firm. (Auditors have found no corresponding entries with the other lawyers or with divergent times for the same meeting.) Conferencing should be limited. Enables junior associates to work efficiently under direction of a supervisor who can narrow the scope of legal research or investigation needed.
- Overstaffing the case (multiple lawyers attending hearing and depositions when one would suffice). The more attorneys who touch a file, the greater the bill amount will be.
- Excessive review and analysis of case (large amounts for "attention to" entries).
- Overresearching or researching on well-established case law.
- Large fees for generating standard form documents such as releases.
- Missing work product or receipts.
- Markups of 100 to 400 percent on fixed-cost items such as meals, faxes, photocopies. (Some law firms charge $0.25 per page for photocopies. Hospitals will charge that amount, but insurers have little control over them.) Don't expect their rate to be as low as commercial copies of $0.03-0.04, but considering the hundreds or thousands of copies that are made over the course of a year, this can amount to a lot of money. Internalize the photocopy function when possible.
- First-class airfare and other miscellaneous items such as clothing and meals at five-star restaurants. Some insurers use per diem guidelines on out-of-town travel.
- Excess time summarizing a deposition.
- Billing more than twenty-four hours in one day.
- Unknown status of individual indicated on bill.
- Overqualified person performing task (ten hours at $245 to make photocopies).
- Overhead costs or day-to-day operating costs that are incurred should not be billed to insurer. These differ from billable items such as out-of-pocket expenses that are traced to a specific client.
- Travel time for more than one attorney when one would have been able to handle the matter.
- A billing rate increase that has not been authorized.

---

for any excuse to reduce the bill even if the legal work was necessary and the charge reasonable; (2) arbitrary judgments are applied as to the time to perform a task when the person doing the review has no familiarity with the file; (3) the same standard of review is applied to each case regardless of its complexity; (4) different litigation and billing guidelines make it inevitable that a mistake will be made in a time entry description that will lead to an automatic reduction in the fee; (5) internal overhead costs have increased significantly in an effort to meet billing requirements; (6) the time it takes to receive payment on a bill has increased dramatically; and (7) the appeal process, if any, is time-consuming and onerous, creating a financial disincentive to challenge write-downs on the bill.[16]

Perhaps the most significant concern about using third-party auditors, and one that is not listed above, is the concern that turning bills over to a third party (a party who is not a client) may breach attorney-client confidentiality and the legal protection of attorney-client privilege.

Normally the work and communications between a client and an attorney are not discoverable by the opposing party under the legal principle called **attorney-client privilege**. The rationale is that clients should be able to trust and confide in legal counsel in order to obtain the best possible defense. However, this protection can be waived (intentionally or unintentionally) if a client shares protected information with others. This is the potential legal problem related to third-party audits. Courts in several districts have held that, by disclosing documents to the auditing agency, the client (unintentionally) waives attorney-client privilege on those *and other* documents.[17]

Forwarding billing statements to auditors could result in a breach of the lawyer's duty of confidentiality and may constitute a waiver of the attorney-client privilege. The plaintiffs' counsel may then assert a waiver and successfully pursue discovery of the defense lawyer's billing statements and the underlying information to which defense counsel is privy. This waiver and discovery may happen at an inopportune time and may be damaging to the insured client's case.

Insurers have countered that there is no question that they can perform in-house reviews of the reasonableness of legal fees and that there is no inherent reason insurers should not be permitted to outsource that function to an outside auditor without creating a risk of loss of the privilege. Court opinions, in the context of insurance defense and the tripartite relationship, are still unresolved on this issue. A number of state bar association ethics committees have rendered informal opinions or advisory opinions on the ethical implications of the transmission of detailed legal bills to third-party auditors.[18]

The bottom line is that insurers should audit bills (or at least samples of bills) to ensure that the bills meet their guidelines. The insurer is a client of the defense lawyer and has the right to monitor the cost and effectiveness of the representation it provides to the insured. Arguably, an insurer should be able to seek the advice of an outside auditor to assist in assessing the cost-effectiveness of the representation the insurer is required to provide, but courts may not see it that way. Insurers and claim representatives need to be cognizant of the problems associated with third-party auditors and make sure the benefits outweigh the costs. Insurers that perform their own audits do not run the same risk of breaching attorney-client confidentiality and waiving privilege.

Develop Alternatives to Hourly Billing

Most defense lawyers are accustomed to time-based billing and to charging by the hour for their services. This type of fee arrangement, known as **hourly billing**, originated with requests from insurers to obtain a better breakdown of expenses, rather than the one lump-sum figure that many attorneys used in the past. Billing for the time spent on a case was thought to be the best way of making lawyers accountable for their services.

As explained earlier, some attorneys took advantage of this hourly billing method, and the potential for abuse is one reason companies have looked to alternative billing arrangements. Other, more significant reasons for using alternative billing arrangements include the need to reduce administrative costs for insurers and law firms and to provide a way for law firms to share in the financial benefits of litigation cost control.

To find out what billing arrangements law firms are willing to offer, insurers often send out requests for proposals (RFPs) to outside law firms. Law firms then submit their proposals for alternative billing arrangements. This enables insurers to compare the various proposals.

The following are a number of alternatives to hourly billing that insurers currently use.

The Yearly Retainer

Under the **yearly retainer arrangement**, the defense lawyer or law firm agrees to handle (within certain guidelines) every case for the insurer in return for a fixed lump-sum payment. At the end of the year, the retainer agreement should be reviewed and a fee negotiated for the next year, based on the degree of satisfaction with the arrangement experienced by both the insurer and counsel. Guidelines should be set, taking into account issues such as complexity and volume of cases and case management guidelines desired by the insurer. The insurer will want to see evidence of favorable settlement or jury verdict experience, and the law firm will want to make a profit.

Flat Fee Schedules (Case-Based Fees)

Flat fee schedules contemplate a fixed or flat fee to be paid for work on an entire case file, regardless of the number of hours devoted to it. Over the course of several similar claims, insurers and legal counsel can arrive at fair approximations of what a case should cost. This average figure could serve as a basis for a flat fee arrangement for handling future cases. Flat fee billing eliminates one cost related to time and expense billing: the cost to audit the bill. This arrangement is usually used by larger insurers who can offer law firms large volumes of similar cases. Customarily, half of the fee is paid up front and the second half, on conclusion.

Modified Flat Fee (Task-Based Fees)

Under a **modified flat fee** arrangement, a flat fee is charged for a defined segment of the case. The common, basic legal work on a case, such as answering a complaint, taking depositions, filing and responding to interrogatories, and drafting a release, would all have a fixed price charge. An hourly rate is then charged for additional work such as trial preparation and trial activity.

Capped Fee Arrangement

Under a **capped fee arrangement**, the parties agree to pay an hourly rate for the work done on the matter, but a cap is placed on the total amount of costs for a case.

Blended Hourly Rates

Blended hourly rates signify that billing is done on an hourly basis but at a fixed hourly rate, whether work is done by the most senior partner in the firm or a new associate.

Defense Contingency Fee

Defense contingency fees are sometimes referred to as reverse contingency fees or **outcome-modified billing.** This arrangement gives law firms an opportunity to share in the rewards of controlling costs and insurer loss payouts. If a defense lawyer successfully keeps awards (or settlements) as low as or lower than the agreed-upon advance evaluation, the lawyer is rewarded with a higher fee. Many possible variations exist, but the basic point is that there are incentives for the lawyer to achieve a favorable verdict or settlement—with perhaps additional incentives for succeeding promptly—and disincentives for a settlement or verdict that is higher than predicted.

Volume Discount

With a **volume discount**, a defense lawyer charges a lower hourly rate in consideration for a large volume of work. (A different rate for complex work may be appropriate, in comparison to the rate charged for more routine work.)

Be Educated and Know Each Other's Needs

Good litigation management techniques will not compensate for poorly trained, overworked claim representatives who lack the time or abilities to settle claims before they become lawsuits. Claim representatives are asked to control the cost of litigation and may have to question the use of depositions, set case budgets, help to establish a viable defense plan, and understand the complications that may arise in the course of a lawsuit. This requires knowledgeable, educated people.

If poorly trained claim representatives try to perform litigation management, costs are likely to increase, as the attorney-client relationship will be damaged and insureds may end up getting poor a defense, leading to higher awards. Insurers have business as well as ethical obligations to make sure claim representatives are well informed and educated. Law firms need to make sure that associates understand their clients' business as well. They need to understand the competitive pressures of their clients and their clients' philosophy on settling cases versus trying cases.

Be a Good Client

Claim representatives should set high expectations for attorneys and themselves. A long-standing relationship is essential to good litigation management, and it is based on trust and cooperation. Good litigation management need not be confrontational or accusatory. Despite the misunderstandings that might exist between insurers and legal counsel, most lawyers are ethical and want to obtain the best possible result for the insured and insurer. Besides its being an issue of professional pride, lawyers understand that it is just good business to accommodate clients' needs and expectations.

Law firms need long-term clients to survive, and they know that they cannot achieve long-term relationships without trust. The partners in the law firm know this and try to be vigilant about the actions of associates in the firm and ensure that they do not take advantage of insurers. If a claim practitioner has concerns about the way a lawyer is handling a case, then he or she should contact a law firm partner and express those concerns. This would not be viewed as underhanded or "tattling" because partners want to have every chance to repair a relationship before it suffers. If the partner seems unresponsive, then it may be time to search for new counsel.

Insurers should be good clients. Being a good client means acting professionally, treating lawyers with respect, communicating, encouraging teamwork, and meeting promises made to the law firm. Exhibit 10-7 lists some specific ways to be a good client and to help foster and maintain effective, well-functioning lawyer-insurer relations.

EXHIBIT 10-7

Ways To Be a Good Client

- Phone attorney when concerns arise.

- Meet with attorney or partner in firm.

- Hold periodic meetings with legal counsel.

- Seek "counseling" before divorcing attorney and consider options if lawyer is not working out.

- Don't be a whiny client. (The squeaky wheel gets grease only for a while. Partners will dismiss complaints readily if they are frequent and petty.)

- Make outside counsel aware of organizational philosophy, business goals, and company claim philosophy.

- Invite counsel to hold in-house seminars to help build relationships.

- View lawyer as a teammate. Claim representatives should ask what they can do to help.

- Don't withhold information from attorney, even if the information is damaging to the insured's case. Attorneys can't represent your client with incomplete information. The only information to keep separate is information about coverage disputes with the insured. This should not be mentioned and must be handled separately.

- Pay bills promptly.

- Write letters commending attorneys when they have done a particularly good job on a case.

- Abide by the management principle of being at least as quick to praise as to criticize.

Insurers have a responsibility to manage their claims inventory in an orderly manner. Claim management must ensure adequate staffing of the claims department to allow proper handling of the anticipated workload. The insurer must also be sure that staff are appropriately trained and specialized to handle the claims they are assigned, including claims in litigation. Claim representatives who send files to attorneys with simple instructions such as "Handle as warranted" are asking for problems.

Claim representatives should meet their end of the litigation management bargain by providing timely coverage analysis, complete factual investigations, and early case evaluations. When a lawsuit is filed, the insurer should promptly review the case and determine what needs to be done, including consideration of alternatives to litigation. This analysis should be communicated promptly to legal counsel for further review and feedback.

The claim representative and the attorney, working as a team, should agree on what must be done to prepare the case for further evaluation, including recommendations for settlement or for trial. They need to establish a list of specific items to be accomplished, along with realistic due dates, and make periodic checks. All such efforts should be recorded in the file notes. The claim representative and the attorney should continue to communicate closely and be prepared to adjust schedules as the case proceeds.

> They will maintain regular contact, advising each other of changes and objectives for the claim's disposition.[19]

In the past, claim representatives simply handed over their claim file to legal counsel when a suit was filed. The responsibility and monitoring the work went to defense counsel. Today, in most cases, the claim representative must have the training, the staff support, and the assertiveness necessary to enable him or her to be a "co-manager" of the defense and work toward the efficient management of litigation and its costs. The claim representative must always be looking to identify the most cost-effective way to resolve a dispute and must pursue that resolution.

In a limited number of situations, the interests of the insurer and the insured will diverge. In such situations, separate, independent insurance counsel may be needed for the insured.

Ethical Issues in Litigation Management

Ethical issues abound between legal counsel and insurers. As mentioned earlier, the same attorney who represents an insured cannot represent the insurer on a coverage issue on the claim. Insurers must appoint separate legal counsel, and in some states, such as California, the insured has the right to choose his or her own legal counsel and have the insurance company pay the bill.

As mentioned in Chapter 1, some insurers set guidelines to reduce the appearance of impropriety in dealing with law firms. Law firms should be selected based on their professional criteria, not on how well lawyers promote the law firm through social events.

Insureds and insurers are co-clients, and liability insurance companies can— and, indeed must be able to—direct the scope and extent of legal representation by defense counsel. This scope is subject to insurance laws, bad faith laws, agency law, and the law of professional responsibility. Attorneys must take care not to benefit one client to the detriment of another. Insurer guidelines should not interfere with the attorneys' performing their obligations to insureds.

Any alternative fee arrangement must be designed to enable the insurer and defense counsel to discharge the contractual obligations owed by the insurer and the ethical obligations owed by defense counsel. The insurer must provide a proper defense using competent counsel. Defense counsel must be loyal to the insured client and must zealously protect the client's interests. To minimize the ethical and contractual risk involved, a well-designed alternative fee program should contain certain safeguards. Any significant disparity between the actual fee and equivalent hourly rate invites an allegation that the carrier and attorney did not adequately defend the interests of the insured.[20]

Defense lawyers have ethical obligations in relation to fees; for example: a fee must be reasonable; the fee arrangement must be communicated to the client; the insured client must be informed of any material conflict of interest;[21] and lawyers should give discounts when work involved in a case has been recycled from work performed for another client.

Insurers also have a duty to monitor the behavior of legal bill auditors. Defense attorneys claim that some legal audit firms have practiced unethical conduct by requiring law firms to cut fees even when they found no billing abuse, threatening that the client insurance company would drop the law firm if it did not reduce its fees. Legal audit firms that operate on contingency arrangements, getting a percentage of the savings they achieved from auditing legal bills, are under pressure to find savings. Insurers should make sure that savings are based on true billing abuses. Allowing bill auditors to coerce lawyers to reduce legitimate expenses is condoning an unethical practice.

SUMMARY

Claim representatives should first control the cost of litigation by performing thorough investigations and settling claims through negotiation or another alternative to litigation. They should strive to allow only the claims they choose to enter into litigation, rather than having litigation occur because of the inability or failure to investigate, evaluate, or negotiate a claim. Some circumstances are beyond the control of claim representatives, such as when a lawsuit is the first notice of loss, but choosing litigation as a last resort is a worthy goal.

Once a claim representative receives notice of a lawsuit, he or she must act promptly to forward the lawsuit to defense counsel. If coverage questions remain at the time of the lawsuit, claim representatives must reserve the rights of the insurer while defending the insured. Claim representatives must assess the need for independent counsel when coverage issues are unresolved at the time the lawsuit is assigned to defense counsel.

Claim representatives need to submit file material in an orderly fashion and request an initial case evaluation from defense counsel. This initial evaluation should form the basis for how the lawsuit should proceed through the litigation process and for the decision of whether the claim should be settled. Claim representatives should work with defense counsel to establish a litigation plan and budget. They should assist with discovery as much as possible and work with legal counsel to determine the extent and type of discovery required for the given case. Legal counsel should be discouraged from performing unnecessary discovery or engaging in tactics designed to harass or coerce the plaintiff into settlement. Claim representatives should, with the help of legal counsel, continuously look for opportunities to settle the claim throughout litigation.

Before proceeding to trial, claim representatives should ask legal counsel to prepare a trial plan and budget and evaluate them against the cost to settle the case. Settlement of cases in litigation depends on the philosophy of the insurer, and claim representatives should understand their own company's philosophy.

Insurers should review appropriate litigation management tactics to help control litigation but be mindful that the savings from these tactics pale in comparison to the cost of trying a case that should have been settled or the cost of overpaying a claim. Claim representatives need to develop the judgment to distinguish between these two outcomes.

Throughout the litigation process, claim representatives should act professionally and treat legal counsel with respect. The insured is entitled to good legal representation, and this can occur only when the insurer and legal counsel are working together cooperatively.

CHAPTER NOTES

1. Doris Hoopes, *The Claims Environment*, 2d ed. (Malvern, Pa.: Insurance Institute of America, 2000).

2. K. A. Reardon, S. G. Golonkin, and E. F. Dunne, "If You Paid for Legal Services Recently, Chances Are You Paid too Much: Hourly Billing and the 'Reasonable' Attorney Fee Standard," *CPCU Journal*, September 1995, pp. 145, 146. Also see J. Kakalik and N. Pace, *Costs and Compensation Paid in Tort Litigation*, Rand Corp. Study, 1983, pp. vi–vii.

3. See, e.g., Danek v. Hommer, 28 N.J. Super 68, 100 A.2d 198 (1953), aff'd 15 N.J. 573, 105 A.2d 677 (1954); Maryland Casualty Co. v. Willsey, 380 P.2d 254 (Okla. 1963); Ferguson v. Birmingham Fire Ins. Co., 254 Or. 496, 460 P.2d 342 (1969); C. Raymond Davis & Sons, Inc. v. Liberty Mutual Ins. Co., 467 F.Supp. 17 (E.D. Pa. 1979); Sears, Roebuck & Co. v. Reliance Insurance Co., 654 Fed.2d 494 (7th Cir. 1981); Seaboard Surety Co. v. Gillette Co., 64 N.Y.2d 304, 476 N.E. 2d 272 (1984); Continental Casualty Co. v. City of Richmond, 763 F.2d 1076 (9th Cir. 1985); Baron Oil Co. v. Nationwide Mutual Fire Insurance Co., 470 2d 810 (Fla. Dist. Ct. of App. 1985); Trizec Properties, Inc. v. Biltmore Const. Co. Inc., 767 F.2d 810 (11 Cir. 1985); Correll v. Fireman's Fund Ins. Cos., 505 So. 2d 295 (Ala. 1986); Waste Management of Carolinas Inc. v. Peerless Insurance Co., 315 N.C. 688, 340 S.E. 2d 374 (1986), reh'g denied, 316 N.C. 386, 346 S.E.2d 134 (1986); Lusalon, Inc. v. Hartford Accident & Indemnity Co., 400 Mass. 767, 511 N.E. 2d 595 (1987); Feed Store, Inc. v. Reliance Ins. Co., 774 S.W.2d 73 (Tex.App. 1989), writ denied (1989);

American Protection Ins. Co. v. McMahan, 151 Vt. 520, 562 A.2d 462 (1989); Upjohn Co. v. Aetna Casualty & Surety Co., 768 F.Supp. 1186 (W.D. Mi. 1990), recons. denied, 1991 U.S. Dist. LEXIS 662 (W.D. Mich. 1991); Eastern Shore Financial Resources, Ltd. v. Donegal Mutual Ins. Co., 84 Md. App. 609, 581 A.2d 452 (1990); Hecla Mining Co. v. New Hampshire Ins. Co., 811 P.2d 1083 (Colo. 1991); Liberty Mutual Ins. Co. v. SCA Services, Inc., 412 Mass. 330, 588 N.E.2d 1346 (1992).

4. San Diego Naval Federal Credit Union v. Cumis Insurance Society, Inc., 162 Calif. App.3d 358, 208 Cal. Rptr. 494 (1984).

5. Crisci v. Security Insurance Co. 66 Cal.2d 425, 58 Cal. Rptr. 13, 426 P.2d 173 (1967).

6. D. W. Rees and R. F. Hall, 36 For The Defense 4, 8 (September 1994).

7. D. W. Mandt, *We Still Need Each Other*, 36 For The Defense 2, 4 (May 1994).

8. S. G. Morrison, *On Balloons, Value, and Loyalty*, 36 For The Defense 1 (May 1994).

9. American Law Institute (ALI) Restatement of the Law Governing Lawyers Section 215 of the Restatement on May 14, 1998.

10. Mark Shoemaker, *Document Collection, Review and Production*, 37 For The Defense 9 (January 1995).

11. Amy Stevens, "Lawyers and Clients," *Wall Street Journal*, Jan. 7, 1994, p. B4.

12. R. E. Mallen (unpublished manuscript; furnished by For the Defense).

13. Lisa Lerman, "Gross Profits? Questions About Lawyer Billing Practices, *Hofstra Law Review* vol. 22, no. 645, 1994; Lisa Lerman, "Scenes From a Law Firm," *Rutgers Law Review*, vol. 50, no. 2153, 1998; William G. Ros, "The Ethics of Hourly Billing By Attorneys," *Rutgers Law Review*, vol. 44, 1991.

14. American Bar Association, Standing Committee on Ethics and Professional Responsibility, 1993.

15. Harry Maue, J.D., Ph.D., Suart, Maue, Mitchell, James Ltd., St. Louis, Mo., Presentation at ACE Conference, 1998.

16. R. E. Mallen.

17. The concern is highlighted by a federal appellate court decision in United States v. Massachusetts Institute of Technology. MIT attempted to assert the attorney-client privilege in response to a document request by the IRS. The most important issue presented was whether MIT's previous disclosure of some of the documents (including billing statements) to an audit agency caused MIT to lose the privilege. The court cited decisions from the Second, Third, Fourth, Federal, and D.C. Circuits in support of its position "that such limited disclosures do destroy the privilege." The issue was explained in detail in R. E. Scott, Jr., *Insurers' Use of Outside Auditing Firms*, 40 For The Defense 1 (July 1998). See also New York Bar Association, World Wide Web: www.nysba2.org/opinions/opinion716.html, December 2000.

18. As of July 1996, such opinions have been issued in six states: Alabama, Florida, Louisiana, South Carolina, Utah, and Washington. These ethics opinions have focused not on the attorney-client privilege, but on the lawyer's duty of confidentiality and the need for informed consent if that duty is to be waived. The opinions have been based on the controlling principle of Model Rule 1.6 of the ABA Model Rules of Professional Conduct. Model Rule 1.6 provides, in part, that "A lawyer shall not reveal information relating to representation of a client unless the client consents after consultation, except for disclosures that are

implicitly authorized in order to carry out the representation…." The principle of Model Rule 1.6 has been adopted as part of the ethics code of every state. The informal or advisory opinions noted above have been based on the interpretation by each state's ethics committee of its version of Model Rule 1.6.

The opinions have been directed toward the responsibilities of insurance defense counsel who has been directed to send his or her bills to an outside auditor. The opinions have held that it is unethical for the lawyer to send his or her bills to an outside auditor unless the lawyer first obtains the client's informed consent. The writers of ethics opinions seem to have assumed that the insured is the defense lawyer's only client, with the insurer relegated to the position of only a third-party payor.

19. Mandt, *supra* note 5 at 6-7.

20. J. J. Fitts and T. J. Newman, *Alternative Billing: It's a Different World*, 36 For The Defense 20, 23 (September 1994).

21. American Bar Association Model Rules of Professional Conduct, Rule 1.5 (a), (b) and Rule 1.7 (b).

Appendix—Summary of Legal System and Legal Terms*

This appendix provides a foundation for understanding law and the legal system. It describes the court system, litigation phases, and legal terminology.

APPENDIX CONTENTS

*This appendix is a summary of terms and concepts described in the AIC 33 text, *The Claims Environment*, 2d ed. (Malvern, Pa.: Insurance Institute of America, 2000).

Peremptory Challenges
Burden of Proof
Preponderance of the Evidence
Opening Statements
Introduction of Evidence Through Testimony
Cross-Examination
Motion for a Directed Verdict
Bench Conferences
Closing Arguments
Jury Instructions
Jury Deliberations and Verdict
Proceedings After the Verdict
Judgment Notwithstanding the Verdict (judgment *n.o.v.*)
Appeals
Enforcement of Judgments

Court Systems

In the United States, the court system is divided into two systems: state and federal. State systems are created by each state's constitution. The federal system is created by the U.S. Constitution and acts of Congress. Whether a case is heard in state or federal court depends on jurisdiction. This section discusses the jurisdiction of state courts and federal courts.

State Courts

Each state organizes its court system differently. For example, some states separate family law cases from other civil cases and try them in a separate branch of the court system. Other states hear all civil and criminal law cases in one court system. In those states, the same judge could hear cases covering a wide variety of subjects. Each state has several levels in its court system. Each level is distinguished by the amount claimed and sometimes by the need for a jury.

Small claims courts have very limited jurisdiction and are used to resolve minor matters. They are the lowest level of the court system. The limit of jurisdiction for small claims courts might be $10,000 or less in many states. Some television shows depict small claims courts where the parties present their own cases without lawyers and a single judge decides the matter. A small claims court has no jury and can generally award only monetary damages. Some examples of small claims suits include those for unpaid shopping debts, minor injuries or damage, and shoddy mechanics' work.

Courts of limited jurisdiction hear cases in very specific and limited situations. Examples include probate courts (wills and estates); county, municipal, or city courts (civil cases and minor criminal cases); and family or juvenile courts (divorce, custody, child support, visitation and alimony matters, and juvenile cases).

Courts of general jurisdiction hear any type of dispute and are limited only by the dollar value of the dispute. Courts of general jurisdiction, often called district courts, have the power to award monetary damages and equitable relief. These courts often deal with minor criminal matters such as misdemeanors and traffic violations. A typical jurisdictional limit for a district court is $25,000. The right to a jury trial in a district court varies by jurisdiction. (Within the federal court system, courts with unlimited dollar authority are also known as district courts. These are not the same as *state* district courts.)

Trial courts are used to conduct trials and hear evidence provided through witnesses. Small claims, district, and superior courts are all trial courts. These courts might be called superior courts, supreme courts (as in New York), circuit courts, or courts of common pleas.

If one party to a dispute wants to challenge the decision of a trial court, that party must bring its case to an **appellate court**. Depending on the jurisdiction, one or two appellate courts could review the decisions of the lower courts. Appellate courts do not hear new evidence; they make their decisions based solely on evidence presented at trial. Appellate courts do not retry the case. In most instances, appellate courts are restricted to examining the law as it applies to the facts determined by the trial court. What these courts are called varies by state. For example, some first-level appellate courts are called superior courts.

Matters that are decided by a state's highest court become the common law of that state and set a **precedent** for later decisions in lower courts in similar cases. The principle that lower courts must follow precedents set by higher courts is known as **stare decisis** [pronounced **stahr**-ee (or **stair**-ee) di-**sI**-sis, meaning "to stand by things decided"]. Lawyers seek creative ways to distinguish cases from unfavorable precedents and attempt to persuade judges that the precedents do not apply. If a precedent is favorable, lawyers attempt to persuade the judge that the case falls within the precedent even if the comparison is strained. For example, if a precedent-setting case involved an interpretation of a physician's duties to a patient, a lawyer might seek to use this precedent for a case involving a veterinarian's duty to an animal's owner.

Federal Courts

Every state has at least one federal district court (not to be confused with state district courts) that is part of a federal circuit. The results of a trial conducted by a federal district court can be appealed to the appropriate circuit court of appeals. There are eleven regional circuits, each of which serves a specific geographic region, the D.C. circuit, and the federal circuit. For example, the Court of Appeals for the Ninth Circuit hears appeals from the federal district courts of Montana, Idaho, Washington, Oregon, Nevada, California, and Arizona.

Federal courts can hear disputes in two main areas. Federal question jurisdiction involves the interpretation of federal laws. Diversity jurisdiction involves cases in which the dispute is between citizens of different states. For example, a lawsuit might be heard in federal court if persons living in California and Texas were injured by the actions of a corporation with headquarters in Florida and incorporated in Delaware. Having the suit heard in federal court removes any "home field" advantage because local pressures would not influence the case. In addition, using a federal court would avoid problems with different laws among the states. Exhibit A-1 illustrates a typical court system.

EXHIBIT A-1

Typical State Court System

Highest Appellate Court

Court of final resort

(Names: Supreme or Supreme Judicial Court)

↑

Intermediate Appellate Court

Hears appeal from trial courts

(Names: Appeals or Superior Court)

↑

Superior Court

General jurisdiction – no dollar limits and can award equitable remedies

(Names: Supreme, Circuit Court, or Court of Common Pleas)

↑

Trial Courts

General jurisdiction – dollar limits, but can award equitable remedies

(Name: District Court)

↑

Courts of Limited Jurisdiction

Small dollar limits ($25,000 or less), handle minor cases

(Names: Probate, County, Municipal or City, Family, or Juvenile Courts)

↑

Lowest Courts

Small dollar limits ($10,000 or less), handle minor cases

(Names: Small Claims, Justice of the Peace, Magistrate, Police, Traffic, or Mayors' Courts)

Names of courts vary by state.

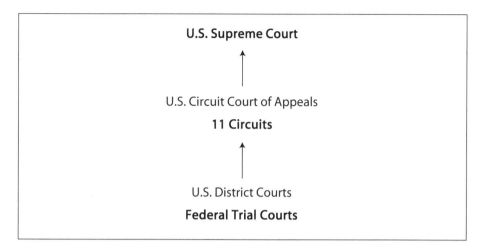

Matters of great significance can be further appealed to the U.S. Supreme Court, although there is no general right to have a case heard by the Supreme Court. Unlike the highest courts in most states, which must hear all cases properly brought before them, the U.S. Supreme Court chooses the cases it reviews. Insurance cases generally do not receive U.S. Supreme Court consideration on appeal because states regulate insurance. For example, coverage issues would rarely receive lower federal court or federal appeals court consideration. However, insurance cases involving federal or constitutional questions or conflict-of-state-law questions might be heard by the U.S. Supreme Court. For example, the Supreme Court decided the United States v. South-Eastern Underwriters Association case.* In that case, the Court decided that Congress had not manifested a clear intention to exempt insurers from federal antitrust laws.

Rules of Civil Procedure

Each state has rules that govern the process of litigation and the form and substance of all documents that must be filed with the court. All parties to the lawsuit must observe these rules, called the **rules of civil procedure**. Most states have rules of civil procedure patterned after the Federal Rules of Civil Procedure, which govern actions brought in federal court. The rules assist with administration of justice and ensure that litigation is conducted in an orderly fashion.

Rules of procedure vary depending on the type of case presented. Usually, states have separate rules for civil and criminal matters. States might have separate rules governing probate litigation, housing matters, and real estate issues. Each tier of the court system has separate rules of procedure that govern the time limits for litigation, when certain matters must be decided, and the conduct of trial. A typical rule is from the Tennessee Rules of Civil Procedure shown below:

Tennessee Rules of Civil Procedure

RULE 3. COMMENCEMENT OF ACTION.

All civil actions are commenced by filing a complaint with the clerk of the court. An action is commenced within the meaning of any statute of

*311 U.S. 533 (1944).

limitations upon such filing of a complaint, whether process be issued or not issued and whether process be returned served or unserved. If process remains unissued for 30 days or is not served or is not returned within 30 days from issuance, regardless of the reason, the plaintiff cannot rely upon the original commencement to toll the running of a statute of limitations unless the plaintiff continues the action by obtaining issuance of new process within one year from issuance of the previous process or, if no process is issued, within one year of the filing of the complaint.

All jurisdictions have similar rules that instruct how an action can be initiated and followed through.

Statutes of Limitation

Each state has statutes that control when a complaint must be filed. After the harm has occurred, the injured party has a specific time within which to begin a lawsuit. Time limits exist for bringing lawsuits so that people (or insurers) know that they cannot be sued after a specified amount of time passes. The law favors certainty, and time limits help to achieve that. These time limits force parties to act on their legal rights while evidence is still fresh and available. The statutes that control time limits are called **statutes of limitation**. The time in which a suit must be brought varies by the type of action (for example, tort or contract) and the jurisdiction. For example, a statute of limitation in one state for contract actions might be six years and for tort actions, two years, while another state might permit ten years for contracts and five years for torts.

The term **toll** has two uses. "Toll" means to annul or take away. "To toll a claim" means to take away the right to pursue the claim. However, "to toll a statute" means to interrupt the running (expiration) of the statute.

Statutes of limitation can be very complicated, and when a statute **tolls** a claim (takes away the right to sue) varies by situation. For example, a statute of limitation for injuries to minors does not begin to toll until the minors reach the age of majority. Thus, if a four-year-old child were injured and the statute of limitation was two years, the child would have until two years after reaching the age of majority to bring a lawsuit. In practice, minors' guardians often pursue lawsuits involving injuries to minors, and the matters are resolved before the minor reaches the age of majority.

Pleadings

Two documents, called pleadings, are used to begin the pretrial phase of litigation. They are called the complaint and the answer. The plaintiff prepares and files a complaint with the court and requests that the court issue a summons. The court issues a summons, along with a copy of the complaint, to the defendant to inform him or her that a lawsuit has commenced. The defendant files an answer in response to the complaint.

Pleadings are formal written statements of the facts and claims of each side in a lawsuit.

A **complaint** lists the allegations of what the defendant has done to harm the plaintiff and the amount of money the plaintiff wants to recover.

A **summons** is a legal document issued by the clerk of the court requiring the sheriff or another officer to notify the person named that an action has commenced against him or her and that he or she must appear on the day named to answer the complaint. Serving the summons begins the lawsuit.

The **answer** provides the defendant's initial response and defenses to the complaint.

Discovery

After the lawsuit has commenced, each party to the litigation discovers the other side's case. Each side attempts to learn everything relevant about the other's case before the trial. This process, called **discovery**, uses five main methods: depositions, interrogatories, requests for the production of documents and things, physical or mental examinations, and requests for admissions. Each of these methods is governed by the court's rules of procedure. Most states have adopted rules of procedure similar to the federal rules. Rule 26 of the Federal Rules of Civil Procedure states the general provisions for discovery as follows:

> Parties may obtain discovery by one or more of the following methods: depositions upon oral examination or written questions; written interrogatories; production of documents or things or permission to enter upon land or other property, for inspection and other purposes; physical and mental examinations; and requests for admissions.

Each of these discovery methods is defined in subsequent rules that govern the scope of discovery, the time limits for the information exchange, and the penalties for noncompliance with the rules. The order in which discovery is conducted (for example, whether depositions are taken before documents are requested) is at the lawyer's discretion. However, according to federal rules and the rules of most states, there is a specific time limit within which all discovery must be completed for the information to be allowed at trial.

Depositions

A **deposition** is a sworn statement a person gives regarding his or her activities or knowledge concerning the subject of a lawsuit. This testimony is typed by a court reporter or videotaped. Depositions are used as trial evidence of what a person saw, heard, or did in relation to the dispute between the parties to the lawsuit. A deposition is generally conducted at the office of the lawyer who requested it.

Depositions have two purposes. First, they allow each party to the litigation to find out what the other party's witnesses know about the facts of the matter. Second, because the testimony is transcribed, the statements a person gives in a deposition cannot be changed later during trial testimony without that person being discredited as a witness or punished for perjury.

Party witnesses (the plaintiff, the defendant, or a representative, such as an employee of a corporation) and nonparty witnesses (all other persons who have knowledge regarding some of the facts of the case) can be deposed.

Under federal rules, the plaintiff or the defendant might request the deposition of the "person with most knowledge" concerning the allegations in the complaint and answer. This rule is frequently applied when the plaintiff or the defendant is a corporation, a partnership, an association, or a government agency. For example, if suing a large corporation, the plaintiff's lawyer might not know which manager was responsible for developing and implementing a particular policy. This rule allows lawyers to depose the appropriate manager. Under the same rule, an insurer might designate a claim representative as its "30(b)(6)" deponent, named after the federal rule.

Interrogatories

Interrogatories are specific written questions or requests that the opposing party must answer in writing. Their primary purpose is to allow each side to discover the other's position regarding its interpretation of the facts of the case and what laws are applicable to that interpretation. Interrogatories are used for the same purposes as depositions. Because there is no chance for follow-up or clarifying questions, interrogatories are especially useful for identifying specific facts and sources of information. The opposing lawyer in an interrogatory, in comparison to in depositions, loses an advantage because there are no opportunities to jump quickly from one question to another or to observe the party's reaction as questions are asked and answered. In addition, interrogatories do not allow the parties to observe nonverbal communications. However, if a witness is out of the United States, interrogatories might be the only way that he or she can be questioned. Interrogatories are a much less expensive form of discovery than are depositions.

Under Rule 33(a) of the Federal Rules of Civil Procedure, answers to interrogatories must be filed within thirty days. Failure to file can result in sanctions (such as fines) or a finding in favor of the interrogating party. The following is an example of interrogatory questions that might be filed:

Question No. 1: Was the defendant legally intoxicated at the time of the accident?

Question No. 2: Did the defendant fail to stop at a stop sign?

Question No. 3: What defenses does the defendant plan to raise?

Question No. 4: What counterclaims, if any, does the defendant plan to raise?

Question No. 5: What physical evidence will the defendant present?

Question No. 6: State the names and addresses of all the witnesses that the defendant will use to testify on behalf of the defendant in the trial of the case.

Requests for Production of Documents

During discovery, each side to the lawsuit usually asks the opposing side to provide all of the documents it has in its possession relating to the facts at issue. The federal rule that requires the production of documents and other tangible evidence is Rule 34 of the Federal Rules of Civil Procedure. Other tangible evidence includes photographs, videotapes, diagrams, computer records, and any other media that are used to transmit or preserve information. If a party has a document in its possession or can obtain it without unreasonable effort, it must produce it on request from the other side. The only exceptions are documents created for or communicated to that party's lawyer in anticipation of litigation. Because parties' communications with their lawyers are protected by attorney-client privilege with few exceptions, such communications can be withheld. The party wishing to withhold documents must identify the document, the communicating parties, and the basis for exercising the privilege (right to prevent disclosure).

Requests for production of documents might require that claim representatives produce copies of their files. The usual procedure is to copy the file and send it to the lawyer representing the insurer or its insured. That lawyer reviews the claim file and removes any documents, or portions of documents, that he or she considers privileged communications. The remaining documents are sent with the request for production of documents.

Requests for Admissions

After all of the depositions have been taken and documents transmitted, but before the end of the discovery period, one party to the lawsuit might request admissions from the opposing side. These **admissions** are factual statements that, unless denied, bind the party at trial. The purpose of this discovery device is to narrow the factual issues to those in contention and reduce the number of facts the court or jury has to determine at trial. Admissions can also serve as the basis for a summary judgment. A **summary judgment** is a final judgment for one side made before trial when the judge finds that there is no factual issue in the case. That decision is based on pleadings and discovery presented before trial.

Pretrial Motions

During litigation, certain matters arise that the court must decide. These matters can include whether certain evidence could be admitted at trial, whether certain persons could be called as witnesses, and whether the lawsuit could be decided without further action by the parties. To bring these matters to the court's attention, lawyers file **motions** with the court. Motions are governed by the rules of civil procedure, which outline when a motion can be brought, the purpose for which a motion can be brought, what must be included in a motion, and the time limits for opposing lawyers' responses to a motion.

Motions that lawyers make include the following:

1. Motion to dismiss
2. Motion *in limine*
3. Motion for summary judgment

Motion to Dismiss

A **motion to dismiss** is a request that the court terminate the action because of settlement, voluntary withdrawal, or some procedural defect.

An example of a procedural defect is the failure of the plaintiff to state a legally recognized cause of action.

Motion *in Limine*

While evidence is gathered during discovery, one party to the lawsuit could request that certain evidence be excluded from the trial. This is done through a motion *in limine* (pronounced **lim**-i-nay). A **motion *in limine*** is a pretrial request to the court by one party to the lawsuit that certain evidence be excluded from the trial. The evidence that lawyers seek to exclude is typically harmful to their case. For example, if photographs showing vehicle damage and bloodstains were offered as evidence, opposing lawyers might attempt to exclude them because they could influence the jury's decision on an award. Although the photographs could be admissible under the rules of evidence, lawyers might convince the court that they should be excluded for the following reasons:

- They are highly prejudicial (bloodstains tend to influence jurors irrespective of determining fault).
- They are cumulative (other photographs demonstrating damage to the vehicle are available that do not show bloodstains).
- The fact is not in controversy (the defendant admits that the car was damaged).

The trial judge decides whether to grant a motion *in limine*.

Motion for Summary Judgment

At the close of discovery, but before trial, the plaintiff or the defendant can file a **motion for summary judgment**, which argues that the other side has failed to meet the legal standard to submit the case to a judge or jury to decide. Courts apply strict standards when reviewing a motion for summary judgment because if the motion is successful, the nonmoving party is deprived of a jury trial. To grant a summary judgment motion, the court must find that there are no genuine issues of material fact in dispute and that the moving party is entitled to judgment as a matter of law.

After the motions and responses have been filed with the court, a hearing is usually held. The court questions the lawyers regarding the basis for their respective motions or oppositions. The court then rules on the motion(s). The court makes its ruling from the viewpoint that all of the pleadings of the opposing party are true. If the motion is denied or covers only some of the issues, the parties proceed to trial.

Pretrial Conference

A **pretrial conference** is a meeting of the judge and the parties' lawyers in the judge's chamber two or three weeks before the trial to narrow the issues to be tried, to stipulate the issues and evidence to be presented at trial, and to help in settling the case.

A pretrial conference is called at the court's discretion when it appears that such a meeting might help settle the case.

Trials

After all discovery has been completed, all pretrial motions have been heard and decided, and no settlement or other action has ended the dispute, the matter proceeds to trial. A trial demands that both sides produce all of their witnesses and physical evidence at a particular time and place. A **trial** is a judicial examination and determination of issues in a court of jurisdiction.

Claim representatives might attend trials to assist lawyers in the evaluation of the case and to observe the actions of lawyers during trial. To evaluate trials effectively, claim representatives must be familiar with the trial process. This section describes jury and nonjury trials, burden of proof, and the trial process from the opening statements through enforcement of judgments.

Jury and Nonjury Trials

Not all civil trials are held before a jury. The right to trial by jury could depend on the amount in controversy or on the particular area of law that applies to the facts of a case. For example, in some states, questions relating to the actions of an insurer investigating a claim are not heard by a jury. They are reserved for determination by a judge. The plaintiff and defendant in a civil trial might agree to have a case heard by a judge alone. A **bench trial**, also called a trial by court or judge, is a trial determined by a judge without a jury.

In trials before a jury, jurors are selected from voter registration lists and drivers' license holders within the court's judicial district, such as a county. Individuals are selected to serve in a jury pool for a period of time. Depending on the cases that are scheduled for trial during that time, a juror could be called to serve on several juries or none at all.

Having been called to a courtroom, potential jurors are questioned by the judge or lawyers concerning the parties to the litigation and the issues to be decided in the case. *Voir dire* (pronounced vwahr-deer) is the process of examining potential jurors concerning their possible interest in the matters presented at trial, their ability to decide the case fairly and without prejudice, and their overall competence to serve as jurors. During this process, lawyers attempt to determine the potential jurors that would most likely be favorable to their clients. Depending on the statute or a court rule, lawyers for each party in the suit are given a set number of **peremptory challenges**, which allow lawyers to exclude a potential juror without stating a reason. After using all of the assigned peremptory challenges, lawyers must state a reason that a potential juror should be excluded from hearing the case.

In some jurisdictions, certain classes of people are automatically excluded from hearing a particular case because of their occupations. For example, lawyers and claim representatives might be excluded from hearing civil trials. Friends, relatives, and acquaintances of the parties are also typically excluded.

Jurors are not informed that an insurer would pay the judgment or that an insurer is paying for a defense (unless, of course, an insured is suing an insurer directly). The existence of insurance to pay the judgment should not affect the judge's or jury's decision regarding fault. Judges and juries should act as though no insurers are involved, even when it is obvious. For example, the parties involved in an automobile accident are likely to have insurance. Thus, insurers are probably involved in civil trials related to such accidents. If any party mentions that an insurer is involved, grounds for a mistrial are established.

Burden of Proof

Burden of proof is a concept that helps to explain the order of events that occur at trial. It is a party's duty to prove the facts that he or she claims are true. Generally, plaintiffs prove that a fact at issue is more probable than not to satisfy their burden of proof. In a civil case, the plaintiff has to prove all of the essential elements of its case by a **preponderance of the evidence**. This phrase means the evidence has greater weight or that it is more credible and convincing than the evidence offered against it. For determining preponderance of evidence, the basis and extent of the witnesses' knowledge, the type and quality of information they possess, and their manner of testifying are more important than the number of witnesses.

Opening Statements

After the jury is assembled, lawyers for each party can make an opening statement. An **opening statement** is not evidence but a summary of the case and of the proof the lawyer intends to present. Because the plaintiff has the burden of proof, he or she goes first. Plaintiff's lawyers use this opportunity to summarize the facts of the case and the issues that the jury will decide. The jury is usually told what witnesses will be called to testify, how this testimony relates to the issues the jury is to decide, and why the jury should decide the case in the plaintiff's favor. After the plaintiff's lawyers make their opening statement, lawyers for the defendant can make an opening statement or reserve the opening until after the close of the plaintiff's case. Whether defendant's lawyers reserve the opening statement is a matter of personal preference.

Introduction of Evidence Through Testimony

After the opening statements, the plaintiff's lawyers introduce evidence through witnesses' testimony. **Testimony** describes the evidence given by witnesses who are called to answer questions by a particular party, such as the plaintiff's or defendant's lawyers. After one party's lawyers elicit sufficient testimony, opposing lawyers are entitled to cross-examine the witness. **Cross-examination** is an essential element of the trial. It allows opposing lawyers to test the truth of the witness's testimony, to further develop the testimony, or to question witnesses for other purposes. Successful cross-examination might discredit testimony or might reduce the weight a jury gives to the evidence.

Motion for a Directed Verdict

After the plaintiff's lawyers have finished presenting their case, defense lawyers can make a motion for a **directed verdict**. This motion argues that the plaintiff has failed to prove his or her case and that the case should be dismissed. The motion is the defense lawyer's argument that the evidence is so clear and convincing that no reasonable trier of fact could find for the plaintiff, based on the plaintiff's case. If a motion for a directed verdict is granted, the judge's verdict favors the defendant and the trial is concluded. However, the plaintiff frequently appeals this finding. A directed verdict is rarely granted because it is uncommon for the plaintiff's evidence to be so defective that it warrants such a ruling.

Bench Conferences

During the trial, matters arise concerning the conduct of the trial that the trial judge must decide. These matters might include whether a particular piece of evidence should be presented to the jury, the scheduling of the proceedings, and the estimated duration of the trial. Because these issues do not concern the jury, and in some cases must be excluded from the jury, the judge and lawyers hold a bench conference. For example, if lawyers want to introduce a piece of evidence and opposing lawyers object, the judge hears arguments from both lawyers on why the evidence should be admitted or excluded. The jury is barred from hearing these arguments to prevent prejudice should the judge decide to exclude the evidence. The jury ignores bench conferences when making its decision on the case. Bench conferences might be recorded by the court reporter so that if one side wants to challenge the court's ruling, a transcript is available. However, a bench conference is not necessarily made a part of the trial's written record.

Closing Arguments

After all evidence has been presented, lawyers for each side are given an opportunity to address the jury. In these **closing arguments**, lawyers typically summarize the facts presented in a light most favorable to their client. As with opening statements, closing arguments are not evidence. Lawyers are not allowed to give opinions about the evidence. However, because closing arguments promote a particular position, lawyers attempt to influence the jury's decision by characterizing evidence adverse to their client's position as being "without weight."

Jury Instructions

After the closing arguments, the judge instructs the jury regarding the law to use in deciding the case. For example, in an automobile accident, a judge instructs the jury regarding the principles of negligence and fault. The judge explains which party has the burden of proving facts. Lawyers usually submit written proposals for instructions, and the judge decides whether to incorporate those proposals in the jury instructions.* If the judge instructs the jury incorrectly, the losing party might have grounds for appealing the case.

---

*An example of model civil jury instructions can be found at http://www.ce9.uscourts.gov/web/sdocuments.nsf/civil+jury, January 2000.

Jury Deliberations and Verdict

After the jury has received the judge's instructions on the law, it retires to the jury room to decide the case. A jury selects a foreperson who acts as the leader. The jury's deliberations have no set time period and continue until a verdict is reached. After the jurors reach a verdict, they return to the courtroom, where the judge asks for their verdict. The verdict is read in open court, usually by a court officer or the jury foreperson.

Proceedings After the Verdict

The court usually accepts the jury's verdict and enters a judgment to that effect. On rare occasions, the court can act on its own initiative or on a motion of the losing party and enter a **judgment notwithstanding the verdict (judgment n.o.v.**[†]**).** This means that the judgment is made in favor of one party even though the verdict favored the other party. Sometimes a motion for a directed verdict is required before a judge can grant a judgment *n.o.v.*

The court can grant a new trial on its own initiative or on a motion of the losing party. Typical grounds for a new trial include insufficient evidence, erroneous rulings on instructions, newly discovered evidence, and a verdict contrary to the instructions. Trial judges seldom grant new trials.

The court can adjust the damages awarded by the jury. If the damages are too high or too low in the judge's opinion, he or she can decrease the award (an action called remittur) or raise it (an action called additur). This typically happens when a jury awards an extraordinarily high judgment that is disproportionate to the damages. The following is an example of a judgment:

> This action having been before the court and jury, and the jury having rendered its verdict for the plaintiff and against the defendant on plaintiff's claim and for the plaintiff and against the defendant on defendant's counterclaim:

> It is ordered and adjudged that the defendant pay the plaintiff the sum of $250,000, together with interest and the costs of this action.

> This 31st day of January, 20X1.

Appeals

A losing party or a winning party can appeal a verdict to a higher court. However, an appeals court does not overturn a judgment because it would have determined the facts differently. Appellate courts usually limit their opinions to a review of the application of law to the facts decided by the jury. Appeals courts hear no new evidence from witnesses.

The appeals process is lengthy. It requires a complete trial transcript to be certified and transmitted to the appeals court, along with all physical evidence introduced at trial. After the parties file appeals briefs, lawyers for each party argue for or against the appeal and answer questions raised by the

[†] The initials "n.o.v." stand for the Latin *non obstante veredicto,* meaning "not withstanding the verdict."

appellate justices at a hearing. After a state appeals court renders a decision, it is final and concludes the matter.

Enforcement of Judgments

In cases in which the defendant loses and has sufficient financial resources to pay damages, the plaintiff is rarely concerned with enforcing the judgment. However, collecting from uninsured or indigent defendants is difficult. If the defendant refuses or is unable to pay, the plaintiff goes to court to enforce the judgment.

Auto Liability Claims

The Initial Phase of the Claim

Analyzing Auto Law and Liability

Vicarious Liability in Auto Claims

PIP and Limited-Tort Laws

Auto Liability Claim Investigations

Case Study—The Auto Liability Accident

Appendix—Automobile Accident Statement Guideline

Auto Liability Claims

For auto liability claims, claim representatives must (1) determine whether the auto coverage applies, (2) gather evidence, (3) assess the liability, and (4) evaluate the extent of damages owed. These phases involve activities such as taking statements, obtaining police reports, and gathering other evidence. Claim representatives must sort through the evidence and apply the law to it.

Chapters 1 and 2 dealt with auto coverage issues that should be considered when analyzing auto liability claims. The elements and concepts of negligence, explained in Chapter 5, also apply to auto liability claims, as do the rules of evidence described in Chapter 7.

The purpose of this chapter is to give examples of how the legal and investigative aspects covered in previous chapters apply to auto liability claims. This chapter begins with some fundamental information about auto liability claims and then concludes with a case study that guides students through a challenging auto liability claim from beginning to end.

THE INITIAL PHASE OF THE CLAIM

In the initial phase of an auto liability claim, a claim assignment is made to the claim representative and he or she sets an initial claim reserve shortly after receiving the assignment. Generally, claims are assigned and reserves are set based on the seriousness of the damages resulting from an auto accident. Sometimes the seriousness of an accident is difficult to determine from an initial loss notice because of the lack of information communicated from insureds to their agents or insurance company call centers. Loss notices commonly have little more than short notations such as "Insured injured in rear-end accident" or "Insured injured when he lost control of car."

Unfortunately, claim managers must assign claims to claim representatives, and claim representatives must set initial reserves and establish a scope of investigation, based on such sketchy information. Several factors show a high correlation to accident severity, and it may help claim managers and claim representatives in their initial decision making to consider them. The following are examples of such factors identified in one recent study:[1]

Accidents that occurred in rural areas were more likely to result in major vehicle damage, disability, and serious injuries than accidents that occurred in more heavily populated cities and suburbs.

Single vehicle crashes tended to result in more serious damage to the vehicle and injury to the claimant than multiple-vehicle accidents.

Frontal impact crashes and rollovers were associated with the greatest amount of vehicle damage, highest rates of disability, and most serious injuries. Rear impact collisions tended to be the least severe.

Accidents that occurred during overnight hours or on weekends were generally more severe in terms of vehicle damage and injury than accidents occurring on weekdays.

Another task in the initial phase of the claim is determining coverage. Claim representatives must ask the following questions:

- Was the policy in effect at the time of the accident?
- Is the driver or owner "an insured"?
- Is the vehicle covered?
- Does the incident fall within the insuring agreement of the policy? (Covered situation and covered damages)
- Do any exclusions apply?
- Have all the policy conditions been met?

Auto liability investigations are discussed later in this chapter, but before considering investigative actions, claim representatives should understand some of the fundamentals of auto law. Claim representatives should consider how liability may apply under various possible circumstances in order to know what investigative actions to take and what questions to ask.

ANALYZING AUTO LAW AND LIABILITY

As mentioned in Chapter 5, negligence occurs when (1) a party owes a duty to another, (2) fails to meet that duty, and (3) the failure causes compensable damages to the other party.

Drivers and owners of autos owe a duty to others to use their autos in a "reasonable, prudent" manner and exercise care for the safety of others. However, this does not necessarily mean that the driver or owner must violate a written statute to be liable. Unlike for other types of liability claims, an extensive number of written rules of the road or traffic ordinances exist to help determine liability.

In addition to following the rules of the road, drivers of motor vehicles have a duty to exercise care not only in the operation of the vehicle, but also with its maintenance. For example, a driver who knowingly operates a vehicle with faulty brakes, lights, or tires is liable to a passenger who may be injured in an accident related to such defects.[2]

Auto liability claim representatives should, at a minimum, be familiar with the rules for motorists, passengers, and pedestrians. They should be able to recognize and assess how vicarious liability or negligent entrustment might apply to a claim. They should understand the basics of personal injury protection (PIP) or limited tort systems and know how liability investigations should be conducted.

Rules of the Road for Motorists

As mentioned earlier, motorists must operate vehicles in a reasonable, prudent manner. Reasonable, prudent people maintain vehicles in a safe condition, obey the rules of the road, conform to highway regulations, obey traffic controls, keep vehicles under control, and do everything possible to avoid accidents.[3]

One rule of the road common to all states is the duty to **keep a clear, assured distance** behind other vehicles. This means leaving enough distance in order to stop or avoid an accident. This distance depends on the speed of the vehicle and the visibility of the surroundings. Drivers in urban areas frequently violate this rule, especially during periods of heavy traffic. The fact that this rule is commonly violated would not likely prevent a driver from being found negligent unless the driver could prove that he or she was maintaining a safe distance until another vehicle cut in front before the driver could react. Such a situation might mitigate, if not eliminate, liability.

Motorists have a duty to comply with traffic controls. More than 3,000 Americans died in 1999 as a result of running a red light or a stop sign.[4] Traffic control violations have become so prevalent at some intersections that "red light cameras" are placed on the traffic lights to photograph drivers who disregard traffic controls.

State laws maintain that "No person shall fail, neglect, or refuse to comply with any *lawful* traffic control *displayed* on any road." Usually, the issue for claim representatives to resolve is *which* party violated the traffic control, not *whether* it was violated. However, sometimes the issue is *whether* a party violated a traffic control (usually a stop or yield sign). For a sign to be lawful, it must be erected by a proper governing authority *and* it must be properly **"displayed."** To be properly displayed, it must be readable and visible. If a sign is damaged by weather or vandals, or if it is obscured from view by weeds or shrubbery, then it is not properly displayed. This does not relieve a driver of exercising care in driving. Even if a sign has been blown over by the wind, a reasonable driver would not approach an "uncontrolled" intersection without exercising caution.

An uncontrolled intersection (one without any sign) is sometimes encountered in rural areas or in parking lots. Vehicles that arrive first at the intersection normally have the right of way over those that enter later. However, traffic on side roads must yield to traffic on main roads. When two vehicles come to an uncontrolled or a similarly controlled intersection (intersections with four-way stop signs), the driver on the right-hand side normally has the right-of-way.

Negligence is typically presumed of drivers who violate crosswalks, railroad crossings, and school bus stop signs. Similarly, drivers who cause accidents by failing to yield to emergency vehicles are likely to be found negligent. However, drivers of emergency vehicles are not permitted to blatantly disregard traffic controls. Most state statutes require them to sound warnings and proceed with caution through intersections. Police cars are granted limited authority to disregard traffic controls when pursuing criminals, but drivers of police cars must still assess the hazards and exercise proper care based on the situation.

Liability Involving Parked Vehicles

A number of state and local ordinances describe how motorists must legally park vehicles. Usually they must park vehicles within six inches of a curb or within a defined parking space. Generally, parking is prohibited on bridges, within twenty-five feet of an intersection, in a lane of traffic alongside another vehicle (double parked), and in spaces designated "No Parking."

The fact that a motorist illegally parked a car does not necessarily make the motorist liable for accidents involving the illegally parked car. To be liable, the driver of the illegally parked vehicle must have caused or contributed to the accident. The illegal parking must be the proximate cause of the accident. Consider a car that was parked illegally in a fire lane and was struck by an inattentive driver who veered into the fire lane. The driver would not be able to successfully allege negligence against the party who illegally parked the car because the proximate cause of the accident was the driver's own inattention, not the illegally parked car.

However, if the illegal parking of the car is the cause of an accident, then the driver who parked the car is negligent. If, for example, an accident is caused by a car parked in the traveled portion of a busy street just around a "blind" bend in the road, the illegal parking would likely be considered the proximate cause of the accident.

Liability Involving Disabled Vehicles

When a vehicle is parked on the traveled portion of a road, the driver is presumed to have parked the vehicle negligently and therefore has the burden of proving any extenuating circumstances that prevented him or her from parking the vehicle elsewhere.

To establish a viable defense to negligence, the driver must prove that (1) an emergency occurred that caused the vehicle to be parked in the road and (2) the driver used due care in leaving the vehicle. The first criterion involves proving that an event beyond the driver's control occurred and the driver had no viable options other than to abandon the car where it was. Also, the driver would need to prove that no warning signs occurred, such as engine trouble, that he or she ignored.

Examples of emergencies are a car's unexpected stalling in a traffic jam when the car cannot be moved off the road or a car engine's sudden breakdown while the car was crossing a long bridge that has no shoulder. The driver must also prove that after the car was parked, he or she did everything possible to prevent the parked car from being hit, such as turning on emergency flashers or lighting flares and immediately calling the police. As with other illegally parked vehicles, the driver of a disabled vehicle is not automatically liable, but the driver would have the burden of proving that any accident was caused by others' negligence.

Liability Involving Passengers

Nearly 30 percent of auto claimants are passengers.[5] Passengers have specific rights and duties, many of which vary by state. Two situations can occur that might make the passenger liable for an accident or at least liable for some of his or her injuries. First, if a passenger's actions cause the driver to lose control of the vehicle, such as a passenger who turns around and bumps the driver's arms, then the passenger can be held liable. The same holds true if a passenger distracts the driver. These actions not only reduce the liability of the driver for any injuries sustained to a passenger but also can make the passenger liable to third parties.

A more common situation is when the actions of the passenger show a disregard for the passenger's own safety. If a passenger knowingly entrusts his or her safety to an incompetent driver, such as an obviously intoxicated driver, then the passenger might not be able to successfully make claim against the driver for any injuries sustained by the passenger in an accident caused by the incompetent driver. This defense is based on either assumption of risk or comparative negligence, concepts that were discussed in Chapter 5.

Passengers would not be responsible for third-party injuries caused by an incompetent driver. For example, if an intoxicated driver injured people in a car that was in an oncoming lane of traffic, the people in the other car could not successfully allege that the passenger was liable for failing to stop the intoxicated driver from driving. Some courts make an exception to this rule when the passenger is a parent or guardian of a minor driving the car or if the passenger is the owner of the vehicle.

A few inventive claimants have sued passengers who are involved in share-the-expense car pools, arguing that all the parties, including the passengers, are engaged in a "joint venture" with the driver. At least one court has accepted this theory, ruling that the use of one vehicle by two or more persons for any common purpose is a joint venture. Consequently, the parties are jointly and individually liable. The prevailing view is that share-the-expense arrangements are not joint ventures unless the parties have a mutual ownership interest or right of control over the vehicle. Therefore, most share-the-expense arrangements would not be considered a "joint venture."

A few states have **guest statutes.** These statutes require passengers to prove that the driver was more than just ordinarily negligent when the driver is transporting the passengers without payment of any kind. The purpose of these laws is to discourage collusion. Most of the states that had guest statutes have now repealed them, but a few states have retained them in an effort to control litigation.

The Effect of Seat Belt Laws on Auto Liability

Almost every state requires occupants of vehicles to wear seat belts. However studies show that only between 69 and 80 percent of people comply with seat belt laws.[6] Courts vary widely on whether not wearing seat belts is a viable defense. States' positions on the **seat belt defense** fall into the following three categories:

- States that do not recognize nonuse of seat belts as negligence
- States that recognize nonuse of seat belts as negligence but set strict limitations on how this defense reduces recovery
- States that permit defendants to assert negligence against claimants for their nonuse of seat belts if they can prove that seat belts would have prevented or minimized the injuries

Most states do not recognize the failure to use seat belts as a viable defense. However, a number of states allow it to be used as a defense but set strict limitations on how this defense can reduce a claimant's recovery. These states may permit reducing injury damages by a small percentage (typically between 1 and 5 percent of the damages claimed).[7] Considering the subjective nature of general damages in injury cases, the deduction of such small percentages is somewhat illusory because injury claims are not normally precisely valued.

A few states allow defendants to argue that failing to wear seat belts is either comparative negligence or a "failure to mitigate damages." These states still require defendants to prove that wearing the seat belts would have made a difference. If, for example, the driver of a small car was killed when a truck ran over the car while it was stopped at a traffic light, the fact that the driver of the small car was not wearing a seat belt probably made no difference. The driver would have died either way. However, if a person who was not wearing a seat belt was involved in a moderate-impact accident and the claimant's head went through the windshield, then the defendant might successfully argue that the head injuries could have been prevented by the use of seat belts. Expert witnesses are usually required to show what effect the nonuse of seat belts had on the claimant's injuries.

Similar issues apply with motorcyclists who are injured while not wearing helmets. A few states permit defendants to raise this as a defense, but most do not.

Pedestrians and Bicyclists—Rights and Duties

About 5 percent of auto liability claims involve pedestrians, bicyclists, or motorcyclists.[8] Pedestrians have the right-of-way when walking on sidewalks or crossing in a crosswalk when they have a green light. Pedestrians have a right to assume that motorists will obey the law, but pedestrians are expected to exercise reasonable care for their own safety and should not walk carelessly into traffic as soon as a light turns green.

When crossing streets that have no pedestrian traffic controls, pedestrians have a greater duty to exercise care. Many statutes require pedestrians to cross at street corners rather than jaywalking between intersections. Pedestrians at uncontrolled intersections should anticipate danger and look for vehicles in all directions. A large percentage of pedestrian accidents involve children darting out from behind parked cars. Even though the children are at fault for these accidents, juries are often sympathetic to children and are known to look for ways to assess some degree of liability on the driver in order to justify a payment to the injured child. This is especially true if the driver observed children playing in the area and failed to foresee children running into the street.

Bicyclists have the same duty as motorists to obey traffic controls and the rules of the road when they travel on roadways. Even bicyclists who are minors are required to observe the rules of the road.[9] When bicyclists are on sidewalks or in crosswalks, they have the same rights as pedestrians.[10] Auto-bicycle accidents have become so common that a number of experts specialize in analyzing them.

Commercial Vehicles

Drivers of commercial vehicles may have additional or different duties from those of private passenger vehicles. Commercial vehicles may be governed by state statutes or federal Department of Transportation (DOT) regulations through the Federal Motor Carrier Safety Administration (FMCSA). The following are examples of differences in laws that may govern commercial drivers:

- Lower speed limits for larger commercial vehicles
- Prohibited use of some streets and tunnels
- Restricted lengths of time a commercial driver can drive without a break
- Specific limits on how much weight they may carry

Statutes forbid loading commercial vehicles in such a way that their contents may be scattered or dropped on streets. In addition, vehicles projecting materials require flags in the daytime or lights at night that clearly identify the projections. Commercial vehicles must also indicate when they are carrying wide loads, hazardous materials, or flammable materials.

VICARIOUS LIABILITY IN AUTO CLAIMS

Claim representatives sometimes encounter situations in which someone, in addition to the driver of the vehicle, is legally liable for an auto accident involving the vehicle. Ordinarily, the owner of a motor vehicle is not responsible for the negligence of someone else using the vehicle; however, a few exceptions exist. Exceptions are made when the person using the vehicle is working or performing an errand on behalf of the owner (is acting as the owner's agent) or when state statutes hold owners legally liable for damage caused by people driving their vehicles. Under the family purpose doctrine still used in a few states, minor children are presumed to be performing errands on behalf of their parents when driving the family vehicle.

Vicarious Liability of Vehicle Owners

In the vast majority of states, the owner is liable only when the driver is an agent of the owner, such as when an employee is driving on behalf of an employer or a child is performing an errand for a parent. A few states impose liability on the owner of a vehicle when the owner's vehicle causes an accident, as long as the vehicle is driven with the owner's consent. The extent of this vicarious liability varies by state. Some states presume that the driver is an agent of the owner, and the owner would have to prove that this was not true in order to escape liability. A few states set monetary limits on the amount for which the owner can be held liable.

Negligent Entrustment of Auto

The claim of **negligent entrustment of an automobile**, while not new in terms of the law, has increased in recent years. Negligent entrustment of an automobile occurs when the owner permits an incompetent person to drive the car. The driver might be incompetent because of age, intoxication, or some mental infirmity.

In one case,[11] a person gave the car keys to a fourteen-year-old friend who was told only to listen to the radio and run the heater while waiting during a work break. Instead, the fourteen-year-old took the car for a joyride and was involved in an accident. The court ruled that this was negligent entrustment, arguing that, based on previous actions of the teenager, the owner should have foreseen that the teenager might take the car on public roads and that she might drive negligently.

One all-too-common example of negligent entrustment is when an owner entrusts a motor vehicle to a driver whom he knows or suspects is intoxicated. The person who entrusts the vehicle to such a person could be liable to third parties who are injured by the intoxicated driver. Courts are aware of the political side of this issue and point to "fundamental fairness and morality" as well as public policy issues in holding car owners liable for accidents caused by drunk drivers using their cars.[12]

PERSONAL INJURY PROTECTION (PIP) AND LIMITED-TORT LAWS

As mentioned in Chapter 10, one of the most significant tort reforms has been the introduction of personal injury protection (PIP) "no-fault" statutes that help to reduce litigation by preventing lawsuits for less serious automobile-related bodily injury claims. In addition to this reform, a number of states have enacted legislation that limits what noneconomic damages claimants can collect for less serious injuries. In both PIP or limited-tort states, noneconomic general damages such as pain and suffering are permitted only for serious injury claims. The definition of a "serious injury" varies by state.

Under traditional PIP plans, insurance consumers were not offered a choice of full tort (which permits claims for noneconomic damages for all) or limited tort (which restricts noneconomic damage). Responding to consumer requests and constitutional concerns about limiting the rights to sue, a number of states implemented laws that permit insurance buyers to choose whether they want full tort or limited tort at the time they purchase their insurance. For a significantly reduced premium, people can purchase the limited-tort option, which means that their recovery is limited to only economic losses such as medical expenses and wage loss for less serious injuries. Under both PIP and limited-tort laws, recovery for noneconomic losses, such as pain and suffering, is allowed for injuries that qualify as "serious injuries." The purpose of both PIP and limited-tort plans is to reduce litigation on less serious injury claims.

Thresholds for Exempting Tort Claims

In general, under PIP or limited tort statutes, a claimant cannot sue the wrong-doer unless a specified **threshold** has been exceeded. Two types of thresholds exist in PIP statutes: verbal and monetary. Exhibit 11-1 shows a table describing various verbal and monetary thresholds in PIP and limited-tort states.

EXHIBIT 11-1		

Examples of Thresholds in Select States Having Tort Exemptions[13]

State	Threshold	PIP or Limited-Tort Law
KS	Recovery for noneconomic losses is permitted when "reasonable and necessary medical expenses exceed $2,000 or if there is permanent injury, fracture of a weight-bearing bone, or permanent disfigurement."	PIP
MI	Recovery for noneconomic losses is permitted when the injured person has suffered death or serious impairment of a body function.	PIP
MN	Accident victims cannot assert a claim for noneconomic damages unless they meet one of the statutory thresholds: (1) an injury resulting in death; (2) a permanent injury or disfigurement; (3) a disability for sixty days or more; or (4) more than $4,000 in medical expenses.	PIP
NJ	Recovery of noneconomic losses is restricted to specific types of injuries: death; dismemberment; significant disfigurement; a fracture; loss of a fetus; permanent loss of use of a body function or system; a medically determined injury or impairment of a nonpermanent nature that prevents the person from performing substantially all of the material acts that constitute that person's usual customary daily activities for not less than 90 days during the 180 days immediately following the occurrence of the injury or impairment.	Limited tort
PA	A "serious injury" is a personal injury resulting in death, serious impairment of a body function, or permanent serious disfigurement.	Limited tort

Verbal thresholds permit claimants to sue only when injuries "qualify" as serious injuries. The exact wording varies by state, but permanent injuries are always exempted from limitations, and therefore claimants suffering permanent injuries are entitled to sue tortfeasors for their loss.

Some PIP states, in addition to having verbal thresholds, have a **monetary threshold** that allows claimants to sue tortfeasors when medical expenses have exceeded a specified dollar amount. These thresholds are seen as less restrictive than the pure verbal thresholds. The idea behind monetary thresholds is that the amount of medical expenses is an indicator of the seriousness of the injury. Therefore, if a claimant incurs medical expenses greater than the threshold amount, the claimant is entitled to sue the tortfeasor. The amount of the threshold varies by state from $2,000 to $50,000.

Critics of monetary thresholds argue that low monetary thresholds only encourage buildup of medical expenses by claimants until they exceed the threshold amount.

Benefits Provided Under PIP

Personal injury protection (PIP) plans provide for various types of economic loss. The categories of benefits provided vary slightly by state, but in general they provide five types of benefits:

- Medical and rehabilitation expense
- Wage loss
- Replacement services
- Death benefits to survivors
- Funeral expenses

States with PIP laws establish minimum amounts of medical expense and wage loss benefits that insureds must purchase. These minimums vary dramatically. Colorado, for example, has one of the most generous benefits, providing medical expense benefits for up to $50,000, plus an additional $50,000 for rehabilitation, and up to fifty-two weeks of wage loss. Many PIP states permit insureds to purchase higher than state minimum PIP limits, which may be as low as $2,500.

Medical expense benefits under PIP plans include medical treatments, surgical or dental treatment, nursing services, rehabilitation expenses, prosthetic devices, and prescriptions. Most states also permit chiropractic expenses, and a few states include expenses related to religious healing.

Replacement services benefits provide for the necessary, reasonable expenses of hiring help to provide essential services such as cooking, cleaning, shopping, and laundering while a person is unable to perform those duties.

Death benefits to survivors pay up to a specified limit for the income loss incurred by a survivor of a person killed in an auto accident.

Some claims that involve these benefits exceed PIP thresholds, so insureds or survivors may also have the option to sue defendants for general damages, too, when the defendants are liable.

Claim Administration and Subrogation Under PIP

Under PIP laws, claims are paid to the injured party by his or her own insurance carrier. This is fairly simple compared to full-tort liability claims. Some claims can be "sleepers" in that they initially appear to be minor claims that will not exceed the threshold but eventually turn into more serious, full-tort claims. This situation is especially common in states having monetary thresholds.

The subrogation rights of insurers who pay PIP claims vary by state. A number of states permit insurers to collect from the tortfeasor or tortfeasor's insurance carrier when the threshold has been exceeded. Generally, subrogation is not permitted when the PIP benefits paid to the injured insured do not exceed the threshold.

Claims can also be complicated when a person from a PIP state travels to, and is injured in, a full-tort state. In such situations, the insured is usually still permitted to collect PIP benefits because he or she paid a premium for them. State laws often prevent subrogation of those payments of PIP benefits in full-tort states because they may be seen as "assignments" of bodily injury claims. Chapter 2 explains the issues surrounding assignments of medical payments claims.

For claims involving insureds from full-tort states traveling in PIP states, the "Other States" provision in auto policies gives insureds basic PIP protection based on the laws of the PIP state.

AUTO LIABILITY CLAIM INVESTIGATIONS

Having confirmed coverage, claim representatives can gather evidence and begin to assess liability.

Unlike product liability claims or general liability claims that can involve complex legal issues, the vast majority of auto liability claims involve simple legal issues, based on basic rules of the road. The challenge in auto liability claims is generally not in determining, for example, whether speeding or running a stop light constitutes negligence, but instead in determining which party ran the red light and how fast the parties were going. In other words, the factual investigation is usually the heart of auto liability claim practices.

Auto investigations can be as simple as phone interviews with insureds or as complex as investigations involving evidence gathered by accident reconstruction experts. Statements and police reports are the most common types of evidence gathered in auto liability claims. Claim representatives take statements from insureds, claimants, and witnesses. The usefulness of police reports in the liability investigation depends on the extent of the police report. Some police reports are detailed and include descriptions of accident scenes, diagrams of accidents, and summaries of statements of witnesses. Other police reports are perfunctory and list barely more than the names of the parties involved and the location of the accident.

To help understand the accident, it is advisable for claim representatives to draw a diagram of the accident scene. For in-person interviews, it is advisable for insureds, claimants, or other witnesses to draw their own diagrams and then sign them so that they can be included as evidence in the claim file. Exhibit 11-3 at the end of this chapter shows a sample diagram of an auto accident drawn by a police officer as part of the officer's accident investigation.

Diagrams are demonstrative evidence designed to help people understand what happened and should show the following:

- The position and course of the vehicles before impact
- The lines and lanes on the road
- Any obstructions to the view of drivers
- Traffic controls
- Hills and turns
- Position and direction of the vehicles at impact
- Position and direction of where the vehicles (or bodies) came to rest
- Location of any witnesses
- Length and distance of skid marks or gouges in the road

When investigating auto accidents, claim representatives must target questions to gather facts that would help to determine liability and assess the nature and extent of the damages claimed.

Chapter 7 discussed the basics of statements and the admissibility of statements and police reports. In today's claim environment, a majority of auto liability claims are concluded by claim representatives taking recorded telephone statements and obtaining police reports. Appendix item 11-A at the end of this chapter shows an auto accident statement guideline.

In investigating auto liability claims, claim representatives should think about the time of day, where the drivers were coming from, and where they were going. These are all items that should be covered in the statements. Drivers entering busy streets from side roads or waiting to make left turns at busy intersections often lose patience and take risks. Traffic intersections that have no green turn arrows are another common source of driver frustration, especially when the driver is in a hurry.

These examples illustrate why it is important for claim representatives to find out the circumstances leading up to the accident. Determining that a person was driving to work and was late could establish a motive for the driver to be in a hurry. Motives can be important because the facts of auto accidents are commonly disputed. For example, two parties are involved in an intersection accident and each party claims to have had the green light. If one party admits to being late for work and the other party had no similar time pressure, then barring other evidence to the contrary, juries are likely to believe that the party who was late for work was "rushing to beat the light."

Proximate Cause and Auto Liability

Determining whether an insured's actions were the proximate cause of an accident can sometimes be challenging. Consider, for example, a person who drives a car at an excessive speed and runs into a strip mall building. The impact directly causes damage to the building. If the retailers in the building cannot conduct business while repairs to the building are being made, they will likely have a loss of income. The proximate cause of the building damage and the income loss is the auto accident because such a loss would be reasonably foreseeable. If drivers passing by gaze at the accident scene and consequently cause accidents on the passing road, the proximate cause of the other accidents is not the original strip mall accident but is instead the inattention of the passing driver.

Consider the case of Allen, who collides with the rear of Katy's car and injures her. His failure to maintain control of his vehicle is the cause of her injuries. If Katy is taken to the hospital and treated with penicillin and she has a severe allergic reaction, then Allen would be responsible for this allergic reaction because it was a natural part of a foreseeable treatment. The allergic reaction is part of an unbroken chain of events stemming from Allen's accident with Katy. Katy would not have received the penicillin if not for the auto accident. If, after being released from the hospital, Katy walks home and trips on a crack in the sidewalk, Allen would not be responsible for any injuries related to the slip-and-fall accident because it is an intervening act. Courts look at two issues in determining causation: foreseeability and intervening acts. The damages caused must be foreseeable by a reasonable person, and no intervening act must occur between the original act of negligence and the ultimate damages to the claimant.

One doctrine sometimes used in auto accidents is the **last clear chance doctrine.** This doctrine states that if the defendant fails to take advantage of a clear opportunity to avoid the injury-causing event, then the defendant is liable, even if the claimant acted negligently before this last clear chance occurred. Consider a driver, Chris, who is waiting to make a left turn at a busy intersection. While the traffic slows, she pulls out into the intersection waiting for traffic to clear. The light turns red while she is waiting in the intersection. A second driver, who now has a green light, sees Chris's car blocking his path. The second driver has a clear chance to avoid hitting the vehicle blocking his lane of traffic and is not permitted to seize upon this opportunity and run into her. This is true even if Chris was negligent in entering the intersection and was blocking traffic, because the second driver had the last clear chance to avoid the accident. Consequently, he must allow Chris to extricate herself from the situation.

Historically, the last clear chance doctrine was used to avoid recovery in states that followed contributory negligence principles. Today, most states have comparative negligence laws, so this doctrine is not applied as commonly. However, the same arguments would be used to show comparative negligence against a party who failed to take an opportunity to avoid an accident.

Some defendants have successfully argued that their accidents were unavoidable. The most likely situation for the **unavoidable accident defense** to succeed would be when the driver suffers a sudden and unexpected stroke or heart attack. Drivers in these situations might be asked to prove that they had no prior warning signs that would have alerted them to the possibility of a stroke or heart attack. If such a driver is under treatment for a heart condition, he or she might not be able to use this defense. Occasionally, defendants can prove that the circumstances were such that they could not have done anything to prevent their accidents. In one case, a driver successfully proved that an overpass obstructed his view of a stopped car and created an unavoidable accident.[14] This angle of the unavoidable accident defense is difficult to prove, because laws require drivers to maintain an appropriate lookout and keep their vehicles under control.

Road defects relate to the improper design, maintenance, or construction of the road. Sometimes these defects cause or contribute to an accident. As mentioned in Chapter 5, states and municipalities vary in how governmental immunity applies to road work. Usually the governmental entity is liable once it receives notice of a problem and fails to correct it. Sometimes the immunity is waived only to the extent of liability insurance coverage. For serious accidents involving road defects, claim representatives should ask the government entity for its road maintenance schedules and record of letters or calls complaining of road problems, in order to determine whether the government entity knew of the problem.

The Use of Experts in Auto Liability Claims

An expert is a skilled, experienced, and educated person who has special knowledge. Experts used in auto accidents include doctors who perform independent medical examinations, mechanics who can determine what parts failed, specially trained police officers who can perform scene investigations, and engineers who can perform accident reconstructions.

Engineers who piece together evidence that helps determine what happened to cause an accident are known as forensic engineers. A **forensic engineer** can examine the vehicles, the skid marks on the pavement, and other physical evidence and then make calculations regarding the speed and position of the vehicles at impact. Forensic engineers can be helpful in determining, for example, which party crossed over the center line in a head-on collision.

About 20 percent of auto accidents reported to the police involve low-speed, rear-end accidents. Unfortunately, claims arising from these types of minor accidents lead to a disproportionate share of injury claims and litigation. In response, a newly developed field of expertise combining accident reconstruction, physics, biomechanics, and computer modeling has developed. Experts in this field can help determine the likely effect a given auto impact would have on the body of an occupant in a vehicle. **Biomechanics** is the science of determining how various forces affect the body. Biomechanics has the following three components, which may be used to analyze any type of injury claim from a slip-and-fall claim to an auto accident:

1.   The physical workings of the human body
2.   The design and materials of the human body (bones, joints, and tissue)
3.   The effect of outside forces on the body and its parts[15]

Experts in low-speed auto accident analysis have successfully proved that occupants in a vehicle could not have sustained the injuries claimed based on the speed of their vehicle, the impact to all vehicles in the accident, and the effect (or lack of effect) these impacts had on the occupants. This type of analysis can be expensive and is usually reserved for defending against claims by multiple parties who are alleging significant injuries from a minor impact (often less than five miles per hour).

Experts are sometimes used to establish that an auto part was defective and that the defective part contributed to the accident. Seat belts, brakes, air bags, and tires are the most common sources of auto defect allegations.

Evidence in Auto Liability Claims

In evaluating liability and damages, claim representatives may need to consider a wide variety of evidence, depending on the claim. Because auto liability claim representatives usually handle a large number of claims, they must learn what evidence is critical for a given claim. Learning how to properly set the scope of an auto liability investigation is important. Exhibit 11-2 lists the categories of evidence that might be used in determining liability in auto claims. Simple auto liability claims may require only two or three different types of evidence.

EXHIBIT 11-2

List of Evidence Used in Determining Auto Liability

A. Statements (or testimony)
   1. Statement of insured
   2. Statement of adverse driver
   3. Statements of passengers
   4. Statements of other witnesses
   5. Negative statements from people confirming that they did not see anything or were not injured in an accident

B. Documentary evidence
   1. Police reports
   2. Photographs of the accident scene
   3. Photographs of damaged vehicles
   4. Traffic court proceedings (especially guilty pleas)
   5. Weather reports
   6. Transit authority reports (if taxicabs or buses are involved)
   7. Newspaper accounts and photographs

C. Demonstrative evidence
   1. Diagrams of accident scene
   2. Videos of traffic light sequence

D. Physical (real) evidence
   1. A blown tire
   2. A defective auto part

E. Expert reports
   1. Accident reconstruction report
   2. Mechanic's report
   3. Biomechanical engineer's report

The categories are listed in order of those most commonly used and usually most critical in auto liability investigations. This list includes just evidence used for determining liability. As described in Chapters 7 and 8, other evidence, such as medical reports and wage loss statements, must be obtained to evaluate and value damages.

CASE STUDY—THE AUTO LIABILITY ACCIDENT

This chapter concludes with the following auto liability claim that presents several challenging issues. This case study requires readers to understand and apply information covered in this chapter and presented in Chapters 1, 2, 5, 6, and 7 of this text. Auto liability claim representatives should be able to handle auto liability claims with similar issues. Readers are encouraged to analyze the claim representatives' actions in this case and judge how well they handle their claims.

Twenty-Two Tattoos

Tom Schmidt and Lenny Roberts were looking forward to the weekend. Townsville was having its annual Oktoberfest with polka bands, soccer tournaments, and other recreational activities. The local restaurants and taverns participated by preparing special food, hiring bands, and selling buckets of beer. On Saturday night, the streets of Townsville would be filled with revelers.

Tom and Lenny borrowed a car from Tom's parents and drove to the downtown area (about a twenty-minute drive down the interstate) where the Oktoberfest celebration was going to take place. At about 7:30 P.M., they bought dinner from a street vendor and began drinking buckets of beer. The streets began to swell with celebrants. Tom and Lenny met up with some friends from high school, and they all decided to "get tattooed on the loop." The loop featured four blocks of twenty-two restaurants and taverns, and during Oktoberfest each had its own unique drink and "tattoo" (ink stamp made specially for the event). When a person bought a drink, the waiter, waitress, or bartender tattooed the person (if he or she wanted). The object of "doing the loop" was to get as many tattoos as possible by getting a drink at each establishment. It was a legendary accomplishment to make it through all twenty-two places. Tom and Lenny had set their sights on attaining that dubious distinction.

As the evening turned to early morning, Tom and Lenny and a few die-hard stragglers were still in pursuit of the twenty-two tattoos. As they approached the Bad Dog Café, the twenty-second establishment, Tom was having difficulty walking. When Tom entered the Bad Dog Café, he could barely ask for a beer and a tattoo. The bartender was reluctant to serve him, but Lenny and some of the others convinced him to sell Tom the beer to complete his quest. The bartender agreed, and Lenny had to help Tom drink the beer.

After the Bad Dog Café, Tom and Lenny headed for the car. Although Lenny had been drinking heavily, too, he seemed to be in better shape than Tom, so he took the keys from Tom's coat pocket. Lenny poured Tom into the back seat and headed for home. After Lenny had traveled on the interstate for about ten minutes, the effects of fatigue and alcohol caused him to get sleepy. He quickly pulled the car over to the right, turned off the engine, turned on the emergency flashers, and fell asleep. This took place at approximately 2:00 A.M. At 2:10 A.M., their car was struck in the rear by a small two-door car driven by Cassandra Holloway.

Cassandra's car hit the rear of Tom's parents' car and spun out of control down the interstate. It ended up across the right and middle lanes of the interstate. Fortunately, the cars following Cassandra were able to avoid hitting her by moving into the far left lane of traffic. Tom's parents' car was forced down a hill. See Exhibit 11-3 showing the police officer's diagram of the accident.

Both Tom and Lenny sustained minor back and neck injuries. Lenny also suffered an injury to his jaw. Cassandra Holloway suffered fractures to her arm and shoulder and also a concussion. She lost consciousness temporarily and was still disoriented when the emergency medical team arrived. All three parties were taken to the hospital by ambulance.

Insurance Coverages

Cassandra's insurance policy had lapsed, so she was uninsured at the time of the accident.

Tom was twenty-one years old and lived at home with his parents. Tom's parents owned two cars. The vehicles were insured by Premium Insurance Company for $100,000 single limit liability coverage; $100,000 single limit of uninsured motorists (UM) coverage; and $5,000 medical payments coverage.

Lenny was twenty-two and lived at home with his parents. They owned two cars insured with Conglomerate Insurance. Both cars were insured for the state minimum of $25,000 liability insurance and $25,000 uninsured motorists (UM) coverage. They also had $2,000 medical payments coverage.

Patty Hampshire was assigned the claim at Premium Insurance, and Nathan Parker was the claim representative for Conglomerate.

The Liability Investigation

Both Patty and Nathan took statements from Tom and Lenny. Cassandra Holloway was still in the hospital and unavailable to give a statement. Tom remembered nothing about the accident. His statements to Patty and Nathan were brief and mainly related to the festivities that took place before midnight. Patty was able to obtain from Tom the names and phone numbers of some of the other people who were "doing the loop" with Tom and Lenny.

Lenny's version of the evening was that he and Tom had gone to the Oktoberfest to eat, drink, and join in the festivities. Lenny stated that as they were leaving, Tom decided that he didn't feel up to driving, so he gave Lenny the keys. Lenny did his best to drive home but started to feel sleepy, so he did the prudent thing and pulled off to the side of the road. He claimed that he turned on the emergency flashers and went to sleep. The next thing he remembered was waking up after the car was struck in the rear by Cassandra Holloway.

Based on Lenny's statement to the police and the officer's scene investigation, the police cited Cassandra for "driving too fast" and "inattention." The police indicated that she was unable to provide insurance information.

Exhibit 11-3 shows the police officer's diagram of the accident.

EXHIBIT 11-3

Excerpt From Police Report

Police Report

Accident Date: 10-17-2000	Accident Time: 2:10 A.M.
Location: I-999	Townsville
Speed limit: 60 mph	Weather Conditions: Clear

C O D E S	Injury	Safety Devices
	1. Fatal	1. None used
	2. Disabling	2. Seat Belt
	3. Evident - Not disabling	3. Air Bag
	4. None apparent	4. Child Restraint

Name	Date of Birth	Injury	Safety Devices	Vehicle
Cassandra Holloway	6-7-57	2	2	1
Tom Schmidt	9-9-79	2	1	2
Leonard Roberts	10-1-78	2	2	2

Probable Contributing Circumstances:

V1	V2	
❑	❑	Vehicle Defect
☒	❑	Speeding
❑	❑	Signal Violation
❑	❑	Improper Turn
❑	❑	Drinking
❑	❑	Drugs
❑	❑	Wrong Way
❑	❑	Failed To Yield
☒	❑	Improper Lane Use
❑	❑	Improper Passing
❑	❑	Following Too Closely
☒	❑	Inattention

Diagram of Accident:

Interstate 999

North ➤➤

Officer's Statement:

Driver #1 (Cassandra Holloway) was traveling north on I-999 when her vehicle (Vehicle #1) struck the rear of Vehicle #2, which was parked on the shoulder of I-999. According to Driver #2 (Leonard Roberts), he had pulled off the interstate because he felt tired and wanted to rest before continuing. While the driver was resting, Vehicle #2 was struck in the rear by Vehicle #1, forcing Vehicle #2 off the shoulder and down an embankment. The passenger, Tom Schmidt, was resting in the back seat of the vehicle at the time of the accident. Driver #1 was disoriented after the accident and could not give a statement. All three individuals were taken by ambulance to Townsville Memorial Hospital for treatment.

Analyzing the Loss Exposures

Patty and Nathan confirmed that Cassandra was uninsured. In setting reserves, Patty and Nathan had to determine the various potential claims and the coverages that apply to them. Conglomerate Insurance had just gone through a major reorganization of its claim department, which had centralized Conglomerate's claim operations. Consequently, Nathan was now required to handle four new states, and he was unfamiliar with the state where this accident occurred. Nathan knew that state laws affect coverage, so he talked with his supervisor, Amelia Rhodes, to find out what coverage differences might exist in this state.

Nathan: Hi, Amelia. Hope you don't mind my bothering you right now, but I've got a fairly serious uninsured motorists claim, and I need to set reserves on it today. With my new territorial assignments, I'm still learning this state's laws. We've got a situation in which our insured was in, actually he was driving, another person's car, and I want to find out how uninsured motorists coverage applies in this state. I am hoping you can help me find out. (Nathan hands the loss notice to Amelia.)

Amelia (Looking over the loss notice): Oh, yes, I'm glad you asked. This state allows stacking of uninsured motorists coverage. Lenny Roberts is insured under two autos with us, so he would have up to $50,000 uninsured motorists coverage. I have a folder of information we just put together about several states. (Amelia pages through a folder.) We are getting ready to put all of this information on our company intranet site, so I have it all right here ready to go. Oh, yes, uninsured motorists coverages stack, and here's another thing—our uninsured motorists coverage is NOT excess; we have to apply it by equal shares with Other Insurance. I assume the car he was riding in has UM coverage.

> Note: See Chapter 2 for a discussion on why the Other Insurance provision of the Uninsured Motorists Coverage varies by state.

Nathan: Yes, UM and Med Pay, too. So let me get this straight—we are going to have to pay half of this uninsured motorists claim from dollar one up to the limits of both UM coverages stacked?

Amelia: Yes. We could end up paying as much as $50,000. How much insurance does the other party have on the car that Mr. Roberts was driving?

Nathan: I'm not sure how much coverage Premium has on this. I'll have to call their claim rep. and find out. Anything else?

Amelia: Yeah, this state does allow offsets for payments made under the Med Pay coverage to apply to the UM claim. But let's not get confused here; our Med Pay coverage would apply only on an excess basis over the Med Pay coverage on the vehicle he was in.

Nathan: Right, the Med Pay coverage applies on an excess basis, just like the policy reads, but we are going to pay half of the uninsured motorists claim because of the state's interpretation of the UM coverage. OK, I think I've got it now.

Amelia: And so does the liability coverage, too. We would be excess over the limits on the car he was driving.

To help better understand the standard policy wording relating to other insurance, the following excerpt from the Other Insurance provision in the Part A–Liability Coverage of the personal auto policy (PAP) is provided. This provision describes how other insurance normally applies when there is no law to contravene the policy.

OTHER INSURANCE

If there is other applicable liability insurance we will pay only our share of the loss. Our share is the proportion that our limit of liability bears to the total of all applicable limits. However, any insurance we provide for a vehicle you do not own shall be excess over any other collectible insurance.

In this claim, three of Conglomerate's and Premium's coverages apply: Part C–Uninsured Motorists, Part B–Medical Payments, and Part A–Liability coverage. The law in the state where this accident occurred requires both insurance companies to share equally in the Uninsured Motorists claim even though standard policy language does not support that. The law does not affect the Part B–Medical Payments coverage or the Part A–Liability coverage. Conglomerate's Medical Payments and Liability coverage is excess over Premium's.

Nathan returned to his office to set the reserves. Across town at Premium Insurance, Patty Hampshire was going through the same analysis. Both Tom and Lenny are "insureds" under their own parents' policy because they reside with their parents. To Patty and Nathan's knowledge, Lenny was a permissive user of Tom's parents' car or, more accurately, Lenny had a "reasonable belief" that he was entitled to drive the car, which makes him an insured under Tom's parents' policy for that car.

As occupants in Tom's parents' car, both Tom and Lenny are entitled to Medical Payments coverage and Uninsured Motorists Coverage provided by Premium Insurance Company. The state law permits UM coverage limits to be stacked. This gives Tom up to $200,000 (2 × $100,000) in UM coverage.

Lenny is covered under Premium Insurance Company's policy for up to $5,000 medical payments (Med Pay) and $100,000 uninsured motorists coverage because he was an occupant of Tom's parents' car. He is also covered under his own parents' policy with Conglomerate for $2,000 Med Pay (on an excess basis) and $50,000 uninsured motorists coverage. The state requires Conglomerate to pay equal shares (in this case, half) of the uninsured motorist claim for Lenny. This is an exception to the general rule that the primary insurance "follows the vehicle." The Med Pay coverage follows the rule and applies only on an excess basis over other Med Pay coverage. Claim representatives need to be aware of these types of coverage exceptions based on state law.

Exhibit 11-4 summarizes how insurance coverages would apply to Lenny's and Tom's claims.

EXHIBIT 11-4

Summary of Coverage Applications to Lenny's and Tom's BI Claims

Lenny Roberts's Injury Claim		Tom Schmidt's Injury Claim	
Insurer	**Coverage**	**Insurer**	**Coverage**
Premium Ins. Co.	Up to $5,000 primary coverage for Med Pay	Premium Ins. Co.	Up to $5,000 primary coverage for Med Pay
Premium Ins. Co.	One-half of UM up to $100,000 limit	Premium Ins. Co.	Up to $200,000 coverage (two UM limits stacked)
		Premium Ins. Co.	Up to $100,000 liability insurance
Conglomerate Ins. Co.	Up to $2,000 Med Pay coverage (on an excess basis)		
Conglomerate Ins. Co.	One-half of UM claim up to $50,000 (two UM coverage limits stacked)		
		Conglomerate Ins. Co.	Up to $25,000 liability coverage (on an excess basis)

Cassandra's Claim

After leaving the hospital, Cassandra Holloway retained an attorney. She alleged that Tom's parents' car was parked illegally and was at least partially in her lane of traffic. Because she was coming over the crest of a hill, she did not see the vehicle until it was too late. She also alleged that the vehicle did not have its emergency flashers on at the time of the accident.

Nathan was also beginning to question his insured's version. The diagram in the police report seemed to be inaccurate, and recent information made Lenny seem less credible. After Nathan obtained (with proper authorization) Lenny's medical records to document his UM claim, Nathan saw the results of a blood test the hospital had performed while he was in the emergency room. The test indicated that Lenny had a blood alcohol level of .22, more than twice the legal limit, at the time of the accident. This wouldn't have any liability significance if the car had truly been parked as Lenny described, but Nathan was beginning to wonder how well Lenny had parked the car.

Nathan discussed his concerns with his supervisor, Amelia. Nathan explained the UM claim potential, and they agreed to have the forensic engineer do an accident reconstruction. They obtained permission from all parties to examine the two vehicles. The engineer would also go to the accident scene.

Cassandra incurred more than $25,000 in medical expenses and was expected to lose about two months of wages. Her annual salary was $40,000. Her total injury claim has a value of around $80,000 (unadjusted for liability factors), and her $5,000 car was a total loss.

Lenny's Injuries and Damages

Lenny's injury diagnosis was for temporomandibular joint syndrome (TMJ). This is normally a lingering injury with treatment that is expected to last about six months. It requires Lenny to wear a corrective device to help re-establish proper alignment of his jaw. Lenny was also treated by a chiropractor for a soft tissue injury to his neck and back. In the venue where this accident took place, Lenny's total injury claim has a value of around $30,000 (unadjusted for liability factors). This includes his $4,500 in past and future medical expenses.

Patty called Nathan to discuss how the two insurers could settle Lenny's uninsured motorist claim.

Patty: Hi, Nathan. This is Patty Hampshire from Premium Insurance. I'm calling you back about the Lenny Roberts UM claim. I guess you've received the same information from Mr. Roberts as I have. I was going to see whether we could conclude his uninsured motorist claim. He has lowered his demand to $30,000 plus his $4,500 medical expense claim, and that seems reasonable to me. What do you think?

Nathan: Oh, yes. I have all the reports and paperwork on this, too. I think his overall claim value is probably around $30,000, too, but. . . .

Patty: OK, since he's your real insured, do you mind taking the lead on this, and we'll chip in $15,000?

Nathan: Hold on a second. I was going to say, I'm not convinced yet that Lenny is free of liability for this accident. Cassandra Holloway is alleging that he was not parked on the shoulder, and we're still investigating that. I think there might be something to her story. As you know, we're having a forensic engineer do an accident reconstruction on this.

Patty: I don't know why you want to open that can of worms. The police report was pretty clear. I hope you're wrong. If he's partially liable for this, then this claim is going to get really complicated.

Nathan: Well, if we have a liability exposure, we ought to address it now rather than later.

Patty: That sounds nice, but as I'm sure you realize, we would likely end up paying any liability claim against your Mr. Roberts because he was driving our car and we're primary on the liability coverage. So if you prove that Lenny was liable, it would just reduce his uninsured motorist claim. I doubt that your insured would be too happy about it.

Nathan: Let's find out what the engineer says. Our job is to call it the way it is.

Let's see what the accident reconstruction report shows and then let the chips fall where they may.

Patty: That's easy for you to say. Let me know when you get the report. I'll talk to you later.

The Uninsured Motorists Coverage pays for compensatory damages that an insured is legally entitled to recover from the owner or operator of an uninsured motor vehicle. If the facts proved that Lenny and not Cassandra was liable for the accident, then Lenny would have no uninsured motorist claim. If Lenny was partially liable, his uninsured motorist claim would also be reduced. If the facts indicate that Lenny is liable, then Conglomerate might have to pay Cassandra for her damages, but, as Patty stated, Cassandra's claim would not affect Conglomerate unless her claim exceeds Premium's $100,000 limit.

Because Nathan had learned about Lenny's blood alcohol content from a lab report he had obtained using an authorization Lenny specifically gave to Conglomerate Insurance Company, Nathan did not share this information with Patty. Patty had some information about Lenny's drinking based on Tom's statement to her. She decided to contact Tom's and Lenny's friends to find out more about the drinking that had taken place and whether there was any possibility of getting one or more of the drinking establishments to contribute some settlement money to this claim.

The Accident Reconstruction Expert

The engineer that Conglomerate hired examined both of the vehicles in the accident. He went to the scene, and the skid marks on the highway and ruts in the embankment next to the road were still visible. The engineer made two findings. First, the position of the vehicles and the angle of the impact indicated in the police report were inaccurate. The engineer explained that in order for Tom's parents' car to take the course it did after the impact, it would have to have been turned slightly toward the embankment. More importantly, the engineer concluded from the angle of impact, the skid marks, and the place where Cassandra's car came to rest that Tom's parents' car would have to have protruded between eighteen inches and three feet into the right lane of the interstate. This confirmed Cassandra's claim to some extent. However, the engineer was able to determine, by examining the light bulb filaments of the emergency flashers, that the flashers were on at the time of the impact. Based on the skid marks and the impact to the vehicles, the engineer estimated Cassandra's speed to be somewhere between seventy and eighty miles per hour. The speed limit at this location of the interstate is only sixty miles per hour.

Exhibit 11-5 shows the engineer's diagram of the accident.

The engineer's determination about the angle of impact differs from that in the police report. This is no reflection on the competence of the police officer who did the report. Police officers have a number of other responsibilities, and the officer drew the diagram based on the information that he had time to investigate.

EXHIBIT 11-5

Engineer's Accident Reconstruction Diagram

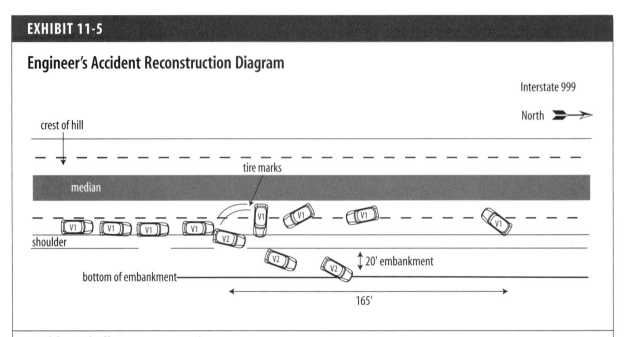

Accident Findings

The above diagram depicts with reasonable certainty how the accident occurred. This information was derived from the physical evidence of the vehicles and the physical evidence at the scene of the accident. Vehicle #1 was traveling in the east lane of northbound I-999. Vehicle #2 was parked at an angle with the left rear corner of the vehicle protruding slightly into the east lane of I-999. Evidence on both vehicles indicates that Vehicle #1 struck the left rear corner of Vehicle #2. Vehicle #2's wheels were turned toward the embankment east of the shoulder. Vehicle #2 took a direct path to the bottom of the embankment. No evidence exists, either in skid marks on the shoulder or tire wear on Vehicle #2, that would suggest that Vehicle #2 was spun into the embankment by an impact. Furthermore, the impact damage to the bumpers and sheet metal of the vehicles does not support an angled front-to-corner impact. Instead, the impact damage suggests a straight front-to-corner impact as depicted above. It is my professional opinion that the conclusion indicated in the police report that Vehicle #2 was taking corrective action after veering onto the shoulder is erroneous. The point of impact would have been between eighteen and thirty-six inches into the east lane of traffic.

Harvey Cedars, P.E., Ph.D.

Case Conclusion

Nathan went to Amelia and summarized the status of the claim for her as follows:

<u>Coverage:</u>

Although Conglomerate's Med Pay, UM, and Liability coverages all potentially apply, it appears that only the UM coverage will be used because the Med Pay and Liability coverages apply on an excess basis.

- Lenny's medical expenses are less than the $5,000 Med Pay limit on Tom's parents' car.

- Although Cassandra Holloway suffered substantial injuries, her claim against Lenny does not look like it will exceed the $100,000 Liability coverage limit on Tom's parents' car, especially if Cassandra is partially liable for the accident. Tom, as Lenny's passsenger, suffered only minor injuries, and he had assumed the risk by giving Lenny the keys and riding in the car with Lenny. (Nobody refuted this version.)

Liability:

It appears from the forensic engineer's report that Lenny is at least 50 percent liable for this accident. According to the report, Lenny did not properly park the vehicle on the shoulder of the road, but instead left it partially blocking the right lane of traffic on the interstate. Lenny had also been drinking. Cassandra Holloway had been driving too fast and could be found comparatively negligent for the accident.

The tavern owners' liability insurance companies may be willing to contribute to Cassandra Holloway's claim because she was an innocent victim. They would not be willing to contribute to the injury claims of Lenny or Tom.

Based on the accident reconstruction report, Premium, Conglomerate, and the attorney for Cassandra Holloway agreed that Cassandra and Lenny were equally liable for the accident.

Nathan and Patty agreed that Lenny should receive 50 percent of his damages under the Uninsured Motorists Coverage. Lenny was less willing to accept this and initially retained an attorney to fight this decision. He later fired the attorney and, faced with an engineer's report and the prospect of testifying about the details of the evening, accepted $15,000 ($7,500 each from Conglomerate and Premium) plus $4,500 from Premium Insurance for his Med Pay claim.

Patty was willing to pay 50 percent of Cassandra's damages, but she believed that the Townsville drinking establishments should also contribute based on liquor liability laws. For recovery from a tavern or restaurant to take place under liquor liability laws in this state, the law requires that the establishment serve someone who is a minor or someone who was obviously intoxicated.

Patty obtained statements from the friends of Tom and Lenny who had accompanied them through the loop. The witnesses were not as helpful as Patty had hoped. Although they all vividly recalled Tom's difficulties in walking and talking and described how he was obviously intoxicated when he was served alcohol at three or four establishments, nobody could recall any similar incidents with Lenny, although Lenny seemed to be keeping the same drinking pace. This information probably would not, by itself, be enough to establish liability in this state.

However, Patty remembered the tattoos. After inquiring with some of Tom's friends again, she learned that Lenny had twenty-two tattoos that were quite visible on his arms. Anyone serving Lenny would have easily been able to see how much he had consumed, even if he was not acting in the same manner as Tom and some of the others. Patty had witnesses who saw Lenny served at the last two establishments, and, when questioned a second time by Patty, one witness recalled that the bartender of the Bad Dog Café congratulated Lenny about the number of tattoos he had garnered.

Patty presented her evidence to the insurers of two of the drinking establishments that Tom and Lenny had patronized toward the end of their quest. Patty had discussed with her claim manager the possibility of having Lenny examined under oath by legal counsel to get more details about the drinking in order to bolster the case of liquor liability. Before this occurred, the two insurers she contacted offered to "chip in" up to $5,000 each "to avoid litigation and bad PR" with the stipulation that they be included on release of liability for the claims of Cassandra Holloway and Tom Schmidt.

Patty called Cassandra's attorney and explained the offers to settle. Cassandra concluded her liability claim against all parties for $47,500, including the loss to her car. The insurers of two of the drinking establishments contributed $10,000, and Premium paid the rest.

Premium concluded Tom's claim with payments under the Med Pay coverage, under the Liability coverage (for Lenny's liability), and under the Uninsured Motorists Coverage. Patty paid half of Tom's claim under the liability and uninsured motorists coverage and took a general release for the Liability coverage payment and a UM release and trust agreement for the Uninsured Motorists Coverage payment. Tom's claim was fairly minor. Not only were his injuries minor, but his liability claim against Lenny was suspect because it was presumed that Tom had assumed some of the risk when he let Lenny drive. Neither Tom nor Lenny corrected this misconception.

Following a number of complaints and several newspaper editorials, Townsville officials toned down the Oktoberfest, and the establishments on the loop ended their practice of tattooing patrons.

CHAPTER NOTES

1. Insurance Research Council, *Characteristics of Auto Accidents, An Analysis of Auto Injury Claims* (Malvern, Pa.: IRC, 2001), pp. 2–3.

2. Donald Hirsch, *Casualty Claim Practice* (Chicago, Ill.: Irwin Publications, 1996), p. 245.

3. Hirsch, p. 227.

4. Dangerous Intersection Study. State Farm Insurance study of 2.5 million accident reports, www.statefarm.com; June 15, 2000.

5. *Characteristics of Auto Accidents*, p. 4.

6. *Characteristics of Auto Accidents*, p. 4.

7. Morton Daller, *Tort Law Desk Reference, Fifty-State Compendium* (New York: Aspen Law and Business, 2000).

8. *Characteristics of Auto Accidents*, p. 4.

9. Cates v. Kinnard 193 Ill Dec. 460, 255 Il App. 3d 952, 626 NE 2d 770 (1994).

10. Chernetski v. American Family Mutual Ins. Co. 183 Wis. 2d 68, 515 NW 2d 283 (1994).

11. Mutual of Ins. Co. v. Hambleton, 84 Or. App. 343, 733 P.2d 948 (1987), review denied, 303 Or. 534, 738 P.2d 977.

12. Lombardo v. Hoag, 237 N.J. Super. 87 566 A.2d 1185 (1989).

13. *Tort Law Desk Reference*.

14. Reinhart v. Young, 874 S 2d 773 (Tx. App. 1994).

15. Alan Watts, Dale Atkinson, and Corey Hennessey, *Low Speed Automobile Accidents* (Tuscon, Ariz.: Lawyers and Judges Publishing Company, Inc., 1996), p. 4.

APPENDIX — AUTOMOBILE ACCIDENT STATEMENT GUIDELINE

11-A AUTOMOBILE RECORDED STATEMENT GUIDE (IN PERSON)[1]

INTRODUCTION (By Claim Representative):

"My name is _____, and I am speaking with _____.

Today's date is _____, and it is (time)_____.

The address here is _____.

This interview concerns an accident that occurred on _____ at _____."

PERMISSION:

"You realize that I am recording this interview?"

"And you have given me permission to record the interview?"

WITNESS DATA:

Name (check spelling), address, age, marital status—spouse's name, occupation, place of employment, home and business phones, and Social Security number.

ACCIDENT DATA:

1. Date, Time and Place of Accident. Number of lanes and their direction. Upgrade, downgrade, level, curve—direction of curve. Road surface, lane dividers, weather conditions, and lighting.

2. Exact Location of Witness at Time of Accident. Specific location when accident occurred. Distance from accident. Direction from which witness viewed the scene.

3. "What, if anything, attracted your attention to this accident?"

ACCIDENT DESCRIPTION:

1. "In your own words, please describe how the accident occurred." (Make notes for follow-up.)

   a. Speed and direction of cars?

   b. Are there any traffic controls?

   c. Which car entered intersection first?

   d. Where in intersection did cars make contact? Points of impact?

   e. Who hit whom?

   f. Parts of cars that were damaged?

   g. Position of cars following the accident?

  h. Were there any attempts to stop by either party?

  i. Were there any skid marks?

  j. Can you identify the drivers or passengers in the vehicles?

  k. Conversations after the accident?

  l. Are you related to any of the parties to the accident?

  m. Do you know any of the parties?

  n. Was anyone's attention distracted that you know of?

2. Police Report:

  a. Authority responding and making reports?

  b. Anyone cited for violation?

3. Any other witnesses? Identify by name and address.

4. To whom, if anyone, did you give your name as a witness to the accident?

INJURY:

1. Any complaints of injuries?

2. Describe injuries.

3. Ambulance at scene?

4. Identify doctors, hospitals, if known.

CLOSING:

(Before concluding, check your notes or diagram to see whether any additional questions or issues need to be asked or clarified.)

1. "Is there anything further you would like to add concerning this accident?"

2. "Have you understood all the questions asked?"

3. "Were your answers true to the best of your knowledge?"

4. "Did you understand that our conversation was being recorded? Was this with your permission?"

5. "Thank you, (*name of person*)."

This concludes the recorded interview. The time now is _____.

                 (A.M. or P.M.)

APPENDIX NOTE

1. Robert J. Prahl and Stephen Utrata, *Liability Claim Concepts and Practices* (Malvern, Pa.: Insurance Institute of America, 1985), p. 272.

Premises Liability Claims

PREMISES LIABILITY CLAIMS

Chapter 5 explained the elements of negligence. Those same elements of negligence apply in premises liability claims, which are made against business owners, apartment owners or renters, homeowners, property managers, and others who own, occupy, or control land. Negligence in premises liability claims is less well defined than negligence in auto liability claims, covered in Chapter 11. In auto liability claims, a driver's duty to others is often based on numerous statutes (rules of the road) governing the conduct of auto owners and operators. Few statutes exist in premises liability claims; common law derived from court cases is used in determining premises liability.

The most common premises liability claims are filed by people who slip and fall on others' property. In a slip-and-fall claim, claim representatives are unlikely to find statutes describing wrongful conduct of landowners toward others. Instead, claim representatives must investigate the circumstances surrounding the slip-and-fall accident and determine whether the insured's conduct was reasonable. Case Study One at the end of this chapter guides readers through a slip-and-fall claim.

Dog-bite claims, another common type of premises liability claim, have reached nearly epidemic proportions in some regions of the United States. Claim representatives should understand the unique legal and investigative challenges related to dog-bite claims. Several examples in this chapter explain how negligence might apply in such claims.

Premises security liability claims are becoming increasingly common for schools and businesses. In this type of claim, a person is injured by an assailant at someone else's property. Sometimes the assailant is an employee of a business; other times the assailant is a third party unknown to the victim or business owner. In either situation, the claimant makes the claim against the property owner or manager for not doing enough to prevent the attack. Case law on premises security liability is still evolving and varies dramatically by state, but this chapter describes some fundamental liability issues.

NEGLIGENCE IN PREMISES LIABILITY CLAIMS

As mentioned earlier, premises liability claims are made against landowners, tenants, landlords, and property managers. For simplicity, this chapter uses the all-inclusive term "the land possessor" or simply "the insured" to mean any party that owns, occupies, controls, or has responsibility for the premises.

This chapter explains how the elements of negligence such as (1) the duty owed, (2) a breach of the duty owed, (3) a proximate cause, and (4) damages relate to premises liability claims.

General Duties Owed in Premises Liability

Under common law, individuals who enter onto the property of others fall into one of three categories: (1) trespassers, (2) licensees, and (3) business invitees. The individual's category depends on his or her purpose for being on the premises and determines the individual's legal rights. In most states, the duty of care that the land possessor owes to the individual claimant varies according to the individual's legal status.

A **trespasser** is one who wrongfully enters another's property. Under common law, the only duties that landowners owe to trespassers is to not intentionally harm them and to not deliberately set traps for them. Generally, a trespasser assumes the risks inherent in entering the land, except under the following circumstances:

- When young children are lured onto the land by an attractive nuisance
- When the land possessor knows and tolerates trespassers
- When limited trespassing is permitted on specific parts of the land

Children who are trespassers are entitled to greater protection than adults, based on the **attractive nuisance doctrine**. Under this doctrine a landowner is liable if an enticing condition or item exists on the premises and induces children to enter the premises. Construction sites, for example, have many items, such as lumber, ladders, and piles of sand or gravel, that children find attractive. Under this doctrine, land possessors can be found liable to a trespassing child when all of the following circumstances exist:

1. The possessor of the land has reason to know that the attractive item is in an area where children are likely to trespass.
2. The possessor knows of the attractive item and knows it poses a serious risk to children.
3. The children who trespass are too young to understand the danger posed by the attractive item.
4. The benefit that the item has to the possessor is slight compared to the risk it poses to the children.
5. The possessor fails to use reasonable care to eliminate the danger or protect the children.

When these five criteria are met, the land possessor may be liable based on the doctrine of attractive nuisance.

Common examples of objects considered to be attractive nuisances include swimming pools and large piles of sand. Young children may not recognize the danger of the swimming pool or may not understand that the piles of sand can shift and cause them to be buried alive.

The attractive nuisance doctrine applies only to conditions or items created or maintained by the land possessor. Thus, one defense to the attractive nuisance doctrine is that the item's or condition's existence occurs naturally. Examples would include natural conditions such as rivers or cliffs. Finding ways to protect unsupervised children from these natural risks is often impossible. Another defense is that the child was able to recognize and understand the danger involved. For example, most children would understand that they can get hurt falling from heights or that fire burns.

A **limited trespasser** is an individual who uses a portion of a premises that the possessor knows is frequented by people. For example, children might use a path near the edge of a property as a shortcut to school, and the shortcut is known and tolerated by the land possessor. The land possessor would need to take reasonable care to not place hazards on or near that path.

If a land possessor is aware of a particular individual's trespassing and tolerates it, then the individual is considered to be a **known trespasser**. The owner has a duty to warn the known trespasser of any hidden dangers on the land possessor's property. Basically, the known trespasser is elevated to the status of "licensee."

A **licensee** has a legal status one step above that of a trespasser. The most common example of a licensee is a social guest of a land possessor. A neighbor who walks over to a homeowner's property as a social guest is a licensee. People with implied permission to be on other people's property, such as mail carriers and couriers, are also licensees. Even door-to-door salespersons can be considered licensees. The possessor owes a duty to warn a licensee of any *known, hidden* hazards that the guest may not anticipate. Examples might include toys left on stairs, oil spilled on the driveway, or small sinkholes in the yard. The licensee is required to keep a lookout for hazards, but if lighting conditions or the position of a hazard makes it hard to see, then the possessor of the land must warn the licensee. However, land possessors have no duty to periodically inspect their premises to ensure the safety of licensees.

People who go to a premises to conduct business transactions are known as **business invitees.** The majority of slip-and-fall claims involves business invitees. Business invitees might be customers purchasing groceries at a grocery store, pumping gas at a service station, or visiting an office to talk to their financial consultant. People using ATM machines or pay phones at businesses have been considered business invitees if they have a general business relationship with the land possessor.[1]

Business owners owe a duty to business invitees to exercise due care to keep the property in a reasonably safe condition. Business owners must remedy any unsafe condition in the property that they know about or *that they should have known about.* This duty requires businesses to make reasonable inspections of the premises. It is this additional duty that gives business invitees a more protected legal status than licensees.

"Notice" is an important legal consideration in claims involving business invitees. In legal terms, notice signifies knowledge. Notice may be actual or constructive. An **actual notice** in premises liability occurs when the possessor is directly given the information about a hazard on the premises. Actual knowledge is established through evidence that the land possessor or the possessor's employee caused, created, or knew of a hazardous condition. If, for example, a customer reports a spill to a stock clerk at a grocery store, then the grocery store owner is said to have actual notice of the spill. Actual notice occurs when any store employee learns of a problem. It is not necessary that the owner or management have knowledge for actual notice to occur. When a claim occurs after actual notice is given, liability usually exists unless the land possessor had no reasonable time to remedy the problem.

Constructive notice, or interpreted notice, exists when circumstances are such that the possessor should have known about a hazard through reasonable observation or inspection. Constructive knowledge is established through evidence that a hazardous condition existed for a sufficient length of time so that the land possessor should have known about it. The most controversial liability issues in premises liability claims usually pertain to whether a possessor had constructive notice of a hazard, because no law specifies exactly what constitutes a "sufficient length of time." The length of time that a hazard can exist before the land possessor should have known about it depends on the nature and location of the hazard. One court said that twenty minutes was not sufficient to establish constructive notice for grapes that had fallen on a supermarket floor,[2] and another court said that thirty minutes for a piece of candy that had fallen on a supermarket floor was also not a sufficient length of time.[3] However, if a larger item falls in a conspicuous area, constructive notice might exist in less than twenty minutes.

A number of stores today are warehouse stores that are essentially self-service. Such stores might have more items left in aisles by customers than do stores that have clerks to assist customers. The self-service stores, therefore, may have a higher duty to inspect for items left in the aisles because it is foreseeable that this would result from self-service operations.[4] In such operations, the length of time is not as important in establishing constructive notice as is the store's method of merchandising.

If a business invitee enters into part of a premises not open to the public, then the individual may lose his or her business invitee status and become a trespasser. If, for example, a customer cannot find what he or she wants on the shelf and decides to go to the back storage area marked "Employees Only," then he or she becomes a trespasser. The duty the store then owes to this customer changes. A business invitee who engages in criminal activities on the premises would also lose the business invitee protection.

Exhibits 12-1 and 12-2 give sample jury instructions for claims involving licensees and business invitees.

The majority of states still uses the three categories of trespasser, licensee, and business invitee in determining the duty owed by the land possessor. However, a significant number of states has blurred or eliminated the distinctions among these categories by no longer formally recognizing the categories. California is an example of a state that has eliminated category distinctions. Its statute specifies that negligence occurs in premises liability claims when a person is injured "by the want of care, or skill in the management of the property, unless the person brings the injury upon himself or herself."[5] In states that make no category distinctions, the courts judge the standard of care in terms of reasonable care and the foreseeability of the injury. Even in these states, what constitutes "reasonable care" varies according to the purpose that the individual has for being on the premises.

EXHIBIT 12-1

Sample Jury Instruction for Licensee[6]

Your verdict must be for the plaintiff if you believe:

First, there was (describe condition on property causing the injury) on the defendant's premises, and as a result the premises were not reasonably safe, and

Second, defendant knew of this condition and knew that such condition was not reasonably safe, and

Third, defendant knew or had information from which defendant, in the exercise of ordinary care, should have known that persons such as plaintiff would not discover such condition or realize the risk of harm, and

Fourth, defendant failed to use ordinary care either to make the condition reasonably safe or to adequately warn of it, and

Fifth, as a direct result of such failure, plaintiff sustained damage.

EXHIBIT 12-2

Sample Jury Instructions for Business Invitees[7]

Your verdict must be for the plaintiff if you believe:

First, there was (describe substance on the floor causing the fall) on the floor of the defendant's store, and as a result the floor was not reasonably safe, and

Second, the defendant knew, or by using reasonable care should have known, of this condition, and

Third, defendant failed to use ordinary care to (remove it, barricade it, or warn of it), and

Fourth, as a direct result of such failure, plaintiff sustained damage.

The following example illustrates how fluid the duty owed can be and how contingent it is upon the relationship between the parties.

A security guard is stationed at an all-night convenience store. The security guard owes a duty of *slight care* to pedestrians across the street in another store's parking lot. The security guard would have a duty not to shoot at them, but he (and his employer) would have no legal duty to protect those pedestrians from potential assailants or even to help them if they were in distress. If the pedestrians cross the street and walk onto the property of the guard's convenience store, the level of duty that the guard owes to these strangers might change to *ordinary care* as they become licensees with implied permission to cross through the store's parking lot. The pedestrians might even be considered business invitees, depending on whether they intend to conduct business at the store. The security guard would at the least be required to inform the pedestrians of any known, hidden hazards on the premises. If the pedestrians enter the store to make purchases, then they would become customers, *and* the level of care and their legal status would, without question, be those of business invitees. These customers would have the right to expect that the store management has maintained and inspected the premises to protect them from hazardous conditions there. If one of these people decides to rob the convenience store clerk, the person's legal status would change again, and the only duty the security guard would owe the robber would be the duty to *not* use *unreasonable* force in stopping the robbery. The guard could and should use reasonable force.

As mentioned in Chapter 5, statutes and ordinances create specific duties. Violations of these duties create negligence per se. Some municipalities have ordinances that require dog owners to keep their dogs on a leash. A state or municipality might also have a statute requiring property owners to clear snow from walkways within a given period of time. These are examples of how statutory laws establish specific duties. In general, determining the duty owed in premises liability claims is highly contingent on the exact circumstances preceding the accident and supports the need for claim representatives to take detailed statements from insureds and claimants to determine all the relevant facts.

Breach of Duty Owed

Once a claim representative has established that a land-possessor insured owed a duty to a claimant, then the claim representative must determine whether the insured breached the duty owed. This is perhaps the most contentious issue in the four elements of negligence in premises liability claims.

Unlike in many auto liability claims, in premises liability claims the claimant cannot point to a specific law or statute that the insured violated, but instead the claimant must prove that the insured's conduct was not reasonable under the circumstances. The fact that a claimant tripped over a crack in the insured's parking lot, or slipped on a grape that had fallen on a grocery store's floor, does not necessarily mean that the insured is legally liable. Land possessors are *not* responsible for every mishap that occurs on their premises. To be liable, they must, through their actions or inaction, have done something "wrong." They must have breached a duty owed to the claimant.

The land possessor's conduct must be evaluated at the time the accident occurred. The issue of foreseeability of harm, discussed in Chapters 5 and 11, is essential to assessing premises liability. Although almost every accident would be preventable with perfect knowledge of what was going to happen, courts cannot hold land possessors to such a high standard. Instead, foreseeability is based on what the insured could have reasonably known before an accident and what the insured could reasonably have done. The following four factors relate to the issue of foreseeability and are used by judges and juries in evaluating liability:

1. What is the probability that harm would occur from the defendant's actions (or failure to take action)?

2. How serious would the harm likely be?

3. What precautions could the defendant have taken to prevent harm?

4. How burdensome would these precautions have been to the defendant?

Consider a claim in which a teenager tripped over some pieces of discarded ice from a soft drink spilled on the pavement of a restaurant's large parking lot. With reference to the first foreseeability factor, the probability that anyone would step on the ice before it melts is somewhat small because of the size of the parking lot, and in most cases the spill would not cause someone to fall. But if one assumes that it caused the teenager to slip and fall, the likelihood of *serious* harm is also low (factor 2). In most cases, a scraped knee or elbow would be the likely extent of the injury. Regarding what precautions the owner could take (factor 3) to prevent such occurrences, the restaurant could hire a number of workers to constantly patrol the parking lot (where they would have little opportunity to assist customers) looking for spilled drinks and similar hazards. However, the cost of such efforts would pose an unreasonable financial burden on the restaurant, given the potential risks of injuries arising from spilled drinks (factor 4). In examining the four factors as they apply to this situation, a court would not likely assess liability against the restaurant owner. The failure to find and clean up the ice from the spilled soft drink would not be a breach of duty to the customer.

Consider a second scenario involving an elderly woman who tripped over a crack in a retirement community's patio. The crack had existed for several weeks. Retirement-community residents and friends frequently gather at the patio. In this scenario, the likelihood of harm is much greater than in the soft drink spill in the parking lot. Uneven pavement on a patio is likely to cause people to trip—especially elderly people who might have poor eyesight or difficulty walking. The potential for harm is also much greater for elderly people who might be susceptible to suffering fractures (like broken hips) from a fall. If this incident could have been prevented by a daily, five-minute inspection of the patio, then courts would not likely consider such a daily inspection to have been burdensome. Consequently, courts would likely rule that the retirement community's owner and/or management had breached its duty.

Uneven pavement is a common complaint, but uneven pavement does not always constitute a "defect" or breach of duty if the unevenness is very slight (one court established this as less than a one-inch variance).[8] Courts also consider the condition of the overall premises and whether the uneven pavement is in an area frequented by pedestrians. Pitted parking lots with small holes may be considered dangerous because the hazard is not as open and obvious as a large crack or raised area. A person wearing high heels might not see the pits and get a heel caught in one of the small holes.[9]

Warnings of known hazards can help reduce the likelihood of injury (which addresses factor 2). If, for example, an area of a store has just been mopped, and bright orange cones are placed around the mopped areas, then the hazard is more visible and less likely to result in an accident. Furthermore, such actions may be the only reasonable precautions that the store can take, as stationing employees around mopped areas would be cost prohibitive. These are important defenses that courts consider.

Warnings might not always be sufficient to preclude liability. Posting warning signs may help reduce, but not necessarily eliminate, liability to business invitees. For instance, a defendant who owned a greenhouse nursery was held liable for a slip-and-fall claim even though he had posted the following sign:

> Please watch where you are going. This is a nursery where plants grow.
>
> There is four seasons: summer and winter, cold and hot,
>
> rain, and icy spots. Flower petals always falling on the floor,
>
> Leaves always on the floor.
>
> We are dealing with nature and we are hoping for the best.
>
> We are not responsible for anyone get hurt on the premises.
>
> Thank you.[10]

Despite the posting, the court in this case found the defendant liable for not anticipating an unreasonable risk of harm and failing to take reasonable steps to prevent the harm of patrons falling. The court did not address whether the result would have been different if the warning had been clearer.

Causation

Another potentially controversial element is determining whether the breach of duty actually caused the claimant's injury or damages. Commonly, the claimant's own negligence or an intervening, or preexisting, factor is the substantial cause of the claimant's injury. Consider a customer who was injured exiting a convenience store parking lot late at night. The customer was intoxicated and had difficulty walking. The customer tripped over a doormat that had a slight kink in it. Surveillance camera footage showed that hundreds of customers had successfully maneuvered over the mat during the day despite the mat's slight problem. The substantial factor contributing to this claimant's fall was not the mat but the claimant's own intoxication.

As with other liability claims, a chain of related events may lead to injury. The concept of proximate cause was discussed in Chapters 5 and 11, but it is worth repeating in this chapter because the issue of proximate cause is important in premises liability. Consider a waitress who negligently spills hot coffee on a customer who is eating breakfast. The customer jumps up and accidentally flings a fork through the crowded restaurant, and the fork strikes another customer in the eye. The actual cause of the injury to the other customer's eye is the thrown fork. However, a court might deem that the customer's reaction to the spilled coffee was a natural reaction and would therefore consider the spilled coffee to be the proximate cause of the other customer's eye injury. If the eye injury is the result of an unbroken chain of events, then the original initiating cause is the proximate cause. In this situation, the restaurant could be held liable for the eye injury. (The customer that flung the fork might also be included as a codefendant if the customer's reaction was also negligent.)

Damages

The special and general damages described in Chapter 8 apply to premises liability claims. The damages must be (1) caused by the defendant's breach of duties and (2) compensable.

Sometimes claimants make premises liability claims for preexisting injuries. As mentioned in Chapter 8, aggravations of preexisting conditions are compensable, but natural occurrences related to preexisting conditions are not. Consider a person who, because of arthritis, needed to have a knee replacement. If the person's knee "goes out," and the person falls onto a store's floor, the store owner is not responsible for ensuing injury. Commonly, people who make claims against stores have some kind of preexisting condition. Determining whether the insured's action (or inaction) caused an accident that aggravated the condition is often difficult and requires careful documentation. Sometimes an independent medical examination is required to establish whether damages are related to an accident.

Claims must also be compensable. As mentioned in Chapters 3 and 8, pure emotional injuries may not be compensable in every state. Furthermore, pure emotional injuries do not always meet the definition of "bodily injury" as defined in insurance policies. Consider a customer at a restaurant who sees a rat run across the restaurant's dining room floor. The customer has an emotional response and makes a claim for her "trauma" because she can no longer eat at restaurants without thinking about the rat. Such a pure emotional injury claim might be attributed to the restaurant owner's negligence, but the injury itself might not be compensable.

Liability insurance that covers premises liability claims generally includes Medical Payments coverage. As mentioned in Chapter 3, this coverage pays for necessary and reasonable medical expenses of customers injured on the insured's premises. This coverage is usually limited to $5,000 or less, but it provides benefits to the injured party regardless of liability. So if a man trips over his own feet and falls on a store's floor, the store's insurance company could still pay the man's medical expenses up to the limit of liability for the Medical Payments coverage. Customers and even insured business owners sometimes have difficulty understanding that Medical Payments coverage applies even if the damages are not caused by the insured's negligence.

Investigating Premises Liability Claims

Probably more than any other type of liability claim, premises liability claims need scene investigations. It is often difficult to assess whether an insured breached a duty to a claimant without observing where the accident took place and determining how it happened. Once these facts are gathered, it becomes easier to determine what the likelihood of injury and the potential for harm were at the time of the accident.

For claims involving business invitees, claim representatives should determine how frequently the area involved is inspected. Employees at stores are supposed to make regular rounds looking for items that have fallen or spilled onto the floor. Claim representatives should ask the store manager for inspection logs that would demonstrate that the insured's employees made regular rounds and cleaned up items as needed. These are handwritten logs that employees prepare when they have walked through or swept the store aisles to monitor and prevent slip-and-fall hazards. Seven out of ten grocery stores surveyed reported using sweep/aisle-walk logs in their stores and striving to maintain a clean, safe environment through routine inspection practices. Unfortunately, these records may not be kept in good order. Many stores leave themselves vulnerable to slip-and-fall liability claims by not maintaining consistent records of their efforts. Grocery stores are somewhat notorious for not keeping good inspection records. The following findings of one study describe the problems with relying on store records.[11]

- Fewer than 40 percent of inspection logs examined in the study were accurate.
- When there were spills and subsequent cleanup, the amount of detail recorded varied by store. (Forty-three percent noted the type of hazards that existed (wet spills, dry spills, etc.), while 54 percent did not keep such details or did not know.
- The frequency with which managers verified logs varied considerably.

In addition to inspecting the scene of an accident, claim representatives must take detailed statements from parties having any knowledge of the accident. In store accidents, obtaining such information may mean coordinating interviews and on-site investigations with the work schedules of employees who were on the scene at the time of the accident. Failing to coordinate interviews and inspections with key people can lead to making more than one scene investigation of the store or ending up with less information than what could have been gained from having key witnesses interviewed at the scene.

Appendix A gives a general statement guideline that could be used in investigating premises liability claims. Key points of the statement relate to the issues of (1) how much notice the insured had regarding the hazard leading to the accident, (2) what actions or precautions the insured could have taken to warn or remedy the condition, *and* (3) what measures the claimant could have taken to avoid the accident or reduce his or her own injuries. Other sections of the statement relate to contact information, injury information, and other information similar to that found in other liability statement guidelines.

Slip-and-Fall Claims With Ice and Snow

Most of the United States has some ice or snow. Ice and snow lead to slip-and-fall claims. Claim representatives should consider several legal and investigative issues related to slip-and-fall claims caused by these weather conditions.

First, land possessors have no duty to clear off snow while it is falling. They have a reasonable amount of time after the precipitation stops to remove the ice or snow. In several states, sidewalks are considered parts of the street, and the responsibility for removing snow from sidewalks rests with the municipality. If an accident occurs on the sidewalk, claim representatives should notify the municipality as soon as possible because some states or municipalities will accept liability only if a claim is brought to their attention within a specified number of days (commonly ninety days) from the date of the accident. Other municipalities require property owners to remove ice and snow from sidewalks, but courts disagree as to whether violations of these snow-removal ordinances constitute negligence per se.

One viable defense is that the snow or ice was a general condition of the community and that the hazards on the insured's premises were no worse than those in any other area in the community at the time. Another defense is that the insured made every reasonable effort to remove the snow or ice. Quite often, some residual snow or ice remains even after removal. Ice melts and then refreezes. Pedestrians have a duty to anticipate this and watch where they are walking. Claim representatives must document what efforts the insureds took to remove the ice or snow. Comparative negligence is the most common defense. If a hazard was "open and obvious," then a claimant's own liability would reduce or eliminate any damage claim against the land possessor.

Timeliness is important in investigating slip-and-fall claims because the alleged hazards will soon melt. On serious injury claims, claim representatives should conduct an initial scene investigation as soon as it is safe to do so. Photographs showing the snow or ice that caused the fall and photographs showing the general condition of the community would have to be taken shortly after the accident. On serious claims, claim representatives can order weather reports that describe the dates, times, and accumulation of snow or ice. Those reports can help in determining whether the property owner had reasonable time to remedy the condition.

If the snow or ice has melted and the condition has improved, claim representatives must find out from property owners or employees whether any ruts or hidden slick spots existed at the time of the accident.

DOG-BITE CLAIMS

A growing number of people are purchasing larger, more aggressive breeds of dogs, which has led to an increase in the number and severity of dog bites. In Los Angeles, for example, dog-bite injuries have reached epidemic levels. In Detroit, dog-bite claims increased 38 percent from 1996 to 1997.[12] In 1998, 4.5 million dog bites occurred in the United States (up from 585,000 in

1986), costing more than $1 billion in claim settlements. One insurer paid nearly $80 million in one year for dog-bite claims. (This amount rose from $31 million ten years earlier.[13]) Of the 4.5 million dog-bite victims, 73 percent were children, making dog bites the leading cause of children's being admitted to emergency rooms.[14] Because of the nature of these incidents and the tender age of the claimants, settlement values in dog-bite claims vary dramatically from other premises liability claims. Special training and preparation are required of claim representatives so that they can properly handle dog-bite claims.

Investigating Dog-Bite Claims

Claim representatives investigating dog-bite claims must keep personal safety in mind and understand the psychological dynamics involved in pet ownership. Many people view their dogs as family members and are reluctant to believe that their dogs are capable of hurting others. They may tell a claim representative that the dog will not bother anyone. Claim representatives should approach such statements with a healthy degree of skepticism. Much like parents discussing their children, dog owners tend to recall only the dog's good characteristics and overlook the bad ones. When investigating dog-bite claims, claim representatives must determine the following:

- Has the dog bitten anyone previously (before the incident under investigation)?
- Has the dog shown vicious propensities towards other people (such as chasing or growling at other people)?
- Does the municipality have a leash law requiring owners to keep dogs on leashes when they are not behind fences?
- Were there circumstances before the attack that might have caused the dog to act aggressively (such as the dog's having puppies or being injured)?
- Did the claimant do anything to provoke the dog?
- What was the status of the claimant (trespasser versus licensee)?
- What is the dog's breed?

Dangerous Dogs

Historically, dog owners were liable only if their dogs had already bitten somebody before. The rationale was that the owners were "on notice" of the danger the dog posed once it had bitten someone, but before that occurrence the danger was not foreseeable to the owner. Over the years, courts began to allow claimants to introduce other evidence of **vicious propensities**. Evidence that the dog had previously chased people, snapped at people, or acted in other menacing ways could be used by claimants to establish that the dog had vicious propensities, which made it foreseeable that the dog might bite someone. Exhibit 12-3 shows an excerpt from one state's definition of vicious propensities.

More recently, some courts have allowed evidence that certain breeds of dogs are more aggressive and prone to attacks and that, therefore, the owners of these dogs are already "on notice" that their dogs pose a danger.

EXHIBIT 12-3

Control of Dangerous Dogs[15]

A. It shall be unlawful for any person to own or allow to be upon a premises under his or her control, any dog of a dangerous, vicious, or ferocious disposition with such a dog being confined to and within the property lines of the premises behind a fence or enclosure from which it cannot escape, or securely fastened to a chain limiting movements of such a dog to an area of ten (10) feet within the property lines of the premises of such a person.

B. For purposes of this section, a dog of a dangerous, vicious, or ferocious disposition means any dog … which demonstrates any of the following behavior:

   1. An attack which requires a defensive action by any person to prevent bodily injury or property damage when such person is conducting himself or herself peacefully and lawfully.

   2. An attack which results in property damage or in an injury to a person when the person is conducting himself or herself peacefully.

   3. An attack on another animal, livestock, or poultry which occurs on property other than that of the owner of the attacking dog.

   4. Any behavior which constitutes a threat of bodily injury to a person when such a person is conducting himself or herself peacefully and lawfully.

Claim representatives should determine the breed of the dog involved in the attack. In some northern states, mixed breeds of wolf-dogs are kept as pets. These dogs pose safety hazards for their owners and for surrounding neighbors, and, as explained in Chapter 5, the owners of these kinds of "wild animals" may be strictly liable for injuries that the animals cause. Certain breeds of dogs such as pit bulls, Rottweilers, chow chows, German shepherds, and bull terriers are known to have a propensity for attacks. Because of jury attitudes towards these more aggressive breeds of dogs, claims involving such dogs might have a higher likelihood of having damages awarded against the dog owners.

Dog Facts

In one year, pit bulls* accounted for 67 percent of all fatal dog attacks even though pit bulls represented less than 1 percent of the dog population.[16] Chow chows were listed by veterinarians as the least suitable breed of dog for a pet because of their aggressive nature. But their bites are not as serious as those of pit bulls, so they might not be considered as dangerous as pit bulls.[17] German shepherds have consistently led in the number of bites, but their attacks are also not usually as serious as those of pit bulls.[18]

* "Pit bulls" refers to the American pit bull terrier, the Staffordshire bull terrier, and the American Staffordshire terrier.

Leash Laws

Most urban and suburban areas have animal-control regulations that specify how dog owners must restrain their dogs. The following regulation is a common example:

> Sec. 3.03.003 RESTRAINT AND CONTROL REQUIRED[19]
>
> A. The owner of any dog shall keep his or her dog under restraint at all times.

These types of regulations are referred to as **leash laws**. Leash laws require that the dog be kept on a leash, in a cage, or behind a fence at all times. Violation of a leash law is negligence per se. As described in Exhibit 12-3, the law may require greater precautions for dogs that are dangerous or have vicious propensities.

Extenuating Circumstances

Claim representative must determine whether any extenuating circumstances caused the dog to attack. Sometimes young children tease dogs by hitting them with sticks or throwing rocks at them. At other times, dogs attack others out of instinct, such as to protect their young. Such extenuating circumstances may reduce the potential for liability awards against the owners. However, claim representatives should also determine whether the dog owners were aware of any extenuating circumstances and find out what, if any, precautions the owners took to prevent dog attacks once they were aware of the circumstances.

Claimant Legal Status

Claim representatives should determine whether the claimant was a trespasser. If the person was trespassing on the insured's property, then the owner was not violating the leash law, and negligence per se would not apply. Trespassing also makes foreseeability less likely, and a lack of foreseeability could be a viable defense if the owner took precautions to make sure the dog was restrained and had no reason to believe anyone would enter the property without permission. As mentioned earlier, this defense may not apply to known trespassers such as children who frequently jump over a homeowner's fence to retrieve balls. On serious dog-bite claims, claimant lawyers will canvass the neighborhood looking for people who might have witnessed the dog in question acting viciously toward people. Ignorance is not bliss when it comes to setting reserves and assessing liability on serious dog-bite claims. Claim representatives should be prepared for claimants' allegations by conducting independent investigations that go beyond just what the insured says. Appendix B gives a statement guideline for investigating dog-bite claims.

Misrepresentations on Insurance Applications

The dog-bite claims trend affects insurance company underwriting decisions. Many insurers are now refusing to write insurance for homeowners with particular breeds of dogs, or they charge an additional premium. Many companies now include questions about dog ownership on their insureds' applications for homeowners insurance. One insurer's CEO described why it no longer insures people who own aggressive breeds of dogs: "Our position is that if you have one of those aggressive breeds of dogs in your household, we will not insure you because we believe there's no way to match the risk with the rate."[20]

As part of their investigations on dog-bite claims, claim representatives should review the information given by insureds on their insurance applications. This adds one more investigative issue for claim representatives: material misrepresentations on applications. If insureds misrepresent their dog ownership on their applications when they purchase their policies, then the policy could be voided *ab initio* (from the beginning). Therefore, coverage would not apply to a claim in which the insured had lied about the type of dog he or she owned. This situation presents an investigative issue that might not have been considered in the past.

CLAIM ALERT!

Canceling a policy is often the purview of the underwriting department. In fact, a few jurisdictions do not permit claim representatives to examine underwriting files. In some states, claim representatives would only submit a report to the underwriting department notifying it about the dog-bite claim. The underwriting department would then be obligated to take further action. Claim representatives should consult with claim management when encountering dog-bite claims that might potentially involve a material misrepresentation by the insured.

PREMISES SECURITY LIABILITY CLAIMS

Premises security liability is the civil liability of property owners for the foreseeable criminal acts of third parties. It arises when a property owner or manager fails to provide a reasonably safe environment and, as a result, someone is victimized by a criminal. Frequently the assailant is known neither to the victim nor to the property owner and is not apprehended.[21] Although the number of these types of claims is increasing quickly, these claims are still not as common as other types of premises liability claims such as slip-and-falls or dog-bites.

Premises security liability claims fall into two broad categories: crimes committed by employees and crimes committed by third parties. In both categories of claims, the employer's or land possessor's foreseeability of the criminal attack is a key liability issue. This is especially true for attacks committed by third parties.

Liability for Crimes Committed by Employees

Crimes committed by employees are less common than crimes committed by third parties, but liability for these claims is easier to understand. If a business negligently hires or retains an employee who is known to be violent, and the employee then hurts one of the business's customers or tenants, the employer could be liable. Consider the following case:

An apartment-building owner hired a resident property manager. The property manager used his passkey to enter the apartment of a woman in the apartment building and raped her at knifepoint. Evidence revealed that the man's application had not been fully completed, and the building owner had not performed a proper background check, which would have shown that the man was on parole for armed robbery. The apartment owner was held liable for the woman's rape.[22]

Negligent hiring occurs when an employer fails to use due diligence in checking employees' backgrounds. With such relevant information easily available to them for a small fee, employers are expected to conduct a reasonable investigation into an employee's background before hiring him or her. This inquiry may take the form of an extensive employment application, a job interview, pre-employment testing, a criminal records check, and a references check. The type and quality of the background investigation to be done are largely dependent on the nature of the job that the prospective employee is to perform. Certainly, someone applying for a job as a child daycare worker or an airline pilot would require a more extensive background investigation than would someone applying for a job as an assembly line worker.

Negligent retention occurs when an employer fails to discharge an employee who is known to pose a danger to others. Once it has been determined that an employee may be dangerous to others, employers may be liable for subsequent attacks committed by these employees. For example, if a school discovers that one of its coaches has a history of violence against children, then the school could be liable for retaining the coach. For claims brought against employees, claim representatives should ask the following questions:

- What type of job application and background check procedure does the insured employer follow, and was this procedure followed on the employee in question?

- Does the employee have any history of violence or other potential security problems that could have been discovered by exercising due diligence in performing a background check?

Liability for Criminal Attacks Committed by Third Parties

This second category of premises security liability is more common and much more controversial. It poses many more legal challenges than claims involving employees. Liability for criminal attacks by third parties is based on one of the following legal theories:

1. The defendant had a special relationship with the claimant that required offering a higher level of security.

2. The defendant voluntarily assumed liability for the claimant's safety.

3. The defendant violated a statute requiring certain security measures.

4. Special circumstances existed that would make criminal attacks more likely so that the defendant should have foreseen and tried to prevent a particular attack.

In general, the victim must prove that the land possessor failed to provide adequate security for the given circumstances. These kinds of claims are commonly known as **inadequate security claims.** Inadequate security might be alleged based on such factors as an inadequate number of security personnel, poor lighting in parking lots, faulty locks, inadequate maintenance of security records, or failure to maintain or repair security equipment.

Rape and sexual assault account for 44 percent of inadequate security claims, followed by assault and battery at 25 percent, and wrongful death claims at 18.5 percent. About 30 percent of inadequate security claims arise from incidents in parking lots. Restaurants have 18 percent of inadequate security claims, followed by hotel rooms at 12 percent. Awards for these types of claims can range into the millions of dollars, especially for cases of rape or wrongful death.[23]

The duties owed to certain individuals may be higher because of the **special relationship** between the parties. For example, schools have a duty to protect students from violence because the schools have a special relationship with their students.[24] Hotel and motel operators, nursing home and apartment building owners, and common carriers (train, plane, and bus owners) have a high duty of care to protect their patrons. Students, patients, tenants, and people staying overnight at hotels or traveling on trains, planes, or buses give up some independence and are somewhat vulnerable. They must entrust their safety to others. Consequently, organizations catering to such people owe a high duty to protect these kinds of customers.

A **statutory duty to provide security** may be created by an ordinance or a statute. Examples of such ordinances may be an ordinance requiring abandoned buildings to be boarded up, statutes requiring proper lighting in dark parking lots, and ordinances requiring locks and deadbolts on hotels, motels, or apartments. If an attack occurs as a result of a violation of a statute or an ordinance, then liability exists as negligence per se. If a motel fails to repair a broken deadbolt on one of its doors and an intruder breaks in and attacks a customer because the door did not have the deadbolt, then the motel owner would be liable as matter of law.

Special circumstances exist when the land-possessor insured knows of previous security problems on the insured's premises that make future criminal attacks foreseeable. The law defining special circumstances as it has evolved to date is described as follows:

> Since the possessor is not an insurer of the visitor's safety, he is ordinarily under no duty to exercise any care until he knows or has reason to know that the acts of the third person are occurring or are about to occur. He may, however, know of or have reason to know, from past experience, that there is a likelihood of conduct on the part of any particular individual. If the place or character of his business, or his past experience, is such that he should reasonably anticipate careless or criminal conduct on the part of third persons, either generally or at some particular time, he may be under a duty to take precautions against it, and to provide a sufficient number of servants to afford a reasonable protection.[25]

Therefore, if the insured is aware of previous security problems that make future security problems foreseeable, the insured has a duty to provide appropriate security based on these special circumstances.

The first legal hurdle that a claimant must clear in a security liability claim is that the incident must have taken place on property owned or controlled by the insured. The rationale is that a property owner cannot be held liable for criminal conduct that occurs on others' property. Even companies that have their own security guards do not have the same authority as law-enforcement personnel. Land possessors are not responsible for crimes committed on neighboring properties (with rare exceptions). Consequently, one of the first investigative issues that claim representatives must determine is where the crime took place.

The second investigative issue addresses the foreseeability of criminal attacks on the insured's premises. To help determine this, claim representatives must learn whether crimes, especially violent crimes, have been committed on or near the insured's premises. Claim representatives can obtain this information from police records.

The duty owed by the insured may also be based on the insured's **voluntary assumption of a duty to provide security** even if an insured has no duty to provide security or if no special circumstances exist. In several states, the insured voluntarily assumes the duty of providing security when the insured directs a customer to perform an act that places the customer in danger. For instance, the insured decides to hire security guards for the premises, but an attack on a customer occurs because of the negligence of a security guard who was engaged in personal business instead of performing his or her job. As another example, an insured directs a customer around to the back of the store for a delivery. Such direction may be considered to be a voluntary assumption of the duty to provide security because the business should not be directing customers to potentially unsafe areas.

In investigating inadequate security liability claims, claim representatives should address the following questions:

- Does the insured have any knowledge of previous security problems at the property where the loss took place, and do the insured's patrons customarily use this property?

- Does the industry in which the insured works have a special relationship with its patrons requiring a higher level of security?

- Has the insured voluntarily provided any security measures?

- Do any applicable statutes and ordinances require the insured to provide any form of security, and were there any violations of these laws? (For example, must the fire alarm system be operational whenever the insured business is open?)

- Does the insured advertise any security measures that it does not live up to? (For instance, "ABC Apartments have twenty-four-hour, on-premises, state-of-the-art security.")

Answers to these questions could help determine whether the insured had inadequate security or misled people about the extent of security it offered.

Premises security liability claims are complicated, and the law regarding these types of claims is evolving and varies widely among states. Claim representatives should consult management or legal counsel before conducting extensive investigations on these types of claims.

CASE STUDY ONE—PREMISES LIABILITY CLAIM

Eric Campbell, a claim representative at National Farm, received a loss notice from one of National's nationwide accounts, Floor-Mart. The loss notice indicated that a woman had injured herself when she slipped and fell inside the insured's store. Eric confirmed coverage and contacted the insured's store manager to get some information about the claim in order to set up the file and establish a reserve.

Eric: Hi, this is Eric Campbell. I'm a claim representative with National Farm. I'm calling about a woman who was injured at your store last Friday. I understand you are the store manager, and I was hoping you could give me some brief information about this.

Store Manager (Barney): Hello, I'm Barney Henderson, and I'm the unit manager at Floor-Mart. I wasn't here at the time, but my assistant manager told me what happened.

Eric: And what's your assistant manager's name?

Barney: Betty Brown. She could give you the details on this, but she doesn't get here until 3:30.

Eric: That's OK; I can talk with her when I come out to the store. I'm just trying to get some basic information right now.

Barney: Well, according to Betty, the fall occurred over in our fabric department. Betty said she was an older woman. She fell and couldn't get back up. Betty called an ambulance, and it took her to the hospital.

Eric: Do you know the extent of the injury or what caused the fall?

Barney: You'd have to talk to Betty. I believe she said she slipped on some candy wrapper or something that was on the floor. But let me tell you, we keep a clean store here, and we make regular inspections to look for those things. But we can't be everywhere.

Eric: Do you keep records of those inspections and when you clean or sweep the floors?

Barney: Absolutely. That's something I insist on.

Eric: Well, I'll call Betty and set up a time to meet with her, photograph the scene, and look at the inspection logs. Thank you for your time.

Barney: No problem.

Eric contacted Betty and arranged to meet with her and photograph the scene. He tried contacting the claimant, Etta Green, but she was not home and did not have an answering machine. Eric sent her a card with his contact information, requesting that she contact him to talk about the incident.

Eric met with Betty later in the week. Betty explained that one of Floor-Mart's clerks, Cara Hart, had found the woman lying on the floor moaning in pain. She had evidently slipped on an open packet of breath mints. Eric asked Betty to describe the breath mints. The store does sell the type of mints. They are found on a stand near the checkout counters. The fabric department is near the middle of the store. The fall occurred more than fifty feet away from the closest checkout counter. Eric looked at the store's inspection log, which indicated that an inspection of the area had been made just *ten minutes before the fall occurred*. Eric commented to Betty on how clear and complete the inspection logs were.

Betty: Yeah, Barney is a real stickler about keeping the store clean. He really went off on Cara when he heard that a lady had slipped on some trash in her area. But he apologized later when he saw that she had made an inspection just before the accident.

Eric: When did Cara write down that she inspected the area?

Betty: Oh, you do that immediately after the inspection.

Eric: OK. Could I speak with Cara? Is she working today?

Betty: No, Cara quit. Somebody said they saw her waiting tables over at the Filmore Diner.

Eric tried unsuccessfully again to contact Ms. Green by phone. A week later, he received an attorney's lien letter advising Eric that Ms. Green would be represented by Jon Morgan.

Eric called Mr. Morgan. Mr. Morgan stated that Ms. Green had sustained serious injuries to her back and neck resulting from her fall at the Floor-Mart. Mr. Morgan alleged negligence on the part of Floor-Mart because it left trash on the floor, which Ms. Green slipped on. Eric learned that Ms. Green had incurred more than $30,000 in medical expenses. Her most serious injury was a cracked vertebra. She is retired, so she had no lost wages. Eric told the attorney that he did not see any liability because a store employee had made an inspection of the area only ten minutes earlier. Mr. Morgan argued that the inspection must not have been reasonable or the employee would have discovered the trash on the floor. Mr. Morgan made a demand for $275,000 and sent Eric a settlement package documenting Ms. Green's injury claim.

Eric evaluated the claim using the settlement template below:

Steps in calculating settlement range:
1. Probable verdict range for a "perfect" case.
   $150,000 to $200,000
2. The chances of a defense verdict (against the claimant) on the claim (zero liability).
   (9 out of 10) = 90%
3. Calculate the risk amount based on line #2.
   Reduce award range amounts to reflect risk to claimant.
   $150,000 – (.90 × $150,000) = $15,000

$200,000 - (.90 \times \$200,000) = \$20,000$

4. Calculate the risk-modified award range.

$150,000 - \$135,000 = \$15,000$ low

$200,000 - \$180,000 = \$20,000$ high

Risk-modified award range: $15,000 - \$20,000$

5. Estimated percentage of fault of defendant: 10%

(For not maintaining careful lookout. Normally this might be

a greater percentage, but the item was somewhat obscured from view.)

6. Liability adjusted verdict range (range less percentage of fault):

$13,500 to \$18,000

7. Percent increase or decrease based on case variables.

Insured is corporate defendant.	+ 15 %
Claimant is elderly in community of elderly people.	+5 %
Venue is somewhat liberal.	+ 10 %
Total percentage adjustment for variables	+ 30 %

8. Variable adjusted verdict range:

$(\$13,500 \times 1.4) = \$18,900$ low

$(\$18,000 \times 1.4) = \$25,200$ high

9. Estimated defense costs through trial: $12,000

10. Expected Medicare medical lien for $30,000. Settlement is problematic.

The Medicare lien would not likely be negotiable, and even though neither the insured nor Eric had received a medical lien from Medicare, Eric knew that he could not pay this claim without including the lien. At some point Medicare would likely file a lien, and Eric knew that, unlike private insurers, Medicare could enforce a lien even if payment had been issued before Medicare notified his company. This claim settlement would be problematic. Ms. Green and her attorney have little to gain by settling the case for less than $30,000.

Eric made offers within the settlement range, which were rejected. After a few weeks, Ms. Green filed suit against Floor-Mart, and the case was assigned to legal counsel. During discovery, Cara, the former Floor-Mart employee, was located and subpoenaed to give a deposition. In her deposition, she stated that she had thoroughly inspected her area and recorded her inspection on the store's "clean and sweep log." She further stated that on her way back to her area, she saw a woman with her two children arguing about eating some candy in the store. The child threw the candy, a package of mints, on the floor near the fabrics. Cara was going to pick up the candy when she was interrupted by a customer asking for help locating linens. Cara showed the woman where the linens were and returned to her area. She had forgotten about the candy on the floor. About five minutes later, an elderly woman (identified as Etta Green) fell near where the candy had been discarded. The woman blamed the package of open mints for her fall. Cara felt badly that she had not picked up the breath mints. She knew that her boss would be upset with her. Cara quit her job at the store the next day.

This deposition changed everything! Before it occurred, the claimant would have had to prove that the store had *constructive* knowledge of the candy hazard on the floor. This would not have been easy to prove, considering that the candy had only been on the floor for about ten minutes. Now, the facts indicate that Cara knew of the hazard, which meant that the store (through its employee Cara), had *actual* notice of the hazard and failed to take action. In one statement, the claim had changed from one with doubtful liability to one with clear liability.

Case One—Conclusion

Eric and the insured's lawyer, Tom Hanson, discussed the possibility of arguing that the item was open and obvious and that therefore the claimant shared at least partial responsibility for the accident. However, the candy was somewhat hidden under a fabric stand, so that argument would probably not hold up. Instead of arguing liability issues, and potentially angering a jury by appearing obstinate, Eric and Tom decided that if the case went to trial, a better approach would be to refute some of the questionable or excessive medical treatments that Ms. Green received from her doctors and chiropractor. Ms. Green was likely to have some residual medical problems with her back for the rest of her life. Those injuries may require future physical therapy or other treatments.

The case did not go to trial. Eric settled with Ms. Green for $195,000 plus $5,000 for the Medical Payments coverage that Eric had already paid to Ms. Green. The settlement was on the high side of settlements for this type of injury, but Eric factored in that the insured was a corporate defendant and that Ms. Green was likely to engender sympathy. Also, Ms. Green would have to pay Medicare over $30,000, so after that payment and paying her attorney fees, she would net about $105,000 (including the $5,000 Medical Payments coverage amount).

CLAIM ALERT!

This case was abbreviated for instructional purposes. In a real case, much more documentation would have been required to justify such a large payment.

CASE STUDY TWO—PREMISES SECURITY LIABILITY CLAIM

Helen Robbins left work late and decided to stop at a fast-food restaurant, The Sandwich King, on her way home. Like many businesses in this urban neighborhood, The Sandwich King had a security guard. The restaurant had been the site of three armed robberies in the past year. They all occurred in the evening. Gang members roamed the area and sometimes harassed customers and snatched purses, especially before The Sandwich King hired a security guard.

While Helen was in The Sandwich King ordering her dinner, some young teenage boys (suspected gang members) crossed over the street and went into the parking lot of The Sandwich King. The security guard made no attempt to ask the youths to leave, but he did escort customers to their cars. Helen stayed in the restaurant and ate her dinner. After about fifteen minutes, she decided to go to her car. While the security guard escorted Helen to her car, a car drove down the street in front of The Sandwich King. Several other teenage boys were in the car yelling profanities out the window at the teenage boys milling around on The Sandwich King parking lot. It was then that Helen noticed that one of the boys in the car was brandishing a gun. He opened fire on the teenagers in the parking lot. Bullets struck two of the teenagers, and an errant bullet struck Helen in the head.

Helen and the two boys were rushed to the hospital. With serious brain damage, Helen clung to life for three days, but when she slipped into a coma, her family asked that she be taken off life-support systems. She died the next day.

Helen's family members hired a lawyer and sued The Sandwich King. They argued that (1) The Sandwich King restaurant was a "gang hangout" and a "crime magnet," which the owners knew because of previous gang problems on the premises; (2) the management of The Sandwich King should have warned customers or should have had more effective security measures; (3) The Sandwich King voluntarily assumed responsibility for the safety of its customers by having security guards escort them; and (4) the restaurant owners should have recognized that these gang members would attract violence and that the restaurant's security guard should have asked the gang members to leave the parking lot or should have at least called the police. Helen's family believed that the restaurant's owners were negligent and responsible for Helen's death.

The family filed suit against the Sandwich King. The insurer for The Sandwich King denied liability, arguing that (1) The Sandwich King had no duty to protect customers from drive-by shootings that occur off the insured's premises, (2) the cause of the injury was the act of a third party unrelated to The Sandwich King, (3) the security at The Sandwich King was adequate, and (4) the restaurant had not assumed any duty to ensure the safety of customers even though it had taken every reasonable precaution to protect customers. The Sandwich King argued that asking the youths to leave would have been a waste of time and that the police in this area would not have responded unless the youths had been committing crimes before the shooting.

Case Two—Conclusion

The judge reviewed the complaint and a written motion filed by the lawyer representing The Sandwich King asking the judge to grant a summary judgment in favor of The Sandwich King. The plaintiff's complaint stated that Helen was killed by a bullet that came from a location off the defendant's premises. Based on the facts stipulated, the judge granted the defense a summary judgment and dismissed the case because the law in this state did not require land possessors to protect customers from acts occurring off the defendant's premises. The plaintiff's appeal was denied. The Sandwich King's insurer paid its limit of $4,000 under the Medical Payments portion of the policy.

Helen's family filed an Uninsured Motorist claim with Helen's personal auto insurance company. The law in this state on this issue was a bit more favorable to Helen's family's case. Some courts had permitted uninsured motorists claims for drive-by shootings, depending on the circumstances. Rather than deny coverage and litigate the coverage issue (and potentially make bad law), the company agreed to pay Helen's family the $25,000 Uninsured Motorists Coverage limit.

The application of Uninsured Motorists coverages to these types of claims was discussed in Chapter 2. Not all states would accept UM coverage for such an incident.

CHAPTER NOTES

1. Campbell v. Weathers, 111 P. 2d 72 (Kan. 1941).
2. Grant v. National Supermarket Inc. 741 S.W. 2d 895 (Mo. App. 1987).
3. Carraway v. National Supermarkets Inc., 611 S.W. 2d 357 (Mo. App. 1980).
4. Sheil v. T.G. & Y. Stores, 781 S.W. 2d 778 (Mo. Banc 1989).
5. California Civil Code 1714 (a).
6. MAI 32.28 (1989); MAI 11.05 (1965). Provided by Russell Watters, Brown and James Law Firm, St. Louis, Mo.
7. MIA 33.05; McVicar v. W.R. Arthur & Co., 312 S.W. 2d 805 (Mo. 1958).
8. Sepulveda v. Duckwall-Alco Stores, 708 P.2d 171 (Kan. 1985).
9. Priviteria v. Coastal Mart, Inc. 908 S.W.2d 779, Mo. App. W.D., 1995.
10. Linda Edwards and Stanley Edwards, *Tort Law for Legal Assistants* (Albany, N.Y.: West Legal Studies, 1999), p. 78.
11. The Gleason Group, Research shows supermarkets have room for improvement at reducing slip and falls, www.PropertyandCasualty.com, January 31, 2001.
12. Charlie Cain, "Dog bites threaten home insurance," July 8, 1998, *The Detroit News*, detnews.com/1998/metro/9807/08/07080110.htm.
13. Jeffrey Sacks, "Dog Bites: How Big a Problem?" *Injury Prevention 1996*, Vol. 2, pp. 52–54. These were the amounts paid out by State Farm Insurance.
14. *NBC Nightly News*, November 2, 1998, www.msnbc.com/news/208918.asp.
15. City Code of Independence, Missouri. Animals and Fowl. Article 3. Licensing and Control of Dogs and Cats. 1987. Sec. 3.03.005.
16. "Beware of This Dog, The Pit Bull Terrier," *Sports Illustrated*, July 7, 1987, p. 75.
17. As reported by the Northeast Louisiana Chapter of the CPCU Society, "Liability Concerns of Dog Owners and Their Insurers," *CPCU Journal*, Sept. 1992, p. 187, citing a study done by *Pet Veterinarian* magazine in November 1990.
18. Ibid; p. 185.
19. Ibid; City Code of Independence, Mo. Sec. 3.03.003.
20. Cain, quoting Richard Bernstein, Vice President MetLife, Auto & Home.

21. Norman D. Bates and Susan J. Dunnell, *Major Developments in Premises Security Liability* (Framingham, Mass.: Liability Consultants, Inc., 1994), p. 1.

22. Ponticas v. KMS Investments, 331 N.W. 2d 907 (Minn. Supreme Ct. 1983).

23. Bates and Dunnell, p. 8.

24. Fazzolari by and through Fazzolari v. Portland School District, 734 P. 2d 1326 (Ore. 1987).

25. Bates and Dunnell, p. 11., citing the Third Restatement of Torts, sec. 344, comment f.

APPENDIX A—STATEMENT GUIDELINE FOR PREMISES LIABILITY CLAIM (CLAIMANT)[1]

INTRODUCTION:

My name is _____, and I am calling from telephone number _____.

Today's date is _____, and it is _____.

I am speaking to _____ at _____.

This interview concerns an accident which occurred on _____ at _____.

PERMISSION:

"You realize that I am recording this interview?"

"And you have given me your permission to record the interview?"

CLAIMANT DATA:

1. What is your full name?
2. How do you spell your last name?
3. May I have your age, please?
4. What is your mailing address and phone number?
5. What is your Social Security number?
6. Are you married? (If so) What is your spouse's name?
7. Do you have any children? (If so) What are their names and ages?
8. Where do you work? What is the address? What do you do there? Can you be reached there by telephone? What is the telephone number?
9. Did you miss any time from work? (If so) What is your present income? (Hourly, weekly, monthly, or annually)
10. Retirement. (How long retired and outside source of income—how much?)

ACCIDENT DATA:

1. Date. (Month, day, and year)
2. Time of accident.
3. Exact location of accident. (Sidewalk, driveway, entrance to house or building, steps, stairway, in house, store, etc.)
4. Weather conditions. (If outside)
   a. Raining, snowing, sleeting, etc.
   b. Condition of premises affected by weather?

ACCIDENT DESCRIPTION:

"In your own words, please describe how the accident occurred." (Make notes for follow-up.)

1. Condition of accident scene.

    a. *If outside*

       (1) Composition and condition of surface. Give its general condition, e.g., uneven, full of holes, broken edges, etc.

       (2) Give approximate measurements of location around accident site, e.g., measurements of driveway, sidewalk, steps, etc.

       (3) Is accident scene actually part of insured premises? (If not, determine owner of property, e.g., city, neighbor.)

    b. *If inside*

       (1) Give room or location where fall took place. Dimensions.

       (2) Condition of floor—carpeted, linoleum, heavily waxed floor, throw rugs on top of waxed floor or linoleum floor, terrazzo, etc.

       (3) Lighting conditions.

       (4) If foreign substance or debris, get description.

2. Were you alone at time of accident? (If not, obtain name, age, address, and relationship of other person or persons present.)

3. What was the purpose of your being at the location of accident scene? (House guest, visitor, baby-sitting, door-to-door selling, customer, etc.?)

4. Exact route traveled to point of accident.

5. Actions before accident. (Walking, running, looking at ground or floor, looking upward, in process of sitting down, etc.)

6. Describe how fall occurred. (Which foot slipped first?)

7. How did you fall? (Forward, backward, sideways, etc.)

8. Position after fall. (On back, on side, on face, and near what object?)

9. Observation of floor or area *after* the fall. (Invite subject to give any peculiarities observed.)

10. Was a specific cause of the fall noted? (Banana peel on floor, toys, marbles, or any other item or substance on the floor that may have caused fall?)

11. Skid marks or any other evidence of fall?

12. What kind of shoes were you wearing? (Rubber or leather soles, height of heels, type of shoe.)

13. Previous falls when same shoes were worn?

14. Bundles or objects carried or pushed? (Describe in what hand or arm, weight, size, etc.)

15. Do you wear glasses? (If so, worn at time of fall? Are glasses with or without bifocals?)

16. Did subject use any artificial aids? (Cane, crutches, artificial limbs, etc.)

17. Witnesses? Identity. (Did they observe hazard involved?)

18. Any remarks made by witnesses? (Obtain verbatim details.)

19. Assistance needed to get up? (Who helped, or what assistance in general?)

20. Was ambulance called? (If so, by whom and what ambulance? Where was claimant taken?)

21. If no ambulance was called, describe how subject left premises.

22. Any drinking or drugs involved?

23. Was there any prior notice of hazard?

24. General condition of accident area OTHER than accident scene, e.g., rest of floor or floors clean and free of debris?

25. Were police called? Obtain details.

INJURY:

1. Any complaints of injuries?

2. Describe injuries.

3. Ambulance at scene?

4. Identify doctors, hospitals, dates, and type of treatment; in particular, date of first treatment.

5. Doctor's diagnosis and prognosis.

6. If employed, any lost time from work?

   a. Extent of time lost.

   b. Is employer continuing to pay wages?

7. Any prior accidents, injuries, or serious illness?

8. What was the extent of your injuries received in the accident?

9. Was any other part of your body injured in this accident? (If yes, follow up.)

CLOSING:

(Before concluding, check your notes or diagram to see whether any additional questions or issues must be asked or clarified.)

1. "Is there anything further you would like to add concerning this accident?"

2. "Have you understood all the questions asked?"

3. "Were your answers true to the best of your knowledge?"

4. "Did you understand that our conversation was being recorded? Was this with your permission?"

5. "Thank you, (*name of person*)."

This concludes the recorded interview. The time now is _____ (A.M. or P.M.).

APPENDIX NOTE

1. Robert J. Prahl and Stephen Utrata, *Liability Claim Concepts and Practices* (Malvern, Pa.: Insurance Institute of America, 1985), pp. 273–274.

APPENDIX B—STATEMENT GUIDELINE FOR DOG-BITE CLAIM (INSURED)

Use the same introduction and conclusion as given in Appendix A.

1. Is your yard fenced (and is fence in good repair)?

2. What type of fence?

3. How high?

4. Do you own a dog?

5. If not now, did you ever?

6. What kind is it?

7. What name does it answer to?

8. How big is it?

9. How old is it?

10. When did you get it?

11. Did the dog ever bite anyone?

12. If yes, get all details.

13. Did the dog ever act viciously toward anyone or any other animal?

14. Did anyone ever complain about the dog?

15. Was the dog kept chained (and where was the chain)?

16. What type of chain?

17. Did the dog ever get loose from the chain? (If yes, when and how?)

18. Did the chain ever break?

19. Did you ever repair the chain?

20. Did anyone else?

21. Were you at home when the dog allegedly bit _____?

22. Who first reported the dog bite to you?

23. What exactly was said?

24. Has the person who was bitten ever been on your property before?

25. Do you have a "beware of dog" sign posted (and why did you put sign up)?

26. Has your dog been vaccinated for rabies?

Product Liability

Product Liability

Product liability claims can be costly and complicated. Product liability cases account for nearly half of all jury-verdict awards over one million dollars, with some awards exceeding $100 million.[1] This chapter begins with an overview of the fundamentals of product liability laws and concepts and concludes with a case study illustrating how a claim representative would handle a product liability claim.

PRODUCT LIABILITY LAWS AND CONCEPTS

The case that follows demonstrates key product liability issues. A manufacturer produces inexpensive plastic toys that are sold to a fast-food establishment distributing the toys to children in a "kid's meal" package sold by the fast-food establishment. Unfortunately, several children choke to death on a small removable part that comes with one of the plastic toys. In most of the cases, the parents of the children who died had purchased the kid's meal toys, but in a few cases, the children were playing with the toys at the homes of other children.

This case elicits several important questions related to product liability claims. After finishing this section, readers should be able to answer the following questions:

- Under what theory(ies) could the manufacturer be held liable for the children's deaths?

- Could the fast-food establishment also be held liable for the deaths if it did not alter the toys or the package the toys came in?

- If the fast-food establishment is sued, could it require the manufacturer to pay for its defense costs?

- Would all of the families of the children who died be able to make a product liability claim, or only those whose parents purchased the kid's meal toys?

- What defenses might the manufacturer or fast-food establishment have in these claims?

Product liability refers to the liability of a manufacturer, a distributor, a retailer, or another type of seller that, because of a product defect, harms a product user, consumer, or—in some cases—bystander. The three theories of liability that claimants might use in making product liability claims are

1. Negligence
2. Warranty
3. Strict Liability

NEGLIGENCE AND PRODUCT LIABILITY

Manufacturers, component suppliers, distributors, and retailers of products can be negligent in various ways. As mentioned in Chapter 5, negligence involves conduct that creates an unreasonable risk of harm to another. The following are some examples of negligent activities for which manufacturers have been held liable:

*   Negligent design
*   Negligent labeling and packaging
*   Negligence in providing warnings or instructions
*   Negligent inspection and testing
*   Negligent assembly

Consider a manufacturer of lawn and garden fertilizer. To make the fertilizer, the manufacturer combines chemicals that will promote growth in grasses and plants. The chemicals must be carefully and accurately mixed to be safe and effective. A computer operator at one of the manufacturer's production plants misprograms a machine that mixes the chemicals and causes a batch of fertilizer to be so strong that it kills grasses and plants. The manufacturer could be found negligent for such harm caused to the consumers of this batch of fertilizer. In addition to being liable for negligently mixing the chemicals forming the fertilizer, the manufacturer might also be held negligent for not making a reasonable inspection of the product to catch product defects.

Negligent design is another common product liability claim. Consider an auto manufacturer that designs a vehicle with a gas tank that proves likely to explode if the vehicle is involved in a collision. Even though the vehicle runs perfectly well, the design would likely be considered defective because it is foreseeable that automobiles will occasionally collide with other vehicles or objects. This element of foreseeability is important in product liability claims because many claims involve the use of a product in an unintended manner.

Manufacturers have a duty to foresee the probable results of the normal use of a product or even a likely misuse of the product that can reasonably be anticipated. Manufacturers should take into consideration the human weaknesses of the users, and thus the possibilities of misuse and accidents. It may also be expected of manufacturers to anticipate whether a product will be used by—for example—a small child, a skilled surgeon, or a semi-skilled office worker. However, manufacturers are not obligated to foresee all of the absurd, dangerous uses of a product.[2] In the case presented involving the children who choked on parts from plastic toys, manufacturers could have reasonably foreseen that the removable parts posed a choking hazard. In such a case, the manufacturer might be negligent in the design of the toys, especially because it knew that small children would be the primary users of the products.

Another potential area of negligence is the **failure to warn**. Manufacturers cannot always design away all the potential hazards of a product or create safeguards that will absolutely prevent accidents. Many products such as cars, lawn mowers, or toys have potential dangers. These products have utility to society, and it would not benefit society to have them all removed from public use. Because a manufacturer possesses a high degree of technical knowledge about a product, the way that product will be used, and the potential dangers related to its use, the manufacturer must warn the user of these dangers.

In the earlier case involved with the plastic toys that came with the kid's meal, the manufacturer should have foreseen that the toys would fall into the hands of small children. Knowing this, the manufacturer should have included with the toys a warning about the toys' potential choking hazards, in addition to designing the toys to reduce the possibility of their parts being swallowed by small children:

At a minimum, a **product warning label** should have the following characteristics:

1. It should be readable.
2. It should be printed in a way to catch the user's attention.
3. Its content should be understandable to the average user of the product, and it should accurately convey the nature of the danger.

Consider the warning on a lawn mower. It is placed on the body of the lawn mower, in large print, in a different color than that of the lawn mower, and it explains that death or serious injury can result if hands and feet are caught in the lawn mower blade. Such a warning meets the criteria of being noticeable and readable (large print, clear language, different color), explaining how a person can become injured by the product (getting hands or feet caught in the blade) and listing the potential consequences (death or serious injury).

The following is part of an example of a *recall* warning issued for a toy included with a "BURGER KING®️ kids meal." The warning is in large yellow and black print and uses simple words and drawings to convey what product is dangerous and the serious potential risk of harm associated with the use of the product. As a recall warning, it also explains what users should do with the affected products they might have in their possession. The accompanying message seems to address the issue of foreseeability of misuse by younger siblings of purchasers of BURGER KING®️ Big Kids Meals.

Exhibit 13-1 shows an example of a message from the Consumer Product Safety Commission (CPSC). This level of detail is required in order for such warnings to be effective. The photo assists consumers in identifying the product.

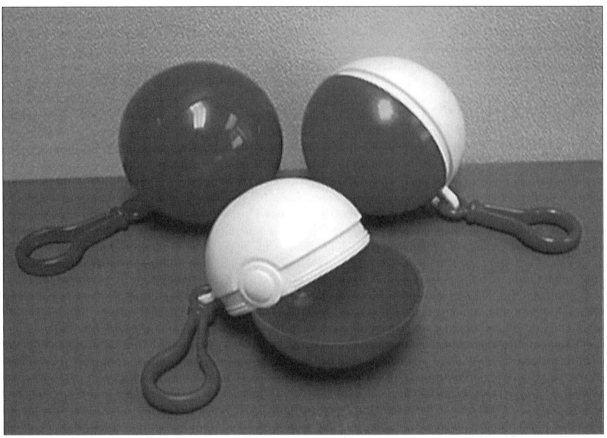

Pokemon balls described in recall warning.

EXHIBIT 13-1

Message From Consumer Product Safety Commission[3]

In Wake of Second Death, CPSC and Burger King Again Urge Consumers to Destroy and Discard Pokemon Balls

WASHINGTON, D.C. The U.S. Consumer Product Safety Commission (CPSC) and Burger King Corp. are again urging consumers to immediately destroy and discard Pokemon balls distributed with Burger King kids meals in November and December 1999. On January 25, 2000, a 4-month-old boy in Indianapolis, Ind., reportedly suffocated when one-half of a Pokemon ball that was in his crib became stuck on his face.

Burger King Corp., in cooperation with CPSC, issued a voluntary recall of more than 25 million Pokemon balls on December 27, 1999. The balls pose a suffocation hazard to children under three years of age.

In December, a 13-month-old girl reportedly suffocated when one-half of a Pokemon ball covered her nose and mouth. Also in December, an 18-month-old girl nearly suffocated when a ball-half got stuck over her face. On the second attempt, the girl's father was able to pull the ball-half from her face.

Pokemon balls are plastic, ball-shaped containers between 2.75 and 3 inches in diameter. They pull apart to reveal one of 57 different Pokemon toys inside. The balls were distributed in a variety of colors including red and white, and hot pink. Packaging described them as safety tested and recommended for all ages of children.

Burger King restaurants nationwide distributed the Pokemon balls inside Burger King big kids meals and regular kids meals from early November through December 1999.

Consumers should immediately take the balls away from children under the age of three. They should discard the ball or return both halves of the ball and the clip to a Burger King restaurant for a free order of small fries. Children can continue to use the Pokemon toy that came inside the ball.

As part of the voluntary recall effort, more than 8,100 Burger King restaurants posted recall notices in both English and Spanish. When the recall was first announced, Burger King placed an ad in *USA Today*, and CPSC broadcast a video news release so local television stations could use video tape showing the danger. CPSC Chairman Ann Brown also announced the recall on the *Today Show* reaching millions of viewers.

In addition, Burger King worked with the CPSC to send recall notices to 56,000 pediatricians' offices, 10,000 emergency room directors and 25,000 emergency health care clinics across the country. Notices were posted on the CPSC and Burger King web sites, and on web sites frequented by Pokemon fans and parents. Recall notices will be posted on tray liners, carry-out bags and french fry bags as well.

Burger King also will purchase national cable and network television advertisements to alert consumers to the recall. Burger King's Consumer Relations phone number is 305-378-3535, which operates Monday through Friday, 9:00 a.m. to 6:00 p.m. east coast time.

Supplier's Negligence

A manufacturer might use component parts prepared by others. This often occurs with many products such as cars and personal computers. The supplier of the component part is liable to the manufacturer for defective parts or material provided to the manufacturer. Some questions exist as to whether the supplier of component parts owes a duty to the ultimate user if the manufacturer accepts the responsibility to inspect the part and include it in the finished product. Because the primary responsibility to inspect the part and to assemble it correctly rests with the manufacturer and the ultimate user has a recourse against the manufacturer, the user normally has no need to seek other sources for recovery. However, in the event that the manufacturer is bankrupt or has inadequate insurance, a user who suffers harm from a component can assert a claim against the component supplier.

Retailer's Negligence

Retailers, as well as manufacturers, may in some circumstances be found negligent. Depending on the circumstances, retailers can be held negligent for the following:

1.   Failure to inspect a product

2. Failure to warn of the dangers of a product
3. Failure to properly assemble a product
4. Negligent sales or sales in violation of a statute

The sale of a defective product is not enough, by itself, to prove negligence against a retailer. Retailers have no duty to open boxes and inspect products. Grocery stores are not required to open canned goods, and appliance stores are not required to open boxes to check microwave ovens. Some retailers may have a responsibility to at least make superficial inspections when they find goods that are *not* in a closed container. Auto dealers would have a duty to at least make a visual inspection of the cars they sell. In some cases, retailers assemble some of the goods they sell. For example, if a home-improvement store sells and assembles tool sheds and outdoor swings, the home-improvement store could be held liable for the improper assembly or installation of these items. Other types of sellers may also be held liable under negligence. Rental-car companies could be held liable for renting defective cars, and a plumber who sells and installs a water heater in violation of a plumbing code could be found liable.[4]

Many states have adopted **negligent misrepresentation** as a cause of action in product liability. This occurs when

1. The seller represents that the product is free from defects, and
2. The seller has no grounds to base the representations that the product is not defective, and the seller knows that a significant danger exists if there is a defect, and
3. The purchaser relies on the representation made by the seller, and
4. The product contains a defect that harms the user.

In one case, an auto dealer assured a buyer that clicks in a car's steering wheel, noticed by the buyer, would eventually go away. Later the steering wheel locked and caused the car to crash. The dealer was held liable under the theory of negligent misrepresentation.

Sales in Violation of a Statute

Sometimes sellers can be held liable if they violate a law in selling a product. In a negligence action based on a statutory violation, the following requirements should be present:

1. The statute must have been enacted to protect a class of persons that includes the claimant.
2. The injury must be of a type that the statute seeks to protect against.
3. The party charged with negligence must have violated the statute.
4. The statutory violation must be the proximate cause of the injury.

Liability in these cases is often negligent sales or sales in violation of a statute.

Consider, for example, a law that prohibits selling gasoline in unapproved containers. Assume that a ten-year-old boy pumps gasoline into a milk carton. On the boy's way home, a cigarette from a passing car catches the gasoline on fire and burns the boy. The gas station that sold the gas in the unapproved container would be liable for negligent sales. Many states have enacted statutes holding the vendor or manufacturer of certain foods and drugs responsible for accidents arising from their use or distribution. Vendors that sell contaminated food that is unfit for human consumption would be in violation of pure food laws.

Consumers who make product liability claims against retailers usually make their claims under warranty or through strict liability theories rather than through proof of negligence. These theories are discussed later in the chapter.

Negligence Defenses for Product Liability

Defendants of product liability claims employ defenses such as

- No defect in their product, or
- Misuse or alteration of the product by the claimant.

In addition to these defenses unique to product liability claims, some of the defenses for negligence claims in general also apply to negligence for product liability. Some of those defenses mentioned in Chapter 5 that might apply are the following:

- Duty owed to claimant was not breached
- No proximate cause of action to injury
- Unforeseeability of harm
- Intervening cause of harm
- Acts of God
- Contributory/comparative negligence on the part of the product user
- Assumption of risk by the product user
- Statutes of limitation

No proximate cause is a defense (described in Chapter 5) in negligence claims that can be used in product cases as well. The defendants actions must be the cause of the claimant's injuries.

Consider the following cases involving product liability claims based on negligence and the defenses successfully used in each case. Keep in mind these defenses are used to counter claims based on negligence. *Some of these claims might have succeeded if they had been based on strict liability (a theory discussed in the following section).*

A mother notices her seven-year-old son playing with matches near some rubbing alcohol. The mother warns the boy about the potential fire hazard and takes the matches away from him. The boy later finds the matches and ignites the alcohol and himself. Because the alcohol container had no danger warning, the parents sued the manufacturer. Because the mother already knew and even warned her son of the fire danger, the lack of warning by the manufacturer was not the cause of the fire, and the manufacturer was therefore not negligent.[5] Thus, the lack of warning was not the proximate cause, and the claimant was comparatively at fault.

A drug manufacturer diligently tests one of its drugs and determines that it is safe and free of adverse reactions. The drug caused a serious adverse reaction in one of its users. The manufacturer did not list this reaction as a possible side effect. The court stated that because the manufacturer, after exercising due care in testing for adverse reactions, had no way of knowing the type of reaction suffered by the claimant would occur, the manufacturer had no duty to warn of the risk.[6] This risk of harm was unforeseeable by the manufacturer.

A manufacturer of a lawn mower successfully argued that a lawn mower operator was guilty of contributory negligence in an accident in which the operator was injured when she ran into a pipe while operating the lawn mower.[7] The claimant's own negligence barred recovery.

Consider the following hypothetical case illustrating the assumption of risk defense and comparing it to contributory/comparative negligence.

A worker detects a defect in an industrial machine. He recognizes the defect as a dangerous hazard but continues to use it, thinking that he can avoid injury if he is cautious. If he then is injured as a result of the defect, the manufacturer could raise the assumption of risk defense. Compare this to another situation in which the worker was injured after he noticed a problem with the machine but continued to use it because he did not recognize the danger posed by the problem. In this second situation, the worker might have been guilty of contributory or comparative negligence because he should have stopped and checked to see what the problem was. However, the worker did not assume the risk entirely because he did not understand the danger.

These are a few examples of defenses that could be raised for product liability claims based on negligence. These defenses might not be successful if used in warranty or strict liability claims.

WARRANTY AND PRODUCT LIABILITY

Consumers usually think of a warranty as being a written document explaining how long, and to what extent, the manufacturer is responsible for product defects. This is one type of warranty, but it is not necessary for the warranty or guarantee to be in writing. Certain warranties are implied simply by the sale of the item. The following are types of **implied warranties**:

1. Warranty of title
2. Warranty of merchantability
3. Warranty of fitness for a particular purpose

Implied warranties are automatic as part of a sales transaction. Courts have imposed obligations on the seller of products to warrant, or guarantee, certain things about the item sold. When a seller fails to live up to a warranty, the seller is said to have committed a **breach of warranty**.

People often think of warranties as being used to seek recourse to obtain refunds for the amount of the defective item purchased or to obtain replacements for defective products. Recovery can actually be much broader than just those economic damages. Recovery under warranty theories of liability, as in cases of negligence, can also be for property damage and personal injuries resulting from the defective product. In claims in which the damages are limited only to economic losses associated with the loss or performance failure of the product, courts may look only to warranty law to apply a remedy. These courts reserve tort law for claims involving physical injury to a person or property. Warranty law is the only remedy for pure economic losses.

Implied Warranty of Title

When an article is offered for sale, the seller guarantees that it has the authority to sell the item. It is implied in the sales transaction that the seller is able to pass on a title and ownership to the buyer. If some other party actually has ownership of the article, the buyer would have recourse against the seller based on a breach of an **implied warranty of title.**

Implied Warranty of Merchantability

When an article is offered for sale, the seller guarantees that the items are of quality good enough to be reasonably fit for the ordinary purposes for which the goods are used and to conform to the promises made on the container or label. The seller implies, for instance, that bottles will not leak, garden hoses will allow water to flow through them, and lawn mowers will cut grass. These are examples of reasonable expectations of consumers and are **implied warranties of merchantability** because they need not be expressed in writing in order for the consumer to have a recourse against the seller.

Warranty of Fitness for a Particular Purpose

A **warranty of fitness for a particular purpose** is created when a seller, who knows what a buyer wants and how the buyer would use the product, makes a recommendation that the buyer relies on. Consider a customer who goes to a hardware store looking for a sander to use to sand all of the wood floors in her house. After explaining her needs to the salesman, he recommends a sander for her to purchase. She takes the sander home, and after using it for two hours, the motor in the sander burns out. The woman takes the sander back to the store and was told by the store manager that the sander she purchased lacked the power to do the work she required. The store could be held liable for a breach of warranty of fitness for a particular purpose because of the salesman's specific recommendation to her regarding the appropriate product for her purpose. This would be considered a breach of an *expressed* warranty because of the salesman's assertions.

Expressed Warranties

There are two types of warranties: implied and expressed. With an **expressed warranty,** the seller specifically represents that the goods sold possess certain qualities. A typical example is a seller that sells "shatterproof" glass. If the glass breaks and shatters into tiny pieces, the seller has committed a breach of an expressed warranty because the glass was expressly represented as being shatterproof. Expressed warranties are often found with products that exceed expectations of other similar products on the market. A seller that sells a waterproof camera would be liable if the camera leaked.

Uniform Commercial Codes

Warranty law is affected by the Uniform Commercial Code (UCC), which deals with warranties on a statutory basis. The UCC is a codified form of the law related to sales transactions and covers such areas as implied warranties, expressed warranties, sales contracts, disclaimers, and damages. Exhibit 13-2 shows an example of wording found in a section of the Uniform Commercial Code that explains an **implied warranty of merchantability**.

EXHIBIT 13-2

Section of Uniform Commercial Code (400.2-314)

Implied warranty- merchantability- usage of trade

(1) Unless excluded or modified (section 400.3-316), a warranty that the goods shall be merchantable is implied in the contract for sale if the seller is a merchant with respect to the good of that kind. Under this section the serving for value of food or drink to be consumed either on the premises or elsewhere is a sale.

(2) Goods to be merchantable must be at least such as

   (a) pass without objection in the trade under the contract description; and

   (b) in the case of fungible goods, are fair average quality with the description; and

   (c) are fit for ordinary purposes for which such goods are used; and

   (d) run, within the variations permitted by the agreement, of even kind, quality and quantity within each unit and among all units involved; and

   (e) are adequately contained, packaged, and labeled as the agreement may require; and

   (f) conform to the promises of affirmations of fact made on the container or label if any.

(3) Unless excluded or modified (section 400.2-314) other implied warranties may arise from course of dealing or usage of trade.

Warranty Defenses

Some defenses to negligence may not succeed with breach of warranty claims. For example, contributory negligence would not be a valid defense to a breach of warranty action.[8] Warranty liability is not based on fault, and therefore the fault of either party is irrelevant. Sellers do have defenses to claims made under the various breach of warranty theories. Common warranty defenses include the following:

- The warranty was fulfilled.
- The alleged expressed warranty was just exaggerated "sales talk."
- The warranty included appropriate disclaimers.
- The claimant assumed the risk.

Sometimes courts may rule that an expressed warranty was fulfilled, even though the product failed. Consider the following case.

A used car dealer told the buyer that the car being considered "was in good shape." At the time of the sale, the car had been driven more than 90,000 miles. Shortly after the buyer purchased the car, the alternator failed. The court stated that this did not constitute a breach of warranty because the buyer could not expect new car performance.[9]

Another factor that courts consider is whether a statement made by a seller is just "puffery" or a sales representative's opinions versus an affirmative statement of warranty. A statement such as "This is a wonderful, trouble-free vacuum cleaner that you'll just love" would not be considered an expressed warranty. The buyer cannot reasonably rely on this recommendation and assume that no repairs or complications will be associated with the vacuum cleaner's use.

Disclaimers are another warranty defense. Consider a paint sprayer that a contractor purchases from a hardware store to paint a large commercial building. The paint sprayer had a noticeably large disclaimer that read as follows:

THIS PAINT SPRAYER IS NOT WARRANTED FOR COMMERCIAL USE.

In such an instance, the seller would have a warranty defense based on this disclaimer. As a rule, sellers try to avoid any liability for *implied* warranties by specifically disclaiming all warranties except the expressed warranties explicitly set forth in the purchase agreement.

Assumption of risk, unlike contributory negligence, is generally viewed by courts as a defense in a warranty action. Courts have applied assumption of risk to the use of machinery that claimants recognized as dangerous.[10] Certainly in cases in which the alleged product defect is inadequate warning, assumption of risk is a complete defense.

Other defenses, such as the defect's not being the proximate cause of injuries and the defense that no defect existed, may sometimes be raised in breach of warranty claims.

STRICT LIABILITY FOR PRODUCTS

The basic rule for strict liability for products is that claimants injured by defective products need not prove that the "seller" was negligent in order to collect damages for their loss. As used in making claims under strict liability, the term **"seller"** is not limited to retailers that sell the goods to the ultimate consumer but can include any party in the chain of selling, including component suppliers, manufacturers, distributors, bailors, and even builders of housing developments.[11] In addition to purchasers and users of products, bystanders can also (in some states) sue for their injuries. If, for example, a pedestrian is struck by a car that had a defective steering mechanism, the pedestrian-bystander could also make a claim under the theory of strict liability for products.

According to Section 402 A of the Restatement (Second) of Torts, in order for a "seller" to be found liable under the theory of strict liability, the following rule must be met: [12]

> The "seller" is subject to liability if it sells the product in a defective condition, that is unreasonably dangerous to the user or consumer, and causes harm to the user or consumer (or to his property), if
>
> (a) the seller is engaged in the business of selling such a product, and
>
> (b) it is expected to reach the consumer or user without substantial change in the condition in which it is sold.

Strict liability applies even if the seller exercised all possible care in the preparation and sale of the product. As mentioned earlier, the party harmed by the product does not have to have purchased the product or entered into a contract with the seller in order to pursue a claim. (In legal terms, the claimant does not have to have privity.) Disclaimers, either in a written contract or otherwise, are not effective defenses in strict liability claims.

For someone to make a claim under the theory of strict liability, a product must contain a defect when it leaves the seller's hands. But what constitutes a defect?

A defect could include any weakness or flaw in the product that later causes harm. A shirt that has bad stitching would be a product defect but not one that would meet the criteria for a claim under strict liability because the defect does not pose an unreasonable danger of harm to the consumer (except perhaps to the consumer's fashion sense). If a new car leaked windshield-washer fluid, it would be defective, but that defect would probably not be considered unreasonably dangerous. In reality, courts are often ready to accept the argument that a defect is unreasonably dangerous if it causes serious harm to the user.

If the product has been altered, and this alteration causes the defect, the "seller" might not be liable. Consider a television that had numerous mechanical failures and repairs until one day the television finally exploded and set the owner's house on fire. If the repairs were made each time by representatives of the seller, then courts would likely consider the "seller" to still be liable because after each repair the television should have been in substantially the same condition as it was when it was purchased.[13] If, on the other hand, the owner or another independent repairperson had made repairs that altered the television and caused or contributed to the defect, the seller would likely not be liable.

Application of strict liability for defective products does *not mean that sellers are absolutely liable for all claims*. Some products cannot perform their essential function without posing some danger. Consider power saws. Anything that can cut through building materials can also cut fingers. The "seller" is not an insurer of all potential harm caused by the use of a product. Consider, for example, a man who claimed that he had run over his foot with his lawn mower while maneuvering the lawn mower in a way that it distributed grass in a "nice even pattern." The man claimed that the lawn mower was defective because it shot grass out in a random pattern that made the lawn look unkempt to the owner.

In such a situation, strict liability would not apply. First, the seller could argue that the lawn mower had no defect. Second, if the random distribution of grass was a defect, it was not unreasonably dangerous. If, during the investigation of the case, it was discovered that the man had dropped the lawn mower on his foot while trimming hedges, the seller could argue that the product was not used in a manner reasonably anticipated.

In review, a seller is only liable under strict liability if (1) the product has a defect, (2) the defect is unreasonably dangerous, (3) the defect was the proximate cause of the claimant's injuries, and (4) the product was used in a manner reasonably anticipated.[14]

Courts sometimes permit product claims to be made under the theory of strict liability if the misuse of the product was reasonably foreseeable. Consider, for example, sharp, heavy yard darts that are sold as toys for children. The yard darts have sharp points on them that could pierce a child's skull. It would be reasonably foreseeable that the children would misuse the product by not accurately throwing the darts or possibly by throwing the darts at each other.

Market-Share Liability

Market-share liability has been imposed in some jurisdictions. This theory of liability is used when identification of the culpable product is not possible. This typically arises in cases involving generic drugs when a drug could have more than one possible manufacturer. If someone is harmed by a defect of the drug, it may be impossible to trace down the exact manufacturer that produced the drugs taken by the claimant. In such cases, some states have allowed claimants to make a claim against all the manufacturers and recover from each based on the proportion of the sales that each manufacturer has in the market. Not all states have accepted this theory of liability.

Strict Liability Defenses for Product Liability

Because many product liability claims are based on the theory of strict liability, claim professionals must know and apply the defenses to strict liability. The defenses most commonly raised in strict product liability claims are the following:

- Criteria for strict liability claim not met
- Contributory negligence
- Assumption of risk
- Misuse of the product
- State of the art defense
- Government specifications

As mentioned earlier, the criteria for a strict product liability claim require that

- A product be manufactured or sold by the defendant (as opposed to a service).
- The product have a defect (when it left the defendant's hands).
- The defect be *unreasonably* dangerous.
- The defect cause the claimant's injuries.
- The product be used in a manner reasonably anticipated.

If these criteria are not met, the theory of strict liability cannot be successfully used. This is the first line of defense in strict product liability claims.

A contributory/comparative negligence defense can be used in strict liability claims if the basis for such a defense is the user's actions, such as altering the product, misusing the product, or failing to read a warning.

Assumption of risk is also a valid defense in strict liability claims. In general, "if the user or consumer discovers the defect and is aware of the danger, and nevertheless proceeds to make use of the product and is injured by it, he is barred from recovery."[15]

Another defense in strict liability for products is the state of the art defense. If the product was conformed to the prevailing industry standards at the time it was designed or built, it should not be considered defective even though industry standards increase in subsequent years, based on technological gains. This is known as the **state of the art defense.** For example, a car made in 1960 might have a metal dashboard, no seat belts, and windshields that shatter on impact. Cars with these characteristics would be considered defective by modern industry standards, but the manufacturers of these old cars cannot be held to new standards if the cars met the prevailing safety standards of 1960. The cars would not be considered defective, even if they are still on the road today.

Sometimes manufacturers rely on **government specifications** in designing, building, or labeling products. For example, the Environmental Protection Agency (EPA) requires manufacturers of pesticides to place EPA-approved warnings on the labeling and packaging produced by the manufacturer. If a claimant makes a product liability claim against the manufacturer based on an inadequate warning label, the manufacturer could rely on the government's specification as a defense.

RETAILER DEFENSES AND RECOVERIES

A claimant can recover from a retailer on the theory of breach of warranty or strict liability. This is true even if the product involved was sold in the exact same condition as it arrived in from the manufacturer. In such cases, the retailer must pay the claimant, but the retailer may have an action of **indemnification** against the manufacturer to recover the damages paid the claimant. The Uniform Commercial Code governing this situation requires the retailer to notify the manufacturer of the claim. This requirement gives the manufacturer the opportunity to step in and take over the defense of the claim. If the manufacturer does not do this, then the retailer is permitted to seek recovery from the manufacturer (indemnification).

APPLICATION OF PRODUCT LIABILITY

A product liability case involving plastic toys sold at a fast-food establishment and related questions were presented at the beginning of this section. After reading the previous sections, the answers to the following questions should be apparent.

- Under what theory(ies) could the manufacturer be held liable for the deaths of the children?

- Could the fast-food establishment also be held liable for the deaths if it did not alter the toys or the package the toys came in?

- If the fast-food establishment is sued, could it require the manufacturer to pay for its defense costs?

- Would all of the families of the children who died be able to make a product liability claim, or only those whose parents purchased the kid's meal toys?

- What defenses might the manufacturer or fast-food establishment have in these claims?

A claim could be made against the manufacturer under the theory of negligent design because it designed toys with small removable parts that posed choking hazards even though the known users were children. If it did not intend that the parts be removed, then it failed to properly construct the toys (or inspect the toys for defects). It might also be negligent for failing to warn of these hazards. The manufacturer probably breached a duty of implied warranty of fitness for a particular purpose because the toys were not suitable for inclusion in a kid's meal that would be used by small children. The manufacturer would also be liable under strict liability theories because the product was defective; the use of the toys posed an unreasonably dangerous risk given the intended users; the defect caused the choking hazard; although the children misused the product, this misuse was reasonably foreseeable; and the children were too young (younger than three years old) to have the assumption of risk defense applied against them.

The fast-food establishment could be held liable under both warranty and strict liability theories but probably not under the theory of negligence if the toys came in sealed packages. Once the fast-food establishment discovered the hazard, it would then have to make every effort to warn consumers and withdraw the toys from the kid's meals. The fast-food establishment would notify the manufacturer that it was being sued and would be indemnified by the manufacturer if the manufacturer did not take over the handling of the claims. (The only thing that might change this is if the fast-food establishment had a contract with the manufacturer that stated something contrary to this position.)

All of the children who died were users of the toys, and their families were therefore able to make claims under negligence, warranty, and strict liability. The manufacturer, if sued, would raise several defenses such as the product was not defective and the defect did not exist when it left the manufacturer. It is unlikely that these defenses would be successful. The retailer fast-food establishment would have good defenses for avoiding negligence claims, but warranty and strict liability claims would probably succeed against it.

PRODUCT LIABILITY—CASE STUDY

The following case is designed to help the reader understand the real-world issues involved in handling a product liability claim. The educational objective for this case study is for the reader, given a product liability claim scenario, to learn how to investigate and assess liability and evaluate damages. The actions taken by the characters portrayed in this case may not be the preferred actions at every insurance company, and other approaches may be equally valid.

The Notice of Loss

National Farm Insurance insures Rock N Roll Music, a musical instrument and equipment dealer, under a commercial general liability policy (CGL). National Farm has recently received a copy of a letter from an attorney representing the parents of a man who was electrocuted while singing at a homeowner's party while using musical equipment rented from Rock N Roll Music. The letter stated that the electrocution was caused by defective musical equipment. The ground wire for the electrical outlet plug had been cut off, and the microphone had been wired to stay in the "on" position at all times. Because of the serious nature of the claim (a fatality), Susan Williams, the claim supervisor for National Farm, calls in Eric Campbell, the claim representative, to discuss this new claim and how it should be handled.

Eric, who normally handles premises slip-and-fall claims, cannot believe that a product liability claim was filed against the retailer, the insured, and does not see much need for an investigation. The loss notice indicates that the singer, a member of a local band, was electrocuted while standing in a puddle of beer and water in the living room of a local residence. Eric's initial thought is that there was obviously no liability against the retailer and that if any liability existed, it should be with the homeowner but not their insured, the music instrument dealer.

Eric asks Susan incredulously, "Are you sure you've got the right claim here? They're making a claim against our insured, Rock N Roll music? That doesn't seem right."

Susan nods and explains, "Yes, that's who the parents of the kid are making a claim against. I've already checked coverage issues on this, so you don't have to worry about that. The insured has a CGL policy in force, and that provides coverage for product liability that includes renting musical instruments. I know you've mainly handled auto and premises liability claims, but I'm confident you'll be able to handle this. I'll be supervising it closely."

Susan addresses Eric's concerns and discusses the possible allegations as set forth in the attorney's letter with regard to the claim under a product liability lawsuit. Susan explains that a claim could potentially be made against the manufacturer under the theory of *negligent design* because musical equipment should have safeguards to prevent electrocution even with possible misuses of the equipment. She speculates that the plaintiff's attorney might argue that the manufacturer knew or should have known that the likely users of the product would be young musicians who might not exercise caution when they play. Susan explains that the insured, Rock N Roll Music, could be held liable for its own negligence in modifying the instruments or assembling the equipment improperly. It might also have failed to provide the proper warnings or instructional literature, which came with the equipment, when they rented it, to make sure it would not be used in an unsafe manner.

She theorizes that the claimants might allege that the manufacturer of the musical instruments, or the Rock N Roll music store, might also be negligent for a *failure to warn* of certain hazards such as using the equipment outside, in the rain, or where water exists.

In addition, both warranty and strict liability theories might apply. She summarizes the criteria for establishing *strict liability* as

1. The product was defective.
2. It posed an unreasonably dangerous risk.
3. The product misuse was reasonably foreseeable because of the likely users.

At this point in the meeting, Eric interrupts Susan and asks, "How can the music store be liable for somebody misusing its product?"

Susan responds, "The law requires sellers to anticipate foreseeable misuse of their product. I just read of a case recently where the manufacturer of airplane glue was held liable for the deaths of three teenagers who died sniffing the glue. The plaintiffs showed that the manufacturer could have foreseen this misuse and prevented the injuries by altering their product with material that would have made the boys sick instead of killing them. I suspect the young age of the boys made a difference, too, and that's something to keep in mind with this claim."

"What a legal system!" Eric complains.

"Well, there are reasons for these laws, and like them or not, we have to play by these rules. In order to do a proper investigation, we have to anticipate the allegations that may be made," concedes Susan.

"Don't get me wrong, a number of defenses could also apply depending upon how the electrocution took place, so we need to look at those as well," advises Susan.

Susan goes on to explain that the manufacturers of the equipment could raise several defenses, such as

*   The product was not defective, and
*   The defect did not exist when the equipment left the manufacturer, but

it was changed or modified when it was rented by the musical equipment store.

Susan suggests that Eric investigate the allegations of negligent repair against the musical equipment store because one of the electrical outlet plugs was cut off and the microphone was repaired to stay in the "on" position at all times. She reminded Eric to write down all identification information about who manufactured each of the products involved. He also must determine the intended use of each piece of musical equipment in order to assess whether it had been misused.

"You said something about breach of warranty, Susan. Do I need to get the warranty papers on all this equipment?" Eric asks.

"Yeah, you should do that, too, but I would like to know what the insured said to the guy when they rented the equipment. Did they change or alter the equipment to meet some particular performance need? Also, find out what repairs might have been made, either at the equipment store or at some other facility after the equipment was rented. Each one of these areas must be thoroughly investigated," concludes Susan.

Eric leaves the meeting, conceding that this is a much more complicated claim than he had originally thought.

The Investigation

The plaintiff's attorney alleges that this is a product liability case. Two reasons for this are that the manufacturer and retailer have "deeper pockets" (greater financial resources) than the homeowner's. Also, the plaintiff's attorney happens to specialize in product liability cases. Eric does not know whether a claim has been brought against the manufacturer or homeowner yet. What he will learn is that the attorney is pursuing this case against Rock N Roll, the equipment rental company, because the attorney's initial findings revealed that some of the equipment's manufacturers are no longer in business. Because the equipment was purchased some time ago, and manufactured even earlier than that, some of the possible defendants are no longer viable targets. In an application of the theory of joint and several liability, each one of the possible responsible parties would be liable separately or as a group. The injured party has the option to pick which parties to pursue. If the other manufacturers are no longer available, then Rock N Roll could be required to pay the entire claim.

Normally, one tortfeasor would seek *contribution* from the other joint tortfeasors, such as the manufacturers, distributors, or other parties involved, but these parties might not have insurance or be in business to pay their share of the claim. For that reason, even a small percentage of liability for this claim could be costly for Rock N Roll Music and its insurer, National Farm.

Eric commences the investigation by obtaining statements from persons at the party and from four individuals in the band. He learns that the plaintiffs' attorney has not yet notified the homeowner and his daughter who hosted the party that he plans to bring them into the lawsuit, so Eric starts his investigation with the owner of the home and his teenage daughter, who threw the party.

Eric drives to the homeowner's house and speaks with the homeowner, Joel, and his two daughters, Cindy and Heather, who threw the party. The homeowner was out of town at the time of the accident, but Eric questions him anyway and learns that when the homeowner purchased the home, grounding outlets were put in the kitchen and bath areas, but not in the living room, where the band, The Vamps, was playing at the time of the accident. The homeowner did not believe it was necessary to put ground outlets in the entire home, but instead only where the code required them (places where water is present), such as the bathrooms and kitchen.

The scene investigation further reveals that the amplifier, guitar, and microphone were still present at the house. Eric dutifully photographs the equipment and records all relevant information about it. He also takes custody of Rock N Roll Music's equipment left at the house. Eric would later safely store it at his claim office because it might need to be inspected later by other parties involved in litigation of this claim.

After talking to the father, Eric turns his attention to Joel's daughter Cindy and takes her statement. Her father was raising her since her mother had passed away some time ago. Her older sister, Heather, was returning from college after her first year. Joel, the father, was busy making plans for his cruise to Mexico with his new girlfriend, and he thought it would be safe for his eighteen-year-old daughter Cindy to remain at home because his older daughter was coming home for the summer. Cindy's boyfriend, Johnny Vamp, was the singer in a local high-school band called The Vamps. Because her father was leaving town for the weekend, Cindy and her boyfriend thought they could make a few bucks by hosting The Vamps and charging $5.00 admission.

They decided to invite fifty teenagers from the high school and handed out flyers. The flyers had coupons so that if the teenagers paid early, they would have to pay only $5.00. If they did not have a ticket when they showed up, they would have to pay $10.00 at the door. Cindy tearfully shows Eric a picture of four members in the group The Vamps, along with the lead singer, Johnny Vamp. On the night of the party, Cindy got a call from her sister, who told Cindy that her plane was delayed and that she would not be home until Sunday. Because her father had already left on Thursday night for his Mexican cruise, Saturday night seemed like a good opportunity to host the party.

When Saturday arrived, it started to rain, but because this was the end of the high-school year, people came anyway. Cindy had stated on the invitation that kegs of beer would be available, which also attracted attention. As the party continued, more people than Cindy had expected arrived. They originally had the band set up outside, but because of the rain and excess water, they decided to move the band inside. As the teenagers kept coming in and out of the house, they were tramping in excess water, as well as much spilled beer.

Heather, the older sister, arrived home and was shocked to see that more than 150 people were in the house and that the carpet was entirely soaked with water and beer.

She saw the band in the middle of the living room, with the singer swinging the microphone around by the cord and grabbing it and then sticking it in his mouth while intermittently shouting and singing.

During Eric's interview of Heather, she recalls that Johnny Vamp had worn moccasins, but that eventually one of the moccasins was in the doorway to keep the door from closing completely. Rainwater and beer were soaking the entire house. Heather noticed that Johnny had one bare foot, along with wearing just one soaked moccasin. Heather yelled at her sister that her father would kill them if he found out that they were having a party with alcohol and that the house was being trashed. Apparently, no one was older than twenty-one, and the living room was becoming a fairly violent dance pit.

Cindy then went up to the microphone to tell people they needed to leave. Apparently, the microphone had quit working, and she handed it to Johnny Vamp. When she gave him the microphone, he was holding a guitar, and he tried to help his girlfriend to get people to leave. He could not get the microphone to work at this time, and then suddenly he fell back into the drum set. The following is an excerpt from Cindy's statement describing the scene:

Eric: Were your parents present during the party?

Cindy: No.

Eric: Where were they?

Cindy: My father was on a cruise to Mexico for the weekend with his new girlfriend.

Eric: Did they give you permission to have the party?

Cindy: Yes.

Eric: How many people were present at the party?

Cindy: That's the problem. Fifty were invited, but more than 150 people came to the party. When I grabbed the microphone from Johnny to ask everyone to please leave, the microphone didn't work for me. I gave the microphone to Johnny to help me ask people to leave, because the party was getting out of hand. After he grabbed the microphone, he was trying to get it to work again and was asking people to leave. All of a sudden he fell backwards into the drum set, along with the guitar he was holding in one hand and the microphone in the other. He then got up and walked to the kitchen and was grabbing his neck and asking for water. He was walking kind of crazed and grabbing his neck like he had been in the desert or something. Then he fell on the floor and never woke up.

(Eric pauses while Cindy regains her composure)

Eric: Did you see where the microphone was plugged in?

Cindy: Yes. The guitar was plugged into one of the big blue amplifiers there.

Eric: You mean this one called SUNSATION?

Cindy: Yes, that's the one. And the microphone was plugged into the other amplifier, the one called MOON.

Eric: Do you recall what Johnny was wearing?

Cindy: He had on a long, puffy-sleeved shirt, like pirates wear, black leather pants that were real tight, and a leather moccasin on one foot that went up to his knee area, and nothing on the other foot. The carpet was soaked from all of the beer and water that was coming in since it had been raining outside.

Eric: How old are you, Cindy?

Cindy: Eighteen.

Eric: I see that the musical equipment was left here. Did someone ask you to leave it over there in the corner?

Cindy: After the incident happened, the police told us that we should keep the instruments here since Johnny's parents live out of state and my father's insurance company might want to inspect them.

After the statements are taken, Eric goes to the amplifiers, guitar, and microphone. On the back of one amplifier is a label that has "Rock N Roll Music" and the address of the insured written on it. The microphone was manufactured by TV Shack, and the guitar had the name of "BUMPER" on it. Eric writes down the name, the manufacturer, and serial numbers of each piece of equipment and takes photographs of all of the equipment. He then takes the equipment into his custody so that there would not be any **spoliation of evidence** issues because the insurance company now has the duty to preserve the evidence for inspection by either the plaintiffs or the insurance company's own expert, as well as the multiple parties that will eventually be brought into the case as defendants.

> Spoliation—The tort of destroying, erasing, or altering evidence. Traditionally, spoliation claims were permitted only when the destruction or alteration was done in bad faith. More recently these claims have been alleged for negligently failing to preserve evidence.

Eric contacts the insured and asks for information regarding whether the store repairs amplifiers, microphones, and such. The store owner advises that the store does and that it frequently rents merchandise to local rock bands, such as The Vamps, and did so in this case. The store often has trouble with these groups damaging the equipment, but the store overcomes such losses by making the groups pay substantial damage deposits. The store owner indicates that it has the instruction manuals on each piece of equipment and agrees to provide copies to Eric.

The appendix to this chapter provides a checklist of investigative activities that claim representatives should consider with product liability claims.

Analyzing Liability

Eric goes back to his supervisor, Susan, and updates her about the investigation. In discussing the investigation, they make a joint decision to notify the homeowner's insurance company of a cross-complaint for negligent entrustment, as well as negligence with regard to the electrical system in the home. They also discuss with their local outside counsel, Tom Hanson, the possibility of filing cross-complaints against the manufacturers of the microphone, the two different amplifier companies, as well as the guitar company, BUMPER. They then revisit the theories of liability that might be alleged against their insured and analyze each one according to what Eric had learned from his initial investigation. Because Rock N Roll Music rents and repairs instruments, it would most likely be held liable under all three theories of product liability, consisting of negligence, breach of warranty, and strict liability.

Duty To Warn

Susan gives Eric an example of jury instructions commonly used in product liability cases. Eric looks over the following instructions, which succinctly describe the law and would guide a jury in its determination of negligence:

> PRODUCTS LIABILITY NEGLIGENCE—SUPPLIER'S DUTY TO WARN
>
> "One who supplies a product, directly or through a third person, for another to use, which the supplier knows, or has reason to know, is dangerous, or is likely to be dangerous, for the use for which it is supplied, has a duty to use reasonable care to give warning of the dangerous condition of the product, or of facts which make it likely to be dangerous to those whom the supplier should expect to use the product, or to be endangered by its probable use, if the supplier has reason to believe that they will not realize its dangerous condition. A failure to fulfill that duty is negligence. This rule applies to a retailer, manufacturer or repair facility of a product."

Rock N Roll was a supplier of the equipment. Susan and Eric analyze this failure-to-warn issue. First, they considered the issue of the altered equipment. Eric's investigation revealed that the ground plug on one of the amplifier cords was cut off. However, in speaking with the insured, the insured advised Eric that the store employees would never send an amplifier out in that condition. Furthermore, the insured also stated that the store always puts a warning label on the electrical cords to indicate not to cut off the grounding plug. Rock N Roll Music also stated that the store employees inspect and test each amplifier, guitar, and microphone by making sure that the equipment is working properly before it is rented. Eric contacted each one of the band members, and all members indicated that when they rented the equipment, the ground plug was cut off.

"All the guys in the band thought it was easier to plug in the equipment with that one prong missing because a lot of the garages they played in had only two holes to plug the equipment into. They had no idea what that round little plug on top was and thought it had something to do with the sound being louder. Doesn't that get the insured off the hook on this? It seems like it should count for something. Don't they have an obligation to know what they are using?" demands Eric.

Susan responds, "That's true, but if they all testify that the plug was like that when they rented it, it doesn't make the insured look good. The insured shouldn't rent out potentially unsafe equipment. I'm not sure how much their ignorance helps us."

Continuing their analysis, they consider whether their insured might be held liable in failing to warn or give instructions in making sure that the electrical amplifiers were plugged into grounded outlets. In checking the records, Eric learns that this equipment had been rented out for more than six months and that no product warning labels indicated that the microphone and guitar should not be plugged into separate amplification devices when they are not grounded. This was potentially a liability problem but not as bad as if the music dealer had sent equipment that was obviously defective.

With regard to the allegations against the manufacturers for negligence, the jury instructions read:

PRODUCTS LIABILITY—DUTY OF MANUFACTURER

"The manufacturer of a product that is reasonably certain to be dangerous if negligently made, has a duty to exercise reasonable care in the design, manufacture, testing and inspection of the product, and in the testing and inspection of any component parts made by another, so that the product may be safely used in a manner and for a purpose for which it was made. A failure to fulfill that duty is negligence."

Susan calls one of National Farm's defense lawyers, Tom Hanson, to discuss this issue. Susan, Eric, and Tom conference on the claim. They discuss the negligence standard described above and agree that *negligence* in the design or inspection might be difficult to prove. Tom indicates that the retailer or manufacturer might more likely be held liable under theories of strict liability or *failure to warn*.

Tom explains, "In order to prove liability for failure to warn, the claimant must prove the following: The insured failed in that (1) the MOON amplifier had its ground plug cut off, and (2) this made the product defective; (3) the product defect caused injury to the claimant; and (4) the claimant's injury resulted from a use of the product that was reasonably foreseeable to your insured."

Tom continues, "Also keep in mind that if the manufacturer of the amplifier is liable under strict liability, then your insured is also liable. That means even if you proved that it came directly from the manufacturer with that defect, then your insured is still on the hook. Now, your insured would likely be able to get indemnification from the manufacturer, but technically the insured is still on the hook. And if the manufacturer is no longer in business, your insured could get stuck paying this whole thing. Now if it can be proven that the rental equipment went out with the ground plug cut off, then your insured alone as the retailer would be subject to strict liability for placing the consumer in an unreasonably dangerous situation."

"Our insured says it didn't send it out like that and that store employees inspect their equipment before sending it out," Eric explains.

"Good. Is your insured going to be a credible witness?" asks Tom.

"I'd say more so than the kids in the band," snaps Eric. "I guess I should have looked around the house to see whether a little metal piece was lying around. I'm sure one of those kids cut it off just so it would fit into the two-pronged outlet. They couldn't find one of those little adapters, so they just cut off the third prong."

"Well, it would be helpful if you could prove that, but your insured still wouldn't be off the hook completely. Let me describe the liability situation in legal terms. A product is defective if it's used by the person in a reasonably foreseeable manner. *And* the product involves a substantial danger that would not be readily recognized by the ordinary user of the product. *And* the seller knows, or should have known, of the danger, but failed to give adequate warning of such a danger," Tom explained.

Eric summarizes, "So what the law is saying is that a manufacturer and also our insured, as a retailer, had a duty to provide an adequate warning for any use of the product that would involve a substantial danger?"

"That's right. In your claim, the manufacturer may have failed to put a warning near the end of the plug indicating that it would be unsafe to cut the ground plug off or to warn that the amplifier should not be plugged into an electrical outlet unless it is properly grounded. We need to contact the manufacturer to learn whether, in fact, any such warning was placed on the cord. If the manufacturer placed a warning label on the cord and your insured removed it, then your insured could be liable for failure to warn."

"It's possible that the manufacturers of the amplifier, guitar, and microphone might also be responsible for failing to warn about the cutting off of ground plugs," advises Tom.

Tom advises both Eric and Susan that all of the equipment should be tested to see whether it has any other problems that might have led to the electrocution.

"We need to find out whether the manufacturer is still in business and who insures it…. Maybe even who used to insure it when it made the product. I'd like to know about what kind of warning labels it normally puts on its equipment," Tom states.

They all agree. The three then begin to discuss possible defenses.

Assessing Defenses

Several defenses might apply to this claim, including improper use, comparative negligence, and assumption of risk.

Improper Use

"Tom, do you recall the Powermart case we had with the guy who did target practice with a nail gun? We won that case on the improper use defense. I still have the jury instructions on that case here. I wonder if that would apply in this claim?" inquires Susan, showing Eric the jury instructions that follow.

> "Any *warranty* of the goods involved in this case was based on the assumption that they would be used in a reasonable manner, appropriate to the purpose for which they were intended."

"If you should find that Johnny's injury resulted solely from his improper use of the goods involved, then he cannot recover damages, at least not under the breach of warranty theory," advises Tom.

During the investigation, Eric learns that Johnny would continuously twirl the microphone briskly in a circular fashion and then grab the microphone and shove it in his mouth while screaming during his performance. Tom cited numerous cases denying recovery when there was "abnormal use" of the product by the user, and he states that this is the insured's strongest defense.

After hearing of Johnny's exploits from Eric, Tom says, "I think you've got a textbook case of improper use."

However, Susan is less convinced. "Tom, I don't know about the microphone-down-the-throat part, but the singer for one of my favorite groups, the Rolling Bones, does that twirling-mike thing, and I suspect a lot of others do that, too."

Tom concurs that such actions might then be a *foreseeable* use or misuse of the product, especially given the people who might be using the product. Thus "improper use" might not be as strong a defense as he originally thought. The manufacturer of this microphone should have known that many singers do this and should have anticipated this type of use (or misuse).

Tom reflects for a while. "Perhaps the most viable defense on this claim is comparative negligence," he concludes.

Comparative Negligence

"Let me give you a brief legal definition of comparative negligence," Tom begins. "Comparative fault is on the part of the plaintiff which—combining with the fault of a defendant (or wrongful conduct of others)—contributes to cause the injury. Comparative fault on the plaintiff's part does not completely bar recovery by the plaintiff. However, the total amount of the plaintiff's damages is reduced by the percentage that the plaintiff contributed to his or her own injury. For example, if Johnny is 90 percent responsible for this accident, then his parents can collect only 10 percent from other parties. Unfortunately for National Farm, in this claim, 10 percent could be a fairly substantial sum."

Tom continues, "With regard to the negligence issue, Johnny may very well be held responsible for *comparative fault* because he was standing in a puddle of water with only one shoe on and holding electrical equipment. Depending on his experience, he should know that if you are touching or holding electrical equipment, then you should be standing in a dry area.

"Also, if it's true that Johnny cut off the ground plug, it could be argued that his actions were the proximate cause of his own injuries. Even if he didn't know the dangers, once he learned that the microphone was not operating properly when Cindy was using it, he should have known that there might be a problem. That's why I think comparative negligence is your insured's strongest defense."

Assumption of Risk

Assumption of risk by the product user could also be argued if, in fact, Johnny Vamp was aware that by cutting off the ground plug and standing in water, he could possibly be electrocuted but consciously decided to stand in the water while handling the equipment. If he knew that a short was in either the guitar, amplifier, or microphone and continued to stand in the water, then he was arguably *assuming the risk*.

As mentioned earlier in Chapter 5, "Determining Liability," this traditional defense is not viable in all jurisdictions. Some jurisdictions believe that comparative negligence is the appropriate defense for these kinds of situations. Tom discusses the significance of the jurisdiction and the application of the assumption of risk defense in this claim.

Tom explains, "The application of this defense varies by state. Even though Johnny's parents, as plaintiffs, live in different states, the law where the incident occurred and where Johnny and the other defendants reside would control the venue and determine the state law that would apply. However, because numerous manufacturers from different states are involved and both his parents live in different states, the case would most likely be filed in federal court. This is significant because if it were proved that Johnny assumed the risk, then his claim would be completely barred under federal laws. It would have to be proved that Johnny voluntarily assumed a known risk to completely bar a negligence claim.

"However, assuming a known risk is different from misusing a product, and proving that Johnny knew anything at all about the risk of electrical shock by misusing the product could be difficult. It would be easier to prove that he misused or altered a product and that he was aware that standing in water might cause him harm. That's probably not going to bar his parents' claims, but it would likely reduce their claims considerably because of his comparative fault."

Susan summarizes, "So to make an assumption of risk defense stick, we would have to prove that he had actual knowledge of the danger of electrocution and voluntarily chose to ignore that risk and continue playing. It seems like it might be difficult to establish his intent because he is dead and we can't ask him what he was thinking."

Tom confirms, "Yes, you're right. A court would have to speculate on his knowledge and willingness to assume the potential risk."

Other Responsible Parties

In discussing the remainder of the claim, Susan and Eric consider other possible responsible parties. Although the liability of others may not relieve the insured of liability, the other parties might be other "targets" for the plaintiffs to sue and might help share in some settlement offer.

Eric learns that the retailer subcontracted much of its repair work to Musical Repairs Electronics, Inc. Eric learns that this business had repaired the microphone switch in a way that made the switch always "on." This condition would not allow the operator of the microphone to turn the microphone off. According to Musical Repairs, the insured knew this. If, in fact, the repair company altered the microphone on/off switch system and the insured failed to properly warn or change the system, the insured would also share in the responsibility for allowing the repaired item to be placed in the chain of custody for the general public. This defect might be considered to be an unreasonable modification that would most likely cause harm to the consumer/user.

Susan and Eric ask Tom how the liability of this subcontractor, Musical Repairs, would affect the claim against the insured. Tom explains that the party ultimately responsible for causing the defect, Musical Repairs, would pay the largest portion of any settlement or judgment, but the insured could still have some liability.

Eric finds that some of the musical equipment manufacturers are still in business. However, the manufacturers' attorneys contended that there was an indemnity agreement with the retailer and that the retailer, Rock N Roll Music, would agree to hold the manufacturer harmless and indemnify the manufacturer for attorney's fees and any judgment or settlement *if* the retailer altered, changed, or modified any of the equipment before its sale or rental (which is one of the plaintiff's contentions). This appears to be the key issue not only for proving liability against Rock N Roll but also for determining whether Rock N Roll would pay for the manufacturers' defense costs, too.

Some liability would be assessed to the homeowner, Joel, and his daughter. He allowed his minor daughter to have a party while he was gone, and her actions contributed to the accident as well. Furthermore, questions remained regarding the grounding of the house and whether the electrical condition of the house was safe.

Evaluating the Damages

Eric and Susan talk to Hanson about the value of the case and the possible jury verdict in order to assess the proportional amounts that might be charged against the various responsible parties. The following is their evaluation of the damages.

Damages

The decedent, Johnny Vamp, had been working at an auto-repair shop and was earning $25,000 a year. Of this $25,000, he was giving $5,000 to his mother for her support. Because his parents were divorced, he spent most of his time with his mother, and his father had not seen or heard from him in five years. Therefore, the loss of life of the son was much more meaningful, both economically and noneconomically, to the mother.

In the state where this claim occurred, the emotional loss of an adult son could be included as party of the parents' damages. Johnny's mother was devastated. She was never going to see her son again, was never going to see him perform with his band again, and was never going to see him open the auto-repair shop that he had dreamed of owning. The case could not be settled until both the mother and the father agreed on the claim value. In evaluating the case, Eric and Susan look at recent jury verdicts to see what juries in the area had awarded for the loss of an adult child. They see that the verdicts ranged from $100,000 to more than $2 million. They then must decide what makes this case different from or similar to the other cases to establish a range of values that a jury could award to Johnny's parents for emotional loss of their son.

Tom Hanson advises the claim representative and supervisor that the jury instructions regarding measure of damages for the death of an adult child are fairly uniform. He faxes them the following jury instructions that describe the factors a jury is permitted to consider:

The plaintiffs are the heirs of _____, deceased, and are the real parties in interest in this action; they are mother and father, the parents of the deceased. If you find that plaintiffs are entitled to recover against the defendants, you will award such damages as under all circumstances of the case will be just compensation for the loss that each heir has suffered by reason of the death of _____, deceased.

In determining such loss, you may consider the financial support, if any, which each of said heirs would have received from the deceased, except for such death, and the right to receive support, if any, which each of said heirs has lost by reason of such death.

The right of one person to receive support from another is not destroyed by the fact that the former does not need the support, nor the fact that the latter has not provided it.

You may also consider:

- The age of the deceased, and each heir;

- The health of the deceased, and each heir, immediately prior to death;

- The respective life expectancy of the deceased, and each heir;

- Whether deceased was kindly, affectionate, or otherwise;

- The disposition of the deceased to contribute financially to support the heirs;

- The earning capacity of the deceased;

- The deceased's habits of industry and thrift; and

- Any other factors shown by the evidence indicating what benefits each heir might reasonably be expected to receive from the deceased had he lived.

With respect to life expectancies, you will only be concerned with the shorter of two, that of an heir or that of the decedent, as one can derive a benefit from the life of another only so long as both are alive.

> Also, you will award reasonable compensation for the loss of love, companionship, comfort, affection, society, solace or moral support.
>
> In determining the loss which each heir has suffered, you are not to consider (1) any pain or suffering of the decedent; (2) any grief or sorrow of the heirs; or (3) the poverty or wealth of any heir.
>
> Also, you shall include in your award, an amount that will compensate for reasonable expenses paid out or incurred for funeral services in memory of the decedent and for burial of the body. In determining that amount, you shall consider the decedent's station in life and the financial condition of the estate, as these circumstances have been shown by the evidence.

Tom reminds Eric and Susan, however, that the damages to the heirs must be reduced in proportion to the negligence attributable to the decedent, Johnny Vamp.

Johnny Vamp was thirty years of age. If he had not died in the accident, he likely would have continued to give the same amount of money to his mother for the rest of her life, which would have been at least an additional fifteen years, according to mortality table guidelines.

Because Johnny made no monetary contribution to his father, the father's damages would be for the emotional loss of his son, whom he had not seen for five years. Furthermore, Eric learned through discussions with the band that the son had disowned his father because the father did not want him playing in the band and wanted him to get on with his automobile-repair career.

In talking with band members and Johnny's girlfriend, Cindy, Eric learned that pictures of Johnny and The Vamps were hung throughout Johnny's old bedroom in the home that he grew up in. His mother was apparently so devastated that she could not even go into the bedroom anymore because she did not want to see the pictures. She also had to cover up the car that he built in the garage since he would no longer be able to complete his overhaul work on it. His mother sent all of the musical recordings that her son had made to his girlfriend because the mother cannot cope with listening to him after his death. Johnny had written one of the songs for his mother. It was called "Mother, I Will Always Be With You." This song was expected to engender a great deal of sympathy and would be compelling evidence of his mother's loss, and Eric figured all of these factors into the assessment of damages that Johnny's mother would claim for her emotional loss.

Some jurisdictions measure each wrongful death beneficiary separately, basing the award on specific evidence of loss or injury to each claimant. In the state where this claim was made, the wrongful death statute calculates damages as a lump sum to all people who qualify as "beneficiaries" and then apportions the settlement or award according to the loss suffered by each. This state's wrongful death statute probably helps Johnny's father because he would not likely be able to prove damages if his claim had to stand on its own merits. The lump-sum amount is apportioned by the court according to the damages suffered. Because Johnny's mother's loss is greater, her share of the award or settlement should be greater than the father's award or settlement. It is likely that the father would receive some percentage of the settlement.

In defense, Tom Hanson finds out during discovery that the singer was an avid user of cocaine and heroin. He shows that this would lower the claim value because the health of the deceased is an important factor in determining damages in a wrongful death case. Tom also points out that of the $5,000 that Johnny was giving to his mother for support, he apparently owed her $15,000 for his auto-repair shop education as well as for money she lent to him to buy all of the component pieces he used in the band.

Defense-Cost Issues

Susan, Eric, and Tom next discuss the legal costs in the case because, not only would the retailer, repair facility, and each one of the manufacturers of the pieces of equipment be brought into the case, but also the homeowner would be brought in, and possibly the school, because the party invitations were handed out at school on the day of the incident.

With regard to legal counsel, the retailer and manufacturer would definitely need separate counsel because the manufacturer is alleging modifications and alterations of the products after they were shipped out of the chain of custody. It would be a conflict of interest for one attorney to represent them both, because they have opposite allegations against each other. If, however, an indemnity agreement existed between them, then a conflict might not exist and legal counsel could possibly represent the retailer, as well as the manufacturer, if they were not alleging separate fault.

The homeowner would require separate counsel, as would the repair shop and each of the manufacturers for the guitar, amplifiers, and microphone. Each of these has separate interests, and most likely they will blame each other for the accident.

Case Conclusion

A consensus of all the defendants is reached. The defendants believe Johnny's parents' claim is worth $500,000 total but believe that Johnny was 50 percent at fault for his own injuries. Therefore they agree to offer $250,000 collectively. They agree to divide this as follows:

- The greatest percentage of defendant fault was with the repair shop for modifying the microphone. Its insurer, Premium Insurance, agrees to pay 60 percent of the defendant's share of the liability and offers $150,000 to settle the case. Premium therefore takes the lead in approaching the plaintiffs and trying to negotiate a settlement.

- All defendants generally agree that it would be difficult for the plaintiffs to prove that the manufacturers were negligent for not placing a warning device on the electrical cord and for not notifying the user of the hazards of cutting off the ground plug. No previous cases had existed on this issue. The manufacturers of all the equipment offer to Johnny's parents only 5 percent collectively and agree to contribute $12,500 just to have the case settled.

- The homeowner's insurer agrees to settle for 25 percent of the claim up to its policy limit of $500,000. It contributes $62,500 to the initial offer. The homeowner allowed the daughter to have the party, and she let it get out of hand, leading to the beer and excess water. This led to the grounding problems that made it more likely that the incident would occur. Also, the short circuit would not have occurred if proper grounds were in the electrical outlets.

- Eric and Susan agree that Rock N Roll would accept 10 percent of all defendants' responsibility, and National Farm offers $25,000.

The attorneys for Johnny's parents believe that the defendants' offer is reasonable but are having a difficult time getting them to understand that Johnny was at least 50 percent responsible and, more important, getting them to accept anything less than $1 million as the value of their son. After a few weeks, it appears that the father's claim is about to settle and that the mother is going to continue to pursue the case in court. However, before concluding with the father, the defendants hear startling news that could complicate the case. Cindy's father has just learned that Cindy is pregnant. She claims that Johnny is the child's father. The blood type is the same as Johnny's. The child could be another potential claimant and perhaps a more sympathetic one.

Everyone else waits until after the child is born to continue settlement negotiations. Forensic DNA tests are performed comparing the child's DNA to Cindy's DNA and the DNA of Johnny's parents (because Johnny's DNA was not readily available). The test concludes that Johnny was indeed the child's father.

After some legal wrangling as to whether the child was a living beneficiary at the time of Johnny's death, the consensus is that the child was a viable fetus at the time of his death and is therefore entitled to make claim. In theory, the number of years of support that Johnny would have provided to the child (both monetary and emotional) greatly exceeds the contribution that Johnny would have made to his mother or father. For that reason, the three plaintiffs agreed to apportion 75 percent of the loss to the child, 20 percent to the mother, and 5 percent to the father. The defendants raise their combined offer to $300,000 in recognition of the sympathy that the child might engender with a jury. The claims are settled with $225,000 going to a court-approved structured settlement that the child, Johnny, Jr., would collect when he reached the age of eighteen. The future value of this settlement totals nearly $800,000. Johnny's mother receives a payment for $60,000, and his father receives $15,000.

This case incorporated elements from several chapters in this text. The case illustrates a fairly challenging type of claim that liability claim representatives may encounter. The purpose of this case and other cases presented in the last three chapters is to help claim representatives to better understand how claims are methodically analyzed and evaluated, and settled. The exact evaluation amounts will vary by region and by company philosophy. The framework for analysis, evaluation, and settlement should be consistent from one claim to the next to maintain the integrity of the claim process. As illustrated by the cases presented in this text, the world of liability claims is often characterized by human drama, requiring claim professionals to apply their knowledge to help resolve a range of business and personal issues.

CHAPTER NOTES

1. Jury Verdict Research, *Personal Injury Handbook, Current Trends in Personal Injury* (Horsham, Pa.: LRP Publications, 1998), p. 15.

2. Thibault v. Sears, Roebuck & Co., 395 A. 2d. 843 (N.H. 1978).

3. Consumer Product and Safety Commission, http://www.cpsc.gov.

4. Citizens Gas & Coke Utility v. American Economy Ins. Co., 477 N.E. 2d 329 (Ind. Ct. App. 1985), vacated on other grounds, 486 N.E. 2d 998 (Ind.).

5. Patrick v. Perfect Parts Company, 515 S.W. 2d 554 (Mo. En banc 1974).

6. Johnson v. Upjohn C., 442 S.W. 2d 93 (Mo. App. 1969).

7. Means v. Sears, Roebuck, & Co. 550 S.W. 2d 780 (Mo. En banc 1977).

8. Collins v. B.F. Goodrich Co., 558 F. 2d 908 (8th Cir. 1977).

9. Guess v. Lorenz, 612 S.W. 2d 831 (Mo. App. 1981), Mack Truck, Inc. 569 S.W. 2d 243 (Mo. App. 1978).

10. Williams v. Deere & Co., 598 S.W. 2d 609 (Mo. App. 1980).

11. Donald Hirsch, *Casualty Claim Practice*, 6th ed. (Homewood, Il.: Irwin/McGraw Hill, 1996), p. 204.

12. Adapted from 402A of the *Restatement (Second) of Torts*.

13. Winters v. Sears, Roebuck and Co., 554 S.W. 2d 565 (Mo. App. 1977).

14. Rogers v. Toro Manufacturing Co., 522 S.W. 2d 632 (Mo. App. 1975).

15. *Restatement of Torts*, 402A, comment n.

APPENDIX—CHECKLIST FOR PRODUCT LIABILITY INVESTIGATIONS

- Identify the product that caused the injury by brand name, model, year, and serial number.
- Determine when the product was made and how old it is.
- Obtain all advertising and instructional manuals for the product.
- Determine the name of all parties that may have sold the alleged defective product, assembled it, installed it, or supplied component parts for it.
- Determine who assembled the part, who supplied component parts, and how parts were installed.
- Determine how the product was tested for safety.
- Check with the Consumer Product Safety Commission (www.cpsc.gov) to learn whether the product has been recalled.
- Get copies of any purchase documentation.
- Determine whether the product was purchased second-hand or sold to the buyer "as is."
- Determine whether the product was sold in a closed container or whether it had been inspected by the retailer.
- Attempt to determine the name of the salesperson who sold the product and determine what, if any, recommendations or promises were made relating to the product.
- Assess how dangerous the product is compared to the benefit it provides.
- Determine what, if anything, could reasonably have been done to make the product safer. (Were warnings adequate?)
- Determine whether the product was properly used by the claimant.
- Determine whether product was inspected by the claimant.
- Examine the product for visible outward signs of defects.
- Obtain permission to preserve the product for future examination by an expert in order to avoid accusation of spoliation of evidence.
- Find out whether the insured had any prior problems with the product.
- Determine whether the insured or insured's employees altered or repaired the product.

Index

1

C

Y